MW00651771

50% OFF Online TExES Core Subjects EC-6 Prep Course

Dear Customer,

We consider it an honor and a privilege that you chose our TExES Core Subjects EC-6 Study Guide. As a way of showing our appreciation and to help us better serve you, we have partnered with Mometrix Test Preparation to offer **50% off their online TExES Core Subjects EC-6 Prep Course**. Many TExES courses are needlessly expensive and don't deliver enough value. With our course, you get access to the best TExES Core Subjects EC-6 prep material, and **you only pay half price**.

Mometrix has structured their online course to perfectly complement your printed study guide. The TExES Core Subjects EC-6 Prep Course contains **in-depth lessons** that cover all the most important topics, **390+ video reviews** that explain difficult concepts, over **800 practice questions** to ensure you feel prepared, and **over 1,250 digital flashcards**, so you can study while you're on the go.

Online TExES Core Subjects EC-6 Prep Course

Topics Covered:

- TExES Core Subjects EC-6 Sections
  - English Language Arts and Reading
  - Mathematics
  - Social Studies
  - Science
  - Fine Arts, Health, and Physical Education

Course Features:

- TExES Core Subjects EC-6 Study Guide
  - Get content that complements our best-selling study guide.
- Full-Length Practice Tests
  - With over 800 practice questions you can test yourself again and again.
- Mobile Friendly
  - If you need to study on the go, the course is easily accessible from your mobile device.
- TExES Core EC-6 (391) Flashcards
  - Our course includes a flashcard mode with over 1,250 content cards to help you study.

To receive this discount, visit them at mometrix.com/university/texes391 or simply scan this QR code with your smartphone. At the checkout page, enter the discount code:
TPBTEXEC50

SCAN HERE

If you have any questions or concerns, please contact Mometrix at support@mometrix.com.

Sincerely,

Test Prep Books in partnership with Mometrix TEST PREPARATION

STOP

TExES Core Subjects EC-6 391 Study Guide

Test Prep with Practice Exam Questions [Updated for the New Outline]

Joshua Rueda

Written and edited by TPB Publishing.

ISBN 13: 9781637750605
ISBN 10: 1637750609

Table of Contents

Quick Overview

As you draw closer to taking your exam, effective preparation becomes more and more important. Thankfully, you have this study guide to help you get ready. Use this guide to help keep your studying on track and refer to it often.

This study guide contains several key sections that will help you be successful on your exam. The guide contains tips for what you should do the night before and the day of the test. Also included are test-taking tips. Knowing the right information is not always enough. Many well-prepared test takers struggle with exams. These tips will help equip you to accurately read, assess, and answer test questions.

A large part of the guide is devoted to showing you what content to expect on the exam and to helping you better understand that content. In this guide are practice test questions so that you can see how well you have grasped the content. Then, answer explanations are provided so that you can understand why you missed certain questions.

Don't try to cram the night before you take your exam. This is not a wise strategy for a few reasons. First, your retention of the information will be low. Your time would be better used by reviewing information you already know rather than trying to learn a lot of new information. Second, you will likely become stressed as you try to gain a large amount of knowledge in a short amount of time. Third, you will be depriving yourself of sleep. So be sure to go to bed at a reasonable time the night before. Being well-rested helps you focus and remain calm.

Be sure to eat a substantial breakfast the morning of the exam. If you are taking the exam in the afternoon, be sure to have a good lunch as well. Being hungry is distracting and can make it difficult to focus. You have hopefully spent lots of time preparing for the exam. Don't let an empty stomach get in the way of success!

When travelling to the testing center, leave earlier than needed. That way, you have a buffer in case you experience any delays. This will help you remain calm and will keep you from missing your appointment time at the testing center.

Be sure to pace yourself during the exam. Don't try to rush through the exam. There is no need to risk performing poorly on the exam just so you can leave the testing center early. Allow yourself to use all of the allotted time if needed.

Remain positive while taking the exam even if you feel like you are performing poorly. Thinking about the content you should have mastered will not help you perform better on the exam.

Once the exam is complete, take some time to relax. Even if you feel that you need to take the exam again, you will be well served by some down time before you begin studying again. It's often easier to convince yourself to study if you know that it will come with a reward!

Test-Taking Strategies

1. Predicting the Answer

When you feel confident in your preparation for a multiple-choice test, try predicting the answer before reading the answer choices. This is especially useful on questions that test objective factual knowledge. By predicting the answer before reading the available choices, you eliminate the possibility that you will be distracted or led astray by an incorrect answer choice. You will feel more confident in your selection if you read the question, predict the answer, and then find your prediction among the answer choices. After using this strategy, be sure to still read all of the answer choices carefully and completely. If you feel unprepared, you should not attempt to predict the answers. This would be a waste of time and an opportunity for your mind to wander in the wrong direction.

2. Reading the Whole Question

Too often, test takers scan a multiple-choice question, recognize a few familiar words, and immediately jump to the answer choices. Test authors are aware of this common impatience, and they will sometimes prey upon it. For instance, a test author might subtly turn the question into a negative, or he or she might redirect the focus of the question right at the end. The only way to avoid falling into these traps is to read the entirety of the question carefully before reading the answer choices.

3. Looking for Wrong Answers

Long and complicated multiple-choice questions can be intimidating. One way to simplify a difficult multiple-choice question is to eliminate all of the answer choices that are clearly wrong. In most sets of answers, there will be at least one selection that can be dismissed right away. If the test is administered on paper, the test taker could draw a line through it to indicate that it may be ignored; otherwise, the test taker will have to perform this operation mentally or on scratch paper. In either case, once the obviously incorrect answers have been eliminated, the remaining choices may be considered. Sometimes identifying the clearly wrong answers will give the test taker some information about the correct answer. For instance, if one of the remaining answer choices is a direct opposite of one of the eliminated answer choices, it may well be the correct answer. The opposite of obviously wrong is obviously right! Of course, this is not always the case. Some answers are obviously incorrect simply because they are irrelevant to the question being asked. Still, identifying and eliminating some incorrect answer choices is a good way to simplify a multiple-choice question.

4. Don't Overanalyze

Anxious test takers often overanalyze questions. When you are nervous, your brain will often run wild, causing you to make associations and discover clues that don't actually exist. If you feel that this may be a problem for you, do whatever you can to slow down during the test. Try taking a deep breath or counting to ten. As you read and consider the question, restrict yourself to the particular words used by the author. Avoid thought tangents about what the author *really* meant, or what he or she was *trying* to say. The only things that matter on a multiple-choice test are the words that are actually in the question. You must avoid reading too much into a multiple-choice question, or supposing that the writer meant something other than what he or she wrote.

5. No Need for Panic

It is wise to learn as many strategies as possible before taking a multiple-choice test, but it is likely that you will come across a few questions for which you simply don't know the answer. In this situation, avoid panicking. Because most multiple-choice tests include dozens of questions, the relative value of a single wrong answer is small. As much as possible, you should compartmentalize each question on a multiple-choice test. In other words, you should not allow your feelings about one question to affect your success on the others. When you find a question that you either don't understand or don't know how to answer, just take a deep breath and do your best. Read the entire question slowly and carefully. Try rephrasing the question a couple of different ways. Then, read all of the answer choices carefully. After eliminating obviously wrong answers, make a selection and move on to the next question.

6. Confusing Answer Choices

When working on a difficult multiple-choice question, there may be a tendency to focus on the answer choices that are the easiest to understand. Many people, whether consciously or not, gravitate to the answer choices that require the least concentration, knowledge, and memory. This is a mistake. When you come across an answer choice that is confusing, you should give it extra attention. A question might be confusing because you do not know the subject matter to which it refers. If this is the case, don't eliminate the answer before you have affirmatively settled on another. When you come across an answer choice of this type, set it aside as you look at the remaining choices. If you can confidently assert that one of the other choices is correct, you can leave the confusing answer aside. Otherwise, you will need to take a moment to try to better understand the confusing answer choice. Rephrasing is one way to tease out the sense of a confusing answer choice.

7. Your First Instinct

Many people struggle with multiple-choice tests because they overthink the questions. If you have studied sufficiently for the test, you should be prepared to trust your first instinct once you have carefully and completely read the question and all of the answer choices. There is a great deal of research suggesting that the mind can come to the correct conclusion very quickly once it has obtained all of the relevant information. At times, it may seem to you as if your intuition is working faster even than your reasoning mind. This may in fact be true. The knowledge you obtain while studying may be retrieved from your subconscious before you have a chance to work out the associations that support it. Verify your instinct by working out the reasons that it should be trusted.

8. Key Words

Many test takers struggle with multiple-choice questions because they have poor reading comprehension skills. Quickly reading and understanding a multiple-choice question requires a mixture of skill and experience. To help with this, try jotting down a few key words and phrases on a piece of scrap paper. Doing this concentrates the process of reading and forces the mind to weigh the relative importance of the question's parts. In selecting words and phrases to write down, the test taker thinks about the question more deeply and carefully. This is especially true for multiple-choice questions that are preceded by a long prompt.

9. Subtle Negatives

One of the oldest tricks in the multiple-choice test writer's book is to subtly reverse the meaning of a question with a word like *not* or *except*. If you are not paying attention to each word in the question, you can easily be led astray by this trick. For instance, a common question format is, "Which of the following is...?" Obviously, if the question instead is, "Which of the following is not...?," then the answer will be quite different. Even worse, the test makers are aware of the potential for this mistake and will include one answer choice that would be correct if the question were not negated or reversed. A test taker who misses the reversal will find what he or she believes to be a correct answer and will be so confident that he or she will fail to reread the question and discover the original error. The only way to avoid this is to practice a wide variety of multiple-choice questions and to pay close attention to each and every word.

10. Reading Every Answer Choice

It may seem obvious, but you should always read every one of the answer choices! Too many test takers fall into the habit of scanning the question and assuming that they understand the question because they recognize a few key words. From there, they pick the first answer choice that answers the question they believe they have read. Test takers who read all of the answer choices might discover that one of the latter answer choices is actually *more* correct. Moreover, reading all of the answer choices can remind you of facts related to the question that can help you arrive at the correct answer. Sometimes, a misstatement or incorrect detail in one of the latter answer choices will trigger your memory of the subject and will enable you to find the right answer. Failing to read all of the answer choices is like not reading all of the items on a restaurant menu: you might miss out on the perfect choice.

11. Spot the Hedges

One of the keys to success on multiple-choice tests is paying close attention to every word. This is never truer than with words like almost, most, some, and sometimes. These words are called "hedges" because they indicate that a statement is not totally true or not true in every place and time. An absolute statement will contain no hedges, but in many subjects, the answers are not always straightforward or absolute. There are always exceptions to the rules in these subjects. For this reason, you should favor those multiple-choice questions that contain hedging language. The presence of qualifying words indicates that the author is taking special care with his or her words, which is certainly important when composing the right answer. After all, there are many ways to be wrong, but there is only one way to be right! For this reason, it is wise to avoid answers that are absolute when taking a multiple-choice test. An absolute answer is one that says things are either all one way or all another. They often include words like *every*, *always*, *best*, and *never*. If you are taking a multiple-choice test in a subject that doesn't lend itself to absolute answers, be on your guard if you see any of these words.

12. Long Answers

In many subject areas, the answers are not simple. As already mentioned, the right answer often requires hedges. Another common feature of the answers to a complex or subjective question are qualifying clauses, which are groups of words that subtly modify the meaning of the sentence. If the question or answer choice describes a rule to which there are exceptions or the subject matter is complicated, ambiguous, or confusing, the correct answer will require many words in order to be expressed clearly and accurately. In essence, you should not be deterred by answer choices that seem excessively long. Oftentimes, the author of the text will not be able to write the correct answer without offering some qualifications and modifications. Your job is to read the answer choices thoroughly and completely and to select the one that most accurately and precisely answers the question.

13. Restating to Understand

Sometimes, a question on a multiple-choice test is difficult not because of what it asks but because of how it is written. If this is the case, restate the question or answer choice in different words. This process serves a couple of important purposes. First, it forces you to concentrate on the core of the question. In order to rephrase the question accurately, you have to understand it well. Rephrasing the question will concentrate your mind on the key words and ideas. Second, it will present the information to your mind in a fresh way. This process may trigger your memory and render some useful scrap of information picked up while studying.

14. True Statements

Sometimes an answer choice will be true in itself, but it does not answer the question. This is one of the main reasons why it is essential to read the question carefully and completely before proceeding to the answer choices. Too often, test takers skip ahead to the answer choices and look for true statements. Having found one of these, they are content to select it without reference to the question above. Obviously, this provides an easy way for test makers to play tricks. The savvy test taker will always read the entire question before turning to the answer choices. Then, having settled on a correct answer choice, he or she will refer to the original question and ensure that the selected answer is relevant. The mistake of choosing a correct-but-irrelevant answer choice is especially common on questions related to specific pieces of objective knowledge. A prepared test taker will have a wealth of factual knowledge at his or her disposal, and should not be careless in its application.

15. No Patterns

One of the more dangerous ideas that circulates about multiple-choice tests is that the correct answers tend to fall into patterns. These erroneous ideas range from a belief that B and C are the most common right answers, to the idea that an unprepared test-taker should answer "A-B-A-C-A-D-A-B-A." It cannot be emphasized enough that pattern-seeking of this type is exactly the WRONG way to approach a multiple-choice test. To begin with, it is highly unlikely that the test maker will plot the correct answers according to some predetermined pattern. The questions are scrambled and delivered in a random order. Furthermore, even if the test maker was following a pattern in the assignation of correct answers, there is no reason why the test taker would know which pattern he or she was using. Any attempt to discern a pattern in the answer choices is a waste of time and a distraction from the real work of taking the test. A test taker would be much better served by extra preparation before the test than by reliance on a pattern in the answers.

Bonus Content

We host multiple bonus items online, including both practice tests in digital format. Scan the QR code or go to this link to access this content:

testprepbooks.com/bonus/texes-core

SCAN ME

The first time you access the page, you will need to register as a "new user" and verify your email address.

If you have any issues, please email support@testprepbooks.com.

Introduction for the TExES 391

Function of the Test

The Texas Examinations of Educator Standards (TExES) are a series of tests administered by the Educational Testing Service (ETS) and recognized by the Texas Education Agency (TEA). They measure the test taker's ability to meet the required educator standards necessary to obtain certification to teach in Texas public schools. The TExES Core Subjects EC-6 (test code 391) is specifically designed to evaluate the readiness of entry-level teachers in five core subject areas for grade school students up to grade six: English Language Arts and Reading (ELAR) & Science of Teaching Reading (STR); Mathematics; Social Studies; Science; and Fine Arts, Health, and Physical Education.

The exam is designed for first time teachers seeking initial certification in the state of Texas. Before registering for the test, prospective test takers should confer with their preparation program or prospective employer to determine whether this exam is appropriate for their certification needs.

Test Administration

Because this exam is designed for meeting Texas state certification standards, the majority of testing centers are located in Texas. However, testing centers can also be found throughout the United States and in Mexico and Puerto Rico. Refer to the TExES website for a full list of testing centers.

The TExES Core Subjects EC-6 tests are offered on a continuous basis throughout the year via a computer administered test (CAT) format. The complete test lasts for five hours and is offered in the morning and in the afternoon. For certification purposes, test takers must pass all five subjects; if they fail in any subject area, prospective educators can retake individual subject areas or the entire test after waiting a period of 45 days. Test takers have five attempts to pass the TExES Core Subjects EC-6 tests for certification; after the fifth attempt, any further scores will not be counted towards certification.

On the testing day, test takers will need to bring an admissions ticket (available via their ETS testing account) and two forms of photo ID. They are not permitted to bring any personal belongings or electronics to the testing area. However, testing accommodations are available for test takers with documented disabilities. Available accommodations include extended test time, access to food and beverages, and Braille format exams.

Test Format

The TExES Core Subjects EC-6 tests comprise five different areas of competency for incoming instructors. All exams take place on a computer and all question types are selected response (also referred to as multiple choice). The number of questions and time limits vary between subjects:

Test Name	Test Code	Number of Questions	Test Time
English Language Arts and Reading	901	45	1 hour and 10 minutes
Mathematics	902	40	1 hour and 10 minutes
Social Studies	903	40	50 minutes
Science	904	45	55 minutes
Fine Arts, Health, and Physical Education	905	40	35 minutes
TOTAL	**391**	**210**	**5 hours**

The exam contents align with educator standards for the state of Texas, including both subject area content and pedagogical topics. A complete list of competencies covered in the exam can be found in the official TExES preparation manual.

Scoring

Each subject test is scored on a range of 100-300 with a minimum passing score of 240. An overall score for the combined TExES Core Subjects EC-6 tests is not reported because it is necessary to pass every individual subject test for certification purposes. Instead, overall test results are simply designated as "pass" or "not pass" depending on whether or not the test taker earned five scores at or over 240. Scores are available online through the test taker's ETS testing account 7 days after taking the exam.

Points are given for correct answers and no penalty is given for incorrect answers (in other words, there is no penalty for guessing on the exam).

Recent/Future Developments

The TExES Core Subjects EC-6 tests are the most up-to-date exams recognized by the TEA for certification. TExES exam policies were updated in 2015 to limit the number of exam attempts to five (including the first attempt and four retakes). For future test development purposes, additional questions may appear on the exam that do not count towards the test taker's score.

Beginning on January 1, 2022, the TExES Core Subjects EC-6 (391) replaced the 291 version of the same test. For certification purposes, teacher candidates also need to take the Science of Teaching (293) test.

Study Prep Plan for the TExES 391

1 **Schedule** - Use one of our study schedules below or come up with one of your own.

2 **Relax** - Test anxiety can hurt even the best students. There are many ways to reduce stress. Find the one that works best for you.

3 **Execute** - Once you have a good plan in place, be sure to stick to it.

One Week Study Schedule

Day 1	English Language Arts and Reading
Day 2	Mathematics
Day 3	Social Studies
Day 4	Science
Day 5	Fine Arts, Health, and Physical Education
Day 6	Practice Test
Day 7	Take Your Exam!

Two Week Study Schedule

Day 1	English Language Arts and Reading	Day 8	Science
Day 2	Vocabulary Development	Day 9	Concepts and Processes
Day 3	Mathematics	Day 10	Reproduction and the Mechanisms of Heredity
Day 4	Geometry and Measurement	Day 11	Fine Arts, Health, and Physical Education
Day 5	Probability and Statistics	Day 12	Practice Test
Day 6	Social Studies	Day 13	Answer Explanations
Day 7	Economics	Day 14	Take Your Exam!

One Month Study Schedule

Day 1	English Language Arts and Reading	Day 11	Mathematical Processes	Day 21	Energy Transformations and Conservation
Day 2	Reading Fluency	Day 12	Social Studies	Day 22	Reproduction and the Mechanisms of Heredity
Day 3	Vocabulary Development	Day 13	Basic Concepts of Culture	Day 23	Structure and Function of Earth Systems
Day 4	Viewing and Representing	Day 14	Geography and Culture	Day 24	Solar System and the Universe
Day 5	Mathematics	Day 15	Economics	Day 25	Fine Arts, Health, and Physical Education
Day 6	Ratios and Unit Rates	Day 16	Government and Citizenship	Day 26	Health
Day 7	Patterns and Algebra	Day 17	Science	Day 27	Physical Education
Day 8	Geometry and Measurement	Day 18	History and Nature of Science	Day 28	Practice Test
Day 9	Tessellations and Symmetry	Day 19	Concepts and Processes	Day 29	Answer Explanations
Day 10	Probability and Statistics	Day 20	Forces and Motion	Day 30	Take Your Exam!

Build your own prep plan by visiting:
testprepbooks.com/prep

English Language Arts and Reading

Oral Language

Basic Linguistic Concepts

Oral language skills are important for students to have in order to thrive in an English-speaking environment. Beyond comprehending spoken English, understanding oral language structure helps students comprehend the context of what they are reading and how to respond appropriately. All languages utilize grammar, vocabulary, phonology, morphology, discourse, and pragmatics; these concepts combine to make words on a page actually form communication—the foundation of sentences.

As an instructor, it's important to be mindful of how comfortable the class is with oral language. Native speakers may be more proficient than those who are learning English as a second language; the latter may need more differentiated instruction to build their conceptual knowledge. No matter the range of student experiences, reading instructors should incorporate drills and lessons that frequently review oral language components throughout the course. This will ensure that core skills such as grammar and word formation remain fresh in students' minds as they continue to progress in reading proficiency. This can be done in a variety of ways and activities using both teacher-based and student-based grouping instruction.

Strategically, it's best to promote oral language by having students isolate and identify different aspects of sentences such as grammar and even vocabulary terms. Reviewing **phonology**, the sounds of English, and **morphology**, how words are formed, is also important. One way to review these aspects would be to present a sample of text and then have students deconstruct the sentences to identify these structures.

Discourse, which studies how language is used in communication, and **pragmatics**, which reflects the correct use of the language, can be reviewed through text examination and interactive activities. It's important to alter and differentiate instruction to review reading principles in different ways and expand critical-thinking skills. One method for reviewing discourse and pragmatics would be for the instructor to write or speak a sentence and then have the class discuss the discourse and pragmatics together. Students can also create the sentences themselves, demonstrating their ability to replicate correct language structure and recognize incorrect sentence components. When reviewing language structure, instructors should continue to assess how students are grasping the material and monitor progress. It's important to remember that reading improvements begin with a strong understanding of language fundamentals.

Types of Assessments

Entry-level assessments, progress monitoring, and summative assessments need to be administered in order to determine students' phonological and phonemic awareness. Appropriate assessments for such purposes include:

The Yopp-Singer Test of Phonemic Segmentation

The **Yopp-Singer Test of Phonemic Segmentation** is an oral entry-level or summative assessment of phonemic awareness during which a teacher reads one of twenty-two words aloud at a time to a single student. The student is to break each word apart by stating the word's sounds in the order that the sounds are heard or said, and the teacher records the student's responses. Correctly segmented letter sounds are circled, and incorrect responses are noted. If a student does well, then he or she is likely to do well in other phonemic areas. Upon poor student performance, the sound(s) with which a student struggles should be emphasized and/or retaught shortly after the time of the assessment.

After the Yopp-Singer Test, the blending of words, syllabification, and/or onset-rime identification should be assessed. The last set of phonological and phonemic skills to be assessed is composed of isolation, blending, deletion, and substitution.

Recognizing Rhyme Assessment

Word awareness, specifically awareness of onset-rime, can be assessed as a progress-monitoring activity. During the **recognizing rhyme assessment**, the teacher says two words. Students are to point their thumbs up if the words rhyme and down if the words do not rhyme. Immediate feedback and remediation are provided if the majority of the students respond incorrectly to a word pair.

Isolation or Matching Games

Games can be used to identify initial, medial, and final phonemes. During a **phoneme-isolation activity**, the teacher says one word at a time. The student is to tell the teacher the first, medial, or last sound of the word. During **phoneme-matching activities**, a teacher reads a group of words. The student is to say which two words from the group begin or end with the same sound. A similar activity can be completed to assess deletion and/or substitution (e.g., "What word would result if we replaced the /c/ of *cat* with an *h*?"). In this way, teachers can assess if remediation or extra instruction on initial, medial, or final phonemes is required, and lessons can be developed accordingly.

Phoneme Blending Assessment

In the **phoneme blending assessment**, a teacher says all the sounds within a word and a student listens to the teacher and is asked for the word that they hear when the sounds are put together quickly. This skill will be needed when students learn letter-sound pairs and decipher unknown words in their reading. Thus, mastery of this assessment can be used as an indicator to the teacher that the students are ready to learn higher-level phonological and/or phonemic tasks.

Please note that student results should be recorded, analyzed, and used to determine if students demonstrate mastery over the assessed skill and/or identify the needs of students. If mastery is not demonstrated, then the assessments should be used to determine exactly which letter-sound combinations or other phonemes need to be remediated. Any of the strategies earlier addressed (rhyming, blending, segmenting, deleting, substituting) can be used for such purposes.

Activities to Build on Oral Language Skills

While there are countless creative ways to integrate language skills in the classroom, here are some of the more common methods:

Role play is an entertaining and low-stress way for students to practice speaking. Students playing store can practice vocabulary. Students acting out a book that the class has just read can practice to summarizing a text. Role play can take place with the class as a whole or in small groups.

Literature circles are groups of students who read the same text independently and meet to discuss it. The teacher groups students based on their level or interests and allows them to choose an appropriate book. The teacher may also assign each student a different role, such as leading discussion or collecting new vocabulary words. The helps keep the group on track and teaches leadership skills. Literature circles foster social connection and critical thinking skills, but they are not suitable for very young students.

Discussion circles are similar to literature circles, but they focus on discussing topics, issues, or ideas rather than the text itself. In an ESL classroom or lower grade, teachers may guide students to discuss a general topic rather than a text. For example, if the theme of the book is overcoming obstacles, students might reflect on obstacles they've encountered in their own lives and discuss their experiences. For students with more advanced language skills, discussion circles are a place to practice persuasive skills and debate more abstract topics such as issues of morality and ethical principles.

In **jigsaw discussions**, the teacher assigns each student or small group a different reading. After everyone has read their assignment, the students meet and present their findings to the group. For example, students might each read about a different country in South America before reconvening to give mini-presentations and combine their information into a travel guide. By summarizing material in front of a group, students practice comprehension, speaking, and critical thinking skills. Jigsaw discussions also help students learn to collaborate effectively, and can encourage notetaking.

Language games help students practice their language skills while providing a break from more serious class activities. Games can involve anything from Simon Says to reading a word and then drawing it for the other students to guess.

Questioning has immeasurable value in the reading process. Answering questions about a text gives purpose for reading to students and focuses them on reading to learn information. Similarly, generating questions about a text for others to answer enables a student to analyze what is important to learn in the text and glean summarizing skills. Keeping Bloom's Taxonomy in mind, teachers can scaffold students toward increased critical thinking capabilities. Bloom's Taxonomy shows the hierarchy of learning progressing through the following stages:

- Remembering
- Understanding
- Applying
- Analyzing
- Evaluating
- Creating

Diversity and Inclusivity in the Classroom

The classroom must be a place that emphasizes respect for all individuals as well as collaboration to achieve a successful learning environment. In addition to teaching reading skills, the instructor is expected to be a model of tolerance and inclusiveness for all students, thus encouraging them to be open-minded toward others. In the United States, it's likely that instructors will have students from a broad range of cultural and linguistic backgrounds. Obviously, these students must be made to feel welcome, and any linguistic difficulties they have should be treated as simply another step in the learning process, not a result of their background. Any difficulty is an opportunity for the whole class to learn and grow.

Encouraging polite and respectful behavior is key. An instructor doesn't necessarily need to explain polite behavior, but rather, should serve as a role model for the class. When addressing students' issues, the teacher should be sensitive to how they feel and be encouraging no matter their religious or ethnic background. It's also important to monitor how students act and respond to one another. Proper language and behavior should be enforced when necessary, and if there is ever anything rude or insensitive said or done, it must be addressed and corrected. Teachers should emphasize the idea that, while everyone is different, they are all equal. Therefore, students must be treated respectfully. Teachers should observe whether students are listening to other students and not being distracted or showing signs of disrespect. Tone and physical behavior must also be monitored; there's no excuse for rudeness. When disrespect occurs, steps should be taken to ensure it isn't repeated. It's important to remember that behaviors and lessons in early learners will inform how children grow and mature.

Reading and writing activities can also provide lessons in respect and collaboration. For instance, students can do group work on a text that discusses respectful behavior for reading practice, and also talk about the meaning of the written content. Other lessons can look at readings from different cultures to expand the students' appreciation and interest in diversity.

Using Oral Language to Aid in Comprehension

Oral or spoken language is important when understanding a text. If proficient, a reader's speech will aid their ability to understand and comprehend words, sentences, paragraphs, and a variety of complex texts. Oral language activities, such as purposeful read-alouds, allow students to focus on comprehension skills. Listening skills can promote and serve as a great foundation for comprehension skills. Understanding a text advances students' comprehension skills. When an instructor reads aloud, a student does not need to decode words for fluency. This allows students to listen and focus solely on the text for comprehension. Teacher read-alouds also provide students the opportunity to learn how to emphasize voice and tone while reading.

Teaching Students to Speak to Various Audiences for Various Purposes

Early childhood educators are instrumental in developing effective communication skills in their students. Verbal and nonverbal communication skills are important in setting a positive, educational, supportive environment to optimize learning. They are equally important for students to master for use in their own daily lives. When communicating with others, students should be fully attentive, make eye contact, and use encouraging facial expressions and body language to augment positive verbal feedback. Postures including hands on hips or crossed over the chest may appear standoffish, while smiling and nodding enhance the comfort and satisfaction of the other party. Active listening is the process of trying to understand the underlying meaning in someone else's words, which builds empathy and trust. Asking open-ended questions and repeating or rephrasing in a reflective or clarifying manner is a form of active listening that builds a positive, trusting relationship.

An important skill for children is the ability to communicate effectively with adults, and developing this comfort from a young age will be helpful throughout life. Educators can facilitate this through providing experiences where children need to talk to adults in the community. For example, educators may take the class on a field trip to the local community library, where students must ask the librarian for help locating certain health resources. Students might also prepare a health fair and invite parents, community members, and those from senior centers to come learn from posters, demonstrations, and presentations. Children can also work on developing communication skills using an array of technologies such as telephone, written word, email, and face-to-face communication.

Teaching Students to Evaluate Their Own Messages and the Messages of Others.

Metacognition is thinking about your own thoughts or learning process. For example, a student who thinks, "When I think ___, I am making an assumption," is practicing metacognition. Metacognition is important because it enables people to evaluate their ideas objectively and determine whether they are valid. Metacognition can also help students think about the way they learn and improve their learning strategies. For example, a student who realizes that they can memorize things faster by writing them down can implement that technique to study efficiently.

Here are some techniques that you can use to help your students develop metacognition:

When students pose an opinion, ask them why they have that opinion. For example, ask, "You've said that you really disliked the novel. Why do you think you feel that way?" This technique provides a way for students to think through their own thought process. However, teachers should be wary of asking too many questions; if students have to defend every single opinion, they will become frustrated.

Model metacognition by talking through your own thought processes. For example, you might write textual evidence on the board and then map your thoughts as you analyze it.

Ask students about how they experience learning and encourage them to use their observations to study more efficiently. For example, you could ask your students to think about whether they are more visual or auditory learners, and then ask them to brainstorm ways that they could use their strengths to learn new vocabulary words.

Word Analysis and Identification Skills

Phonemic Awareness

A **phoneme** is the smallest unit of sound in a given language and is one aspect under the umbrella of skills associated with phonological awareness. A child demonstrates phonemic awareness when identifying rhymes, recognizing alliterations, and isolating specific sounds inside a word or a set of words. Students who demonstrate basic phonemic awareness will eventually also be able to independently and appropriately blend together a variety of phonemes.

Some classroom strategies to strengthen phonemic awareness may include:

- Introduction to nursery rhymes and word play
- Introduces speech discrimination techniques to train the ear to hear more accurately
- Repeated instruction connecting sounds to letters and blending sounds
- Use of visual images coupled with corresponding sounds and words
- Teaching speech sounds through direct instruction
- Comparing known to unfamiliar words
- Practicing pronunciation of newly introduced letters, letter combinations, and words
- Practicing word decoding
- Differentiating similar sounding words

Age-appropriate and developmentally appropriate instruction for phonological and phonemic awareness is key to helping children strengthen their reading and writing skills. Phonological and phonemic awareness, or PPA, instruction works to enhance correct speech, improve understanding and application of accurate letter-to-sound correspondence, and strengthen spelling skills. Since skill-building involving phonemes is not a natural process but needs to be taught, PPA instruction is especially important for children who have limited access and exposure to reading materials and who lack familial encouragement to read. Strategies that educators can implement include leading word and sound games, focusing on phoneme skill-building activities, and ensuring all activities focus on the fun, playful nature of words and sounds instead of rote memorization and drilling techniques.

Word Recognition and Analysis Skills

Automatic Word Recognition

Word recognition occurs when students are able to correctly and automatically recognize and read a word. Phonics and sight word instruction help with the promotion of accurate and automatic word identification and word recognition. Once students are able to readily identify and recognize words, their attention is not devoted toward the dissection of word interpretation, and they can focus on the meaning of the text, supporting reading comprehension skills.

Phonics instruction stresses letter-sound correspondences and the manipulation of phonemes. Through phonics instruction, students discover the different sounds of a spoken language and how a written language's letters and symbols relate to one another. It is through the application of phonics principles that students are able to decode words. When a word is **decoded**, the letters that make up the printed word are translated into sounds. When students are able to recognize and manipulate letter-sound relationships of single-syllable words, they are able to apply such relationships to decode more complex words. In this way, phonics aids reading fluency and reading comprehension.

Sight words, sometimes referred to as **high-frequency words**, are words that are used often but may not follow the regular principles of phonics. Sight words may also be defined as words that students are able to readily recognize and read without having to sound them out. Students are encouraged to memorize words by sight so their reading fluency is not deterred through the frequent decoding of regularly-occurring irregular words. In this way, sight word recognition aids reading fluency and reading comprehension.

Applying Word-Analysis Skills

Phonics and decoding skills aid the analysis of new words. **Word analysis** is the ability to recognize the relationships between the spelling, syllabication, and pronunciation of new and/or unfamiliar words. Having a clear understanding of word structure, orthography, and the meaning of morphemes also aid in the analysis of new words. However, not all words follow predictable phonics patterns, morphology, or orthography. Such irregular words must be committed to memory and are called sight words. Phonics skills, syllabic skills, structural analysis, word analysis, and memorization of sight words lead to word recognition automaticity. **Word recognition** is the ability to correctly and automatically recognize words in or out of context. Word recognition is a prerequisite for fluent reading and reading comprehension.

Contextual Analysis

Reference materials are the most obvious way students can independently learn the definition and pronunciation of new vocabulary terms.

When using **contextual strategies**, students are introduced to new words indirectly within a sentence or paragraph. Contextual strategies require students to infer the meaning of a word by utilizing semantic and contextual clues.

The use of appositives and parenthetical elements can be very effective contextual strategies. **Appositives** are words or a group of words that add meaning or define a term that directly precedes them. An example of a sentence that includes apposition is: "Strawberries, heart-shaped and red berries, are delicious when eaten right off of the vine." In this sentence, the definition of strawberries ("heart shaped and red berries") directly follows the term and is introduced with and closes with a comma. **Parenthetical elements** are specific types of appositives that add details to a term but not necessarily a definition. For example: "My cat, the sweetest in the whole world, didn't come home last night." In this sentence, the parenthetical element ("the sweetest in the whole world") further describes the cat but does not provide a definition of the word "cat."

Structural analysis skills are beneficial in the pronunciation of new words. When readers use **structural analysis**, they recognize affixes or roots as meaningful word parts within a word. When a new word doesn't contain parts that are recognized by a student, the reader can use phonic letter–sound patterns to divide the word into syllables. The word parts can then be combined to yield the proper pronunciation.

Word maps are visual organizers that promote structural analysis skills for vocabulary development. **Word maps** may require students to define or provide synonyms, antonyms, and pictures for given vocabulary terms. Alternatively, **morphological maps** may be used to relate words that share a common morpheme.

Similarly, **word webs** are used to compare and classify a list of words. Word webs show relationships between new words and a student's background knowledge. With the main concept placed centrally within the word web, secondary and tertiary terms stem off from this central concept.

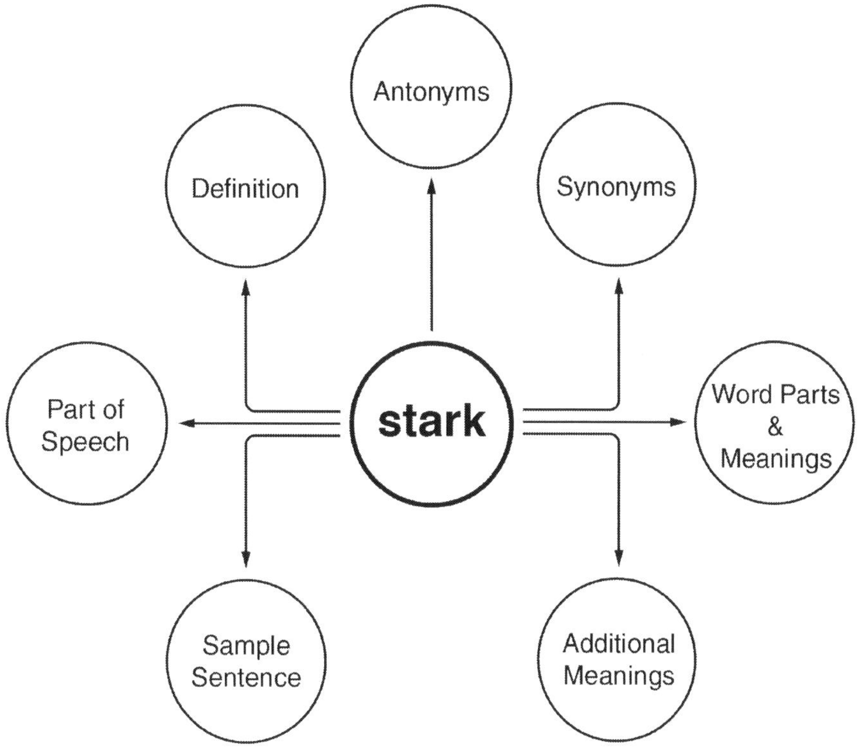

The table below identifies additional ways in which teachers can help students independently define unfamiliar words or words with multiple meanings:

Strategy	Examples
By Definition: Look up the word in a dictionary or thesaurus. Helps students realize that a single word can have multiple meanings.	Her favorite fruit to eat was a date. He went on a date with his girlfriend.
By Example: Invite students to offer their own examples, or to state their understanding following your own examples.	A myth is a story attempting to explain a natural phenomenon, such as the story of Prometheus to understand fire.
By Synonym: Understand that words have many different meanings. Some words are better synonyms than others.	She was very happy that day; her face was *radiant* with joy.
By Antonym: Teach student to look for words that have opposite meanings if the context of the sentence calls for its opposite.	Hannah was not happy that day; she was, in fact, very *depressed*.
By Apposition: Apposition is when the definition is given within the sentence.	The mango, a round, yellow, juicy fruit with an enormous seed in the middle, was ripe enough to eat.
By Origin: Identify Greek and Latin roots to figure out meanings of words.	In the word *hypertension*, the root "*hyper*" is a Greek word meaning "above" or "over."
By Context: Identifying what a word means by the surrounding text.	Water evaporates when it becomes hot, and the liquid turns into gas.

Semantics

Semantics is the branch of linguistics that studies meanings of words. Morphemes, words, phrases, and sentences all carry distinct meanings. The way these individual parts are arranged can have a significant effect on meaning. In order to construct language, children must be able to use semantics to arrange and rearrange words to achieve the particular meaning they are striving for. Activities that teach semantics revolve around teaching the arrangement of word parts (morphology) and root words, and then the teaching of vocabulary. Moving from vocabulary words into studying sentences and sentence structure leads children to learn how to use context clues to determine meaning and to understand anomalies such as metaphors, idioms, and allusions.

There are five types of semantic relationships that are critical to understand:

Hyponyms refer to a relationship between words where general words have multiple more-specific words (hyponyms) that fall into the same category (e.g., horse: mare, stallion, foal, Appaloosa, Clydesdale).

Meronyms refer to a relationship between words where a whole word has multiple parts (meronyms) that comprise it (e.g., horse: tail, mane, hooves, ears).

Synonyms refer to words that have the same meaning as another word (e.g., instructor/teacher/educator, canine/dog, feline/cat, herbivore/vegetarian).

Antonyms refer to words that have the opposite meaning as another word (e.g., true/false, up/down, in/out, right/wrong).

Homonyms refer to words that are spelled the same (**homographs**) or sound the same (**homophones**) but mean different things (e.g., there/their/they're, two/too/to, principal/principle, plain/plane, (kitchen) sink/ sink (down as in water)).

Sight Word Instruction

The goal of **sight word instruction** is to help students readily recognize regular and irregular high-frequency words in order to aid reading fluency and comprehension. Several factors affect the sequence of instruction for specific sight words. For example, before a child is exposed to sight words, he or she needs to be able to fluently recognize and say the sound of all uppercase and lowercase letters. Also, students need to be able to accurately decode target words before they recognize sight words. When irregular words are introduced, attention should be drawn to both the phonetically regular and the phonetically irregular portions of the words.

Before sight word instruction can begin, teachers need to identify high-frequency words that do and do not follow normal spelling conventions, but are used often. Teachers may choose to select words that are used often within their students' reading materials, words that students have an interest in learning, or content-specific words. Alternatively, grade-level standardized sight word lists, such as the Dolch word lists, can be referenced.

Sight Word Activities

Repetition and exposure through guided and independent practice are essential in student retention of sight words. Each lesson should introduce only three to five new sight words and also review words from previous lessons. Visually similar words should not be introduced in proximity to one another. Sample activities through which sight words can be taught are listed below.

Students can practice reading decodable texts and word lists.

Teachers should read text that contains the sight words that a class is currently learning. As a teacher reads aloud, they should pause, point to, and correctly pronounce the words. Instead of pointing to the words, teachers can underline or highlight the words as they appear in sentences that are read.

Flashcards can be used to practice sight word recognition.

Games are fun and motivating avenues through which sight words can be practiced. Examples of games that can be used to practice sight words include Bingo, Go Fish, and Memory.

As students learn new sight words, they can write them in a sight word "dictionary." Students should be asked to write a sentence using each sight word included within the dictionary.

High-Frequency Sight Word Activities

The spelling of high-frequency words should be taught after students have been exposed to the words, can readily recognize the words, and can read the words. The following multisensory strategies can be used to help students master the spelling of high-frequency sight words.

Spell reading: Spell reading begins when a student says the high-frequency word. Then, the student spells out the letters in the word. Lastly, the student reads the word again. Spell reading helps commit the word to a student's memory when done in repetition.

Air writing: When air writing, a student uses their finger to write the letters of a word in the air.

Arm tapping: During arm tapping, a student says the word, spells the word's letters on their arm, and then reads the word again.

Table writing: Students write the word on the table. A substrate, where the word is written in sand or shaving cream, can be added to the table.

Letter magnet spelling: Arranging letter magnets on a metal surface, such as a cookie sheet, is a fun way for students to learn how to spell sight words. Because this strategy is seen as a game to the student, letter magnet spelling increases student motivation to write words.

Material writing: Students can use clay, play dough, Wikki sticks, or other materials to form letters that are used to spell the words.

Decoding Complex Words and Syllabication

Decoding More Advanced Words

Students in grades K–5 should be able to decode increasingly complex letter combinations and phonics elements. They should know the vowel-vowel (VV) syllable division pattern and should have progressive knowledge of the ways that words are divided into syllables. They must be able to spell advanced words. They should have advanced knowledge of prefixes and suffixes.

Syllabication

Syllabic analysis, or **syllabication**, is a skill that teaches students how to analyze words and separate them into syllables. **Syllables** are phonological units that contain a vowel sound. Teaching students how to break apart multisyllabic words into morphological and phonological units can greatly help them not to be intimidated by long words, since these tools will help them use syllable types to make longer words seem like a series of smaller words. The identified syllables can then be blended, pronounced, and/or written together as a single word. This helps students learn to decode and encode the longer words more accurately and efficiently with less anxiety. Thus, syllabic analysis leads to the rapid word recognition that is critical in reading fluency and comprehension.

The following table identifies the six basic syllable patterns that should be explicitly taught during syllabic instruction:

Basic Syllable Patterns		
Name of Syllable Type	Characteristics of Syllable Type	Examples
Closed	A syllable with a single vowel closed in by a consonant.	lab, bog, an
Open	A syllable that ends with a single vowel. Note that the letter *y* acts as a vowel.	go, me, sly
Vowel-Consonant-Silent *e*	A syllable with a single vowel followed by a consonant then *e*.	like, rake, note, obese
Vowel Teams	A syllable that has two consecutive vowels. Note that the letters *w* and *y* act as vowels.	meat, pertain, bay, toad, window
R-controlled	A syllable with one or two vowels followed by the letter *r*.	car, jar, fir, sir, collar, turmoil
Consonant *le (-al, -el)* Also called final stable	A syllable that has a consonant followed by the letters *le*, *al*, or *el*.	puddle, stable, uncle, bridal, pedal
Other final stable syllables	A syllable at the end of words can be taught as a recognizable unit such as *cious, age, ture, tion*, or *sion*.	pension, elation, puncture, stumpage, fictitious

Reference Materials

Dictionary

Dictionaries are readily available in print, digital formats, and as mobile apps. A dictionary offers a wealth of information to users. First, in the absence of spell-checking software, a dictionary can be used to identify correct spelling and to determine the word's pronunciation—often written using the International Phonetic Alphabet (IPA). Perhaps the best-known feature of a dictionary is its explanation of a word's meanings, as a single word can have multiple definitions. A dictionary organizes these definitions based on their parts of speech and then arranges them from most to least commonly used meanings or from oldest to most modern usage. Many dictionaries also offer information about a word's etymology and usage. With all these functions, then, a dictionary is a basic, essential tool in many situations. Students can turn to a dictionary when they encounter an unfamiliar word or when they see a familiar word used in a new way.

There are many dictionaries to choose from, but perhaps the most highly respected source is the *Oxford English Dictionary* (OED). The OED is a historical dictionary, and as such, all entries include quotes of the word as it has been used throughout history. Users of the OED can get a deeper sense of a word's evolution over time and in different parts of the world. Another standard dictionary in America is *Merriam-Webster*.

Thesaurus

Whereas a dictionary entry lists a word's definitions, a **thesaurus** entry lists a word's synonyms and antonyms—i.e., words with similar and opposite meanings, respectively. A dictionary can be used to find out what a word means and where it came from, and a thesaurus can be used to understand a word's relationship to other words. A thesaurus can be a powerful vocabulary-building tool. By becoming familiar with synonyms and antonyms, students will be more equipped to use a broad range of vocabulary in their speech and writing. Of course, one thing to be aware of when using a thesaurus is that most words do not have exact synonyms. Rather, there are slight nuances of meaning that can make one word more appropriate than another in a given context. In this case, it is often to the user's advantage to consult a thesaurus side-by-side with a dictionary to confirm any differences in usage between two synonyms. Some digital sources, such as *Dictionary.com*, integrate a dictionary and a thesaurus.

Generally, though, a thesaurus is a useful tool to help writers add variety and precision to their word choice. Consulting a thesaurus can help students elevate their writing to an appropriate academic level by replacing vague or overused words with more expressive or academic ones. Also, word processors often offer a built-in thesaurus, making it easy for writers to look up synonyms and vary word choice as they work.

Glossary

A **glossary** is similar to a dictionary in that it offers an explanation of terms. However, while a dictionary attempts to cover every word in a language, a glossary only focuses on those terms relevant to a specific field. Also, a glossary entry is more likely to offer a longer explanation of a term and its relevance within that field. Glossaries are often found at the back of textbooks or other nonfiction publications in order to explain new or unfamiliar terms to readers. A glossary may also be an entire book on its own that covers all of the essential terms and concepts within a particular profession, field, or other specialized area of knowledge. Thus, for learners seeking general definitions of terms from any context, a dictionary is an appropriate reference source, but for students of specialized fields, a glossary will usually provide more in-depth information.

Collaboration with Families and Communities

Family Collaboration

Educate caregivers on reading techniques and offer them resources for teaching at home. For example, you could host workshops on teaching phonics so that caregivers know how to help their children sound out words when reading at home. Suggesting supplemental resources for both parents and students is also a great idea. Parents can benefit from recommendations of literacy activities, books to read with their children, or books and websites that teach them how to help their students succeed in reading.

Make opportunities for caregivers to join your classroom. For example, you could have parents come and read aloud to students in class; alternatively, you could invite caregivers who work in fields that relate to your reading to come and answer questions. When parents spend time in the classroom, they gain a better understanding of their child's abilities and needs. Classroom involvement may also inspire caregivers to spend more time working with their children at home.

Communicate regularly with caregivers. Newsletters, parent/teacher meetings, and meetings where the teacher meets with both the parent and the student are all useful. Communication regarding the class's progress and children's individual needs gives caregivers the information they need to help their students succeed. Communication also encourages caregivers to take an active part in their child's education.

Community Collaboration

Being proactive in the community will help when seeking which groups may be interested in collaboration. Reading specialists should look for partners that share similar values, such as promoting reading, education, or outreach. Common places where people gather, such as a community gym or even a theater company, are ideal because both depend on the community being proactive and prosperous. For example, an independent theater company is a great place to promote literacy programs because plays are both a dramatic and written art form. Organizing a collaborative partnership could bring positive attention to both groups. The students' program would be highlighted and garner support, while the theater company would gain more attention, not only for their performances but also for giving back to the community. Partnerships can be established by any kind of agency, from local charities to large or small businesses.

Connecting with the community is key; one has to engage potential partners in order to assess whether a collaboration can even be possible. Maintaining contact lists will enable the reading specialists to have a pool of potential groups to reach out to and partner with at all times. It is also important to have a clear form of collaboration in place. Will the partner in question sponsor an event, hand out pamphlets on the importance of reading, or host a field trip? Planning collaborative efforts in advance is essential to both parties.

Reading Fluency

Reading Fluency and Comprehension

Reading fluency has been traditionally defined as a student's ability to read accurately, quickly, and with appropriate expression. This definition only accounts for reading aloud, however, so it has been expanded to include silent reading. **Silent reading fluency** is the ability to read more than one word at a time without having to vocalize one's reading. If readers are able to derive the accurate meaning and message from a reading passage without involving too much labor of reading mechanics, they are said to be reading with fluency. Reading fluency is automatic, with less attention and effort spent on decoding, allowing the reader to concentrate fully on reading comprehension. When a reader reaches the fluency stage, reading becomes a much more enjoyable activity.

Generally, fluent readers do not need to reread passages for understanding and have developed a fairly large inventory of sight-word vocabulary. Fluent readers are usually able to self-correct and employ a number of reading strategies. Signs that a child is having difficulty with reading fluency include reading slowly, focusing on only one word at a time, needing to reread the passage for understanding, and stopping often to decipher and decode unknown words. There are three main focus areas that relate to reading fluency: accuracy, rate, and prosody. When children read accurately with steady, consistent speed and appropriate expression, reading comprehension is likely to strengthen.

As children's reading fluency strengthens, they are able to interact on a much higher level with a variety of texts. It is important for educators to recognize that reading fluency acts as a bridge to reading comprehension and that time devoted to the individual components of reading fluency benefits a child's overall reading comprehension.

Accuracy, Rate, and Prosody

Accuracy

Accuracy refers to the frequency of pronunciation errors a student might make when reading. When students make frequent pronunciation errors while reading, guess at the pronunciation of unknown words, or ignore words altogether, they are showing signs of **dysfluency**. Reading accurately requires the reader to read words correctly with minimal to no errors. When errors do occur, readers who read with accuracy are generally able to self-correct and continue reading without interrupting the flow of the reading.

Rate

Rate refers to a student's ability to recognize words automatically without having to spend any time on decoding them. This manifests in their ability to read texts at a steady and consistent rate. Both accurate reading and reading at a consistent rate greatly strengthen a reader's overall reading comprehension.

Prosody

Prosody refers to appropriate expression when reading—showing emotions, such as excitement, panic, or sorrow that accurately matches the intended emotions of the text. Readers may be able to read texts with accuracy and at a steady and consistent rate, but if they are unable to vocalize any expression in their reading or if the expression used does not match the intended expression of the text, their overall comprehension will be negatively affected. Readers who engage in an emotional or personal level with the text will experience greater reading comprehension and fluency.

Strategies to Improve Fluency

Reading accuracy requires that students have a strong understanding of letter-sound correspondence and the ability to accurately blend the sounds together. Providing systematic, explicit instruction in phonemic awareness, phonics, and decoding skills will cultivate such accuracy. When students are readily able to identify high-frequency sight words, their accuracy improves. Therefore, instructors should provide ample opportunities to practice these words.

Reading aloud has proven effective in strengthening reading fluency. Whisper-reading accompanied by teacher monitoring has also proven effective for students who don't yet display automaticity in their decoding skills. Timed reading of sight phrases or stories also improves fluency with respect to rate. During a **timed-reading** exercise, the number of words read in a given amount of time is recorded. Routinely administering timed readings and displaying the results in graphs and charts has been shown to increase student motivation.

Timed-repeated readings, where a student reads and re-reads familiar texts in a given time, is a commonly used instructional strategy to increase reading speed, accuracy, and comprehension. Students read and re-read the passage until they reach their target rate.

Encouraging Independent Reading

Teachers are required to have a classroom library, which should be an inviting environment for students. Small lamps make the area warmer—like home rather than school—and provide extra light for reading. Furniture—such as beanbag chairs, pillows, and small chairs—allows students to get comfortable, rather than reading at their desk. Not only is the environment important, but the reading center must also be an organized, designated space. If books are disorganized in the classroom library, students may be deterred from using the space appropriately, simply because they cannot find what they are looking for or out of sheer frustration. Organizing books by theme or genre helps students search for the books they desire. For students in younger grades, books should be grouped in plastic tubs using picture and word category labels like "animals" or "holidays." This organization method is especially helpful to those learning to read.

Having a bookshelf with the teacher's or students' text selections may encourage readers to select a good book quickly. Some students enjoy re-reading a book from a teacher read-aloud; therefore, placing it in the "teacher's pick" area may encourage developing readers to pick it up. Students also like to follow their classmates. Therefore, teachers should have a section where students can place a book that they want to recommend to their friends. Older students can fill out brief recommendation sheets that briefly list a few of the book's main themes so that potential readers can see if they are interested in reading it. Reading from basal readers and school texts does not necessarily encourage reading for pleasure, as these texts are chosen by the school and instructor. For this reason, silent reading time is so important. Silent reading time gives students options and a chance to make their own choices. Students can choose the book and the appropriate reading pace when reading independently.

Independent reading strategies promote healthy reading for pleasure and enjoyment. Hopefully, these strategies promote a lifelong love of reading. Students should be given daily, independent reading time in the classroom. Teachers phrase this time as **D.E.A.R.** or "Drop Everything and Read" time. Typically, this time can be incorporated into a teacher's reading block. It is suggested that students have about 20 minutes of D.E.A.R. time daily. Students can read a book from home, the library, or one selected from the variety of books found within the classroom.

Reading Comprehension and Applications

Basics of Reading Comprehension

Comprehension is defined as the level of understanding of content that a child demonstrates during and after the reading of a given text. Comprehension begins well before a child is able to read. Adults and educators can foster comprehension by reading aloud to children and helping them respond to the content and relate it to their prior knowledge. Throughout the reading process, the child asks and answers relevant questions confirming her or his comprehension and is able to successfully summarize the text upon completion.

Since reading comprehension encompasses several cognitive processes, including the awareness and understanding of phonemes, phonics, and the ability to construct meaning from text, educators should employ reading comprehension strategies prior to, during, and after reading. Reading comprehension is a lifelong process. As the genres of written text change and written language becomes more complex, it is essential that educators continually reinforce reading comprehension strategies throughout a student's educational career.

Some instructional strategies to consider are:

- Pre-teaching new vocabulary
- Monitoring for understanding
- Answering and generating questions
- Summarizing

Levels of Reading Comprehension

Literal Comprehension

Literal comprehension refers to the reader's ability to understand the actual meaning of texts. This is not meant to be complicated. It means literally understanding the facts, setting, plot, etc. of what is being read.

To bolster literal comprehension, show students how to ask pertinent questions. When they are reading stories, children should learn to ask who the characters are, what happened, where the story is taking place, and in what order the events occurred.

Inferential Comprehension

Inferential comprehension requires students to understand the hidden context or unstated meaning of a text. They should be able to explain why an action occurred and what they think will happen next.

When it comes to inferential comprehension, children need to recall the facts that occurred in the story and what those facts represent. They should ask the following questions:

Why did this happen?
How might the characters feel?
What might happen next?
How important is "X" character?

Evaluative Comprehension

Evaluative comprehension can be a matter of opinion; the student will make a judgment about the moral or definitive meaning of a piece of writing.

Evaluative comprehension involves questions about the moral of the story. Students primarily need to ask, "what does this story teach us?" If there is a conflict in the story, they need to ask, "how can this be solved? Is "X" character right or wrong?" The students should also freely express how they felt about the story and if they like the way it was written.

These three levels of comprehension are all part of critical thinking. Critical thinking allows students to identify if there are any biases in a story. They will be able to organize the information they have learned to form stronger opinions about what they read. They will also become stronger readers.

Critical thinking is difficult to teach because it depends on the comprehension skills of the people doing the thinking. Different types of reading material also call for different types of analysis. As teachers, your best bet is to encourage critical thinking at every opportunity. Standard strategies that encourage critical thinking include assigning various types of reading materials and topics, asking students to recall what they have read, and giving assignments that make them elaborate on the reading.

Transitioning from "Learning to Read" to "Reading to Learn"

To help students transition from "learning to read" to "reading to learn," consider the following well-researched tactics.

Set a Purpose for Reading

Students are motivated to read when they have a purpose for doing so. They are more likely to pay attention to the text and observe important details that they may have glossed over otherwise.

To help students set a purpose for reading, consider setting a few guidelines for them. For example, you could ask them to read until a certain point in the story, then ask them to identify the setting, main characters, and/or problem in the story. This can also ensure that the students have comprehended what they've read so far.

Reinforce what your students have read by assigning activities. Ask them to recount the stories in their own words, draw pictures of what happened in the stories, take notes as they go along, or write down details of how certain characters change over the course of the stories.

Eventually, students will learn to set a purpose for reading on their own. Remind them that there are different reasons to read, such as enjoyment or learning more about a topic.

Apply Knowledge of Text Structures

Many students struggle with identifying text structures such as sequences, comparisons, descriptions, problems, solutions, causes, and effects. Recognition of these structures helps students process what they read.

To help students identify text structures, you can teach them to identify key details in each sentence. Questions like, "What is the problem presented in this sentence?" or, "What are the keywords in this statement?" are helpful. Testing students on the vocabulary used in the texts they read and having them write summaries can also help them understand text structures.

Use Text Features

Text features help readers identify the primary ideas being presented in the text. Common features include titles, headings, introductory and closing paragraphs, the first sentence in a paragraph, and questions at the end of the text. Visuals, like photos, maps, tables, and charts are also text features.

Each of these features helps inform the reader of what is happening in the text. If students are having trouble understanding the subject matter they are reading, remind them to go back and re-read each feature. Ask them questions about what they've read or observed. You can create text feature cards for them to fill out as they read, like the following:

Text Feature: What information does this feature tell me?	Text Feature: What information does this feature tell me?
Text Feature: What information does this feature tell me?	Text Feature: What information does this feature tell me?

Strategies to Enhance Reading Comprehension

Structural Patterns of a Text

Teaching students text structure helps them to search for information when answering questions about the text. This again integrates reading and writing strategies when learning about comprehension. Text needs should be written in a logical way. Consistent and logical written thoughts aid in comprehension and help readers find information easier within the text, especially when trying to locate answers to comprehension questions. Students should recall that the broader meaning of text is located at the beginning of a story, and more specific details are provided throughout the text. Subtitles will help students locate information they are seeking.

Author's Point of View

It is important for readers to understand an author's purpose for writing a text. They need to identify the author's opinion in order to appropriately identify the facts that are being presented. Many standardized tests require students to identify an author's point of view and perspective and requires the use of inferential reading comprehension skills.

Generalizing the Knowledge Learned from Texts to Other Areas of Learning

Reading comprehension strategies are essential when studying other subject areas. Reading, writing, and language are built upon each other. In addition to these, social studies and the sciences are more complex disciplines that require basic knowledge of comprehension. Students who have mastered areas of reading, writing, and language will often perform better in other more difficult subject areas than those who have yet to obtain comprehension skills.

Identifying Similarities and Differences Between Texts

Oftentimes students need to compare and contrast different texts. As noted previously, Venn diagrams are a great way to compare and contrast texts. Venn diagrams allow students to relate information across a wide range of texts. This helps reading comprehension, as students need to utilize higher thinking skills and identify the relationships amongst more than one text.

Different Types of Texts

Writing can be classified under four passage types: narrative, expository, descriptive (sometimes called technical), and persuasive. Though these types are not mutually exclusive, one form tends to dominate the rest. By recognizing the *type* of passage you're reading, you gain insight into *how* you should read. If you're reading a narrative, you can assume the author intends to entertain, which means you may skim the text without losing meaning. A technical document might require a close read because skimming the passage might cause the reader to miss salient details.

1. **Narrative** writing, at its core, is the art of storytelling. For a narrative to exist, certain elements must be present. First, it must have characters. While many characters are human, characters could be defined as anything that thinks, acts, and talks like a human. For example, many recent movies, such as *Lord of the Rings* and *The Chronicles of Narnia*, include animals, fantastical creatures, and even trees that behave like humans. Second, it must have a plot or sequence of events. Typically, those events follow a standard plot diagram, but recent trends start *in medias res* or in the middle (near the climax). In this instance, foreshadowing and flashbacks often fill in plot details. Finally, along with characters and a plot, there must also be conflict. Conflict is usually divided into two types: internal and external. Internal conflict indicates the character is in turmoil and is presented through the character's thoughts. External conflicts are visible. Types of external conflict include a person versus nature, another person, or society.

2. **Expository** writing is detached and to the point. Since expository writing is designed to instruct or inform, it usually involves directions and steps written in second person ("you" voice) and lacks any persuasive or narrative elements. Sequence words such as *first*, *second*, and *third*, or *in the first place*, *secondly*, and *lastly* are often given to add fluency and cohesion. Common examples of expository writing include instructor's lessons, cookbook recipes, and repair manuals.

3. Due to its empirical nature, **technical** writing is filled with steps, charts, graphs, data, and statistics. The goal of technical writing is to advance understanding in a field through the scientific method. Experts such as teachers, doctors, or mechanics use words unique to the profession in which they operate. These words, which often incorporate acronyms, are called *jargon*. Technical writing is a type of expository writing but is not meant to be understood by the general public. Instead, technical writers assume readers have received a formal education in a particular field of study and need no explanation as to what the jargon means. Imagine a doctor trying to understand a diagnostic reading for a car or a mechanic trying to interpret lab results. Only professionals with proper training will fully comprehend the text.

4. **Persuasive** writing is designed to change opinions and attitudes. The topic, stance, and arguments are found in the thesis, positioned near the end of the introduction. Later supporting paragraphs offer relevant quotations, paraphrases, and summaries from primary or secondary sources, which are then interpreted, analyzed, and evaluated. The goal of persuasive writers is not to stack quotes but to develop original ideas by using sources as a starting point. Good persuasive writing makes powerful arguments with valid sources and thoughtful analysis. Poor persuasive writing is riddled with bias and logical fallacies. Sometimes logical and illogical arguments are sandwiched together in the same piece. Therefore, readers should display skepticism when reading persuasive arguments.

Making Connections Between Multiple Texts

When analyzing two or more texts, there are several different aspects that need to be considered, particularly the styles (or the artful way in which the authors use diction to deliver a theme), points of view, and types of argument. In order to do so, one should compare and contrast the following elements between the texts:

- Style: narrative, persuasive, descriptive, informative, etc.
- Tone: sarcastic, angry, somber, humorous, etc.
- Sentence structure: simple (1 clause) compound (2 clauses), complex-compound (3 clauses)

- Punctuation choice: question marks, exclamation points, periods, dashes, etc.
- Point of view: first person, second person, third person
- Paragraph structure: long, short, both, differences between the two
- Organizational structure: compare/contrast, problem/solution, chronological, etc.

The following two passages concern the theme of death and are presented to demonstrate how to evaluate the above elements:

Passage I

Death occurs in several stages. The first stage is the pre-active stage, which occurs a few days to weeks before death, in which the desire to eat and drink decreases, and the person may feel restless, irritable, and anxious. The second stage is the active stage, where the skin begins to cool, breathing becomes difficult as the lungs become congested (known as the "death rattle"), and the person loses control of their bodily fluids.

Once death occurs, there are also two stages. The first is clinical death, when the heart stops pumping blood and breathing ceases. This stage lasts approximately 4-6 minutes, and during this time, it is possible for a victim to be resuscitated via CPR or a defibrillator. After 6 minutes however, the oxygen stores within the brain begin to deplete, and the victim enters biological death. This is the point of no return, as the cells of the brain and vital organs begin to die, a process that is irreversible.

Passage II

It was her sister Josephine who told her, in broken sentences; veiled hints that revealed in half concealing. Her husband's friend Richards was there, too, near her. It was he who had been in the newspaper office when intelligence of the railroad disaster was received, with Brently Mallard's name leading the list of "killed." He had only taken the time to assure himself of its truth by a second telegram, and had hastened to forestall any less careful, less tender friend in bearing the sad message.

She did not hear the story as many women have heard the same, with a paralyzed inability to accept its significance. She wept at once, with sudden, wild abandonment, in her sister's arms. When the storm of grief had spent itself she went away to her room alone. She would have no one follow her.

There stood, facing the open window, a comfortable, roomy armchair. Into this she sank, pressed down by a physical exhaustion that haunted her body and seemed to reach into her soul.

Excerpt from "The Story of an Hour" by Kate Chopin

Now, using the outline above, the similarities and differences between the two passages are considered:

1. **Style:** Passage I is an expository style, presenting purely factual evidence on death, completely devoid of emotion. Passage II is a narrative style, where the theme of death is presented to us by the reaction of the loved ones involved. This narrative style is full of emotional language and imagery.

2. **Tone:** Passage I has no emotionally-charged words of any kind, and seems to view death simply as a process that happens, neither welcoming nor fearing it. The tone in this passage, therefore, is neutral. Passage II does not have a neutral tone—it uses words like "disaster," "killed," "sad," "wept," "wild abandonment," and "physical exhaustion," implying an anxiety toward the theme of death.

3. **Sentence Structure:** Passage I contains many complex-compound sentences, which are used to accommodate lots of information. The structure of these sentences contributes to the overall informative

nature of the selection. Passage II has several compound sentences and complex sentences on their own. It's also marked by the use of many commas in a single sentence, separating modifying words. Perhaps this variety is meant to match the sporadic emotion of the character's discovery of her husband's death.

4. **Punctuation Choice:** Passage I uses only commas and periods, which adds to the overall neutral tone of the selection. Passage II mostly uses commas and periods, and then one semicolon. Again, the excess of commas and semicolon in the first sentence may be said to mirror the character's anxiety.

5. **Point of View:** Passage I uses third-person point of view, as it avoids any first- or second-person pronouns. Passage II also uses third-person point of view, as the story is being told by a narrator about characters separate from the narrator.

6. **Paragraph Structure:** The first passage is told in an objective way, and each paragraph is focused on the topic brought up in the first sentence. The second passage has no specific topic per paragraph. It is organized in a sequential way, so the paragraphs flow into the next in a chronological order.

7. **Organizational Structure:** The structure of Passage I is told in a very objective, organized way. The first paragraph tells of the stages before death, and the second paragraph tells of the stages after death. The second passage is told in chronological order, as a sequence of events, like in a fictional story.

When analyzing the different structures, it may be helpful to make a table and use single words to compare and contrast the texts:

Elements	**Passage I**	**Passage II**
Style	Expository	Narrative
Tone	Neutral	Emotional
Sentence Structure	Long	Long/Sporadic
Punctuation Choice	.	. and ,
Point of View	Third	Third
Paragraph Structure	Focused	Sequential
Organizational Structure	Objective/Logical	Chronological

The main differences between the two selections are style, tone, and structure. Possibly the most noticeable difference is the style and tone, as one tone is more neutral, and the other tone is more emotional. This is due to the word choice used and how each passage treats the topic of death. These are only a handful of the endless possible interpretations the reader could make.

Summarizing and Paraphrasing

A summary is a shortened version of the original text, written by the reader in their own words. In order to effectively summarize a more complex text, it is necessary to fully understand the original source, and to highlight the major points covered. It may be helpful to outline the original text to get a big picture view of it, and to avoid getting bogged down in the minor details. For example, a summary wouldn't need to include a specific statistic from the original source unless it was the major focus of the piece. Also, it's important for readers to use their own words, but to retain the original meaning of the passage. The key to a good summary is to emphasize the main idea without changing the focus of the original information.

Paraphrasing calls for the reader to take a small part of the passage and list or describe its main points. Paraphrasing is more than rewording the original passage, though. As with summary, a paraphrase should be written in the reader's own words, while still retaining the meaning of the original source. The main difference between summarizing and paraphrasing is the length of the original passage. A summary would be appropriate for a much larger piece, while paraphrase might focus on just a few lines of text. Effective paraphrasing will indicate an understanding of the original source, yet still help the reader expand on their interpretation. A paraphrase should neither add new information nor remove essential facts that will change the meaning of the source.

Facts and Opinions

It is important to distinguish between facts and opinions when reading a piece of writing. When an author presents **facts**, such as statistics or data, readers should be able to check those facts to verify that they are accurate. When authors share their own thoughts and feelings about a subject, they are expressing their **opinions**.

Authors often use words like *think, feel, believe,* or *in my opinion* when expressing an opinion, but these words won't always appear in an opinion piece, especially if it is formally written. An author's opinion may be backed up by facts, which gives it more credibility, but that opinion should not be taken as fact. A critical reader should be wary of an author's opinion, especially if it is only supported by other opinions.

Fact	Opinion
There are nine innings in a game of baseball.	Baseball games run too long.
James Garfield was assassinated on July 2, 1881.	James Garfield was a good president.
McDonald's® has stores in 118 countries.	McDonald's® has the best hamburgers.

Critical readers examine the facts used to support an author's argument. They check the facts against other sources to be sure those facts are correct. They also check the validity of the sources used to be sure those sources are credible, academic, and/or peer-reviewed. When an author uses another person's opinion to support his or her argument, even if it is an expert's opinion, it is still only an opinion and should not be taken as fact. A strong argument uses valid, measurable facts to support ideas. Even then, the reader may disagree with the argument.

An authoritative argument may use the facts to sway the reader. In the example of global warming, many experts differ in their opinions of which alternative fuels can be used to aid in offsetting it. Because of this, a writer may choose to only use the information and experts' opinions that supports his or her viewpoint. For example, if the argument is that wind energy is the best solution, the author will use facts that support this idea. That same author may leave out relevant facts on solar energy. The way the author uses facts can influence the reader, so it's important to consider the facts being used, how those facts are being presented, and what information might be left out.

Authors can also demonstrate **bias** if they ignore an opposing viewpoint or present their side in an unbalanced way. A strong argument considers the opposition and finds a way to refute it. Critical readers should look for an unfair or one-sided presentation of the argument and be skeptical, as a bias may be present. Even if this bias is unintentional, if it exists in the writing, the reader should be wary of the validity of the argument.

Readers should also look for the use of stereotypes that refer to specific groups. **Stereotypes** are often negative connotations about a person or place and should always be avoided. When a critical reader finds stereotypes in a piece of writing, he or she should immediately be critical of the argument and consider the validity of anything the author presents. Stereotypes reveal a flaw in the writer's thinking and may suggest a lack of knowledge or understanding about the subject.

Metacognitive Skills

Metacognitive Skills

Metacognitive strategies ask the student to decode text passages. In part, they require the student to preview text, be able to recognize unfamiliar words, then use context clues to define them for greater understanding. In addition, meta-cognitive strategies in the classroom employ skills such as being able to decode imagery, being able to predict, and being able to summarize. If a student can define unfamiliar vocabulary, make sense of an author's use of imagery, preview text prior to reading, predict outcomes during reading, and summarize the material, he or she is achieving effective reading comprehension. When approaching reading instruction, the teacher who encourages students to use phrases such as *I'm noticing*, *I'm thinking*, and *I'm wondering* is teaching a meta-cognitive type strategy.

Strategies to Help Read New and/or Difficult Words

Children who are developing reading fluency and comprehension skills can become frustrated when presented with unfamiliar words in a given text. With direct phonics instruction, educators can teach children to decode words and then use context clues to define the words while reading. If children have a strong enough understanding of language structures, including nouns and verbs, educators can ask them to consider what part of speech the unknown word might be based on and where it might fit into the sentence. Other useful strategies involve **self-monitoring**, in which children are asked to think as they read and ask themselves if what they have just read makes sense. Focusing on visual clues, such as drawings and photographs, may give children valuable insight into deciphering unknown words. Looking for the word in another section of the text to see how it relates to the overall meaning could give a clue to the new vocabulary word. Spelling the word out loud or looking for word chunks, prefixes, and suffixes, as well as demonstrating how to segment the unknown word into its individual syllables, may also be effective strategies to employ.

One of the most valuable strategies, however, for helping children to read and understand new words is pre-teaching. In this strategy, educators select what they evaluate to be the unfamiliar words in the text and then introduce them to the class before reading. Educators using this method should be careful not to simply ask the children to read the text and then spell the new words correctly. They should also provide clear definitions and give the children the opportunity to read these words in various sentences to decipher word meaning. This method can dramatically reduce how often children stop reading in order to reflect on unknown words. Educators are often unsure as to whether to correct every mispronounced word a child makes when reading. If the mispronounced word still makes sense, it is sometimes better to allow the child to continue to read, since the more the child stops, the more the child's reading comprehension and fluency are negatively affected.

Selecting Diverse Texts

In recent years, there has been a growing emphasis on including diverse texts in the classroom. Diverse texts are books that include characters from minority groups. There are two central reasons for this change. First, students have an easier time relating to characters who share their culture and background; hence, diverse texts help students from minority groups feel included in the classroom and engage with the readings. Diverse texts empower minority students by giving them representation in the classroom, and they also help majority students expand their horizons and develop cultural awareness.

Here are some important criteria to consider when choosing diverse texts for the classroom.

The book should depict cultural differences accurately. Books that reinforce stereotypes or contain false information will do more harm than good.

While the diversity of the students in your classroom can guide your choice of books, it should not limit the scope of the diverse literature you choose. Books about any culture in your community, country, or even the world will help students understand and empathize with other people.

One purpose of diverse literature is to teach children how to correctly interact with people from different cultures. Books should model positive interactions and/or provide meaningful engagement with social issues.

While diverse literature is an essential component of any curriculum, it is best to intersperse these texts with books that feature characters and settings that are familiar to the majority of your students. Since students are most engaged when they can relate to the characters about whom they are reading, not every book needs to be about different cultures.

Teachers should also take their students' interests into account when choosing texts. Consider the surrounding community, as well as any common interests that your students share. Do most of your students live on farms, or are you teaching in an urban community? Are your students always talking about a certain topic or animal? Think about your students' interests, and then choose books that involve those issues.

Various Literary Genres

Fictional Prose

Fiction written in prose can be further broken down into **fiction genres**—types of fiction. Some of the more common genres of fiction are as follows:

- **Classical fiction**: a work of fiction considered timeless in its message or theme, remaining noteworthy and meaningful over decades or centuries—e.g., Charlotte Brontë's *Jane Eyre*, Mark Twain's *Adventures of Huckleberry Finn*
- **Fables**: short fiction that generally features animals, fantastic creatures, or other forces within nature that assume human-like characters and has a moral lesson for the reader—e.g., *Aesop's Fables*
- **Fairy tales**: children's stories with magical characters in imaginary, enchanted lands, usually depicting a struggle between good and evil, a sub-genre of folklore—e.g., Hans Christian Anderson's *The Little Mermaid, Cinderella* by the Brothers Grimm
- **Fantasy**: fiction with magic or supernatural elements that cannot occur in the real world, sometimes involving medieval elements in language, usually includes some form of sorcery or witchcraft and sometimes set on a different world—e.g., J.R.R. Tolkien's *The Hobbit*, J.K. Rowling's *Harry Potter and the Sorcerer's Stone*, George R.R. Martin's *A Game of Thrones*
- **Folklore**: types of fiction passed down from oral tradition, stories indigenous to a particular region or culture, with a local flavor in tone, designed to help humans cope with their condition in life and validate cultural traditions, beliefs, and customs—e.g., William Laughead's *Paul Bunyan and The Blue Ox*, the Buddhist story of "The Banyan Deer"

- **Mythology**: closely related to folklore but more widespread, features mystical, otherworldly characters and addresses the basic question of why and how humans exist, relies heavily on allegory and features gods or heroes captured in some sort of struggle—e.g., Greek myths, Genesis I and II in the Bible, Arthurian legends

- **Science fiction**: fiction that uses the principle of extrapolation—loosely defined as a form of prediction—to imagine future realities and problems of the human experience—e.g., Robert Heinlein's *Stranger in a Strange Land*, Ayn Rand's *Anthem*, Isaac Asimov's *I, Robot*, Philip K. Dick's *Do Androids Dream of Electric Sheep?*

- **Short stories**: short works of prose fiction with fully-developed themes and characters, focused on mood, generally developed with a single plot, with a short period of time for settings—e.g., Edgar Allan Poe's "Fall of the House of Usher," Shirley Jackson's "The Lottery," Isaac Bashevis Singer's "Gimpel the Fool"

Drama

Drama refers to a form of literature written for the purpose of performance for an audience. Like prose fiction, drama has several genres. The following are the most common ones:

- **Comedy**: a humorous play designed to amuse and entertain, often with an emphasis on the common person's experience, generally resolved in a positive way—e.g., Richard Sheridan's *School for Scandal*, Shakespeare's *Taming of the Shrew*, Neil Simon's *The Odd Couple*

- **History**: a play based on recorded history where the fate of a nation or kingdom is at the core of the conflict—e.g., Christopher Marlowe's *Edward II*, Shakespeare's *King Richard III*, Arthur Miller's *The Crucible*

- **Tragedy**: a serious play that often involves the downfall of the protagonist. In modern tragedies, the protagonist is not necessarily in a position of power or authority—e.g., Jean Racine's *Phèdre*, Arthur Miller's *Death of a Salesman*, John Steinbeck's *Of Mice and Men*

- **Melodrama**: a play that emphasizes heightened emotion and sensationalism, generally with stereotypical characters in exaggerated or realistic situations and with moral polarization—e.g., Jean-Jacques Rousseau's *Pygmalion*

- **Tragi-comedy**: a play that has elements of both tragedy—a character experiencing a tragic loss—and comedy—the resolution is often positive with no clear distinctive mood for either—e.g., Shakespeare's *The Merchant of Venice*, Anton Chekhov's *The Cherry Orchard*

Poetry

The genre of **poetry** refers to literary works that focus on the expression of feelings and ideas through the use of structure and linguistic rhythm to create a desired effect.

Different poetic structures and devices are used to create the various major forms of poetry. Some of the most common forms are discussed in the following chart.

Type	Poetic Structure	Example
Ballad	A poem or song passed down orally which tells a story and in English tradition usually uses an ABAB or ABCB rhyme scheme	William Butler Yeats' "The Ballad of Father O'Hart"
Epic	A long poem from ancient oral tradition which narrates the story of a legendary or heroic protagonist	Homer's *The Odyssey* Virgil's *The Aeneid*
Haiku	A Japanese poem of three unrhymed lines with five, seven, and five syllables (in English) with nature as a common subject matter	Matsuo Bashō "An old silent pond ... A frog jumps into the pond, splash! Silence again."
Limerick	A five-line poem written in an AABBA rhyme scheme, with a witty focus	From Edward Lear's *Book of Nonsense*: "There was a Young Person of Smyrna Whose grandmother threatened to burn her ..."
Ode	A formal lyric poem that addresses and praises a person, place, thing, or idea	Edna St. Vincent Millay's "Ode to Silence"
Sonnet	A fourteen-line poem written in iambic pentameter	Shakespeare's Sonnets 18 and 130

Literary Nonfiction

Nonfiction works are best characterized by their subject matter, which must be factual and real, describing true life experiences. There are several common types of literary non-fiction.

Biography

A **biography** is a work written about a real person (historical or currently living). It involves factual accounts of the person's life, often in a re-telling of those events based on available, researched factual information. The re-telling and dialogue, especially if related within quotes, must be accurate and reflect reliable sources. A biography reflects the time and place in which the person lived, with the goal of creating an understanding of the person and his/her human experience. Examples of well-known biographies include *The Life of Samuel Johnson* by James Boswell and *Steve Jobs* by Walter Isaacson.

Autobiography

An **autobiography** is a factual account of a person's life written by that person. It may contain some or all of the same elements as a biography, but the author is the subject matter. An autobiography will be told in first person narrative. Examples of well-known autobiographies in literature include *Night* by Elie Wiesel and *Margaret Thatcher: The Autobiography* by Margaret Thatcher.

Memoir

A **memoir** is a historical account of a person's life and experiences written by one who has personal, intimate knowledge of the information. The line between memoir, autobiography, and biography is often muddled, but generally speaking, a memoir covers a specific timeline of events as opposed to the other forms of nonfiction. A memoir is less all-encompassing. It is also less formal in tone and tends to focus on the emotional aspect of the presented timeline of events. Some examples of memoirs in literature include *Angela's Ashes* by Frank McCourt and *All Creatures Great and Small* by James Herriot.

Journalism

Some forms of **journalism** can fall into the category of literary non-fiction—e.g., travel writing, nature writing, sports writing, the interview, and sometimes, the essay. Some examples include Elizabeth Kolbert's "The Lost World, in the Annals of Extinction series for *The New Yorker* and Gary Smith's "Ali and His Entourage" for ***Sports Illustrated***.

Vocabulary Development

Effective Methods for Teaching Vocabulary

The TEKS for ELAR provide requirements for helping students in kindergarten through grade 6 with their vocabulary development. Here is some of the advice as laid out in chapter 110.

1. Texts should grow more challenging over the course of the school year to improve vocabulary.

   Students should be exposed to a variety of literature to help grow their vocabularies. Along the way, they should be learning basic sentence structure and grammar.

2. Special attention should be given to **English language learners (ELLs)**, or students for whom English is a second language.

   These students are exposed to grammar in multiple languages, which can either put them at an advantage or disadvantage. Incorporate elements from their native languages to help them engage in decoding exercises and discourse.

3. Employ different word-learning strategies to help students of varying abilities increase their vocabularies.

   Use flash cards, pop quizzes, or visual images so that children can associate words with certain images or actions. They should learn how to look up terms in dictionaries, thesauruses, and web search engines.

The TEKS for ELAR go on to describe the importance of frequent exposure to new vocabulary. Repeated exposure increases students' comprehension levels and response skills. This will prompt clearer communication with adults and their peers. They will also learn various nuances of language, such as inflection.

The guidelines frequently mention integrating the seven strands of knowledge into lesson plans. Doing so will make students more proficient learners, especially when it comes to language arts. Ultimately, children in kindergarten through grade 6 should feel confident enough to work on their self-sustained reading. Regular instruction focused on vocabulary development will meet the TEKS guidelines for ELAR as well as help children become better students.

Vocabulary in Informational Texts

Vocabulary used throughout informational texts is generally quite different than vocabulary found in fictional print. For this reason, it is imperative that educators help children strengthen and increase their vocabulary inventory so that they can eventually become successful at reading and understanding informational text.

For instance, educators can point out *signal words* throughout texts to help children more readily and accurately identify the author's purpose. Authors employ specific vocabulary that spotlight their intent. For instance, if authors wish to list examples to support a main idea, they may use vocabulary such as *for example*, *such as*, or *as illustrated*. When displaying the chronological order of events, authors may use *first*, *lastly*, *before*, and *finally*. Some common compare and contrast vocabulary words include *but*, *same as*, *similar to*, *as opposed to*, and *however*. There are several key phrases that signal cause and effect relationships, including *because of*, *as a result of*, and *in order to*.

By using word walls and personal dictionaries, sorting vocabulary words according to theme, introducing text maps, and teaching children to become familiar with sidebars and glossaries in informational texts, educators will help expand their students' vocabularies and strengthen their abilities to read and comprehend informational texts successfully.

Range of Vocabularies

There are three tiers of vocabulary:

Tier 1 is composed of basic vocabulary words that appear often in everyday speech (for example, "cat," "run," "almost"). Teachers do not usually need to teach these words, as children know them before entering grade school. Because they are so familiar, they make excellent words for new readers.

Tier 2 features words that occur fairly often in English but are more complicated than Tier 1 words or have multiple meanings. For example, "profitable," "eager," and "execute" are all Tier 2 words. This is the level of vocabulary in which students progress furthest during their education, and it is often used to measure student progress.

Tier 3 includes words that appear only in specialized contexts. Students typically learn these words in context; for example, students learn "heterozygous" in biology class and "Industrial Revolution" in history.

There are also two types of vocabulary knowledge:

Recognition refers to a student's ability to understand a word. For example, a student who understands the word "heinous" when it appears but would be unable to think of the word without reading or hearing it demonstrates recognition.

Production is the capacity to use the word properly without reading or hearing it. A student who can use the word "aptitude" correctly without being prompted is said to be *producing* the word. Production necessitates a deeper level of vocabulary knowledge than recognition, as the student must remember the word well enough to think of it by themselves.

Reinforcing Activities

When teaching your students new words, the most important factor is timing. Teaching words before students encounter them in a text helps students avoid confusion while reading. This method is useful for students who struggle with reading comprehension, and it can help make complex texts less overwhelming. For example, you might want to pre-teach words before your students read a book that includes many new scientific words. However, this teaching method can easily become boring. Make sure to engage students by giving examples, using the word in context, and using pictures for younger students.

Teaching students words as they encounter them in the text is useful because it is easier to learn words in context instead of relying on a definition. However, this method will be too disruptive if the text is full of new words. So while a teacher could certainly teach words like "simultaneous" as they appear in a novel, teaching a long list of scientific words as they appear would break up the reading too much and frustrate the students.

Teaching words after students have completed the reading is useful when you are teaching children how to define new words by themselves. For example, the teacher could have students write down words they do not understand and look them up in a dictionary.

Teachers should also teach students word learning strategies so that they can gain vocabulary by themselves. Here are some effective strategies.

Teaching students how to use **dictionaries** enables them to learn words independently. You can engage students by having them collect and define new words in a text, or by holding competitions to see who can use the dictionary faster.

Contextual clues are the elements of a text that surround a word and hint at its meaning. For example, consider the following sentence: "He decided to litigate, so he hired a lawyer." A student could guess that "litigate" means "sue" by recognizing the cause-and-effect relationship between "decided to litigate" and "hired a lawyer." In this case, "so" is the contextual clue. Another example of a contextual clue is contrast. If a student reads that "dogs are energetic, but cats are lethargic," they can use the word "but" to determine that "lethargic" is the opposite of "energetic."

Morphemic analysis is defining words by breaking them into parts. A morpheme is a word part or unit of meaning; for example, the word "tirelessness" includes the morphemes "tire," "less," and "ness." If students know that "less" means "without" and "ness" turns adjectives into nouns, they can deduce the meaning of "tirelessness."

Reading, Inquiry, and Research

Types of Sources

With a wealth of information at people's fingertips in this digital age, it's important to know not only the type of information one is looking for, but also in what medium one is most likely to find it. Information needs to be specific and reliable. For example, if someone is repairing a car, an encyclopedia would be mostly useless. While an encyclopedia might include information about cars, an owner's manual will contain the specific information needed for repairs. Information must also be credible, or trustworthy. A well-known newspaper may have reliable information, but a peer-reviewed journal article will have likely gone through a more rigorous check for validity. Determining **bias** can be helpful in determining credibility. If the information source (person, organization, or company) has something to gain from the reader forming a certain view on a topic, it's likely the information is skewed. For example, if trying to find the unemployment rate, the Bureau of Labor Statistics is a more credible source than a politician's speech.

Primary sources are best defined as records or items that serve as historical evidence. To be considered primary, the source documents or objects must have been created during the time period in which they reference. Examples include diaries, newspaper articles, speeches, government documents, photographs, and historical artifacts. In today's digital age, primary sources, which were once in print, are often embedded in secondary sources. **Secondary sources**—such as websites, history books, databases, or reviews—contain analysis or commentary on primary sources. Secondary sources borrow information from primary sources through the process of quoting, summarizing, or paraphrasing.

Today's students often complete research online through **electronic sources**. Electronic sources offer advantages over print and can be accessed on virtually any computer, while libraries or other research centers are limited to fixed locations and specific catalogs. Electronic sources are also efficient and yield massive amounts of data in seconds. The user can tailor a search based on key words, publication years, and article length. Lastly, many

databases provide the user with instant citations, saving the user the trouble of manually assembling sources for a bibliography.

Although electronic sources yield powerful results, researchers must use caution. While there are many reputable and reliable sources on the internet, just as many are unreliable or biased sources. It's up to the researcher to examine and verify the reliability of sources. *Wikipedia*, for example, may or may not be accurate, depending on the contributor. Many databases, such as *EBSCO* or *SIRS*, offer peer-reviewed articles, meaning the publications have been reviewed for the quality and accuracy of their content.

Instructional Strategies for Comprehension of Abstract Content in Written Materials

It is important for students to be exposed to a variety of texts, reading materials, and resources. To become well-rounded readers, teachers should provide students with expository texts in addition to the classroom textbooks. Key characteristics of informational and expository texts include informative facts about a specific topic. Since these are nonfiction texts, diagrams or other graphic aids may be used to assist in understanding the text. Other forms of informational text include news articles, research journals, educational magazines with informational text, and websites. These texts can be used in small groups or can be introduced in whole group instruction, and then further explored in small intervention groups. Intervention groups are useful because they allow small groups of students to focus more intently on a particular problem, area of instruction, or topic than can be achieved by the group as a whole. They can be used both to address particular issues experienced by readers who are less fluent and to allow more advanced students to explore a particular topic of interest in greater depth.

Fact-based understanding and the use of textual evidence is imperative in expository and informational texts. Students should be able to compare and contrast two different texts and identify problems and solutions as well as cause and effect. Graphic organizers arranged chronologically can help students take notes when covering nonfiction texts. Students need to have the correct order of events in a nonfiction piece in order to identify the cause of an event, as well as the effect it had on problems and solutions. At times, students may need to compare and contrast two texts to identify the similarity of facts, the differences in reported facts, or note any bias from the author. Using knowledge of writing standards and instruction can aid students' understanding of informational text. When comprehending an informative text's objective, students should utilize their prior knowledge of the topic, prior writing assignments, and concluding sentences in the text. This is another example of how reading comprehension and writing go hand-in-hand in the learning process, and how writing and language become important to student comprehension.

Elements That Aid in Interpretation and Comprehension

Graphic Features

Graphics always help interpret a story or text. Younger learners rely on pictures to help tell the story, while older students use diagrams, maps, and charts to aid in understanding texts. Even for adults, graphic features assist with visualizing the text. Charts and diagrams help organize information into clear and concise patterns. Maps help understand specific places and locations. Illustrations help visualize a fictional story. Furthermore, illustrations with captions help visualize nonfiction and fiction texts, particularly when paired with captions that provide an explanation of why the illustration is important.

Locating Information

In informational texts, certain features function to organize the information and also act as guides, which in turn supports the reader's overall comprehension.

Headings include titles and subtitles that identify the topic of study. They also help a reader to arrive at a clearer understanding with regard to the text's main idea. Headings can help readers make connections between background knowledge and the information in the text, which helps them make predictions before reading begins. Headings also strategically organize a text into sections so that one section at a time can be studied.

Sidebars are found in the right or left margins of informational texts. Sidebars often provide the reader with helpful, additional information about a topic that appears on that particular page. By providing examples, interesting facts, definitions of key terms, and more, sidebars emphasize important information that the author wishes to convey.

Hyperlinks are in-text links to specific website addresses that a reader may wish to visit to further their understanding of a specific topic. When authors insert hyperlinks into modern informational texts, they create a text that is more interactive, providing further resources for children to strengthen their comprehension of a given topic.

Using Inquiry and Research Skills

While teachers have access to an ever-increasing volume of sources, not every source is reliable. Some research is biased and presents facts that are not necessarily true; other sources are not researched at all and are based purely on personal experience. Teachers need to evaluate their sources for credibility before using them in the classroom, particularly when using material from the internet.

Here are some helpful questions you can ask yourself to determine whether a source is credible.

Is the source published by a reputable organization? If you are not sure, research the publisher and make sure that it is trustworthy. Some examples of reputable sources are research journals, academic presses, and well-known organizations (such as libraries or museums). If you are conducting research online, you will find that these sources typically have web addresses that end with .edu or .gov. Some research journals are especially reliable because they have been **peer-reviewed**, which means that they have been vetted by a team of experts before publication. Sources that are not reliable include personal blogs and social media posts: online, these sources will usually be on websites ending with .com.

Who is the author, and what are their credentials? The best advice comes from experienced researchers and professionals. Information about personal experience, such as a post on a teaching blog, may help teachers brainstorm new ideas, but it is not as reliable as source material for research.

Does the source use evidence to back its claims? Good research is grounded in fact, not speculation.

What is the date of the source? Research is always advancing, so older sources are typically not as reliable as newer ones.

Is the source's writing of a high quality? Numerous grammar mistakes, typos, and other errors indicate that the author or organization is not credible.

Is the source unbiased? This question is particularly important when evaluating the findings from studies. For example, consider a study on the risks and benefits of teaching reading with computers and tablets. If this study is conducted by a major electronics company, it is not unbiased: the researchers have a considerable stake in the findings, and they may design a study that favors computer use.

Research Process

The following list depicts the steps relevant to the research process. Each step should be performed in chronological order, as they depend on each other for optimal work. For example, without the "Revise and edit" step, step 8 would be a poorly written first draft.

- Step 1: Decide on a topic to research
- Step 2: Set the purpose of the research
- Step 3: Locate sources of information—print, digital, experts
- Step 4: Evaluate the sources
- Step 5: Summarize information and cite sources
- Step 6: Write draft
- Step 7: Revise and edit
- Step 8: Publish writing

Developing a Topic Sentence and Using Evidence to Support Conclusions

Developing a Topic Sentence

Good writers get to the point quickly. This is accomplished by developing a strong and effective topic sentence that details the author's purpose and answers questions such as *What does the author intend to explain or impress?* or *What does the author want the reader to believe?* The **topic sentence** is normally found at the beginning of a supporting paragraph and usually gives purpose to a single paragraph. When reading, critical readers should find the topic sentence in each paragraph. If all information points back to one sentence, it's the topic sentence.

Use of Evidence to Support Conclusions

Using only one form of supporting evidence is not nearly as effective as using a variety to support a claim. Presenting only a list of statistics can be boring to the reader, but providing a true story that's both interesting and humanizing helps. In addition, one example isn't always enough to prove the writer's larger point, so combining it with other examples in the writing is extremely effective. Thus, when reading a passage, readers should not just look for a single form of supporting evidence.

For example, although most people can't argue with the statement, "Seat belts save lives", its impact on the reader is much greater when supported by additional content. The writer can support this idea by:

- Providing statistics on the rate of highway fatalities alongside statistics of estimated seat belt usage.

- Explaining the science behind car accidents and what happens to a passenger who doesn't use a seat belt.

- Offering anecdotal evidence or true stories from reliable sources on how seat belts prevent fatal injuries in car crashes.

Another key aspect of supporting evidence is a **reliable source**. Does the writer include the source of the information? If so, is the source well-known and trustworthy? Is there a potential for bias? For example, a seat belt study done by a seat belt manufacturer may have its own agenda to promote.

Writing Conventions

Stages of Acquiring Writing Conventions

The following table lists the stages in writing conventions:

Developmental Stages of Writing	Description	Grade-Appropriate Continuum
Scribbling	Random marks, circles, and lines that may not resemble print, but represent ideas for the young writer.	Praise the children's creativity and ask them to explain their work to you. Consider adding a sentence at the bottom of their work based on the children's ideas.
Letter-like symbols	Letter-like symbols start to randomly appear and may be mixed in with numbers and scribbles.	Praise the children's creativity and point to the letter-like symbols for discussion. Consider adding a sentence at the bottom of the work based on the children's ideas.
Strings of letters	Using strings of letters in a row, children are demonstrating the preliminary understanding of letter-to-sound relationships.	Praise the children's efforts in attempting to use letters to represent sounds. Ask the children to tell you the story or to read you the sentences and consider writing what they say at the bottom.
The emergence of beginning sounds	Children begin to use letters to represent actual words and may string the letters together in a row that can tell a story.	Praise the children's efforts in attempting to use letters to represent actual words. Help with spacing, building sound-letter correspondence, and expanding vocabulary.
Words represented by consonants	Children begin to leave spaces between words with a possible mixture of uppercase and lowercase letters.	Praise children's work as a prompt for further explanation of the story. Prompt children to use more details and to build more sentences.

Developmental Stages of Writing	Description	Grade-Appropriate Continuum
Initial, middle, final sounds	Children begin to write some basic sight words and familiar names, but all other words are spelled the way they sound.	Praise children's progress and continue to build vocabulary. Help children to organize writing with structure and sentence variety.
Transitional phase	Writing is beginning to approach conventional spelling.	Praise children's progress and model the use of effective wording by using specific vocabulary to expand ideas.
Standard spelling	Children begin to spell most words correctly, with a basic understanding that the spelling of many words is connected to the meaning.	Praise children's progress and challenge them to begin writing more complex sentences, expand ideas, and establish a clear purpose for writing.

Opportunities to Use and Develop Spelling Skills

Letter-Sound Assessments

During phoneme and **letter-sound correspondence assessments**, teachers point to random letters or phonemes. The student is to then say the sound of the letter or phoneme and the teacher records the student's responses. Letter-sound combinations and phonemes with which a student, group, or class needs additional instruction and/or practice can be identified. The teacher can use this information to create lessons that emphasize the identified letter-sound correspondences and/or phonemes.

Phonics Assessments

Examples to test a student's ability to decode words or readily read sight words include Sylvia Green's Informal Word Analysis Inventory, Test of Word Reading Efficacy (TOWRE), and the CORE Phonics Survey. In these types of assessments, students are given a list of words and/or phonics patterns. Initially, high-frequency words that follow predictable phonics patterns are presented. Examples of **predictable phonics patterns** may include blending, word patterns, digraphs, etc. The words presented become more challenging as a student masters less difficult words. For example, a child may be assessed on his or her ability to decode nonsense words.

The nonsense word assessments progress from decoding common sounds to less common sounds. Multisyllabic words within the assessments can reveal how well learners can chunk word parts through syllabication. As with other assessments discussed, the student's responses are recorded on a teacher's record sheet. In this way, the teacher can identify which word analysis principles and sight words a single student, a group of students, or an entire class is having difficulty with. These sight words, word parts, letter combinations, blending patterns, and/or syllabication principles can then be reinforced, retaught, reviewed, and practiced in future lessons. Additionally, the results of the assessment can be used to form instructional groups.

Informal Word Analysis Inventories

These can be used to assess encoding (spelling) of single-syllable words in the traditional manner. Students write the words that are read aloud by their teacher on a sheet of paper. In the early stages of spelling development, students are assessed on lists of words that are common to everyday language, share a word pattern or theme, and/or follow common orthographic patterns. The word lists become more complex as students demonstrate proficiency. The teacher can then plan instruction that targets the letter combinations and patterns with which students are struggling. Such assessments can also be used to form instructional groups of students who share the same approximate developmental stage of spelling to better facilitate differentiated instruction.

As a general rule of thumb, isolated phonics tests should be given every four to six weeks. Spelling assessments can be given weekly or biweekly. Remediation should be implemented when students miss two or more questions on a five-question assessment and three or more questions on a ten-question assessment.

Contextualized Decoding Assessments

Despite the popularity of isolated decoding assessments, decoding should also be assessed in context. The **Word Recognition in Context** subtest of the Phonological Awareness Literacy Screening (PALS) is an example of an assessment that can be used for this purpose. During such assessments, passages that can be read by a student with 90 to 97 percent accuracy at acceptable rates are selected. The student reads these passages aloud to the teacher.

By analyzing students' approaches to figuring out unknown words and students' errors when reading a grade-appropriate passage, teachers are better able to determine which of the following three decoding strategies to emphasize during instruction:

Meaning cues should be emphasized when a student fails to use context, story background, or pictures to assist in the decoding of new words.

Structural cues are emphasized when a student does not use grammar or syntax to figure out an unknown word.

Visual cues are emphasized when a student does not use grapheme or phoneme information to decode an unknown word. For example, a student may only read the beginning, middle, or end of words correctly (e.g., read hat as cat). A student may leave off a suffix or use incorrect yet similar letter combinations, indicating that visual cues need to be retaught.

Spelling Assessments

Similarly, spelling should be assessed within the context of a student's writing samples. When a student's spelling is assessed in the context of a writing assignment, a teacher is able to detect patterns of misconceptions and areas that need remediation. Not only can such assessments be used to detect the proper encoding of words, but also a student's vocabulary, diction, and syntax. By using a rubric, teachers are better able to determine which developmental stage of spelling (the pre-phonetic stage, the semiphonetic stage, the phonetic stage, the transitional stage, and the conventional stage) of each student. Spelling instruction that targets each student's individual strengths, weaknesses, and developmental stage of spelling can then be created and implemented by the teacher.

Please note that once a student's areas of need are determined, any of the previously suggested phonics, sight word, or spelling strategies can be used for remediation and re-teaching of the identified skills.

Helping Students Use English Writing Conventions

Writing Development

Like with any complicated processes, writing development begins with the simplest form of indiscernible scribbles and progresses to fully formed words and, finally, to clearly written sentences and paragraphs. This is actually a complicated cognitive process that takes time and instruction to improve.

With very young students, emphasis can focus on simply making letters clear. After all, letter and word formation are the starting blocks of written language. The next phase in development can focus on actually creating words and making sure they are spelled correctly. When students are at the sentence development stage, grammar and linguistic rules become a priority. The foundations of the English language need to be firm in order for students to have good writing. When students have progressed to more advanced levels and are composing fully formed sentences with a specific purpose, it's time to incorporate content-related feedback.

Feedback at all levels of writing development is crucial; this is how students will learn to correct mistakes and strengthen growing skills. Instructor feedback must be clear while also being sensitive to the students' struggles or backgrounds. Differentiated instruction may be required to bolster students' writing skills. A good starting point for overall writing instruction is to introduce students to the stages of writing an original piece.

The goal with the stages of writing is to build on the previous work. The prewriting stage is the time for students to write down ideas and plan on how they will approach the topic at hand. The actual writing stage then dovetails on this fluidly because the student already has a framework of what the writing will focus on and how they will present information. In addition to practicing physical writing, these stages focus on critical-thinking and planning skills and may lessen the student's stress before they write and receive feedback. Feedback on the initial writing, or first draft, is key. The instructor should be able to assess any difficulties and then steer the student toward improving their writing in the revision stage. After revisions, instructors should examine how effective their feedback was in helping the writing improve overall.

Effective Composing

Good writing is composed of several key elements: development, focus, clarity and coherence, grammatical proficiency, and originality. Different institutions and individual instructors will list such qualities differently, but good composition will have these basic qualities.

Strong compositions have well-developed ideas that are explained clearly throughout the piece. Good writing seems to have been planned and executed without any gaps or confusion. Through their writing, students must essentially develop an idea and line of reasoning that leave readers clear about the focus of the piece. This also means that paragraphs must be arranged in a way that they enhance and expand on the central focus of the paper, using evidence sensibly.

A writer's focus is the central point. A successful composition will not only contain a clear focus but carry the focus throughout the piece. The reader should never lose the focus or be confused by it. The way in which the content is presented throughout the text, while remaining focused on the central idea, is key. This is done by the tactical use of evidence surrounding and supporting claims relating to the central idea.

Language can be elegant and creative, but it must be used in a way the reader can understand. Much of a writer's success will depend on the coherence of the written piece. Paragraphs and the ideas within them should not be random but connect together, seamlessly blending into the next section to advance the focus of the writing. Each paragraph should strengthen the claim. Unnecessary paragraphs disrupt the flow of the writing and distract the reader, ultimately weakening the piece. Naturally, the writing should also be grammatically correct and proofed for accurate spelling and sentence structure.

Originality is the defining aspect of a well-written piece. Students should not parrot the writing style or ideas of others but instead write something that is unique. Ideas, and the way they are presented, should be fresh and approach topics in a way that offers a new perspective to the reader.

Effective Written Expression

Written expression refers to the ability of the writer to fluidly communicate meaning and purpose throughout the composition. Essentially, this refers not only to how clear the central focus of the piece is but how well the ideas surrounding the central focus are presented. If the writer can't successfully express the meaning and implications of the idea, the writing will not be strong.

Effective written expression utilizes detailed, clear communication. A writer doesn't need to unload elaborate diction throughout the paragraphs. Such an embellishment can be distracting to the reader, which actually defeats the principles behind effective writing. Sentences should be direct and emphasize language that, while engaging, remains simple enough for the audience to understand. This doesn't mean abstaining from using advanced words but rather keeping sentences direct and to the point. Students should avoid rambling line after line. Avoiding exaggerating language or overdramatic phrasing is also important. Not only can this confuse the reader, it can also harm the reader's credibility.

A simple formula for effective writing is to introduce an idea, discuss it, and then make a conclusion. This applies for the written piece as a whole but must also be used within individual paragraphs. If a writer just introduces idea after idea with no substance, the reader is left with unsubstantiated claims. Without supporting evidence to understand the view, the reader is left with only opinion. With the implementation of facts and supporting details, this opinion is strengthened. Thus, the reasoning behind the central idea is clearly executed and can be considered seriously. This helps the writer achieve credibility.

Paragraph coherence is vital for effective written expression. Paragraph sequencing and information placement are essential to streamlining the entire piece. Evidence and supporting information should be used to transition from one section to another, up to the conclusion. This enables the information to be clearly expressed. The author should strive to write in a way that, as the piece progresses, the focus becomes clearer and more convincing. By the conclusion of the written piece, the author should also restate his or her thesis to solidify their views and reasoning.

Different Types of Spoken English

Register

Despite the fact that a standardized form of English is used in published academic and scientific language, several varieties of spoken and written English also exist. There are differences in how one speaks at home, with friends, to teachers, and to colleagues. In each social setting, a person's *register*—his or her level of formality—will likely change in order to appropriately address the audience. Written registers also vary, depending on a number of factors. For instance, when writing a research paper for professional purposes, formal language will be used, but when writing a letter to a friend, a person is more apt to employ a more casual register. The following statements indicate differences in register:

> *Call me back when you get this message.*
>
> *I look forward to hearing back from you at your earliest convenience.*

Although both statements express the writer's desire to further communicate with the receiver of the message, the degree of formality, the register, is strikingly different.

Dialect

A language also has several dialects, which are dependent on a great many factors. *Dialects* have specific grammatical rules and patterns that often differ from the standard rules of the language. For instance, within Britain, Canada, and the United States, there are several dialects of the English language. One need only travel from Newfoundland, in eastern Canada, to Louisiana, in the southern United States, to witness a striking difference in how the English language is spoken.

Written dialects and registers also exist. They vary, based on the type of written work, when it was created, where it was written, by whom it was written, for what purposes, and for what audience it was intended. Authors of dramas, stories, and poetry employ the use of dialect for a multitude of reasons. For instance, when authors wish to develop a clear picture of the setting and characters within a drama, dialect plays a significant role. Here are some examples of dialect:

> "Bess, you is my woman now..."—from George Gershwin's opera, *Porgy and Bess*

> "That ain't no matter."—from Mark Twain's novel, *Huckleberry Finn*

With the careful and skillful placement of written dialect, the author conveys the character's personality, situation, and social class.

Factors of Writing

High-quality writing takes more than simply good writing skills and a knowledge of vocabulary. High-quality writing takes a lot of planning, writing, and revising in order to meet the standards of the audience. Many factors go into high-quality writing, but some major ones, including content, voice, and word choice, are listed below:

Content

The **content** of a piece of writing includes the ideas, structure, language, and effect of a particular text. Content begins with a writer being able to effectively brainstorm and research their topic in order to obtain credibility as an author. Thorough research of a topic and proper citation is the first step in creating good content. Organization of the text is also important to high-quality content, as is knowledge of vocabulary and sentence structure. Finally, good writing content will have an intended effect on the audience, whether that be persuading the audience to act or informing them of how something is done.

Voice

The voice an author selects is also important to note. An author's **voice** is that element of style that indicates their personality. It's important that authors move us as readers; therefore, they will choose a voice that helps them do that. An author's voice may be satirical or authoritative. It may be light-hearted or serious in tone. It may be silly or humorous as well. Voice, as an element of style, can be vague in nature and difficult to identify, since it's also referred to as an author's tone, but it is that element unique to the author. It is the author's "self." A reader can expect an author's voice to vary across literary genres. A non-fiction author will generally employ a more neutral voice than an author of fiction, but use caution when trying to identify voice. Do not confuse an author's voice with a particular character's voice.

Word Choice

An author's **word choice** helps to convey meaning in a particular way. Through diction, an author can convey a particular tone—e.g., a humorous tone, a serious tone—in order to support the thesis in a meaningful way to the reader.

Connotation

Connotation is when an author chooses words or phrases that invoke ideas or feelings other than their literal meaning. An example of the use of connotation is the word *cheap*, which suggests something is poor in value or negatively describes a person as reluctant to spend money. When something or someone is described this way, the reader is more inclined to have a particular image or feeling about it. Thus, connotation can be a very effective language tool in creating emotion and swaying opinion. However, connotations are sometimes hard to pin down because varying emotions can be associated with a word. Generally, though, connotative meanings tend to be fairly consistent within a specific cultural group.

Denotation

Denotation refers to words or phrases that mean exactly what they say. It is helpful when a writer wants to present hard facts or vocabulary terms with which readers may be unfamiliar. Some examples of denotation are the words *inexpensive* and *frugal*. *Inexpensive* refers to the cost of something, not its value, and *frugal* indicates that a person is conscientiously watching his or her spending. These terms do not elicit the same emotions that *cheap* does.

Authors sometimes choose to use both, but what they choose and when they use it is what critical readers need to differentiate. One method isn't inherently better than the other; however, one may create a better effect, depending upon an author's intent. If, for example, an author's purpose is to inform, to instruct, and to familiarize readers with a difficult subject, his or her use of connotation may be helpful. However, it may also undermine credibility and confuse readers. An author who wants to create a credible, scholarly effect in his or her text would most likely use denotation, which emphasizes literal, factual meaning and examples.

Correct Pencil Grip

Learning how to grip a pencil correctly is a fundamental skill that all students must learn as soon as possible. While most older students will do this well, many younger students will need assistance with developing this skill. Here are some ways to teach correct pencil grip.

Encourage further development of students' fine motor skills with other activities besides writing. Coloring, cutting construction paper, drawing lines, and opening containers are good ways to strengthen the muscles in their hands and practice using them a certain way. Completing mazes is also a good way for students to practice holding writing utensils correctly.

Other methods for teaching students to hold pencils correctly include having them hide something, like a marble, under their pinky and ring fingers while writing with a pencil or giving them shorter pencils to write with (both of which make it more difficult to use incorrect gripping methods). There are also various pencil grippers that slide onto the pencil and guide the student to where to place their fingers.

Another technique is called the "pinch and flip." To perform this trick, students pinch the sharpened end of a pencil and then flip it until it lands in the space between their thumb and forefingers.

Pinch and Flip Technique

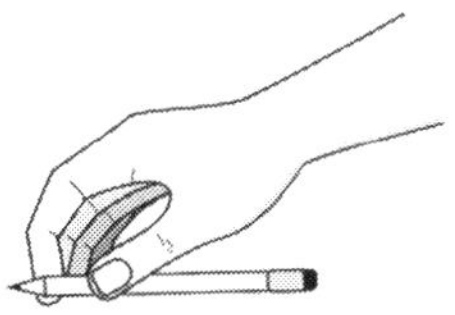

With the sharpened end of the pencil pointing away from you, pinch the top of the pencil where the paint begins.

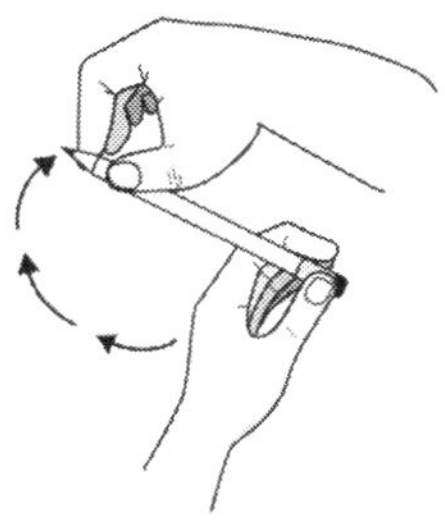

With your other hand, grasp the other end of the pencil and twist it until it rests on your hand.

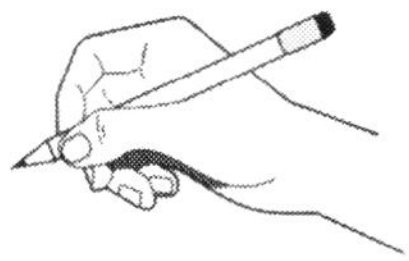

Correct pencil grip

Written Communication

Purposeful Writing

Purposeful writing practices have a significant effect on writing development. **Purposeful writing** refers to intentional writing practices for the purpose of communicating. Through learning to write well, students can begin to use writing as a method of thinking through issues and solving problems. They become more adept with questioning and investigation. Students learn to accurately convey and critique information. They can more readily express real or imagined experiences to others. Through the varied writing purposes, students learn to focus on what the audience understands, while at other times, they focus on the topic and what information they are trying to impart. Other situations call for focus on their own thinking and feelings. Writing as a whole becomes more effective and accessible as students glean skills for writing with purpose. Some of the writing purposes are as follows:

- Letter writing
- Poetry and Songs
- Creative and Narrative writing
- Informative writing
- Opinion writing
- Persuasive writing
- Compare and Contrast writing
- Explanatory/Expository writing
- Problem and Solution writing

Providing Many Opportunities to Read and Write

Children who receive regular and consistent encouragement to write and whose environment is rich with writing materials and resources will be more apt to strengthen their writing proficiency. Research suggests that at least an hour a day of writing practice, including skilled instruction, is necessary. Writing projects should be chosen that also involve the subjects of science, social studies, reading, or mathematics to give students well-rounded views of the purposes for writing. Piece by piece, students practice writing skills in all subjects, and collectively it should add up to more than an hour a day.

Providing Instruction in Various Stages of Writing

POWER Strategy

The **POWER strategy** helps all students to take ownership of the writing process by prompting them to consciously focus on what they are writing.

The POWER strategy is an acronym for the following:

- Prewriting or Planning
- Organizing
- Writing a first draft
- Evaluating the writing
- Revising and rewriting

Prewriting and Planning

During the Prewriting and Planning phase, students learn to consider their audience and purpose for the writing project. Then they compile information they wish to include in the piece of writing from their background knowledge and/or new sources.

Organizing

Next, students decide on the organizational structure of their writing project. There are many types of organizational structures, but the common ones are: story/narrative, informative, opinion, persuasive, compare and contrast, explanatory, and problem/solution formats. Often graphic organizers are an important part of helping students complete this step of the writing process.

Writing

In this step, students write a complete first draft of their project. Educators may begin by using modeled writing to teach this step in the process. It may be helpful for beginning writers to work in small groups or pairs. Verbalizing their thoughts before writing them is also a helpful technique.

Evaluating

In this stage, students reread their writing and note the segments that are particularly strong or need improvement. Then they participate in peer editing. They ask each other questions about the piece. The peers learn to provide feedback and constructive criticism to help the student improve. Scoring rubrics are a helpful tool in this phase to guide students as they edit each other's work.

Revising and Rewriting

Finally, the student incorporates any changes she or he wishes to make based on the evaluating process. Then students rewrite the piece into a final draft and publish it however it best fits the audience and purpose of the writing.

Technology and Writing Instruction

Teachers are learning to adapt their writing instruction to integrate today's technology standards and to enhance engagement in the writing process. The key is to still build a strong foundation of the fundamentals of writing while using current technology. Gone are the days when writing relied solely on handwritten pieces and when the tools of the trade were pencils, paper, hardback dictionaries, and encyclopedias. Online resources are now the backbone of the writing experience. It is now possible to integrate photo, video, and other interactive components into a completed project to provide a well-rounded engagement with media. In order to have an education conducive to college and career readiness and success, students need online research and digital media writing skills.

There are many compelling reasons to teach students to be digitally aware and prudent users of technology when it comes to their writing. With current digital technology, the writing process has become a much more collaborative experience. In higher education and in career settings, collaborative skills are essential. Publishing and presenting are now simplified such that completed work is often read by a wide variety of audiences. Writing can be instantly shared with parents, peers, educators, and the general public, including experts in the field. Students are more apt to take an interest in the writing process when they know that others are reading their writing. Feedback is also simplified because so many platforms allow comments from readers. Teachers can be interactive with the students throughout the process, allowing formative assessment and integration of personalized instruction. Technology is simply a new vehicle for human connection and interactivity.

A student may be exposed to a plethora of technology, but this does not mean that she or he necessarily knows how to use it for learning. The teacher is still responsible for guiding, monitoring, and scaffolding the students toward learning objectives. It is critical that educators teach students how to locate credible information and to reliably cite their sources using bibliographies. Platforms and apps for online learning are varied and plentiful. Here are some ideas for how to use technology for writing instruction in the classroom:

- Use a projector with a tablet to display notes and classwork for the group to see. This increases instructional time because notes are already available rather than having to be written in real-time. This also provides the ability to save, email, and post classwork and notes for students and parents to access on their own time. A student can work at his or her own pace and still keep up with instruction. Student screens can be displayed for peer-led teaching and sharing of class work.

- More technology in class means less paperwork. Digital drop-boxes can be used for students to turn in assignments. Teachers can save paper, keep track of student revisions of work, and give feedback electronically.

- Digital media can be used to differentiate instruction for multiple learning styles and multiple skill levels. Instead of using standardized textbook learning for everyone, teachers can create and collect resources for individualizing course content.

- Inquiry- and problem-based learning is easier with increased collaborative capabilities provided by digital tools.

- Digital textbooks and e-readers can replace hardback versions of text that are prone to damage and loss. Students can instantly access definitions for new words, as well as annotate and highlight useful information without ruining a hardbound book.

- Library databases can be used to locate reliable research information and resources. There are digital tools for tracking citation information, allowing annotations for internet content, and for storing internet content.

- Mobile devices may be used in the classroom to encourage reading and writing when students use them to text, post, blog, and tweet.

- PowerPoint and other presentation software can be used to model writing for students and to provide a platform for presenting their work.

- Students can create a classroom blog, review various blog sites, and use blogs as they would diaries or journals. They can even write from the perspective of the character in a book or a famous historical person.

- Web quests can be used to help guide students on research projects. They can get relevant information on specific topics and decide what pieces to include in their writing.
- Students can write about technology as a topic. They can "teach" someone how to use various forms of technology, specific learning platforms, or apps.
- Students can create webpages, make a class webpage, and then use it to help with home-school communication.
- Online feedback and grading systems can be used. There are many to choose from. This may allow students to see the grading rubric and ask questions or receive suggestions from the teacher.
- Students and teachers can use email to exchange ideas with other schools or experts on certain topics that are being studied in the classroom.
- Game show-style reviews can be created for units of study to use on computers or on an overhead projector.
- A wiki website can be created that allows students to collaborate, expand on each other's work, and do peer editing and revision.
- Publishing tools can be used to publish student work on the web or in class newspapers or social media sites.

Writing Style

An author's *writing style*—the way in which words, grammar, punctuation, and sentence fluidity are used—is the most influential element in a piece of writing, and it is dependent on the purpose and the audience for whom it is intended. Together, a writing style and mode of writing form the foundation of a written work, and a good writer will choose the most effective mode and style to convey a message to readers.

Writers should first determine what they are trying to say and then choose the most effective mode of writing to communicate that message. Different writing modes and *word choices* will affect the tone of a piece—that is, its underlying attitude, emotion, or character. The argumentative mode may utilize words that are earnest, angry, passionate, or excited whereas an informative piece may have a sterile, germane, or enthusiastic tone. The tones found in narratives vary greatly, depending on the purpose of the writing. *Tone* will also be affected by the audience—teaching science to children or those who may be uninterested would be most effective with enthusiastic language and exclamation points whereas teaching science to college students may take on a more serious and professional tone, with fewer charged words and punctuation choices that are inherent to academia.

Sentence fluidity—whether sentences are long and rhythmic or short and succinct—also affects a piece of writing as it determines the way in which a piece is read. Children or audiences unfamiliar with a subject do better with short, succinct sentence structures as these break difficult concepts up into shorter points. A period, question mark, or exclamation point is literally a signal for the reader to stop and takes more time to process. Thus, longer, more complex sentences are more appropriate for adults or educated audiences as they can fit more information in between processing time.

The amount of *supporting detail* provided is also tailored to the audience. A text that introduces a new subject to its readers will focus more on broad ideas without going into greater detail whereas a text that focuses on a more specific subject is likely to provide greater detail about the ideas discussed.

Writing styles, like modes, are most effective when tailored to their audiences. Having awareness of an audience's demographic is one of the most crucial aspects of properly communicating an argument, a story, or a set of information.

Writing Conventions and Documentation

Writing Conventions

Writing conventions, including spelling, capitalization, punctuation, and grammar, make writing readable. Each of these conventions is important. Spelling, capitalization, punctuation, and correct grammar are skills that are useful in our everyday lives.

There are also specific conventions that apply to different types of writing. For example, narrative writing's conventions are the plot, setting, and characters. Expository writing is meant to explain or instruct; its conventions include introductory paragraphs, thesis statements, and conclusions. Descriptive writing uses vivid vocabulary that appeals to your senses. And finally, persuasive writing presents facts to sway readers' opinions.

Documentation

Students need to know when to use appropriate forms of documentation to acknowledge sources. Keep reading to learn what those forms of documentation are and how you can teach them.

Quotations

Students should learn how to incorporate quotations into their writing. They can practice this by transcribing their own conversations into dialogue. They will also need to learn how to format quotations correctly. Consider providing students with the following checklist, which contains the necessary elements of quotation formatting:

Quotation Checklist
✓ Started a new line to begin quotation
✓ Indented new line of dialogue
✓ Applied quotation marks around dialogue

Bibliographical information

Citing sources helps prevent writers from being accused of plagiarism. Therefore, learning to cite them correctly is important. Students will also need to learn that not all bibliographies look the same. A bibliography in the Modern Language Association (MLA) style will not look like one in the American Psychological Association (APA) style or Chicago Manual Style (CMS).

Teach students the different parts of citations. Then, create a sort of puzzle for them by cutting a citation up and having them piece it back together in order.

Paraphrasing vs. Plagiarism

Paraphrasing is using different words to recreate a writer's original statements. Plagiarizing is using a writer's exact words as if they are your own.

Paraphrasing can be a difficult skill to master, but it's important that students understand how to do it so that they do not plagiarize sources. Make sure that they understand that plagiarizing content has consequences, especially in the classroom, such as receiving a failing grade.

To teach paraphrasing, you can use speaking exercises. Have a student make a statement, then call on another student to rephrase what they said. Then, call on another student to rephrase what the second student said, and so forth. This basic exercise is a great introduction to paraphrasing.

Viewing and Representing

Using Media to Influence and Inform

Many of today's students are saturated with technology in their everyday lives. With the availability of iPads, iPods, personal computers, and smartphones, children as early as the primary grades are not only familiar with modern technology, but are becoming confident practitioners. Therefore, integrating technology in the classroom is a logical approach to helping children connect to the learning process and engage their interests.

With regard to English language arts instruction, technology can provide ample opportunities for educators to help strengthen students' critical thinking, oral communication, and reading comprehension skills. Since stories have always been used as a way of helping to explain the world and our place in it, they continue to be an integral part of any society's culture. The same story can be shared orally, in print, in film, or onstage, and each presentation provides similarities and differences with regard to the story's elements and to the audience's interpretation. By allowing children to compare and contrast various presentations of the same story, educators can increase students' motivation in English language arts.

Isolated scenes in films or documentaries can be used to begin a class discussion on a given topic. Children can openly discuss what version of the story they prefer and why. They can become detectives as they watch carefully for differences and similarities in the story's elements, such as setting, plot, and character traits. Educators who introduce a film or stage version of a literary work may wish to introduce the elements of lighting, dialogue, or special effects and begin a class discussion about how these elements, much like points of view, setting, and details in print, are critical to a film's structure.

If used strategically and with careful planning, the use of films, plays, and various technology-based story presentations can prove to be a very effective instructional strategy that strengthens students' understanding and appreciation of English language arts.

Using Different Types of Media and Technology in the Classroom

Students in a modern classroom have access to a wide variety of instructional resources. From teacher-led instruction and classroom activities, traditional textbooks, encyclopedias, nonfiction magazines, and customized classroom libraries to desktop computers, iPads, tablets, laptops, online tutorials, and smart boards, there is a plethora of information waiting to be discovered. Learning how to integrate traditional written, visual, and oral information to other information provided on a multimedia platform can prove challenging, but it is well worth the effort. Since the vast majority of children from the primary school years and older are well equipped at using a variety of technology-based resources, educators who integrate technology in the classroom will likely succeed in helping children to progress both academically and socially. The classroom is as much a social setting as it is academic, and as society changes, so must the instructional approaches. Teachers must find a way to incorporate both traditional resources and technology in a complementary way in the classroom.

For instance, one effective approach is to instruct children to ensure that every research project involves a minimum of two textbook sources as well as a minimum of two technology-based sources. When introducing new topics or reinforcing a lesson, educators are still highly encouraged to use visual aids in the classroom, including word walls, personal dictionaries, and classroom labels. Modeling the effective use of hand-held books, reference guides, and magazines also provides children the opportunity to see how valuable written information continues to be in the world of education.

In order for children to experience a well-rounded, quality education, instructional days should be divided between effective, quality instruction, independent exploration and learning, and positive social interaction. Since the needs of children vary in each classroom, as well as their academic and social levels, each educator's decision on how to divide instructional time will also vary. However, having access to technology is paramount in every classroom and at every grade level.

Technology in the classroom helps children to become more actively engaged and encourages independent learning with the use of student-centered, project-based activities. From virtual math tools to collaborative class blogs, there are many ways for students to effectively engage in technology in the classroom.

Although technology plays an important role in the modern classroom, it is still important for educators to guide children, helping them use the technology in an effective, efficient, and responsible manner. Teaching children about cyber-bullying, copyright, plagiarism, and digital footprints will inevitably strengthen their ability to responsibly and safely conduct themselves online.

Educators also use technology for lesson planning, assessments, and evaluation. With a number of online programs available, educators are able to provide students, colleagues, administration, and parents with effective feedback and to develop and evaluate high-quality formative and summative assessments in an efficient manner.

By combining the use of technology along with teacher-centered instruction and traditional textbooks, educators will undoubtedly help to create a classroom with children who are actively engaged throughout the instructional day.

Utilizing Visual Images from Various Types of Media

Studies continue to show a strong correlation between language development and the use of visual aids. From the primary years of education through the post-secondary years, the use of visual aids as a way to enhance reading comprehension has proven to be very effective. In the primary grades, picture books provide students with visual cues that help them to decode unknown words and strengthen reading comprehension. Visual aids support and clarify meaning, helping to make the learning and reading process more enjoyable and more interactive. When educators engage the students in a *picture walk*, skimming through picture books prior to reading, children become more motivated to read. Even reluctant readers, struggling readers, and English language learners are more apt to pick up a picture book and attempt to read it from cover to cover, enjoying the graphics and using them as powerful clues to the text's overall meaning.

Graphic novels are also becoming a popular addition to classroom and school libraries. With a structural approach that is similar to comic books, graphic novels have a strong appeal to children in the middle school years, teen years, and beyond. The visual images within graphic novels help children to make immediate connections to a story's plot and help them to understand potentially more challenging information.

As a universal learning tool, visual aids help all learners to comprehend the meaning behind the words and strengthen their ability to retain information over a longer period of time.

Multimedia Presentations

Multimedia presentations, such as PowerPoint or SlideShare, have been traditionally most effective at the higher education levels. However, as young children are more and more exposed to a world of technology, educators at the primary years are beginning to employ multimedia presentations in the classroom.

If carefully planned out, multimedia presentations can be used to enhance comprehension on virtually any subject. Using powerful graphic imagery that is directly relevant to the topic—coupled with effective textual language or audio—has been particularly effective in a growing number of classrooms.

Presenting students with the challenge of creating their own multimedia presentations can also be very rewarding for educators and students alike. Either independently, in pairs, or in groups, children take the learning process into their own hands with the opportunity to demonstrate the knowledge of a given subject by employing relevant written text and graphics.

Using Technology to Produce Various Types of Communications

Students should be educated through many mediums that appeal to various interests and learning styles. Modern technology has allowed for the incorporation of many mediums in the classroom, such as newspapers, multimedia projects, and video presentations.

Newspapers are effective teaching tools. One reason they're so effective is because they feature topics that appeal to almost anyone, whether that's sports and comics or news and weather. They're great for strengthening children's vocabularies. For example, you can ask students to highlight words they do not know in a specific passage, and then work with them to define those words. Later, quiz the students on the words they've learned. Creating a class newspaper is a good way to help students develop their writing, citation, and storytelling skills.

Multimedia reports help students develop their presentation and public speaking skills. They'll learn how to operate presentation devices and troubleshoot technical issues that may occur. Multimedia reports allow students to be creative; they can incorporate photos, audio, video clips, or graphics into their presentations.

Like multimedia reports, video reports also allow students to develop presentation skills and be creative. Recording videos with cameras or their phones is just one way for students to use this medium. Virtual video calls have also become a regular part of many classrooms. You can teach students how to use tools like Zoom or Skype by requiring them to host meetings and share their screens with the rest of the class.

These different types of technology can assist you, the instructor, with classroom engagement. Use them often, not only to show your students how they work, but also to provide variety in your curriculum and stave off student boredom. Using different mediums also helps educate students at various skill levels.

Assessment of Developing Literacy

Common Types of Assessments

Educators should incorporate a range of assessments into their curriculum because doing so creates a balanced, fair, and comprehensively informative system. Routinely administering the same type of assessment (such as a summative multiple-choice test) robs some students from an understanding of the material. It also eliminates valuable tools from the educator's arsenal, which would otherwise help guide content and instructional methods and lead to better student outcomes.

The following, which are some of the most common types of assessments used in classrooms, should be designed and built into elementary reading programs:

- **Performance Assessments**: Used to strengthen a student's higher-order thinking by measuring the ability to apply skills and learned material or to complete a process.
- **Self-Assessments**: Involve students' evaluation of themselves personally. These are useful for helping students develop the ability to monitor their own progress and learning, identify their strengths and weaknesses, and learn when to seek help.
- **Formal Assessments**: Include standardized tests, criterion-referenced tests, norm-referenced tests, essay tests, and achievement tests. These are used to obtain scores and evaluation material for students. They contain material that has been taught and learned and reveal data that can be used to support the analyses of the test. A student's result can be used to determine proficiency of the content and/or achievement in a specific standard.
- **Informal Assessments**: Used spontaneously throughout the day, unit, or school year, these are driven by performance and content rather than data. Teachers may observe students, collect journal responses, ask questions, administer exit tickets, etc. to gather informal assessment information.
- **Formative Assessments**: Used at the beginning of the school year or unit of study to inform teaching by establishing students' starting points and readiness levels.
- **Interim Assessments**: Used periodically throughout the school year or unit of study to evaluate progress toward learning, inform necessary instruction modifications, predict students' needs and areas of weakness, and provide students with feedback about their comprehension and skill attainment.
- **Summative Assessments**: Used at the end of the school year or unit of study; measures student success along with the efficacy of instructional method and/or curriculum materials; informs future learning and teaching.

Formative and Summative Assessments

Identifying Research-Based Approaches to Formative and Summative Assessment

It is almost as important to provide feedback and evaluate a student's skill level as it is to teach. Most classes utilize both formative and summative assessments as a grading template. Although assessment and grading are not the same thing, assessments are often used to award a grade. A **formative assessment** monitors the student's progress in learning and allows continuous feedback throughout the course in the form of homework and in-class assignments, such as quizzes, writing workshops, conferences, or inquiry-based writing prompts. These assessments typically make up a lower percent of the overall grade. Alternatively, a **summative assessment** compares a student's progress in learning against some sort of standard, such as against the progress of other students or by the number of correct answers. These assessments usually make up a higher percent of the overall grade and come in the form of midterm or final exams, papers, or major projects.

One evidence-based method used to assess a student's progress is a rubric. A **rubric** is an evaluation tool that explicitly states the expectations of the assignment and breaks it down into different components. Each component has a clear description and relationship to the assignment as a whole. For writing, rubrics may be **holistic**, judging the overall quality of the writing, or they can be **analytic**, in which different aspects of the writing are evaluated (e.g., structure, style, word choices, and punctuation).

Rubrics can be used in all aspects of a curriculum, including reading comprehension, oral presentations, speeches, performances, papers, projects, and listening comprehension. They are usually formative in nature but can be summative depending on the purpose. Rubrics allow instructors to provide specific feedback and allow students to understand the expectations for an assignment.

An example of an analytic rubric is displayed below:

Name ______________________________ **Date** ______________________________

Essay Rubric	4 Mastery	3 Satisfactory	2 Needs Improvement	1 Poor
Writing Quality	- Excellent usage of voice and style - Outstanding organizational skills - Wealth of relevant information	- Style and voice of essay was interesting - Mostly organized - Useful amount of information	- Inconsistent style and voice - Lacked clear organization - Small amount of useful information	- No noticeable style or voice - Virtually no organization - No relevant information
Grammar Conventions	- Essentially no mistakes in grammar - Correct spelling throughout	- Minor amount of grammar and spelling mistakes	- Many errors in grammar conventions and spelling	- Too many grammatical errors to understand the meaning of the piece

Another research-proven strategy is **conferencing**, in which students participate in a group discussion that usually involves the teacher. Students learn best when they can share their thoughts on what they've read or written and receive feedback from their peers and instructors. For writing, conferencing is frequently done in the revision stage. Through discussion, students are also able to enhance their listening and speaking skills. Conferences can be done in a one-on-one setting, typically between a student and instructor, or in a small group of students with guidance from the instructor. They are useful in that they provide an atmosphere of respect where a student can share his or her work and thoughts without fear of judgment. They increase motivation and allow students to explore a variety of topics and discussions. Conferences also allow the instructor to provide immediate feedback or prompt students for deeper explanations of their ideas. The most successful conferences have these characteristics:

- Have a set structure
- Focus on only a few points—too many are confusing or distracting
- Are solution based
- Allow students to both discuss their thoughts/works and receive/provide feedback for others
- Encourage the use of appropriate vocabulary
- Provide motivation and personal satisfaction or pleasure from reading and writing
- Allow a time where questions can be asked and immediately answered

Rubrics and conferencing are both methods that provide useful **feedback**, one of the most important elements in the progress of a student's learning. Feedback is essentially corrective instruction delivered in writing, either verbally or non-verbally. Research has shown that the following techniques are the most effective when giving feedback:

Being Specific

For a student to know exactly how he or she is doing, feedback should be directed towards specific components of a student's writing, listening, or speaking skills, not a holistic overview. For example, writing "Excellent!" on a student's paper or homework is not useful information as it's unclear what was done well. A paper should provide useful comments throughout the body of the work, for example, "Wording is confusing here," or "Great use of adjectives." However, instructor comments should not overwhelm the student's writing; they should be used to focus their attention on specific areas of success or improvement. This encourages the student to keep doing what he or she is doing well and work on what needs improvement without being overwhelmed.

Being Sensitive

Giving feedback is precarious in nature as it entirely depends upon the emotional and mental states of the receiver. Some students do well with "tough love," while others may be discouraged and disheartened to see a slew of comments on their paper. Teachers should pay attention to how a student reacts to feedback. As a general rule, feedback should focus more on the positives so as not to damage self-esteem, while teaching students new techniques for self-correction, instead of simply criticizing what they've done. Also, it's important to try and be aware of the types of feedback each student responds the most effectively to, for example, providing oral feedback for students who don't read well.

Being Prompt

Feedback should be presented sooner rather than later, so that students will not have time to repeat mistakes they are unaware of that may become habitual. Studies have shown that students who are given immediate feedback display a greater increase in performance than those who were given feedback later in the term. As soon as the action has happened, it is important give the appropriate praise or critique so that the student associates the feedback with the action.

Being Explicit

It is important to explain the purpose of the feedback before it is given so that a student does not feel controlled, too closely examined, or competitive. This can cause the learner to feel self-conscious and discourage him or her from performing his or her best. The importance of feedback and how it is meant to improve on a personal skill set should be explained to the student.

Being Focused

Teachers should try and keep the feedback in alignment with the goal the student is expected to achieve. Too much feedback, especially if it is unrelated to the goal, can be overwhelming and distracting from the purpose of the assignment or paper.

Here are some other tips to consider when giving feedback:

- Teachers should be aware of their body language and facial expressions when giving feedback—a frown or grimace can be very discouraging, even if the written feedback was mostly positive.
- It's conducive to concentrate on one thing at a time. If a student submits a paper with a lot of errors, for example, it may be helpful to identify a prevalent pattern of error and work through strategies to correct it so that student does not feel overwhelmed.
- Using effective rubrics can make all the difference—letting students know exactly what is expected will provide them with a basis on which to model their techniques and skills.

- Students should be educated on giving feedback. This can be demonstrated by example and through instruction how to give feedback in a positive, constructive way and correct any behavior that trends toward disrespect or excessive competition. Students should also provide feedback to the teacher as well.
- Teachers should not give the same comments to every student, but make them personal.
- When offering criticism, teachers should always offer tips for how the student can improve.
- It's important to avoid personal comments, e.g., "You're so smart!" or "Math isn't your best subject." Rather, the comments should focus on the writing: e.g., "The organization of this paper is clear."
- Students shouldn't be compared to each other, e.g., "Look how perfectly Victor composed this sentence!" This can galvanize the students into competing with one another.

Evaluating the Effectiveness of Research-Based Approaches to Formative and Summative Assessment

Most research has already been done to evaluate the effectiveness of certain strategies of formative and summative assessments. Because there are innumerable approaches to the art of teaching, the only real way one can evaluate a strategy's effectiveness is to monitor how the students improve over time with any given approach. If one strategy does not seem to show much improvement, then a different one should be used. Because each student has individual needs, a teacher may need to utilize several different techniques tailored to the needs of each student.

To monitor student process, the following approaches should be considered:

- Asking questions in the classroom during and after a lecture
- Cultivating a classroom environment that encourages student questions
- Circulating around the classroom and engaging in one-on-one conferences during in-class assignments
- Giving periodic quizzes
- Leaving sufficient time for questions at the end of a lecture
- Assigning and collecting homework and returning the corrected material immediately
- Giving midterms and final exams
- Conducting regular reviews of student progress through the above methods and adjusting teaching strategies accordingly

Another strategy to assess student knowledge and identify areas in need of development is to create a K-W-L chart in preparation for a lesson that introduces a new topic. First, students are prompted for what they already know (K). Then, they are asked to consider what they want to know (W). The instructor may then choose to adjust the lesson by spending less time on areas that students are already proficient in and by spending more time on areas that students want to know more about. Finally, after the lesson, students can be asked to reflect on what they learned (L). A K-W-L chart lets students know that they are active participants in their own learning.

Involving Students in the Evaluation of Assessment Results

Because elementary students are young, early in their educational careers, and still developing in every facet of their lives, educators may fail to see the importance and usefulness of involving their young students in the evaluation and assessment process. A common assumption is that children at these ages are unable to take responsibility in their learning and are uninterested in hearing what is expected of them. However, the truth is that most young pupils thrive on feeling like they have some ability to take care of themselves, make their own choices, and demonstrate their autonomy. Moreover, children tend to respond well when expectations and objectives are clear. For these reasons, it's not only effective, but also helpful, to communicate evaluation criteria and assessment results to students. The task of the educator is to communicate in a way that their young students can understand the purpose of evaluation in general, the specific criteria against which the students will be assessed and why, and how well an individual student is achieving the goals and what he or she can do to improve. Satisfying these outcomes will facilitate a successful assessment process and can help students develop their own self-assessment skills.

Scoring rubrics are particularly helpful in explicitly describing the evaluation criteria and the various benchmarks of performance along the continuum. Teachers should explain performance standards and use examples of anonymous or fabricated finished work to demonstrate models of the different levels of achievement of the standards. After using the rubric and evaluating a student's work or effort, the educator should take the time to explain the outcomes to each student. After several evaluation experiences, students should be given the opportunity to use the same rubric and practice evaluating their own work.

Teachers can lead this process by prompting students to consider what concepts they think they did well in, which concepts they are still working on, and what areas are particularly confusing. It is especially important to place significant evaluative emphasis on a student's effort and attitude in the early elementary years because it will plant the seeds of studiousness, the desire to learn, and self-efficacy in one's own learning. Students can then see that even if they aren't grasping concepts as readily or easily as peers, they aren't "failures." Finally, teachers who involve students in the evaluation process help them develop the ability to constructively critique the work of their peers. As students move through their schooling, the ability to gauge their comprehension becomes imperative for monitoring their mastery, identifying study needs, and learning when to seek additional help.

Differentiation

Whether an instructor uses informal or formal assessment, data will be produced from the assessment. This data, both written or gained through observation, is highly valuable in diagnosing whether to change teaching methods in order to accelerate students' reading skills development. Data-driven instruction guides reading improvement for all students simply because the data provides clear indications of where students are facing reading challenges or demonstrating strengths.

Differentiated instruction acknowledges that, while a group of students may be learning the same subject, the way each student learns and processes the subject is different. This technique looks at the different learning methods and reading areas that students respond best to in order to effect change. Therefore, an educator can then tailor, or differentiate, lessons to build on these skills and expedite the learning process. Differentiated instruction is divided into interest-based and ability-based instruction.

Much of a student's performance is based on their interest in the subject at hand. Sometimes a student may show difficulty reading because he or she isn't engaged in the material. One way to encourage reading growth is to allow students to choose their learning activities. This will give students ownership over their own education, enabling them to have fun while learning and to use specific activities they feel help them improve their reading abilities. For example, students more interested in visual activities may find reading more beneficial than listening to oral reading exercises.

Ability-based differentiation focuses on three core focus areas that determine reading proficiency and build skill. The first area of focus examines students' conceptual understanding of reading. If a teacher uses vocabulary or reading comprehension exercises in class, they will be able to examine how students are performing and modify instruction to address any confusion. This can also indicate students' preferences as well. The second differentiation looks at how students analyze and use the reading. Instructors must look at how students respond to questions and whether their interpretation is accurate. The final differentiation looks at how students evaluate and perform reading, creating a reaction that responds to the reading. The third differentiation looks at interpretation with the added step of using this knowledge to write or say something without being prompted. Identifying issues in one of these areas will narrow down where more emphasis must be placed to improve reading skills. Each reading area will affect the other two; improving one differentiated area will impact the others.

Determining Students' Independent, Instructional, and Frustration Reading Levels

Frequent assessment ensures that students are grouped together according to their ability and their performance on state standards and benchmarks. Thus, different groups may be practicing different skills. Some may be practicing the same skills, but at different paces. Also, some students may need more than one skill retaught. These students may be in more than one intervention group at times.

As small groups work with one another, the teacher should be formatively observing and assessing performance. A teacher should be able to recognize a student's frustration reading level. Heightened frustrations occur when a student cannot understand or pronounce 90 percent of the words in the text. Frustration may also occur when a student cannot answer at least 60 percent of grade-level comprehension questions. A child will not develop reading skills productively at this level. Thus, students performing at this level need additional assistance or may benefit from a higher-leveled text being read aloud to them.

Self-Assessment and Peer-Review of Writing

Writing assessment is a critical part of instruction. Teachers can help students improve their writing skills by assessing areas that need improvement, teaching students helpful writing strategies, and reinforcing new writing skills with activities and helpful feedback.

The more students write, the better they become at assessing their own writing and that of their peers. These assessments ensure that their writing is interesting and easy to understand.

Introduce students to the plan, organize, write, edit, and revise (POWER) writing process. The POWER model helps teach good writing skills. Teachers can use it to review students' work, and students can refer to the model when they are self- or peer-reviewing. Below is a brief description of each step in the process:

Plan: Determine what to write about, research it, take notes, and collect sources.
Organize: Decide the order in which to write about the information you found. Create an outline.
Write: Using the outline for guidance, write about the chosen topic.
Edit: Check for spelling, grammar, syntax, and other errors.
Revise: Rewrite areas that need better clarification. Add more supportive information if needed.

The POWER model can also be used to review students' work.

1. Plan: Did the student provide sources for their work? Is there supportive evidence in their writing that shows they've done their research?
2. Organize: Ask for a copy of the outline. Does it make sense, and/or is it organized clearly?
3. Write: Did the student write according to the outline, or are they missing information?
4. Edit: Check their spelling, grammar, syntax, etc.
5. Revise: If revisions are needed, provide clear feedback about what sections of the students' work need to be rewritten.

Assess students' writing regularly. Frequent assessment helps track students' writing progress throughout the school year, and it highlights areas where they need improvement.

Responding to Individual Students' Needs

In any classroom, there will be students who fall behind or are at risk for struggling in the future. Here are some ways to recognize these students, preventing failure before it happens and helping students who are behind get back on track.

Implement screening assessments at the start of the school year. For example, you might administer the Informal Reading Inventory during the first few weeks of class to determine whether any of your students are at risk and would benefit from intervention.

Build communication with your students' parents, and suggest ways for parents of at-risk students to improve their children's performance, such as reading with them or supervising their homework. Often, parents who know that their child is struggling at school can take steps to help the student work through these issues at home before they become a bigger problem. For example, telling a couple that their son is performing poorly on spelling tests might enable the parents to motivate their child to practice at home and catch up with the rest of the class.

Make sure that at-risk students are receiving adequate peer support. **Peer support** is the help that students receive from other students. For example, if a struggling student asks another student to explain something, they are asking for peer support. Peer support is important because it increases the engagement in your classroom and builds a sense of community and responsibility. You can encourage students to help each other by seating at-risk students near high performers, implementing a buddy system, and breaking students into groups.

Scaffolding is a method of making students' workload seem less overwhelming by dividing it into manageable sections. Instead of assigning all the work at once and letting students either accomplish it or fail, teachers break the learning into steps and help students accomplish each one. For example, a teacher might scaffold by teaching the unfamiliar vocabulary in a text before the students read it. Scaffolding is a great way of preventing confusion and helping students with poor organization skills stay on track.

Multisensory instruction is a method of integrating touch, sight, and hearing to teach new skills. For example, a teacher might have a student draw new vocabulary words after reading them or hearing them. By appealing to multiple areas of the brain, multisensory instruction builds strong memory cues and puts students with different strengths (for example, visual learners and auditory learners) on an equal playing field.

Informal and Formal Feedback

Students need to know what they are doing well and what needs improvement. There should be no mystery about the learning targets. They need a positive self-image fostered by repeated success. Feedback should be positive and specific. Giving clear and effective feedback communicates to the student that her or his work is worthwhile, and that someone cares enough to review and consider it.

Informal feedback is part of formative assessment and should let students know where they are in the learning process and what they should do next. They should be able to formulate a plan for improvement and a vision of the next success they can achieve. Informal feedback is often oral and interactive.

Formal feedback is driven by objectives and rubrics that students should be given prior to a learning task. This gives them a clear goal for the activity and outlines expectations. Formal feedback should be presented in writing or another tangible format. Formal feedback is often summative in nature and may or may not be tied to grades and final assessments.

Feedback strategies are variable. Individualized adjustments can be made regarding timing, amount, mode, and audience. The timing may be immediate or delayed and given frequently or infrequently. Feedback might describe progress on many points or just a few, and it may go into great detail or be generalized. It may be oral, written, or demonstrative. It might be addressed to the individual, a small group, or the entire class. Feedback content is also infinitely variable. Feedback might focus on the work itself, the process, or the student's self-regulation but never on the student personally. Feedback comparisons might be criterion-, norm-, or self-referenced. It may function as a description of the work or an evaluation of the work but should not be judgmental. It can be both positive and negative, but any negative comments should be accompanied by suggestions for improvement. Feedback should be understandable to the student and developmentally appropriate. In some cases, feedback can be too specific so that it becomes difficult for a student to apply it to other situations. It can also be overly general, which does not give the student enough information to help with correction. Finally, feedback should communicate respect, activate motivation, and inspire thought.

Response to Intervention

Response to Intervention (RTI) is a process designed to help struggling students catch up through intervention and monitoring in a general education classroom. Students who suffer from undiagnosed reading disorders, attention issues, or even ELL students struggling to learn the language may begin to fall behind the rest of the students in reading skills. RTI is an informal intervention process done by the school that focuses on utilizing research and technology to help the student "catch up" to the rest of the class. The school's RTI teams will review assessments taken of each child in the classroom to determine which students need these instructional interventions. Teachers track students through **progress monitoring**, a process that measures whether or not the interventions are making a difference.

Although there are various ways to do RTI, it is usually set up as a three-tier system of support, also known as **multi-tier system of supports (MTSS)**. The tiers below are in order of least intense to most intense.

Tier 1: High-Quality Classroom Instruction, Screening, and Group Interventions

In **Tier 1 interventions**, the entire classroom is assessed using universal screening, where everyone's skillset is measured in a general education classroom by using methods that have been proven to be effective. Students who receive Tier 1 support are generally divided into small groups based on their skill level. Many students receive Tier 1 support because their math or reading skills are not quite at grade level. Progress of Tier 1 instruction is monitored, and many students are able to effectively catch up to grade level.

Tier 2: Targeted Interventions

Tier 2 interventions are for students who do not yet reach the potential of Tier 1 intervention. Targeted interventions give more detailed attention to the student who is struggling in addition to the regular classroom instruction. Since targeted interventions are done in addition to the regular classroom instruction, they are sometimes conducted during extracurricular activities or electives.

Tier 3: Intensive Interventions and Comprehensive Evaluation

The **Tier 3 Interventions** of the RTI process is intensive intervention. Intensive interventions are often done one-on-one or in small groups with other special-needs children. Usually only one or two students in a classroom will need this kind of instruction, so one-on-one help is more readily available for this tier.

Practice Quiz

1. Writing practice for the sole purpose of communicating refers to what kind of writing?
    a. Persuasive
    b. Informational
    c. Narrative
    d. Purposeful

2. A second-grade student brings a book to read to a group. It is about a caterpillar counting its food each day of the week before becoming a butterfly. Realizing the group is very familiar with their days and numbers, the teacher uses the story to explore the "moral" of the story and proper nutrition. This is an example of what?
    a. Modeling
    b. Encouragement
    c. Acknowledgement
    d. Challenging

3. A student is struggling with reading, especially aloud. When it is his turn to read to the class, the teacher offers an easier book she knows the student likes and is very familiar with. When the student reads aloud well and with enthusiasm, the teacher praises him to the class, then gives a more challenging book the next time. What is this called?
    a. Acknowledgement
    b. Providing feedback
    c. Encouragement
    d. Effective assistance

4. Preparation, Presentation, Application, and Evaluation are the four steps of what?
    a. Demonstration
    b. Modeling
    c. Explanation
    d. Challenging

5. Students are asked to pretend to prepare a meal. At various classroom stations, they must draw a picture, engage in pretend play, or write a list of instructions: one for grocery shopping, cooking, and cleanup. The teacher helps each student choose which task to pair with which station, encouraging autonomy and self-motivation. This is an example of what instruction technique?
    a. Challenging
    b. Modeling
    c. Giving feedback
    d. Giving assistance

See answers on next page.

Answer Explanations

1. D: Intentional writing practice for the purpose of communicating refers to purposeful writing. Students can use this as a method of thinking through issues and solving problems related to writing.

2. C: Considering prior knowledge before instruction is part of acknowledgement. For teachers, it begins with understanding where students are coming from and the experiences they bring with them to the classroom. When a teacher considers prior knowledge before beginning instruction, they are being considerate of each student's time and intellect.

3. B: Providing feedback is a way to build positive self-image and encourage success. A positive self-image is fostered by repeated success. Giving clear and effective feedback communicates to the student that her or his work is worthwhile and that someone cares enough to review and consider it.

4. A: Demonstration includes the four steps: Preparation, Presentation, Application, and Evaluation. Demonstration is when a teacher not only models and explains how to do a task but also engages in thinking through the task with the students. Effective teachers narrate their thinking processes when modeling a strategy.

5. D: Autonomy and self-motivation are the goals of giving assistance. Students need assistance and guidance in a classroom; however, knowing how much help to offer is always a balancing act. If teachers give too much assistance, they end up doing the work for students, who then do not learn. If teachers do not offer enough assistance, students become lost, overwhelmed, and do not learn.

Mathematics

Mathematics Instruction

Applying Research-Based Theories of Learning Mathematics

The most effective teachers apply research-based theories and principles into their classroom. Some examples of such theories and principles are the following:

1. Begin each day with a quick review of the previous lesson. Reviewing allows students to make connections between old and new material.

2. Present new material in short intervals afterwards in which students get a chance to practice each step. It is proven that students can only grasp so much information at once, and breaking up the lesson allows for there to be a better chance of the material being placed in one's memory.

3. Ask many questions throughout the lecture to see if the students understand the material. Students need time to practice the material in class, and seeing if they are getting correct responses allows for the teacher to determine if more instruction is necessary.

4. Provide models that supplement word problems. Worked out examples allow for students to see the step-by-step process necessary to solve problems, and this approach requires less strain on their memory and more emphasis on understanding.

5. Provide more instructional support on difficult tasks that are assigned. Examples of such support could be guidance through steps from the teacher or checklists, and once some problems are completed, the idea would be to eventually withdraw the instructional support. In conclusion, many theories and principles tend to overlap some ideas, but all have been heavily researched and studied to show their success with use in the classroom.

Linguistic, Cultural, and Socioeconomic Diversity of Students

In the classroom, teachers can aim to close the achievement gap that currently exists between students of different cultures and socioeconomic backgrounds. They can honor the diversity of their students by using it to their advantage. Students will have different backgrounds in literature, art, music, languages, politics, entertainment, and food. Teachers have the ability to introduce diverse and new concepts to students, and in doing so, it will make them better suited for the real world. Collaborative activities amongst students of different backgrounds should be welcomed and integrated into daily activities. Teachers can show that they genuinely care about the diversity of their students by taking time to learn about their different cultures, which supports their students' individual needs. Once they learn a little more about each student, that individualized information can be used to create lessons that relate to students on a more personal level.

In mathematics, word problems and problems involving real-world applications such as units of measurement are what relates instructional material to the real world. Teachers have the ability to create their own word problems based on cultural values of their students. For example, when teaching students how to use a clock to tell time, if there are students who speak Spanish in the classroom, the teacher could introduce the process in both English and Spanish. In that case, numbers from 1 to 12 could be reviewed in Spanish as well. Also, simple word problems focusing on different mathematical concepts can be changed to represent a scenario relating to some of the students' cultural backgrounds.

Concrete, Symbolic, and Abstract Representations of Mathematical Knowledge

When concepts are introduced into the mathematics classroom, there is a three-part strategy that can be used for instruction purposes. This strategy involves breaking up instruction into the concrete, symbolic, and abstract phase.

In the concrete phase, the teacher introduces the concept using tangible ideas and real models so that the idea can be seen in a physical sense. For example, when learning how to find the area of a rectangle, an actual rectangle composed of unit blocks can be used. The area of the rectangle would be found by counting the number of blocks. Also, at this point it could be shown that the number of blocks on the side representing its length times the number of blocks on the side representing its height equals this same quantity.

The second stage, known as the symbolic stage, involves the teacher using other types of representations such as drawings, graphs, and charts, of the concrete idea to support further introduction of the concept. In the area idea, this would involve drawing a rectangle on the board and noting the length of each side. Perhaps, the actual multiplication of the length times width could be written on the board now.

Finally, the last stage involves the abstract stage, in which the teacher introduces the idea on a symbolic level only. Only mathematical expressions consisting of numbers, variables, and operations are used here. In the area example, the formula of the area of the rectangle would be introduced: Area is equal to length times width, or $A = l \times w$. This three-step process is designed so that each student understands the connections between each type of representation. Research has shown that students who learn in this manner are more engaged and are more likely to be able to apply the concepts in the real world.

Manipulatives and Technological Tools

Manipulatives and technological tools are items that need to be introduced early into the mathematics classroom. They are important because they allow for other ways besides paper and pencil problems for students to enhance their understanding of mathematics. Their use allows the students to develop concrete examples that apply to abstract concepts while providing fun and engaging ways to learn math concepts. For example, base ten blocks can be used to learn addition and place value. The visualization of the math concepts and actual physical manipulation of the objects allow for great ways to conceptualize and understand the concepts being taught. Manipulatives also allow students to develop common language between their peers in the classroom and the teachers. They provide a fun and interesting way to learn new vocabulary while matching up each new term to a concrete, tangible idea. Research has also shown that classrooms that utilize manipulatives have students who are more interested in mathematics and who find more enjoyment in problem solving. Other types of manipulatives are tangrams, which consist of seven flat shapes that can be rearranged to form new shapes to teach geometry, interlocking cubes, pattern blocks, and fraction strips.

Mathematical Tasks in Individual, Small-Group, and Large-Group Settings

In the classroom, teachers can vary instruction techniques by introducing tasks to be completed individually and in small and large-group settings. To actively engage students in each type of setting, different monitoring approaches can be used. In individualized tasks, specific questions can be asked to both challenge the student and assess their progress. For example, in this setting it would be appropriate to ask how the student came up with the solution procedure on their own, to ask what patterns they saw along the way, and to ask how they relate the situation to other scenarios that have been seen before both in and out of the classroom.

In small and large-group settings, questions can be asked relating to how the group organized their thoughts, how they came up with their solution approach, if they think it is the best approach, if there is anything they would do differently, and if any members agreed or disagreed at any point along the way. There will probably be more disagreement in larger groups and more situations in which some students see different approaches as being better due to the larger group size. Each different type of setting is a chance for the students to use both their communication and math skills in various ways.

Tools to Strengthen Students' Mathematical Understanding

Many tools need to be introduced into the classroom by the teacher these days, and the large number of tools might seem discouraging. Basic tools involve chalkboard and chalk and pencil and paper. Very young students can be first introduced to base ten blocks, which allow for understanding of place value in numbers, and a 100-bead basic abacus, which allows for practice counting numbers. Then measurement devices, or manipulatives, such as protractors, compasses, and rulers, need to be used because of their applicability in the real world. Time measurement devices such as clocks and stopwatches and anything relating to counting money are also applicable to the real world.

Simultaneously, computer software and interactive lessons are used in the classroom. Today, some software exists that replaces physical measurement devices. For example, software can replace ruler or compass measurements that would originally be completed on paper so that it is done on the screen. In many ways, the software allows a student to better visualize the process. Older students can support the process of learning how to plot points and graph lines with graphing software and graphing calculators. It is important that once each tool is introduced into the classroom, it is fully understood by the students before introducing another tool. All of these tools will help strengthen students' mathematical understanding. However, full understanding of a few tools is more beneficial to students than being introduced to a multitude of tools while having little understanding of each item.

Mathematics in the Texas Essential Knowledge and Skills (TEKS)

In order to engage the students, a math teacher should utilize various methods of instruction. The material should be introduced using an assortment of ways, or else most students will get bored. If every day were spent taking notes and solving problems with pencil and paper, many students would have a hard time staying motivated. Lecture is an important part of classroom time, but other items can be mixed in. Group work is a great technique to break up the monotony. Working with peers allows for the concepts to be better understood, and it provides a chance for students to practice using their new vocabulary. Technology is another way to change the traditional lecture style. Items such as mathematical software and graphing calculators are great ways to see the concepts in a new way. Also, self-guided lectures can be utilized as ways for students to learn new material by teaching the material to themselves. Depending on the situation and the students, this can be a great technique to really allow the material to sink in. Finally, visuals such as diagrams, graphs, videos, and charts should be utilized whenever possible to create a link between the abstract and a tangible idea.

Reevaluate Instruction Based on the Mathematics in the TEKS

Each teacher needs to ask the question, what do I want my students to know at the end of their time in the classroom? Lesson plans should be created that are centered around the mathematical concepts necessary to be taught throughout the year. However, a little bit of flexibility should be allowed. It is important to make sure all the necessary topics are covered; however, if an instruction technique is not working in a given classroom, there should always be a chance for adjustment. It is important to keep updating the lesson plans throughout the year. As assessments are completed, teachers can adjust their lessons based on student interest and performance, making sure to adhere to the topics listed in the TEKS. For example, if the students are not reacting well to a certain tool such as mathematical software, and it is not something that the students need to learn, the teacher should take the opportunity to find a new instruction method that replaces the software. The mathematical concepts being introduced are more important than the instruction methods.

Mathematics and Other Disciplines Such as Art, Music, Science, Social Science, and Business

The problem-solving process involves applying the skills learned in the classroom to situations in the real world. Mathematics reasoning can appear in many scenarios and in many other disciplines, such as art, music, science, social science, and business. In art, mathematical concepts like symmetry, proportion, linear perspective, and recursion appear as well as various geometric figures and properties. In music, concepts such as intervals, counting, tempo, fractions, patterns, and symbols appear, and an understanding of mathematics is required to both read and write sheet music as well as when playing a musical instrument. For example, the length of notes relates to fractions. When playing a musical instrument or singing, whole notes, half notes, quarter notes, eighth notes, and sixteenth notes are used. A whole note can be thought of as a whole pie, the number 1, or 100%. Each subsequent note is a piece of the pie. For example, an eighth note is equivalent to the fraction $\frac{1}{8}$ or the percentage 12.5%. In relation to a pie, if a pie were cut into eight equal parts, an eighth note would be one piece of the pie.

Traditionally, more time in the classroom is spent on how mathematics relates to other disciplines such as science and business. However, it is very important to show how math is used in the arts and music. Traditional word problems that relate to science applications are those that involve Newton's Second Law of motion where force is equal to mass times acceleration, population growth and decay, and calculus problems that relate an equation of motion with its velocity and acceleration through derivatives and integrals. Social science problems involve anything relating to economics, sociology, and political science. Real world situations are modeled using math equations and formulas. Finally, in business, traditional problems involve formulas involving interest.

Encouraging Mathematical Discourse

In the classroom, the teacher should pose different types of questions relating to the mathematical concepts being discussed. Each question should be both engaging and challenging and the teacher should use questions that require both oral and written response types. The teacher should also determine when it is appropriate to provide helpful information and when to let the students deal with the difficulty on their own. For example, in some scenarios, students can be allowed to ask questions to gather more information necessary to provide a solution, as in a case study environment. However, this scenario would not be appropriate in a test situation that asks specific questions that involve evaluating expressions and solving equations. Also, especially in early mathematics, testing should involve a combination of both vocabulary and skill, to ensure that the students can not only work with the concepts being taught but verbally communicate within the subject as well.

Common Misconceptions and Error Patterns

A range of assessments exists that allow a teacher to evaluate how his or her students are performing in the classroom. They can be grouped into two categories: formal and informal. Formal methods can be used to place scores on each student's achievement levels. They are a way to judge how well students have learned concepts throughout the year. Some examples would be chapter tests, quizzes, and final exams. Each formal assessment is administered and graded in a formal manner. Each student is graded the same way, and each problem is either right or wrong, unless partial credit is given, in which a student can be right in some steps of the problem. Teachers can also utilize informal assessments throughout the year. These include any way of measuring the success of students besides a formal testing procedure. Some examples of informal assessments are experiments, group projects, and presentations. Each one of these does not have a formal method of evaluation; however, they are still beneficial tools that allow teachers to measure success in the classroom. An advantage of informal processes is that they also give the teachers a chance to assess both communication skills in addition to the mathematics material.

Relationship Between Assessment and Instruction

In the classroom, assessment should be used to guide instruction. Assessments are utilized to judge how well students are retaining the concepts being taught, while instruction is the process in which they actually learn the concepts. Assessments and instruction should be designed together in order to enhance one other. If both are not designed with each other in mind, it can impact student learning and achievement in a negative way. Each type of learning method has its own optimal assessments and assessments that do not work.

For example, a vocabulary lesson in which new mathematics terms are introduced are best assessed through questions that allow the students to recall terms and definitions. Such question types are multiple-choice, matching, and fill-in-the blank. Lessons involving problem solving in which students need to apply techniques should use different assessment techniques. Multiple-choice problems should not be utilized for long problems, and assessments that involve more of an open-response problem set are better suited. In this way, the student does not focus on the answer, but instead the focus is on what process is the best approach in order to solve the problem. If multiple-choice questions are given to assess problems that involve many steps, the teacher will not be able to see where the student went wrong. The assessment should be used as a tool to help guide instruction in addition to its traditional use of giving out scores and grades.

Various Assessments in Mathematics, Including Formative and Summative Assessments

Throughout the year, different types of assessments come into play, and it is important to utilize the correct type when necessary. First, a diagnostic test can be utilized at the beginning of the year. This type of test provides insight as to how much each student knows going into the year. Teachers can plan their lessons accordingly. Formative assessment is then used throughout the year, mostly in the form of tests and quizzes, that provide regular insight on how well each student is retaining the information being taught.

Formative assessments are most useful in recognizing student error patterns and can assist teachers by highlighting what skills and topics need to be revisited in their instruction. Summative assessment is testing completed at the end of the year, and it can provide a final score that summarizes how well each student did in the class. Finally, standardized testing is completed in some years, and these types of tests ask the same questions to every student of the same age at a national level. Their results provide an individual comparison of each student to national averages. Each type of assessment has its own benefits, but the formative assessments are the most useful throughout the year for teachers.

Uses of Mathematics in Careers and Professions

A great way to engage students in the mathematics classroom is to show them how math is used in the workplace. For example, teachers of younger students can introduce examples that relate to counting money and act as if they are working within a banking environment. This provides a fun way to link the classroom to a day-to-day use. Teachers of older students have the ability to introduce word problems that actually occur in a workplace. These types of situations provide practice with problem solving as well as a chance to motivate students by allowing them to see the usefulness of the problems. The question "why do I need to know this" is a common one in math classes, and any chance a teacher has to answer it with a tangible example should be taken.

A great example involves the medical field and calculating dosages for medication. For example, a nurse needs to administer 450 mg of a medication that comes as 150 mg diluted in 3 ml of fluid. The rule is to divide the total needed by the amount per measure, times the amount of liquid that comes in. Therefore, they would need to administer $\frac{450}{150} \times 3 = 9$ ml of the medication to the patient. Banking settings also provide great examples that show how math is used in professions. In lower level mathematics, simple counting can be used to highlight what a teller does, and in higher-level classes, compound interest problems can be worked through to show what a financial advisor does.

Number Concepts and Operations

Basic Operations

Problem Situations for Operations

Addition and subtraction are *inverse operations*. Adding a number and then subtracting the same number will cancel each other out, resulting in the original number, and vice versa. For example, $8+7-7=8$ and $137-100+100=137$. Similarly, multiplication and division are inverse operations. Therefore, multiplying by a number and then dividing by the same number results in the original number, and vice versa. For example, $8 \times 2 \div 2 = 8$ and $12 \div 4 \times 4 = 12$. Inverse operations are used to work backwards to solve problems. In the case that 7 and a number add to 18, the inverse operation of subtraction is used to find the unknown value ($18-7=11$). If a school's entire 4th grade was divided evenly into 3 classes each with 22 students, the inverse operation of multiplication is used to determine the total students in the grade ($22 \times 3 = 66$). Additional scenarios involving inverse operations are included in the tables below.

There are a variety of real-world situations in which one or more of the operators is used to solve a problem. The tables below display the most common scenarios.

Addition & Subtraction

	Unknown Result	Unknown Change	Unknown Start
Adding to	5 students were in class. 4 more students arrived. How many students are in class? $5+4=?$	8 students were in class. More students arrived late. There are now 18 students in class. How many students arrived late? $8+?=18$ Solved by inverse operations $18-8=?$	Some students were in class early. 11 more students arrived. There are now 17 students in class. How many students were in class early? $?+11=17$ Solved by inverse operations $17-11=?$
Taking from	15 students were in class. 5 students left class. How many students are in class now? $15-5=?$	12 students were in class. Some students left class. There are now 8 students in class. How many students left class? $12-?=8$ Solved by inverse operations $8+?=12 \rightarrow 12-8=?$	Some students were in class. 3 students left class. Then there were 13 students in class. How many students were in class before? $?-3=13$ Solved by inverse operations $13+3=?$

	Unknown Total	Unknown Addends (Both)	Unknown Addends (One)
Putting together/ taking apart	The homework assignment is 10 addition problems and 8 subtraction problems. How many problems are in the homework assignment? $10 + 8 = ?$	Bobby has \$9. How much can Bobby spend on candy and how much can Bobby spend on toys? $9 = ? + ?$	Bobby has 12 pairs of pants. 5 pairs of pants are shorts, and the rest are long. How many pairs of long pants does he have? $12 = 5 + ?$ Solved by inverse operations $12 - 5 = ?$
	Unknown Difference	**Unknown Larger Value**	**Unknown Smaller Value**
Comparing	Bobby has 5 toys. Tommy has 8 toys. How many more toys does Tommy have than Bobby? $5 + ? = 8$ Solved by inverse operations $8 - 5 = ?$ Bobby has \$6. Tommy has \$10. How many fewer dollars does Bobby have than Tommy? $10 - 6 = ?$	Tommy has 2 more toys than Bobby. Bobby has 4 toys. How many toys does Tommy have? $2 + 4 = ?$ Bobby has 3 fewer dollars than Tommy. Bobby has \$8. How many dollars does Tommy have? $? - 3 = 8$ Solved by inverse operations $8 + 3 = ?$	Tommy has 6 more toys than Bobby. Tommy has 10 toys. How many toys does Bobby have? $? + 6 = 10$ Solved by inverse operations $10 - 6 = ?$ Bobby has \$5 less than Tommy. Tommy has \$9. How many dollars does Bobby have? $9 - 5 = ?$

Multiplication and Division

	Unknown Product	Unknown Group Size	Unknown Number of Groups
Equal groups	There are 5 students, and each student has 4 pieces of candy. How many pieces of candy are there in all? $5 \times 4 = ?$	14 pieces of candy are shared equally by 7 students. How many pieces of candy does each student have? $7 \times ? = 14$ Solved by inverse operations $14 \div 7 = ?$	If 18 pieces of candy are to be given out 3 to each student, how many students will get candy? $? \times 3 = 18$ Solved by inverse operations $18 \div 3 = ?$

	Unknown Product	Unknown Factor	Unknown Factor
Arrays	There are 5 rows of students with 3 students in each row. How many students are there? $5 \times 3 = ?$	If 16 students are arranged into 4 equal rows, how many students will be in each row? $4 \times ? = 16$ Solved by inverse operations $16 \div 4 = ?$	If 24 students are arranged into an array with 6 columns, how many rows are there? $? \times 6 = 24$ Solved by inverse operations $24 \div 6 = ?$

	Larger Unknown	Smaller Unknown	Multiplier Unknown
Comparing	A small popcorn costs \$1.50. A large popcorn costs 3 times as much as a small popcorn. How much does a large popcorn cost? $1.50 \times 3 = ?$	A large soda costs \$6 and that is 2 times as much as a small soda costs. How much does a small soda cost? $2 \times ? = 6$ Solved by inverse operations $6 \div 2 = ?$	A large pretzel costs \$3 and a small pretzel costs \$2. How many times as much does the large pretzel cost as the small pretzel? $? \times 2 = 3$ Solved by inverse operations $3 \div 2 = ?$

Remainders in Division Problems

If a given total cannot be divided evenly into a given number of groups, the amount left over is the remainder. Consider the following scenario: 32 textbooks must be packed into boxes for storage. Each box holds 6 textbooks. How many boxes are needed? To determine the answer, 32 is divided by 6, resulting in 5 with a remainder of 2. A remainder may be interpreted three ways:

- Add 1 to the quotient
  How many boxes will be needed? Six boxes will be needed because five will not be enough.

- Use only the quotient
  How many boxes will be full? Five boxes will be full.

- Use only the remainder
  If you only have 5 boxes, how many books will not fit? Two books will not fit.

Rational Numbers and Their Operations

Irregular Products and Quotients

The following shows examples where multiplication does not result in a product greater than both factors, and where division does not result in a quotient smaller than the dividend.

If multiplying numbers where one or more has a value less than one, the product will not be greater than both factors. For example, $6 \times \frac{1}{2} = 3$ and $0.75 \times 0.2 = 0.15$. When dividing by a number less than one, the resulting quotient will be greater than the dividend. For example, $8 \div \frac{1}{2} = 16$, because division turns into a multiplication problem, $8 \div \frac{1}{2} \rightarrow 8 \times \frac{2}{1}$. Another example is $0.5 \div 0.2$, which results in 2.5. The problem can be stated by asking how many times 0.2 will go into 0.5. The number being divided is larger than the number that goes into it, so the result will be a number larger than both factors.

Composing and Decomposing Fractions

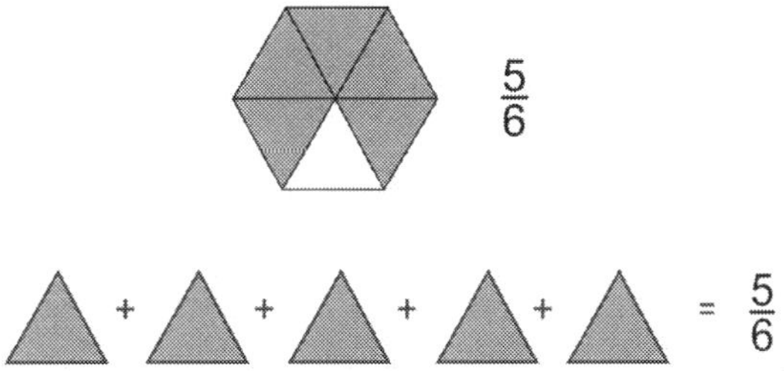

Fractions can be broken apart into sums of fractions with the same denominator. For example, the fraction $\frac{5}{6}$ can be decomposed into sums of fractions with all denominators equal to 6 and the numerators adding to 5. The fraction $\frac{5}{6}$ is decomposed as: $\frac{3}{6}+\frac{2}{6}$; or $\frac{2}{6}+\frac{2}{6}+\frac{1}{6}$; or $\frac{3}{6}+\frac{1}{6}+\frac{1}{6}$; or $\frac{1}{6}+\frac{1}{6}+\frac{1}{6}+\frac{2}{6}$; or $\frac{1}{6}+\frac{1}{6}+\frac{1}{6}+\frac{1}{6}+\frac{1}{6}$.

A unit fraction is a fraction in which the numerator is 1. If decomposing a fraction into unit fractions, the sum will consist of a unit fraction added the number of times equal to the numerator. For example, $\frac{3}{4}=\frac{1}{4}+\frac{1}{4}+\frac{1}{4}$ (unit fractions $\frac{1}{4}$ added 3 times). Composing fractions is simply the opposite of decomposing. It is the process of adding fractions with the same denominators to produce a single fraction. For example, $\frac{3}{7}+\frac{2}{7}=\frac{5}{7}$ and $\frac{1}{5}+\frac{1}{5}+\frac{1}{5}=\frac{3}{5}$.

Decrease in Value of a Unit Fraction

A unit fraction is one in which the numerator is 1 ($\frac{1}{2},\frac{1}{3},\frac{1}{8},\frac{1}{20}$, etc.). The denominator indicates the number of *equal pieces* that the whole is divided into. The greater the number of pieces, the smaller each piece will be. Therefore, the greater the denominator of a unit fraction, the smaller it is in value. Unit fractions can also be compared by converting them to decimals. For example, $\frac{1}{2}=0.5, \frac{1}{3}=0.\overline{3}, \frac{1}{8}=0.125, \frac{1}{20}=0.05$, etc.

Use of the Same Whole When Comparing Fractions

Fractions all represent parts of the same whole. Fractions may have different denominators, but they represent parts of the same one whole, like a pizza. For example, the fractions $\frac{5}{7}$ and $\frac{2}{3}$ can be difficult to compare because they have different denominators. The first fraction may represent a whole divided into seven parts, where five parts are used. The second fraction represents the same whole divided into three parts, where two are used. It may be helpful to convert one or more of the fractions so that they have common denominators for converting to equivalent fractions by finding the LCM of the denominator. Comparing is much easier if fractions are converted to the equivalent fractions of $\frac{15}{21}$ and $\frac{14}{21}$. These fractions show a whole divided into 21 parts, where the numerators can be compared because the denominators are the same.

Conversions Between Fractions, Decimals, and Percents

To convert a fraction to a decimal, the numerator is divided by the denominator. For example, $\frac{3}{8}$ can be converted to a decimal by dividing 3 by 8 ($\frac{3}{8}=0.375$). To convert a decimal to a fraction, the decimal point is dropped, and the value is written as the numerator. The denominator is the place value farthest to the right with a digit other than zero. For example, to convert .48 to a fraction, the numerator is 48, and the denominator is 100 (the digit 8 is in the hundredths place). Therefore, $0.48=\frac{48}{100}$. Fractions should be written in the simplest form, or reduced. To reduce a fraction, the numerator and denominator are divided by the largest common factor. In the previous example, 48 and 100 are both divisible by 4. Dividing the numerator and denominator by 4 results in a reduced fraction of $\frac{12}{25}$.

To convert a decimal to a percent, the number is multiplied by 100. To convert .13 to a percent, .13 is multiplied by 100 to get 13 percent. To convert a fraction to a percent, the fraction is converted to a decimal and then multiplied by 100. For example, $\frac{1}{5}=0.20$ and 0.20 multiplied by 100 produces 20 percent.

To convert a percent to a decimal, the value is divided by 100. For example, 125 percent is equal to 1.25 ($\frac{125}{100}$). To convert a percent to a fraction, the percent sign is dropped, and the value is written as the numerator with a denominator of 100. For example, $80\%=\frac{80}{100}$. This fraction can be reduced ($\frac{80}{100}=\frac{4}{5}$).

Prime Factorization

Prime and Composite Numbers

Whole numbers are classified as either prime or composite. A prime number can only be divided evenly by itself and one. For example, the number 11 can only be divided evenly by 11 and one; therefore, 11 is a prime number. A helpful way to visualize a prime number is to use concrete objects and try to divide them into equal piles. If dividing 11 coins, the only way to divide them into equal piles is to create 1 pile of 11 coins or to create 11 piles of 1 coin each. Other examples of prime numbers include 2, 3, 5, 7, 13, 17, and 19.

A composite number is any whole number that is not a prime number. A composite number is a number that can be divided evenly by one or more numbers other than itself and one. For example, the number 6 can be divided evenly by 2 and 3. Therefore, 6 is a composite number. If dividing 6 coins into equal piles, the possibilities are 1 pile of 6 coins, 2 piles of 3 coins, 3 piles of 2 coins, or 6 piles of 1 coin. Other examples of composite numbers include 4, 8, 9, 10, 12, 14, 15, 16, 18, and 20.

To determine if a number is a prime or composite number, the number is divided by every whole number greater than one and less than its own value. If it divides evenly by any of these numbers, then the number is composite. If it does not divide evenly by any of these numbers, then the number is prime. For example, when attempting to divide the number 5 by 2, 3, and 4, none of these numbers divide evenly. Therefore, 5 must be a prime number.

Factors and Multiples of Numbers

The factors of a number are all integers that can be multiplied by another integer to produce the given number. For example, 2 is multiplied by 3 to produce 6. Therefore, 2 and 3 are both factors of 6. Similarly, $1 \times 6 = 6$ and $2 \times 3 = 6$, so 1, 2, 3, and 6 are all factors of 6. Another way to explain a factor is to say that a given number divides evenly by each of its factors to produce an integer. For example, 6 does not divide evenly by 5. Therefore, 5 is not a factor of 6.

Multiples of a given number are found by taking that number and multiplying it by any other whole number. For example, 3 is a factor of 6, 9, and 12. Therefore, 6, 9, and 12 are multiples of 3. The multiples of any number are an infinite list. For example, the multiples of 5 are 5, 10, 15, 20, and so on. This list continues without end. A list of multiples is used in finding the least common multiple, or LCM, for fractions when a common denominator is needed. The denominators are written down and their multiples listed until a common number is found in both lists. This common number is the LCM.

Prime factorization breaks down each factor of a whole number until only prime numbers remain. All composite numbers can be factored into prime numbers. For example, the prime factors of 12 are 2, 2, and 3 ($2 \times 2 \times 3 = 12$). To produce the prime factors of a number, the number is factored, and any composite numbers are continuously factored until the result is the product of prime factors only. A factor tree, such as the one below, is helpful when exploring this concept.

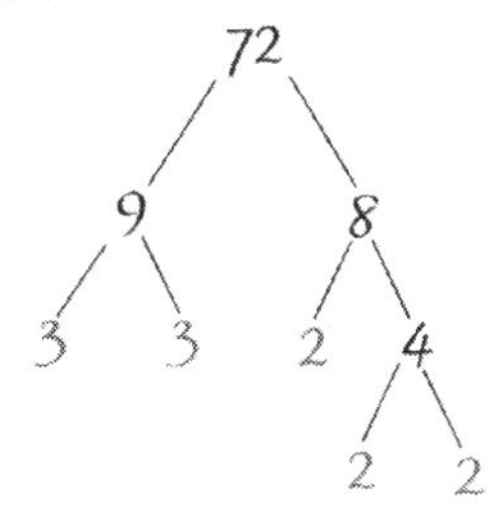

72 = 3 x 3 x 2 x 2 x 2

Ratios and Unit Rates

A ratio is a comparison of two quantities that represent separate groups. For example, if a recipe calls for 2 eggs for every 3 cups of milk, this is expressed as a ratio. Ratios can be written three ways:

- With the word "to"
- Using a colon
- As a fraction.

In the previous example, the ratio of eggs to cups of milk is written as 2 to 3, 2:3, or $\frac{2}{3}$. When writing ratios, the order is very important. The ratio of eggs to cups of milk is not the same as the ratio of cups of milk to eggs, 3:2.

In simplest form, both quantities of a ratio should be written as integers. These should also be reduced just as a fraction is reduced. For example, 5:10 is reduced to 1:2. Given a ratio where one or both quantities are expressed as a decimal or fraction, multiply both by the same number to produce integers. To write the ratio $\frac{1}{3}$ to 2 in simplest form, both quantities are multiplied by 3. The resulting ratio is 1 to 6.

A problem involving ratios may give a comparison between two groups. The problem may then provide a total and ask for a part, or provide a part and ask for a total. Consider the following: The ratio of boys to girls in the 11th grade class is 5:4. If there are a total of 270 11th grade students, how many are girls? The total number of *ratio pieces* should be determined first. The total number of 11th grade students is divided into 9 pieces. The ratio of boys to total students is 5:9, and the ratio of girls to total students is 4:9. Knowing the total number of students, the number of girls is determined by setting up a proportion: $\frac{4}{9} = \frac{x}{270}$.

A rate is a ratio comparing two quantities expressed in different units. A unit rate is a ratio in which the second quantity is one unit. Rates often include the word *per*. Examples include miles per hour, beats per minute, and price per pound. The word per is represented with a / symbol or abbreviated with the letter *p* and units abbreviated. For example, miles per hour is written as mi/h. When given a rate that is not in its simplest form (the second quantity is not one unit), both quantities are divided by the value of the second quantity. If 99 heartbeats were recorded in $1\frac{1}{2}$ minutes, both quantities are divided by $1\frac{1}{2}$ to determine the heart rate of 66 beats per minute.

Models and Objects for Representing Numbers

Concrete Models

Concrete objects are used to develop a tangible understanding of operations of rational numbers. Tools such as tiles, blocks, beads, and hundred charts are used to model problems. For example, a hundred chart (10×10) and beads can be used to model multiplication. If multiplying 5 by 4, beads are placed across 5 rows and down 4 columns producing a product of 20. Similarly, tiles can be used to model division by splitting the total into equal groups. If dividing 12 by 4, 12 tiles are placed one at a time into 4 groups. The result is 4 groups of 3. This is also an effective method for visualizing the concept of remainders.

Representations of objects can be used to expand on the concrete models of operations. Pictures, dots, and tallies can help model these concepts. Utilizing concrete models and representations creates a foundation upon which to build an abstract understanding of the operations.

Rational Numbers on a Number Line

A number line typically consists of integers (...3, 2, 1, 0, -1, -2, -3...), and is used to visually represent the value of a rational number. Each rational number has a distinct position on the line determined by comparing its value with the displayed values on the line. For example, if plotting -1.5 on the number line below, it is necessary to recognize that the value of -1.5 is 0.5 less than -1 and 0.5 greater than -2. Therefore, -1.5 is plotted halfway between -1 and -2.

Number lines can also be useful for visualizing sums and differences of rational numbers. Adding a value indicates moving to the right (values increase to the right), and subtracting a value indicates moving to the left (numbers decrease to the left). For example, $5 - 7$ is displayed by starting at 5 and moving to the left 7 spaces, if the number line is in increments of 1. This will result in an answer of -2.

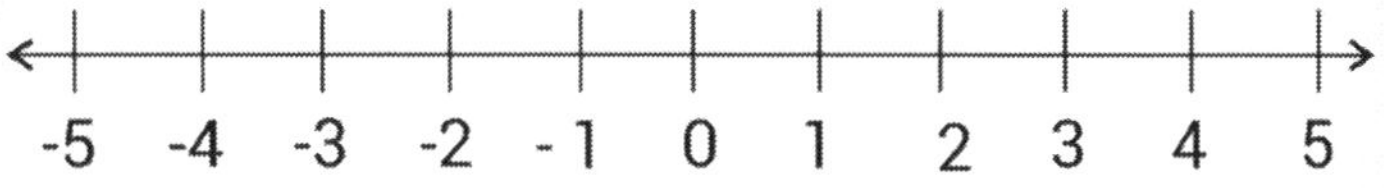

Multiplication and Division Problems

Multiplication and division are inverse operations that can be represented by using rectangular arrays, area models, and equations. Rectangular arrays include an arrangement of rows and columns that correspond to the factors and display product totals.

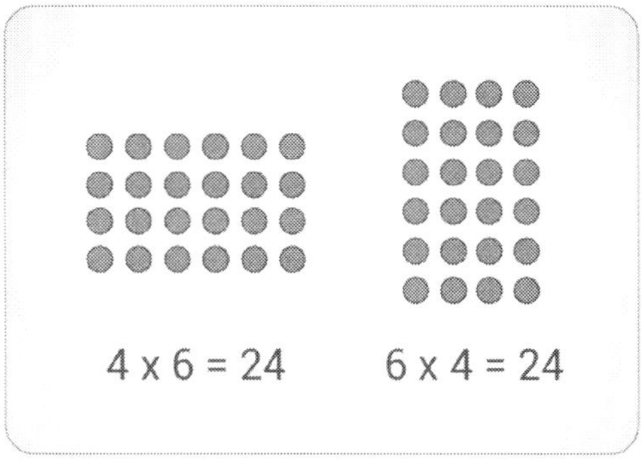

Another method of multiplication can be done with the use of an *area model*. An area model is a rectangle that is divided into rows and columns that match up to the number of place values within each number. Take the example 29×65. These two numbers can be split into simpler numbers: $29 = 25 + 4$ and $65 = 60 + 5$. The products of those 4 numbers are found within the rectangle and then summed up to get the answer. The entire process is:

$$(60 \times 25) + (5 \times 25) + (60 \times 4) + (5 \times 4) = 1{,}500 + 240 + 125 + 20 = 1{,}885$$

Here is the actual area model:

	25	**4**
60	60x25 1,500	60x4 240
5	5x25 125	5x4 20

```
  1,500
    240
    125
+    20
  -----
  1,885
```

Dividing a number by a single digit or two digits can be turned into repeated subtraction problems. An area model can be used throughout the problem that represents multiples of the divisor. For example, the answer to $8{,}580 \div 55$ can be found by subtracting 55 from 8,580 one at a time and counting the total number of subtractions necessary.

However, a simpler process involves using larger multiples of 55. First, $100 \times 55 = 5{,}500$ is subtracted from 8,580, and $3{,}080$ is leftover. Next, $50 \times 55 = 2{,}750$ is subtracted from $3{,}080$ to obtain 380. $5 \times 55 = 275$ is subtracted from 330 to obtain 55, and finally, $1 \times 55 = 55$ is subtracted from 55 to obtain zero. Therefore, there is no remainder, and the answer is $100 + 50 + 5 + 1 = 156$.

Here is a picture of the area model and the repeated subtraction process:

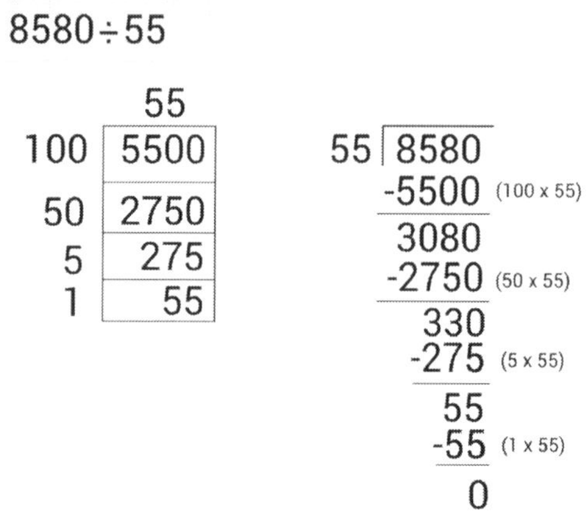

Counting Techniques

A great visualization tool for counting is the number line. For example, counting by 1's would require moving one number to the right. Counting one unit to the right from 8 results in the next value of 9. This idea can be utilized with both counting and adding. Adding 3 + 2 involves starting with 3 on the number line and moving two places to the right, resulting in 5.

A similar approach is used with counting backward, which is done by moving to the left on the number line. Counting backward leads to the more complicated process of subtraction. For instance, the number line can be used to subtract $5 - 3$. Start with 5 and move 3 places to the left, which result in the answer of 2.

Skip counting involves counting forward by numerical values other than 1. For example, 10, 20, 30, 40, etc., is skip counting by 10. Notice that each value is obtained by adding 10 to the previous value. Finding even numbers is another form of skip counting. The pattern 2, 4, 6, 8, 10, etc., is found by adding 2 to the previous number. As long as an even number is first in the sequence, another even number will be obtained. Odd numbers can be found in the same manner. As long as an odd number is the starting value, adding 2 each time will result in a sequence of odd numbers such as 1, 3, 5, 7, etc.

Skip counting can be also visualized using a number line. For instance, to skip count by 5, move a number 5 units to the right on the number line. Skip counting is a good lead into learning multiplication tables. For instance, counting by 5, such as in the sequence 5, 10, 15, 20, etc., allows one to learn multiplication by 5. The first number is 1 times 5, the second number is 2 times 5, and the third number is 3 times 5, etc.

Counting how many ways something can happen when order does not matter is called a combination. For example, determining how many ways to select 3 students out of 10 to participate in a science fair would make use of a combination. The factorial symbol n! represents multiplying each natural number from *n* down to 1. For instance,

$4! = 4 \times 3 \times 2 \times 1$. The formula for a combination is the following: the number of ways to select k items from a group of n items, where order does not matter, is $\binom{n}{k} = \frac{n!}{k!(n-k)!}$. Therefore, the number of ways 3 students out of 10 could be selected is $\binom{10}{3} = \frac{10!}{3!(10-3)!} = \frac{10!}{3!7!} = \frac{10\times9\times7}{3\times2\times1} = 120$.

Place Value and Rounding

Place Value

The number system that is used consists of only ten different digits or characters. However, this system is used to represent an infinite number of values. The place value system makes this infinite number of values possible. The position in which a digit is written corresponds to a given value. Starting from the decimal point (which is implied, if not physically present), each subsequent place value to the left represents a value greater than the one before it. Conversely, starting from the decimal point, each subsequent place value to the right represents a value less than the one before it.

The names for the place values to the left of the decimal point are as follows:

Billions	Hundred-Millions	Ten-Millions	Millions	Hundred-Thousands	Ten-Thousands	Thousands	Hundreds	Tens	Ones

*Note that this table can be extended infinitely further to the left.

The names for the place values to the right of the decimal point are as follows:

Decimal Point (.)	Tenths	Hundredths	Thousandths	Ten-Thousandths	...

*Note that this table can be extended infinitely further to the right.

When given a multi-digit number, the value of each digit depends on its place value. Consider the number 682,174.953. Referring to the chart above, it can be determined that the digit 8 is in the ten-thousands place. It is in the fifth place to the left of the decimal point. Its value is 8 ten-thousands or 80,000. The digit 5 is two places to the right of the decimal point. Therefore, the digit 5 is in the hundredths place. Its value is 5 hundredths or $\frac{5}{100}$ (equivalent to .05).

Rounding

Rounding is an important concept dealing with place value. **Rounding** is the process of either bumping a number up or leaving it the same, based on a specified place value. First, the place value is specified. Then, the digit to its right is looked at. For example, if rounding to the nearest hundreds place, the digit in the tens place is used. If it is a 0, 1, 2, 3, or 4, the digit being rounded to is left alone. If it is a 5, 6, 7, 8 or 9, the digit being rounded to is increased by one.

All other digits before the decimal point are then changed to zeros, and the digits in decimal places are dropped. If a decimal place is being rounded to, all subsequent digits are just dropped. For example, if 845,231.45 was to be rounded to the nearest thousands place, the answer would be 845,000. The 5 would remain the same due to the 2 in the hundreds place. Also, if 4.567 was to be rounded to the nearest tenths place, the answer would be 4.6. The 5 increased to 6 due to the 6 in the hundredths place, and the rest of the decimal is dropped.

Fractions

A **fraction** is a part of something that is whole. Items such as apples can be cut into parts to help visualize fractions. If an apple is cut into 2 equal parts, each part represents ½ of the apple. If each half is then cut into two parts, the apple now is cut into quarters. Each piece now represents ¼ of the apple. In this example, each part is equal because they all have the same size. Geometric shapes, such as circles and squares, can also be utilized to help visualize the idea of fractions. For example, a circle can be drawn on the board and divided into 6 equal parts:

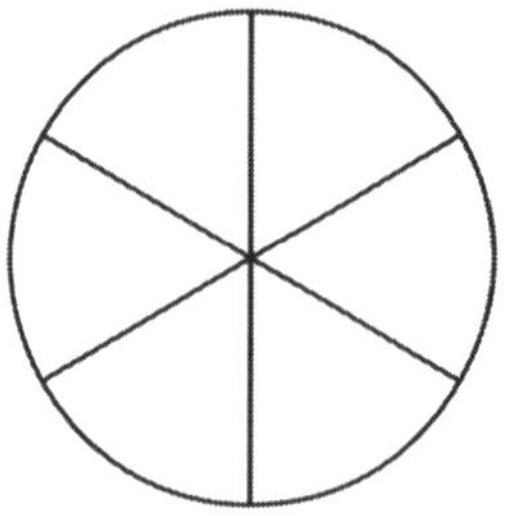

Shading can be used to represent parts of the circle that can be translated into fractions. The top of the fraction, the **numerator,** can represent how many segments are shaded. The bottom of the fraction, the **denominator,** can represent the number of segments that the circle is broken into. A pie is a good analogy to use in this example. If one piece of the circle is shaded, or one piece of pie is cut out, $1/_6$ of the object is being referred to. An apple, a pie, or a circle can be utilized in order to compare simple fractions. For example, showing that $\frac{1}{2}$ is larger than $\frac{1}{4}$ and that $\frac{1}{4}$ is smaller than $\frac{1}{3}$ can be accomplished through shading. A **unit fraction** is a fraction in which the numerator is 1, and the denominator is a positive whole number. It represents one part of a whole—one piece of pie.

Imagine that an apple pie has been baked for a holiday party, and the full pie has eight slices. After the party, there are five slices left. How could the amount of the pie that remains be expressed as a fraction? The numerator is 5 since there are 5 pieces left, and the denominator is 8 since there were eight total slices in the whole pie. Thus, expressed as a fraction, the leftover pie totals $\frac{5}{8}$ of the original amount.

Fractions come in three different varieties: proper fractions, improper fractions, and mixed numbers. **Proper fractions** have a numerator less than the denominator, such as $\frac{3}{8}$, but **improper fractions** have a numerator greater than the denominator, such as $\frac{7}{2}$. **Mixed numbers** combine a whole number with a proper fraction, such as $3\frac{1}{2}$. Any mixed number can be written as an improper fraction by multiplying the integer by the denominator, adding the product to the value of the numerator, and dividing the sum by the original denominator. For example:

$$3\frac{1}{2} = \frac{3 \times 2 + 1}{2} = \frac{7}{2}$$

Whole numbers can also be converted into fractions by placing the whole number as the numerator and making the denominator 1. For example, $3 = \frac{3}{1}$.

The bar in a fraction represents division. Therefore $\frac{6}{5}$ is the same as $6 \div 5$. In order to rewrite it as a mixed number, division is performed to obtain $6 \div 5 = 1 \text{ R } 1$. The remainder is then converted into fraction form. The actual remainder becomes the numerator of a fraction, and the divisor becomes the denominator. Therefore, $1 \text{ R } 1$ is written as $1\frac{1}{5}$, a mixed number. A mixed number can also decompose into the addition of a whole number and a fraction.

For example:

$$1\frac{1}{5} = 1 + \frac{1}{5} \text{ and } 4\frac{5}{6} = 4 + \frac{1}{6} + \frac{1}{6} + \frac{1}{6} + \frac{1}{6} + \frac{1}{6}$$

Every fraction can be built from a combination of unit fractions.

One of the most fundamental concepts of fractions is their ability to be manipulated by multiplication or division. This is possible since $\frac{n}{n} = 1$ for any non-zero integer. As a result, multiplying or dividing by $\frac{n}{n}$ will not alter the original fraction since any number multiplied or divided by 1 doesn't change the value of that number. Fractions of the same value are known as equivalent fractions. For example, $\frac{2}{8}$, $\frac{25}{100}$, and $\frac{40}{160}$ are equivalent, as they are all equal to $\frac{1}{4}$.

Like fractions, or **equivalent fractions**, are the terms used to describe these fractions that are made up of different numbers but represent the same quantity. For example, the given fractions are $\frac{4}{8}$ and $\frac{3}{6}$. If a pie was cut into 8 pieces and 4 pieces were removed, half of the pie would remain. Also, if a pie was split into 6 pieces and 3 pieces were eaten, half of the pie would also remain. Therefore, both of the fractions represent half of a pie. These two fractions are referred to as like fractions. **Unlike fractions** are fractions that are different and do not represent equal quantities. When working with fractions in mathematical expressions, like fractions should be simplified. Both $\frac{4}{8}$ and $\frac{3}{6}$ can be simplified into $\frac{1}{2}$.

Comparing fractions can be completed through the use of a number line. For example, if $\frac{3}{5}$ and $\frac{6}{10}$ need to be compared, each fraction should be plotted on a number line. To plot $\frac{3}{5}$, the area from 0 to 1 should be broken into 5 equal segments, and the fraction represents 3 of them. To plot $\frac{6}{10}$, the area from 0 to 1 should be broken into 10 equal segments, and the fraction represents 6 of them.

It can be seen that $\frac{3}{5} = \frac{6}{10}$

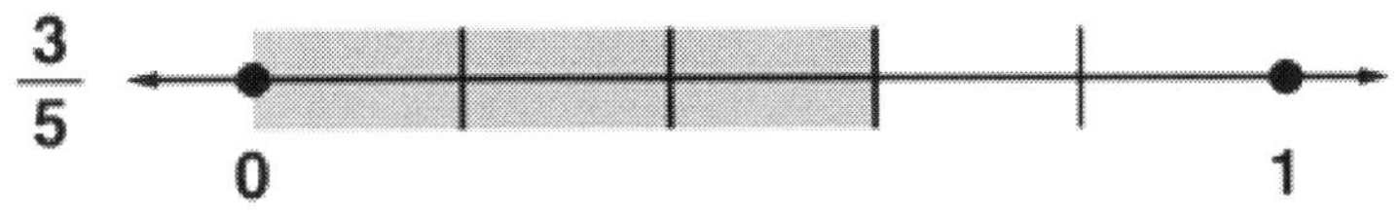

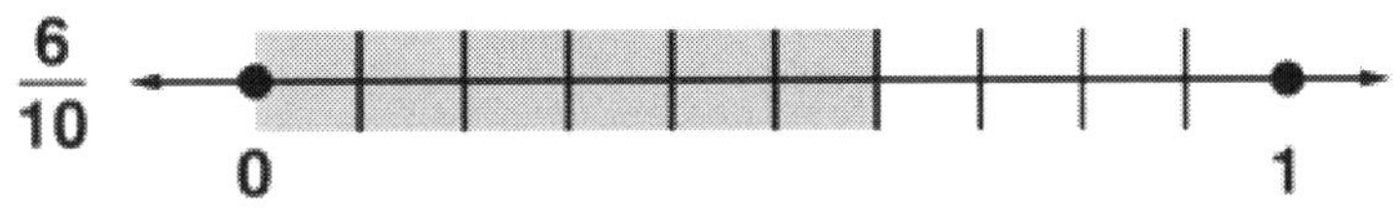

Like fractions are plotted at the same point on a number line. Unit fractions can also be used to compare fractions. For example, if it is known that:

$$\frac{4}{5} > \frac{1}{2}$$

and

$$\frac{1}{2} > \frac{4}{10}$$

Then, it is also known that:

$$\frac{4}{5} > \frac{4}{10}$$

Also, converting improper fractions to mixed numbers can be helpful in comparing fractions because the whole number portion of the number is more visible.

Adding and subtracting mixed numbers and fractions can be completed by decomposing fractions into a sum of whole numbers and unit fractions. For example, the given problem is:

$$5\frac{3}{7} + 2\frac{1}{7}$$

Decomposing into:

$$5 + \frac{1}{7} + \frac{1}{7} + \frac{1}{7} + 2 + \frac{1}{7}$$

This shows that the whole numbers can be added separately from the unit fractions. The answer is:

$$5 + 2 + \frac{1}{7} + \frac{1}{7} + \frac{1}{7} + \frac{1}{7} = 7 + \frac{4}{7} = 7\frac{4}{7}$$

Although many equivalent fractions exist, they are easier to compare and interpret when reduced or simplified. The numerator and denominator of a simple fraction will have no factors in common other than 1. When reducing or simplifying fractions, divide the numerator and denominator by the greatest common factor. A simple strategy is to divide the numerator and denominator by low numbers, like 2, 3, or 5 until arriving at a simple fraction, but the same thing could be achieved by determining the greatest common factor for both the numerator and denominator and dividing each by it. Using the first method is preferable when both the numerator and denominator are even, end in 5, or are obviously a multiple of another number. However, if no numbers seem to work, it will be necessary to factor the numerator and denominator to find the GCF. Here are some examples:

1) Simplify the fraction $\frac{6}{8}$:

Dividing the numerator and denominator by 2 results in $\frac{3}{4}$, which is a simple fraction.

2) Simplify the fraction $\frac{12}{36}$:

Dividing the numerator and denominator by 2 leaves $\frac{6}{18}$. This isn't a simple fraction, as both the numerator and denominator have factors in common. Dividing each by 3 results in $\frac{2}{6}$, but this can be further simplified by dividing by 2 to get $\frac{1}{3}$. This is the simplest fraction, as the numerator is 1. In cases like this, multiple division operations can be avoided by determining the greatest common factor (12, in this case) between the numerator and denominator.

3) Simplify the fraction $\frac{18}{54}$ by dividing by the greatest common factor:

First, determine the factors for the numerator and denominator. The factors of 18 are 1, 2, 3, 6, 9, and 18. The factors of 54 are 1, 2, 3, 6, 9, 18, 27, and 54. Thus, the greatest common factor is 18. Dividing $\frac{18}{54}$ by 18 leaves $\frac{1}{3}$, which is the simplest fraction. This method takes slightly more work, but it definitively arrives at the simplest fraction.

Adding and Subtracting Fractions

Adding and subtracting fractions that have the same denominators involves adding or subtracting the numerators. The denominator will stay the same. Therefore, the decomposition process can be made simpler, and the fractions do not have to be broken into unit fractions.

For example, the given problem is:

$$4\frac{7}{8} - 2\frac{6}{8}$$

The answer is found by adding the answers to both

$$4 - 2 \text{ and } \frac{7}{8} - \frac{6}{8}$$

$$2 + \frac{1}{8} = 2\frac{1}{8}$$

A common mistake would be to add the denominators so that $\frac{1}{4} + \frac{1}{4} = \frac{1}{8}$ or to add numerators and denominators so that $\frac{1}{4} + \frac{1}{4} = \frac{2}{8}$. However, conceptually, it is known that two quarters make a half, so neither one of these are correct.

If two fractions have different denominators, equivalent fractions must be used to add or subtract them. The fractions must be converted into fractions that have common denominators. A **least common denominator** or the product of the two denominators can be used as the common denominator. For example, in the problem $\frac{5}{6} + \frac{2}{3}$, either 6, which is the least common denominator, or 18, which is the product of the denominators, can be used. In order to use 6, $\frac{2}{3}$ must be converted to sixths. A number line can be used to show the equivalent fraction is $\frac{4}{6}$. What happens is that $\frac{2}{3}$ is multiplied by a fractional form of 1 to obtain a denominator of 6. Hence:

$$\frac{2}{3} \times \frac{2}{2} = \frac{4}{6}$$

Therefore, the problem is now:

$$\frac{5}{6} + \frac{4}{6} = \frac{9}{6}$$

which can be simplified into $\frac{3}{2}$. In order to use 18, both fractions must be converted into having 18 as their denominator. $\frac{5}{6}$ would have to be multiplied by $\frac{3}{3}$, and $\frac{2}{3}$ would need to be multiplied by $\frac{6}{6}$.The addition problem would be:

$$\frac{15}{18} + \frac{12}{18} = \frac{27}{18}$$

which reduces into $\frac{3}{2}$.

It is always possible to find a common denominator by multiplying the denominators. However, when the denominators are large numbers, this method is unwieldy, especially if the answer must be provided in its simplest form. Thus, it's beneficial to find the **least common denominator** of the fractions—the least common denominator is incidentally also the **least common multiple**.

Once equivalent fractions have been found with common denominators, simply add or subtract the numerators to arrive at the answer:

1) $\frac{1}{2} + \frac{3}{4} = \frac{2}{4} + \frac{3}{4} = \frac{5}{4}$

2) $\frac{3}{12} + \frac{11}{20} = \frac{15}{60} + \frac{33}{60} = \frac{48}{60} = \frac{4}{5}$

3) $\frac{7}{9} - \frac{4}{15} = \frac{35}{45} - \frac{12}{45} = \frac{23}{45}$

4) $\frac{5}{6} - \frac{7}{18} = \frac{15}{18} - \frac{7}{18} = \frac{8}{18} = \frac{4}{9}$

Multiplying and Dividing Fractions

Of the four basic operations that can be performed on fractions, the one that involves the least amount of work is multiplication. To multiply two fractions, simply multiply the numerators together, multiply the denominators together, and place the products of each as a fraction. Whole numbers and mixed numbers can also be expressed as a fraction, as described above, to multiply with a fraction.

Because multiplication is commutative, multiplying a fraction by a whole number is the same as multiplying a whole number by a fraction. The problem involves adding a fraction a specific number of times. The problem $3 \times \frac{1}{4}$ can be translated into adding the unit fraction three times:

$$\frac{1}{4} + \frac{1}{4} + \frac{1}{4} = \frac{3}{4}$$

In the problem $4 \times \frac{2}{5}$, the fraction can be decomposed into $\frac{1}{5} + \frac{1}{5}$ and then added four times to obtain $\frac{8}{5}$. Also, both of these answers can be found by just multiplying the whole number by the numerator of the fraction being multiplied.

The whole numbers can be written in fraction form as:

$$\frac{3}{1} \times \frac{1}{4} = \frac{3}{4}$$

$$\frac{4}{1} \times \frac{2}{5} = \frac{8}{5}$$

Multiplying a fraction by a fraction involves multiplying the numerators together separately and the denominators together separately. For example:

$$\frac{3}{8} \times \frac{2}{3} = \frac{3 \times 2}{8 \times 3} = \frac{6}{24}$$

This can then be reduced to $\frac{1}{4}$.

Dividing a fraction by a fraction is actually a multiplication problem. It involves flipping the divisor and then multiplying normally. For example:

$$\frac{22}{5} \div \frac{1}{2} = \frac{22}{5} \times \frac{2}{1} = \frac{44}{5}$$

The same procedure can be implemented for division problems involving fractions and whole numbers. The whole number can be rewritten as a fraction over a denominator of 1, and then division can be completed.

A common denominator approach can also be used in dividing fractions. Considering the same problem, $\frac{22}{5} \div \frac{1}{2}$, a common denominator between the two fractions is 10. $\frac{22}{5}$ would be rewritten as $\frac{22}{5} \times \frac{2}{2} = \frac{44}{10}$, and $\frac{1}{2}$ would be rewritten as:

$$\frac{1}{2} \times \frac{5}{5} = \frac{5}{10}$$

Dividing both numbers straight across results in:

$$\frac{44}{10} \div \frac{5}{10} = \frac{44/_5}{10/_{10}} = \frac{44/_5}{1} = \frac{44}{5}$$

Many real-world problems will involve the use of fractions. Key words include actual fraction values, such as *half, quarter, third, fourth*, etc. The best approach to solving word problems involving fractions is to draw a picture or diagram that represents the scenario being discussed, while deciding which type of operation is necessary in order to solve the problem. A phrase such as "one fourth of 60 pounds of coal" creates a scenario in which multiplication should be used, and the mathematical form of the phrase is $\frac{1}{4} \times 60$.

Multi-Step Problems

In solving multi-step problems, the first step is to line up the available information. Then, try to decide what information the problem is asking to be found. Once this is determined, construct a strip diagram to display the known information along with any information to be calculated. Finally, the missing information can be represented by a **variable** (a letter from the alphabet that represents a number) in a mathematical equation that the student can solve.

For example, Delilah collects stickers, and her friends gave her some stickers to add to her current collection. Joe gave her 45 stickers, and Aimee gave her 2 times the number of stickers that Joe gave Delilah. How many stickers did Delilah have to start with, if after her friends gave her more stickers, she had a total of 187 stickers?

In order to solve this, the given information must first be sorted out. Joe gives Delilah 45 stickers, Aimee gives Delilah 2 times the number Joe gives (2×45), and the end total of stickers is 187.

A strip diagram represents these numbers as follows:

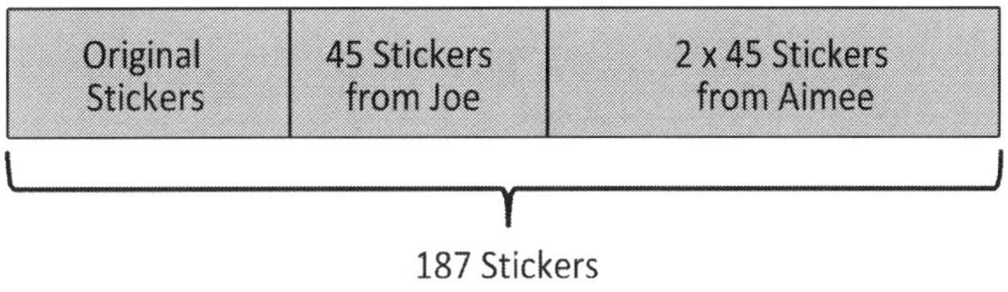

The entire situation can be modeled by this equation, using the variable s to stand for the original number of stickers:

$$s + 45 + (2 \times 45) = 187.$$

Solving for s would give the solution, as follows:

$$s + 45 + 90 = 187$$

$$s + 135 = 187$$

$$s + 135 - 135 = 187 - 135$$

$$s = 52 \text{ stickers}$$

Word problems take concepts that are learned in the classroom and turn them into real-life situations. Some parts of the problem are known and at least one part is unknown. There are three types of instances in which something can be unknown: the starting point, the change, or the final result. These can all be missing from the given information.

For solving problems with unknown factors, it is often easiest to set up an array to visualize the grouping of the information. In these problems, set up the initial numbers in uniformly sized groups, so the solution can be determined by inspection of the grouping.

Find the missing number (?) in the following equation:

$$? \times 5 = 35$$

Knowing that one of the factors is to be multiplied is 5 allows the groupings to be made in sets of five columns. In this case, there 5 columns of items are created, until the desired number (35) is reached.

Here, the number of 35 is reached with the seventh row of items. Therefore, the missing factor is 7.

$$5 \times 7 = 35$$

The same problem could be demonstrated with the equation:

$$5 \times ? = 35$$

This would simply require the information to be grouped into five rows, and items added evenly until the desired number (35) is reached.

Again, the solution is:

$$5 \times 7 = 35.$$

This demonstrates the commutative property of multiplication by showing the missing factor could be the number of rows or the number of columns, and yet result in the same solution.

Patterns and Algebra

Graphing Algebraic Functions and Relations

To graph relations and functions, the Cartesian plane is used. This means to think of the plane as being given a grid of squares, with one direction being the *x*-axis and the other direction the *y*-axis. Generally, the independent variable is placed along the horizontal axis, and the dependent variable is placed along the vertical axis. Any point on the plane can be specified by saying how far to go along the *x*-axis and how far along the *y*-axis with a pair of numbers (x, y). Specific values for these pairs can be given names such as $C = (-1, 3)$. Negative values mean to move left or down; positive values mean to move right or up. The point where the axes cross one another is called the **origin**. The origin has coordinates $(0, 0)$ and is usually called *O* when given a specific label. An illustration of the Cartesian plane, along with the plotted points $(2, 1)$ and $(-1, -1)$, is below.

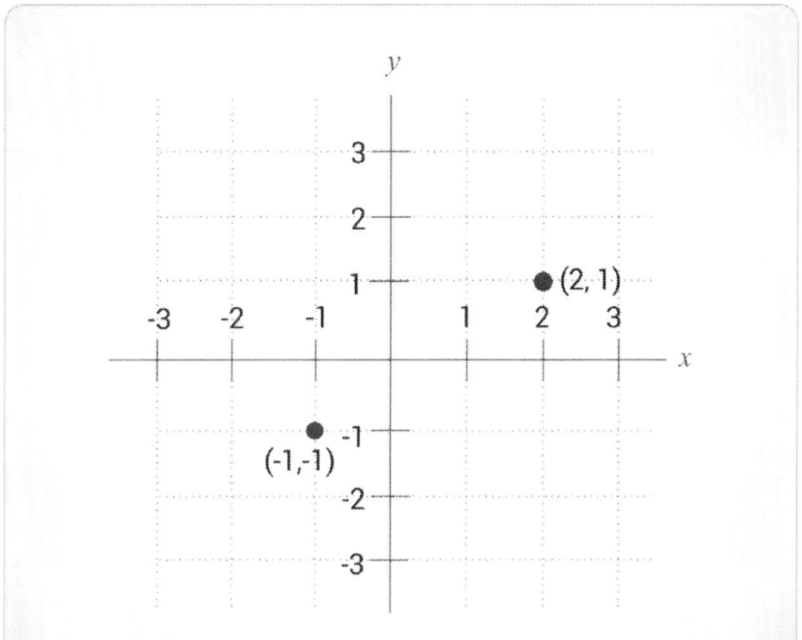

Relations also can be graphed by marking each point whose coordinates satisfy the relation. If the relation is a function, then there is only one value of y for any given value of x. This leads to the **vertical line test**: if a relation is graphed, then the relation is a function if any possible vertical line drawn anywhere along the graph would only touch the graph of the relation in no more than one place. Conversely, when graphing a function, then any possible vertical line drawn will not touch the graph of the function at any point or will touch the function at just one point. This test is made from the definition of a function, where each x-value must be mapped to one and only one y-value.

Using Patterns to Make Predictions

An arithmetic or geometric sequence can be written as a formula and used to determine unknown steps without writing out the entire sequence. (Note that a similar process for repeating patterns is covered in the previous section.) An arithmetic sequence progresses by a **common difference**. To determine the common difference, any step is subtracted by the step that precedes it. In the sequence 4, 9, 14, 19 ... the common difference, or d, is 5. By expressing each step as a_1, a_2, a_3, etc., a formula can be written to represent the sequence. a_1 is the first step. To produce step two, step 1 (a_1) is added to the common difference (d):

$$a_2 = a_1 + d$$

To produce step three, the common difference (d) is added twice to a_1:

$$a_3 = a_1 + 2d$$

To produce step four, the common difference (d) is added three times to a_1:

$$a_4 = a_1 + 3d$$

Following this pattern allows a general rule for arithmetic sequences to be written. For any term of the sequence (a_n), the first step (a_1) is added to the product of the common difference (d) and one less than the step of the term ($n - 1$):

$$a_n = a_1 + (n - 1)d$$

Suppose the 8th term (a_8) is to be found in the previous sequence. By knowing the first step (a_1) is 4 and the common difference (d) is 5, the formula can be used:

$$a_n = a_1 + (n - 1)d \rightarrow a_8$$

$$4 + (7)5 \rightarrow a_8 = 39$$

In a geometric sequence, each step is produced by multiplying or dividing the previous step by the same number. The *common ratio*, or (r), can be determined by dividing any step by the previous step. In the sequence 1, 3, 9, 27 ... the common ratio (r) is 3 ($\frac{3}{1} = 3$ or $\frac{9}{3} = 3$ or $\frac{27}{9} = 3$). Each successive step can be expressed as a product of the first step (a_1) and the common ratio (r) to some power. For example:

$$a_2 = a_1 \times r; a_3 = a_1 \times r \times r$$

or

$$a_3 = a_1 \times r^2; a_4 = a_1 \times r \times r \times r$$

or

$$a_4 = a\_1 \times r^3$$

Following this pattern, a general rule for geometric sequences can be written. For any term of the sequence (a_n), the first step (a_1) is multiplied by the common ratio (r) raised to the power one less than the step of the term ($n - 1$):

$$a_n = a_1 \times r^{(n-1)}$$

Suppose for the previous sequence, the 7th term (a_7) is to be found. Knowing the first step (a_1) is one, and the common ratio (r) is 3, the formula can be used:

$$a_n = a_1 \times r^{(n-1)}$$

$$a_7 = (1) \times 3^6$$

$$a_7 = 729$$

Sequences and Patterns

Number and Shape Patterns

Patterns within a sequence can come in 2 distinct forms: the items (shapes, numbers, etc.) either repeat in a constant order, or the items change from one step to another in some consistent way. The core is the smallest unit, or number of items, that repeats in a repeating pattern. For example, the pattern oo▲oo▲o... has a core that is oo▲. Knowing only the core, the pattern can be extended. Knowing the number of steps in the core allows the identification of an item in each step without drawing/writing the entire pattern out. For example, suppose the tenth item in the previous pattern must be determined. Because the core consists of three items (oo▲), the core repeats in multiples of 3. In other words, steps 3, 6, 9, 12, etc. will be ▲ completing the core with the core starting over on the next step. For the above example, the 9th step will be ▲ and the 10th will be o.

The most common patterns in which each item changes from one step to the next are arithmetic and geometric sequences. An arithmetic sequence is one in which the items increase or decrease by a constant difference. In other words, the same thing is added or subtracted to each item or step to produce the next. To determine if a sequence is arithmetic, determine what must be added or subtracted to step one to produce step two. Then, check if the same thing is added/subtracted to step two to produce step three. The same thing must be added/subtracted to step three to produce step four, and so on.

Consider the pattern 13, 10, 7, 4 ... To get from step one (13) to step two (10) by adding or subtracting requires subtracting by 3. The next step is checking if subtracting 3 from step two (10) will produce step three (7), and subtracting 3 from step three (7) will produce step four (4). In this case, the pattern holds true. Therefore, this is an arithmetic sequence in which each step is produced by subtracting 3 from the previous step. To extend the sequence, 3 is subtracted from the last step to produce the next. The next three numbers in the sequence are 1, -2, -5.

A geometric sequence is one in which each step is produced by multiplying or dividing the previous step by the same number. To determine if a sequence is geometric, decide what step one must be multiplied or divided by to produce step two. Then check if multiplying or dividing step two by the same number produces step three, and so on. Consider the pattern 2, 8, 32, 128 ... To get from step one (2) to step two (8) requires multiplication by 4. The next step determines if multiplying step two (8) by 4 produces step three (32), and multiplying step three (32) by 4 produces step four (128). In this case, the pattern holds true. Therefore, this is a geometric sequence in which each step is produced by multiplying the previous step by 4. To extend the sequence, the last step is multiplied by 4 and repeated. The next three numbers in the sequence are 512; 2,048; 8,192.

Although arithmetic and geometric sequences typically use numbers, these sequences can also be represented by shapes. For example, an arithmetic sequence could consist of shapes with three sides, four sides, and five sides (add one side to the previous step to produce the next). A geometric sequence could consist of eight blocks, four blocks, and two blocks (each step is produced by dividing the number of blocks in the previous step by 2).

Conjectures, Predictions, or Generalizations Based on Patterns

An arithmetic or geometric sequence can be written as a formula and used to determine unknown steps without writing out the entire sequence. (Note that a similar process for repeating patterns is covered in the previous section.) An arithmetic sequence progresses by a **common difference**. To determine the common difference, any step is subtracted by the step that precedes it. In the sequence 4, 9, 14, 19 ... the common difference, or d, is 5. By expressing each step as a_1, a_2, a_3, etc., a formula can be written to represent the sequence. a_1 is the first step. To produce step two, step 1 (a_1) is added to the common difference (d):

$$a_2 = a_1 + d$$

To produce step three, the common difference (d) is added twice to a_1:

$$a_3 = a_1 + 2d$$

To produce step four, the common difference (d) is added three times to a_1:

$$a_4 = a_1 + 3d$$

Following this pattern allows a general rule for arithmetic sequences to be written. For any term of the sequence (a_n), the first step (a_1) is added to the product of the common difference (d) and one less than the step of the term ($n - 1$):

$$a_n = a_1 + (n - 1)d$$

Suppose the 8th term (a_8) is to be found in the previous sequence. By knowing the first step (a_1) is 4 and the common difference (d) is 5, the formula can be used:

$$a_n = a_1 + (n - 1)d \rightarrow a_8 = 4 + (7)5 \rightarrow a_8 = 39$$

In a geometric sequence, each step is produced by multiplying or dividing the previous step by the same number. The **common ratio**, or (r), can be determined by dividing any step by the previous step. In the sequence 1, 3, 9, 27

... the common ratio (r) is 3($\frac{3}{1} = 3$ or $\frac{9}{3} = 3$ or $\frac{27}{9} = 3$). Each successive step can be expressed as a product of the first step (a_1) and the common ratio (r) to some power. For example:

$$a_2 = a_1 \times r$$

$$a_3 = a_1 \times r \times r \text{ or } a_3 = a_1 \times r^2$$

$$a_4 = a_1 \times r \times r \times r \text{ or } a_4 = a\_1 \times r^3$$

Following this pattern, a general rule for geometric sequences can be written. For any term of the sequence (a_n), the first step (a_1) is multiplied by the common ratio (r) raised to the power one less than the step of the term ($n - 1$):

$$a_n = a_1 \times r^{(n-1)}$$

Suppose for the previous sequence, the 7th term (a_7) is to be found. Knowing the first step (a_1) is one, and the common ratio (r) is 3, the formula can be used:

$$a_n = a_1 \times r^{(n-1)} \to a_7 = (1) \times 3^6 \to a_7 = 729$$

Corresponding Terms of Two Numerical Patterns

When given two numerical patterns, the corresponding terms should be examined to determine if a relationship exists between them. Corresponding terms between patterns are the pairs of numbers that appear in the same step of the two sequences. Consider the following patterns 1, 2, 3, 4 ... and 3, 6, 9, 12 ... The corresponding terms are: 1 and 3; 2 and 6; 3 and 9; and 4 and 12. To identify the relationship, each pair of corresponding terms is examined and the possibilities of performing an operation (+, −, ×, ÷) to the term from the first sequence to produce the corresponding term in the second sequence are determined.

In this case:

$1 + 2 = 3$ or $1 \times 3 = 3$

$2 + 4 = 6$ or $2 \times 3 = 6$

$3 + 6 = 9$ or $3 \times 3 = 9$

$4 + 8 = 12$ or $4 \times 3 = 12$

The consistent pattern is that the number from the first sequence multiplied by 3 equals its corresponding term in the second sequence. By assigning each sequence a label (input and output) or variable (x and y), the relationship can be written as an equation. If the first sequence represents the inputs, or x, and the second sequence represents the outputs, or y, the relationship can be expressed as $y = 3x$.

Consider the following sets of numbers:

a	2	4	6	8
b	6	8	10	12

To write a rule for the relationship between the values for a and the values for b, the corresponding terms (2 and 6; 4 and 8; 6 and 10; 8 and 12) are examined. The possibilities for producing b from a are:

$2 + 4 = 6$ or $2 \times 3 = 6$

$4 + 4 = 8$ or $4 \times 2 = 8$

$6 + 4 = 10$

$8 + 4 = 12$ or $8 \times 1.5 = 12$

The consistent pattern is that adding 4 to the value of a produces the value of b. The relationship can be written as the equation $a + 4 = b$.

Algebraic Expressions and Equations

Differentiating between Algebraic Expressions and Equations

An algebraic expression is a statement about an unknown quantity expressed in mathematical symbols. A variable is used to represent the unknown quantity, usually denoted by a letter. An equation is a statement in which two expressions (at least one containing a variable) are equal to each other. An algebraic expression can be thought of as a mathematical phrase and an equation can be thought of as a mathematical sentence.

Algebraic expressions and equations both contain numbers, variables, and mathematical operations. The following are examples of algebraic expressions: $5x + 3, 7xy - 8(x^2 + y)$, and $\sqrt{a^2 + b^2}$. An expression can be simplified or evaluated for given values of variables. The following are examples of equations: $2x + 3 = 7$, $a^2 + b^2 = c^2$, and $2x + 5 = 3x - 2$. An equation contains two sides separated by an equal sign. Equations can be solved to determine the value(s) of the variable for which the statement is true.

Adding and Subtracting Linear Algebraic Expressions

An algebraic expression is simplified by combining like terms. A term is a number, variable, or product of a number and variables separated by addition and subtraction. For the algebraic expression $3x^2 - 4x + 5 - 5x^2 + x - 3$, the terms are $3x^2$, $-4x$, 5, $-5x^2$, x, and -3. Like terms have the same variables raised to the same powers (exponents). The like terms for the previous example are $3x^2$ and $-5x^2$, $-4x$ and x, and 5 and -3. To combine like terms, the coefficients (numerical factor of the term including sign) are added, and the variables and their powers are kept the same. Note that if a coefficient is not written, it is an implied coefficient of 1 ($x = 1x$). The previous example will simplify to:

$$-2x^2 - 3x + 2$$

When adding or subtracting algebraic expressions, each expression is written in parenthesis. The negative sign is distributed when necessary, and like terms are combined. Consider the following: add $2a + 5b - 2$ to $a - 2b + 8c - 4$. The sum is set as follows:

$$(a - 2b + 8c - 4) + (2a + 5b - 2)$$

In front of each set of parentheses is an implied positive one, which, when distributed, does not change any of the terms. Therefore, the parentheses are dropped and like terms are combined:

$$a - 2b + 8c - 4 + 2a + 5b - 2 = 3a + 3b + 8c - 6$$

Consider the following problem: Subtract $2a + 5b - 2$ from $a - 2b + 8c - 4$. The difference is set as follows:

$$(a - 2b + 8c - 4) - (2a + 5b - 2)$$

The implied one in front of the first set of parentheses will not change those four terms. However, distributing the implied -1 in front of the second set of parentheses will change the sign of each of those three terms:

$$a - 2b + 8c - 4 - 2a - 5b + 2$$

Combining like terms yields the simplified expression:

$$-a - 7b + 8c - 2$$

Using Fractions to Solve for Ratios and Percentages

Using Ratio Reasoning to Convert Rates

Ratios and rates can be used together to convert rates into different units. For example, if someone is driving 50 kilometers per hour, that rate can be converted into miles per hour by using a ratio known as the **conversion factor**. Since the given value contains kilometers and the final answer needs to be in miles, the ratio relating miles to kilometers needs to be used. There are 0.62 miles in 1 kilometer. This, written as a ratio and in fraction form, is $\frac{0.62 \text{ miles}}{1 \text{ km}}$. To convert 50 km/hour into miles per hour, the following conversion needs to be set up:

$$\frac{50 \text{ km}}{\text{hour}} \times \frac{0.62 \text{ miles}}{1 \text{ km}} = 31 \text{ miles per hour}$$

Proportional Relationships

Much like a scale factor can be written using an equation like $2A = B$, a **relationship** is represented by the equation $Y = kX$. X and Y are **proportional** because as values of X increase, the values of Y also increase. A relationship that is **inversely proportional** can be represented by the equation $Y = \frac{k}{X}$, where the value of Y decreases as the value of x increases and vice versa.

Proportional reasoning can be used to solve problems involving ratios, percentages, and averages. Ratios can be used in setting up proportions and solving them to find unknowns. For example, if a student completes an average of 10 pages of math homework in 3 nights, how long would it take the student to complete 22 pages? Both ratios can be written as fractions. The second ratio would contain the unknown.

The following proportion represents this problem, where x is the unknown number of nights:

$$\frac{10 \text{ pages}}{3 \text{ nights}} = \frac{22 \text{ pages}}{x \text{ nights}}$$

Solving this proportion entails cross-multiplying and results in the following equation: $10x = 22 \times 3$. Simplifying and solving for x results in the exact solution: $x = 6.6$ nights. The result would be rounded up to 7 because the homework would actually be completed on the 7th night.

The following problem uses ratios involving percentages:

If 20% of the class is girls and 30 students are in the class, how many girls are in the class?

To set up this problem, it is helpful to use the common proportion: $\frac{\%}{100} = \frac{is}{of}$. Within the proportion, % is the percentage of girls, 100 is the total percentage of the class, *is* is the number of girls, and *of* is the total number of students in the class. Most percentage problems can be written using this language. To solve this problem, the proportion should be set up as $\frac{20}{100} = \frac{x}{30}$, and then solved for x. Cross-multiplying results in the equation $20 \times 30 = 100x$, which results in the solution $x = 6$. There are 6 girls in the class.

Ratios can be used to solve problems that concern length, volume, and other units. For example, a problem may ask for the volume of a cone to be found that has a radius, $r = 7$ m and a height, $h = 16$ m. Referring to the formulas provided on the test, the volume of a cone is given as:

$$V = \pi r^2 \frac{h}{3}$$

r is the radius and h is the height. Plugging $r = 7$ and $h = 16$ into the formula, the following is obtained:

$$V = \pi(7^2)\frac{16}{3}$$

Therefore, the volume of the cone is found to be approximately 821 m^3. Sometimes, answers in different units are sought. If this problem wanted the answer in liters, 821 m^3 would need to be converted. Using the equivalence statement $1 \text{ m}^3 = 1{,}000 \text{ L}$, the following ratio would be used to solve for liters:

$$821 \text{ m}^3 \times \frac{1{,}000 \text{ L}}{1 \text{ m}^3}$$

Cubic meters in the numerator and denominator cancel each other out, and the answer is converted to 821,000 liters, or 8.21×10^5 L.

Other conversions can also be made between different given and final units. If the temperature in a pool is 30°C, what is the temperature of the pool in degrees Fahrenheit? To convert these units, an equation is used relating Celsius to Fahrenheit. The following equation is used:

$$T_{°\text{F}} = 1.8T_{°\text{C}} + 32$$

Plugging in the given temperature and solving the equation for T yields the result:

$$T_{°\text{F}} = 1.8(30) + 32 = 86°\text{F}$$

Units in both the metric system and U.S. customary system are widely used.

Here are some more examples of how to solve for proportions:

1) $\frac{75\%}{90\%} = \frac{25\%}{x}$

To solve for x, the fractions must be cross multiplied: ($75\%x = 90\% \times 25\%$). To make things easier, let's convert the percentages to decimals: ($0.9 \times 0.25 = 0.225 = 0.75x$). To get rid of x's coefficient, each side must be divided by that same coefficient to get the answer $x = 0.3$. The question could ask for the answer as a percentage or fraction in lowest terms, which are 30% and $\frac{3}{10}$, respectively.

2) $\frac{x}{12} = \frac{30}{96}$

Cross-multiply: $96x = 30 \times 12$

Multiply: $96x = 360$

Divide: $x = 360 \div 96$

Answer: $x = 3.75$

3) $\frac{0.5}{3} = \frac{x}{6}$

Cross-multiply: $3x = 0.5 \times 6$

Multiply: $3x = 3$

Divide: $x = 3 \div 3$

Answer: $x = 1$

You may have noticed there's a faster way to arrive at the answer. If there is an obvious operation being performed on the proportion, the same operation can be used on the other side of the proportion to solve for x. For example, in the first practice problem, 75% became 25% when divided by 3, and upon doing the same to 90%, the correct answer of 30% would have been found with much less legwork. However, these questions aren't always so intuitive, so it's a good idea to work through the steps, even if the answer seems apparent from the outset.

Solving Ratio and Percent Problems

Questions dealing with percentages can be difficult when they are phrased as word problems. These word problems almost always come in three varieties. The first type will ask to find what percentage of some number will equal another number. The second asks to determine what number is some percentage of another given number. The third will ask what number another number is a given percentage of.

One of the most important parts of correctly answering percentage word problems is to identify the numerator and the denominator. This fraction can then be converted into a percentage, as described above.

The following word problem shows how to make this conversion:

A department store carries several different types of footwear. The store is currently selling 8 athletic shoes, 7 dress shoes, and 5 sandals. What percentage of the store's footwear are sandals?

First, calculate what serves as the 'whole,' as this will be the denominator. How many total pieces of footwear does the store sell? The store sells 20 different types ($8 \text{ athletic} + 7 \text{ dress} + 5 \text{ sandals}$).

Second, what footwear type is the question specifically asking about? Sandals. Thus, 5 is the numerator.

Third, the resultant fraction must be expressed as a percentage. The first two steps indicate that $\frac{5}{20}$ of the footwear pieces are sandals. This fraction must now be converted into a percentage:

$$\frac{5}{20} \times \frac{5}{5} = \frac{25}{100} = 25\%$$

Linear Equations and Functions

Defining Linear Equations

A function is called **linear** if it can take the form of the equation $f(x) = ax + b$, or $y = ax + b$, for any two numbers *a* and *b*. A linear equation forms a straight line when graphed on the coordinate plane. An example of a linear function is shown below on the graph.

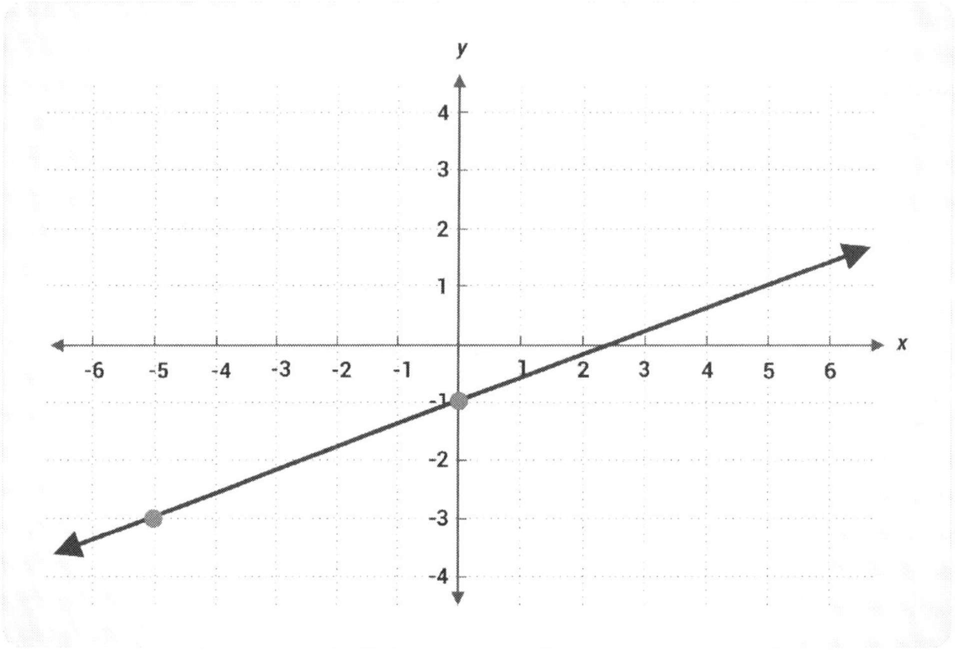

This is a graph of the following function: $y = \frac{2}{5}x - 1$. A table of values that satisfies this function is shown below.

x	y
-5	-3
0	-1
5	1
10	3

These points can be found on the graph using the form (x, y). For more on graphing in the coordinate plane, refer to the Graphing section below.

Forms of Linear Equations

When graphing a linear function, note that the ratio of the change of the y-coordinate to the change in the x-coordinate is constant between any two points on the resulting line, no matter which two points are chosen. In other words, in a pair of points on a line, (x_1, y_1) and (x_2, y_2), with $x_1 \neq x_2$ so that the two points are distinct, then the ratio $\frac{y_2 - y_1}{x_2 - x_1}$ will be the same, regardless of which particular pair of points are chosen. This ratio, $\frac{y_2 - y_1}{x_2 - x_1}$, is called the **slope** of the line and is frequently denoted with the letter m. If slope m is positive, then the line goes upward when moving to the right, while if slope m is negative, then the line goes downward when moving to the right. If the slope is 0, then the line is called **horizontal**, and the y-coordinate is constant along the entire line. In lines where the x-coordinate is constant along the entire line, y is not actually a function of x. For such lines, the slope is not defined. These lines are called **vertical** lines.

Linear functions may take forms other than $y = ax + b$. The most common forms of linear equations are explained below:

1. Standard Form: $Ax + By = C$, in which the slope is given by $m = \frac{-A}{B}$, and the y-intercept is given by $\frac{C}{B}$.

2. Slope-Intercept Form: $y = mx + b$, where the slope is m and the y-intercept is b.

3. Point-Slope Form: $y - y_1 = m(x - x_1)$, where the slope is m and (x_1, y_1) is any point on the chosen line.

4. Two-Point Form: $\frac{y-y_1}{x-x_1} = \frac{y_2-y_1}{x_2-x_1}$, where (x_1, y_1) and (x_2, y_2) are any two distinct points on the chosen line. Note that the slope is given by $m = \frac{y_2-y_1}{x_2-x_1}$.

5. Intercept Form: $\frac{x}{x_1} + \frac{y}{y_1} = 1$, in which x_1 is the x-intercept and y_1 is the y-intercept.

These five ways to write linear equations are all useful in different circumstances. Depending on the given information, it may be easier to write one of the forms over another.

If $y = mx$, y is directly proportional to x. In this case, changing x by a factor changes y by that same factor. If $y = \frac{m}{x}$, y is inversely proportional to x. For example, if x is increased by a factor of 3, then y will be decreased by the same factor, 3.

Solving Linear Equations

Sometimes, rather than a situation where there's an equation such as $y = ax + b$ and finding y for some value of x is requested, the result is given and finding x is requested.

The key to solving any equation is to remember that from one true equation, another true equation can be found by adding, subtracting, multiplying, or dividing both sides by the same quantity. In this case, it's necessary to manipulate the equation so that one side only contains x. Then the other side will show what x is equal to.

For example, in solving $3x - 5 = 2$, adding 5 to each side results in $3x = 7$. Next, dividing both sides by 3 results in $x = \frac{7}{3}$. To ensure the calculated results of x is correct, this calculated value can be substituted into the original equation and solved to see if it makes a true statement. For example, $3(\frac{7}{3}) - 5 = 2$ can be simplified by cancelling out the two 3s. This yields $7 - 5 = 2$, which is a true statement.

Sometimes an equation may have more than one x-term. For example, consider the following equation:

$$3x + 2 = x - 4$$

Moving all of the x-terms to one side by subtracting x from both sides results in $2x + 2 = -4$. Next, subtract 2 from both sides so that there is no constant term on the left side. This yields $2x = -6$. Finally, divide both sides by 2, which leaves $x = -3$.

Inequalities and Systems

Linear Inequalities

Solving linear inequalities is very similar to solving equations, except for one rule: when multiplying or dividing an inequality by a negative number, the inequality symbol changes direction. Given the following inequality, solve for x: $-2x + 5 < 13$. The first step in solving this equation is to subtract 5 from both sides. This leaves the inequality: $-2x < 8$. The last step is to divide both sides by -2. By using the rule, the answer to the inequality is $x > -4$.

Since solutions to inequalities include more than one value, number lines are often used to model the answer. For the previous example, the answer is modelled on the number line below. It shows that any number greater than -4, not including -4, satisfies the inequality.

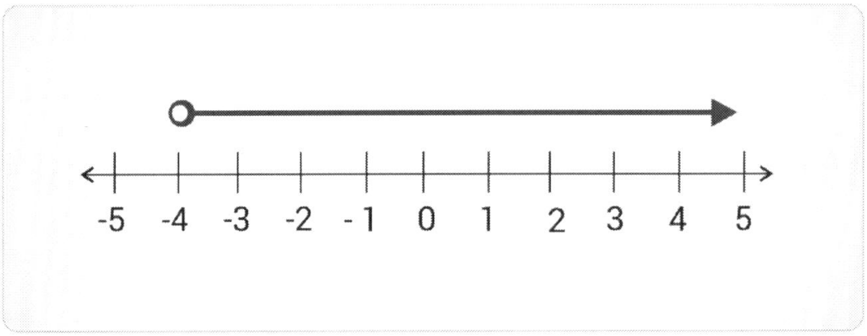

Linear Systems of Equations

A problem sometimes involves multiple variables and multiple equations. These are called **systems of equations**. In this case, try to manipulate them until an expression is found that provides the value of one of the variables. There are a couple of different approaches to this, and some of them can be used together in some cases. The three basic rules to keep in mind are the following.

1. Manipulate a set of equations by doing the same operation to both equations, just as is done when working with just one equation.

2. If one of the equations can be changed so that it expresses one variable in terms of the others, then that expression can be substituted into the other equations and the variable can be eliminated. This means the other equations will have one less variable in them. This is called the method of substitution.

3. If two equations of the form $a = b, c = d$ are included, then a new equation can be formed by adding the left sides and adding the right sides, $a + c = b + d$, or $a - c = b - d$. This enables the elimination of one of the variables from an equation. This is called the method of elimination.

The simplest case is the case of a **linear** system of equations. Although the equations may be written in more complicated forms, linear systems of equations with two variables can always be written in the form $ax + by = c, dx + ey = f$. The two basic approaches to solving these systems are substitution and elimination.

Consider the system $3x - y = 2$ and $2x + 2y = 3$. This can be solved in two ways.

1. By substitution: start by solving the first equation for y. First, subtract $3x$ from both sides to obtain $-y = 2 - 3x$. Next, divide both sides by -1, to obtain $y = 3x - 2$. Then substitute this value for y into the second equation. This yields:

$$2x + 2(3x - 2) = 3$$

This can be simplified to $2x + 6x - 4 = 3$, or $8x = 7$, which means $x = \frac{7}{8}$. By plugging in this value for x into $y = 3x - 2$, the result is

$$y = 3\left(\frac{7}{8}\right) - 2 = \frac{21}{8} - \frac{16}{8} = \frac{5}{8}$$

So, this results in $x = \frac{7}{8}, y = \frac{5}{8}$.

2. By elimination: first, multiply the first equation by 2. This results in $-2y$, which could cancel out the $+2y$ in the second equation. Multiplying both sides of the first equation by 2 gives results in $2(3x - y) = 2(2)$, or $6x - 2y = 4$. Adding the left sides and the right sides of the two equations and setting the results equal to one another results in:

$$(6x + 2x) + (-2y + 2y) = 4 + 3$$

This simplifies to $8x = 7$, so again $x = \frac{7}{8}$. Plug this back into either of the original equations and the result is $3\left(\frac{7}{8}\right) - y = 2$ or:

$$y = 3\left(\frac{7}{8}\right) - 2 = \frac{21}{8} - \frac{16}{8} = \frac{5}{8}$$

This again yields $x = \frac{7}{8}, y = \frac{5}{8}$.

As this shows, both methods will give the same answer. However, one method is sometimes preferred over another simply because of the amount of work required. To check the answer, the values can be substituted into the given system to make sure they form two true statements.

Properties of Real Numbers

Properties of operations exist that make calculations easier and solve problems for missing values. The following table summarizes commonly used properties of real numbers.

Property	Addition	Multiplication
Commutative	$a + b = b + a$	$a \times b = b \times a$
Associative	$(a + b) + c = a + (b + c)$	$(a \times b) \times c = a \times (b \times c)$
Identity	$a + 0 = a;\ 0 + a = a$	$a \times 1 = a;\ 1 \times a = a$
Inverse	$a + (-a) = 0$	$a \times \frac{1}{a} = 1;\ a \neq 0$
Distributive	$a(b + c) = ab + ac$	

The commutative property of addition states that the order in which numbers are added does not change the sum. Similarly, the commutative property of multiplication states that the order in which numbers are multiplied does not change the product. The associative property of addition and multiplication state that the grouping of numbers being added or multiplied does not change the sum or product, respectively. The commutative and associative properties are useful for performing calculations. For example, $(47 + 25) + 3$ is equivalent to $(47 + 3) + 25$, which is easier to calculate.

The identity property of addition states that adding zero to any number does not change its value. The identity property of multiplication states that multiplying a number by one does not change its value. The inverse property of addition states that the sum of a number and its opposite equals zero. Opposites are numbers that are the same with different signs (ex. 5 and -5; $-\frac{1}{2}$ and $\frac{1}{2}$). The inverse property of multiplication states that the product of a number (other than zero) and its reciprocal equals one. Reciprocal numbers have numerators and denominators that are inverted (ex. $\frac{2}{5}$ and $\frac{5}{2}$). Inverse properties are useful for canceling quantities to find missing values (see algebra content). For example, $a + 7 = 12$ is solved by adding the inverse of 7 (which is -7) to both sides in order to isolate a.

The distributive property states that multiplying a sum (or difference) by a number produces the same result as multiplying each value in the sum (or difference) by the number and adding (or subtracting) the products. Consider the following scenario: You are buying three tickets for a baseball game. Each ticket costs $18. You are also charged a fee of $2 per ticket for purchasing the tickets online. The cost is calculated: $3 \times 18 + 3 \times 2$. Using the distributive property, the cost can also be calculated $3(18 + 2)$.

Geometry and Measurement

Characteristics of Geometric Figures

Three-Dimensional Figures with Nets

A net is a construction of two-dimensional figures that can be folded to form a given three-dimensional figure. More than one net may exist to fold and produce the same solid, or three-dimensional figure. The bases and faces of the solid figure are analyzed to determine the polygons (two-dimensional figures) needed to form the net.

Consider the following triangular prism:

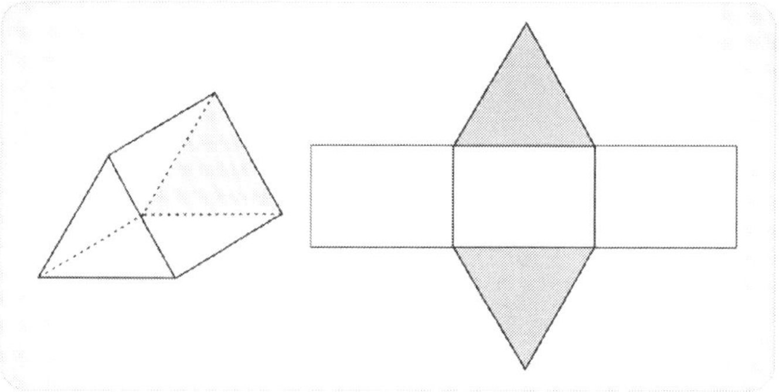

The surface of the prism consists of two triangular bases and three rectangular faces. The net beside it can be used to construct the triangular prism by first folding the triangles up to be parallel to each other, and then folding the two outside rectangles up and to the center with the outer edges touching.

Consider the following cylinder:

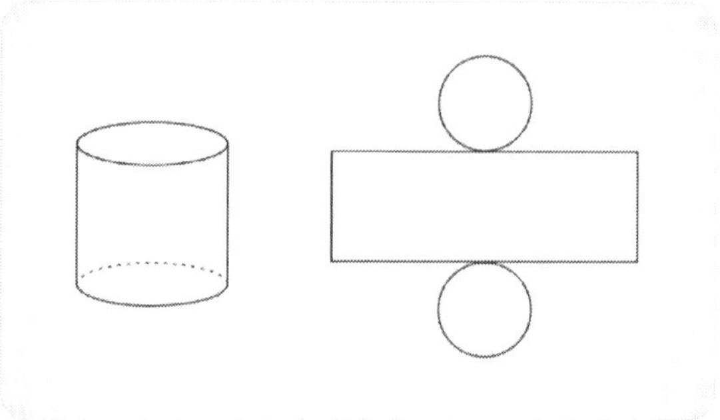

The surface consists of two circular bases and a curved lateral surface that can be opened and flattened into a rectangle. The net beside the cylinder can be used to construct the cylinder by first folding the circles up to be parallel to each other, and then curving the sides of the rectangle up to touch each other. The top and bottom of the folded rectangle should be touching the outside of both circles.

Consider the following square pyramid below on the left. The surface consists of one square base and four triangular faces. The net below on the right can be used to construct the square pyramid by folding each triangle towards the center of the square. The top points of the triangle meet at the vertex.

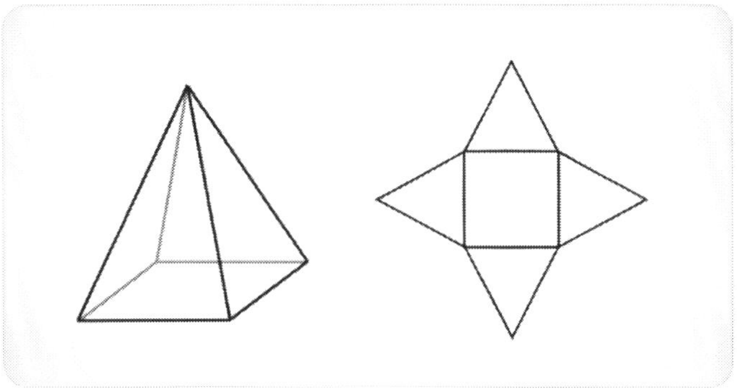

Surface Area of Three-Dimensional Figures

The area of a two-dimensional figure refers to the number of square units needed to cover the interior region of the figure. This concept is similar to wallpaper covering the flat surface of a wall. For example, if a rectangle has an area of 10 square centimeters (written $10\ \text{cm}^2$), it will take 10 squares, each with sides one centimeter in length, to cover the interior region of the rectangle. Note that area is measured in square units such as: square centimeters or cm^2; square feet or ft^2; square yards or yd^2; square miles or mi^2.

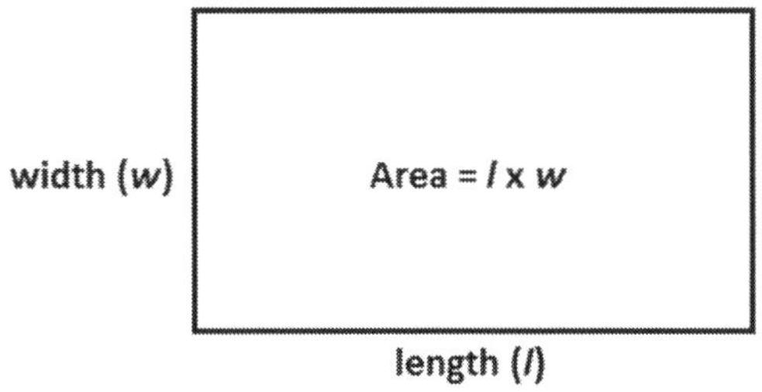

The surface area of a three-dimensional figure refers to the number of square units needed to cover the entire surface of the figure. This concept is similar to using wrapping paper to completely cover the outside of a box. For example, if a triangular pyramid has a surface area of 17 square inches (written $17\ \text{in}^2$), it will take 17 squares, each with sides one inch in length, to cover the entire surface of the pyramid. Surface area is also measured in square units.

Many three-dimensional figures (solid figures) can be represented by nets consisting of rectangles and triangles. The surface area of such solids can be determined by adding the areas of each of its faces and bases. Finding the surface area using this method requires calculating the areas of rectangles and triangles. To find the area (A) of a rectangle, the length (l) is multiplied by the width:

$$(w) \rightarrow A = l \times w$$

The area of a rectangle with a length of 8 cm and a width of 4 cm is calculated:

$$A = (8\text{ cm}) \times (4\text{ cm}) \rightarrow A = 32\text{ cm}^2$$

To calculate the area (A) of a triangle, the product of $\frac{1}{2}$, the base (b), and the height (h) is found:

$$A = \frac{1}{2} \times b \times h$$

Note that the height of a triangle is measured from the base to the vertex opposite of it forming a right angle with the base. The area of a triangle with a base of 11 cm and a height of 6 cm is calculated:

$$A = \frac{1}{2} \times (11\text{ cm}) \times (6\text{ cm}) \rightarrow A = 33\text{ cm}^2$$

Consider the following triangular prism, which is represented by a net consisting of two triangles and three rectangles.

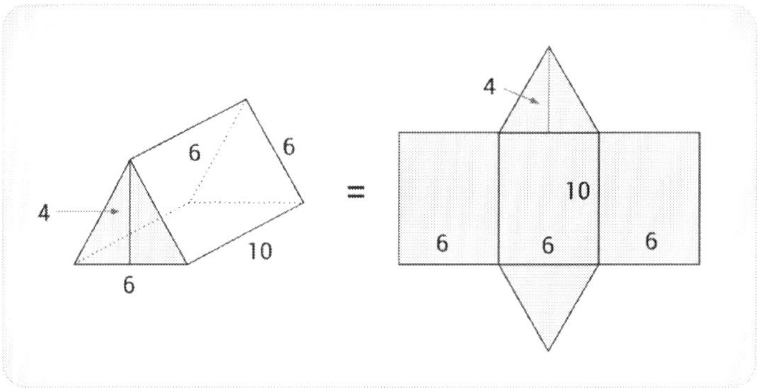

The surface area of the prism can be determined by adding the areas of each of its faces and bases.

$$surface\ area\ (SA) = area\ of\ triangle + area\ of\ triangle + area\ of\ rectangle + area\ of\ rectangle + area\ of\ rectangle.$$

$$SA = \left(\frac{1}{2} \times b \times h\right) + \left(\frac{1}{2} \times b \times h\right) + (l \times w) + (l \times w) + (l \times w)$$

$$SA = \left(\frac{1}{2} \times 6 \times 4\right) + \left(\frac{1}{2} \times 6 \times 4\right) + (6 \times 10) + (6 \times 10) + (6 \times 10)$$

$$SA = (12) + (12) + (60) + (60) + (60)$$

$$SA = 204\text{ square units}$$

Area and Perimeter of Polygons

Perimeter is the measurement of a distance around something or the sum of all sides of a polygon. Think of perimeter as the length of the boundary, like a fence. In contrast, **area** is the space occupied by a defined enclosure, like a field enclosed by a fence.

When thinking about perimeter, think about walking around the outside of something. When thinking about area, think about the amount of space or **surface area** something takes up.

Squares

The perimeter of a square is measured by adding together all of the sides. Since a square has four equal sides, its perimeter can be calculated by multiplying the length of one side by 4. Thus, the formula is $P = 4 \times s$, where s equals one side. For example, the following square has side lengths of 5 meters:

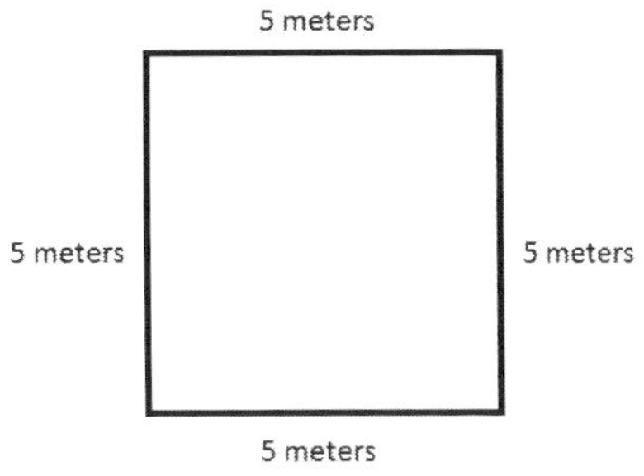

The perimeter is 20 meters because 4 times 5 is 20.

The area of a square is the length of a side squared. For example, if a side of a square is 7 centimeters, then the area is 49 square centimeters. The formula for this example is $A = s^2 = 7^2 = 49$ square centimeters. An example is if the rectangle has a length of 6 inches and a width of 7 inches, then the area is 42 square inches:

$$A = lw = 6(7) = 42 \text{ square inches}$$

Rectangles

Like a square, a rectangle's perimeter is measured by adding together all of the sides. But as the sides are unequal, the formula is different. A rectangle has equal values for its lengths (long sides) and equal values for its widths (short sides), so the perimeter formula for a rectangle is:

$$P = l + l + w + w = 2l + 2w$$

l equals length
w equals width

The area is found by multiplying the length by the width, so the formula is $A = l \times w$.

For example, if the length of a rectangle is 10 inches and the width 8 inches, then the perimeter is 36 inches because:

$$P = 2l + 2w = 2(10) + 2(8) = 20 + 16 = 36 \text{ inches}$$

Triangles

A triangle's perimeter is measured by adding together the three sides, so the formula is $P = a + b + c$, where a, b, and c are the values of the three sides. The area is the product of one-half the base and height so the formula is:

$$A = \frac{1}{2} \times b \times h$$

It can be simplified to:

$$A = \frac{bh}{2}$$

The base is the bottom of the triangle, and the height is the distance from the base to the peak. If a problem asks to calculate the area of a triangle, it will provide the base and height.

For example, if the base of the triangle is 2 feet and the height 4 feet, then the area is 4 square feet. The following equation shows the formula used to calculate the area of the triangle:

$$A = \frac{1}{2}bh = \frac{1}{2}(2)(4) = 4 \text{ square feet}$$

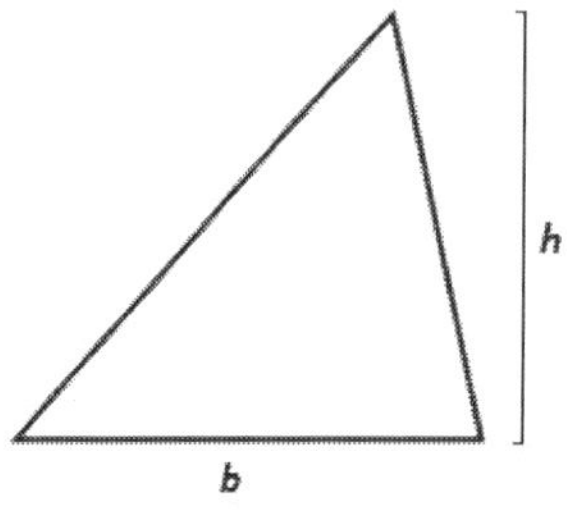

Circles

A circle's perimeter—also known as its circumference—is measured by multiplying the diameter by π.

Diameter is the straight line measured from a point on one side of the circle to a point directly across on the opposite side of the circle.

π is referred to as pi and is equal to 3.14 (with rounding).

So, the formula is $\pi \times d$.

This is sometimes expressed by the formula $C = 2 \times \pi \times r$, where r is the radius of the circle. These formulas are equivalent, as the radius equals half of the diameter.

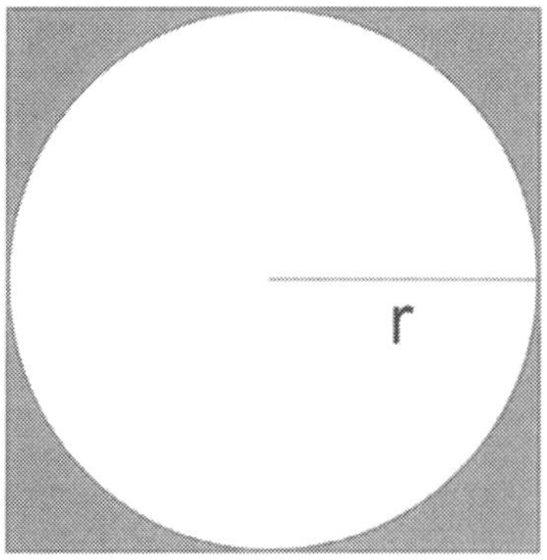

The area of a circle is calculated through the formula:

$$A = \pi \times r^2$$

The test will indicate either to leave the answer with π attached or to calculate to the nearest decimal place, which means multiplying by 3.14 for π.

Arc

The **arc of a circle** is the distance between two points on the circle. The length of the arc of a circle in terms of **degrees** is easily determined if the value of the central angle is known. The length of the arc is simply the value of the central angle. In this example, the length of the arc of the circle in degrees is 75°.

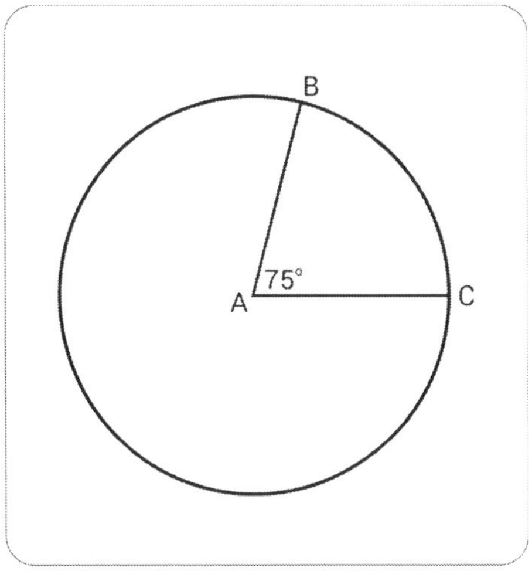

To determine the length of the arc of a circle in distance, the values for both the central angle and the radius must be known. This formula is:

$$\frac{central\ angle}{360°} = \frac{arc\ length}{2\pi r}$$

The equation is simplified by cross-multiplying to solve for the arc length. In the following example, to solve for arc length, substitute the values of the central angle (75°) and the radius (10 inches) into the equation above.

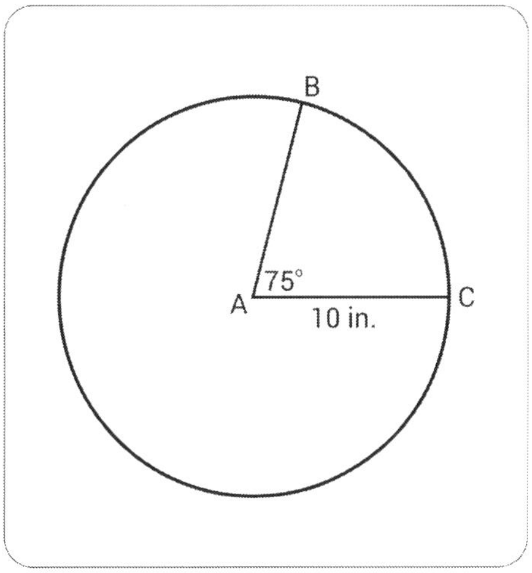

$$\frac{75°}{360°} = \frac{arc\ length}{2(3.14)(10\text{ in.})}$$

To solve the equation, first cross-multiply: $4{,}710 = 360(arc\ length)$. Next, divide each side of the equation by 360. The result of the formula is that the arc length is 13.1 (rounded).

Parallelograms

Similar to triangles, the height of the parallelogram is measured from one base to the other at a 90° angle (or perpendicular).

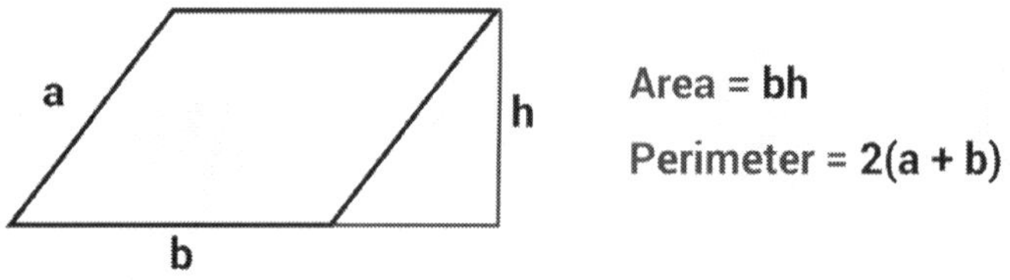

Trapezoid

The area of a trapezoid can be calculated using the formula: $A = \frac{1}{2} \times h(b_1 + b_2)$, where h is the height and b_1 and b_2 are the parallel bases of the trapezoid:

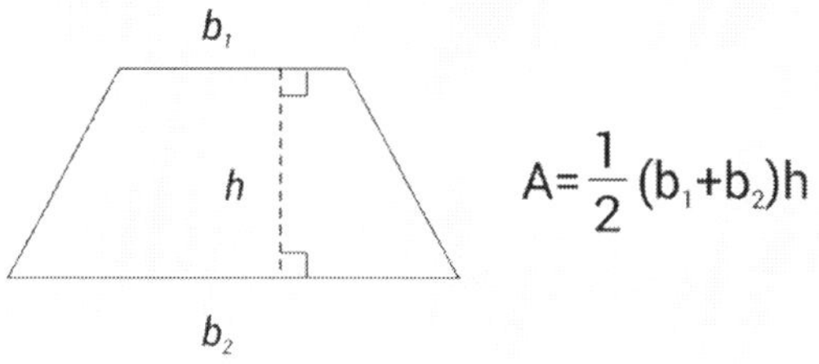

Regular Polygon

The area of a regular polygon can be determined by using its perimeter and the length of the apothem. The apothem is a line from the center of the regular polygon to any of its sides at a right angle. (Note that the perimeter of a regular polygon can be determined given the length of only one side.) The formula for the area (A) of a regular polygon is $A = \frac{1}{2} \times a \times P$, where a is the length of the apothem, and P is the perimeter of the figure. Consider the following regular pentagon:

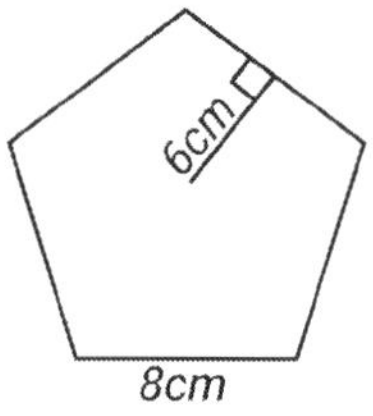

To find the area, the perimeter (P) is calculated first: $8\text{ cm} \times 5 \to P = 40\text{ cm}$. Then the perimeter and the apothem are used to find the area (A):

$$A = \frac{1}{2} \times a \times P \to A = \frac{1}{2} \times (6\text{ cm}) \times (40\text{ cm}) \to A = 120\text{ cm}^2$$

Note that the unit is $\text{cm}^2 \rightarrow \text{cm} \times \text{cm} = \text{cm}^2$.

Irregular Shapes

The perimeter of an irregular polygon is found by adding the lengths of all of the sides. In cases where all of the sides are given, this will be very straightforward, as it will simply involve finding the sum of the provided lengths. Other times, a side length may be missing and must be determined before the perimeter can be calculated.

Consider the example below:

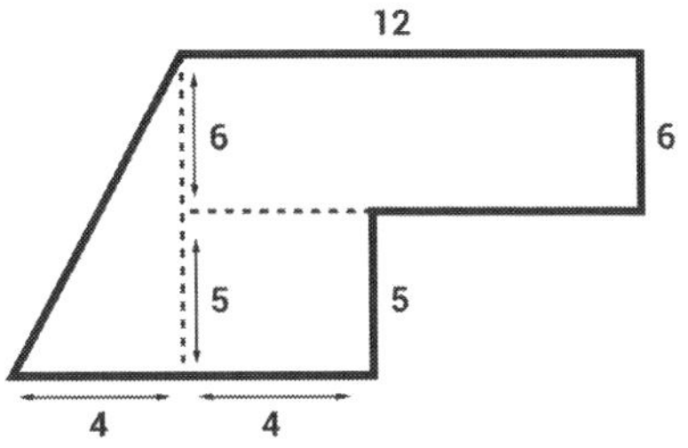

All of the side lengths are provided except for the angled side on the left. Test takers should notice that this is the hypotenuse of a right triangle. The other two sides of the triangle are provided (the base is 4 and the height is $6 + 5 = 11$). The Pythagorean Theorem can be used to find the length of the hypotenuse, remembering that:

$$a^2 + b^2 = c^2$$

Substituting the side values provided yields:

$$(4)^2 + (11)^2 = c^2$$

Therefore:

$$c = \sqrt{16 + 121} = 11.7$$

Finally, the perimeter can be found by adding this new side length with the other provided lengths to get the total length around the figure:

$$4 + 4 + 5 + 8 + 6 + 12 + 11.7 = 50.7$$

Although units are not provided in this figure, remember that reporting units with a measurement is important.

The area of irregular polygons is found by decomposing, or breaking apart, the figure into smaller shapes. When the area of the smaller shapes is determined, the area of the smaller shapes will produce the area of the original figure when added together. Consider the earlier example:

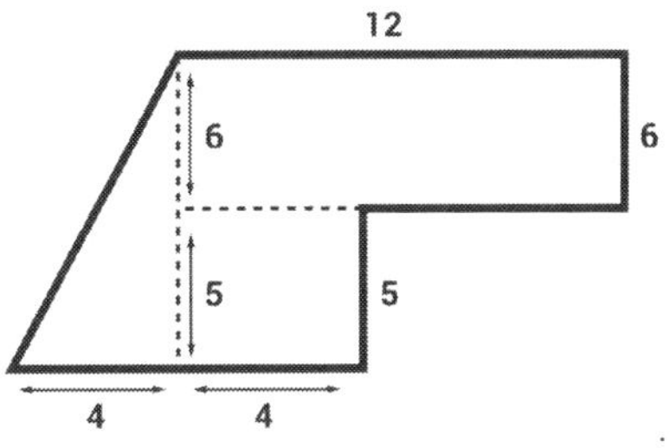

The irregular polygon is decomposed into two rectangles and a triangle. The area of the large rectangle ($A = l \times w \rightarrow A = 12 \times 6$) is 72 square units. The area of the small rectangle is 20 square units ($A = 4 \times 5$). The area of the triangle ($A = \frac{1}{2} \times b \times h \rightarrow A = \frac{1}{2} \times 4 \times 11$) is 22 square units. The sum of the areas of these figures produces the total area of the original polygon:

$$A = 72 + 20 + 22 \rightarrow A = 114 \text{ square units}$$

Here's another example:

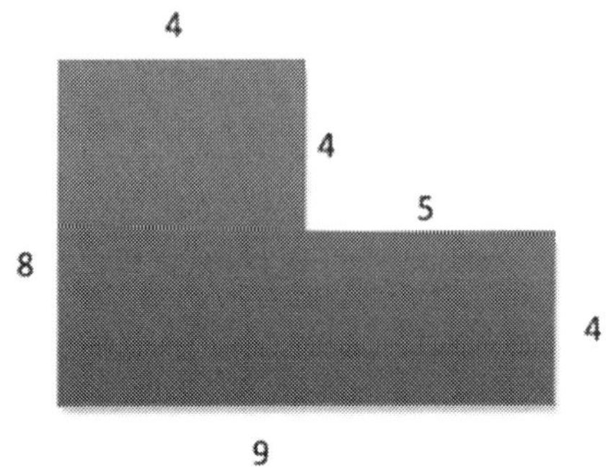

This irregular polygon is decomposed into two rectangles. The area of the large rectangle ($A = l \times w \rightarrow A = 8 \times 4$) is 32 square units. The area of the small rectangle is 20 square units ($A = 4 \times 5$). The sum of the areas of these figures produces the total area of the original polygon:

$$A = 32 + 20 \rightarrow A = 52 \text{ square units}$$

Right Rectangular Prisms

A right rectangular prism consists of:

- Two congruent (same size and shape) rectangles as the parallel *bases* (top and bottom).
- Two congruent rectangles as the *side* faces.
- Two congruent rectangles as the *front and back* faces.

It is called a right prism because the base and sides meet at right angles.

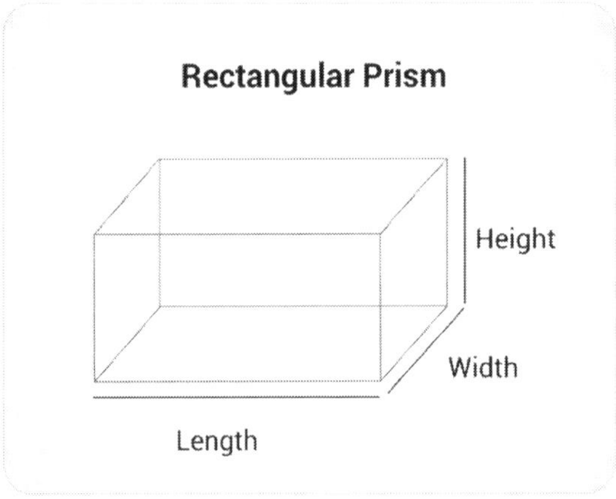

The length and width of the prism is the length and width of the rectangular base. The height of the prism is the measure from one base to the other.

The surface area of three-dimensional figures can be found by adding the areas of each of its bases and faces. The areas of a right rectangular prism are found as follows: two bases $\rightarrow A = l \times w$; front and back faces $\rightarrow A = l \times h$; two side faces $\rightarrow A = w \times h$. The sum of these six areas will equal the surface area of the prism. (Surface area = area of 2 bases + area of front and back + area of 2 sides). This is true for all right rectangular prisms leading to the formula for surface area:

$$SA = 2 \times l \times w + 2 \times l \times h + 2 \times w \times h$$

$$SA = 2(l \times w + l \times h + w \times h)$$

Given the right rectangular prism below, the surface area is calculated as follows:

$$SA = 2\left(3\frac{1}{2}\text{ft}\right)\left(2\frac{1}{2}\text{ft}\right) + 2\left(3\frac{1}{2}\text{ft}\right)\left(1\frac{1}{2}\text{ft}\right) + 2\left(2\frac{1}{2}\text{ft}\right)\left(1\frac{1}{2}\text{ft}\right) \rightarrow SA = 35.5\text{ft}^2$$

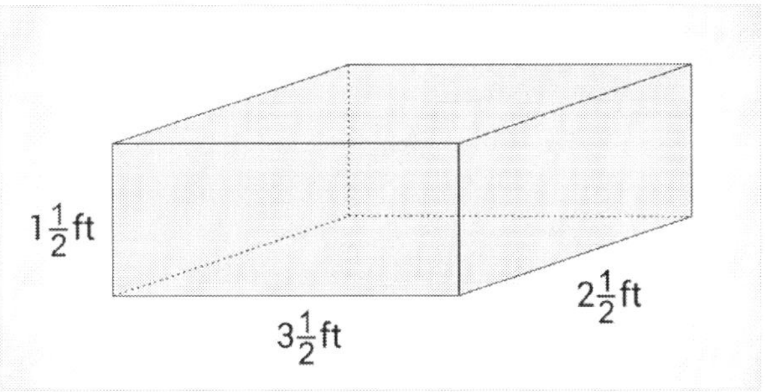

The volume of a solid (three-dimensional figure) is the number of cubic units needed to fill the space that the figure occupies. This concept is similar to filling a box with blocks. Volume is a three-dimensional measurement. Therefore, volume is expressed in cubic units such as cubic centimeters (cm^3), cubic feet (ft^3), and cubic yards (yd^3). If a rectangular prism has a volume of 30 cubic meters (30 m^3), it will take 30 cubes, each with sides one meter in length, to fill the space occupied by the prism. A simple formula can be used to determine the volume of a right rectangular prism. The area of the base of the prism ($l \times w$) will indicate how many "blocks" are needed to cover the base. The height (h) of the prism will indicate how many "levels" of blocks are needed to construct the prism.

Therefore, to find the volume (V) of a right rectangular prism, the area of the base ($l \times w$) is multiplied by the height (h):

$$V = l \times w \times h$$

The volume of the prism shown above is calculated:

$$V = \left(3\frac{1}{2}\text{ ft}\right) \times \left(2\frac{1}{2}\text{ ft}\right) \times \left(1\frac{1}{2}\text{ ft}\right) \rightarrow V = 13.125\text{ ft}^3$$

Effects of Changes to Dimensions on Area and Volume

Similar polygons are figures that are the same shape but different sizes. Likewise, similar solids are different sizes but are the same shape. In both cases, corresponding angles in the same positions for both figures are congruent (equal), and corresponding sides are proportional in length. For example, the triangles below are similar. The following pairs of corresponding angles are congruent: $\angle A$ and $\angle D$; $\angle B$ and $\angle E$; $\angle C$ and $\angle F$. The corresponding sides are proportional:

$$\frac{AB}{DE} = \frac{6}{3} = 2$$

$$\frac{BC}{EF} = \frac{9}{4.5} = 2$$

$$\frac{CA}{FD} = \frac{10}{5} = 2$$

In other words, triangle ABC is the same shape but twice as large as triangle DEF.

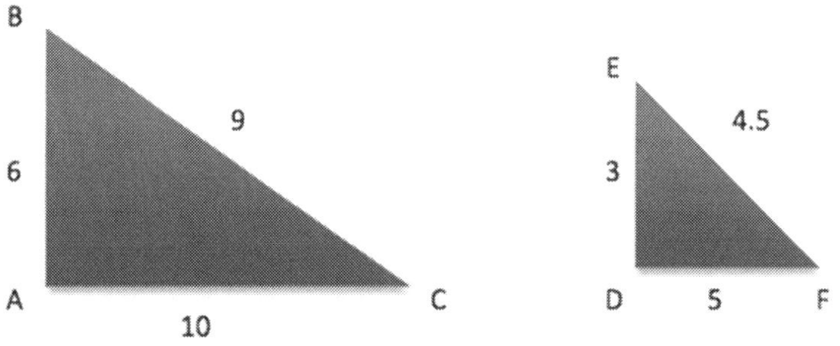

An example of similar triangular pyramids is shown below.

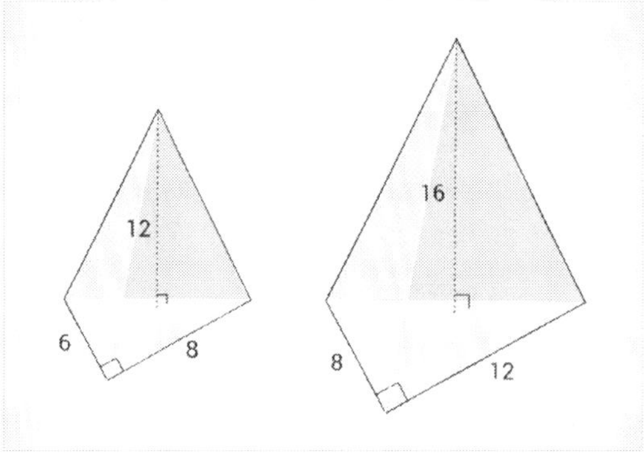

Given the nature of two- and three-dimensional measurements, changing dimensions by a given scale (multiplier) does not change the area of volume by the same scale. Consider a rectangle with a length of 5 centimeters and a width of 4 centimeters. The area of the rectangle is 20 cm^2. Doubling the dimensions of the rectangle (multiplying by a scale factor of 2) to 10 centimeters and 8 centimeters *does not* double the area to 40 cm^2. Area is a two-dimensional measurement (measured in square units). Therefore, the dimensions are multiplied by a scale that is squared (raised to the second power) to determine the scale of the corresponding areas. For the previous example, the length and width are multiplied by 2. Therefore, the area is multiplied by 2^2, or 4. The area of a $5 \text{ cm} \times 4 \text{ cm}$ rectangle is 20 cm^2. The area of a $10 \text{ cm} \times 8 \text{ cm}$ rectangle is 80 cm^2.

Volume is a three-dimensional measurement, which is measured in cubic units. Therefore, the scale between dimensions of similar solids is cubed (raised to the third power) to determine the scale between their volumes. Consider similar right rectangular prisms: one with a length of 8 inches, a width of 24 inches, and a height of 16 inches; the second with a length of 4 inches, a width of 12 inches, and a height of 8 inches. The first prism, multiplied by a scalar of $\frac{1}{2}$, produces the measurement of the second prism. The volume of the first prism, multiplied by $\left(\frac{1}{2}\right)^3$, which equals $\frac{1}{8}$, produces the volume of the second prism. The volume of the first prism is $8 \text{ in} \times 24 \text{ in} \times 16 \text{ in}$ which equals $3{,}072 \text{ in}^3$. The volume of the second prism is $4 \text{ in} \times 12 \text{ in} \times 8$ in which equals 384 in^3:

$$3{,}072 \text{ in}^3 \times \frac{1}{8} = 384 \text{ in}^3$$

The rules for squaring the scalar for area and cubing the scalar for volume only hold true for similar figures. In other words, if only one dimension is changed (changing the width of a rectangle but not the length) or dimensions are changed at different rates (the length of a prism is doubled, and its height is tripled) the figures are not similar (same shape). Therefore, the rules above do not apply.

Congruent Triangles

Triangles are similar if they have the same angle measurements, and their sides are proportional to one another. Triangles are **congruent** if the angles of the triangles are equal in measurement and the sides of the triangles are equal in measurement.

There are five ways to show that triangles are congruent:

1. SSS (Side-Side-Side Postulate) – when all three corresponding sides are equal in length, then the two triangles are congruent.

2. SAS (Side-Angle-Side Postulate) – if a pair of corresponding sides and the angle in between those two sides are equal, then the two triangles are congruent.

3. ASA (Angle-Side-Angle Postulate) – if a pair of corresponding angles are equal and the side lengths within those angles are equal, then the two triangles are equal.

4. AAS (Angle-Angle-Side Postulate) – when a pair of corresponding angles for two triangles and a non-included side are equal, then the two triangles are congruent.

5. HL (Hypotenuse-Leg Theorem) – if two right triangles have the same hypotenuse length, and one of the other sides in each triangle are of the same length, then the two triangles are congruent.

If two triangles are discovered to be similar or congruent, this information can assist in determining unknown parts of triangles, such as missing angles and sides.

The example below involves the question of congruent triangles. The first step is to examine whether the triangles are congruent. If the triangles are congruent, then the measure of a missing angle can be found.

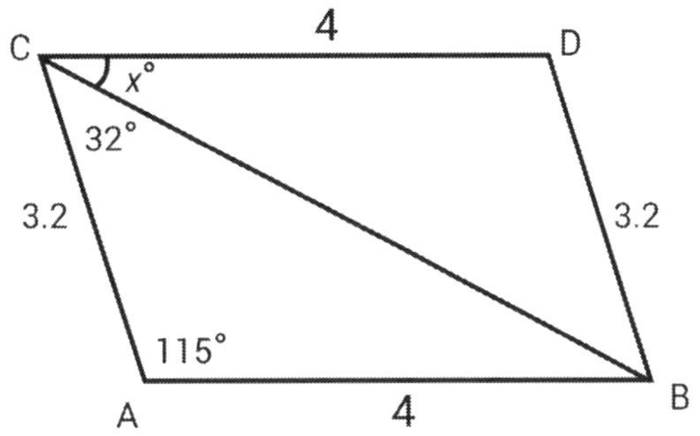

The above diagram provides values for angle measurements and side lengths in triangles CAB and CDB. Note that side CA is 3.2 and side DB is 3.2. Side CD is 4 and side AB is 4. Furthermore, line CB is congruent to itself by the reflexive property. Therefore, the two triangles are congruent by SSS (Side-Side-Side). Because the two triangles are congruent, all of the corresponding parts of the triangles are also congruent. Therefore, angle x is congruent to the inside of the angle for which a measurement is not provided in triangle CAB. Thus, $115^{\circ} + 32^{\circ} = 147^{\circ}$. A triangle's angles sum to 180°, therefore, $180^{\circ} - 147^{\circ} = 33^{\circ}$. Angle $x = 33^{\circ}$, because the two triangles are reversed.

Points, Lines, and Angles

Lines, Rays, and Line Segments

The basic unit of geometry is a point. A point represents an exact location on a plane, or flat surface. The position of a point is indicated with a dot and usually named with a single uppercase letter, such as point A or point T. A point is a place, not a thing, and therefore has no dimensions or size. A set of points that lies on the same line is called collinear.

A set of points that lies on the same plane is called coplanar.

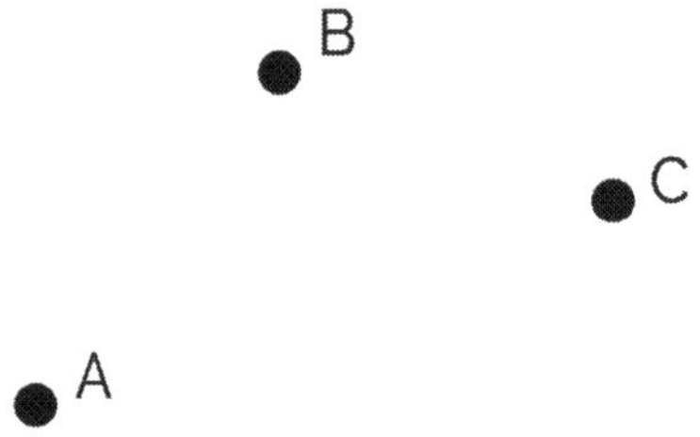

The image above displays point A, point B, and point C.

A line is as series of points that extends in both directions without ending. It consists of an infinite number of points and is drawn with arrows on both ends to indicate it extends infinitely. Lines can be named by two points on the line or with a single, cursive, lower case letter. The two lines below could be named line AB or line BA or $\overleftrightarrow{AB}$ or $\overleftrightarrow{BA}$; and line m.

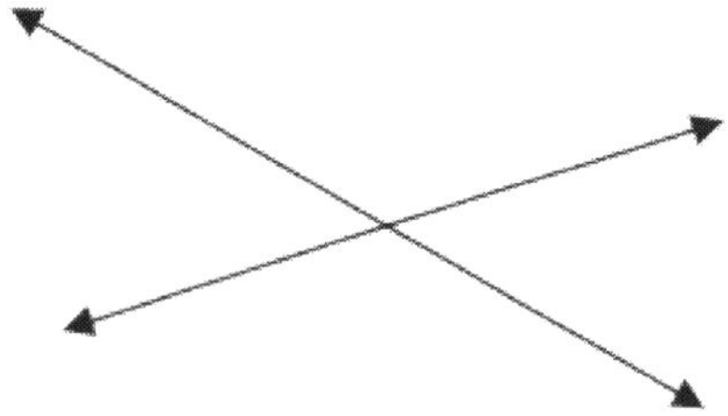

Two lines are considered parallel to each other if, while extending infinitely, they will never intersect (or meet). Parallel lines point in the same direction and are always the same distance apart. Two lines are considered perpendicular if they intersect to form right angles. Right angles are 90°. Typically, a small box is drawn at the intersection point to indicate the right angle.

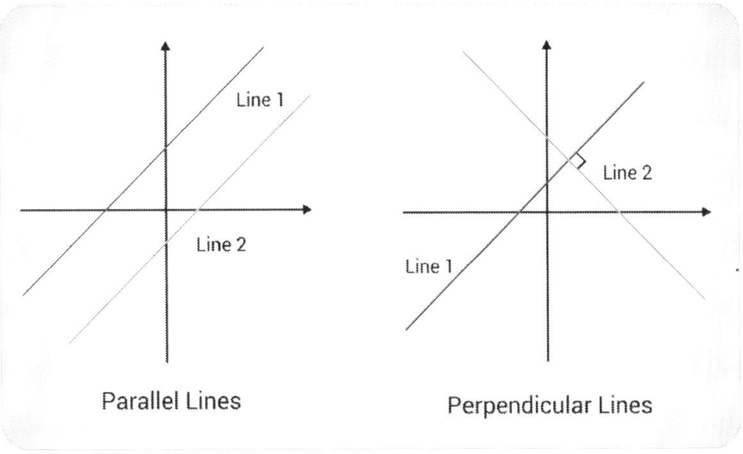

Line 1 is parallel to line 2 in the left image and is written as $\text{line } 1 \parallel \text{line } 2$. Line 1 is perpendicular to line 2 in the right image and is written as $\text{line } 1 \perp \text{line } 2$.

A ray has a specific starting point and extends in one direction without ending. The endpoint of a ray is its starting point. Rays are named using the endpoint first, and any other point on the ray. The following ray can be named ray AB and written $\overrightarrow{AB}$.

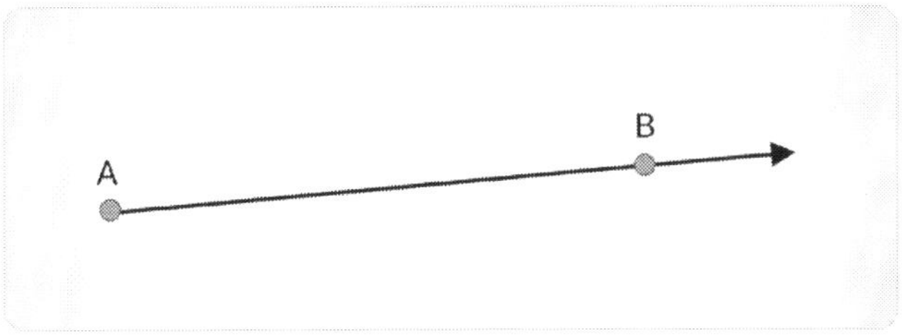

A line segment has specific starting and ending points. A line segment consists of two endpoints and all the points in between. Line segments are named by the two endpoints. The example below is named segment KL or segment LK, written $\overline{KL}$ or $\overline{LK}$.

Classification of Angles

An angle consists of two rays that have a common endpoint. This common endpoint is called the vertex of the angle. The two rays can be called sides of the angle. The angle below has a vertex at point B and the sides consist of ray BA and ray BC. An angle can be named in three ways:

1. Using the vertex and a point from each side, with the vertex letter in the middle.
2. Using only the vertex. This can only be used if it is the only angle with that vertex.
3. Using a number that is written inside the angle.

The angle below can be written $\angle ABC$ (read angle ABC), $\angle CBA$, $\angle B$, or $\angle 1$.

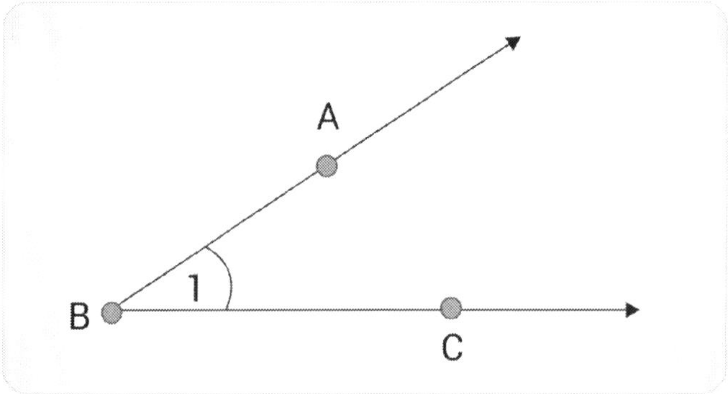

An angle divides a plane, or flat surface, into three parts: the angle itself, the interior (inside) of the angle, and the exterior (outside) of the angle. The figure below shows point M on the interior of the angle and point N on the exterior of the angle.

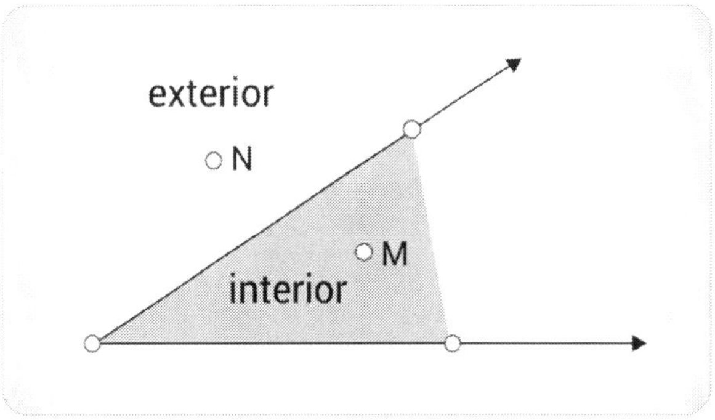

Angles can be measured in units called degrees, with the symbol °. The degree measure of an angle is between 0° and 180° and can be obtained by using a protractor.

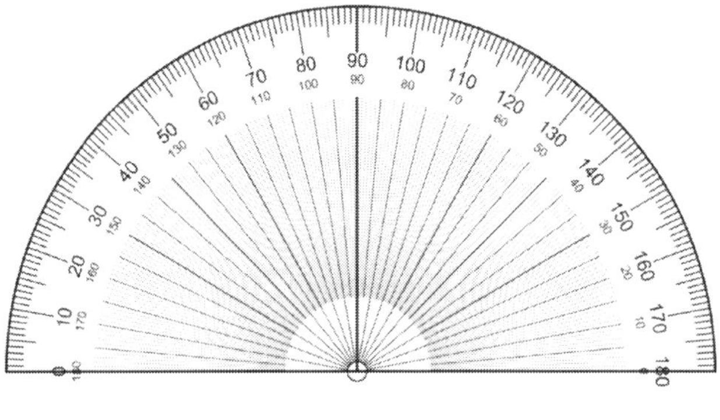

A straight angle (or simply a line) measures exactly 180°. A right angle's sides meet at the vertex to create a square corner. A right angle measures exactly 90° and is typically indicated by a box drawn in the interior of the angle. An acute angle has an interior that is narrower than a right angle. The measure of an acute angle is any value less than 90° and greater than 0°. For example, 89.9°, 47°, 12°, and 1°. An obtuse angle has an interior that is wider than a right angle. The measure of an obtuse angle is any value greater than 90° but less than 180°. For example, 90.1°, 110°, 150°, and 179.9°.

- Acute angles: Less than 90°
- Obtuse angles: Greater than 90°
- Right angles: 90°
- Straight angles: 180°

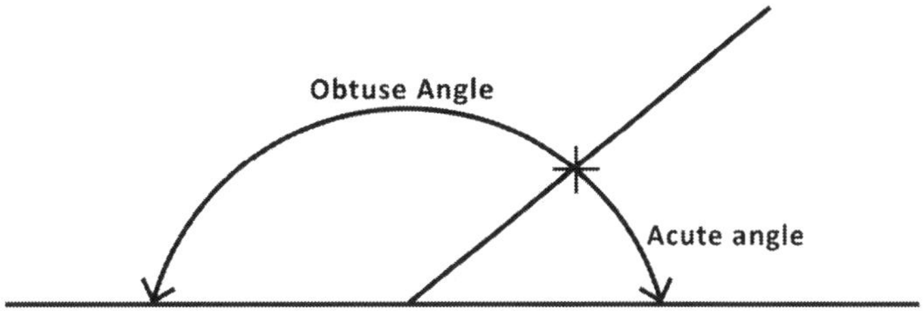

Two- and Three-Dimensional Figures

A polygon is a closed geometric figure in a plane (flat surface) consisting of at least 3 sides formed by line segments. These are often defined as two-dimensional shapes. Common two-dimensional shapes include circles, triangles, squares, rectangles, pentagons, and hexagons. Note that a circle is a two-dimensional shape without sides.

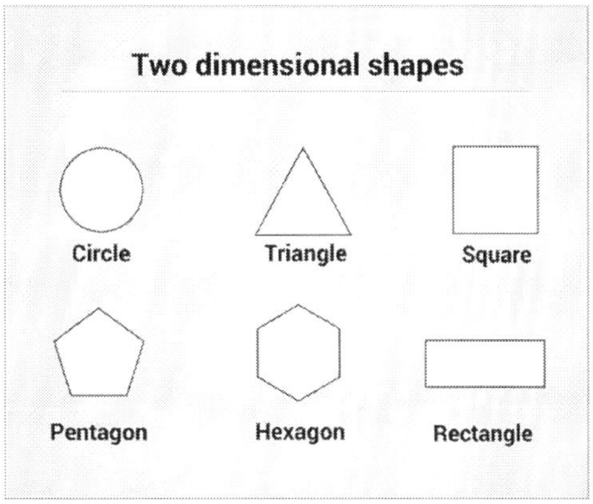

A solid figure, or simply solid, is a figure that encloses a part of space. Some solids consist of flat surfaces only while others include curved surfaces. Solid figures are often defined as three-dimensional shapes. Common three-dimensional shapes include spheres, prisms, cubes, pyramids, cylinders, and cones.

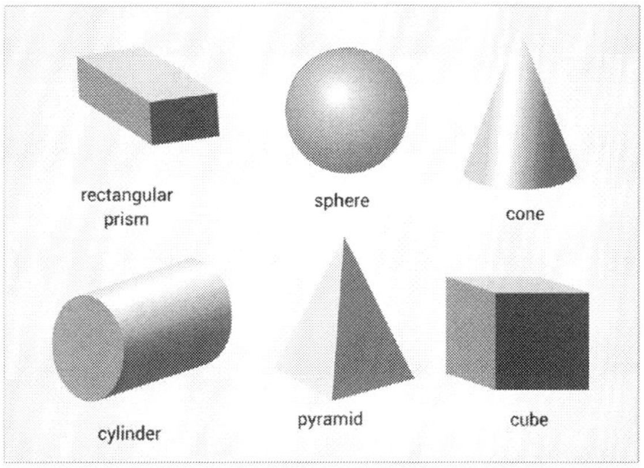

Composing two- or three-dimensional shapes involves putting together two or more shapes to create a new larger figure. For example, a semi-circle (half circle), rectangle, and two triangles can be used to compose the figure of the sailboat shown below.

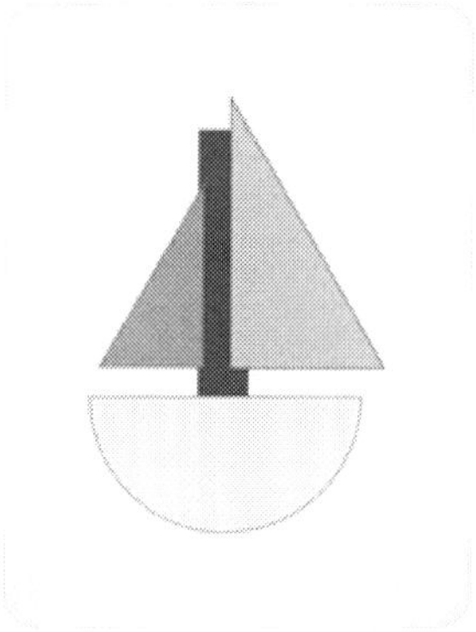

Similarly, solid figures can be placed together to compose an endless number of three-dimensional objects.

Decomposing two- and three-dimensional figures involves breaking the shapes apart into smaller, simpler shapes. Consider the following two-dimensional representations of a house:

This complex figure can be decomposed into the following basic two-dimensional shapes: large rectangle (body of house); large triangle (roof); small rectangle and small triangle (chimney). Decomposing figures is often done more than one way. To illustrate, the figure of the house could also be decomposed into: two large triangles (body); two medium triangles (roof); two smaller triangles of unequal size (chimney).

Tessellations and Symmetry

A tiling exists when individual shapes are placed to fill a flat space with no gaps or overlapping. A tiling is also known as a tessellation. Some can have repeating patterns, and some do not. If they repeat, they are known as a periodic tiling. Some can also be symmetric because if it is folded over a line of symmetry, the pattern represents two mirror images.

If an object can be split in half by a line and flipped over that line to lie directly on top of itself, it is said to have **line symmetry**. An example is seen below.

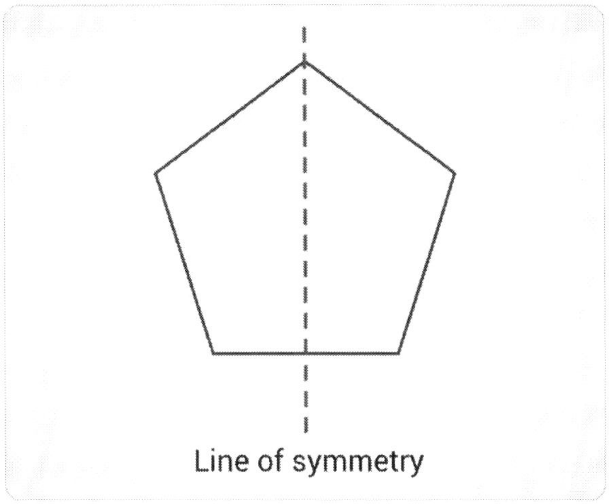

If an object can be rotated about its center to any degree smaller than 360, and it lies directly on top of itself, the object is said to have **rotational symmetry**. An example of this type of symmetry is shown below. The pentagon has an order of 5.

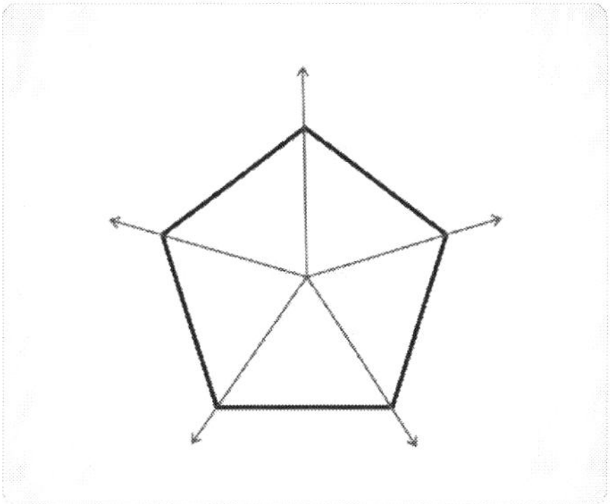

The rotational symmetry lines in the figure above can be used to find the angles formed at the center of the pentagon. Knowing that all of the angles together form a full circle, at 360 degrees, the figure can be split into 5 angles equally. By dividing the 360° by 5, each angle is 72°.

Given the length of one side of the figure, the perimeter of the pentagon can also be found using rotational symmetry. If one side length was 3 cm, that side length can be rotated onto each other side length four times. This would give a total of 5 side lengths equal to 3 cm. To find the perimeter, or distance around the figure, multiply 3 by 5. The perimeter of the figure would be 15 cm.

If a line cannot be drawn anywhere on the object to flip the figure onto itself or rotated less than or equal to 180 degrees to lay on top of itself, the object is asymmetrical. Examples of these types of figures are shown below.

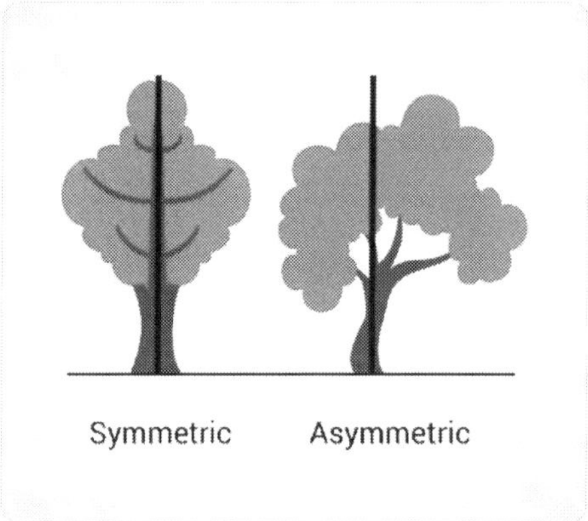

Estimation

There is a difference between an exact answer and an estimation. Sometimes answering a question with an estimate is good enough; however, an exact answer is often required. Also, using an estimate as a ballpark to tell if an exact answer is reasonable is sometimes a good technique to use as well. For example, consider the situation if a student has to buy lunch at school, and they only have $5 to do so. A sandwich is $2.29, a piece of fruit is $0.75, and a drink is $1.25. An estimate might be enough to tell if he or she had enough money. A good estimate would be to round each cost to whole dollar amounts. Therefore, the estimate would be that lunch would cost $2.00 for the sandwich, $1.00 for the fruit, and $1.00 for the drink, which adds up to $4.00.

The estimate would be that $5.00 is enough to pay for lunch. The exact amount is $4.29, so the estimate does the trick. However, sometimes estimation could steer someone in the wrong direction. Consider a situation where the sandwich was $2.45, the fruit was $1.25, and the drink was $1.35. Rounding to the nearest dollar would still result in an estimate of $4.00; however, the exact amount in this scenario is $5.05. Therefore, the student would not have enough money. Perhaps rounding to the nearest $0.50 would be a better estimation process. Exact calculations are usually the best, but estimations are useful if they are done correctly.

Problems Involving Time, Volume, Money, Length, and Mass

Problems that involve measurements of length, time, volume, etc. are generally dependent upon understanding how to manipulate between various units of measurement, as well as understanding their equivalencies. They also require determining which operations (addition, subtraction, multiplication, and division) should be performed, and using and/or converting the proper unit for the scenario.

The following table lists key words that can be used to indicate the proper operation:

Addition	Sum, total, in all, combined, increase of, more than, added to
Subtraction	Difference, change, remaining, less than, decreased by
Multiplication	Product, times, twice, triple, each
Division	Quotient, goes into, per, evenly, divided by half, divided by third, split

Problems Involving Time

Time is measured in units such as *seconds, minutes, hours, days*, and *years*. For example, there are 60 seconds in a minute, 60 minutes in each hour, and 24 hours in a day.

When dealing with problems involving elapsed time, break the problem down into workable parts. For example, suppose the length of time between 1:15pm and 3:45pm must be determined. From 1:15pm to 2:00pm is 45 minutes (knowing there are 60 minutes in an hour). From 2:00pm to 3:00pm is 1 hour. From 3:00pm to 3:45pm is 45 minutes. The total elapsed time is 45 minutes plus 1 hour plus 45 minutes. This sum produces 1 hour and 90 minutes. 90 minutes is over an hour, so this is converted to 1 hour (60 minutes) and 30 minutes. The total elapsed time can now be expressed as 2 hours and 30 minutes.

To illustrate time intervals, a clock face can show solutions.

For example, Ani needs to complete all of her chores by 1:50 p.m. If she begins her chores at 1:00 p.m., can she finish the following? Vacuuming (15 minutes), dusting (10 minutes), replacing light bulbs (5 minutes), and degreasing the garage floor (25 minutes).

A blank clock face is useful in illustrating the time lapse necessary for all of Ani's tasks.

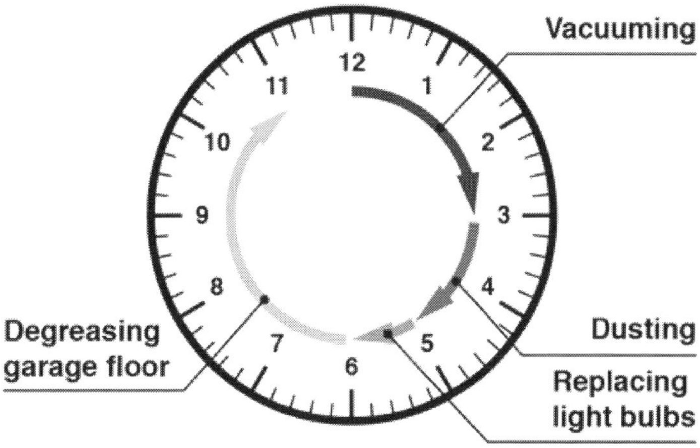

It is easy to see that the chores will span beyond 50 minutes after the hour, so no, Ani could not complete the chores in the given time frame.

When dealing with problems involving elapsed time, breaking the problem down into workable parts is helpful. For example, suppose the length of time between 1:15pm and 3:45pm must be determined. From 1:15pm to 2:00pm is 45 minutes (knowing there are 60 minutes in an hour). From 2:00pm to 3:00pm is 1 hour. From 3:00pm to 3:45pm is 45 minutes. The total elapsed time is 45 minutes plus 1 hour plus 45 minutes. This sum produces 1 hour and 90 minutes. 90 minutes is over an hour, so this is converted to 1 hour (60 minutes) and 30 minutes. The total elapsed time can now be expressed as 2 hours and 30 minutes.

Problems Involving Volume

Volume is how much space something occupies. That "something" can be liquid or solid. Essentially, volume is a measurement of capacity. Whereas area is calculated by counting squares within a two-dimensional object, volume is calculated by counting cubes within a three-dimensional object. It is a measure of the space a figure occupies. Volume is measured using cubic units, such as cubic inches, feet, centimeters, or kilometers. Centimeter cubes can be utilized in the classrooms in order to promote understanding of volume.

For instance, if 10 cubes were placed along the length of a rectangle, with 8 cubes placed along its width, and the remaining area was filled in with cubes, there would 80 cubes in total, which would equal a volume of 80 cubic centimeters. Its area would equal 80 square centimeters. If that shape was doubled so that its height consists of two cube lengths, there would be 160 cubes, and its volume would be 160 cubic centimeters. Adding another level of cubes would mean that there would be $3 \times 80 = 240$ cubes. This idea shows that volume is calculated by multiplying area times height. The actual formula for volume of a three-dimensional rectangular solid is $V = l \times w \times h$, where l represents length, w represents width, and h represents height. Volume can also be thought of as area of the base times the height.

The base in this case would be the entire rectangle formed by l and w. Here is an example of a rectangular solid with labeled sides:

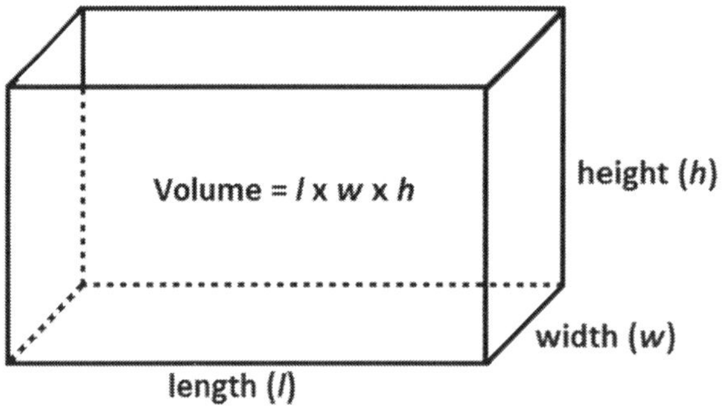

A **cube** is a special type of rectangular solid in which its length, width, and height are the same. If this length is s, then the formula for the volume of a cube is $V = s \times s \times s$.

The U.S. customary units for volume of liquids, from smallest to largest, are: fluid ounces (fl oz), cup (c), pint (pt), quart (qt), and gallon (gal). The metric units for volume of liquids, from smallest to largest, are: milliliter (mL), centiliter (cL), deciliter (dL), liter (L), and kiloliter (kL.).

A problem involving liquid volume would be: If Mart needed 2 quarts of liquid for a recipe and only has a measuring cup, how could he measure out 2 quarts?

The solution would involve Mart measuring out 2 quarts by filling the cup 8 times.

Problems Involving Money

Let's consider a problem involving change. Gwen wants to purchase a number of items at the school supply store. Prices are as follows:

Erasers are \$0.05
Highlighters are \$0.20
Pencils are \$0.10
Pens are \$0.15

Gwen wants to buy 1 highlighter, 5 erasers, 2 pencils, and 3 pens. Would she be able to use the following coins, and if so, what are possible combinations Gwen could use?

To begin, add the total value of the coins:

$$2 \text{ quarters} + 5 \text{ dimes} + 2 \text{ nickels}$$

$$(2 \times \$0.25) + (5 \times \$0.10) + (2 \times \$0.05) = \$1.10$$

Then calculate the total cost of the items Gwen wants to purchase:

Erasers are \$0.05
Highlighters are \$0.20
Pencils are \$0.10
Pens are \$0.15

Gwen wants to buy 1 highlighter, 5 erasers, 2 pencils, and 3 pens.

$$1 \text{ highlighter} + 5 \text{ erasers} + 2 \text{ pencils} + 2 \text{ pens}$$

$$\$0.20 + (5 \times \$0.05) + (2 \times \$0.10) + (2 \times \$0.15)$$

$$\$0.20 + \$0.25 + \$0.20 + \$0.30 = \$0.95$$

Gwen has enough money to purchase all of the items, and there is only one combination that would provide the correct amount of \$0.95: 2 quarters, 4 dimes, and 1 nickel.

Here is another example of a problem involving money that is a bit more difficult:

A store is having a spring sale, where everything is 70% off. You have \$45.00 to spend. A jacket is regularly priced at \$80.00. Do you have enough to buy the jacket and a pair of gloves, regularly priced at \$20.00?

There are two ways to approach this.

Method 1:

Set up the equations to find the sale prices: the original price minus the amount discounted.

$$\$80.00 - (\$80.00\ (0.70)) = sale\ cost\ of\ the\ jacket$$
$$\$20.00 - (\$20.00\ (0.70)) = sale\ cost\ of\ the\ gloves$$

Solve for the sale cost.

$$\$24.00 = sale\ cost\ of\ the\ jacket$$
$$\$6.00 = sale\ cost\ of\ the\ gloves$$

Determine if you have enough money for both.

$$\$24.00 + \$6.00 = total\ sale\ cost$$

\$30.00 is less than \$45.00, so you can afford to purchase both.

Method 2:

Determine the percent of the original price that you will pay.

$$100\% - 70\% = 30\%$$

Set up the equations to find the sale prices.

$$\$80.00\ (0.30) = cost\ of\ the\ jacket$$
$$\$20.00\ (0.30) = cost\ of\ the\ gloves$$

Solve.

$$\$24.00 = cost\ of\ the\ jacket$$
$$\$6.00 = cost\ of\ the\ gloves$$

Determine if you have enough money for both.

$$\$24.00 + \$6.00 = total\ sale\ cost$$

\$30.00 is less than \$45.00, so you can afford to purchase both.

Problems Involving Length

The length of an object can be measured using standard tools such as rulers, yard sticks, meter sticks, and measuring tapes. The following image depicts a yardstick:

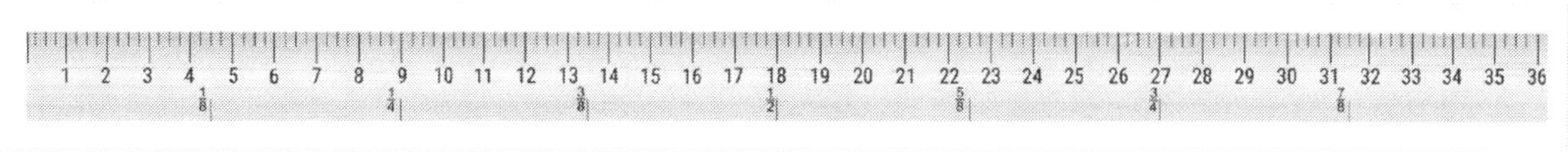

Choosing the right tool to perform the measurement requires determining whether United States customary units or metric units are desired, and having a grasp of the approximate length of each unit and the approximate length of each tool. The measurement can still be performed by trial and error without the knowledge of the approximate size of the tool.

For example, to determine the length of a room in feet, a United States customary unit, various tools can be used for this task. These include a ruler (typically 12 inches/1-foot-long), a yardstick (3 feet/1-yard-long), or a tape measure displaying feet (typically either 25 feet or 50 feet). Because the length of a room is much larger than the length of a ruler or a yardstick, a tape measure should be used to perform the measurement.

When the correct measuring tool is selected, the measurement is performed by first placing the tool directly above or below the object (if making a horizontal measurement) or directly next to the object (if making a vertical measurement). The next step is aligning the tool so that one end of the object is at the mark for zero units, then recording the unit of the mark at the other end of the object. To give the length of a paperclip in metric units, a ruler displaying centimeters is aligned with one end of the paper clip to the mark for zero centimeters.

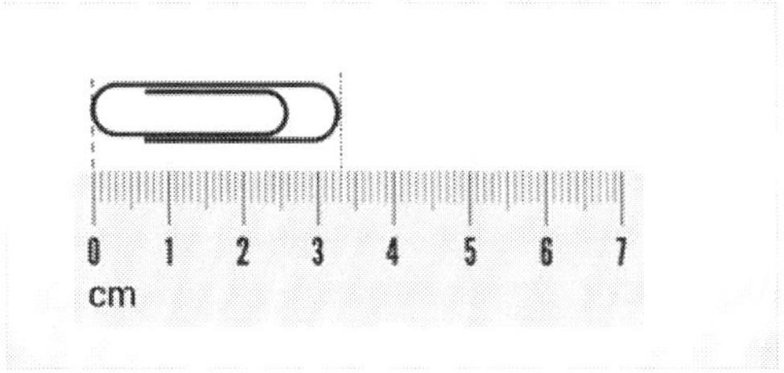

Directly down from the other end of the paperclip is the mark that measures its length. In this case, that mark is two small dashes past the 3-centimeter mark. Each small dash is 1 millimeter (or .1 centimeters). Therefore, the length of the paper clip is 3.2 centimeters.

To compare the lengths of objects, each length must be expressed in the same unit. If possible, the objects should be measured with the same tool or with tools utilizing the same units. For example, a ruler and a yardstick can both measure length in inches. If the lengths of the objects are expressed in different units, these different units must be converted to the same unit before comparing them. If two lengths are expressed in the same unit, the lengths may be compared by subtracting the smaller value from the larger value. For example, suppose the lengths of two gardens are to be compared. Garden A has a length of 4 feet, and garden B has a length of 2 yards. 2 yards is converted to 6 feet so that the measurements have similar units. Then, the smaller length (4 feet) is subtracted from the larger length (6 ft): $6 \text{ ft} - 4 \text{ ft} = 2 \text{ ft}$. Therefore, garden B is 2 feet larger than garden A.

Identifying and utilizing the proper units for the scenario requires knowing how to apply the conversion rates for length. For example, given a scenario that requires subtracting 8 inches from $2\frac{1}{2}$ feet, both values should first be expressed in the same unit (they could be expressed $\frac{2}{3}$ ft & $2\frac{1}{2}$ ft, or 8 in and 30 in). The desired unit for the answer may also require converting back to another unit.

Consider the following scenario that involves length: A parking area along the river is only wide enough to fit one row of cars and is $\frac{1}{2}$ kilometers long. The average space needed per car is 5 meters. How many cars can be parked along the river? First, all measurements should be converted to similar units: $\frac{1}{2}$km = 500m. The operation(s) needed should be identified. Because the problem asks for the number of cars, the total space should be divided by the space per car. 500 meters divided by 5 meters per car yields a total of 100 cars. Written as an expression, the meters unit cancels and the cars unit is left: $\frac{500 \text{ m}}{5 \text{ m/car}}$ the same as $500 \text{ m} \times \frac{1 \text{ car}}{5 \text{ m}}$ yields 100 cars.

Problems Involving Mass

The metric system measures **mass**, which is the quantity of matter within an object. Mass and weight do not measure the same thing. **Weight** is affected by gravity, and deals with how strongly Earth is pulling on an object.

The following is an example of a problem involving mass:

A piggy bank contains 12 dollars' worth of nickels. The mass of a nickel is 5 grams, and the empty piggy bank has a mass of 1,050 grams. What is the total mass of the full piggy bank?

A dollar contains 20 nickels. Therefore, if there are 12 dollars' worth of nickels, there are $12 \times 20 = 240$ nickels. The mass of each nickel is 5 grams. Therefore, the mass of the nickels is $240 \times 5 = 1{,}200$ grams. Adding in the mass of the empty piggy bank, the mass of the filled bank 2,250 grams.

Translations, Rotations, and Reflections

Given a figure drawn on a plane, many changes can be made to that figure, including **rotation**, **translation**, and **reflection**. Rotations turn the figure about a point, translations slide the figure, and reflections flip the figure over a specified line. When performing these transformations, the original figure is called the **pre-image**, and the figure after transformation is called the **image**.

More specifically, **translation** means that all points in the figure are moved in the same direction by the same distance. In other words, the figure is slid in some fixed direction. Of course, while the entire figure is slid by the same distance, this does not change any of the measurements of the figures involved. The result will have the same distances and angles as the original figure.

In terms of Cartesian coordinates, a translation means a shift of each of the original points (x, y) by a fixed amount in the x- and y-directions, to become $(x + a, y + b)$.

Another procedure that can be performed is called **reflection**. To do this, a line in the plane is specified, called the **line of reflection**. Then, take each point and flip it over the line so that it is the same distance from the line but on the opposite side of it. This does not change any of the distances or angles involved, but it does reverse the order in which everything appears.

To reflect something over the x-axis, the points (x, y) are sent to $(x, -y)$. To reflect something over the y-axis, the points (x, y) are sent to the points $(-x, y)$. Flipping over other lines is not something easy to express in Cartesian coordinates. However, by drawing the figure and the line of reflection, the distance to the line and the original points can be used to find the reflected figure.

Example: Reflect this triangle with vertices $(-1, 0)$, $(2, 1)$, and $(2, 0)$ over the y-axis. The pre-image is shown below.

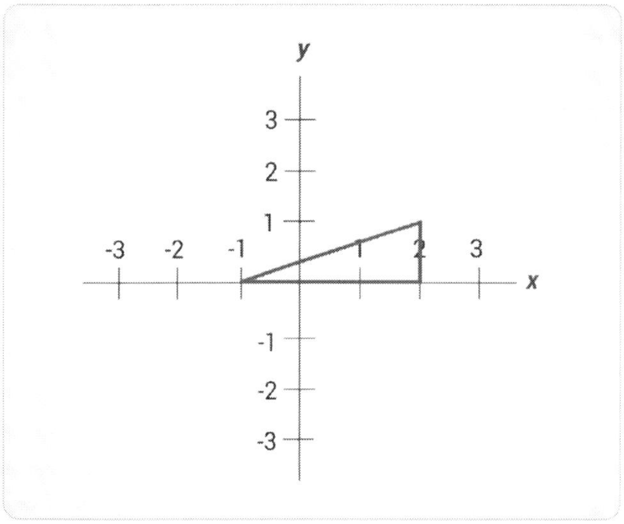

To do this, flip the x-values of the points involved to the negatives of themselves, while keeping the y-values the same. The image is shown here.

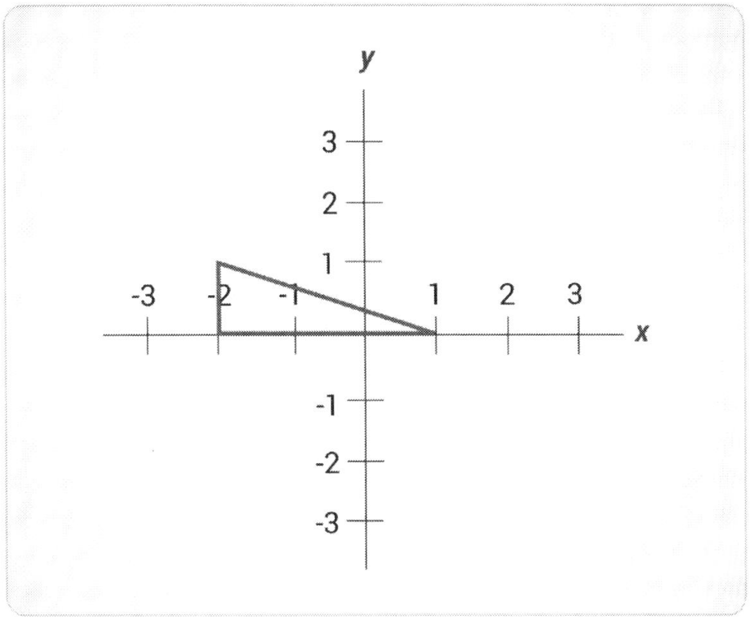

The new vertices will be $(1, 0)$, $(-2, 1)$, and $(-2, 0)$.

Another procedure that does not change the distances and angles in a figure is **rotation**. In this procedure, pick a center point, then rotate every vertex along a circle around that point by the same angle. This procedure is also not easy to express in Cartesian coordinates, and this is not a requirement on this test. However, as with reflections, it's helpful to draw the figures and see what the result of the rotation would look like. This transformation can be performed using a compass and protractor.

Each one of these transformations can be performed on the coordinate plane without changes to the original dimensions or angles.

If two figures in the plane involve the same distances and angles, they are called **congruent figures**. In other words, two figures are congruent when they go from one form to another through reflection, rotation, and translation, or a combination of these.

Remember that rotation and translation will give back a new figure that is identical to the original figure, but reflection will give back a mirror image of it.

To recognize that a figure has undergone a rotation, check to see that the figure has not been changed into a mirror image, but that its orientation has changed (that is, whether the parts of the figure now form different angles with the x-and y-axes).

To recognize that a figure has undergone a translation, check to see that the figure has not been changed into a mirror image, and that the orientation remains the same.

To recognize that a figure has undergone a reflection, check to see that the new figure is a mirror image of the old figure.

Keep in mind that sometimes a combination of translations, reflections, and rotations may be performed on a figure.

Conversions Within and Between Measurement Systems

When working with different systems of measurement, conversion from one unit to another may be necessary. The conversion rate must be known to convert units. One method for converting units is to write and solve a proportion. The arrangement of values in a proportion is extremely important. Suppose that a problem requires converting 20 fluid ounces to cups. To do so, a proportion can be written using the conversion rate of 8fl oz = 1c with x representing the missing value. The proportion can be written in any of the following ways:

$$\frac{1}{8}=\frac{x}{20}\left(\frac{c\ for\ conversion}{fl\ oz\ for\ conversion}=\frac{unknown\ c}{fl\ oz\ given}\right)$$

$$\frac{8}{1}=\frac{20}{x}\left(\frac{fl\ oz\ for\ conversion}{c\ for\ conversion}=\frac{fl\ oz\ given}{unknown\ c}\right)$$

$$\frac{1}{x}=\frac{8}{20}\left(\frac{c\ for\ conversion}{unknown\ c}=\frac{fl\ oz\ for\ conversion}{fl\ oz\ given}\right)$$

$$\frac{x}{1}=\frac{20}{8}\left(\frac{unknown\ c}{c\ for\ conversion}=\frac{fl\ oz\ given}{fl\ oz\ for\ conversion}\right)$$

To solve a proportion, the ratios are cross-multiplied and the resulting equation is solved. When cross-multiplying, all four proportions above will produce the same equation:

$$(8)(x)=(20)(1)\rightarrow 8x=20$$

Divide by 8 to isolate the variable x, the result is $x=2.5$. The variable x represented the unknown number of cups. Therefore, the conclusion is that 20 fluid ounces converts (is equal) to 2.5 cups.

Sometimes converting units requires writing and solving more than one proportion. Suppose an exam question asks to determine how many hours are in 2 weeks. Without knowing the conversion rate between hours and weeks, this can be determined knowing the conversion rates between weeks and days, and between days and hours. First, weeks are converted to days, then days are converted to hours. To convert from weeks to days, the following proportion can be written:

$$\frac{7}{1}=\frac{x}{2}\left(\frac{days\ conversion}{weeks\ conversion}=\frac{days\ unknown}{weeks\ given}\right)$$

Cross-multiplying produces: $(7)(2)=(x)(1)\rightarrow 14=x$. Therefore, 2 weeks is equal to 14 days. Next, a proportion is written to convert 14 days to hours:

$$\frac{24}{1}=\frac{x}{14}\left(\frac{conversion\ hours}{conversion\ days}=\frac{unknown\ hours}{given\ days}\right)$$

Cross-multiplying produces:

$$(24)(14)=(x)(1)\rightarrow 336=x$$

Therefore, the answer is that there are 336 hours in 2 weeks.

Axiomatic Structure of Geometry

An axiomatic system is comprised of a list of axioms, which are true statements that serve as starting points for arguments. The basis of geometry is a list of axioms that can be used to form theorems, which are proven statements based on a sequential combination of axioms. Proving is the fundamental task in geometry. A geometric proof is a list of true statements, or axioms, that show a math concept to be true. The statements are typically listed in two columns: the first column lists the statements, and the second column explains why the statement is known to be true. A direct proof uses true statements that build upon each other to show the truth of the given proposition. A proof by contradiction shows that assuming what is known to be false will inevitably lead to a contradiction, which in turn shows the truth of the original proposition.

Some commonly used axioms in geometry include the following:

A straight line can be drawn between any two points.
Any line segment can be extended indefinitely.
All right angles are equivalent.
A circle can be created from any given center point and radius.

In some cases, theorems can be proved in multiple ways. Consider the Pythagorean Theorem, which states that given a right triangle, the sum of the squares of the two sides is equal to the square of the hypotenuse. A proof using similar triangles exists, which splits the triangle up into two similar triangles. The proof is built on the idea of proportionality between the two triangles. A second way to prove the theorem is through the construction proof. In this proof, squares and triangles are drawn, and axioms and theorems are used to show that the Pythagorean Theorem is always true.

Polygons

A polygon is a closed two-dimensional figure consisting of three or more sides. Polygons can be either convex or concave. A polygon that has interior angles all measuring less than 180° is convex. A concave polygon has one or more interior angles measuring greater than 180°. Examples are shown below.

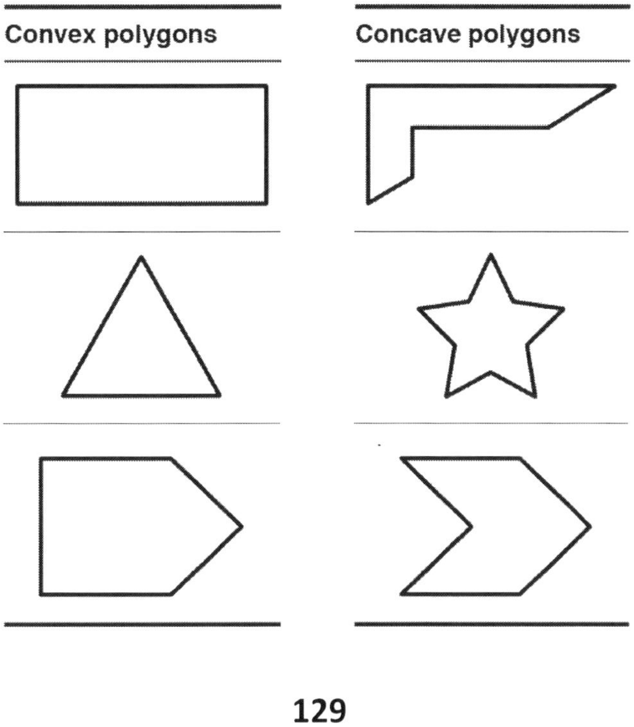

Polygons can be classified by the number of sides (also equal to the number of angles) they have. The following are the names of polygons with a given number of sides or angles:

# of sides	**3**	**4**	**5**	**6**	**7**	**8**	**9**	**10**
Name of polygon	Triangle	Quadrilateral	Pentagon	Hexagon	Septagon (or heptagon)	Octagon	Nonagon	Decagon

Equiangular polygons are polygons in which the measure of every interior angle is the same. The sides of equilateral polygons are always the same length. If a polygon is both equiangular and equilateral, the polygon is defined as a regular polygon. Examples are shown below.

Triangles can be further classified by their sides and angles. A triangle with its largest angle measuring 90° is a right triangle. A triangle with the largest angle less than 90° is an acute triangle. A triangle with the largest angle greater than 90° is an obtuse triangle. Below is an example of a right triangle.

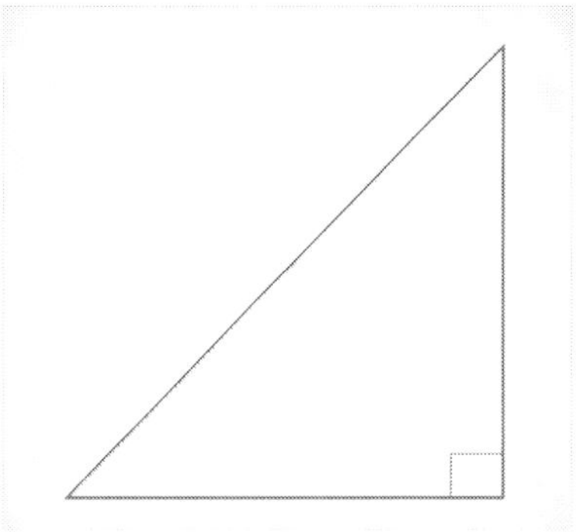

A triangle consisting of two equal sides and two equal angles is an isosceles triangle. A triangle with three equal sides and three equal angles is an equilateral triangle. A triangle with no equal sides or angles is a scalene triangle.

Isosceles triangle:

Equilateral triangle:

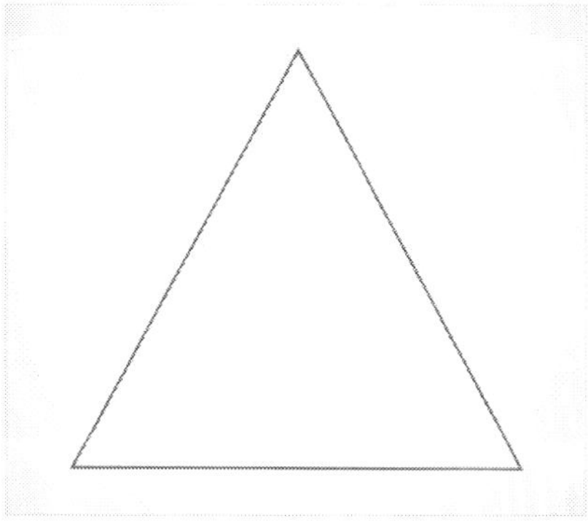

Scalene triangle:

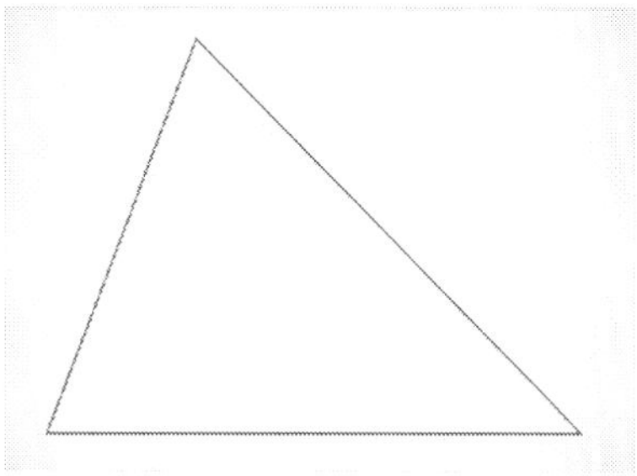

Quadrilaterals can be further classified according to their sides and angles. A quadrilateral with exactly one pair of parallel sides is called a trapezoid. A quadrilateral that shows both pairs of opposite sides parallel is a parallelogram. Parallelograms include rhombuses, rectangles, and squares. A rhombus has four equal sides. A rectangle has four equal angles (90° each). A square has four 90° angles and four equal sides. Therefore, a square is both a rhombus and a rectangle.

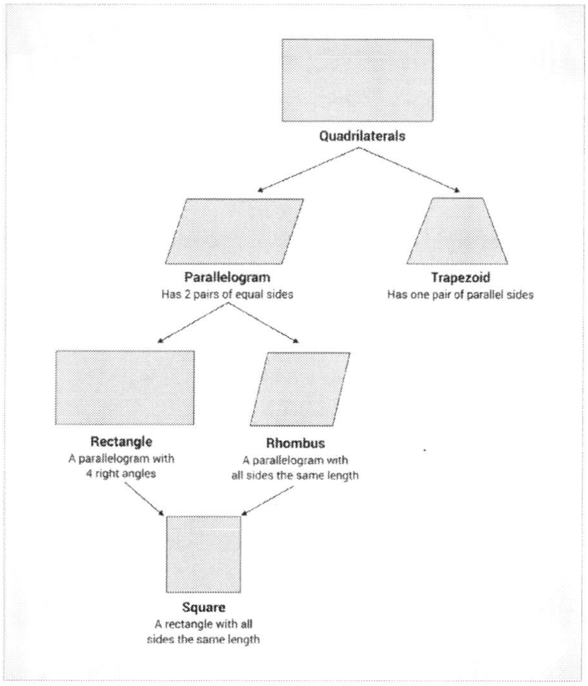

A solid is a three-dimensional figure that encloses a part of space. Solids consisting of all flat surfaces that are polygons are called polyhedrons. The two-dimensional surfaces that make up a polyhedron are called faces. Types of polyhedrons include prisms and pyramids. A prism consists of two parallel faces that are congruent (or the same shape and same size), and lateral faces going around (which are parallelograms).

A prism is further classified by the shape of its base, as shown below:

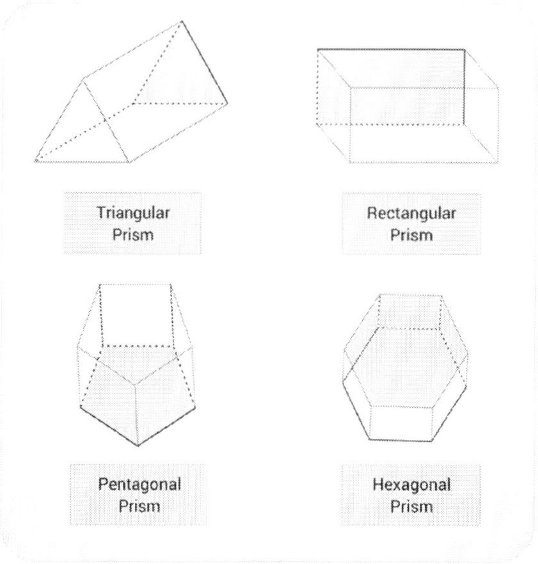

A pyramid consists of lateral faces (triangles) that meet at a common point called the vertex and one other face that is a polygon, called the base. A pyramid can be further classified by the shape of its base, as shown below.

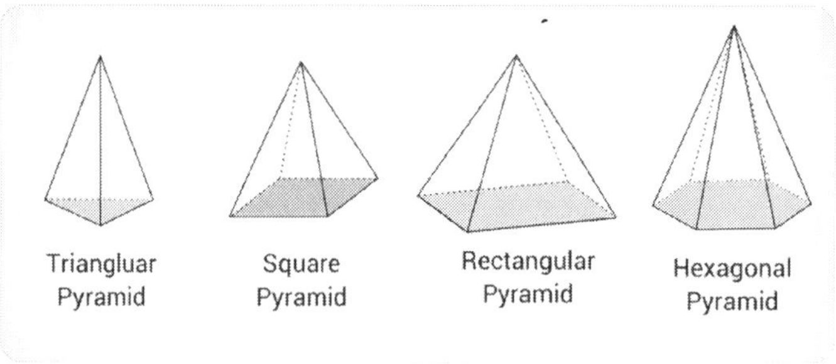

A tetrahedron is another name for a triangular pyramid. All the faces of a tetrahedron are triangles.

Solids that are not polyhedrons include spheres, cylinders, and cones. A sphere is the set of all points a given distance from a given center point. A sphere is commonly thought of as a three-dimensional circle. A cylinder consists of two parallel, congruent (same size) circles and a lateral curved surface. A cone consists of a circle as its base and a lateral curved surface that narrows to a point called the vertex.

Similar polygons are the same shape but different sizes. More specifically, their corresponding angle measures are congruent (or equal), and the length of their sides is proportional. For example, all sides of one polygon may be double the length of the sides of another. Likewise, similar solids are the same shape but different sizes. Any corresponding faces or bases of similar solids are the same polygons that are proportional by a consistent value.

United States Currency

The currency of the United States is the U.S. dollar, which has a symbol of \$. If someone has one dollar, the symbolic form of this amount is \$1 or \$1.00. Dollars are given in paper currency, or bills, and exist in seven different denominations: \$1, \$2, \$5, \$10, \$20, and \$100. Even though it is not as widespread, a dollar can also exist as a coin.

A dollar is made up of 100 cents, and the coin used for a cent is known as a penny. If a person has 50 pennies, they have 50 cents or 50¢. 50 cents is also equal to half of a dollar and can be written as \$0.50. A half dollar coin also exists; however, it is not very prevalent.

Other coins include quarters, dimes, and nickels. A quarter is equal to 25 cents, 25¢, or \$0.25. Four quarters sum to \$1. A dime is equal to 10 cents, 10¢, or \$0.10. Ten dimes add up to \$1. Finally, a nickel is equal to 5 cents, 5¢, or \$0.05. Twenty nickels sum to \$1.

It is important to know the values of coins and bills to give correct change. For example, if something costs \$2.65, and a 5-dollar bill is used to pay for that item, then $\$5 - \$2.65 = \$2.35$ is due back in change. The change would be given as two dollar bills plus \$0.35 in change, which could come in several combinations such as a quarter plus a dime or three dimes plus a nickel.

The Coordinate Plane

X-Axis, Y-Axis, Origin, and Four Quadrants

The coordinate plane, sometimes referred to as the Cartesian plane, is a two-dimensional surface consisting of a horizontal and a vertical number line. The horizontal number line is referred to as the x-axis, and the vertical number line is referred to as the y-axis. The x-axis and y-axis intersect (or cross) at a point called the origin. At the origin, the value of the x-axis is zero, and the value of the y-axis is zero. The coordinate plane identifies the exact location of a point that is plotted on the two-dimensional surface. Like a map, the location of all points on the plane are in relation to the origin. Along the x-axis (horizontal line), numbers to the right of the origin are positive and increasing in value (1,2,3, ...) and to the left of the origin numbers are negative and decreasing in value (-1,-2,-3, ...). Along the y-axis (vertical line), numbers above the origin are positive and increasing in value and numbers below the origin are negative and decreasing in value.

The x- and y-axis divide the coordinate plane into four sections. These sections are referred to as quadrant one, quadrant two, quadrant three, and quadrant four, and are often written with Roman numerals I, II, III, and IV.

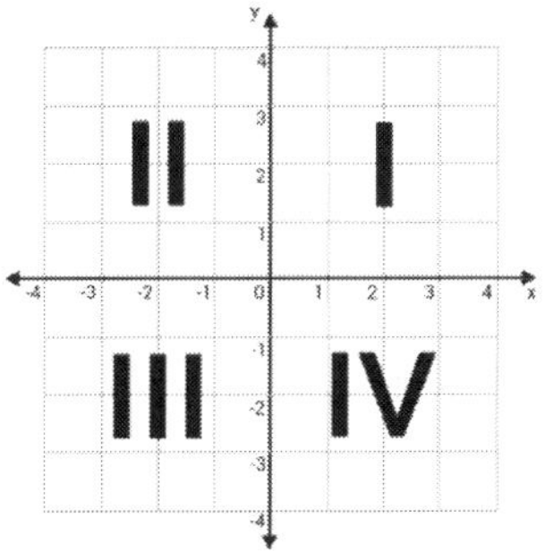

The upper right section is Quadrant I and consists of points with positive x-values and positive y-values. The upper left section is Quadrant II and consists of points with negative x-values and positive y-values. The bottom left section is Quadrant III and consists of points with negative x-values and negative y-values. The bottom right section is Quadrant IV and consists of points with positive x-values and negative y-values.

Solving Problems in the Coordinate Plane

The location of a point on a coordinate grid is identified by writing it as an ordered pair. An ordered pair is a set of numbers indicating the x-and y-coordinates of the point. Ordered pairs are written in the form (x, y) where x and y are values which indicate their respective coordinates. For example, the point $(3, -2)$ has an x-coordinate of 3 and a y-coordinate of -2.

Plotting a point on the coordinate plane with a given coordinate means starting from the origin $(0, 0)$. To determine the value of the x-coordinate, move right (positive number) or left (negative number) along the x-axis. Next, move up (positive number) or down (negative number) to the value of the y-coordinate. Finally, plot and label the point. For example, plotting the point $(1, -2)$ requires starting from the origin and moving right along the x-axis to positive one, then moving down until straight across from negative 2 on the y-axis. The point is plotted and labeled. This point, along with three other points, are plotted and labeled on the graph below.

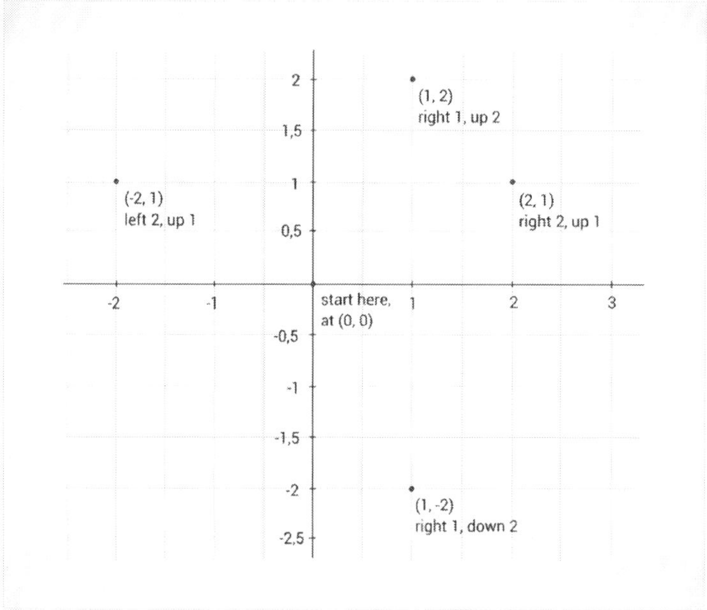

To write the coordinates of a point on the coordinate grid, a line should be traced directly above or below the point until reaching the x-axis (noting the value on the x-axis). Then, returning to the point, a line should be traced directly to the right or left of the point until reaching the y-axis (noting the value on the y-axis). The ordered pair (x, y) should be written with the values determined for the x- and y-coordinates.

Polygons can be drawn in the coordinate plane given the coordinates of their vertices. These coordinates can be used to determine the perimeter and area of the figure. Suppose triangle RQP has vertices located at the points:

$R(-4, 2)$, $Q(1, 6)$, and $P(1, 2)$. By plotting the points for the three vertices, the triangle can be constructed as follows:

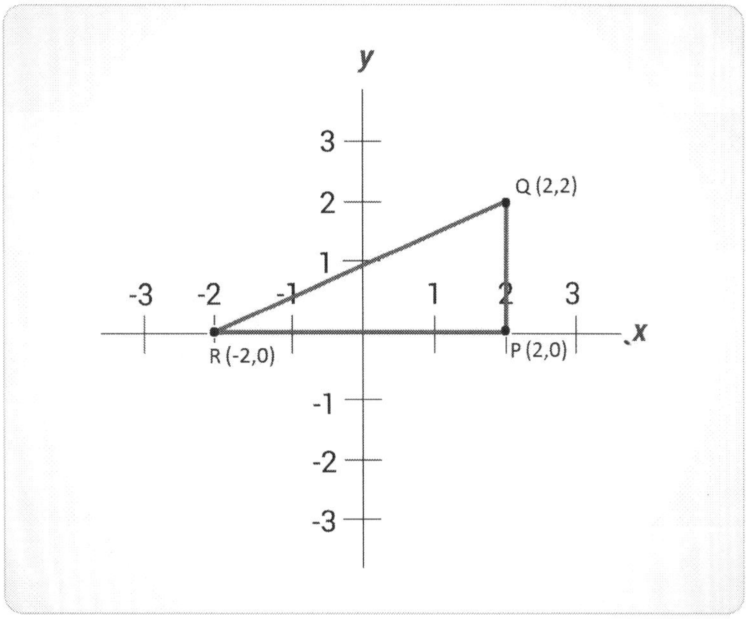

Because points R and P have the same y-coordinates (they are directly across from each other), the distance between them is determined by subtracting their x-coordinates (or simply counting units from one point to the other): $2 - (-2) = 4$. Therefore, the length of side RP is 4 units. Because points Q and P have the same x-coordinate (they are directly above and below each other), the distance between them is determined by subtracting their y-coordinates (or counting units between them): $2 - 0 = 2$. Therefore, the length of side PQ is 2 units. Knowing the length of side RP, which is the base of the triangle, and the length of side PQ, which is the height of the triangle, the area of the figure can be determined by using the formula $A = \frac{1}{2}bh$.

To determine the perimeter of the triangle, the lengths of all three sides are needed. Points R and Q are neither directly across nor directly above and below each other. Therefore, the distance formula must be used to find the length of side RQ.

The distance formula is as follows:

$$d = \sqrt{(x_2 - x_1)^2 + (y_2 - y_1)^2}$$

$$d = \sqrt{(2 - (-2))^2 + (2 - 0)^2}$$

$$d = \sqrt{(4)^2 + (2)^2}$$

$$d = \sqrt{16 + 4}$$

$$d = \sqrt{20}$$

The perimeter is determined by adding the lengths of the three sides of the triangle.

Probability and Statistics

Organizing and Displaying Data

Interpreting Displays of Data

A set of data can be visually displayed in various forms allowing for quick identification of characteristics of the set. Histograms, such as the one shown below, display the number of data points (vertical axis) that fall into given intervals (horizontal axis) across the range of the set. The histogram below displays the heights of black cherry trees in a certain city park. Each rectangle represents the number of trees with heights between a given five-point span. For example, the furthest bar to the right indicates that two trees are between 85 and 90 feet. Histograms can describe the center, spread, shape, and any unusual characteristics of a data set.

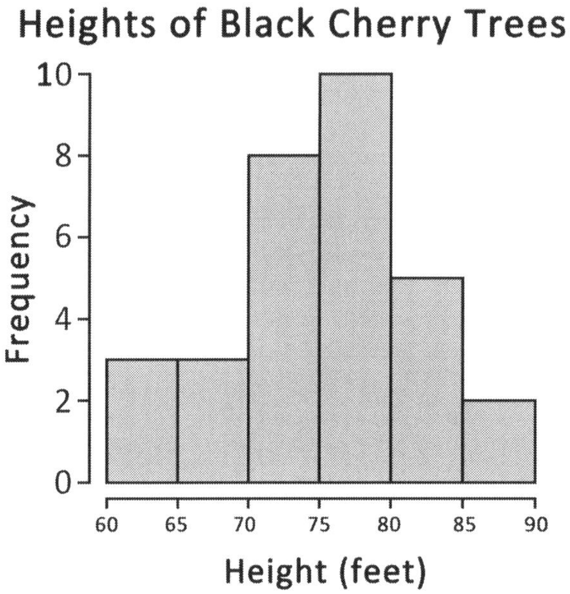

A box plot, also called a box-and-whisker plot, divides the data points into four groups and displays the five-number summary for the set as well as any outliers. The five-number summary consists of:

- The lower extreme: the lowest value that is not an outlier
- The higher extreme: the highest value that is not an outlier
- The median of the set: also referred to as the second quartile or Q_2
- The first quartile or Q_1: the median of values below Q_2
- The third quartile or Q_3: the median of values above Q_2

Calculating each of these values is covered in the next section, *Graphical Representation of Data*.

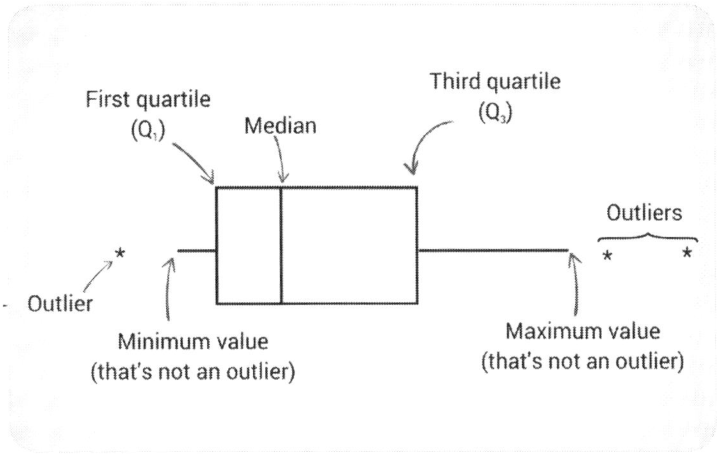

Suppose the box plot displays IQ scores for 12th grade students at a given school. The five number summary of the data consists of: lower extreme (67); upper extreme (127); Q_2or median (100); Q_1 (91); Q_3 (108); and outliers (135 and 140). Although all data points are not known from the plot, the points are divided into four quartiles each, including 25% of the data points. Therefore, 25% of students scored between 67 and 91, 25% scored between 91 and 100, 25% scored between 100 and 108, and 25% scored between 108 and 127. These percentages include the normal values for the set and exclude the outliers. This information is useful when comparing a given score with the rest of the scores in the set.

A scatter plot is a mathematical diagram that visually displays the relationship or connection between two variables. The independent variable is placed on the x-axis, or horizontal axis, and the dependent variable is placed on the y-axis, or vertical axis. When visually examining the points on the graph, if the points model a linear relationship, or if a line of best-fit can be drawn through the points with the points relatively close on either side, then a correlation exists. If the line of best-fit has a positive slope (rises from left to right), then the variables have a positive correlation. If the line of best-fit has a negative slope (falls from left to right), then the variables have a negative correlation. If a line of best-fit cannot be drawn, then no correlation exists. A positive or negative correlation can be categorized as strong or weak, depending on how closely the points are graphed around the line of best-fit.

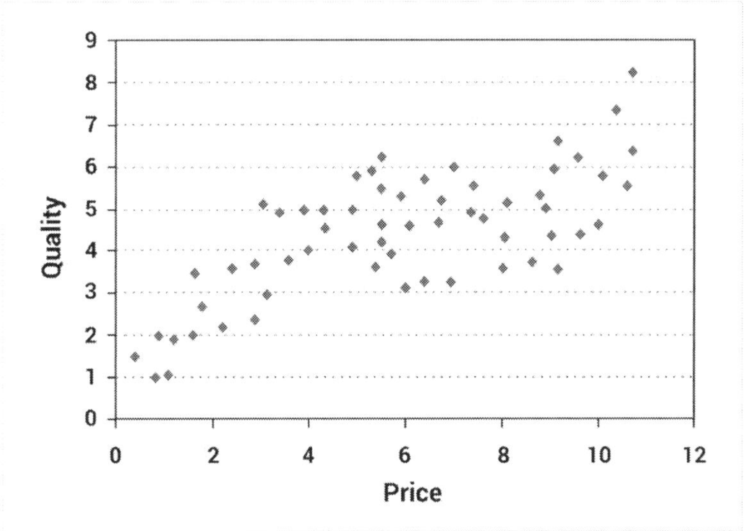

Graphical Representation of Data

Various graphs can be used to visually represent a given set of data. Each type of graph requires a different method of arranging data points and different calculations of the data. Examples of histograms, box plots, and scatter plots are discussed in the previous section *Interpreting Displays of Data*. To construct a histogram, the range of the data points is divided into equal intervals. The frequency for each interval is then determined, which reveals how many points fall into each interval. A graph is constructed with the vertical axis representing the frequency and the horizontal axis representing the intervals. The lower value of each interval should be labeled along the horizontal axis. Finally, for each interval, a bar is drawn from the lower value of each interval to the lower value of the next interval with a height equal to the frequency of the interval. Because of the intervals, histograms do not have any gaps between bars along the horizontal axis.

A scatter plot displays the relationship between two variables. Values for the independent variable, typically denoted by x, are paired with values for the dependent variable, typically denoted by y. Each set of corresponding values are written as an ordered pair (x, y). To construct the graph, a coordinate grid is labeled with the x-axis representing the independent variable and the y-axis representing the dependent variable.

Each ordered pair is graphed.

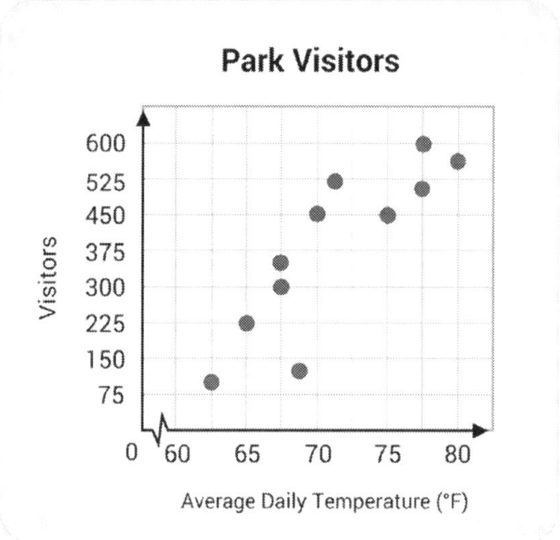

Like a scatter plot, a line graph compares variables that change continuously, typically over time. Paired data values (ordered pairs) are plotted on a coordinate grid with the x- and y-axis representing the variables. A line is drawn from each point to the next, going from left to right. The line graph below displays cell phone use for given years (two variables) for men, women, and both sexes (three data sets).

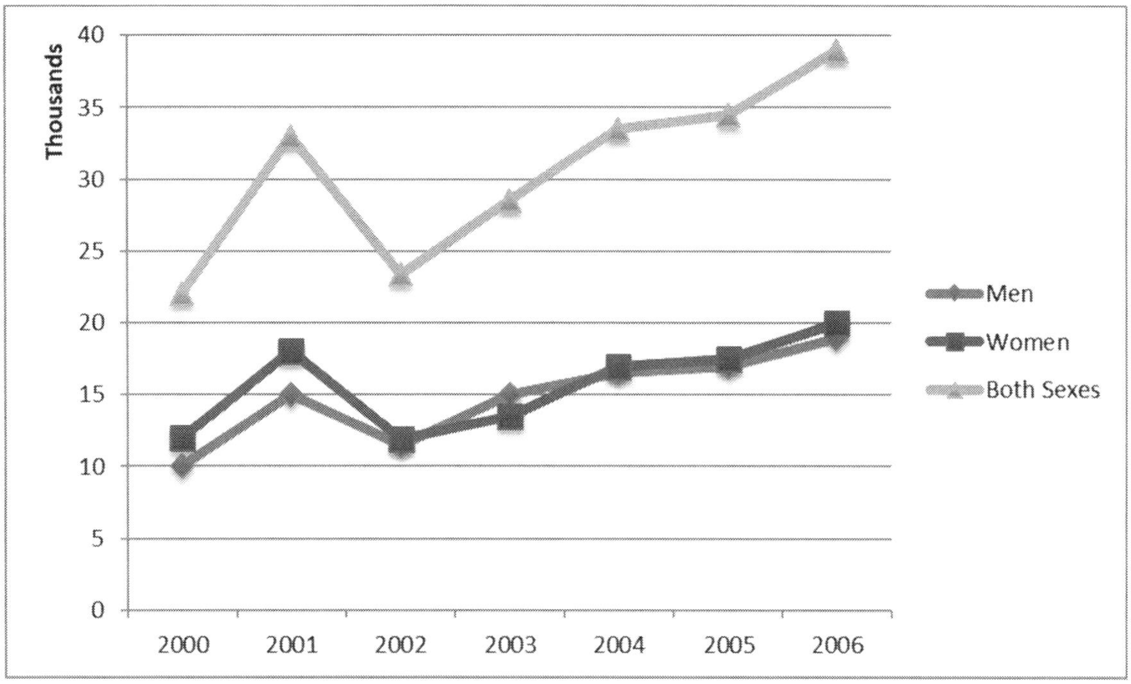

A line plot, also called dot plot, displays the frequency of data (numerical values) on a number line. To construct a line plot, a number line is used that includes all unique data values. It is marked with x's or dots above the value the number of times that the value occurs in the data set.

A bar graph looks similar to a histogram but displays categorical data. The horizontal axis represents each category, and the vertical axis represents the frequency for the category. A bar is drawn for each category (often different colors) with a height extending to the frequency for that category within the data set. A double bar graph displays two sets of data that contain data points consisting of the same categories. The double bar graph below indicates that two girls and four boys like Pad Thai the most out of all the foods, two boys and five girls like pizza, and so on.

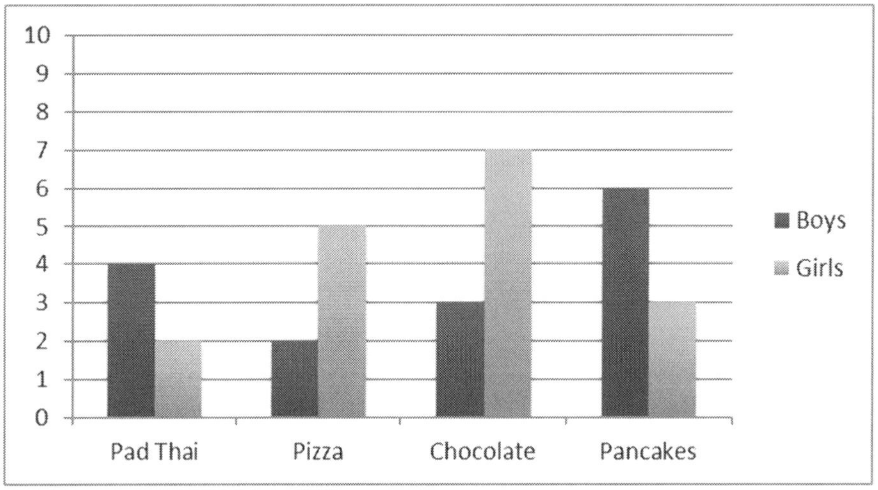

A circle graph, also called a pie chart, displays categorical data with each category representing a percentage of the whole data set. To construct a circle graph, the percent of the data set for each category must be determined. To do so, the frequency of the category is divided by the total number of data points and converted to a percent. For example, if 80 people were asked their favorite pizza topping and 20 responded cheese, then cheese constitutes 25% of the data ($\frac{20}{80} = 0.25 = 25\%$). Each category in a data set is represented by a *slice* of the circle proportionate to its percentage of the whole.

Choice of Graphs to Display Data

Choosing the appropriate graph to display a data set depends on what type of data is included in the set and what information must be displayed. Histograms and box plots can be used for data sets consisting of individual values across a wide range. Examples include test scores and incomes. Histograms and box plots will indicate the center, spread, range, and outliers of a data set. A histogram will show the shape of the data set, while a box plot will divide the set into quartiles (25% increments), allowing for comparison between a given value and the entire set.

Scatter plots and line graphs can be used to display data consisting of two variables. Examples include height and weight, or distance and time. A correlation between the variables is determined by examining the points on the graph. Line graphs are used if each value for one variable pairs with a distinct value for the other variable. Line graphs show relationships between variables.

Line plots, bar graphs, and circle graphs are all used to display categorical data, such as surveys. Line plots and bar graphs both indicate the frequency of each category within the data set. A line plot is used when the categories consist of numerical values. For example, the number of hours of TV watched by individuals is displayed on a line plot. A bar graph is used when the categories consist of words. For example, the favorite ice cream of individuals is displayed with a bar graph. A circle graph can be used to display either type of categorical data. However, unlike line plots and bar graphs, a circle graph does not indicate the frequency of each category. Instead, the circle graph represents each category as its percentage of the whole data set.

Measures of Central Tendency

The center of a set of data (statistical values) can be represented by its mean, median, or mode. These are sometimes referred to as measures of central tendency.

Mean

The first property that can be defined for this set of data is the mean. This is the same as the average. To find the mean, add up all the data points, then divide by the total number of data points. For example, suppose that in a class of 10 students, the scores on a test were 50, 60, 65, 65, 75, 80, 85, 85, 90, 100. Therefore, the average test score will be:

$$\frac{50 + 60 + 65 + 65 + 75 + 80 + 85 + 85 + 90 + 100}{10} = 75.5$$

The mean is a useful number if the distribution of data is normal (more on this later), which roughly means that the frequency of different outcomes has a single peak and is roughly equally distributed on both sides of that peak. However, it is less useful in some cases where the data might be split or where there are some **outliers**. Outliers are data points that are far from the rest of the data. For example, suppose there are 10 executives and 90 employees at a company. The executives make \$1,000 per hour, and the employees make \$10 per hour.

Therefore, the average pay rate will be:

$$\frac{\$1{,}000 \times 10 + \$10 \times 90}{100} = \$109 \text{ per hour}$$

In this case, this average is not very descriptive since it's not close to the actual pay of the executives or the employees.

Median

Another useful measurement is the **median**. In a data set, the median is the point in the middle. The middle refers to the point where half the data comes before it and half comes after, when the data is recorded in numerical order. For instance, these are the speeds of the fastball of a pitcher during the last inning that he pitched (in order from least to greatest):

90, 92, 93, 93, 95, 96, 97, 97, 97

There are nine total numbers, so the middle or *median* number is the 5th one, which is 95.

In cases where the number of data points is an even number, then the average of the two middle points is taken. In the previous example of test scores, the two middle points are 75 and 80. Since there is no single point, the average of these two scores needs to be found.

The average is:

$$\frac{75+80}{2}=77.5$$

The median is generally a good value to use if there are a few outliers in the data. It prevents those outliers from affecting the "middle" value as much as when using the mean.

Since an outlier is a data point that is far from most of the other data points in a data set, this means an outlier also is any point that is far from the median of the data set. The outliers can have a substantial effect on the mean of a data set, but they usually do not change the median or mode, or do not change them by a large quantity. For example, consider the data set (3, 5, 6, 6, 6, 8). This has a median of 6 and a mode of 6, with a mean of $\frac{34}{6}\approx 5.67$. Now, suppose a new data point of 1,000 is added so that the data set is now (3, 5, 6, 6, 6, 8, 1,000). The median and mode, which are both still 6, remain unchanged. However, the average is now $\frac{1{,}034}{7}$, which is approximately 147.7. In this case, the median and mode will be better descriptions for most of the data points.

Outliers in a given data set are sometimes the result of an error by the experimenter, but oftentimes, they are perfectly valid data points that must be taken into consideration.

Mode

One additional measure to define for X is the **mode**. This is the data point that appears most frequently. If two or more data points all tie for the most frequent appearance, then each of them is considered a mode. In the case of the test scores, where the numbers were 50, 60, 65, 65, 75, 80, 85, 85, 90, 100, there are two modes: 65 and 85.

The range of a data set is the difference between the highest and the lowest values in the set. The range can be considered the span of the data set. To determine the range, the smallest value in the set is subtracted from the largest value. The ranges for the data sets A, B, and C above are calculated as follows: A: $14-7=7$; B: $51-33=18$; C: $173-151=22$.

Explores concepts of probability through data collection, experiments and simulations.

Statistical inference, based in probability theory, makes calculated assumptions about an entire population based on data from a sample set from that population.

Population Parameters

A population is the entire set of people or things of interest. For example, if researchers wanted to determine the number of hours of sleep per night for college females in the U.S, the population would consist of *every* college female in the country. A **sample** is a subset of the population that may be used for the study. A sample might consist of 100 students per school from 20 different colleges in the country. From the results of the survey, a sample statistic can be calculated. A **sample statistic** is a numerical characteristic of the sample data including mean and variance. A sample statistic can be used to estimate a corresponding **population parameter**, which is a numerical characteristic of the entire population.

Confidence Intervals

A population parameter estimated using a sample statistic may be very accurate or relatively inaccurate based on errors in sampling. A **confidence interval** indicates a range of values likely to include the true population parameter.

A given confidence interval such as 95% means that the true population parameter will occur within the interval for 95% of samples.

Measurement Error

The accuracy of a population parameter based on a sample statistic may also be affected by measurement error. **Measurement error** can be divided into random error and systematic error. An example of **random error** for the previous scenario would be a student reporting 8 hours of sleep when she actually sleeps 7 hours per night. **Systematic errors** are those attributed to the measurement system. If the sleep survey gave response options of 2,4,6,8, or 10 hours. This would lead to systematic measurement error because certain values could not be accurately reported.

Simple and Compound Events

Probability is a measure of how likely an event is to occur. Probability is written as a fraction between zero and one. If an event has a probability of zero, the event will never occur. If an event has a probability of one, the event will definitely occur. If the probability of an event is closer to zero, the event is unlikely to occur. If the probability of an event is closer to one, the event is more likely to occur. For example, a probability of $\frac{1}{2}$ means that the event is equally as likely to occur as it is not to occur. An example of this is tossing a coin. The probability of an event can be calculated by dividing the number of favorable outcomes by the number of total outcomes. For example, suppose you have 2 raffle tickets out of 20 total tickets sold. The probability that you win the raffle is calculated:

$$\frac{number\ of\ favorable\ outcomes}{total\ numberof\ outcomes} = \frac{2}{20} = \frac{1}{10}$$

Therefore, the probability of winning the raffle is $\frac{1}{10}$ or 0.1.

Chance is the measure of how likely an event is to occur, written as a percent. If an event will never occur, the event has a 0% chance. If an event will certainly occur, the event has a 100% chance. If an event will sometimes occur, the event has a chance somewhere between 0% and 100%. To calculate chance, probability is calculated, and the fraction is converted to a percent.

The probability of multiple (compound) events occurring can be determined by multiplying the probability of each event. For example, suppose you flip a coin with heads and tails, and roll a six-sided die numbered one through six. To find the probability that you will flip heads AND roll a two, the probability of each event is determined, and those fractions are multiplied. The probability of flipping heads is $\frac{1}{2}\left(\frac{1\ side\ with\ heads}{2\ sides\ total}\right)$, and the probability of rolling a two is $\frac{1}{6}\left(\frac{1\ side\ with\ a\ 2}{6\ total\ sides}\right)$. The probability of flipping heads AND rolling a 2 is:

$$\frac{1}{2} \times \frac{1}{6} = \frac{1}{12}$$

The above scenario with flipping a coin and rolling a die is an example of independent events. Independent events are circumstances in which the outcome of one event does not affect the outcome of the other event. Conversely, dependent events are ones in which the outcome of one event affects the outcome of the second event. Consider the following scenario: a bag contains 5 black marbles and 5 white marbles. What is the probability of picking 2 black marbles without replacing the marble after the first pick?

The probability of picking a black marble on the first pick is $\frac{5}{10}\left(\frac{5\ black\ marbles}{10\ total\ marbles}\right)$. Assuming that a black marble was picked, there are now 4 black marbles and 5 white marbles for the second pick. Therefore, the probability of picking a black marble on the second pick is $\frac{4}{9}\left(\frac{4\ black\ marbles}{9\ total\ marbles}\right)$. To find the probability of picking two black marbles, the probability of each is multiplied:

$$\frac{5}{10} \times \frac{4}{9} = \frac{20}{90} = \frac{2}{9}$$

Basics of Probability

Probability is defined as how likely something is to happen. The most common way to approach this concept is by considering the flip of a coin. When a coin is tossed, it is just as likely to obtain heads or tails. Therefore, the probability of either outcome is the same. Furthermore, consider a six-sided die. If it is rolled one time, the probability of obtaining any of the faces (the values one through six) is also the same. Each outcome is equally as likely. However, consider the probability of obtaining an odd number versus rolling the number three. There are three odd numbers available on a six-sided die: one, three, and five. On the other hand, there is only one out of six options available when rolling for a three.

Therefore, it can be said that rolling an odd number is more likely than rolling the number three. Rolling an even number is just as likely as rolling an odd number on a six-sided die because there are also three available options out of six: 2, 4, and 6. These examples help derive that the probability of a certain event is equal to the number of ways a single event can happen divided by the total number of possible outcomes. For example, the probability of rolling an odd number on one roll of a six-sided die is $\frac{3}{6} = \frac{1}{2}$ because there are three odd numbers and six total options. In the examples with the dice and the coin, each single outcome (heads/tails or the numbers one through six) has an equal chance of occurrence. This type of probability is known as classical or theoretical probability.

Another type of probability is empirical probability, which is based on historical data. For example, the expected (theoretical) result of tossing a coin six times would be heads three times and tails three times, since each outcome is just as likely to occur. However, real-life experiments would probably differ. For instance, an experiment could result in two heads and four tails, which would help in calculating the empirical probability.

Solving Probability Problems

Geometric probability works with continuous variables, such as values on the number line. Consider a number line containing the values from 0 to 8. If a line segment is drawn from 1 to 4 and a random point on the number line is selected, the probability that the point is on the line segment can be computed. Because the line segment contains three numbers, and the overall number line contains eight, the probability that the selected point is on the line segment is $\frac{3}{8}$. This example pertains to a one-dimensional line, and the quantity discussed is length.

Probability can also be calculated given a two-dimensional example in which the quantity discussed is area. For instance, consider a circle that lies within a rectangle. If a point is selected at random inside the rectangle, the probability that the point lies within the circle can be calculated. The desired outcome is that the point is in the circle. Therefore, the area of the circle needs to be calculated. The area of the rectangle is the set of all possible points, so this area needs to be calculated as well. The probability that the selected point lies within the circle is equal to the area of the circle divided by the area of the rectangle.

This idea can even be extended to three-dimensional shapes, where the quantity discussed is volume. Consider a ball or a sphere placed within a large cylinder. If a point is randomly selected within the cylinder, the probability that the point lies within the sphere is equal to the volume of the sphere divided by the volume of the cylinder. The desired outcome is that the point lies within the sphere, and the set of all possible outcomes is the total volume of the cylinder.

In probability, combinations refer to a series of possible outcomes in which order doesn't matter. This differs from permutations, in which order does matter. For instance, determining the probability that three people are elected on a city council is a different calculation than determining how three people out of a group could be elected president, vice president, and secretary. In the first example, order does not matter, so it involves combinations. In the second example, order does matter, so it involves permutations.

Summary Statistics and Graphs

Three typical values when referring to summary statistics are the mean, median, and mode of a data set. The mean, otherwise known as the average, is equal to the total sum of the values divided by the total number of data points. The median is equal to the value in the center of the data set when written in numerical order. If there is an odd number of data points, the median is the value exactly in the center. If there is an even number of data points, the median is the average of the two values in the center. Finally, the mode of a data set is the value that appears the most often. Note that some data sets can have more than one mode, and some have no mode.

Some data sets can have outliers, which are values that are very far removed from the rest of the values in the set. Note that the median is not affected by the outliers. However, the mean is affected by the outliers because they impact the calculation.

Consider the data set $\{1, 3, 5, 7, 9, 9\}$. The mode is 9 because it appears twice. The median is the average of 5 and 7, which is 6. Finally, the mean is the sum of the values divided by 6, or approximately 5.67.

Data sets can also be described visually using graphs. A bar chart can be used to plot categorical data. The different categories are placed along the horizontal axis, and the counts of data values located in each category are placed along the vertical axis. A histogram is similar to a bar chart; however, it is used to plot continuous data. In this case, both the horizontal axis and vertical axis are comprised of numerical values. Here is an example of a bar chart and a histogram:

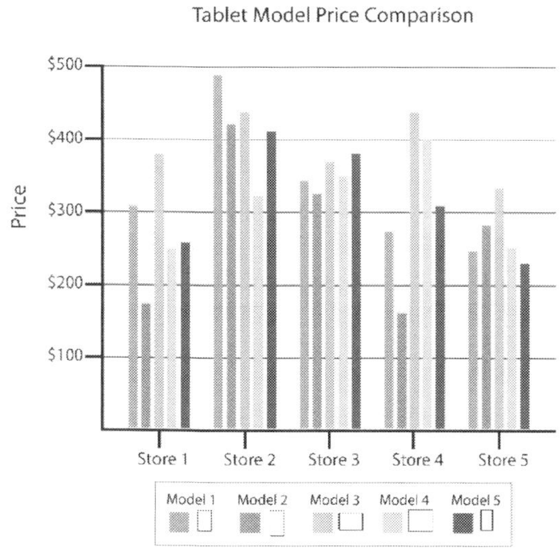

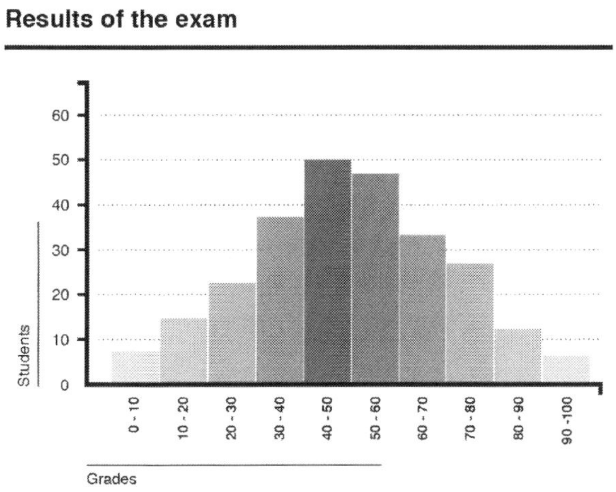

Other graphs that can be used to view one-variable data are box-and-whisker plots, dot charts, and pie charts. However, they are not as widely used as histograms and bar graphs.

Statistical Experiments and Real-World Problems

Real-world problems can be investigated using observational studies, surveys, and experiments. Once a question is asked that can be answered using data, statistical experiments can be designed. These involve collecting, organizing, and analyzing data, then forming a conclusion based on that analysis.

Observational studies involve collecting data purely through observation, and no variables are manipulated by the observer. For instance, in order to determine how many people prefer wheat bread over white bread in a community, the researcher could stand in the bread aisle at the grocery store and count how many bread purchasers buy each type. The data would be collected, and an answer could be made purely by calculation.

A survey is a different type of observational study in which the data is collected by asking people different questions and collecting answers. A survey could be sent out via email to a randomly selected group of people asking their preferences. The data would be collected in a similar manner to the observational study, and the answer would be formulated.

An experiment includes the manipulation of a variable. The researcher assigns people to two groups to see if there is any effect of the variable that has been manipulated. Common experiments involve determining the effectiveness of prescription drugs. One group either receives no treatment or receives a placebo, which would be a "fake" treatment, and the other group would receive the prescription drug. The response of the drug on the people who received it would be measured. The data would then be collected and analyzed to make a conclusion about the effectiveness of the drug.

Using Probability Models

The difference between classical/theoretical and empirical probability can be highlighted using probability models that are simulated in the classroom. For example, let's consider probabilities of different combinations of genders within a family with four kids. A coin could be tossed, with heads (H) representing female (F) and tails (T) representing male (M). To represent genders of the four children, the coin would be tossed four times. One instance could be HHTH, which would imply FFMF: three girls and one boy. Another instance could be TTTH, which would mean MMMF: three males and one female. We could even go one step further and state that the order matters. In the second example, the first three children born would be male, and the last child born would be female.

Other items could be used for the same scenario. For instance, if a student has a 6-sided die, then rolling an even number could represent having a boy and rolling an odd number could represent having a girl. This method works for this simulation because there are only two outcomes with an equal likelihood of being selected: even and odd numbers. Also, if a student has a 52-card deck of cards, then they could randomly select either a black or red card. There is an equal chance of selecting a red or black card. Pulling a red card could represent having a boy and pulling a black card could represent having a girl. It would not work to let a face card represent having a boy and a number card represent having a girl. Since there are more number cards than face cards, the probability of selecting a number card is higher than selecting a face card.

Data Distribution Graphs

A set of data can be described in terms of its center, spread, shape and any unusual features. The center of a data set can be measured by its mean, median, or mode. The spread, or variability, of a data set refers to how far the data points are from the center (mean or median). The spread can be measured by the range or by the quartiles and interquartile range. A data set with all its data points clustered around the center will have a small spread. A data set covering a wide range of values will have a large spread.

When a data set is displayed as a **histogram** or frequency distribution plot, the shape indicates if a sample is normally distributed, symmetrical, or has measures of skewness or kurtosis.

When graphed, a data set with a **normal distribution** will resemble a bell curve.

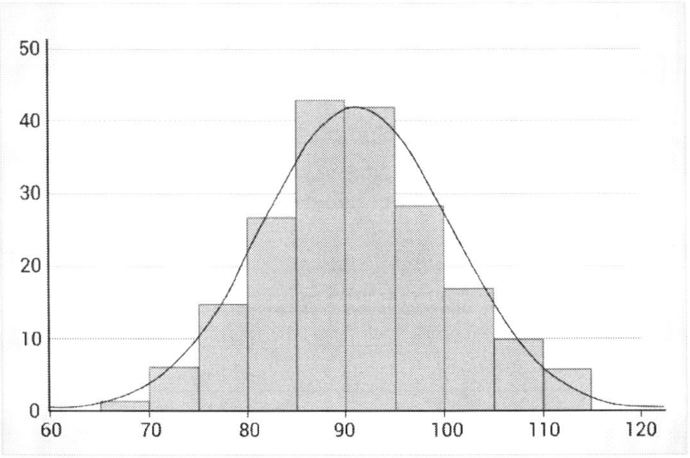

If the data set is symmetrical, each half of the graph when divided at the center is a mirror image of the other. If the graph has fewer data points to the right, the data is **skewed right**. If it has fewer data points to the left, the data is **skewed left**.

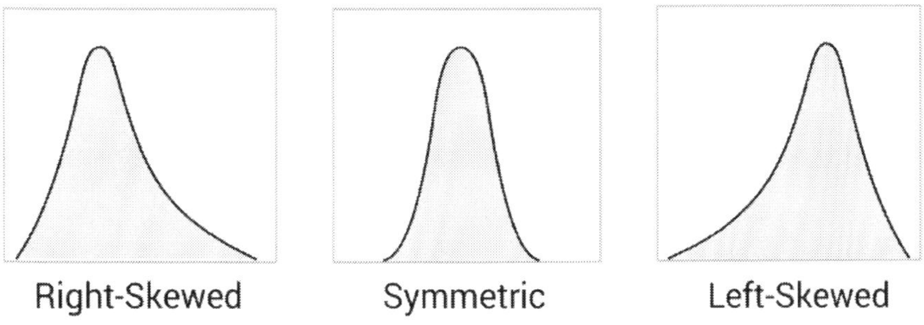

Kurtosis is a measure of whether the data is heavy-tailed with a high number of outliers, or light-tailed with a low number of outliers.

A description of a data set should include any unusual features such as gaps or outliers. A **gap** is a span within the range of the data set containing no data points. An **outlier** is a data point with a value either extremely large or extremely small when compared to the other values in the set.

Mathematical Processes

Logical Reasoning in Mathematics

Reasoning in mathematics involves figuring out how to solve a problem, using a tool or software correctly, or achieving any other type of goal in the classroom. Students learn to determine what is being asked for and decide what they think the best approach will be. Specifically, logic is introduced when determining whether statements and conjectures are true or false. An example of a true statement is "the sum of two even numbers results in an even number." An example of a false statement is "the sum of two even numbers results in an odd number." Logical reasoning can be used to show the first statement is true by a formal proof, and it can also be used to show the second example is false by an example disproving it. Such an example would be $4 + 6 = 10$, and it is known as a counterexample.

Ultimately, formal reasoning is used to prove theorems, and a famous proof that uses such a formalized mechanism is the Pythagorean Theorem. The proof involves a step-by-step logical process of using properties of right triangles to prove that $a^2 + b^2 = c^2$. In the classroom, such formal reasoning is taught in Geometry, Trigonometry, etc., but informal logic is used every day.

Informal reasoning is an important part of the classroom as well. Hands-on activities are great ways to introduce informal reasoning. For example, before geometric shapes are introduced through definitions and theorems, physical representations can be passed around from student to student. In this situation, the students can form their own thoughts and ideas about each shape, which will help them later as they have to conduct the formal reasoning at test time.

Deriving Valid Conclusions from a Set of Premises

The legitimacy of a conclusion is always based on the correctness of the argument. The argument is only deemed to be valid if every single premise is accurately used in a correct order to build the argument. If a premise is wrong, then the entire argument is invalid. This thought process applies to formal proving techniques, such as in geometry, and in other situations such as solving equations in algebra. Each step in the solution procedure involves justification as to why it can be done, and if something is done incorrectly, then the conclusion is most likely wrong.

Teachers should pay attention to the way students think and build their reasoning as they work through problems in the classroom. The process in which a student builds an argument or solves a problem can vary student to student. If the teacher sees a common mistake being made, time should be spent clarifying the error to the entire class so that it does not continue to happen. Also, teachers need to understand that in some situations there are many ways to obtain a solution, and they should make their students aware of that fact as well.

Inductive Reasoning and Deductive Methods to Evaluate Validity of Conjectures

A **deductive** argument is one in which the goal is to show that a conjecture must be true. Logical reasoning is used to find statements and conjectures that are always true to come up with a conclusion that has to be true. Geometry and Trigonometry problems involve deductive reasoning. In order to prove a statement or theorem, facts are used to build an argument that makes up a formal proof. If one of the premises used is incorrect, the entire proof is wrong. Deductive reasoning would be used in the following setting: Every time a train stops at the station, people get off the train. For every person getting off the train, two people board the train. If 13 people get off the train, deductive reasoning is used to determine that 26 people will subsequently board the train. This amount is based on the known premises, so $13 \times 2 = 26$ new passengers.

An **inductive** argument is one in which the goal is to show that the conjecture is probably true. If the premises, meaning the conjectures used to build the argument, are true, then the conclusion is most likely true. Inductive reasoning involves more of an estimation. The premises are observations that are not necessarily true. For example, if a person boards an airplane from Los Angeles to Phoenix, and no children are on the plane, he or she could conclude that children do not fly that route. However, this is based on the one-time observation and is not always going to be a true statement.

Reasonableness of a Solution

Once a math problem is solved, the answer should be checked if possible to see if it is correct. For example, in most equations, once the variable is solved for, it can be checked in the original equation to see if it makes a true statement. If it creates a false statement, then the solution does not work, and a mistake has been made somewhere. If it is not possible to check the answer completely, a sanity check can be completed. For example, the scale of the answer should be considered. Basically, does the size of the answer make sense?

If the problem involved finding a dollar amount necessary to perform a task, and the answer found was less than \$0.00001, then the answer does not really make sense. Similarly, if the task was to build a fence, and the solution stated that over a million feet of fencing was necessary, something was probably incorrect. In either case, the problem-solving steps should be revisited to see if an error was made. All solutions should be deemed reasonable. The teacher should stress this concept in the classroom. Not only is it important to set up and solve the problem correctly, but it is always helpful to make sure the answer makes sense.

Connections Among Concepts in Areas of Mathematics

Coordinate geometry is the link that connects algebra and geometry. Throughout its use, equivalent representations in both fields can be associated. Consider a rectangle in geometry. Typical lessons involve calculating the area and perimeter of the shape and discussing properties of angles and lines that make up the figure.

A rectangle can be inserted into the Cartesian coordinate plane as such:

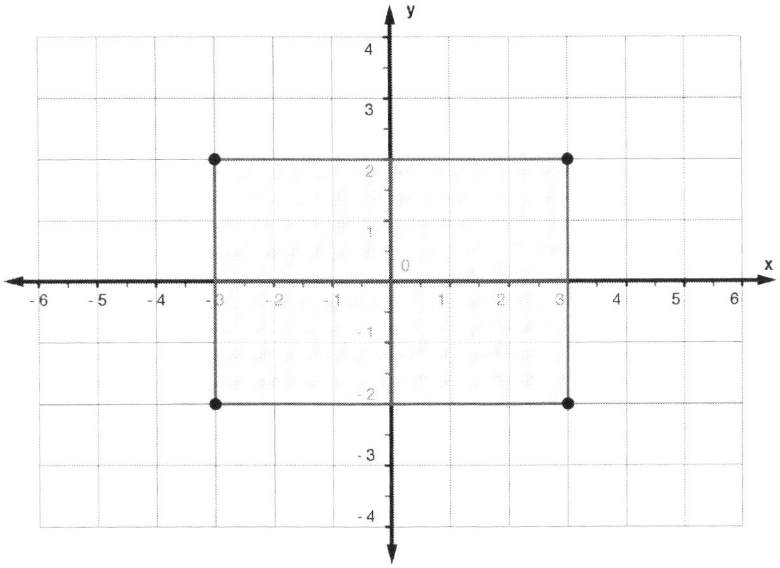

Two of the sides run parallel to the x-axis, and the other two sides run parallel to the y-axis. The length of each side can be determined by counting the number of tick marks on each axis that the shape includes. Each point on the rectangle corresponds to an ordered pair (x, y) in the plane, and the distance between any two points (x_1, y_1), (x_2, y_2) can be calculated using the distance formula $d = \sqrt{(x_2 - x_1)^2 + (y_2 - y_1)^2}$. The equation of each line can be determined using algebraic rules. For example, the bottom line is equivalent to $y = -3, -3 \leq x \leq 3$. All two-dimensional shapes can be inserted into the xy-plane in a similar manner. Some traditional geometric proofs can be completed using algebra using the coordinate system relationship. For example, the Pythagorean Theorem can be proved using traditional side lengths a, b, and c, or a right triangle can be placed inside the xy-plane, and side lengths can be found using the distance formula. Each proof uses the same properties, but different methodologies.

Three dimensional geometric shapes can also be represented in a coordinate system. If a third axis, the z-axis, is introduced into an xy-plane, the three-dimensional world is defined. The x and y axes represent a horizontal plane, and the z-axis runs vertical through the origin. Each point in this space is an ordered triple (x, y, z).

The following shows a pyramid in the three-dimensional coordinate system with vertices labeled and one vertex located at the origin:

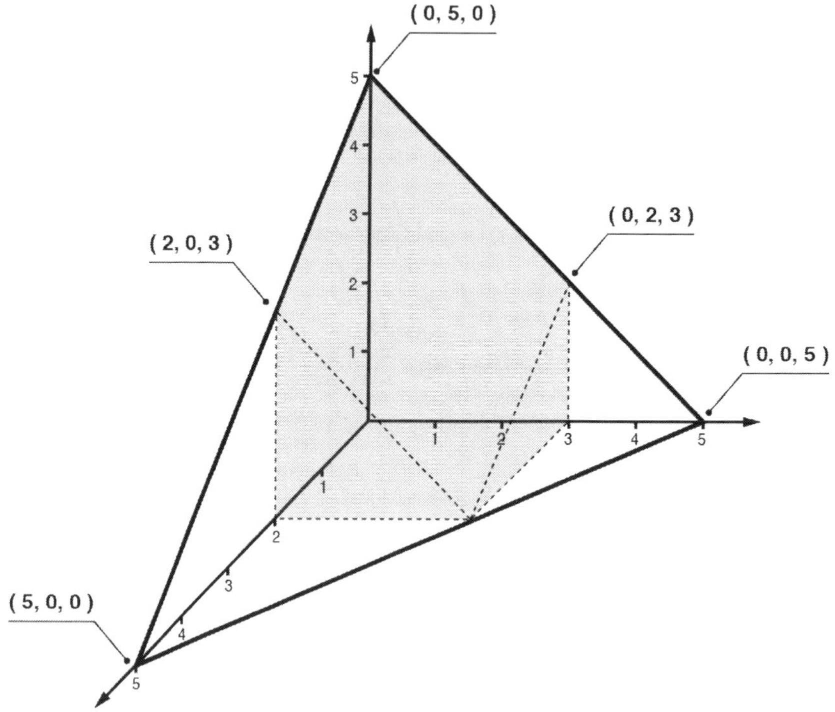

Solving Math Problems

Often, there are a variety of ways to solve a math problem. For example, the perimeter of a rectangle can be found by finding the sum of all four sides or by using the formula $p = 2 \times l + 2 \times w$, where l is the length and w is the width of the rectangle. Also, in many instances, theorems can be proved using different approaches. Premises can be used in an alternate order, or an entirely different set of premises might be used. Sometimes one approach is better than the others, meaning it is probably a faster and more efficient way of doing something. Consider the derivative in Calculus. It is first introduced in its limit definition into the classroom. This is known as the dreaded "long way" to students, and they usually do not enjoy calculating derivatives this way. However, derivative rules, proven with use of the limit definition, such as the product and quotient rules, are used to shorten the process. It is important to understand both techniques, but probably use the quicker method.

Appropriate Mathematical Language

Being able to transition back and forth between mathematical expressions and verbal statements that represent the same concept is an important part of mathematical development. A student should be able to see an equation or an expression and read it as though it is a sentence in the English language. Also, he or she should be able to represent it verbally in more than one way. For example, consider the equation $2x + 3 = 5$. It can be read literally as "two times x plus 3 equals 5." However, it can also be read as "three more than double x is equivalent to 5" or "the sum of two times *x* and 3 is the same as 5." Each mathematical operation translates to multiple words in the English language, and each grade level has its own requirements for what should be understood and used in the classroom.

Expressions that represent the addition process are *sum, in addition to, plus, entire, total, increase, more than, combined,* and *in all*. Expressions that can be used to express subtraction verbally are *minus, difference, less than, decrease, reduce, fewer,* and *remain*. Multiplication can be stated as *product, multiply, times,* and *part of* if fractions are involved. Also, words like *twice, triple, four times,* etc. also represent multiplication. Finally, verbal cues that represent division are *quotient, divide, split, each, per, equal parts, average,* and *shared*. Note that sometimes multiplication and division can be used interchangeably. For example, multiplying times ¼ is the same as dividing by 4. Also, it must be recognized by the student if the statement represents an expression or an equation. An expression just needs to be evaluated and is not set equal to any quantity. A statement representing an equation would need to be solved for the missing quantity, and phrases corresponding to "is equal to" are used in this case.

Representations of Mathematical Ideals

In the classroom, mathematical concepts can be introduced in a number of ways, and each student has a best way in which he or she processes the information. The teacher should utilize all such methods so that the different learning styles are represented. There are visual learners that understand concepts better using pictorial representations such as graphs, charts, animations, and diagrams, quantitative learners who grasp concepts better with symbolic representations such as equations and formulas, and verbal learners who understand the material best through discussion and brainstorming.

Consider the introduction of volume of a sphere in the classroom. Visual learners would do best with seeing a drawing of a sphere, with its diameter and radius labeled. With both labeled, they can see that the diameter is twice the radius. Once graphics are shown, the formula can be introduced. Then, practical applications can be discussed. Real-life scenarios might help some learners grasp the concept more. A fun example might be determining the volume of an orange. It can be cut in half to measure either the radius or diameter so that the formula can be used.

Throughout this lesson, a variety of representations are used and each one appeals to a different type of learner. Also, what can be discussed, depending on the grade level, is how the concept or formula was derived. In the case of volume of a sphere, this would be a Calculus problem, which involves integration. When students are able to see where a concept comes from, it gives them a more concrete understanding of the material. Sometimes it might even help them out when it comes to test time. If they forget a formula at test time, but remember how to derive it, it might save the day if they have to use the formula at some point.

Using Visual Media to Communicate Mathematical Information

Graphs, tables, diagrams, and animations can all be used to show a mathematical relationship between numbers, categories, and objects. A graph shows the relationship using points and lines or differentiated parts of a whole, like in a pie chart. Other graph options include line graphs and bar charts. A pie chart could be used to show favorite types of pizza in a classroom. Each slice of pie would represent the total number of students whose favorite is pepperoni, cheese, etc. The largest slice indicates what type of pizza had the largest number of students claiming it as their favorite.

Tables contain columns and rows and show the relationship between adjoining values and categories. In the pizza example, there could be a column for each type of pizza. Each row could represent the totals for each class in a school listing out their favorite types of pizza. Typically, tables are used first to organize data before creating graphs. The data is arranged in a nice manner so that it can be directly inserted into the graph. From the table, each row could represent a different pie chart or bar graph, or a line graph could be used in which each line represents a different classroom.

Diagrams and animations are more visual representations; they include illustrations and photographs representing the mathematical relationships. Animations are moving images. Size is a common tool used with diagrams and animations to represent mathematical quantities. For example, a small drawing of a pizza could represent the type that the students prefer the least, and a large drawing of a pizza could represent the favorite type.

Estimation

There is a difference between an exact answer and an estimation. Sometimes answering a question with an estimate is good enough; however, an exact answer is often required. Also, using an estimate as a ballpark to tell if an exact answer is reasonable is sometimes a good technique to use as well. For example, consider the situation if a student has to buy lunch at school, and they only have \$5 to do so. A sandwich is \$2.29, a piece of fruit is \$0.75, and a drink is \$1.25. An estimate might be enough to tell if he or she had enough money. A good estimate would be to round each cost to whole dollar amounts. Therefore, the estimate would be that lunch would cost \$2.00 for the sandwich, \$1.00 for the fruit, and \$1.00 for the drink, which adds up to \$4.00.

The estimate would be that \$5.00 is enough to pay for lunch. The exact amount is \$4.29, so the estimate does the trick. However, sometimes estimation could steer someone in the wrong direction. Consider a situation where the sandwich was \$2.45, the fruit was \$1.25, and the drink was \$1.35. Rounding to the nearest dollar would still result in an estimate of \$4.00; however, the exact amount in this scenario is \$5.05. Therefore, the student would not have enough money. Perhaps rounding to the nearest \$0.50 would be a better estimation process. Exact calculations are usually the best, but estimations are useful if they are done correctly.

Mathematical Manipulatives

Mathematical manipulatives and appropriate technological tools can be introduced into the classroom at any age. They consist of innovative ways to allow students to see concepts in a more tangible way and introduce more ways to communicate verbally using the math concepts being discussed. They can be used alongside paper and pencil problems to enhance a student's understanding even more. Common manipulatives include base-ten blocks, tangrams, rulers, protractors, compasses, measuring cups, playing cards, scales, thermometers, and abacuses. Each type of manipulative relates to several math concepts. For example, compasses and protractors can be used throughout many geometry lessons. Blocks can be used in basic addition and in a lesson involving areas of squares and rectangles. In addition to providing concrete examples, manipulatives also promote engagement and interest amongst the students, which results in a positive learning environment.

Technology, in the form of different types of calculators and mathematical software, can also be used to enhance the classroom experience. Graphing calculators can be used to enhance the graphing process and assist in statistics. Scientific calculators are helpful with logarithmic and exponential expressions. Finally, financial calculators can assist with any lesson involving interest problems. Teachers do have to make sure calculators are used as a tool to enhance learning, and not as a substitute for learning the concepts. Students should not rely heavily on them for simple calculations. Software in the classroom has many uses as well. It can help to introduce concepts by showing visualizations, and it can help to reinforce concepts through the use of drills, games, and online homework, quizzes, and tests.

History of Mathematical Concepts

Mathematical concepts stem from ancient Egypt, Babylonia, and Greece. Counting techniques date back to prehistoric times. Ancient artifacts have been found which show that numeral systems were first introduced around 3500 or 4000 B.C. Clay tablets were used to count days, animals, and many other objects. The decimal system, which is the most widely used numeral system today, is dated back to 2000 B.C. Roman numerals were developed in ancient Rome somewhere around the fourth century B.C.

Mathematical calculations stemming from arithmetic and algebra date back to 2,000 B.C. It was during this time that computations, such as addition, subtraction, multiplication, and division, were derived. Also, the technique of measuring objects was introduced. Algebra is based on arithmetic computations, and it involves creating equations to solve for unknown amounts. Ancient algebraic techniques are different than those that we study today. Simple linear equations were the focus of the ancient Egyptians, while more complicated algebra was the work of the Babylonians.

The ancient Egyptians also helped to form the concept of geometry. It was during this time that calculations such as the area of two-dimensional shapes, like triangles and rectangles, and the volume of three-dimensional shapes, like cylinders and rectangular boxes, were derived. The introduction of geometric proofs developed in Greece from about 700 to 500 B.C. It was during this time that some famous theorems were derived, including the concept that the sum of three angles in a triangle is equal to 180 degrees. It was also during this time that construction problems were formulated. Construction problems are those that utilize both a compass and a straightedge. It was during this time that the Greek philosopher Pythagoras derived the Pythagorean theorem, which states that the sum of the squares of two sides in a right triangle is equal to the square of its hypotenuse. The hypotenuse is the side which is opposite the right angle.

Cultural Contributions to Mathematics

Ethnomathematics is the study of connections between culture and mathematics. Different cultures have distinct ways in which they recognize some mathematical concepts, and various human groups also have distinct ways in which they solve math problems. It is important to see how different cultures have helped derive mathematical concepts in various ways. Some cultures have numerous games of skill, which are a fun way to show students the cultural differences. For example, mancala is one of the oldest mathematical games, stemming from ancient Egypt, and it involves using various counting techniques in a game setting.

In Japan, origami is a popular hobby. Mathematical concepts of symmetry and patterns are used in this paper folding technique. Also, geometrical concepts such as the intersection of planes and volume calculations can also appear in origami.

Different cultures have also helped derive the concept of numerals. Roman numerals were formulated to represent positive integers. They are still used today; however, they are not used for extremely large positive integers. The more widespread numeral system in use today is the Arabic numeral system. These numerals were derived in India and can be used to represent positive and negative integers, decimals, and fractions.

The ways that numbers are read also vary culturally. They differ according to language and structure. In English, the way numbers are read varies based on their size. The numbers 1-19 have special words, and the numbers 20 and beyond follow the same structure such as "thirty-seven," "seventy-seven," etc. The tens are read first, and then the ones are read. In the German culture, the number 37 is read with the ones amount first and then the tens amount next as "seven and thirty." In French culture, the multiples of ten are read a bit differently. In English, the number 60 is "sixty," but in French it translates to "sixty-ten," and 80 is read as "four-twenty."

Financial Literacy Concepts

The basic purposes of financial institutions are to boost the economy and improve current living standards. They act as the middle ground between people and/or companies that either have money that they wish to save to accrue interest or want to borrow money. The financial institutions either pay out interest to those people and companies who have loaned them money, or they charge interest to those who have borrowed money. Financial institutions are highly regulated by the government. Banks are the most common type of financial institution. Credit unions are similar to banks, but they offer their services to investors on a smaller scale.

Banks usually have three types of savings options that one can utilize. A regular savings account offers a low interest rate, and the money is readily available. Therefore, withdrawing money from a savings account can be immediate. Common ways to withdraw money from a savings account are checks and debit cards. A money market account is similar to a savings account; however, it typically has a minimum amount that can be invested. They offer higher interest rates than savings accounts and typically are easy to withdraw cash from using a check. A third type of savings option is a certificate of deposit, or a CD. They offer the highest interest rate of all three options, but access to the money is extremely limited. In most cases, the money has to be left in the account for a certain amount of time. Each saving option has its advantages and disadvantages, and it is up to the investor to weigh those options and make the best decision for their investment goals.

In order to make a profit, a company must earn more than they spend. Gross profit, which is also known as gross income, is the total amount of money a company earns before taxes and other types of deductions. They earn this money through selling their goods and services. However, all companies have expenses, such as payroll and utility bills. The net profit, or net income, is equal to gross profit minus all the expenses and deductions. For an individual, gross income is the amount of a paycheck before taxes and deductions, and net income is the actual amount of money going into their pocket once taxes and deductions have been subtracted.

Many types of taxes exist, and they can be classified as income, property, or sales taxes. Income tax is money charged by the government on personal revenue, such as someone's biweekly paycheck. Other types of income taxes can include taxes on investment gains and taxes paid to Social Security and Medicare. Property taxes are paid on owned property, such as a home. Home worth varies every year, so this amount can fluctuate. Finally, sales tax is tax paid to the government on purchased goods and services. Sales tax varies by location. For example, if a 6.5% sales tax exists in a city, then the total purchase at a home goods store would be the total sum of the goods plus 6.5% of the bill added on in sales tax.

Credit cards are another way to borrow money. When someone applies for a credit card, the credit card company gives them an amount of money that they can spend, known as a credit limit. It is from this amount that they can borrow from. Each type of credit card has different fees, interest rates, perks, and interest rates, so those options must be weighed when deciding what card to apply for. Once someone uses their credit card, it will have a balance. Borrowers will have to decide how to pay off their balance. Some people are able to pay off their balance monthly, so no interest is accrued. However, if someone keeps a running balance, the credit card fee will charge interest each month. Paying the balance down quicker is typically the best option.

Application of Mathematics to Finances

In math, a cost function is a formula that is used to model expenses in a given scenario. A common use is to model a cost function for a factory. The total cost is equal to the fixed costs, which are costs that apply regardless of how many items are produced, plus the variable costs, which vary based on the number of items made. Fixed costs could include the electric bill, the gas bill, and rent, while variable costs could include materials necessary for production. As a mathematical function, the cost function is $C(x) = mx + b$, where b is equal to the fixed costs, m is the variable cost per item, and x represents the number of items produced. Notice that mx is equal to the cost per item times the number of items, resulting in the total cost of the production of all items.

The business then sells the items that they produce at a certain amount to obtain their revenue. The revenue function is $R(x) = rx$, where r is equal to the price per item. For the company to make a profit, their revenue has to be greater than their cost. Their total profit is calculated by subtracting cost from revenue, and therefore, $P(x) = R(x) - C(x)$. A company breaks even if their revenue is equal to their costs, and they lose money if their costs are greater than their revenue. The goal is for profit to be greater than zero.

The same thought process can be applied to one's own life. Fixed costs are those that occur each month and do not change. Some of those costs could include a phone bill, cable bill, sewer bill, mortgage, and car payment. Variable costs change each month, and some examples could be the total cost of eating out at restaurants, entertainment expenses, and gas in the car. A monthly budget is useful to keep track of all these different expenses. They can be listed in a spreadsheet or some other organizational method that can be used to find their total.

These financial records can be saved each month and can be used to create a monthly budget. In creating a budget, one would want to make sure that their total expenses are not greater than the amount of money they bring in each month. This is similar to the idea of the company's profit. If one's total expenses are greater than the amount of money they make, they would want to decrease their expenses. Therefore, one would want to think of ways to decrease both fixed and variable costs. In terms of fixed costs, perhaps a less expensive cell phone plan could be found, or home refinancing would be possible so that one's mortgage is decreased. In terms of variable costs, decreasing the number of times one eats out each month and lowering entertainment expenses would be beneficial.

Practice Quiz

1. Which of the following could be used in the classroom to show $\frac{3}{7} < \frac{5}{6}$ is a true statement?
   a. A bar graph
   b. A number line
   c. An area model
   d. Base 10 blocks

2. A teacher is showing students how to evaluate $5 \times 6 + 4 \div 2 - 1$. Which operation should be completed first?
   a. Multiplication
   b. Addition
   c. Division
   d. Subtraction

3. A factor of 36 is defined as:
   a. A whole number that can be divided by 36 and have no remainder
   b. A whole number that 36 can be divided by and have no remainder
   c. A prime number that is multiplied by 36
   d. An even number that is multiplied by 36

4. Which of the following is the definition of a prime number?
   a. A number whose only factors are itself and 1
   b. A number greater than 1 whose only factors are itself and 1
   c. A number less than 10
   d. A number divisible by 10

5. What is the next number in the following sequence? $1, 3, 6, 10, 15, 21, \ldots$
   a. 26
   b. 27
   c. 28
   d. 29

See answers on next page.

Answer Explanations

1. B: This inequality can be seen with the use of a number line. $\frac{3}{7}$ is close to $\frac{1}{2}$. $\frac{5}{6}$ is close to 1, but less than 1, and $\frac{8}{7}$ is greater than 1. Therefore, $\frac{3}{7}$ is less than $\frac{5}{6}$.

2. A: Using the order of operations, multiplication and division are computed first from left to right. Multiplication is on the left; therefore, multiplication should be performed first.

3. B: If 36 can be divided by a whole number and have no remainder, then that number is a factor of 36. In other words, a factor of 36 is a whole number that can be multiplied by another whole number to make 36. The number 36 equals 1×36, 2×18, 3×12, 4×9, and 6×6, so it has nine unique factors: 1, 2, 3, 4, 6, 9, 12, 18, and 36.

4. B: A prime number is a number whose only factors are itself and 1, but only numbers greater than 1 can be considered prime.

5. C: Starting with 1, we get the next number in the sequence by adding 2, then 3, 4, 5, and 6. So to find the next number, we take our latest number and add 7, getting $21 + 7 = 28$.

Social Studies

Social Science Instruction

An early education social studies curriculum should offer content that is comprehensive and thematic, introducing a variety of viewpoints on historical events and highlighting the relevance of connecting the past with the present. Teachers must know how to guide students in obtaining, evaluating, and processing the information associated with these topics. Although the school's textbook is a ready resource, teachers should suggest and encourage alternate sources of information, such as the library, field trips, maps, and other visual material, interviews, and discussions of current events. These opportunities allow students to analyze information and increase their societal understanding. Classroom activities can help students apply previously acquired learning through problem solving, such as performing their own mock election in order to gain a better grasp of the election process. Encouraging students to investigate social studies topics that interest them and involve real-world projects helps them to become objective observers and develop a sense of public duty. When students can interpret, organize, and present what they have learned through a variety of methods, it promotes a deeper understanding and application of wider social studies themes.

Social Studies Content and Performance Standards of the TEKS

In total, the social studies Texas Essential Knowledge and Skills (TEKS) are organized into eight strands: 1) history, 2) geography, 3) economics, 4) government, 5) citizenship, 6) culture, 7) science, technology, and society, and 8) social studies skills. The goal of these eight strands is to prepare students for college-level history, which demands that they analyze history from multiple perspectives. The first five strands introduce students to various fields or disciplines in the social sciences. The sixth and seventh strands introduce students to broader themes that guide each of the fields or disciplines. And the final strand introduces students to skills that allow them to access each of the previous seven strands. These strands are embedded in the vertical alignment of the social studies TEKS, though some grade levels may emphasize certain strands for the sake of vertical progression.

Vertical Alignment of the Social Science in the TEKS

The social sciences Texas Essential Knowledge and Skills (TEKS) are horizontally aligned across several academic disciplines, preparing teachers and students alike for embarking on interdisciplinary studies. In addition, the social sciences TEKS are vertically aligned, paving a curricular pathway from kindergarten-level historical inquiry to college readiness. The social sciences TEKS are meant to be consistent and cumulative across all grade levels so Texas students can gradually gain momentum in their learning trajectory. The social sciences TEKS's vertical alignment allows students to start with the personal (self, family, classroom) and gradually expand outward to a globalized perspective (people and places in the contemporary world). The vertical alignment for the social sciences TEKS is as follows:

- Sixth grade: People and places in the contemporary world
- Fifth grade: United States history
- Fourth grade: Texas in the Western Hemisphere
- Third grade: Communities past and present, including Texas and the nation
- Second grade: Local community, Texas, nation
- First grade: Classroom, school, and local community
- Kindergarten: Self, family, and classroom

The purpose of this broad, multi-context curriculum is to gradually expand students' historical horizons so they are better prepared as engaged family members, community members, and global citizens. One major purpose of this vertical alignment is to promote a variety of civic competencies (microcosmic and macrocosmic) over a seven-year period. The progression from the self to the globe is strategic in drawing connections between personal identity, historical agency, and civic engagement. Overall, the goal is to create active and informed citizens for the state of Texas and the world. Drawing energy from such broad-ranging disciplines as political science, geography, environmental science, economics, education, history, sociology, and psychology, the vertical alignment of social sciences TEKS attempts to prepare students for interdisciplinary college classrooms.

Uses Social Studies Terminology Correctly

Literacy should be a top concern in all K–12 classrooms. However, there is no denying that social studies classrooms are some of the most demanding for students when it comes to literacy and language acquisition. In social studies, students will not only have to comprehend basic verbs, nouns, and adjectives, but they will also have to understand complex social studies terms for particular contexts, places, eras, persons, movements, and groups. Social studies standards across different states typically demand that students obtain a relative amount of terminological specificity. In other words, literacy in a social studies classroom can be hyper-specific, which poses problems with students of all learning types and grade levels. In particular, social studies terminology can pose problems for Section 504 students, special education (SPED) students, and English language learners (ELLs).

It is important that social studies teachers introduce students to best practices such as 1) using study cards, cognitive maps, and organizational charts for understanding social studies terms, 2) finding individualized structures and styles for note-taking, 3) employing memory games and mnemonic devices for recalling important information, and 4) using timelines and charts for understanding the importance of context, time, and sequence when it comes to social studies terms. Understanding and using social studies terminology correctly is almost always contingent on properly understanding the notion of time and context in history.

Stages for Implementing Effective Learning Experiences

Teachers must first assist students with understanding their own identities before they try to expose them to diverse identities and communities within the social sciences. Implementing social and emotional learning (SEL) activities can help students understand themselves as well as their peers. SEL activities, such as personal reflections or class diaries, can help students in the social sciences prepare for interacting within the broader world. SEL activities help students understand the idea of community while also helping them *build* community in the classroom. Student growth and development in the social sciences should begin with identity and gradually branch out to classroom community, family, and personal community. Once students understand themselves better and the ways in which their ideas and emotions operate, then they will be more ready to comprehend the similarities and differences they have with their teachers and peers. As the complex components of the in-class community are more readily understood, students should be ready to deconstruct their relationships to their individual families and communities.

Teachers should prompt students to understand the *why* of their beliefs and emotions as well as the source. This is crucial in a social sciences classroom because students are consistently analyzing identity, culture, society, and social relations. Without this basic foundation, it is difficult for students to respect their own cultures. Moreover, it may be difficult for them to share about their own cultures and collaborate with people who may reside outside of their cultures. The routines and expectations of every social sciences classroom should therefore be mandated by some sort of community agreement or constitution. To design and implement effective learning experiences, the entire community must "buy into" a particular social contract. Teachers should create nonnegotiable aspects of class culture, but they should also call upon students as experts and engineers of their own context. Social science classes with poor management typically fail to implement "student voice and choice" when it comes to routines and expectations, especially for working cooperatively within the community.

Current Technology as a Tool for Teaching

Computer technology – especially with regard to the Internet, smartphones, tablets, and social media – is progressing at a rate that is often difficult for teachers to "keep up" with what is pertinent, effective, and relevant for their students. With the world becoming increasingly connected (and separated) by technology, it is important for every student in the social sciences to be exposed to contemporary techniques and practices for incorporating technology into the classroom. Students must know how to use the Internet, smartphones, tablets, and social media in their social sciences classroom to adequately prepare for the next era of college learning and professional research.

Teachers must acquaint themselves with up-to-date, research-based practices for incorporating technology in the classroom. Specifically, in a social studies classroom, students must be prepared to access sources online and differentiate whether they are primary or secondary sources. More importantly, students must be able to assess whether the sources are legitimate enough to incorporate into research or presentations. Teachers should explicitly teach students how to research on technological devices while also teaching them how to assess the validity of sources and databases. In an increasingly digitized world, it is important to expose students to digital museums and databases. It is also important to use technology – specifically social media and smartphone apps – to "hook" students onto a particular topic or area of inquiry.

Applies Developmentally Appropriate Instructional Practices

Teachers should strive to move beyond textbooks in the classroom, introducing students to a variety of primary and secondary sources. Written secondary sources can include professional monographs, popular histories, historical fiction, magazines, newspapers, and scholarly journals and articles. Written primary sources can include journals, diaries, newspaper clippings, government documents, context-specific literature, letters, biographies and autobiographies, folklore, and cultural mythology. Students should also be exposed to visual sources such as political cartoons, artwork, ads, signs, graphs, charts, tables, photographs, and videos. Students can also be introduced to relevant musical works. As digital archives and histories are becoming more relevant in 21st century classroom, it's important that students are exposed to computer-based resources.

Promoting Use of Social Science Skills

In social studies, vocabulary terms typically focus on particular people, places, groups, or features that happened or existed in the past (or present). Social studies vocabulary terms can be particularly challenging because there is a certain specificity that goes along with complex identities, groups, and events. To promote student understanding of these complex vocabulary terms, it is important that teachers connect the terms to larger concepts (i.e., "words or phrases that refer to categories of information"). Concepts allow social studies students to organize large amounts of information using historical context and change over time. When analyzing concepts, students should pay close attention to the definition of the concept and examples of the concept. For example, one concept that can be bequeathed to students is the concept of "war in American history." Under the umbrella of this concept, students can chronologically or thematically organize such disparate vocabulary terms as *French and Indian War, American Revolution, War of 1812, Mexican-American War, Civil War, Spanish-American War, World War I,* and *World War II.* Students may even broaden this concept to include such terms as *Cold War* and *War on Drugs*.

To promote study skills in the classroom, teachers can introduce students to such strategies as using study cards. This is particularly helpful for visual learners who need to see a certain term or concept to make an impression in their minds. Additionally, teachers can introduce students to the "art of note-taking," which will help them succeed in both K–12 and higher-education classrooms. Students should be explicitly taught how to underline, highlight, color-code, and take notes in the margins. Test-taking skills should also be explicitly taught to students—students should know the E.R.A. approach to standardized tests that encourages them to "Examine the Question," "Recall What They Know," and "Apply What They Know." Lastly, students should be exposed to research tools such as libraries, databases, archives, citation styles, and public museums. To be prepared for the twenty-first century, students should also be exposed to digital versions of these tools. It is quite possible that students can even go on "digital tours" of museum collections, thanks to the Internet and computer technologies.

Instruction that Relates Skills and Ideas Across Different Social Science Disciplines

Over the course of the last twenty-five years, the K–12 and higher-education systems in the United States have been gradually adopting interdisciplinary practices that encourage teachers and students to integrate skills, concepts, and ideas across a variety of different disciplines. This has become especially true in the social sciences at the K–12 level, where teachers and students must continually combine theories and practices from such disparate fields as history, political science, social studies, geography, psychology, government, ethics, economics, environmental studies, and sociology. Additionally, twenty-first-century teachers and students will be expected to make connections between the social sciences, sciences, arts, and mathematics.

While teachers should strive to enrich their knowledge of content in their particular field of inquiry, they should also strive to make connections between fields. This means they should employ instructional practices in the classroom that explicitly and implicitly expose students to the interconnected nature of all learning. One way this could be accomplished is through collaboration with colleagues who are experts in other fields. Another way is by introducing textbooks, articles, and materials from other fields into content-specific social science classrooms. Lastly, teachers can help students to relate skills, concepts, and ideas across different social science disciplines by incorporating project-based learning (PBL) activities into the classroom that require students to analyze/approach/solve real-world problems through collaboration with peers, professionals, and public agencies with unique, discipline-specific experiences. PBL activities ensure that students not only grasp interdisciplinary content, but also *apply* this content to real-life problems, projects, and scenarios.

Making Connections Between Knowledge in the Social Sciences and Other Areas

As mentioned earlier, teachers must extend interdisciplinary study to include fields and content areas that exist outside the traditional social sciences (i.e., history, political science, social studies, geography, psychology, government, ethics, economics, environmental studies, and sociology). The future of the social sciences depends heavily on communication with fields that traditionally fall under the STEM (Science, Technology, Engineering, and Math) or STEAM (Science, Technology, Engineering, Art, and Math) categories. Disassociating the social sciences from these other fields is not beneficial for young students. In an increasingly technological world, students must be prepared to incorporate skills, ideas, concepts, and practices from STEM and STEAM courses into their social science classrooms. It is difficult to imagine future historians, political scientists, social studies teachers, geographers, psychologists, government officials, ethicists, economists, environmentalists, and sociologists functioning without science, technology, engineering, art, and mathematics. Future historians, for example, will likely have to be forensic computer scientists who sift through old files and data to better understand history and historical agents. Whenever possible, teachers should explicitly expose students to the ways in which these fields perpetually affect each other within the global economy and popular culture.

Uses Effective Instructional Strategies

Besides traditional lectures, textbook work, PowerPoints, and direct instruction, teachers can diversify pedagogical methods in their classrooms by incorporating inquiry-based practices, project-based learning, field work, role plays, sociodramas, skits, simulations, field trips, student-specific academic interventions, debates, and identity-based social-emotional learning activities into social science courses. The goal is to differentiate sources, instruction, and assessments so all students have access to social science content.

Social Science Issues and Trends

Social science students should not solely be focused on history and the past. Students should be exposed to disciplines such as political science, social studies, geography, psychology, government, ethics, economics, environmental studies, and sociology. These disciplines all emphasize present-day issues and trends in society; students should use these disciplines to determine the essence of their own historical context. Students must be able to not only understand social science concepts, but also apply the problem-solving and decision-making skills of the social sciences to the real world. Even history can help students better understand the present and have enough foresight to protect the future. The social sciences, in this sense, are as much about civic engagement as they are about content acquisition.

Maps and Other Graphics

Students should not only be able to analyze maps and other infographics, but they should also be able to create graphs, charts, tables, documents, maps, timelines, and other visual materials to represent geographic, political, historical, economic, and cultural features. Students should be made aware of the different options they have to present data. They should understand that maps visually display geographic features, and they can be used to illustrate key relationships in human geography and natural geography. Maps can indicate themes in history, politics, economics, culture, social relationships, demographic distributions, and climate change. Students can also choose to display data or information in a variety of graphs: Bar graphs compare two or more things with parallel bars; line graphs show change over time with strategic points placed carefully between vertical and horizontal axes; and pie graphs divide wholes into percentages or parts. Likewise, students can choose to use timelines or tables to present data/information. Timelines arrange events or ideas into chronological order, and tables arrange words or numbers into columns or rows. These are just some of the visual tools teachers and students can use to help visually convey their historical questions or ideas.

Methods for Assessing Social Science Concepts

Differentiated assessments are crucial for tailoring the educational environment for individual learning types. Teachers must be aware and sensitive to the neurodiversity in their classrooms. When designing social science assessments, teachers should keep in mind the unique learning types and cognitive skills of English Language Learners (ELLs), Section 504 students, Gifted and Talented (GT) students, and Special Education (SPED) students. In addition, teachers in K-6 social science classrooms must be sensitive to culture. Whenever possible, social science teachers should make their materials and assessments personally and culturally relevant.

Students should be comfortable exploring and expressing their identities in social science classrooms. For students to excel at historical inquiry, it's important that they understand their own genders, sexual orientations, races, ethnicities, political affiliations, religious beliefs, and socioeconomic statuses to better understand how these categories drive the decisions of historical actors and even their peers. The TEKS performance standards act as a means for assessing the needs of each student; moreover, the TEKS performance standards encourage cultural diversity. Contrary to popular belief, these standards don't limit one's ability to implement varied assessments; rather, the TEKS were created as guideposts for implementing diverse assessments that account for the varied interests and skills present in every classroom. Whenever possible, use the TEKS for direction, and employ kinesthetic-, auditory-, oral-, written-, and visual-based assessments for every student. Also try to vary assessments by incorporating design-thinking, inquiry-based learning, project-based learning, and student voice and choice. Inevitably, a good teacher will respond to student needs and concerns and offer alternative assessments without diminishing the crucial nature of the TEKS.

Value of Social Studies Education

Teachers and students must also engage parents/caregivers, colleagues/peers, and the community to convey the overall importance of a social studies education. When challenged about the importance of a social studies education, teachers and students can illustrate the ways in which a social studies education can help people become better writers, researchers, and presenters. Moreover, a quality social studies education will also make teachers and students better problem solvers, decision makers, and civic engagers. A knowledge of social studies can help teachers and students understand many problems faced in present-day global society. Politicians, businessmen, and common citizens all could benefit from enriching their historical consciousness so that they can effectively diagnose and implement positive changes for their government, customers, families, or fellow citizens. Social studies can help rebuild communities and prevent international conflicts; it can help teachers and students become better citizens in an often-conflicted global society.

History

Historical Points of Reference

Texas history can be divided into nine categories: 1) pre-colonial Texas, 2) first contact and colonial Texas, 3) the Mexican National Period, 4) revolution and the Republic of Texas, 5) U.S. annexation and the Mexican-American War, 6) antebellum slavery and the Civil War, 7) Reconstruction and post-Reconstruction, 8) 20th Century advancement, and 9) immigration and migration to the Sunbelt south.

Pre-Colonial Texas

Texas was home to Paleoindians during the prehistoric period. In fact, people have lived in Texas for over 12,000 years. Anthropologists and archaeologists working in Texas have discovered artifacts of the Clovis culture that developed in North America some 11,000–12,000 years ago. During the First Agricultural Revolution, many hunter-gatherers of nomadic Paleoindian groups began to settle permanently or semi-permanently in Texas. These earliest Native American groups included the Karankawas, the Coahuiltecans, the Caddos, the Witchitas, the Atakapas, the Jumanos, the Tonkawas, and the Apaches. Additionally, many Native Americans resettled in Texas during the era of Indian Removal and Manifest Destiny. These included the Comanches and Kiowas.

First Contact and Colonial Texas

In the 1500s, Spanish conquistadors and French settlers began exploring the Gulf Coast region. In 1519, Spanish explorer Alonso Alvarez de Pineda became one of the first conquistadors to probe the Texas coast. There is no evidence that he reached the Texas mainland, but his expedition increased Spanish interest in Texas. Spanish explorer Panfilo de Narvaez's expedition became the first to explore the Texas mainland, albeit accidentally. During this expedition, Narvaez's ships wrecked, and explorer Alvar Nunez Cabeza de Vaca was taken in by Karankawa Indians. This first contact, which occurred in 1528, encouraged Cabeza de Vaca to continue his travels, even after he was captured and placed in captivity by Coahuiltecan Indians. Between 1528 and 1536, Cabeza de Vaca and a band of other shipwrecked survivors wandered across Texas and modern-day Mexico. Eventually they reached Mexico City in 1536 with the help of Spanish soldiers they encountered on their journey.

Cabeza de Vaca later published an account of his expedition, which caught the attention of Spanish viceroys and explorers. This led conquistador Francisco Vasquez de Coronado to embark on a journey with a force of over 1,300 men in 1540 in search of gold. While Coronado never found gold, he and his men did become some of the first Europeans to see the Grand Canyon and travel through modern-day West Texas. By the 1600s, after years of expeditions, the Spanish colonial government began establishing missions along the frontiers of modern-day Mexico, New Mexico, California, and Texas. Some settlements sprouted up along the Rio Grande in South Texas. French explorer Robert de La Salle led several expeditions in East Texas in the 1680s.

Control over East Texas shifted hands from the Spanish and French on multiple occasions in the late 1600s and early 1700s until Spain took possession due to the missionary efforts of men like Father Francisco Hidalgo, a Franciscan priest who established missions in East Texas for the Spanish crown. Throughout the 1700s, Spain continued to establish missions, presidios, and ranches throughout Texas. Life in Spanish Texas during this era was marked by extreme isolation, loose government control, and border skirmishes. The Spanish crown had a hard time controlling the region based on its remoteness and a lack of manpower.

The Mexican National Period

Following Mexican independence from Spain in September 1821, Texas became part of the new Republic of Mexico. Young Tejano ranchers, now generations removed from their grandparents' settlement in the region, became the new lifeblood of Texas under Mexican national rule. During this era, Texas became a key frontier for both Mexico and the United States. The Mexican government created plans to colonize the region while many Anglo-Americans also founded frontier homes on Mexican land. Catalyzed by the free labor of slaves, farming and ranching became the economic cornerstones of the regions. Gradually, Texans established a unique cultural identity that resisted the loose control of the Mexican Republic.

Revolution and the Republic of Texas

Eventually, Mexican and Texan identities became so distinct that the Texans decided to rebel against the centralist Mexican government. The ensuing Texas Revolution, which took place in 1835 and 1836, allowed Texas to declare independence from Mexico. A flood of United States volunteers assisted in helping Texans find the Republic of Texas, which officially received its independence via the Consultation of 1836. The Republic of Texas was a short-lived nation because its people quickly accepted annexation by the United States of America in 1845.

U.S. Annexation and the Mexican-American War

President John Tyler initiated an annexation bill in March 1845, which President James K. Polk officially signed in December 1845. The Republic of Texas officially revoked its sovereignty, lawfully agreeing to become the 28th state of the Union in February 1846. The Mexican-American War (1846–1848), in many ways, was a direct response to President Polk's annexation of Texas. The war ended in the Treaty of Guadalupe, which resulted in a Mexican Cession that officially brought parts of Texas, New Mexico, Arizona, and California within the territory of the United States. One social impact of U.S. annexation and the Mexican-American War was increased political tensions over the role of slavery in new territories.

Significant Events and Issues in Texas History

Antebellum Slavery and the Civil War

Texas became part of the South's valuable cotton belt, a regional plantation economy built on the free labor of slaves. Growing national divisions over slavery divided the nation. Most Texas politicians were tied to the cotton economy and sided with the pro-slavery politicians of the broader South. Additionally, these slavery advocates emphasized state-based sovereignty, choosing to believe the rights of states outweighed the overreach of federal government. The state of Texas joined the Confederates States of America on March 2, 1861 as the seventh state to secede from the Union. Texas troops proved to be a cornerstone of the Confederate militia during the Civil War.

Reconstruction and Post-Reconstruction

After the Civil War, the United States entered an era known as Reconstruction. During Reconstruction, the Texas government, like many Southern states, passed black codes that denied civil rights to former slaves. In the wake of emancipation, freed African-Americans were once again second-class citizens. Texas politics became intermingled with the violence of the Ku Klux Klan (KKK), as many Texans participated in the public murder of freed blacks. Many Republican politicians, such as Texas Governor Edmund J. Davis, chose to fight the intimidation tactics of the KKK and assist African-Americans in protecting their civil rights. Davis was a fervent advocate of using public funding to educate African-Americans as equals. Nevertheless, as Reconstruction waned in the South, Texas joined other

Southern states in adopting segregationist Jim Crow laws. Segregation (the separation of whites and blacks in public spaces) became a keystone of Texas politics well into the 1950s and 1960s. The Civil Rights Movement of that era ended legal segregation in the South.

20th Century Advancement

The 20th century not only witnessed the extension of voting rights to women in Texas, but also the civil liberties of African-Americans. Economically, the 20th century saw Texas become a gas and petroleum powerhouse. During the Cold War, Houston joined Cape Canaveral as an epicenter of NASA's space race. The oil and space industries carried Texas well into the 21st century, bringing millions of professionals to the Sunbelt South. Population increases during this era paved the way for environmental devastation. Today, Texas cities still struggle to cope with the rampant excesses of 20th century industrialization and urbanization.

Immigration and Migration to the Sunbelt South

In the 20th and 21st centuries, immigration and migration to the Sunbelt South transformed the racial, ethnic, and religious fiber of Texas. Immigration from Mexico and Latin America has helped "Hispanicize" Texas culture. Young professionals from all racial, ethnic, and religious backgrounds gravitate toward the budding tech industries in Austin, Houston, San Antonio, and Dallas. Many Texas cities are bursting at the seams with diversity and population growth. This immigration and migration has made Texas a diverse economic powerhouse, though this rapid influx of new residents has stirred racial tensions and has complicated city planning.

Native American Groups in North America

The first people arrived in North America at least 15,000 years ago by crossing the land bridge from Asia to present-day Alaska. Their descendants are referred to as **Native Americans** or **American Indians**. They gradually made their way through North and South America, adapting to the climate and landscape of the varied regions and splitting off into numerous tribes. There was a great deal of diversity among these tribes with each possessing its own culture and language. Although the different tribes did lay claim to their own specific territories, land within a tribe was considered communal. The concept of individual land ownership was not recognized. This sense of equality was also evident in the way women were generally viewed and treated. They were given some degree of political power and worked in the fields while the men fought wars, hunted, and cleared the land for planting crops.

Indians in the East, upper Midwest, and Northwest sections of North America survived by hunting, gathering, and fishing. Some of them also farmed the land. Their dwellings were wood longhouses, plank houses, or wigwams, which are round, wood-framed, domed huts. Plains Indians hunted buffalo, often following them across the open prairies and living in teepees that were easily moved from place to place to suit their nomadic lifestyle. Indians in the Southwest relied on farming for much of their food and built adobes, which are houses made of dried clay or earth.

European Exploration and Colonization

When examining how Europeans explored what would become the United States of America, one must first examine why Europeans came to explore the New World as a whole. In the fifteenth century, tensions increased between the Eastern and Mediterranean nations of Europe and the expanding Ottoman Empire to the east. As war and piracy spread across the Mediterranean, the once-prosperous trade routes across Asia's Silk Road began to decline, and nations across Europe began to explore alternative routes for trade.

Italian explorer Christopher Columbus proposed a westward route. Contrary to popular lore, the main challenge that Columbus faced in finding backers was not proving that the world was round. Much of Europe's educated elite knew that the world was round; the real issue was that they rightly believed that a westward route to Asia, assuming a lack of obstacles, would be too long to be practical. Nevertheless, Columbus set sail in 1492 after obtaining support from Spain and arrived in the West Indies three months later.

Spain launched further expeditions to the new continents and established *New Spain*. The colony consisted not only of Central America and Mexico, but also the American Southwest and Florida. France claimed much of what would become Canada, along with the Mississippi River region and the Midwest. In addition, the Dutch established colonies that covered New Jersey, New York, and Connecticut. Each nation managed its colonies differently, and thus influenced how they would assimilate into the United States. For instance, Spain strove to establish a system of Christian missions throughout its territory, while France focused on trading networks and had limited infrastructure in regions such as the Midwest.

Even in cases of limited colonial growth, the land of America was hardly vacant, because a diverse array of Native American nations and groups were already present. Throughout much of colonial history, European settlers commonly misperceived native peoples as a singular, static entity. In reality, Native Americans had a variety of traditions depending on their history and environment, and their culture continued to change through the course of interactions with European settlers; for instance, tribes such as the Cheyenne and Comanche used horses, which were introduced by white settlers, to become powerful warrior nations. However, a few generalizations can be made: many, but not all, tribes were matrilineal, which gave women a fair degree of power, and land was commonly seen as belonging to everyone. These differences, particularly European settlers' continual focus on land ownership, contributed to increasing prejudice and violence.

Situated on the Atlantic Coast, the Thirteen Colonies that would become the United States of America constituted only a small portion of North America. Even those colonies had significant differences that stemmed from their different origins. For instance, the Virginia colony under John Smith in 1607 started with male bachelors seeking gold, whereas families of Puritans settled Massachusetts. As a result, the Thirteen Colonies—Virginia, Massachusetts, Connecticut, Maryland, New York, New Jersey, Pennsylvania, Delaware, Rhode Island, New Hampshire, Georgia, North Carolina, and South Carolina—had different structures and customs that would each influence the United States.

Competition among several imperial powers in eastern areas of North America led to conflicts that would later bring about the independence of the United States. The French and Indian War from 1754 to 1763, which was a subsidiary war of the Seven Years' War, ended with Great Britain claiming France's Canadian territories as well as the Ohio Valley. The same war was costly for all the powers involved, which led to increased taxes on the Thirteen Colonies. In addition, the new lands to the west of the colonies attracted new settlers, and they came into conflict with Native Americans and British troops that were trying to maintain the traditional boundaries. These growing tensions with Great Britain, as well as other issues, eventually led to the American Revolution, which ended with Britain relinquishing its control of the colonies.

Britain continued to hold onto its other colonies, such as Canada and the West Indies, which reflects the continued power of multiple nations across North America, even as the United States began to expand across the continent. Many Americans advocated expansion regardless of the land's current inhabitants, but the results were often mixed. Still, events both abroad and within North America contributed to the growth of the United States. For instance, the rising tumult in France during the French Revolution and the rise of Napoleon led France to sell the Louisiana Purchase, a large chunk of land consisting not only of Louisiana but also much of the Midwest, to the United States in 1803. Meanwhile, as Spanish power declined, Mexico claimed independence in 1821, but the new nation became increasingly vulnerable to foreign pressure. In the Mexican-American War from 1846 to 1848, Mexico surrendered territory to the United States that eventually became California, Nevada, Utah, and New Mexico, as well as parts of Arizona, Colorado, and Wyoming.

Even as the United States sought new inland territory, American interests were also expanding overseas via trade. As early as 1784, the ship *Empress of China* traveled to China to establish trading connections. American interests had international dimensions throughout the nation's history. For instance, during the presidency of Andrew Jackson, the ship *Potomac* was dispatched to the Pacific island of Sumatra in 1832 to avenge the deaths of American sailors. This incident exemplifies how U.S. foreign trade connected with imperial expansion.

This combination of continental and seaward growth adds a deeper layer to American development because it was not purely focused on western expansion. For example, take the 1849 Gold Rush; a large number of Americans and other immigrants traveled to California by ship and settled western territories before more eastern areas, such as Nevada and Idaho. Therefore, the United States' early history of colonization and expansion is a complex network of diverse cultures.

Influence of Various Factors on the Development of Societies

As societies, or groups of people living together as communities, develop, the members are better able to identify and achieve what they need to be happy and healthy. Development involves the society's ability to set goals, recognize opportunities for positive change, and use tools to solve problems. A society's ability to develop is impacted by a variety of factors.

Geography and climate affect commodities available to a society (e.g., minerals, ability to grow crops or raise livestock). They also impact whether a society is stationary or nomadic and how openly it can interact with neighboring societies. Migration and trade both encourage development by transferring potentially beneficial skills and ideas, a practice known as spatial exchange. Societies may exchange information on scientific discoveries and new technologies, such as water treatment, that can improve quality of life and promote development.

Societies are also shaped by the environment's physical landscape. In the desert, for example, societies may not easily come into contact with other groups of people, which can limit spatial exchange. Similarly, lacking local access to necessary resources can impact individuals' health and time for opportunities that promote development. For example, if children are malnourished or are needed on the farm for time-consuming chores, they may not be able to attend school, which inhibits development.

Societies are also impacted by the characteristics of people both within their own society and those with whom they may interact. The long-held beliefs of a society, including gender roles and trust of people in power, can also affect health and opportunities that promote development. For example, if females are seen as most useful in childcare or are considered inferior, they will likely lack opportunities to be educated and contribute economically to their society, no matter their own interests.

Characteristics of Communities

Communities are groups of people who have a shared interest or purpose and often live or have fun together. People in communities have incentives to care for each other and feel responsibility for each other's well-being and happiness, as their interests are connected and sometimes dependent on each other. Communities may develop because people live near each other, but many other factors can influence their formation. Historically, communities formed for protection (strength in numbers) and to share in the task of producing food through hunting, gathering, or farming. Others shared religious beliefs, political views, or social ideals. Still other communities were based on gender, race, nationality, class, skills, occupation, or hobbies.

Communities share natural resources in an area (such as clay, coal, oil, or timber) to build homes and schools, create jobs, and trade with others to make money and increase prosperity. With the income earned and resources gained, members meet their needs (things required for survival) and attain their wants (things they would like to have but are not necessary for survival) as they develop their economy. As a community establishes itself and its economy, it also develops means of transportation to move people and goods from one place to another and communication systems to share information internally and with those outside the community.

To stabilize a community and enable it to achieve common goals, the members must establish political, economic, and social customs and policies. Communities share customs that sometimes become formalized as rules or laws and are intended to keep the community functioning in a way that protects the members, their relationships, and their common interests.

Communities change over time due to a number of factors. The beliefs and goals of members may shift with time or as immigration and emigration change the make-up of the community. Economic development, as well as advances in science and technology, may impact the types of jobs and activities community members pursue. As has been the case in Texas history, for example, the economy may shift from labor to more technological pursuits as demand shifts and more community members gain appropriate skills and education.

All people within the community play an important role in supporting its mission and facilitating its maintenance and growth. Particular individuals may feel especially impassioned about their communities and may be noted as historical figures that supported their communities by advancing major causes (e.g., Martin Luther King Jr.'s role in desegregating the United States). History also recognizes patriots who defend their countries against tyranny (e.g., important figures in the American Revolution). But many who help to shape their communities are citizens who will never appear in a history book because their impact, while localized, is relatively small; however, it is still important in shaping their communities. In a community, few roles are too small to have an impact on the greater good.

Basic Concepts of Culture

Cross-cultural interactions are the very heart of world history and must be closely examined to understand the world's historical patterns. One of the main reasons why cross-cultural studies are so important is because cultures are not necessarily synonymous with political entities, such as states. Many countries, ranging from China to Greece, historically have many subcultures that should be considered individually. For example, a study of culture in the United States would need to consider multiple ethnic and regional groups. Even individual states and cities have their own traditions. On the other hand, these multiple cultures often coalesce into a larger, national culture that defines the overall society and politics of the nation. Therefore, cross-cultural studies of different subgroups in a larger body allow people to understand how the different parts of a culture interact and connect with each other.

Furthermore, cultures are not always restricted by the borders of nations, and cultural phenomena may extend through multiple countries. This can be seen in the spread of the Spanish language across Central and South America as well as other regions. The Spanish language and other various traditions tie the different countries together with a common culture. Even so, each nation changes the culture and gives it a unique style. A study of the culture in a single nation may be very insightful, but it would be incomplete if it failed to account for aspects of the culture beyond that country. In addition, this means that different cultures can overlap with each other and that the cultures of different countries may intersect in ways that their borders do not. By examining multiple cultures and how they are linked with each other, larger cultural patterns become apparent, which makes these studies critical in world history.

Throughout history, cultures have not existed in isolation but rather have been affected by other traditions. A key influence in how different cultures develop is not only their setting and history but how they interact with neighboring cultures. For instance, the conflict from 499 to 449 B.C. between the Persian Empire and the Greek city-states helped to influence the course of Greek culture as a whole by creating a national sense of dichotomy between the Greek ideal of freedom and Persian autocracy. Aside from direct impacts such as wars, cultures can influence each other through interactions that spread some concepts while also adopting new ideas from their neighbors. Pasta became a phenomenon in Italy in part because the Silk Road linked Italy with China, which already had similar foods.

The pervasiveness of globalization in the present day has increased the importance of cross-cultural comparison and made it a topic of immediate relevance. The world now has a truly global market in which travel, communications, and trade function on an international scale. This means that people of different cultures can now interact with each other much more easily than in earlier centuries, which allows for a rapid exchange of ideas and goods between cultures. Furthermore, despite the international scope of modern trade, many globalized markets strive to build on the appeal of local cultures. Doing so gives the products a genuine and unique quality that resonates with consumers. Yet it is critical to realize how local cultures are transformed and combined with concepts from other cultures in the global market. For example, sushi is a traditional food in Japan, but its export to other nations has led chefs to create new culinary fusions, such as sushi tacos.

Cross-cultural comparisons also help to reveal common patterns in human society. Sometimes different cultures develop similar concepts without directly interacting with each other. For instance, both the Mayan culture in Central America and the ancient Egyptians independently developed pyramid structures. Although the similarities have sparked rumors that these civilizations were connected, it is most likely that each version originated independently. Close examination of the two types of pyramids and their respective cultures reveals significant differences amidst the similarities. These comparisons are important because they show how human cultures converge and diverge in their patterns of growth. A key function of historical study is to gain a better understanding and appreciation of how humanity develops. By examining the commonalities and differences between cultures, people can begin to theorize what factors influence the course of civilizations. However, such studies must account for the complex manners through which cultures interact with each other.

Effects of Innovations on Political, Economic, Social and Environmental Developments

Science and technology are major factors that drive societal development. Generally, technology makes tasks simpler and provides greater, easier access to resources and income. However, as societies develop, inequity and conflict tend to increase.

The use of simple tools allowed hunter-gatherer societies to grow or raise food as horticultural or pastoral societies, respectively. One advantage to this level of development was being able to store a surplus of food, which opened up trade and allowed for increases in population size. Because this allowed some members to have greater amounts of resources, it became a less equitable society than hunter-gatherers. The difference in individuals' or family groups' amounts of resources created a hierarchy, which can influence health, survival, and influence within the society.

Further advances in technology including the use of plows, other large tools, and animal labor allowed agricultural societies to develop. Members of agricultural societies were capable of having even greater wealth and population sizes than horticultural/pastoral societies; however, the resulting inequity may increase conflict, either within the society or with other societies. Further, agricultural societies amplified gender inequality: much of the labor was physically taxing and male-dominated, which gave them a power advantage over women who contributed by having more children for labor.

When the development of machines and electricity created a shift from agricultural economies toward industrialization, notable changes occurred in nearly every aspect of life. Industrial societies have greater access to wealth than agricultural ones but slightly lower levels of economic and gender inequality. Whereas communities in hunter-gatherer and agricultural societies were bonded more by common interests and goals, social relationships in urban industrial societies are more practical. Neighbors rely on each other more for the services they provide rather than being linked by shared beliefs; this makes industrial societies more prone to disagreements, violence, and uprising. Environmentally, industrial societies heavily consume natural resources and extensively pollute the environment.

Postindustrial societies rely on higher education to prepare members for information technology and service jobs, which dominate manufacturing jobs in the economy. This shift has led many U.S. companies to move manufacturing operations overseas. The lack of domestic manufacturing jobs creates a barrier for individuals without college degrees to secure employment, which increases inequity. Globally, countries that are able to achieve postindustrial development may also have a similar advantage over agricultural and industrial societies.

Formulating Historical Research Questions

As a social science, history requires evidence to support ideas that have become universally accepted facts. Facts that are accepted today are based on research questions that historians have asked for centuries and then used reliable resources to answer.

Teachers should encourage students to conduct historical research, which begins with formulating a question. Good research questions are focused and specific. They often relate to familiar topics, like those that the student has previously learned about or is otherwise interested in. Current events are another good place to look for research questions. A review of the academic literature can highlight areas where more research is necessary, and a question may form from there.

To answer the question, students will need to conduct research. Historical research can use both primary sources developed by a person present at the event and secondary sources written by those who were not there. It likely won't be enough to look at just one set of sources. Research raises new questions and reveals new ideas that may need additional investigation. Research should be evaluated for validity and bias so that it can be analyzed accurately.

Research provides informed answers to historical questions that are rooted in actual experiences of people, which can be accepted as fact.

Conducting Historical Research

Researchers utilize reputable sources including libraries, experts, and reputable academic literature. The two types of sources are primary and secondary sources. Primary sources, including speeches, letters and emails, memoirs, photos, newspaper articles, recordings, and public records, are those recorded during or soon after an event by someone who was there. Secondary sources—like books, reputable internet sites, and academic journals—come from people who were not present for the event but have researched it. Secondary sources tend to be broader and are a good place to start historical research.

When researching in any source, historians must ask the five W's: who, what, when, where, and why. Research may include opinions, facts, and different interpretations, so it's important to identify these characteristics to interpret the different viewpoints without bias and form a better understanding of what happened and why. It is also important to ensure that information is taken from a variety of sources so that it is balanced and validated by multiple sources. Good historians also stay mindful of their own biases relative to the sources they are reading.

Primary and Secondary Source Documents

Traditionally, historical documents have been separated into two major categories: primary sources and secondary sources. Understanding the features of each is crucial for building foundational historical inquiry skills in the K-6 classroom. Students must learn to deconstruct primary and secondary sources to gain a better understanding of historical context and personal perspective.

Primary sources contain firsthand documentation of a historical event or era. Primary sources are provided by people who have experienced an historical era or event. Primary sources capture a specific moment, context, or era in history. They are valued as eyewitness accounts and personal perspectives. Examples include diaries, memoirs, journals, letters, interviews, photographs, context-specific artwork, government documents, constitutions, newspapers, personal items, libraries, and archives. Another example of a primary source is the Declaration of Independence. This historical document captures the revolutionary sentiment of an era in American history.

Authors of secondary sources write about events, contexts, and eras in history with a relative amount of experiential, geographic, or temporal distance. Normally, secondary source authors aren't firsthand witnesses. In some cases, they may have experienced an event, but they are offering secondhand, retrospective accounts of their experience. All scholars and historians produce secondary sources—they gather primary source information and synthesize it for a new generation of students. Monographs, biographies, magazine articles, scholarly journals, theses, dissertations, textbooks, and encyclopedias are all secondary sources. In some rare instances, secondary sources become so enmeshed in their era of inquiry that they later become primary sources for future scholars and analysts.

Teachers and students alike must spend a great deal of time analyzing the relationships between primary sources, secondary sources, and their historical scopes. Juxtaposing primary sources with secondary sources helps teachers and students attain a deeper understanding of the material they are studying.

Problem-Solving Processes

Problem solving includes multiple steps:

- Define the problem
- Analyze the problem
- Develop alternative solutions
- Evaluate possible solutions and make a choice
- Implement the solution and evaluate the choice

A problem must always be clearly defined before a valid solution can be found. Be sure to examine the problem and not a related issue or only a small part of a larger problem. Describing what the problem is includes identifying what specifically must be solved or achieved as well as many details about the problem's cause. Gathering background details makes it easier to identify possible solutions and eventually choose the best one.

Once the problem is identified, analyze the current situation surrounding it, including pros and cons of why things are the way they currently are. Based on that information, develop alternative solutions to the problem. Brainstorming and working with a group of people in this stage can help to create a list of many possible solutions to draw from. Wait until the list is complete before moving on to the next step, which is to evaluate possible solutions and make a choice. When choosing the best solution, consider its pros and cons, the practicality of implementation, and whether it really solves the problem identified in step 1. As a best practice, as you finally implement the solution, evaluate how things are progressing and whether small adjustments should be made to optimize the new approach.

A similar process can be followed to make decisions:

- Identify the decision
- Gather information
- List options
- Choose the best decision
- Enact the decision and evaluate the choice

The first step is to identify the decision that is to be made. Again, it is important to be sure of the main issue is that needs to be addressed. Next, gather data that will inform the decision. It may be helpful to discuss the problem with experts or others who have experienced something similar. Third, list the decision options there are to choose from. Then, examine those alternatives and weigh the pros and cons of each to determine how doable and desirable the options are. Consider asking others to weigh in with their perspectives. Then, make the decision that seems best based on the evidence. Finally, gather the resources necessary and enact the decision. As with the problem-solving process, upon moving ahead with a decision, it's important to occasionally evaluate and tweak the approach as necessary to improve its effectiveness.

Analyzing Historical Information

Reviewing historical data such as population statistics (population size, ages, gender distribution, etc.), patterns of migration, and voting trends allows historians to analyze historical data and make predictions about the future. Once categorized and given a context, data from different categories, times, and places can be compared and contrasted to identify patterns.

With voting trends, for example, historians may categorize election data by political party, voter demographics, year, and location to identify trends. Once trends are analyzed, they can be used to predict future voting outcomes. Historical data can give insight into generalizable effects of beliefs, interests, and demographics on communities' future needs for funding and infrastructure, among other things. Politicians may also use such data to tailor their campaigns and increase their likelihood of being elected.

Population distribution by age and demographics can be analyzed, along with the effects of immigration and emigration on a particular population. The U.S. Census is a well-known analysis of such data. Conducted every 10 years, the Census collects data that the government uses to adjust electoral districts and apportion the seats in the House of Representatives based on population. Census results also guide distribution of federal funding for a variety of programs, including Medicaid and Head Start, from the state to the community level. Business leaders also use data as they make decisions on what products and services are needed in an area, where to open businesses, and how to allocate employees.

As an in-class project, students could research historical census data and examine changes in population in their area over time. Older students could role-play as business owners who must use the Census data to determine the best location for their store, factory, or restaurant, for example.

Sequential Nature of Historical Events

Timelines are useful tools that teachers and students of history use to understand the sequential nature of events. Timelines are essential for listing events in chronological order. Knowing the chronology of events can help teachers and students understand relationships between events, and how historical context can affect human decisions. Often, in a social studies classroom, timelines assist students in understanding cause and effect. There are two basic types of chronologies that teachers can highlight for students: absolute chronology and relative chronology. Timelines are examples of absolute chronologies that arrange events in a specific order based on the dates that events occurred. Relative chronologies are less structured than absolute chronologies and merely list events in order without regarding specific dates.

Foundations of Representative Government in the United States

The path to democracy in the United States began when Europeans colonized the region in the 1500s. It culminated in the mid-1700s when British colonists began to rebel against British rule and its restrictions. Colonists particularly rebelled against the burden of taxation without representation in Parliament. These **Patriots** decided to fight for their freedom, defeated Great Britain in the Revolutionary War, and established a new country they called the United States of America. The US Constitution was drafted in 1787 at the Constitutional Convention in Philadelphia. The goal was to create a government with checks and balances, and by dividing it into three branches, no single branch had ultimate governmental control. They designated the two legislative bodies—the House and Senate—as the Congress. This document is recognized as the world's first formal plan for a modern democracy and the oldest working constitution in existence.

Many people made significant contributions toward expanding the rights and freedoms of Americans by fighting in the Revolutionary War, signing the Declaration of Independence, and serving as delegates to the Constitutional

Convention. The men who shaped the democracy of the United States are often referred to as America's **Founding Fathers**.

This prestigious group includes:

- George Washington
- Alexander Hamilton
- James Madison
- John Adams
- Thomas Jefferson
- James Monroe
- Benjamin Franklin

Washington, Adams, Jefferson, Madison, and Monroe became U.S. Presidents, and Washington, Hamilton, and Madison were instrumental in leading the charge for discussion at the Constitutional Convention.

Westward Expansion

Westward expansion began with the 1803 Louisiana Purchase, which tripled America's land size. Within 50 years, America would gain all the remaining land that currently constitutes the contiguous United States. In 1845, the term *Manifest Destiny* was coined to describe the purported God-given right of Americans to own all land between the Atlantic and Pacific Oceans. Traveling west and annexing new lands allowed the U.S. government to address overcrowding issues in the East while also developing new economic opportunities including agriculture, mining, and timber harvest.

As Americans moved west, they objected to American Indian tribes' use of land and pressured the government to take action. Congress passed the Indian Removal Act in 1830, which moved tribes from their homes to reservations. American Indian tribes, first east of the Mississippi and eventually farther westward, were repeatedly displaced by government actions. One of the most famous displacements is known as the Cherokee Trail of Tears. The U.S. government repeatedly failed to deliver on promises of replacement land, food, and other necessary supplies as tribes were forced to migrate. The toll on American Indian populations was severe.

Following the admission of Texas to the United States, President Polk aggressively pursued and eventually annexed present-day California, Colorado, Arizona, New Mexico, Utah, and Nevada following the Mexican-American War. All of these areas were still inhabited by the Spanish-speaking Mexicans and American Indians who originally inhabited them. And with the white men and women who soon came for the California gold rush, a large population of Chinese migrant workers also arrived to work in mines and on railroads. However, California's state constitution made it clear that only white residents were considered true citizens with civil privileges, excluding and often exploiting American Indians, Mexican Americans, immigrants, and slaves.

Civil War and Reconstruction

Slavery

Slavery was an issue for America from its early days when Africans were brought to Virginia to work in the tobacco fields. In the 1800s, the Underground Railroad was a secret network of tunnels and safe houses that helped slaves escape slavery in the South and gain freedom in the North. Escaped slave Harriet Tubman was its most famous "conductor." Slave owners and abolitionists bitterly debated slavery, and southern leaders began to threaten secession. Slavery became the major focus of the 1860 presidential election, particularly since the South was convinced that Abraham Lincoln would abolish slavery if elected. Lincoln won the election, which only further increased tensions. Southern states began to secede in late 1860. By February 1861, they had formed the new nation of the **Confederate States of America**, electing Jefferson Davis as their president in November of that year.

Civil War

In April 1861, Confederate soldiers fired upon a Union-held ship seeking to reinforce Fort Sumter in Charleston, South Carolina. This signaled the beginning of the Civil War and divided the U.S. into the North (**Union**) and South (**Confederates**). The two sides battled for four years, and the smaller Confederate Army surprised the Union Army with their tenacity. The Confederate Army claimed various victories throughout Virginia from 1861-1863 under the leadership of General Robert E. Lee. These victories included the Battle of Bull Run, Fredericksburg, and Chancellorsville. The turning point was the **Battle of Gettysburg** in Pennsylvania, which resulted in 51,000 troops on both sides being killed, wounded, or declared missing. The Confederate Army suffered a loss of one-third of its soldiers. In 1864, Union General William T. Sherman marched through Georgia, burning Atlanta and devastating much of the landscape. In 1865, he then moved through the Carolinas to Richmond, Virginia where General Lee, who was facing the determined assaults of future president Ulysses S. Grant, surrendered. Five days later, John Wilkes Booth shot President Lincoln who was watching a play at Ford's Theatre in Washington, D.C.; Lincoln died the next morning.

Reconstruction

During the **Reconstruction** period following the Civil War, the North and South continued to wage power and economic struggles. Many African Americans from the South moved north and west to seek more fair treatment. The American frontier provided opportunities for immigrants and others seeking new prospects. Many people made their way west, farming the land and finding jobs in industries such as mining, forestry, and oil. This forced Native Americans to fight for their land or pick up and move to reservations. In the 1876 conflict known as **Custer's Last Stand**, Colonel George Custer's troops were killed by a group of Sioux Indians led by Chiefs Crazy Horse and Sitting Bull. This defeat angered the U.S. government and caused them to increase their efforts against the Indians, which put an end to the Indian Wars. The introduction of the railroad in the mid-nineteenth century provided many jobs and allowed people and goods to travel the vast landscape of North America at a much quicker pace.

Major Reform Movements

Civil Rights Movement

During this time, African Americans were still repressed, particularly in the southern U.S., and segregation was rampant in many public places. When the Supreme Court ruled that school segregation was illegal in 1954 in the revolutionary case **Brown vs. the Board of Education**, the **Civil Rights Movement** was set in motion. This movement continued throughout the 1950s and 1960s and included dozens of nonviolent protests, such as the Montgomery bus boycott in Alabama. The boycott was organized after Rosa Parks was arrested because she refused to give up her seat on the bus to a white man. The Southern Christian Leadership Conference (SCLC) was soon formed as a way to bring African Americans together to help fight segregation in a peaceful way. The Reverend Dr. Martin Luther King, Jr. was its first president. Dr. King and his supporters kept up the fight throughout the 1960s, staging sit-ins at segregated lunch counters, **Freedom Rides** on segregated buses, and marches and protests in segregated cities, such as Birmingham, Alabama. The demonstrations often ended in violence and police brutality, which served to aid the cause and led to the passage of the **Civil Rights Act** in 1964.

Women's Rights Movement

Women gained the right to vote in 1920, but still were not on equal terms with men in many areas. Suffragist leader Alice Paul had introduced the **Equal Rights Amendment (ERA)** in 1923 to help bridge this gap. Congress finally passed the ERA in 1972 and sent it to the states for ratification. However, not all states ratified the amendment, and to date only a total of thirty-five have ratified it, which is three less than the thirty-eight required to pass. In the controversial 1973 court case ***Roe v. Wade***, the Supreme Court gave women the right to legally obtain abortions within the first three months of pregnancy.

Temperance

Temperance, or the Prohibition Movement, evolved from reform movements touting that individuals should not only avoid sin but also work to help others in their communities do so. Known as teetotalers, supporters of this Progressive Era movement considered the prevalence of alcohol consumption at the time, particularly in urban areas dense with Catholic immigrants, to be a significant barrier to avoiding sin. They further blamed alcohol for numerous social problems, including domestic violence, child neglect, and unemployment. Temperance groups, including the Woman's Christian Temperance Union and Anti-Saloon League, lobbied locally and at the state and national levels to ban the sale of alcohol.

Despite the contrary efforts of brewers and distillers among others, the teetotalers' political influence led to the passage of the 18th Amendment in 1919, which made alcohol illegal in the United States. The Amendment would later be repealed in 1933 amidst the growth of organized crime and systemic corruption.

Boom and Bust Cycles

Texas has experienced numerous boom (economic growth) and bust (economic decline) cycles throughout its history. In its earliest years, Texas' economy was dominated by agriculture and cattle ranching. The Texas railroad boom that followed the Civil War allowed for the expansion of markets beyond the state and even into Canada.

Cotton farming started when the first white settlers moved into Texas. Cotton production relied heavily on slave labor before the Civil War, but Mexican labor kept production up following the Emancipation Proclamation. Texas was the leading U.S. producer of cotton by 1890. The introduction of the boll weevil nine years later caused decline, which required the industry to adapt and move westward to compensate.

The stock market crash that led to the Great Depression initiated a bust cycle when the prices of cotton and cattle dropped, a situation made even worse for farmers and ranchers by the severe wind and drought termed the Dust Bowl. Unemployment, hunger, and homelessness rose drastically; many Texans left to find work elsewhere. It wasn't until the New Deal raised cotton prices by adjusting supply that farmers who stayed were able to begin to recover economically.

The discovery of petroleum in 1901 kicked off an era of oil discovery that led to the Texas Oil Boom, the greatest period of economic growth since the Civil War. Oil production rose sharply through the early 1970s. But as investors recognized that the inevitably limited supply would run out eventually, prices soared. Prices eventually leveled off, but with the fall of OPEC, prices fell, and unemployment rose. Despite projections, Texas' oil industry underwent several more booms and busts through recent years.

World War II caused a boom as Texas was made home to military bases, factories, and hospitals, broadening the economy in a more service-oriented direction. Entrepreneurs began using government funds to develop advanced technology in existing sectors moving with oil, for example, from refinement to use in valuable and novel chemicals like synthetic rubber.

Between 1949 and 1957, a severe drought in Texas led to an immense decline of farms and ranches in the state, followed by a period of urbanization and industrialization as rural populations sought greater economic opportunity. With population growth, the state broadened its economic base even further, reducing its economic reliance on oil. Migration within the state and immigration from other areas created large, urban population centers that expanded economic diversity into technology, communications, healthcare, and higher education throughout the twenty-first century.

Twentieth Century Developments

The late nineteenth and early twentieth century not only marked U.S. expansion within North America but also internationally. For instance, after the Spanish-American War in 1898, the United States claimed control over Guam, Puerto Rico, and the Philippines. Rivalries in Europe culminated in World War I, in which great powers ranging from France to Russia vied for control in a bloody struggle. Americans did not enter the war until 1917, but we had a critical role in the final phase of the war. During the peace treaty process, President Woodrow Wilson sought to establish a League of Nations in order to promote global harmony, but his efforts only achieved limited success.

After World War I, the United States largely stayed out of international politics for the next two decades. Still, American businesses continued overseas ventures and strengthened the economy in the 1920s. However, massive speculation in the stock market in 1929 triggered the Great Depression—a financial crisis that spread worldwide as nations withdrew from the global economy. The crisis shepherded in the presidency of Franklin D. Roosevelt, who reformed the Democratic Party and implemented new federal programs known as the New Deal.

The Great Depression had ramifications worldwide and encouraged the rise of fascist governments in Italy and Germany. Highly dictatorial, fascism emphasized nationalism and militarism. World War II began when the Axis powers of Germany, Italy, and Japan built up their military forces and launched invasions against neighboring nations in 1939. As part of the Allies, which also included Britain, France, and the Soviet Union, America defeated the Axis powers in 1945 and asserted itself as a global force.

The Union of Soviet Socialist Republics had emerged through the Bolshevik Revolution in 1917 in Russia and militantly supported Communism—a socialist system of government that called for the overthrow of capitalism. Although the Soviet Union formed an alliance with the United States during World War II, relations chilled, and the Cold War began in 1947. Although no true war was declared between the two nations, both the Union of Soviet Socialist Republics and the United States engaged in indirect conflict by supporting and overthrowing foreign governments.

Meanwhile, the Civil Rights Movement began to grow as marginalized groups objected to racial segregation and abuse by whites across the nation. Civil rights leaders, such as Martin Luther King Jr., argued for nonviolent resistance, but others, such as Malcolm X, advocated more radical approaches. Civil rights groups became increasingly discontented during the Vietnam War because they felt they were being drafted for a foreign war that ignored domestic problems. Even so, significant reforms, such as the Voting Rights Act of 1965, opened up new opportunities for freedom and equality in America.

In 1991, the Soviet Union collapsed, leaving the United States as the dominant global power. However, as the United States struggled to fill the void left by the Soviet Union, questions arose about America's role in the world. Terrorist acts, such as the 9/11 attack on the World Trade Center in 2001, have shed doubt on the United States' ability to enforce its authority on an international scale.

Twentieth-Century Developments in the United States

Although the United States began industrializing in the second half of the nineteenth century, American technology continued to develop in new directions throughout the course of the twentieth century. A key example was the invention of the modern assembly line. Assembly lines and conveyor belts had already become a prominent part of industrial work, but Henry Ford combined conveyor belts with the system of assembly workers in 1913 in order to produce Model T automobiles. This streamlined production system, in which multiple parts were assembled by different teams along the conveyors, allowed industries in the United States to grow ever larger.

Ford's assembly lines also promoted the growth of the automobile as a means of transportation. Early cars were an expensive and impractical novelty and were primarily the toys of the rich. The Model T, on the other hand, was relatively affordable, which made the car available to a wider array of consumers. Many of the automobiles' early issues, such as radiator leaks and fragile tires, were gradually corrected, and this made the car more appealing than horses. With the support of President Eisenhower, the Federal Aid Highway Act of 1956 paved the way for a network of interstates and highways across the nation.

At the same time, a revolutionary approach to transportation was emerging: flight. Blimps and balloons were already gaining popularity by the turn of the twentieth century, but aviators struggled to create an airplane. The first critical success was by the Wright Brothers in 1903, and they demonstrated that aircrafts did not need to be lighter than air. In time, airplanes surpassed the popularity of balloons and blimps, which tended to be more volatile. Aircraft also added a new dimension to warfare, and aircraft carriers became an integral piece of the American navy during World War II.

Furthermore, by demonstrating that heavier-than-air vehicles could actually carry passengers upward, the stage was set for the space race in the second half of the twentieth century. In 1958, the U.S. government created the National Aeronautics and Space Administration (NASA) to head the budding initiative to extend American power into space. After the Soviet Union successfully launched the Sputnik satellite into Earth's orbit in 1957 and sent the first human in space in 1961, the United States intensified its own space program through the Apollo missions. Apollo 11 successfully landed on the moon in 1969 with Buzz Aldrin and Neil Armstrong. Later ventures into space would focus on space shuttles and satellites, and the latter significantly enhanced communications worldwide.

Indeed, the twentieth century also made considerable advancements in communications and media. Inventions such as the radio greatly boosted communication across the nation and world, such that news could be reported immediately rather than take days. Furthermore, motion pictures evolved from black-and-white movies at theaters to full-color television sets in households. From animation to live films, television matured into a compelling art form in popular culture. Live-action footage gave a new layer to news broadcasts and proved instrumental in the public's reaction to events, such as the Civil Rights Movement and the Vietnam War. With the success of the space program, satellites became a fundamental piece of Earth's communications network by transmitting signals across the planet instantaneously.

Further communications advancements resulted from the development of computer technology. The early computers in the twentieth century were enormous behemoths that were too bulky and expensive for anything but government institutions. However, computers gradually became smaller while still storing large amounts of data. A turning point came with the 1976 release of the Apple computer by entrepreneurs Steve Wozniak and Steve Jobs. The computer had a simplistic design that made it marketable for a mass consumer audience, and computers eventually became household items. Similarly, the networks that would become the Internet originated as government systems, but in time they were extended to commercial avenues that became a vibrant element of modern communications.

However, other advancements in American science during the twentieth century were aimed toward more lethal purposes. In response to the multiple wars throughout the century, the United States built up a powerful military force, and new technologies were devised for that purpose. One of the deadliest creations was the atomic bomb, which split molecular atoms to produce powerful explosions; in addition to the sheer force of the bombs, the aftereffects included toxic radiation and electronic shutdowns. Developed and used in the last days of World War II, the nuclear bomb was the United States' most powerful weapon during the Cold War.

On the other hand, the twentieth century also marked new approaches to the natural environments in America. In reaction to the depletion of natural habitats by industrialization and overhunting, President Theodore Roosevelt helped preserve areas for what would become the National Parks in 1916. Laws, such as the Clean Water Act of 1972, helped improve the health of ecosystems, which benefitted not only wildlife but people across the nation. This also led to the development of alternative energy sources such as wind and solar power.

America continues to change and grow into the twenty-first century by building on preexisting ideas but also pioneering new concepts. As globalization becomes an increasingly prominent phenomenon, American businesses strive to adapt their products to consumers worldwide while also funneling in new ideas from other nations. Yet many of the current developments in American enterprises stem in part from earlier events in American history. For instance, the environmental movement has expanded to address new issues such as global warming. NASA continues its space exploration endeavors, but entrepreneurs hope one day to travel to Mars. Therefore, the history of technology within the United States remains an engaging and relevant subject in the present.

Twentieth-Century Development in World History

At the turn of the twentieth century, imperialism had led to powers, such as France, the United States, and Japan, to establish spheres of influence throughout the world. The combination of imperial competition and military rivalries led to the outbreak of World War I when Archduke Ferdinand of Austria was assassinated in 1914. The war pitted the Allies, including England, France, and Russia, against the Central Powers of Austria-Hungary, Germany, and the Ottoman Empire—a large Islamic realm that encompassed Turkey, Palestine, Saudi Arabia, and Iraq. The rapid advances in military technology turned the war into a prolonged bloodbath that took its toll on all sides. By the end of the war in 1918, the Ottoman Empire had collapsed, the Austrian-Hungarian Empire was split into multiple countries, and Russia had descended into a civil war that would lead to the rise of the Soviet Union and Communism.

The Treaty of Versailles ended the war, but the triumphant Allies also levied heavy fines on Germany, which led to resentment that would be accentuated by the Great Depression of the 1930s. The Great Depression destabilized the global economy and led to the rise of fascism, a militarized and dictatorial system of government, in nations such as Germany and Italy. The rapid expansion of the Axis Powers of Germany, Italy, and Japan led to the outbreak of World War II. The war was even more global than the previous conflicts, with battles occurring in Europe, Africa, and Asia. World War II encouraged the development of new technologies, such as advanced radar and nuclear weapons, that would continue to influence the course of future wars.

In the aftermath of World War II, the United Nations was formed as a step toward promoting international cooperation. Based on the preceding League of Nations, the United Nations included countries from around the world and gave them a voice in world policies. The formation of the United Nations coincided with the independence of formerly colonized states in Africa and Asia, and those countries joined the world body. A primary goal of the United Nations was to limit the extent of future wars and prevent a third world war; while the United Nations could not prevent the outbreak of wars, it nevertheless tried to peacefully resolve them. In addition to promoting world peace, the United Nations also helped protect human rights.

Even so, the primary leadership in the early United Nations was held by the United States and its allies, which contributed to tensions with the Soviet Union. The United States and the Soviet Union, while never declaring war on each other, fueled a number of proxy wars and coups across the world in what would be known as the Cold War. Cold War divisions were especially noticeable in Europe, where communist regimes ruled the eastern region and democratic governments controlled the western portion. These indirect struggles often involved interference with foreign politics, and sometimes local people began to resent Soviet or American attempts to influence their countries. For instance, American and Soviet interventions in Iran and Afghanistan contributed to fundamentalist Islamic movements. The Cold War ended when the Soviet Union collapsed in 1991, but the conflict affected nations across the globe and continues to influence current issues.

Another key development during the twentieth century, as noted earlier with the United Nations, was that most colonized nations broke free from imperial control and asserted their independence. Although these nations achieved autonomy and recognition in the United Nations, they still suffered from the legacies of imperialism. The borders of many countries in Africa and Asia were arbitrarily determined by colonists with little regard to the arrangement of native populations. Therefore, many former colonies have suffered conflicts between different ethnic groups; this was also the case with the British colony in India, which became independent in 1947. Violence occurred when it split into India and Pakistan because the borders were largely based on religious differences. In addition, former colonial powers continue to assert economic control that inhibits the growth of native economies. On the other hand, the end of direct imperialism has helped a number of nations, such as India and Iran, rise as world powers that have significant influence on the world as a whole.

Additionally, there were considerable environmental reforms worldwide during the twentieth century. In reaction to the growing effects of industrialization, organizations around the world protested policies that damaged the environment. Many of these movements were locally based, but others expanded to address various environmental threats across the globe. The United Nations helped carry these environmental reforms forward by making them part of international policies. For instance, in 1997, many members of the United Nations signed a treaty, known as the *Kyoto Protocol*, that tried to reduce global carbon dioxide emissions.

Most significantly, the twentieth century marked increasing globalization. The process had already been under way in the nineteenth century as technological improvements and imperial expansions connected different parts of the world, but the late twentieth century brought globalization to a new level. Trade became international, and local customs from different lands also gained prominence worldwide. Cultural exchanges occur on a frequent basis, and many people have begun to ponder the consequences of such rapid exchanges. One example of globalization was the 1993 establishment of the European Union—an economic and political alliance between several European nations.

Impact of Historical Events on Contemporary Societies

Contemporary societies have been shaped by all the historical events that led up to their current status. When societies have been invaded, taken over forcibly in conquests, or colonized by other countries, often the native society, customs, and political and economic structures become suppressed. When more powerful societies move into an area, they may displace native populations and exploit the people and resources.

Consequently, the dominant culture, language, and religion in societies where such events have taken place usually reflect those of the people who took over the area, not those who originally inhabited it. The people of native societies also often suffer repression in the form of slavery and brutality. Their populations may decline as they are exposed to new diseases against which they have no immunity, as was the case the American Indians. The dominant society exploits local resources for their own gain, sometimes polluting, destroying, or eliminating the native societies' resources in the process.

If and when the native society is able to regain control of its area by winning independence, it often lacks the appropriate infrastructure, economic independence, and political organization to promote their own well-being and further development.

Geography and Culture

Key Concepts in Geography

Geography is essential in understanding the world as a whole. This requires a study of spatial distribution, which examines how various locations and physical features are arranged in the world. The most common element in geography is the region, which refers to a specific area that is separate from surrounding ones. Regions can be defined based on a variety of factors, including environmental, economic, or political features, and these different kinds of regions can overlap with each other.

It is also important to know the difference between location and place. A location, defined either through its physical position or through its relation to other locations, determines where something is, and this characteristic is static. A place, on the other hand, describes a combination of physical and human elements in relation to each other; the determination of place is therefore changeable depending on the movement of individuals and groups.

Places and Regions

Both absolute and relative location help humans understand their sense of place. Place is a simple concept that helps to define the characteristics of the world around us. For example, people may create **toponyms** to further define and orient themselves with their sense of place. Toponyms are simply names given to locations to help develop familiarity within a certain location. Although not always the case, toponyms generally utilize geographical features, important people in an area, or even wildlife commonly found in a general location. For example, many cities in the state of Texas are named in honor of military leaders who fought in the Texas Revolution of 1836 (such as Houston and Austin), while other places, such as Mississippi and Alabama, utilize Native American toponyms to define their sense of place.

Regions

Geographers divide the world into regions in order to more fully understand differences inherent with the world, its people, and its environment. Lines of latitude such as the Equator, the Tropics, and the Arctic and Antarctic Circles already divide the Earth into solar regions relative to the amount of either direct or indirect sunlight that they receive. Although not the same throughout, the middle latitudes generally have a milder climate than areas found within the tropics. Furthermore, tropical locations are usually warmer than places in the middle latitudes, but that is not always the case. For example, the lowest place in the United States—Death Valley, California—is also home to the nation's highest-ever recorded temperature. Likewise, the Andes Mountains in Peru and Ecuador, although found near the Equator, are also home to heavy snow, low temperatures, and dry conditions, due to their elevation.

Formal regions are spatially defined areas that have overarching similarities or some level of **homogeneity** or **uniformity.** Although not exactly alike, a formal region generally has at least one characteristic that is consistent throughout the entire area. For example, the United States could be broken down into one massive formal region due to the fact that in all fifty states, English is the primary language. Of course, English isn't the only language spoken in the United States, but throughout that nation, English is heavily used. As a result, geographers are able to classify the United States as a formal region; but, more specifically, the United States is a **linguistic region**—a place where everyone generally speaks the same language.

Functional regions are similar to formal regions in that they have similar characteristics, but they do not have clear boundaries. The best way to understand these sorts of regions is to consider large cities. Each large city encompasses a large **market area,** whereby people in its vicinity generally travel there to conduct business, go out to eat, or watch a professional sporting event. However, once anyone travels farther away from that **primate city**, they transition to a different, more accessible city for their needs. The functional region, or **area of influence**, for that city, town, or sports team transitions, depending upon the availability of other primate cities. For example, New York City has two primary professional baseball, basketball, and football teams. As a result, its citizens may have affinities for different teams even though they live in the same city. Conversely, a citizen in rural Idaho may cheer for the Seattle Seahawks, even though they live over 500 miles from Seattle, due to the lack of a closer primate city.

Influence of Geographic Factors

Across the globe, humans have adapted to the unique conditions of numerous geographical areas, developing shelter and managing food sources based on the physical characteristics of their landscape. Some people groups migrate to ensure that they can meet all their needs, while others adapt to their environment. Those who live in mountainous areas, for example, may terrace their hillsides to allow for agriculture, while those who live in desert areas may develop irrigation systems for the same purpose.

Societies have traditionally settled in areas that are rich in the resources needed to survive. Historically, communities commonly lived near bodies of water, but not just for its life-sustaining necessity. Water serves as a natural border and as a means of uniting societies through transportation and trade. The Port of Galveston, a large port through which many resources arrive in Texas, is an excellent example of how water can impact trade, development, and economy.

In the United States, native populations had their own approaches to the ways they relied on and used the land they called home. However, as the population of white settlers grew and expanded, they saw their relationship with the land differently than the original American Indian inhabitants. While American Indians left large tracts of land undeveloped for hunting and gathering, white American settlers saw this as a waste of resources and preferred instead to divide the land into much smaller tracts used almost exclusively for agriculture. In the Western United States, including Texas, this disagreement combined with the political clout of white settlers led to the displacement, enslavement, and death of thousands of American Indians in the name of Manifest Destiny.

This is one of many global examples of colonialism and conquests by which more powerful societies and nations exploit the resources of an area at the expense of the people living there. Geographic areas where economically valuable natural resources are found (e.g., coal, oil, and diamonds) are particularly vulnerable to tense political relationships and colonialism. Historically, another country assumes power, exploits the resource, and often leaves the native society ill-prepared to govern themselves, while simultaneously imposing their culture on the native people.

In addition to the political and social consequences of humans' use of the natural environment, there are also direct impacts on the environment itself. Pollution of water, air, and soil may result from the mining, refinement, and use of natural resources. Such environmental degradation also has secondary social and political effects. People don't generally want to live in areas where the environment has been degraded to a point where it can be harmful, so those with the lowest incomes typically live closer to such polluted areas. Other effects, such as damming for irrigation, may impact neighboring communities' access to necessary natural resources. Neighboring areas may have to work together to mitigate these issues or navigate the conflicts they cause. They may rely on the government to protect them from such circumstances.

Physical Processes and Their Effects on Environmental Patterns

Weathering and Erosion

Weathering is the process of breaking rock while **erosion** is the process of moving rock. Weathering can be caused by both physical and chemical changes. Mechanical forces such as roots growing, animal contact, wind, and extreme weather cause weathering. Another cause is the water cycle, which includes flowing water, moving glaciers, and liquid ice seeping into rocks and cracking them as water freezes and expands. Chemical weathering actually transforms the regolith into clay and soft minerals. One consequence of chemical weathering is corrosive acid rain.

Continental Drift (Plate Tectonics)

In 1912, Alfred Wegener proposed that at one point in Earth's history, all of the continents were joined in one supercontinent (now known as Pangaea) and gradually separated to form the seven separate continents as they currently exist. The evidence, he argued, was present in the fact that fossils of similar species were found on continents several thousand miles apart. Unfortunately, Wegener had no model to explain the mechanism in which this occurred, so his theory was discarded.

However, Wegener's proposal was the foundation for **plate tectonics**, the theory that Earth's crust is composed of rigid, moving rock plates called the **lithosphere**. They move by gliding slowly over Earth's outer **mantle**, a layer of slowly moving silicate rock propelled by the hot magma below it. As hot rock from Earth's core rises to the surface, it causes the fragmented pieces of the crust to spread apart, moving away from each other. As the hot rock begins to cool, it sinks towards Earth's core, causing the plates above it to sink as well, meanwhile pushing the adjacent plates over the sinking plates. The deep trench created by the sinking and pushing is called the **subduction zone**. This process of spreading and sinking is the underlying cause of the movement of the continents.

Subduction

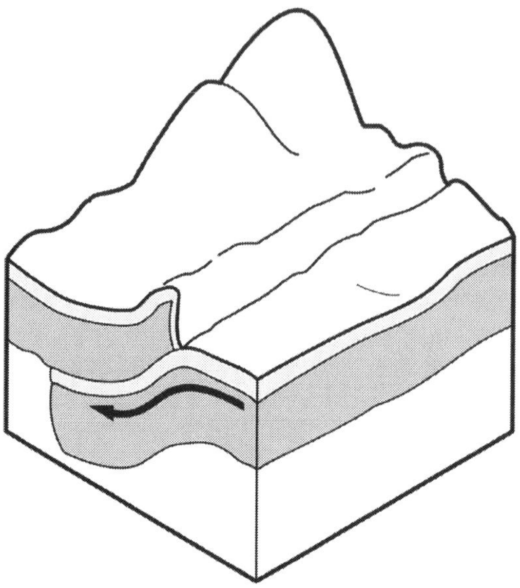

Development and Movement of Weather Patterns

A **weather pattern** is weather that's consistent for a period of time. Weather patterns are created by fronts. A **cold front** is created when two air masses collide in a high-pressure system. A **warm front** is created when a low-pressure system results from the collision of two air masses; they are usually warmer and less dense than high-pressure systems. When a cold front enters an area, the air from the warm front is forced upwards. The temperature of the warm front's air decreases, condenses, and often creates clouds and precipitation. When a warm front moves into an area, the warm air moves slowly upwards at an angle. Clouds and precipitation form, but the precipitation generally lasts longer because of how slowly the air moves.

Impacts of Developments in Science and Technology

Often, science and technology make it easier to access physical resources. Advanced technologies facilitate locating, extracting, refining, and utilizing natural resources, while also creating significantly greater impacts on the natural environment. The extraction and use of fossil fuels, for example, can pollute waterways and soil as well as alter or destroy natural ecosystems. Their use as a fuel, which is extensively relied upon for everything from keeping lights on to charging electronic devices, creates air pollution that has been shown to contribute to climate change.

While the natural environment may suffer, economies often thrive thanks to technological advances. For example, new technology allows for the extraction of natural gas that wasn't accessible 50 years ago, which provides a new source of energy and thus lowers consumer costs. Lower costs usually lead to increased spending, which should promote economic development. With economic development, societies are better able to provide opportunities to their members and help them thrive.

Often, however, the economic growth is not equitable across all members of society. While technology grows, some economic sectors are phased out. For example, computers do make some manual jobs obsolete. Postindustrial information-based societies generally thrive as technological developments advance, but the economies of such societies have significantly more opportunities for people with college educations.

The often generationally repeated lack of access to higher education marginalizes members of society without degrees, making it increasingly difficult for them to find work to maintain or advance their status. Simultaneously, the use of technology allows businesses to leverage human resources from all over the world, as geography is now rarely a barrier to communication and collaboration. This can increase global opportunity while exacerbating local inequity.

Maps and Their Elements

Geography is visually conveyed using maps, and a collection of maps is called an atlas. To illustrate some key points about geography, please refer to the map below.

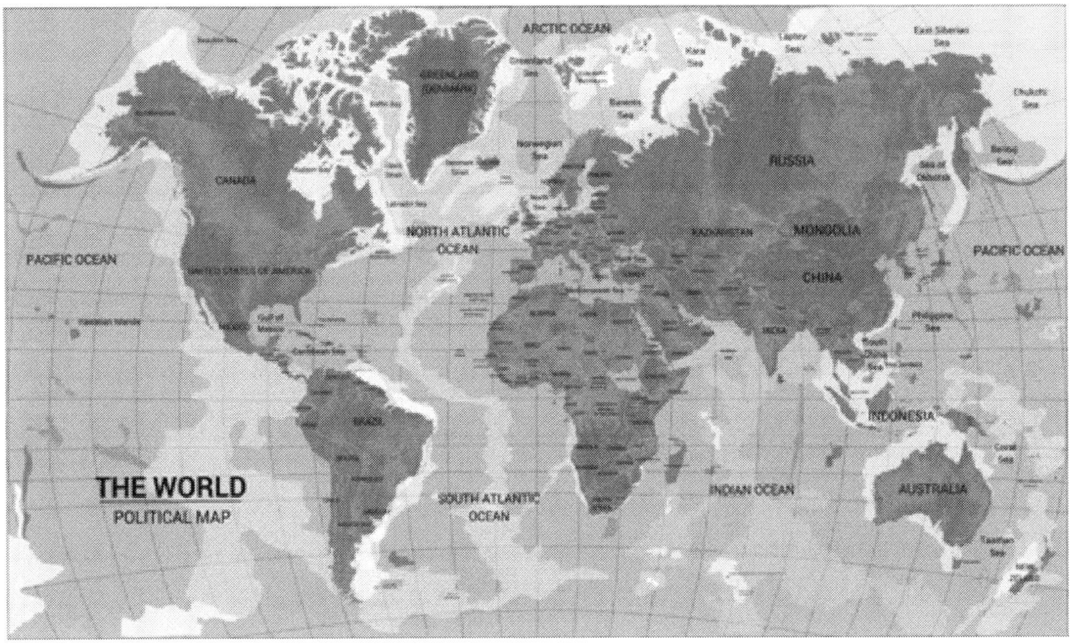

This is a traditional map of the world that displays all of the countries and six of the seven continents. Countries, the most common approach to political regions, can be identified by their labels. The continents are not identified on this map, with the exception of Australia, but they are larger landmasses that encompass most of the countries in their respective areas; the other five visible continents are North America, South America, Europe, Africa, and Asia. The seventh continent, Antarctica, is found at the South Pole and has been omitted from the map.

The absence of Antarctica leads into the issues of distortion, in which geographical features are altered on a map. Some degree of distortion is to be expected with a two-dimensional flat map of the world because Earth is a sphere. A map projection transforms a spherical map of the world into a flattened perspective, but the process generally alters the spatial appearance of landmasses. For instance, Greenland often appears, such as in the map above, larger than it really is.

Furthermore, Antarctica's exclusion from the map is, in fact, a different sort of distortion—that of the mapmakers' biases. Mapmakers determine which features are included on the map and which ones are not. Antarctica, for example, is often missing from maps because, unlike the other continents, it has a limited human population. Moreover, a study of the world reveals that many of the distinctions on maps are human constructions.

Even so, maps can still reveal key features about the world. For instance, the map above has areas that seem almost three-dimensional and jut out. They represent mountains and are an example of topography, which is a method used to display the differing elevations of the terrain. A more detailed topographical map can be viewed below.

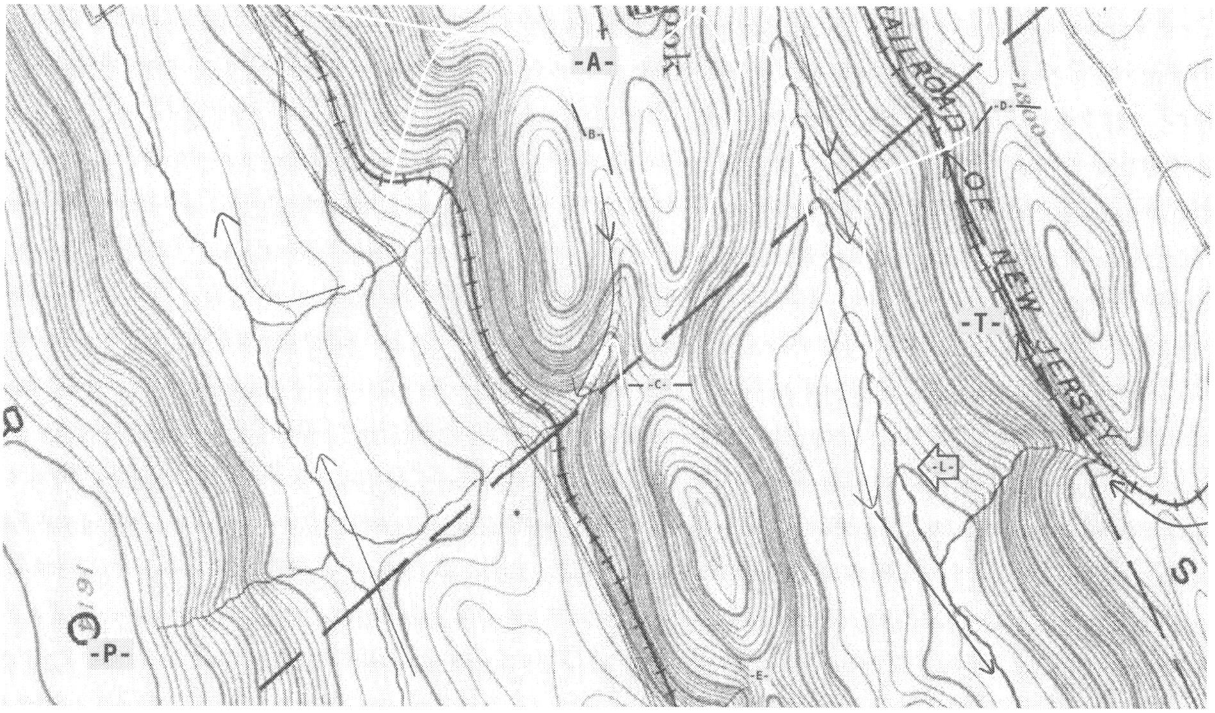

On some colored maps, the oceans, represented in blue between the continents, vary in coloration depending on depth. The differences demonstrate *bathymetry*, which is the study of the ocean floor's depth. Paler areas represent less depth, while darker spots reflect greater depth.

Please also note the many lines running horizontally and vertically along the map. The horizontal lines, known as *parallels,* mark the calculated latitude of those locations and reveal how far north or south these areas are from the equator, which bisects the map horizontally. Generally, with exceptions depending on specific environments, climates closer to the equator are warmer because this region receives the most direct sunlight. The equator also serves to split the globe between the Northern and Southern hemispheres.

Longitude, as signified by the vertical lines, determines how far east or west different regions are from each other. The lines of longitude, known as meridians, are also the basis for time zones, which allocate different times to regions depending on their position eastward and westward of the prime meridian. As one travels west between time zones, the given time moves backward accordingly. Conversely, if one travels east, the time moves forward.

There are two particularly significant longitude-associated dividers in this regard. The prime [Greenwich] meridian, as displayed below, is defined as zero degrees in longitude, and thus determines the other lines. The line, in fact, circles the globe north and south, and it therefore divides the world into the Eastern and Western hemispheres. It is important to not confuse the Greenwich meridian with the International Date Line, which is an invisible line in the Pacific Ocean that was created to represent the change between calendar days. By traveling westward across the International Date Line, a traveler would essentially leap forward a day. For example, a person departing from the United States on Sunday would arrive in Japan on Monday. By traveling eastward across the line, a traveler would go backward a day. For example, a person departing from China on Monday would arrive in Canada on Sunday.

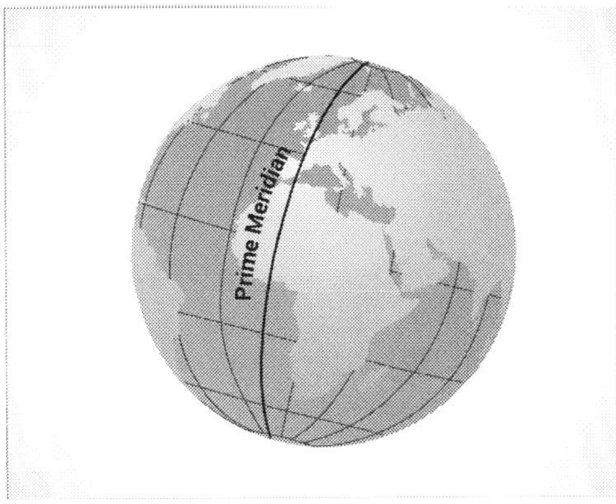

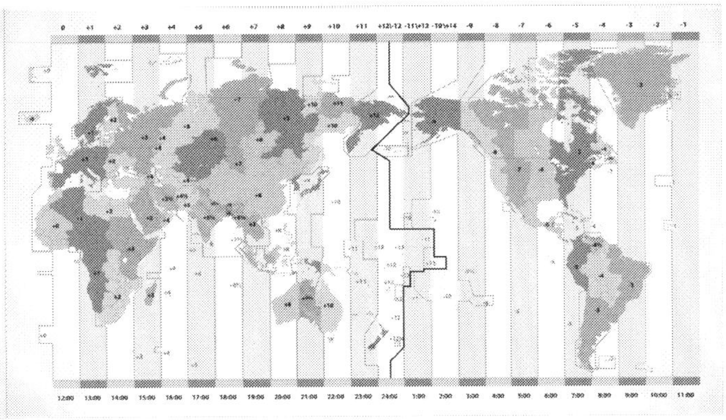

Although world maps are useful in showing the overall arrangement of continents and nations, it is also important at times to look more closely at individual countries because they have unique features that are only visible on more detailed maps.

For example, take the following map of the United States of America. It should be noted that the country is split into multiple states that have their own culture and localized governments. Other countries are often split into various divisions, such as provinces, and while these features are ignored for the sake of clarity on larger maps, they are important when studying specific nations. Individual states can be further subdivided into counties and townships, and they may have their own maps that can be examined for closer analysis.

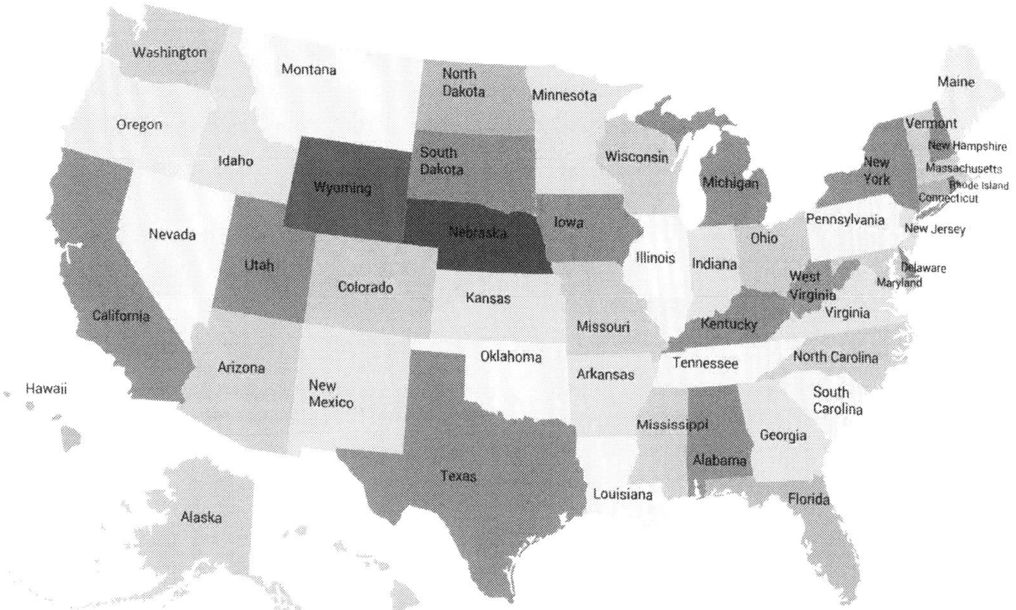

Finally, one of the first steps in examining any map should be to locate the map's key or legend, which will explain what features different symbols represent on the map. As these symbols can be arbitrary depending on the maker, a key will help to clarify the different meanings.

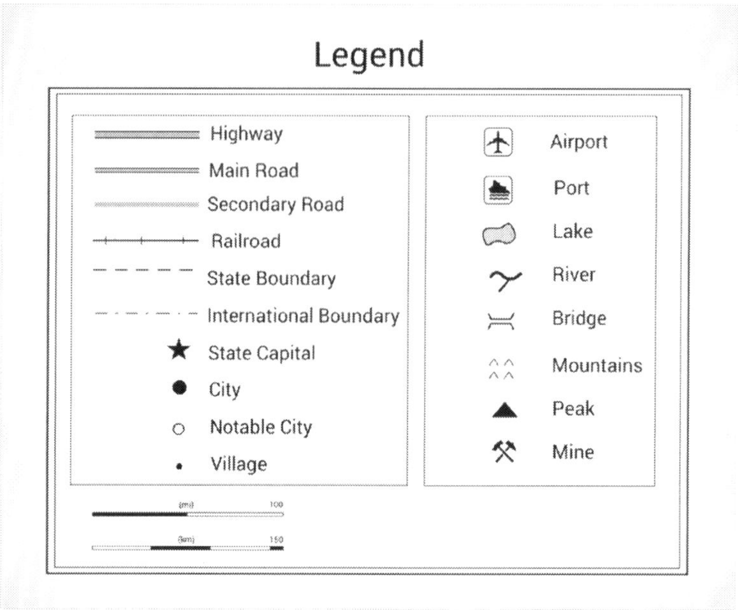

Contributions of Various Civilizations

Various civilizations throughout history have made significant contributions to cultural advancement. Mesopotamia was home to one of the earliest civilizations between the Euphrates and the Tigris rivers in the Near East. The rivers provided water and vegetation for early humans, but they were surrounded by desert. This led to the beginning of irrigation efforts to expand water and agriculture across the region, which resulted in the area being known as the Fertile Crescent.

The organization necessary to initiate canals and other projects led to the formation of cities and hierarchies, which would have considerable influence on the structure of later civilizations. For instance, the new hierarchies established different classes within the societies, such as kings, priests, artisans, and workers. Over time, these city-states expanded to encompass outside territories, and the city of Akkad became the world's first empire in 2350 B.C. In addition, Mesopotamian scribes developed systemized drawings called pictograms, which were the first system of writing in the world; furthermore, the creation of wedge-shaped cuneiform tablets preserved written records for multiple generations.

Later, Mesopotamian kingdoms made further advancements. For instance, Babylon established a sophisticated mathematical system based on numbers from one to sixty; this not only influenced modern concepts, such as the number of minutes in each hour, but also created the framework for math equations and theories. In addition, the Babylonian king Hammurabi established a complex set of laws, known as the Code of Hammurabi, which would set a precedent for future legal systems.

Meanwhile, another major civilization began to form around the Nile River in Africa. The Nile's relatively predictable nature allowed farmers to use the river's water and the silt from floods to grow many crops along its banks, which led to further advancements in irrigation. Egyptian rulers mobilized the kingdom's population for incredible construction projects, including the famous pyramids. Egyptians also improved pictographic writing with their more complex system of hieroglyphs, which allowed for more diverse styles of writing. The advancements in writing can be seen through the Egyptians' complex system of religion, with documents such as the **Book of the Dead** outlining not only systems of worship and pantheons of deities but also a deeper, more philosophical concept of the afterlife.

While civilizations in Egypt and Mesopotamia helped to establish class systems and empires, other forms of government emerged in Greece. Despite common ties between different cities, such as the Olympic Games, each settlement, known as a polis, had its own unique culture. Many of the cities were oligarchies, in which a council of distinguished leaders monopolized the government; others were dictatorships ruled by tyrants. Athens was a notable exception by practicing an early form of democracy in which free, landholding men could participate, but it offered more freedom of thought than other systems.

Taking advantage of their proximity to the Mediterranean Sea, Greek cities sent expeditions to establish colonies abroad that developed their own local traditions. In the process, Greek merchants interacted with Phoenician traders, who had developed an alphabetic writing system built on sounds instead of pictures. This diverse network of exchanges made Greece a vibrant center of art, science, and philosophy. For example, the Greek doctor Hippocrates established a system of ethics for doctors called the Hippocratic Oath, which continues to guide the modern medical profession. Complex forms of literature were created, including the epic poem "The Iliad," and theatrical productions were also developed. Athens in particular sought to spread its vision of democratic freedom throughout the world, which led to the devastating Peloponnesian War between allies of Athens and those of oligarchic Sparta from 431 to 404 B.C.

Alexander the Great helped disseminate Greek culture to new regions. Alexander was in fact an heir to the throne of Macedon, which was a warrior kingdom to the north of Greece. After finishing his father's work of unifying Greece under Macedonian control, Alexander successfully conquered Mesopotamia, which had been part of the Persian Empire. The spread of Greek institutions throughout the Mediterranean and Near East led to a period of Hellenization, during which various civilizations assimilated Greek culture; this allowed Greek traditions, such as architecture and philosophy, to endure into the present day.

Greek ideas were later assimilated, along with many other concepts, into the Roman Empire. Located west of Greece on the Italian peninsula, Rome greatly expanded its territories and grew to be a powerful empire through the conquering of its neighboring civilizations; by 44 B.C., Rome had conquered much of Western Europe, northern Africa, and the Near East. Romans were very creative, and they adapted new ideas and innovated new technologies to strengthen their power. For instance, Romans built on the engineering knowledge of Greeks to create arched pathways, known as aqueducts, to transport water for long distances and devise advanced plumbing systems.

One of Rome's greatest legacies was its system of government. Early Rome was a republic, a democratic system in which leaders are elected by the people. Although the process still heavily favored wealthy elites, the republican system was a key inspiration for later institutions such as the United States. Octavian "Augustus" Caesar later made Rome into an empire, and the senate had only a symbolic role in the government. The new imperial system built on the examples of earlier empires to establish a vibrant dynasty that used a sophisticated legal code and a well-trained military to enforce order across vast regions. Even after Rome itself fell to barbarian invaders in fifth century A.D., the eastern half of the empire survived as the Byzantine Empire until 1453 A.D. Furthermore, the Roman Empire's institutions continued to influence and inspire later medieval kingdoms, including the Holy Roman Empire; even rulers in the twentieth century called themselves Kaiser and Tsar, titles which stem from the word "Caesar."

In addition, the Roman Empire was host to the spread of new religious ideas. In the region of Israel, the religion of Judaism presented a new approach to worship via monotheism, which is the belief in the existence of a single deity. An offshoot of Judaism called Christianity spread across the Roman Empire and gained popularity. While Rome initially suppressed the religion, it later backed Christianity and allowed the religious system to endure as a powerful force in medieval times.

Effects of Race, Gender, and Socioeconomic Class

As societies develop, resource distribution becomes less equitable, which creates or exacerbates social stratification.

Historically, women and ethnic/racial minorities have been viewed as inferior around the world. A good example of this is how Texas formerly belonged to Native Americans and Mexicans who were then marginalized and displaced after white settlers moved into the area. Greater in political clout, though smaller in numbers, white settlers used their self-serving laws and resulting power to relocate and enslave minorities.

With a lack of resources and opportunities to improve their situations, the plight of these people groups was passed down generationally. While the dominant class can meet, if not exceed, their basic needs, they are also more likely to have gainful employment and seek educational opportunities that prepare them to seek employment in more technical fields. This is especially important as societies are transformed from industrial to post-industrial or information societies.

Those who have been historically discriminated against may not even have the resources to meet their families' basic needs. They experience higher levels of unemployment and lower levels of education. Without these opportunities, it is difficult for them to move beyond the oppression their families have faced for generations.

Further, without representation in the government, they have no means to improve their chances of gaining these opportunities, unless someone in the dominant demographic acknowledges their plight and implements effective means of addressing the root causes of inequity.

As an educator, being aware of these inequities is a good step in the direction of helping groups who have been historically or may even currently be discriminated against to get the support they need to transcend the generations of injustice that oppressed them in their societies.

Cultural Customs, Celebrations, and Traditions

School schedules in the United States generally follow an Anglo-Christian calendar with breaks scheduled around holidays in that tradition. However, modern classrooms house students from diverse backgrounds who may celebrate different and/or additional holidays. By identifying students' cultures and customs, teachers may incorporate them into the curriculum and help students to learn about each other's traditions.

Most schools observe breaks for Christmas, a traditionally Christian holiday celebrating the birth of Jesus. As traditionally Catholic, many Mexicans celebrate the nine days before Christmas with the posada ("inn") fiesta. Families join in a celebration that includes reenacting Mary and Joseph's arrival and search for lodging in Bethlehem where Jesus was to be born. Part of the family plays the role of the innkeeper within the house, who eventually welcome the rest of the family representing Mary and Joseph. Together, they celebrate with food, drink, and a piñata.

Jewish students, whose faith does not believe Jesus was divine, may alternatively celebrate Hannukah. This eight-day winter festival of lights celebrates Jews' reclamation of the temple in Jerusalem from the Greeks.

Those in the African American community may celebrate Kwanza, a cultural celebration that runs from December 26th through January 1st. With festivities including feasts, dancing, and music, celebrants reflect on and recommit to The Seven Principles: unity, self-determination, collective work and responsibility, cooperative economics, purpose, creativity, and faith.

Though not all students celebrate these traditions, teaching them about other cultures and religions promotes understanding and acceptance, despite differences.

Roles of Families

Family life has changed as societies have developed from hunter-gatherer to post-industrial. Hunter-gatherer societies were among the most equitable, as the community members worked together, and no one had more than anyone else. All family members were active in the gathering and/or preparation of food. Women typically carried their children with them as they worked in this nomadic lifestyle and were very attentive. Additionally, children learned the ways the community worked and lived through experience.

The shift to an agricultural society created more gender bias. Men conducted much of the labor while women completed domestic work and birthed children. Children were taught to work on the farm from a young age, often at the expense of an education. But with the ability to store food, families no longer needed to be nomadic and were able to settle in one place.

Industrial societies generally provide employment opportunities to both men and women. The ability to work many hours could impact family life by limiting the time spent at home together. Without laws to prevent it, industrial societies might also employ very young children, sometimes for long hours, which limits their access to education.

In post-industrial societies, men and women both have the ability to work. Family life differs depending on how many adult family members in a household work. Post-industrial employment is lucrative enough that children don't need to work. They generally pursue education and often earn college degrees, which allows them to find their own jobs that require higher education or skill levels.

Traditions differ with the type of society. In hunter-gatherer societies, for example, large pieces of game would require many people and hours to process and cook. Food preparation and consumption could easily become a social event. The technology of post-industrial times makes cooking much quicker and easier, and it is also possible to purchase pre-prepared food. In any level of development, however, traditions and customs are important in building a sense of belonging in the family and community. They transfer values and culture from one generation to another and bond family members together.

Native American Groups Before European Colonization

Native American tribes shared many characteristics including a connection with the spirit world, especially related to nature and the resources needed for survival. They varied based on language, how they obtained food, what they wore, and the structures of their homes, which were all often based on the physical characteristics of and resources available in their home ranges. Tribal groups engaged in trade with each other and also experienced conflict, often related to competition.

There were four Native American cultural areas in Texas, as defined by Europeans: Western Gulf, Southeast, Southwest, and Plains. Smaller groups within each of these arbitrarily defined areas were unique and diverse in their cultures and languages. Examples of a few Texan tribes are described below.

The Caddos of East Texas were an agricultural society who lived in permanent wood-framed houses and had social ranking levels. They are recognized as having the most complex societies of Native American Indians in Texas.

The Karankawas of the Gulf coast were nomads who traveled and fished for food in their dugout canoes. They lived in animal skin wigwams set up around a central fire, always near the shoreline, and communicated over distances with smoke signaling.

The Coahuiltecan lived in south Texas, with some living in the Rio Grande delta. They were nomadic hunter-gatherers who lived in small, independent groups of only a few dozen people. Larger groups would congregate in summer to feast on prickly pear and interact socially. Upon settling in a new area to use the available food there, they would build circular huts made of poles covered with woven mats.

Other tribes, including the Cherokee and Shawnee, migrated to Texas as they lost their homes east of the Mississippi to the U.S government.

Diversity Within Cultures

When studying different cultures, it is important to realize that cultures are always changing in response to individuals and groups within it. Therefore, one must avoid stereotyping members of a certain culture or overgeneralizing. For example, American culture is highly diverse with multiple ethnic groups. Many ethnic communities have resided in the United States for generations, so it is incorrect to label them as a foreign culture, yet each group must be closely examined to understand American culture as a whole.

This diversity within larger classifications of cultures can be seen with Native Americans. There are many different tribes of Native Americans, and each has its own unique history and characteristics. Nevertheless, a few general qualities describe most Native American groups. First of all, Native Americans continue to struggle to escape the poverty that they were historically forced into during white settlement of the United States. Many, but not all, tribes have been traditionally matrilineal—with ancestry defined through female lineage—and emphasized communal sharing and a sustainable relationship with nature, but the American government often suppressed these customs. This has led many Native Americans to begin protecting their surviving heritage, including their rights to traditional religious practices and access to historical artifacts.

South of the United States, Mexico has a vibrant yet troubled culture. Mexico was one of the principal colonies of Spain, and the culture is therefore a diverse blend of Spanish and native customs. One enduring legacy of Spain's rule is the prominence of Roman Catholicism, albeit mixed with pre-Spanish concepts; for instance, the traditional Day of the Dead embodies both pre-Columbian and Christian ideals. On the other hand, the Spanish system of large estates created significant class disparities. Furthermore, Mexico's war for independence and conflicts with other nations drastically destabilized its government, and the nation continues to struggle with corruption and violence. Still, Mexico retains a rich culture that celebrates its complex history. Mexican families are generally large and cooperate to help each other.

French national identity is relatively new because regional ties were prevalent until the French Revolution in the 1790s. A rising sense of nationalism unites French culture today, but various regions maintain their own local traditions. Much of France has been traditionally agricultural, but the globalization of the food trade has disrupted local markets and led to mass migration to cities. Reflecting Catholic values, most of France's families follow a nuclear model of a two-parent household with children.

South Africa is culturally and ethnically diverse, but historically white settlers used apartheid to oppress and isolate other groups. However, previously marginalized ethnic groups are now actively working to assert their own identity within South Africa. Rural communities tend to be more traditional, while people within cities have adopted new values. South Africa is largely patriarchal with defined gender roles that give men dominance over women. Efforts to strengthen South Africa's industries have depleted many of its natural resources and created a growing environmental crisis that is particularly devastating to rural populations.

Laying claim to the legacies of ancient Persia, Iran's culture was at the crossroads of trade routes between multiple continents for centuries, which gave it a long and diverse background. Iran is primarily Islamic, with the majority of Muslims belonging to the Shi'a faith. They believe that their religious leaders, imams, are divinely appointed as the religious successors, known as caliphs, to the prophet Muhammad; even so, other religions such as Judaism and Zoroastrianism are also practiced in the country. Iran's patriarchal culture generally restricts the role of women, but women have nevertheless become more involved in the civil service, sciences, and other fields.

Russia's culture is built on a rich history but has been especially influenced by the dominance of communism until the Soviet Union's dissolution in 1991. The use of state police and other agents to enforce government policies led to a sense of paranoia and distrust of anyone outside the family. On the other hand, this situation created strong support networks within families that led to strong relationships with relatives. The Soviet Union's drive to industrialize also led to numerous current environmental issues across Russia.

As with Russia, the People's Republic of China's modern culture is deeply influenced by decades of Communist rule. Under the leadership of Mao, China enacted massive efforts to strengthen Chinese industry and agriculture at the cost of environmental damage; China continues to undergo intense industrial operations in the present, which has caused pollution in the cities. On the other hand, China takes great pride in its long traditions and history that date back thousands of years. China has been traditionally patriarchal, and children have been expected to respect and care for their elders. Chinese culture is not monolithic, and there are many different ethnic groups within the country, including the Han, Manchu, and Uyghur. However, the one-child policy from 1978 to 2015 has destabilized long-term family dynamics by putting considerable pressure on single children to look after their parents.

Japan's family structure has also been disrupted in the modern era. Japanese culture is built on a sense of interdependence within families and the community as a whole, but a low birthrate has led to a rising number of elderly relatives and few children, which has unsettled the traditional foundation. Even so, Japan embraces a blend of modern advancements and traditional customs. Japanese culture is built on multiple layers of social status, and people use different forms of language depending on their relationship with others. As a result, traditional Japanese society is highly formal, but recent generations have become more open to new ideas. As Japan's islands have limited space and resources, it has been at the forefront of many natural conservation efforts, although some controversial traditions, such as whaling, still persist.

Integrating Geography and Cultural Studies with Other Disciplines

From the physical environment of a particular area to the disagreements among societies that neighbor each other geographically, historical events are driven by geography. When a community upstream dams a river and limits water access for a community downstream, geography is creating a conflict that may set a historic precedent for how similar situations are handled in the future.

Similarly, cultures are shaped by their physical environments and the impact of neighboring cultures. Sociology is the social science that studies relationships among the people and institutions of a culture and how they impact each other. Within sociology, people belong to groups based on factors such as race, ethnicity, age, gender, and class. Because each culture views these factors differently, sociologists can study how that unique view impacts life for members of that culture. They may examine, for example, the relationship between gender inequality as a social structure within a culture and how that relates to levels of education and employment.

Anthropology is another social science that studies geography and culture and how they relate to humanity. It aims to better understand humans as a distinct, yet historically and geographically diverse species. Archeology, one branch of anthropology, relies on the use of field work to excavate sites and learn more about how ancient societies lived. An archeologist would be able to discuss the differences between Texan Native American tribes based on the tools they used and food they ate, as evidenced by the artifacts found in their home ranges. Alternatively, cultural anthropologists collect data by interacting with societal groups. They may learn more about Texan Native American tribes by speaking with their descendants.

Geographical and Cultural Research

While physical geography focuses on the natural world and how it is affected by physical processes, human geography focuses on how physical geography shapes people's lives, as well as their interactions with nature and each other. Human geography, also called cultural geography, is more of a social science than physical geography. It uses research to examine how culture is built and how it changes as people travel and move to different geographic areas. Human geographers may study aspects of culture including art, language, religion, governmental structures, and economic systems. Through such data, geographers examine the reasons why particular cultural conventions occur in a specific place, compare those with conventions in other places, and learn more about how and why they differ. Studying different cultures' connections with each other and their environments can provide information on global issues like social inequality, poverty, development, immigration, and human impact on the environment.

Research in human geography uses both quantitative (i.e., measurable, numerical data) and qualitative (i.e., non-numerical data, often personal accounts) methods to collect and analyze data. Both forms aim to find relationships between different aspects of cultures. Often, data collection requires fieldwork. Both quantitative and qualitative data may come from either primary or secondary sources. Primary sources include on-the-ground interviews, questionnaires, and surveys; they are collected directly from the source. Secondary sources include input from others who comment on or interpret primary sources. As with all good research, sources must be evaluated to determine the author's point of view and whether bias may impact the data.

Quantitative forms of research include measurement through experiments, questionnaires, surveys with set response options, and information from databases. Once data are collected, they are analyzed numerically with statistics to identify relationships among different variables. Quantitative data can reveal cause-and-effect relationships. For example, comparing the fertility rate (number of children per woman) in an area with the percentage of women who complete high school may indicate a relationship, or lack thereof, between the two variables. Mapping is frequently used to display data, particularly through geographic information systems (GIS), which allows for the comparison of different map layers and the data they contain.

Qualitative forms of research include interviews, focus groups, observation, oral history, records, and open-ended surveys. Maps and photographs can also be used to gather data for research. Following collection, the researcher will code the data based on themes that were either predetermined or developed afterward based on the data. Qualitative research often seeks details to better understand why a particular behavior or relationship between two variables is observed. In the above example, if fertility rate and education level are linked, researchers could conduct surveys to attempt to find the reason why the relationship exists as such.

One limitation of qualitative research is that the cost and time involved often limit the sample size (the number of data points collected). In scientific study, more data always makes for more reliable conclusions. Further, qualitative data is much more subjective than quantitative. The interpretations and conclusions made are vulnerable to the bias of the researcher.

Analyzing Geographic and Cultural Data

Geographical data includes maps, aerial photographs (taken from the sky), satellite photographs (taken from space), and geographic information system (GIS) data. They may be collected from libraries, image collections, and other databases; many have been digitized.

Aerial and satellite images can be used to compare changes in the natural environment or communities (e.g., urbanization) over time. GIS is a computer-based program that stores data in map layers that can be overlain upon each other to see the relationship among different data types. GIS is useful in comparing two types of data to make a decision. It might be used to identify neighborhoods that could reasonably house a new school by overlaying neighborhoods and school districts. Alternatively, comparing a parks and open spaces layer with one that shows the location of industrial complexes could highlight possible locations for a new park, ensuring that it's not near any air-polluting industrial complexes.

Cultural data include educational, economic (e.g., employment rates, dominant industries), and sociologic data (e.g., racial issues, class stratification, and gender issues) as they relate to a society's culture. Cultural data reveal what languages are used in an area, which health issues are common, and how populations are distributed according to race and class, among other things. Analysis of these data points could provide information on where educational programs should be placed, for example, or how to best advertise (e.g., social media, radio) beneficial programs to a local population.

Both geographic and cultural data may be displayed in infographics, or informational graphics. Infographics transform numerical data into visual representations using pictures and symbols to show patterns and trends. Often, these are easier to interpret by an audience who may be less familiar with a particular topic.

Representation of Culture Through Story and Art

Before descriptions of history and culture were written down, they were passed from one generation to another through oral tradition, which includes stories, folktales, myths, rituals, and songs. Before Europeans arrived in North America, there were no confirmed writing systems used among native people. Instead, oral storytelling served as a way to remember history, share moral boundaries, and establish social norms within a group. Many of the stories taught applicable life lessons through fictional events.

The earliest art identified in Texas is the rock art, or cave paintings, of the Pecos River. Dating back to 2,000 BC, over 300 paintings in this area show symbols, animals, and people that have been interpreted to represent rituals, myths, and history of the cultures that created them.

More recently, art is often used to immerse those who view or experience it in the emotions of a time and place. Like those who share oral traditions, artists capture the history and culture of their subject in sculpture, painting, song, or literature to pass it on to future generations.

Common themes in Texan art follow the state's history and include Native Americans (e.g., the paintings of Friedrich Richard Petri), famous battles including the Alamo (e.g., *The Fall of the Alamo* by Robert Jenkins Onderdonk), cowboy culture (e.g., the sculptures of Frederic Remington), and landscapes (e.g., the bluebonnet paintings of Julian Onderdonk).

Music as an art is as diverse in Texas as the people themselves. In its Mexican roots lies traditional music like mariachi with its elaborate costumes and themes of love, longing, and pride. White settlers first brought primarily Christian sacred music, but in modern times, Texas is very well known for its country music including honky-tonk and Western swing, as well as its Texas blues culture.

Influence of Art

Art is an excellent way to preserve history. For centuries, people have used painting, sculpture, music, literature, and other art forms to express themselves and the sentiments of their time. Beyond the historical facts presented in a textbook, art expresses the emotions of a person or group at a given time in history. Art immerses observers and listeners in the culture and experiences of a different time instead of just informing them about it through reading. In the case of societies that have been eliminated or assimilated, such as with many American Indian tribes, art preserves a first-person account of a culture and way of life that may not exist otherwise.

The earliest human art has been identified in cave paintings. At the time they were created, there was no written language. Historians suspect that early cave paintings were abstract, but later paintings appeared to be meaningful, and perhaps even spiritual, ways of communicating.

Since then, historical art forms have been used to examine and express opinions and emotions surrounding societal changes over time, justice and injustice, and religion. Negro spirituals, songs developed and sung by American black slaves, communicated using information from the Christian religion. In contrast to celebratory songs of redemption sung in white churches, Negro spirituals reflected the oppressive, painful life of slaves. Slaves also used their lyrics as code to communicate with one another, particularly in ways that were forbidden by masters.

Many pieces of literature tell stories in the context of history, making it more relatable and palpable for the reader. The novel *Out of the Dust* by Karen Hesse, for example, doesn't just teach about the Great Depression and the Dust Bowl; it also allows the reader to experience the unconscionable reality of a child living through it.

Art unites people within cultures. It exposes people to and creates an understanding and appreciation of different cultures. It also has the potential to change someone's opinion. In its time, art is often controversial and starts conversations about difficult topics that may lead to change. Art may be produced by or on behalf of marginalized people or groups. Works of art may inspire others to seek change.

Economics

Basic Economic Concepts

Economics form a key component of human society. Studies of economies can be divided between macroeconomics, which considers the larger economy as a whole, and microeconomics, which focuses on the actions of smaller groups, households, and individuals. However, the most basic principle of economics comes down to resources. A resource can be defined as an object or material that can be used for some purpose. Natural resources come directly from the environment, whereas items altered through human activity are considered manufactured goods. Resources can be further divided into renewable resources, which are gradually replenished given enough time and proper circumstances, and nonrenewable resources, which regenerate slowly or not at all. In addition, there are four main types of economic resources: land, which includes most natural resources; labor, the services provided by individuals to create products; capital, which encompasses human-manufactured resources; and entrepreneurship, the process in which individuals utilize available resources for business ventures that generate new products.

Early on, human civilizations functioned using a barter system, where people would trade certain goods for other items. It remains common in some parts of the world today. However, the difficulty of storing and transporting products, such as livestock and minerals, for exchange, led to the development of monetary systems. Money is an object, such as a coin or a paper bill, which can be exchanged for any commercial product given enough money. It is important to note that money on its own often has no worth; paper money, for example, is a rather flimsy material with little actual use outside of its monetary worth. It only has value when members of a society agree that it can be used to make purchases.

Due to the artificial nature of money within societies, prices fluctuate depending on the supply and demand of products. Supply refers to the available quantity of a specific good or resource. In contrast, demand accounts for the quantity that buyers wish to obtain. These two factors influence several economic patterns. The law of supply states that the quantity available for purchase is directly related to the price, while the law of demand states that the price of an item is inversely related to the demand for the item. Thus, raising prices increases supply and reduces demand.

Furthermore, the value of money in part depends on the amount that is circulated in the market. A surplus of money has the potential to devalue the currency, which lowers the worth of each unit of money. This process, called inflation, has a detrimental effect on the economy as prices generally increase. However, the opposite trend, deflation, can also be detrimental; thus, political leaders usually strive to find a stable balance between the two ends of the spectrum. By finding equilibrium between supply and demand, an economy's prices remain relatively stable.

Economies, by nature, have limited access to certain resources, which creates a conflict between supply and demand. Scarcity occurs when the demand for a product exceeds its availability. Scarcity in part depends on the choices of individuals as they determine which products they want more than others. Choices, in turn, are influenced by the perceived costs of pursuing certain options over others. The costs and benefits of specific choices often differ depending on the individuals' perceptions of the options. When people believe that a certain service's or product's benefits outweigh its necessary costs, they may choose to pay more for the desired benefits. It is important to realize that the laws of supply and demand are not absolute, and they may fluctuate depending on the situation.

Supply and demand can be further affected by monopolies, in which an individual or group holds sole or primary access to a given product or service. The individuals controlling a monopoly can limit the supply in a manner that best suits themselves but not necessarily the consumers. Monopolies are often asserted through the creation of barriers that limit access to the resources or services. For instance, patents give exclusive rights for inventions and discoveries to their respective creators or the firms that sponsored them. Without restraints, a monopoly can significantly limit economic development and prosperity of a society.

Economic Systems

Economic systems affect the assets, labor, and trade of a specific place to alter the production of goods and determine how resources are distributed. Goods include any purchasable items as well as education, the environment, and institutions. How these resources, services, and goods are allocated in a region to affect a society's functioning depends on its economic system(s).

There are four types of economic systems that vary based on what goods are produced, how they are produced, and for whom they are produced to meet the society's economic goals:

1. **Traditional economies**: these are the most basic; they involve many people working similar jobs with little specialization. Economic activities depend on the customs of their culture but often include hunting or farming. While this was a common system in ancient cultures, it is less prevalent today and it exists primarily in second and third world countries. With low access to resources, traditional systems are generally unable to create an economic surplus, but goods and services are fairly evenly distributed. This system is efficient and sustainable mainly due to its simplicity and slow growth. However, there is little opportunity for economic growth or technological development.

2. **Command economies**: these are controlled by a central authority, usually the government, which manages production through quotas. They are common in communist countries (e.g., the former Soviet Union). Command economies are most successful when the central authority acts on behalf of the people's welfare and interests; however, they are usually managed in light of the central authority's self-interest. While economically secure, they are not very efficient with poor planning leading to excesses and shortages. Further, people often lack motivation and incentives to work hard.

3. **Market economies**: these lack government control of resources and instead rely on supply and demand, driven by individuals, to dictate production in free markets. Market economies promote economic freedom and fast growth. Without a central authority controlling the economy, private companies have the greatest impact. This reduces economic security and inequity, promoting greater success among those in control.

4. **Mixed economies**, or dual systems: these have features of both market and command economies, with governments controlling select services and other industries remaining private. The extent of the government's involvement varies by country (e.g., universal healthcare vs. private healthcare). Overall, they are more equitable, secure, and sustainable than market economies. Capitalist economies (as in the United States) are mixed economies.

Free-Enterprise System

Free enterprise in free market economies is driven by private businesses and consumers with little to no governmental control. Free markets can exist when resources are predominantly privately owned, giving individuals and companies control over production, exchange, and labor. Industries determine consumer interests and needs, and consumers use their purchasing power to determine the success or failure of a product. Free markets may only exist when financial institutions like banks are present to provide capital and investment services.

While a complete lack of government control doesn't realistically exist, the overall level of regulation is low and usually involves laws like those against monopolies. Further, theoretically those who provide goods and services do so at will in any amount they choose; the government doesn't impose quotas on private business. However, some laws may limit the sale of a product (e.g., age limits on the purchase of tobacco).

Free markets follow supply and demand with buyers and sellers setting the value of goods and services. For example, farmers set the prices for the food they sell, employers set salaries for employees, and those in the service industry (e.g., plumbers) set the fees for their services, all without a central authority dictating those amounts. Conversely, consumers are free to choose what and how much they purchase, as well as what prices they are willing to pay for goods and services. However, the government does impose fees that affect the prices of goods in the form of government-dictated taxes and tariffs on imported products.

A potential drawback of free enterprise is that its ultimate success relies on the morality of industries and businesses to focus not only on profits but also on the needs and well-being of their employees and consumers. When companies cut corners to maximize their profits, their actions may compromise employee or consumer safety (e.g., a faulty product). Market failures, like the Great Depression and the real estate crash of 2008, can also result when individuals or companies make immoral choices. The crash of 2008 occurred when people benefitted from investing in stocks that they knew would pay them when the housing market crashed, causing many people to lose their homes to foreclosure and many investors to lose their livelihood.

Economic Resources

Economics are closely linked with the flow of resources, technology, and population in societies. The use of natural resources, such as water and fossil fuels, has always depended in part on the pressures of the economy. A supply of a specific good may be limited in the market, but with sufficient demand the sellers are incentivized to increase the available quantity. Unfortunately, the demand for certain objects can often be unlimited, and a high price or limited supply may prevent consumers from obtaining the product or service. If the sellers succumb to the consumers' demand and continue to exploit a scarce resource, supply could potentially be exhausted.

The resources for most products, both renewable and nonrenewable, are finite. This is a particularly difficult issue with nonrenewable resources, but even renewable resources often have limits: organic products such as trees and animals require stable populations and sufficient habitats to support those populations. Furthermore, the costs of certain decisions can have detrimental effects on other resources. For example, industrialization provides economic benefits in many countries but also has had the negative effect of polluting surrounding environments; the pollution, in turn, often eliminates or harms fish, plants, and other potential resources.

The control of resources within an economy is particularly important in determining how resources are used. While the demand may change with the choices of consumers, the range of supply depends on the objectives of the people producing the goods. They determine how much of their supply they allot for sale, and in the case of monopolies, they might have sole access to the resource. They might choose to limit their use of the resources or instead gather more to meet the demand. As they pay for the products, consumers can choose which sellers they rely on for the supply. In the case of a monopoly, though, consumers have little influence over the company's decision because there is no alternative supplier. Therefore, the function of supply within an economy can drastically influence how the resources are exploited.

The availability of resources, in turn, affects the human population. Humans require basic resources such as food and water for survival, as well as additional resources for healthy lifestyles. Therefore, access to these resources helps determine the survival rate of humans. For much of human existence, economies have had limited ability to extract resources from the natural world, which restricted the growth rate of populations. However, the development of new technologies, combined with increasing demand for certain products, has pushed resource use to a new level. On the one hand, this led to higher living standards that ensured that fewer people would die. However, this has also brought mass population growth. Admittedly, countries with higher standards of living often have lower birthrates. Even so, the increasing exploitation of resources has sharply increased the world's population as a whole to unsustainable levels. The rising population leads, in turn, to more demand for resources that cannot be met. This creates poverty, reduced living conditions, and higher death rates. As a result, economics can significantly influence local and world population levels.

Technology is also intricately related to population, resources, and economics. The role of demand within economies has incentivized people to innovate new technologies that enable societies to have a higher quality of life and greater access to resources. Entrepreneurs expand technologies by finding ways to create new products for the market. The Industrial Revolution, in particular, illustrates the relationship between economics and technology because the ambitions of businessmen led to new infrastructure that enabled more efficient and sophisticated use of resources. Many of these inventions reduced the amount of work necessary for individuals and allowed the development of leisure activities, which in turn created new economic markets. However, economic systems can also limit the growth of technology. In the case of monopolies, the lack of alternative suppliers reduces the incentive to meet and exceed consumer expectations. Moreover, as demonstrated by the effects of economics on resources, technology's increasing ability to extract resources can lead to their depletion and create significant issues that need to be addressed.

Consumption and Production

Consumption

Consumer economics is a term used to describe the ways in which consumers make decisions about their roles in a capitalist economy. The factors that consumers consider when buying goods and services include satisfaction and utility. Most consumers want to obtain as much satisfaction and/or utility from their purchase as possible; in colloquial terms, they "want the biggest bang for the buck." Consumers also have to consider the quantity of goods and services they are able to purchase at any given time, in accordance with the current price. This phenomenon is known as **demand.** When individual demand combines with aggregate demand, it is called **market demand.** Individual demands and market demands are also factors that consumers must consider when making decisions. These demands – individual and aggregate – drive consumer tastes. Most consumers do not demand goods that do not provide them with utility or satisfaction.

Consumers must also consider supply and scarcity. Consumers do not always have enough time or money to make their purchases, and this is known as scarcity. **Scarcity** basically means that consumers have to make choices: they cannot always have all the goods they want and participate in all their preferred activities. Likewise, all consumers – individuals, households, businesses, and governments – are bound to the supply chains of goods. At times, the actual goods or services might become scarce, meaning there are not enough products or services to meet consumer demand. As a result, consumers might have to consider alternative options for utility or satisfaction.

When an individual decides between possibilities, that individual is making a choice. Choices allow people to compare opportunity costs. ***Opportunity costs*** are benefits that a person could have received, but gave up, in choosing another course of action. What is an individual willing to trade or give up for a different choice? For example, if an individual pays someone to mow the lawn because he or she would rather spend that time doing something else, then the opportunity cost of paying someone to mow the lawn is worth the time gained from not doing the job himself or herself.

Individuals earn an income by trading their labor – both mental and physical – for pay. They then budget their money through spending or saving it. As consumers, every choice has an opportunity cost since they must choose which goods and services they want to buy with a limited income. By purchasing one good or service, they give up the chance to purchase another.

Additionally, consumers have the choice to save money when they don't have enough money to purchase what they want, or when they want to utilize a savings account to use during emergencies or periods of economic difficulty. People also choose to save for **retirement**, a time when they will no longer be working and drawing a salary. Saving money by putting it in a bank is considered low-risk – the bank will pay the saver a low interest rate to keep it safe, but it will not increase much in value. A riskier path is investing money through the purchase of valuable items (or **assets**) in the hopes that they will increase in worth over time and yield returns (or **profits**). Assets can include shares in companies, real estate or land investments, or capital such as money, equipment, and structures used to create wealth.

Production

Product markets are where goods and services are bought and sold. Product markets provide a place for sellers to offer goods and services and for consumers to purchase them. The annual value of goods and services exchanged throughout the year is measured by the Gross Domestic Product (GDP), a monetary measure of goods and services made either quarterly or annually. Department stores, gas stations, grocery stores, and other retail stores are all examples of product markets. However, product markets do not include any raw, scarce, or trade materials.

As the Circular Flow Model below indicates, the role of a product market is quite different from the role of a resource market in a market economy. Both the resource market and product market interact with businesses and households, but their roles in buying and selling are reversed. **Resource markets** function with households selling resources and businesses buying these resources. The role of the product market is quite different: product markets function with businesses (i.e., stores, gas stations, grocery stores, and other retail stores) selling products and households buying these products.

As the Circular Flow Model illustrates, consumption and expenditures are funneled into the product market via households, allowing revenue to flow to the businesses. Goods and services are filtered through the product market and into the households of consumers. Also, goods and services flow into the product market from businesses in exchange for revenue. This is different from resource markets where land, labor, capital, and entrepreneurial ability flow into the resource market from households as money and income (wages, rent, interest, profits) flow back into the households from the resource market. On the business side of resource markets, costs flow from the businesses to the resource market and resources flow from the resource market to the business.

Circular Flow Model

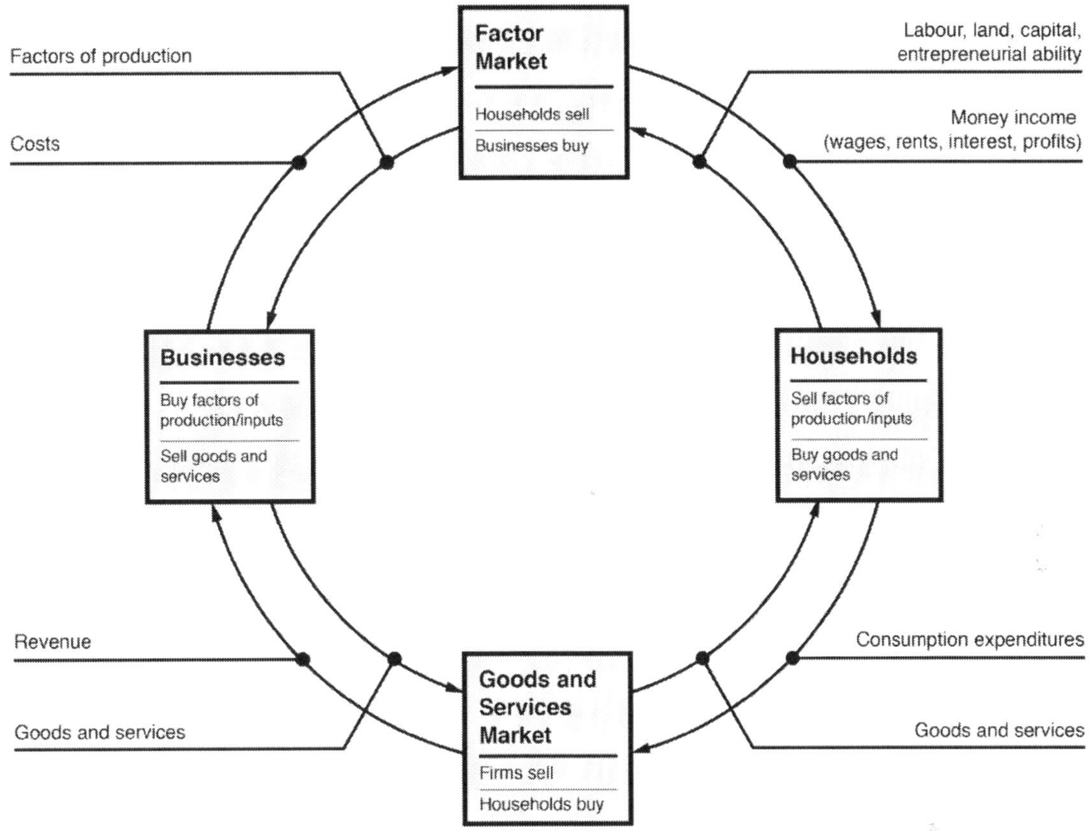

Resources

Productive resources are the means used by a society to succeed and survive. The four types are:

- Natural resources: the raw materials taken from the land, such as corn, beef, lumber, water, oil, and iron.
- Human resources: the human labor, both mental and physical, that are required to produce goods.
- Capital resources: the man-made physical resources used to create products, such as machinery, tools, buildings, and equipment.
- Entrepreneurship: the capability and motivation to cultivate, organize, and oversee the other three resources into a business venture.

Money functions as a method of exchange to obtain goods or services. It replaced the barter system, which was often considered inefficient and disorganized. Economists referred to the barter system as a double coincidence of wants since trades between parties were not always considered equal. Prices of goods are determined by supply and demand. **Inflation** occurs when people have money to spend, but not enough goods can be produced or imported to meet their demand for a product, which causes prices to rise. The amount of money issued by government-controlled central banks and the prices of leading commodities, such as oil, can also affect inflation. **Deflation** can when people save their money and spend less, leaving stores with surplus goods, which causes prices to drop.

Economic Activities and Indicators

An economic activity refers to the production, purchase, sale, or exchange of goods and services. The types of activities are geographically distributed based on factors including the physical environment (e.g., presence of natural resources in an area), culture (e.g., preferences and gender roles), technology (e.g., equipment needed to extract and refine a resource), and the role of government (e.g., tariffs). The four types of economic activities are primary, secondary, tertiary, and quaternary.

Primary activities, like hunting, gathering, fishing, and farming involve obtaining natural resources from the earth. These activities are vital to the rest of the economy because they provide the raw materials for other types of activities.

Secondary activities involve the modification of products to add value, often through manufacturing. One example would be turning cotton into clothing; another is the refinement of oil.

Tertiary activities include services that don't offer a tangible product but give the consumer an amenity that they can't produce on their own. These workers include physicians, lawyers, electricians, and mechanics.

Quaternary activities are knowledge-based activities performed by workers who have specific skills. Banking, information technology, education, and research/development all fall into this category.

Economic indicators measure the health of a country's economy. The most commonly used indicator is Gross Domestic Product (GDP), which uses consumption, investment, government spending, and exports to quantify the size of a country's economy. Other indicators of economic performance include the stock market, retail sales, unemployment rate, and interest rates.

Effects of Government Regulation

Governments have considerable influence over the flow of economies, which makes it important to understand the relationships between them. When a government has full control over the economic decisions of a nation, it is called a command system. This was the case in many absolute monarchies such as eighteenth-century France; King Louis XIV built his economy on the concept of mercantilism, which believed that the state should manage all resources, particularly by accumulating gold and silver. This system of economics discouraged exports and thereby limited trade.

In contrast, the market system is guided by the concept of capitalism, in which individuals and businesses have the freedom to manage their economic decisions. This allows for private property and increases the opportunities for entrepreneurship and trade. Early proponents of capitalism emphasized *laissez-faire* policies, which means "let it be," and argued that the government should not be involved with the economy at all. They believe the market is guided by the concept of self-interest and that individuals will optimally work for their personal success. However, individuals' interests do not necessarily correlate with the needs of the overall economy. For instance, during a financial recession, consumers may decide to save up their money rather than make purchases; doing so helps them in the short run but further reduces demand in a slumping economy. Therefore, most capitalist governments still assert a degree of control over their economies while still allowing for private business.

Likewise, many command system economies, such as monarchical France, still relied heavily on private businesses maintained by wealthy businessmen. With the end of most absolute monarchies, communism has been the primary form of command system economies in the modern era. Communism is a form of socialism that emphasizes communal ownership of property and government control over production. The high degree of government control gives more stability to the economy, but it also creates considerable flaws. The monopolization of the economy by the government limits its ability to respond to local economic conditions because certain regions often have unique resources and needs. With the collapse of the Soviet Union and other communist states, command systems have been largely replaced with market systems.

The U.S. government helps to manage the nation's economy through a market system in several ways. First and foremost, the federal government is responsible for the production of money for use within the economy; depending on how the government manages the monetary flow, it may lead to a stable economy, deflation, or inflation. Second, state and federal governments impose taxes on individuals, corporations, and goods. For instance, a tariff might be imposed on imports in order to stimulate demand for local goods in the economy. Third, the government can pass laws that require additional regulation or inspections. In addition, the government has passed antitrust laws to inhibit the growth of private monopolies, which could limit free growth in the market system. Debates continue over whether the government should take further action to manage private industries or reduce its control over the private sector.

Just as governments can affect the direction of the economy, the state of the economy can have significant implications on government policies. Financial stability is critical in maintaining a prosperous state. A healthy economy will allow for new developments that contribute to the nation's growth and create jobs. On the other hand, an economic crisis, such as a recession or depression, can gravely damage a government's stability. Without a stable economy, business opportunities plummet, and people begin to lose income and employment. This, in turn, leads to frustration and discontent in the population, which can lead to criticism of the government. This could very well lead to demands for new leadership to resolve the economic crisis.

The dangers of a destabilized economy can be seen with the downfall of the French monarchy. The mercantilist approach to economics stifled French trade. Furthermore, regional aristocracies remained exempt from government taxes, which limited the government's revenues. This was compounded by expensive wars and poor harvests that led to criticism of King Louis XIV's government. The problems persisted for decades, and Louis XIV was forced to convene the Estates-General, a legislative body of representatives from across France, to address the crisis. The economic crises at the end of the eighteenth century were critical in the beginning of the French Revolution. Those financial issues, in turn, at least partially stemmed from both the government's control of the economy through mercantilism and its inability to impose economic authority over local regions.

Major Events, Trends, and Issues in Economic History

Economies of the United States and the world have historically followed the pattern of development form hunter-gatherer to agrarian to industrialization to finally information-technology-based societies.

Like their hunter-gatherer predecessors, agrarian societies are primarily rural. One advantage they have, though, is their ability to maintain surpluses. This material security provides a more stable economy and also develops opportunities for economic inequity among society members.

The transition from rural, agrarian societies to urban, industrial ones was driven by access to resources and the introduction of technology. There are two global industrial revolutions commonly recognized by historians. The first started in Britain with the novel use of steam-powered engines. It arrived in the United States and much of the rest of the world by the 1840s. Steam engines allowed for travel and transport by rail and steamship, allowing people to live farther from the sources of the natural resources they depended on (e.g., food, fuel). Advances in textile science and toolmaking during this time also facilitated the development of production lines.

The second industrial revolution (late 19th to early 20th century) saw the use of novel techniques and machinery to mass produce items that had once been made by hand. Factory jobs provided wages for workers to purchase items instead of making them at home. Increasing numbers of consumers were able to afford extravagances, like china. From this group, a middle class began to form.

In the late 19th century, the U.S. government began to intercede in business affairs at the request of small businesses, farms, and organized labor movements. Early laws enacted served to regulate railroads (Interstate Commerce Act) and prevent the formation of monopolies (Sherman Antitrust Act). Increases in tariffs and tax cuts following World War I helped to fuel the prosperous Roaring Twenties of U.S. history. A thriving automobile industry paired with the spread of electricity and telephone service stimulated spending, tourism, and migration to urban centers. But the stock market crash of 1929 led to a global Great Depression.

Franklin Roosevelt's New Deal (1933-1939)—a collection of programs, regulations, reforms, and work projects—focused on economic recovery, economic reform to prevent another depression, and relief for the poor and unemployed. Populations grew, and finances rebounded through the 1950s. Further, the GI Bill offered low-cost loans that made homeownership accessible to millions of eligible veterans. Combined with the development of the interstate highway system, this housing boom led to suburbanization as many people left crowded urban centers. Increases in tourism and shopping along highways created a demand for related services (e.g., restaurants, hotels) and growth in service-related industries, sometimes called deindustrialization. Greater access to higher education and further advances in technology also diversified the economy into more white-collar sectors.

A recession in 1980 led to the election of Ronald Reagan, who instituted deep tax cuts and policies that severely reduced unemployment rates. The resulting economic boom was accompanied by increased spending on many consumer goods including modern electronic devices, like computers and cell phones. The continued increase in digital communications and technology (e.g., the internet) through recent years is sometimes referred to as the third industrial revolution. Some foresee a fourth revolution emerging with the use of artificial intelligence and advanced biotechnology.

Interdependence of Economies

International trade is when countries import and export goods and services. Countries often want to deal in terms of their own currency. Therefore, when importing or exporting goods or services, consumers and businesses need to enter the market using the same form of currency. For example, if the United States would like to trade with China, the U.S. may have to trade in China's form of currency, the *Yuan*, versus the dollar, depending on the business.

The exchange rate is what one country's currency will exchange for another. The government and the market (supply and demand) determine the exchange rate. There are two forms of exchange rates: fixed and floating. Fixed exchange rates involve government interventions (like central banks) to help keep the exchange rates stable. Floating, or "flexible," exchange rates constantly change because they rely on supply and demand needs. While each type of exchange rate has advantages and disadvantages, the rate truly depends on the current state of each country's economy. Therefore, each exchange rate may differ from country to country.

Here is a chart displaying the advantages and disadvantages of fixed and floating exchange rates:

Advantages and Disadvantages of Fixed Versus Floating Exchange Rates			
Fixed Exchange Rate: government intervention to help keep exchange rates stable		Floating or "Flexible" Exchange Rate: Supply and demand determines the exchange rate	
Advantages -Stable prices -Stable foreign exchange rates -Exports are more competitive and in turn more profitable	*Disadvantages* -Requires a large amount of reserve funds -Possibly mispricing currency values -Inflation increases	*Advantages* -Central bank involvement is not needed. -Facilitates free trade	*Disadvantages* -Currency speculation -Exchange rate risks -Inflation increases

Countries may have differing economic statuses and exchange rates, but they rely on one another for goods and services. Prices of imports and exports are affected by the strength of another country's currency. For example, if the United States dollar is at a higher value than another country's currency, imports will be less expensive because the dollar will have more value than that of the country selling its good or service. On the other hand, if the dollar is at a low value compared to the currency of another country, importers will tend to avoid buying international items from that country. However, U.S. exporters to that country could benefit from the low value of the dollar.

Government and Citizenship

Historical Origins of Democratic Forms of Government

Modern democracy originated in Ancient Greece; the word is derived from two Greek words meaning people (*demos*) and rule (*kratos*). It was established on the belief that people should be active in their government and that governmental authority should be transferred peacefully without need for a revolution. This was a notable shift in governance from the monarchies and aristocracies that were common at the time. Monarchies are led by a single person, and aristocracies are led by a privileged or noble class.

The United States' model of democracy has many characteristics that come from the original democracy in Ancient Greece. At the time, Greece was comprised of city-states, including Athens and Sparta, which were governed independently but united in times of national defense. Upon gaining independence from England, the United States maintained the boundaries of the original 13 colonies to allow for state-level independent governing with a federal government to unite the states.

In the earliest democracy of Athens, citizens (i.e., free men, as were defined at the time) were required to participate directly in the government at the risk of being fined. However, the U.S. democracy is a representative democracy, meaning the people elect representatives to vote on laws on behalf of their constituents.

The government of Ancient Greece was the first to have a constitution, which prescribed appropriate behavior as determined by law, as well as consequences for breaking the law. The US Constitution similarly describes the branches of government and individual citizens' rights.

Finally, the U.S. subscribes to the rule of law, a tenant of Greek democracy, which holds that all individuals and even institutions such as the government are subject to the same laws. In other words, no one is immune to the laws developed by the government.

Social, Economic, and Political Rights

The US Constitution is a series of written rules defining the power of the U.S. government and the rights of U.S. citizens. Written in 1787 to create a stronger national government, it is the world's oldest working constitution. It gave Americans more rights than any other country had previously given its people. Collectively referred to as the Bill of Rights, the first ten amendments to the Constitution were added to protect the individual rights of U.S. citizens and to keep the federal government from wielding too much control. These are rights such as freedom of speech, freedom of religion, freedom of the press, and right to a fair trial. The Constitution has been amended twenty-seven times in order to accommodate changes and updates. Some of these amendments were made to be more inclusive to the wide range of American citizens. For example, the 14th Amendment, adopted in 1868, abolished slavery and stated that all citizens must be treated equally under Constitutional law and allowed the same protection within each state.

Basic Structure and Functions of the United States Government

The United States of America's government, as outlined by the Constitution, is designed to serve as a compromise between democracy and preceding monarchical systems. The American Revolution brought independence from Britain and freedom from its aristocratic system of governance. On the other hand, the short-lived Articles of Confederation revealed the significant weaknesses of state-based governance with limited national control. By dividing power between local, state, and federal governments, the United States can uphold its value of individual liberties while, nevertheless, giving a sense of order to the country.

The federal government, which is in charge of laws that affect the entire nation, is split into three main branches: executive, judicial, and legislative. It is important to realize that the three segments of the federal government are intended to stand as equal counterparts to the others, and that none of them are "in charge." The executive branch centers on the president, the vice president, and the cabinet. The president and vice president are elected every four years. Also known as the commander-in-chief, the president is the official head of state and serves as the nation's head diplomat and military leader. The vice president acts as the president of the Senate in the legislative branch, while the president appoints members of the cabinet to lead agencies, including the Treasury and Department of Defense. However, the president can only sign and veto laws and cannot initiate them himself.

Instead, the legislative branch, specifically Congress, proposes and debates laws. Congress is bicameral because it is divided into two separate legislative houses. Each state's representation in the House of Representatives is determined proportionally by population, with the total number of voting seats limited to 435. The Senate, in contrast, has only two members per state and a total of one hundred senators. Members of both houses are intended to represent the interests of the constituents in their home states and to bring their concerns to a national level. Ideas for laws, called bills, are proposed in either chamber and then are voted upon according to the body's rules; should the bill pass the first round of voting, the other legislative chamber must approve it before it can be sent to the president. Congress also has a variety of other powers, such as the rights to declare war, collect taxes, and impeach the president.

The judicial branch, though it cannot pass laws itself, serves to interpret the laws. At the federal level, this is done through several tiers of judicial bodies. At the top, the Supreme Court consists of judges appointed by the president; these judges serve for life, unless they resign from their position or are removed by Congress for improper behavior. The Supreme Court's decisions in trials and other judgments rest on the justices' interpretations of the Constitution and enacted laws. As the Constitution remains fundamental to the American legal system, the Supreme Court's rulings on how laws follow or fail to uphold the Constitution have powerful implications on future rulings. Beneath the Supreme Court, there are a number of other federal judicial bodies—courts of appeals, district courts, and courts of special jurisdiction.

While the federal government manages the nation as a whole, state governments address issues pertaining to their specific territory. In the past, states claimed the right, known as nullification, to refuse to enforce federal laws that they considered unconstitutional. However, conflicts between state and federal authority, particularly in the South in regard to first, slavery, and later, discrimination, have led to increased federal power, and states cannot defy federal laws. Even so, the Tenth Amendment limits federal power to those specifically granted in the Constitution, and the rest of the powers are retained by the states and citizens. Therefore, individual state governments are left in charge of decisions with immediate effects on their citizens, such as state laws and taxes. Like the federal government, state governments consist of executive, judicial, and legislative branches, but the exact configuration of those branches varies between states. For instance, while most states follow the bicameral structure of Congress, Nebraska has only a single legislative chamber. State governments have considerable authority within their states, but they cannot impose their power on other states, nor can they secede from the United States.

Local governments, which include town governments, county boards, library districts, and other agencies, are especially variable in their composition. They often reflect the overall views of their state governments but also have their own values, rules, and structures. Generally, local governments function in a democratic fashion, although the exact form of government depends on its role. Depending on the location within the state, local government may have considerable or minimal authority based on the population and prosperity of the area; some counties may have strong influence in the state, while others may have a limited impact.

Native American tribes are treated as dependent nations that answer to the federal government but may be immune to state jurisdiction. As with local governments, the exact form of governance is left up to the tribes, which ranges from small councils to complex systems of government. Other U.S. territories, including the District of Columbia (site of Washington, D.C.) and acquired islands, such as Guam and Puerto Rico, have representation within Congress, but their legislators cannot vote on bills.

As members of a democracy, U.S. citizens are empowered to elect most government leaders, but the process varies between branch and level of government. Presidential elections at the national scale use the Electoral College system. Rather than electing the president directly, citizens cast their ballots to select electors, who generally vote for a specific candidate, that represent each state in the college. Legislative branches at the federal and state level are also determined by elections, albeit without an Electoral College. In some areas, judges are elected, but in other states judges are appointed by elected officials. It should also be noted that the two-party system was not built into the Constitution but gradually emerged over time.

Key Principles and Ideas in Major Documents and Speeches

With more than two hundred years of history, American leaders have produced a number of important documents and speeches. One of the most essential is the Declaration of Independence, which the Second Continental Congress ratified on July 4, 1776. Although many historians and politicians have drawn upon the words of the Declaration to demonstrate the American ideal of freedom, most of them focus on the preamble, which focuses on the necessity of fair government and the right to overthrow tyrants. The main body of the document consists of a set of grievances against King George III. Still, this document was instrumental in American history because it asserted American independence from Great Britain. Even so, it is important to note that the Declaration did not immediately lead to the United States; the document does not outline the government of the soon-to-be independent colonies, and independence would not become reality until Britain agreed.

The colonies' first blueprint for government was the Articles of Confederation, which was ratified in 1777. The document declared that the confederacy would be called the United States of America and that the individual states would have "a firm league of friendship" with each other. The emphasis on friendship and cooperation highlights how the confederation was a voluntary effort that states could follow or ignore as they saw fit. Still, the document also revealed the importance of obeying decisions made by Congress as a whole; while this was not very effective during the confederation period, the framework would live on to a degree in the following Constitution.

Much like the Declaration of Independence, the 1787 Constitution of the United States is most remembered for the preamble, which takes a more philosophical approach. However, the body of the Constitution is highly complex, and it covers the framework and responsibilities of the different branches of the federal government and the limits to state power. These details are very important and help to define the key institutions within the government. To resolve later issues not addressed in the Constitution, the fifth article in the document establishes a process to modify the government, and the first ten amendments are known as the *Bill of Rights*. Under the Tenth Amendment, powers not specifically allotted to Congress by the Constitution are reserved for the people and to individual states.

George Washington was the first president of the United States, and his administration set many precedents for the nation, particularly with his Farewell Address. In it, he noted the rise of regional feelings, and he urged citizens to uphold their duty to the nation above sectionalism because he felt that America was strongest when united. The issue of regional conflicts and national identity would become increasingly important in years to come, especially during the Civil War. Washington also argued against intervention in European affairs, and this warning would become the cornerstone for advocates of American isolation. On the other hand, his advice that political parties are detrimental to democracy failed to halt the development of the party system.

Washington's fears about sectional conflict were confirmed at the start of the Civil War, when the southern states violently seceded from the Union. As the president during that tumultuous time, Abraham Lincoln was seen by many to embody the Union as a whole. This can be demonstrated through his Gettysburg Address in November of 1863. After the difficult and bloody Battle of Gettysburg ended in a Union victory, crowds gathered for the dedication of the Soldiers' National Cemetery. Although he was not the main speaker of the event, Lincoln's short yet eloquent speech proved to be the most significant. Drawing upon the Declaration of Independence's assertion that "all men are created equal," he argued that the current war was a test of that ideal. More than that, he emphasized the importance of the United States as a whole and argued that it must endure as a Union for the sake of the world.

Earlier that year in January, Lincoln had already indicated his opposition to slavery through the Emancipation Proclamation. Although it was an executive order instead of a law passed by Congress, this document was not challenged by the courts and helped determine the objectives of the Civil War. The proclamation asserted that all slaves in Confederate territories were free. One must note that some southern states remained in the Union, and therefore, were not affected by this proclamation. Even so, the order helped establish a basis for later laws and amendments that would end slavery in the United States.

Another presidential attempt to set a new precedent for American policy was Woodrow Wilson's Fourteen Points, which were outlined in a speech he gave to Congress in 1918 after the United States had entered World War I. Wilson saw the United States as a protector of democracy in the world and said that we could reform world policy by fighting in the war. For instance, Wilson called for an end to private negotiations, which had contributed to the secret alliances behind the war. Most of all, he argued for nations to come together in an international body to determine world policies. The negotiations after the war only partially fulfilled Wilson's ambitions by creating a weak League of Nations, but his vision of U.S. involvement in global affairs would become a key aspect of American foreign policy.

Even as the United States began playing a more active role on the international stage of politics, internal issues such as civil rights remained important, as shown in Martin Luther King Jr.'s "I Have a Dream" speech. A leader in the civil rights movement, King gave his speech as part of the 1963 March on Washington. Drawing on Lincoln's past speech at Gettysburg, King argued that America's journey to true equality was not over yet. His references to biblical passages gave the speech a spiritual tone, but he also mentioned specific locations across the nation to signify how local struggles were tied with national consequences. By emphasizing his optimism, King's speech reflects not only civil rights activism but also the American dream of freedom and progress.

Organization of Government in Colonial America

The American Revolution largely occurred as a result of changing values in the Thirteen Colonies that broke from their traditional relationship with England. Early on in the colonization of North America, the colonial social structure tried to mirror the stratified order of Great Britain. In England, the landed elites were seen as intellectually and morally superior to the common man, which led to a paternalistic relationship. This style of governance was similarly applied to the colonial system; government was left to the property-owning upper class, and the colonies as a whole could be seen as a child dutifully serving "Mother England."

However, the colonies' distance from England meant that actual, hereditary aristocrats from Britain only formed a small percentage of the overall population and did not even fill all the positions of power. By the mid-eighteenth century, much of the American upper class consisted of local families who acquired status through business rather than lineage. Despite this, representatives from Britain were appointed to govern the colonies. As a result, a rift began to form between the colonists and British officials.

Tensions began to rise in the aftermath of the French and Indian War of 1754 to 1763. To recover the financial costs of the long conflict, Great Britain drew upon its colonies to provide the desired resources. Since the American colonists did not fully subscribe to the paternal connection, taxation to increase British revenue, such as the Stamp Act of 1765, was met with increasing resistance. Britain sent soldiers to the colonies and enacted the 1765 Quartering Act to require colonists to house the troops. In 1773, the new Tea Act, which created a monopoly, led some colonists to raid a ship and destroy its contents in the Boston Tea Party.

Uncertain about whether they should remain loyal to Britain, representatives from twelve colonies formed the First Continental Congress in 1774 to discuss what they should do next. When Patriot militiamen at Lexington and Concord fought British soldiers in April 1775, the Revolutionary War began. While the rebel forces worked to present the struggle as a united, patriotic effort, the colonies remained divided throughout the war. Thousands of colonists, known as Loyalists or Tories, supported Britain. Even the revolutionaries proved to be significantly fragmented, and many militias only served in their home states. The Continental Congress was also divided over whether to reconcile with Britain or push for full separation. These issues hindered the ability of the revolutionary armies to resist the British, who had superior training and resources at their disposal.

Even so, the Continental Army, under General George Washington, gradually built up a force that utilized Prussian military training and backwoods guerrilla tactics to make up for their limited resources. Although the British forces continued to win significant battles, the Continental Army gradually reduced Britain's will to fight as the years passed. Furthermore, Americans appealed to the rivalry that other European nations had with the British Empire. The support was initially limited to indirect assistance, but aid gradually increased. After the American victory at the Battle of Saratoga in 1777, France and other nations began to actively support the American cause by providing much-needed troops and equipment.

In 1781, the primary British army under General Cornwallis was defeated by an American and French coalition at Virginia, which paved the way for negotiations. The Treaty of Paris in 1783 ended the war, recognized the former colonies' independence from Great Britain, and gave America control over territory between the Appalachian Mountains and Mississippi River. However, the state of the new nation was still uncertain. The new nation's government initially stemmed from the state-based structure of the Continental Congress and was incorporated into the Articles of Confederation in 1777.

The Articles of Confederation emphasized the ideals of the American Revolution, particularly the concept of freedom from unjust government. Unfortunately, the resulting limitations on the national government left most policies—even ones with national ramifications—up to individual states. For instance, states sometimes simply decided to not pay taxes. Many representatives did not see much value in the National Congress and simply did not attend the meetings. Some progress was still made during the period, such as the Northwest Ordinance of 1787, which organized the western territories into new states; nevertheless, the disjointed links in the state-oriented government inhibited significant progress.

Although many citizens felt satisfied with this decentralized system of government, key intellectuals and leaders in America became increasingly disturbed by the lack of unity. An especially potent fear among them was the potential that, despite achieving official independence, other powers could threaten America's autonomy. In 1786, poor farmers in Massachusetts launched an insurrection, known as Shays' Rebellion, which sparked fears of additional uprisings and led to the creation of the Constitutional Convention in 1787.

While the convention initially intended to correct issues within the Articles of Confederation, speakers, such as James Madison, compellingly argued for the delegates to devise a new system of government that was more centralized than its predecessor. The Constitution was not fully supported by all citizens, and there was much debate about whether or not to support the new government. Even so, in 1788, the Constitution was ratified. Later additions, such as the Bill of Rights, would help protect individual liberty by giving specific rights to citizens. In 1789, George Washington became the first president of the newly created executive branch of the government, and America entered a new stage of history.

Political Processes in the United States

The Processes of the U.S. Legal System

The processes of the U.S. legal system have historically borrowed components from English common law, relying heavily on the role of judicial structures in dictating, developing, and monitoring laws, which are evaluated through the lens of the nation's principal federal governing document, the US Constitution.

In the United States of America, all laws are developed at the federal and state levels. Additionally, local municipal jurisdictions can pass legal codes, so long as they do not interfere with the statutes established in state constitutions and the US Constitution. Statutes can be defined as any law adopted by the legislative bodies of the federal and state governments. The state and federal courts assist in the process by enforcing these statutes and making addenda to these statutes.

Common Law: Common law is different than statutory law because of its focus on individual rights; all common laws are not covered by statutory law.

Federal Statutes: Federal statutes are federal laws enacted by Congress and supported by the US Constitution. The process of making these statutes begins when the Senate or House of Representatives introduces a bill. After sending these bills through committees and subcommittees, which have to resolve differences between the bicameral legislature, the Senate and House approve a uniform version of the bill. This bill is then sent to the president, where it can be vetoed. The Senate and the House can overrule the veto with a two-thirds vote.

Below is a chart explaining the process of how a bill becomes law:

How does a bill become a law?

1. Every law starts with an idea

That idea can come from anyone, even you! Contact your elected officials to share your idea. If they want to try to make it a law, they will write a bill.

2. The bill is introduced

A bill can start in either house of Congress when it's introduced by its primary sponsor, a Senator or a Representative. In the House of Representatives, bills are placed in a wooden box called "the hopper".

Here, the bill is assigned a legislative number before the Speaker of the House sends it to a committee.

3. The bill goes to committee

Representatives or Senators meet in a small group to research, talk about, and make changes to the bill. They vote to accept or reject the bill and its changes before sending it to:

The House or Senate floor for debate

or

to a subcommittee for further research

4. Congress debates and votes

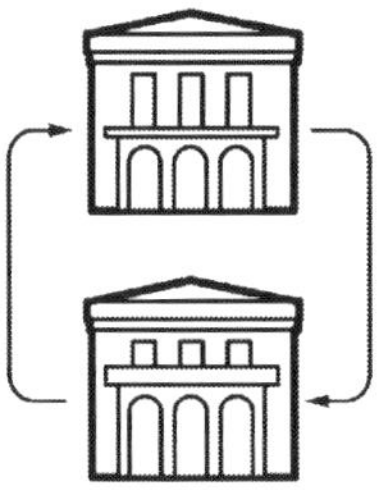

Members of the House or Senate can now debate the bill and propose changes or amendments before voting. If the majority vote for and pass the bill, it moves to the other house to go through a similar process of committees, debates, and voting. Both house have to agree on the same version of the final bill before it goes to the President.

The House uses an electronic voting system while the Senate typically votes by voice, saying "yay" or "nay".

5. Presidential action

When the bill reaches the President, he or she can:

Approve and Pass → The bill is law

The President signs and approves the bill. The bill is law.

Veto

The President rejects the bill and returns it to Congress with the reasons for the veto. Congress can override the veto with 2/3 vote of those present in both the House and the Senate and the bill will become a law.

Choose no action

The President can decide to do nothing. If Congress is in session after 10 days of no answer from the President the bill then automatically becomes law.

Pocket veto

If Congress adjourns (goes out of session) within the 10 day period after giving the President the bill, the President can choose not to sign it and the bill will not become law.

State Statutes: So long as the laws do not conflict with those established by federal statutes and the US Constitution, state legislatures can also pass laws that reside in their jurisdiction or within their shared jurisdiction with Congress. The process for a bill to become a law in each state legislature is very similar to the ways in which bills become laws at the federal level.

The Roles of Courts: U.S. courts can enforce, interpret invalidate, and create laws.

- **Enforce**: If a law is infringed upon, undermined, or disregarded, the courts can oversee a suit to enforce the law.
- **Interpret**: If a definition, statement, or meaning within a law is not adequately defined, then the courts have the right to interpret that law, offering their own definitions, statements, and meanings within parameters of constitutionality.
- **Invalidate**: Using the US Constitution as a "litmus test for legality," courts have the power to invalidate laws if they are deemed unconstitutional.
- **Create**: Courts can create "common laws" that focus on individual rights that are not protected under statutory law.

Types of Courts: There are two major types of federal and state courts, trial courts and appellate courts.

- **Trial Courts**: Any case is tried in a trial court.
- **Appellate Courts**: Trial decisions can be reviewed in appellate courts.

Levels of Federal Court: There are a total of thirteen judicial circuits within the federal court system of the United States of America. These circuit courts handle some appeals, such as patents and claims court cases. Each of the thirteen federal circuit courses has one appellate court, which is referred to as a Court of Appeals. Each federal circuit has lower levels of judicial districts. These districts vary in size, but can be as large as an entire state or as small as one city. The Supreme Court has the power to review all decisions made by the Court of Appeals.

Jurisdiction: Jurisdiction refers to the right each court has to review a particular question or case; for instance, the federal court has jurisdiction over federal cases and federal questions.

Criminal vs. Civil Cases: Criminal cases are a violation of criminal law, such as murder or arson. The defendant in these cases is tried and sentenced by a jury. Civil cases are not criminal infractions; they are legal suits over rights that are based on common laws or statutory laws.

Types of Government

Governments are often classified based on how power is distributed and how people participate in the governmental process. Most countries' governments combine multiple defined types.

In terms of power distribution, government may be unitary, led by a central authority. Alternatively, independent groups that voluntarily work together toward a common goal form a confederation. In a federation, constituents (e.g., states) are formally bound by the federal government.

The level of citizen involvement also affects the type of government. Individuals have little to no power in an autocratic government, which grants a single individual unlimited power (e.g., absolute monarchy, dictatorship). Citizens play a minor role in oligarchic or aristocratic governments run by a small group of people. However, democratic governments aim for maximal citizen involvement either directly or via representatives chosen by the people through elections.

A democratic government is one in which the people have power in the legislative process. Earliest democracies, such as the original in Athens, Greece, directly employed people in the political process. Representative democracies are more common in modern society; citizens elect officials such as Senators and Representatives to act on their behalf and with their interests in mind. Theoretically in democracies, governmental power is passed peacefully through elections, and the rule of law applies to all people and institutions equally.

Totalitarian governments, like the one led by Adolph Hitler in Nazi Germany, are forcibly run by a single political party. The party in power not only rules but maintains absolute power by preventing the formation or election of alternate parties. Totalitarian governments aim to control people through policies and the economy, and they attempt to sway beliefs and values, often through propaganda. Such governments have immense power and great potential for corruption.

Monarchical governments are ruled by a single individual (e.g., king, empress) who likely inherits the position through birthright. Traditionally, monarchies were absolute, where the single leader was exclusively in charge without opposition. Constitutional monarchies, like the United Kingdom and Japan, limit the monarch's control with a democratic government. Most current constitutional monarchies are parliamentary with an elected prime minster leading the government. The democratic side of a constitutional monarchy gives citizens more power in their government.

Changing the United States and Texas Constitutions

Amendments to the Texas Constitution may include additions, deletions, or modifications of text. The process for amending the Constitution is included within the original document itself. Amendment ratification is a two-step process. First, either the Senate or House introduces a joint resolution, which must then pass both chambers of the state legislature by a two-thirds majority vote. To be ratified, the change must win a simple majority of voters in a special election, which occurs on a date determined by the legislature. The proposed amendments, an explanation of their contents, and the date of the election must be publicized ahead of time. They appear as "propositions" on the ballot. If the proposition wins the majority vote, the governor issues a proclamation that the amendment will be included in the Constitution. The Texas Constitution has been amended over 500 times.

The process for amending the US Constitution is outlined therein under Article V. As in Texas, amendment of the US Constitution first requires that a proposal pass in both the House and Senate with a two-thirds majority vote. Unlike Texas, U.S. amendments are ratified via approval by three-quarters of the state legislatures, not by individual voters. The Constitution also provides for Congress's ability to call a national convention of state delegations as a means to pass an amendment, but as of 2021, this approach has never been used. Of the amendments proposed by Congress, twenty-seven have been ratified by the states. Some of the most impactful amendments include the thirteenth, which ended slavery, the nineteenth, which granted women the right to vote, and the eighteenth, which prohibited alcohol (later appealed by the twenty-first amendment).

Landmark Supreme Court Cases

Landmark Supreme Court cases are historic decisions that had a notable and major impact on the country.

In Marbury v. Madison (1803), the Supreme Court ruled that it can act only to review cases decided by judges in lower courts; it may not be the first court to try a case. This case established the role of the Supreme Court in judicial review and interpretation of cases where the constitutionality of a decision is questioned.

Several landmark Supreme Court cases had a direct impact on the changing views of slavery and racial segregation in the United States. In Dred Scott v. Stanford (1857), a slave who moved to a free state with his master sued for his freedom. However, the Court ruled that slaves were denied the right to be considered U.S. citizens and deemed them property instead. This decision fueled mounting support for the U.S. Civil War and was reversed by the Thirteenth Amendment in 1865.

In Plessy v. Ferguson (1896), Homer Plessy was arrested for traveling in a white-designated railroad car because he was one-eighth black. Though he argued that his arrest was in violation of the Thirteenth and Fourteenth amendments, the Supreme Court ruled that the states lawfully offered "separate but equal" treatment under the racial segregation imposed by Jim Crow laws. This idea was eventually challenged by another landmark case, Brown v. Board of Education.

The decision shared in Brown v. Board of Education (1954) ruled that "separate but equal" had "no place" in education, and that separate schools could not be equal. This decision initiated the desegregation of public schools and ended the misguided era validated by the Plessy v. Ferguson decision. Though federal law didn't recognize racial equality until the Civil Rights Act (1964), many credit the Brown decision with creating national momentum toward that cause.

Several other landmark cases include Miranda v. Arizona (1966), which protects defendants from incriminating themselves. Tinker v. Des Moines (1969) granted students freedom of expression in schools when it doesn't disrupt educational activities. Engel v. Vitale (1962) ruled that public institutions, namely schools, may not require prayer.

Leadership in a Constitutional Republic

In a constitutional republic, elected officials represent the people and their interests. The law set forth by the constitution not only informs the representatives' governance, but also limits the government's power and makes it subject to judicial review. The Constitution outlines the government's structure, which is often divided into branches to prevent any one person or group from having too much power. It also describes laws, governing procedures, and the rights of people.

Effective leaders in a constitutional republic abide by and uphold the Constitution. They are held accountable for doing so at the risk of being removed from office. They are charged with preventing the majority from overshadowing the rights of minorities and pursuing a common good, as defined by the Constitution.

Abraham Lincoln is one of the best-known and most revered constitutional leaders in U.S. history. In his role as the president of a country newly divided by states' views on slavery, he was known for listening to different points of view. He understood the difficulty of a constitution-bound republic in effectively pursuing changes appropriate for the people versus maintaining the status quo outlined in the document meant to prescribe the law for the country. However, in his best efforts to preserve the Union in times of war, he pushed the limits of his executive power under what he termed military necessity. This included the issuance of the Emancipation Proclamation, which was a historic step in protecting minorities (slaves) from the majority (pro-slave white people). His constitutional loyalty is evident, though, in his refusal to postpone presidential elections during the Civil War, despite the likelihood that even people in his party were rallying against his reelection.

Customs, Symbols, Landmarks, and Celebrations

As a democratic country that fought for its freedom from Great Britain, America has many symbols, customs, and landmarks that celebrate its identity.

Independence Day, or the Fourth of July, celebrates the day in 1776 on which delegates from the original thirteen colonies adopted the finalized Declaration of Independence, which asserted America's right to form its own government as a newly independent nation. Politicians used early celebrations of Independence Day to foster unity in the young country. Modern celebrations often include parades, concerts, barbeques, and fireworks, a tradition dating back to the first organized Independence Day celebrated in Philadelphia in 1777.

Two national symbols and landmarks of American democracy and freedom include the Liberty Bell and the Statue of Liberty.

The Liberty Bell sat in the tower of Pennsylvania's State House (now Independence Hall), where it called people to meetings, including the first public reading of the Declaration of Independence in 1776. After over 90 years of use, the Liberty Bell became irreparably cracked. It now sits on display near its former home, bearing the famous inscription, "Proclaim Liberty Throughout All the Land Unto All the Inhabitants thereof."

Standing in New York Harbor since 1886, the Statue of Liberty is a globally recognized symbol. From the date on her tablet (July 4, 1776) to the light of her torch to the broken chains under her feet, Lady Liberty represents freedom, hope, and justice. The statue has long welcomed people to the country in a way best described by the poem inscribed on its pedestal: "Give me your tired, your poor, Your huddled masses yearning to breathe free."

Texas history and pride is likewise represented by numerous symbols. The Alamo has been depicted in innumerable works of art as a symbol of Texans' courage in their fight for independence, despite their defeat at the hands of Santa Anna's troops. San Jacinto and the monument dedicated to it memorialize the final battle of the revolution, which won Texas its independence from Mexico.

The Lone Star flag similarly celebrates Texans' fight for freedom with the colors blue (loyalty), red (bravery), and white (purity) along with a single star to represent the peoples' solidarity. It is the only state flag which once represented an independent country.

Individual Rights and Responsibilities in Democratic Societies

Citizens living in a democracy have several rights and responsibilities to uphold. The first duty is that they uphold the established laws of the government. In a democracy, a system of nationwide laws is necessary to ensure that there is some degree of order. Therefore, citizens must try to obey the laws and also help enforce them because a law that is inadequately enforced, such as early civil rights laws in the South, is almost useless. Optimally, a democratic society's laws will be accepted and followed by the community as a whole.

However, conflict can occur when an unjust law is passed. For instance, much of the civil rights movement centered around Jim Crow laws in the South that supported segregation between black and whites. Yet these practices were encoded in state laws, which created a dilemma for African Americans who wanted equality but also wanted to respect the law. Fortunately, a democracy offers a degree of protection from such laws by creating a system in which government leaders and policies are constantly open to change in accordance with the will of citizens. Citizens can influence the laws that are passed by voting for and electing members of the legislative and executive branches to represent them at the local, state, and national levels.

This, however, requires citizens to be especially vigilant in protecting their liberties because they cannot depend solely on the existing government to meet their needs. To assert their role in a democracy, citizens should be active voters and speak out on issues that concern them. Even with these safeguards, it is possible for systems to be implemented that inhibit active participation. For instance, many southern states had laws that prevented blacks from voting. Under such circumstances, civil rights leaders felt that they had no choice but to resist the laws in order to defend their personal rights. Once voting became possible, civil rights groups strove to ensure that their votes counted by changing state and national policy.

An extension of citizens' voting rights is their ability to run as elected officials. By becoming leaders in the government, citizens can demonstrate their engagement and help determine government policy. The involvement of citizens as a whole in the selection of leaders is vital in a democracy because it helps to prevent the formation of an elite cadre that does not answer to the public. Without the engagement of citizens who run for office, voters are limited in their ability to select candidates that appeal to them. In this case, voting options would become stagnant, which inhibits the ability of the nation to grow and change over time. As long as citizens are willing to take a stand for their vision of America, America's government will remain dynamic and diverse.

These features of a democracy give it the potential to reshape itself continually in response to new developments in society. In order for a democracy to function, it is of the utmost importance that citizens care about the course of politics and be aware of current issues. Apathy among citizens is a constant problem that threatens the endurance of democracies. Citizens should have a desire to take part in the political process, or else they simply accept the status quo and fail to fulfill their role as citizens. Moreover, they must have acute knowledge of the political processes and the issues that they can address as citizens.

A fear among the Founding Fathers was the prevalence of mob rule, in which the common people did not take interest in politics except to vote for their patrons; this was the usual course of politics in the colonial era, as the common people left the decisions to the established elites. Without understanding the world around them, citizens may not fully grasp the significance of political actions and thereby fail to make wise decisions in that regard. Therefore, citizens must stay informed about current affairs, ranging from local to national or global matters, so that they can properly address them as voters or elected leaders.

Furthermore, knowledge of the nation's history is essential for healthy citizenship. History continues to have an influence on present political decisions. For instance, Supreme Court rulings often take into account previous legal precedents and verdicts, so it is important to know about those past events and how they affect the current processes. It is especially critical that citizens are aware of the context in which laws were established because it helps clarify the purpose of those laws. For instance, an understanding of the problems with the Articles of Confederation allows people to comprehend some of the reasons behind the framework of the Constitution. In addition, history as a whole shapes the course of societies and the world; therefore, citizens should draw on this knowledge of the past to realize the full consequences of current actions. Issues such as climate change, conflict in the Middle East, and civil rights struggles are rooted in events and cultural developments that reach back centuries and should be addressed.

Therefore, education is a high priority in democracies because it has the potential to instill generations of citizens with the right mind-set and knowledge required to do their part in shaping the nation. Optimally, education should cover a variety of different subjects, ranging from mathematics to biology, so that individuals can explore whatever paths they wish to take in life. Even so, social studies are especially important because students should understand how democracies function and understand the history of the nation and world. Historical studies should cover national and local events as well because they help provide the basis for the understanding of contemporary politics. Social studies courses should also address the histories of foreign nations because contemporary politics increasingly has global consequences. In addition, history lessons should remain open to multiple perspectives, even those that might criticize a nation's past actions, because citizens should be exposed to diverse perspectives that they can apply as voters and leaders.

Practice Quiz

1. What is used to pinpoint location on a map?
    a. Scale and longitude
    b. Contour lines and scale
    c. Latitude and longitude
    d. Latitude and contour lines

2. Third-grade students are debating what are the obligations of citizens under America's democratic form of government. Which of the following is NOT one of these obligations?
    a. Obey the law.
    b. Pay taxes.
    c. Serve on a jury if asked to do so.
    d. Vote in elections.

3. A teacher is preparing a lesson about the dynamic nature of history. Which of the following is a good example of this principle?
    a. The fact that GPS technology was first implemented in the 1960s but now is available on smartphones
    b. The fact there are checks and balances built into the various branches of government
    c. The fact that there are contradictory accounts of certain historical events, such as when Europeans first came to America
    d. The fact that there are twenty-seven amendments to the US Constitution

4. What is the interaction of consumers, households, and companies within individual markets and the relations between them called?
    a. Macroeconomics
    b. Microeconomics
    c. Boom and bust
    d. Economic output

5. What are the types of productive resources used to create products, such as machinery, tools, buildings, and equipment called?
    a. Natural resources
    b. Human resources
    c. Capital resources
    d. Entrepreneurship

See answers on next page.

Answer Explanations

1. C: Latitude—imaginary lines covering the globe from east to west—and longitude—imaginary lines running north to south—are used to pinpoint location on a map. Scale is used to show the relationship between the map measurements and the equivalent distance on the world's surface. Contour lines are used to show detailed elevation on a map.

2. D: Under America's democratic form of government, voting is a right, but it is not an obligation. US citizens are obliged to obey the law, pay taxes, and serve on a jury if asked to do so, making Choices *A*, *B*, and *C* incorrect.

3. D: History is dynamic, meaning that it can change over time. A good example of this is that there are twenty-seven amendments to the US Constitution. The document was not created and then set permanently in stone. It has been changed to reflect changing thoughts and circumstances in the country. The 14th Amendment was adopted in 1868 to abolish slavery. The 18th Amendment was passed in 1919 and prohibited the production and sale of alcoholic beverages, but the 21s Amendment repealed it in 1933. It is true that GPS technology was first implemented in the 1960s and now is available on smartphones, but this is more about improvements in technology and not how the field of history and social sciences itself changes. There are checks and balances built into the various branches of government, but this is an example of balancing power rather than change. Lastly, there are contradictory accounts of certain historical events, such as when Europeans first came to America. This is a good example of considering sources, perspectives, reliability, and circumstances when studying social sciences.

4. B: Microeconomics looks at the interplay of consumers, households, and companies within individual markets and the relationships between them. Macroeconomics, Choice *A*, is the study of entire economies. Booms and busts, Choice *C*, are terms used to describe the cyclical nature of economic activity, typically prompted by extreme changes in the economy. Economic output, Choice *D*, is the total amount of goods and services produced by an *economy.*

5. C: Capital resources are the man-made physical resources used to create products, such as machinery, tools, buildings, and equipment. Natural resources, Choice *A*, are raw materials taken from the land, such as corn, beef, lumber, water, oil, and iron. Human resources, Choice *B*, refer to the human labor – both mental and physical – required to produce goods. Entrepreneurship, Choice *D*, is the capability and motivation to cultivate, organize, and oversee the other three resources into a business venture.

Lab Processes, Equipment, and Safety

Safety Regulations and Guidelines

When conducting experiments and activities in a science classroom, laboratory environment, or field experience, safety should always be the primary concern of a science educator. It is the teacher's responsibility to ensure a safe environment for student learning. Proper direction and supervision greatly reduce the risk of injury. Failure to prepare students with safety precautions and to ensure student safety in the environment can result in the failure to exercise ordinary or reasonable care, or legal negligence. Thus, safety procedures, equipment protocols, directions for disposing of chemicals, rules for complying with mandated classroom layouts, and rules for safely handling living organisms and specimens should be embedded within classroom curricula and routines.

Safety Procedures: Students should be explicitly taught and quizzed on safety procedures in the classroom. Likewise, these procedures should be posted throughout the classroom with adequate cautionary signage. In particular, they should know how to exit in case of an emergency or respond in case of a fire or hazardous spill.

Equipment Protocols: Students must be taught how to properly use all science equipment in the classroom, including, but not limited to: graduated cylinders, Bunsen burners, scales, thermometers, scalpels, safety equipment (i.e., fire extinguishers, fire blankets, and emergency eye-wash stations), microscopes, safety goggles, gloves, storage cabinets for flammable materials, and containers for broken glassware, flammables, corrosives, and wastes.

Storing and Disposing of Chemicals: Chemicals should not be stored near heat sources or in open/active areas of the classroom; all solutions should be disposed of according to local codes and laws; all chemical waste should be disposed of in properly labeled containers and separated from other chemicals.

Compliance with Classroom Layout Rules: Every classroom's spatial layout should be in compliance with local, state, and federal codes; likewise, students should be informed of these safety laws and should understand the function of the spatial layout, the location of emergency accessories, and the procedures for exiting during an emergency.

Safely Handling Living Organisms and Specimens: Biological materials, like chemical materials, should be handled with gloves; biological materials such as living organism and specimens should not be stored near food or water supplies; they should be labeled appropriately and disposed of according to local, state, and federal codes.

Appropriate and Safe Use of Materials

The appropriate and safe use of laboratory materials not only reduces the potential harm to people and the environment, but also minimizes waste and ensures accurate data collection. The following guidelines highlight the crucial skills in safely handling chemical reagents and specimens.

Identifying Hazards

The ability to identify a hazard allows one to take safety measures such as wearing the appropriate clothing and responding appropriately to spills.

Common types of laboratory hazards include:

- Chemical hazards
- Toxins
- Corrosives
- Flammables
- Reactive substances
- Biological hazards
- Animals
- Plants
- Microbes
- Genetically-modified organisms
- Physical hazards
- Extreme heat
- Extreme cold
- Noise
- Heating devices
- Projectiles
- Electrical hazards
- Fire

- Shock
- Radiation hazards
- Ionizing radiation
- Non-iodizing radiation
- Mechanical hazards
- Machinery
- Airborne hazards
- Vapor
- Fume
- Dust

Handling Chemicals and Specimens

A **specimen** is any substance or fluid taken from a plant, animal, or other object, such as urine, blood, saliva, stool, or tissue. To safely handle chemicals and specimens, one should adhere to the following guidelines:

- Always read the safety data sheet that accompanies a chemical.
- Make sure specimens and chemicals are properly stored.
- Ensure that any first-aid equipment, including eye-washing stations, are close and ready for use.
- Keep all work stations clean and sanitized.
- Use the smallest amount of chemical or specimen possible.
- Make sure all containers are properly labeled.
- Use substitutions for more harmful chemicals whenever possible.

Safe Disposal of Materials

The following are basic requirements to follow for the disposal of chemical hazardous waste:

Create a Hazardous Waste Area

- Select an area near the source of the waste, out of the way of normal lab activities, and easily accessible to all lab personnel.

- Label the area "Danger—Hazardous Waste" with the following sign:

Deposit chemicals into the appropriate containers. Make sure that containers into which the chemicals will be discarded are stable enough to hold them—chemicals must not weaken or dissolve the material of the container.

- Acids and bases cannot be stored with metal.
- Hydrofluoric acid cannot be stored with glass.
- Solvents (i.e., gasoline) cannot be stored in polyethylene containers, such as a milk jug.
- Waste containers must come with lids and caps that are resistant to leakage, and containers should be closed at all times, except when opened to add more waste.
- The size of the container should be appropriate for the amount of expected waste.
- Waste containers should be placed inside a larger, empty container to catch any waste that may potentially spill or leak.

Attach a Hazardous Waste Tag

Complete and attach the following hazardous waste tag to all containers:

Hazardous Waste Tag

Front

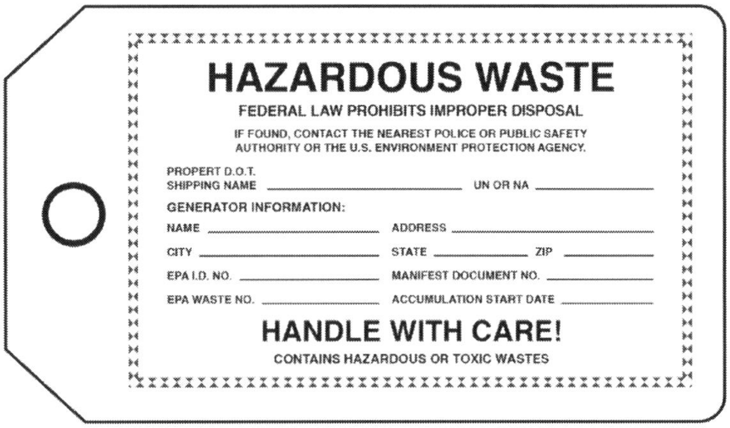
HAZARDOUS WASTE
FEDERAL LAW PROHIBITS IMPROPER DISPOSAL
IF FOUND, CONTACT THE NEAREST POLICE OR PUBLIC SAFETY AUTHORITY OR THE U.S. ENVIRONMENT PROTECTION AGENCY.
PROPERT D.O.T. SHIPPING NAME ________ UN OR NA ________
GENERATOR INFORMATION:
NAME ________ ADDRESS ________
CITY ________ STATE ________ ZIP ________
EPA I.D. NO. ________ MANIFEST DOCUMENT NO. ________
EPA WASTE NO. ________ ACCUMULATION START DATE ________
HANDLE WITH CARE!
CONTAINS HAZARDOUS OR TOXIC WASTES

Back

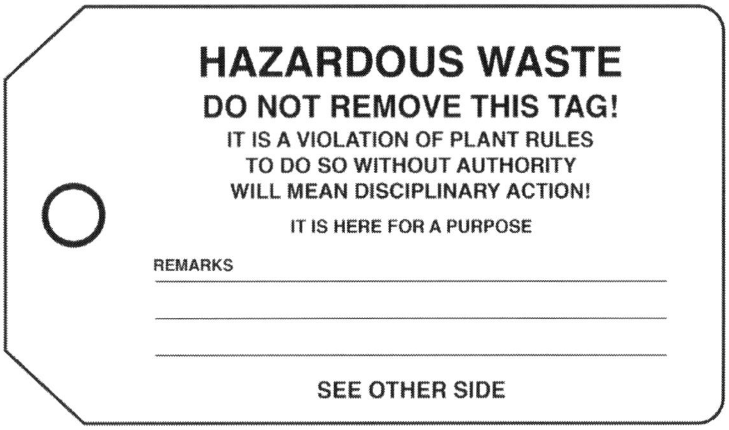
HAZARDOUS WASTE
DO NOT REMOVE THIS TAG!
IT IS A VIOLATION OF PLANT RULES
TO DO SO WITHOUT AUTHORITY
WILL MEAN DISCIPLINARY ACTION!
IT IS HERE FOR A PURPOSE
REMARKS ________
SEE OTHER SIDE

Requirements for Liquid Waste

- Don't overfill containers—be sure to leave at least 10% space between the container opening and the surface of the waste.
- Never mix liquid and solid waste.
- Double-bag small containers, such as vials, in clear plastic bags.
- Bag small containers composed of the same kind of waste.
- Attach a completed hazardous waste tag to all bags and containers.

Requirements for Solid Waste

Chemical solid waste is composed of three different categories: lab trash, dry chemicals, and sharps.

- Lab trash
- Use for waste such as Kim Wipes, disposable gloves, paper towels, and wooden stirrers
- Double-bag in clear bags
- Attach a completed hazardous waste tag to all bags
- Dry chemicals
- Return the chemical waste to the original container in which it was purchased.
- Attach a completed hazardous waste tag.
- Sharps
    - Examples include glass (broken or intact), pipettes and pipette tips, needles, X-ACTO™ knives, or anything capable of piercing, cutting, slicing, or tearing human flesh.
- Discard any used sharps into a designated sharps container with a biohazard sign.

Biohazard container

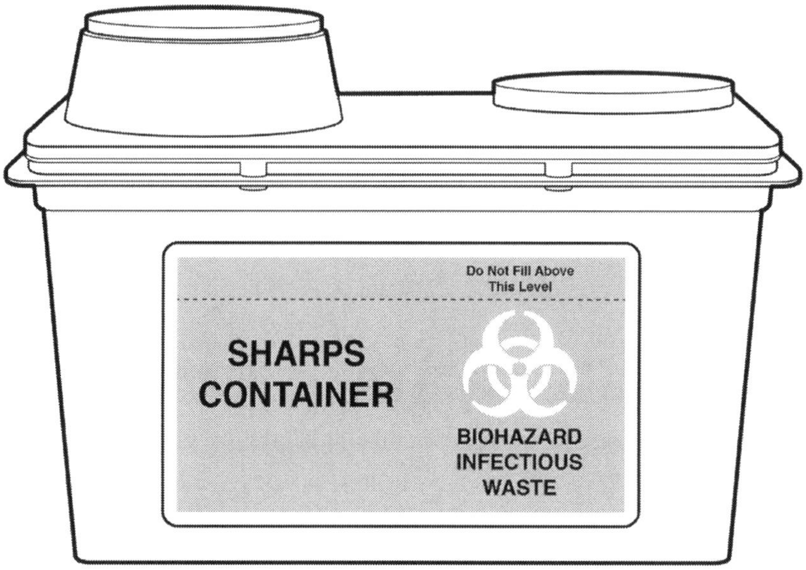

Preparation for Laboratory Experiments

Conducting a science lab is one of the most exciting ways to teach science. It not only allows students to experience science as professionals but also gives them the opportunity to apply learned concepts to real-world scenarios. Before beginning a lab, instructors should:

- Know and clarify the concepts and theories upon which the experiment is based
- Test the experiment and equipment, following along in the student instruction manual to identify any potential issues

The most common preparations a science instructor will conduct are preparing solutions, staining slides, and labeling samples.

Preparing a Solution of a Given Concentration

The primary way that a solution is measured is expressed in terms of **molarity**. A solution's molarity is the number of moles per liter of a pure substance.

$$\text{Molarity (M)} = \text{moles/L}$$

A **mole** is the mass of pure substance (including atoms and all corresponding chemical units, such as elements and particles) containing the same number of constituent units as there are atoms in exactly 12.000 grams of ^{12}C. It's equivalent to 6.022×10^{23} molecules, also known as Avogadro's Number.

Most solutions are made by using a pure solid or by diluting a stock solution.

Using a Pure Solid

Instructors should follow this procedure for making a solution from a pure solid:

1. Determine the molecular mass of the solid.
2. Calculate the mass needed to make the solution.
3. Weigh out the substance and place it in the appropriate flask.
4. Dissolve solute in less water than the desired volume.
5. Fill the flask to the desired amount of solution.

Because standard weighing devices cannot measure a compound in moles, one must determine the molecular mass of a substance, which is expressed in g/mol. The molecular mass of an element can be found in a periodic table.

For example, an experiment calls for 400 mL of a 0.750 M solution of NaOH. To determine the atomic weight of the formula, one must add each element's molecular mass together.

Total molecular weight (NaOH) = 22.990 g/mol + 15.999 g/mol + 1.0078 g/mol = *39.997 g/mol* (the reported molecular weights are in five significant figures).

Once the molecular weight has been determined, the mass needed to make 400 mL of a 0.750 M solution of NaOH can be calculated by multiplying the volume of the solution (400 mL) by the molarity (0.750 mol/L) and the molecular weight of the substance (39.007 g/mol).

By entering the values, the total grams needed are calculated as follows:

Total molecular weight (NaOH) = Na^{11} (Sodium, 22.990) O^{8} (Oxygen, 15.999) H^{1} (Hydrogen, 1.0078) = 39.997 g/mol

Volume needed — Molarity — Molecular weight

$$\text{mL of solution} \times \frac{\text{mol substance}}{\text{1000 mL solution}} \times \frac{\text{g of substance}}{\text{mol of substance}} = \text{grams of substance needed to make solution}$$

$$\text{400 mL NaOH} \times \frac{\text{0.750 mol NaOH}}{\text{1000 mL NaOH}} \times \frac{\text{39.997 g NaOH}}{\text{1 mol NaOH}} = \text{11.999 g NaOH}$$

solution — solution

Because the required solution is given with three significant figures, the weight in grams should be measured at three significant figures as well, so 12.0 grams is necessary for this solution.

Finally, the experimenter will weigh 12.0 grams of NaOH and place it in a 500-mL volumetric flask. About 200 mL of distilled water can be added and mixed until the solute has dissolved. Then more water is added until the flask reads 400 mL.

Using a Stock Solution

Stock solutions are used frequently in labs, as many substances are considered too hazardous to have in their pure form. For example, an experiment calls for a 500 mL solution of 1.25 M of HCl (hydrochloric acid). To save space, a school's stockroom would likely have a bottle of 12.0 M HCl that would then be diluted with water to form the desired concentration. Instructors should follow the procedure below to create the desired solution using a stock:

- Calculate the appropriate volume of stock solution to add to water.
- Add the correct amount of stock to a flask containing some of the required water.
- Dilute with water until desired volume is reached.

To make a 500 mL solution of 1.25 M HCl from a 12.0 M stock of HCl, the appropriate ratio must be set up. Because the total amount of the solute doesn't change when water is added, the moles of solute from the stock solution equal the moles of solute in the dilute solution:

$$Moles\ of\ Solute\ in\ Stock\ Solution = Moles\ of\ Solute\ in\ Dilute\ Solution$$

To calculate the moles of solute, one must multiply the volume (V) of the solution times the molarity (M) of the solution: $M \times V$.

$$M \times V\ (stock) = M \times V\ (dilute)$$

or

$$M_S V_S = M_D V_D$$

$$M_S = 12.0 \quad V_S = ? \quad M_D = 1.25 \quad V_D = 500 \text{ mL}$$

Using algebra, the necessary volume of stock solution can be solved:

$$V_S = \frac{M_D V_D}{M_S}$$

$$V_S = \frac{(1.25 \text{ M})(500 \text{ mL})}{12.0 \text{ M}} = 52.1 \text{ mL}$$

Finally, 52.1 mL of the stock solution can be measured into a volumetric flask containing 200 mL of water. More water should be added until the volume reads 500 mL, and presto! There's 500 mL of a 1.25 M HCl solution. It's important to note that when diluting stock acid solutions, the acid should always be added to the water instead of the reverse. This is to prevent the acid from splashing out of the container and damaging laboratory equipment or causing bodily harm.

Staining Slides

Microscope slides are the mounts that specimens are placed upon in order to observe them under a microscope. Specimens may be **dry mounted**, or placed directly between the slide and cover slip, or they may be **wet mounted**, in which the specimen is suspended in an aqueous solution between the slide and cover slip. Staining a slide requires a wet mount.

To stain a slide, an instructor should follow this procedure:

1. Obtain a clean slide and cover slip.

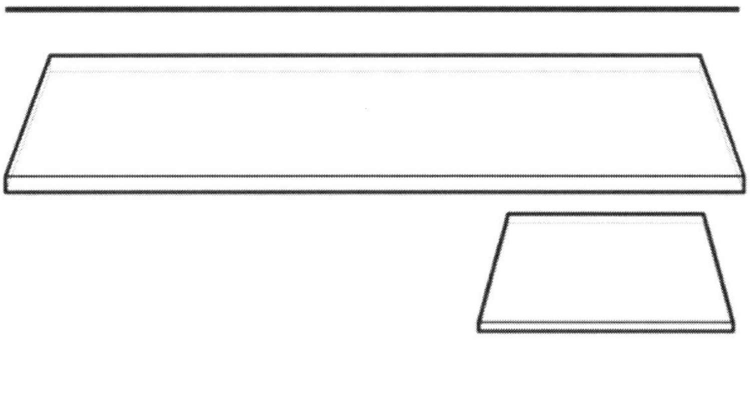

2. Place a *very thin* slice of the specimen directly in the middle of the slide.

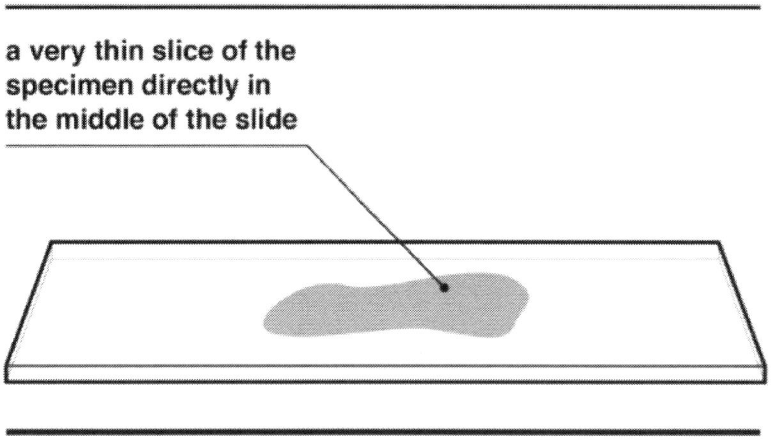

3. Add a drop of water to the specimen using a pipette.

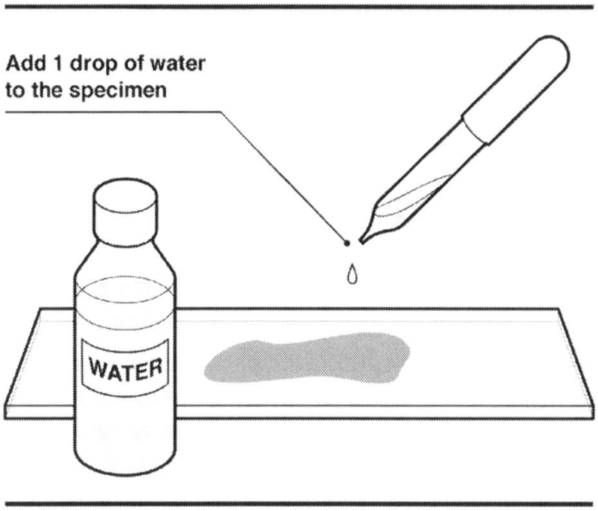

4. Add the cover slip by placing the slip on its edge and lowering it onto the specimen from a 45° angle.

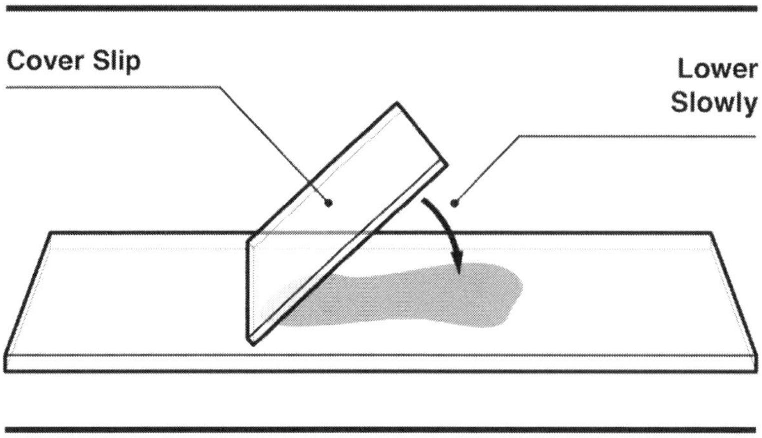

5. Add the appropriate stain (table below) on one side of the cover slip and a piece of paper towel on the other side.

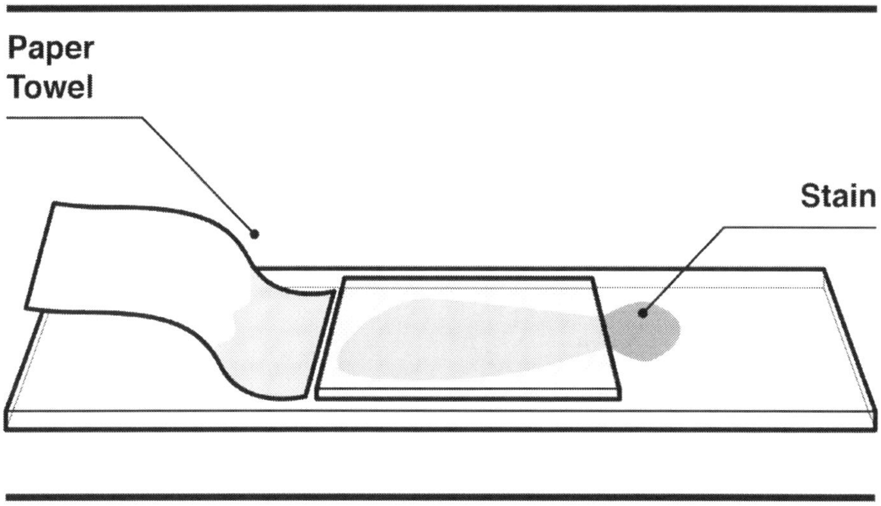

6. Press down on the paper towel so the stain is drawn through the cover slip and specimen.

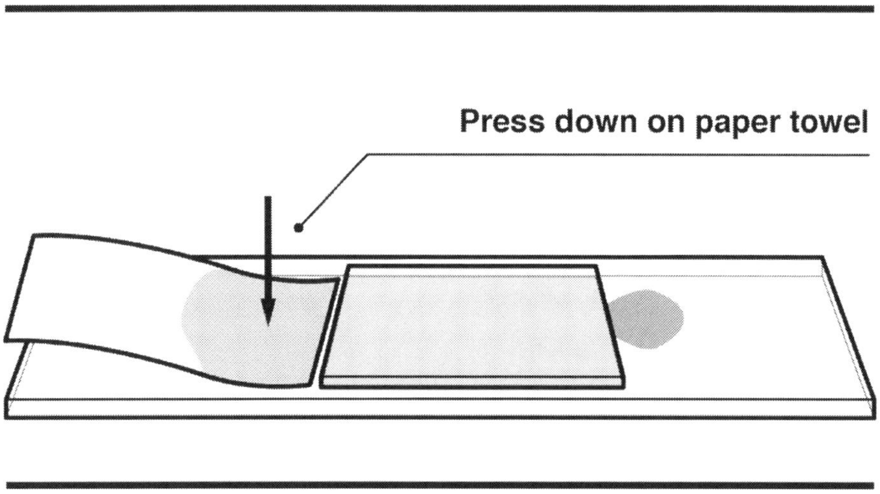

When choosing a stain, this table may be helpful:

Stain	Function	Uses
Eosin Y	Stains pink for alkaline cells (blood, cytoplasm, membranes)	Blood and bone marrow testing
Iodine	Stains brown or bluish-black for carbohydrates	Identify starches in plant and animal specimens
Gram's Stain	Stains purple for bacteria	Identify bacteria
Methylene Blue	Stains blue for acidic cells by allowing them to show against their background	Identifying acidic cell nucleic, DNA

Labeling Samples

All chemicals and collected specimens need appropriate labels to minimize confusion, which could have disastrous results. For samples within a laboratory, the following key information should be included:

- Name or initials of the researcher
- Date sample was prepared or collected
- Identification
- Chemical formula or name
- Identification number (if applicable)
- Any solvents or solutions that a sample is suspended in (such as water or acid)

Precision, Accuracy, and Error

The concepts of precision and accuracy are utilized to show how close certain measurements are to an actual or desired value. Although they seem to be interchangeable terms, they are quite different. Accuracy refers to how close a measurement is to a desired value, and precision refers to the consistency of measurements taken. Precision signifies the reproducibility of a measurement. This concept can be visualized as darts thrown at a dartboard. A dart hitting the bullseye would be an example of an accurate throw. If three darts are thrown and all three hit a ten but miss the bullseye, they are considered precise but not accurate. If three darts are thrown, all hitting the bullseye, these throws would be considered both accurate and precise. Accuracy and precision show the reliability of data.

Measuring error is a way to quantify how reliable data is. An error measurement is the difference between a true or theoretical value and a measured value. Within a scientific experiment, a theoretical value is mathematically determined as what a measurement should be if the experiment is done correctly and efficiently, and the measured value is the actual, recorded result of the experiment. A common way to record error is as percent error. Percent error is the theoretical value subtracted from the measured value, divided by the theoretical value, then multiplied by 100:

$$\%\,Error = \frac{(Theoretical\ value - Actual\ Value)}{Theoretical\ value} \times 100$$

Percent error is the best way to mathematically determine the accuracy and precision of a set of data within a scientific experiment.

Organizing and Displaying Data in a Variety of Ways

Observations made during a scientific experiment are organized and presented as data. Data can be collected in a variety of ways, depending on the purpose of the experiment. In testing how light exposure affects plant growth, for example, the data collected would be changes in the height of the plant relative to the amount of light it received. The easiest way to organize collected data is to use a **data table**.

A data table always contains a title that relates the two variables in the experiment. Each column or row must contain the units of measurement in the heading only. See the below example (note: this is not actual data).

Plant Growth During Time Exposed to Light (130 Watts)	
Time (Hours)	Height (cm)
0	3.2
192	5.0
480	7.9
720	12.1

Data must be presented in a concise, coherent way. Most data are presented in graph form. The fundamental rule for creating a graph based on data is that the independent variable (i.e., amount of time exposed to light) is on the x-axis, and the dependent variable (i.e., height of plant) is on the y-axis.

There are many types of graphs that a person may choose to use depending on which best represents the data.

The **illustrative diagram** provides a graphic representation or picture of some process. Questions may address specific details of the process depicted in the graphic. For example, "At which stage of the sliding filament theory of muscle contraction does the physical length of the fibers shorten (and contract)?"

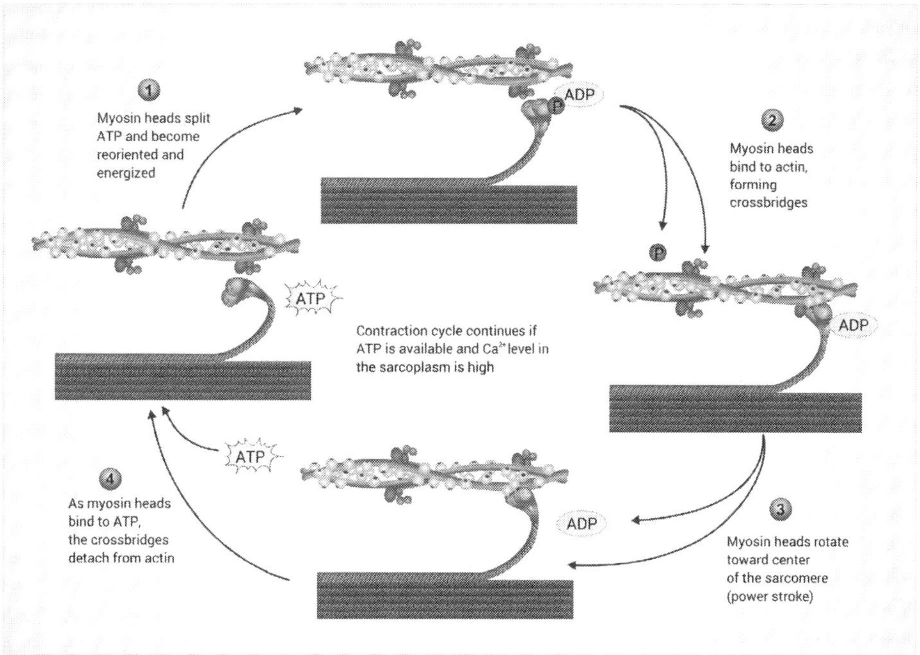

Bar graphs depict the passage data as parallel lines of varying heights. GED bar graphs will be printed in black and white. Data may be oriented vertically or horizontally. Questions may ask, "During the fall season, in what habitat do bears spend the most time?"

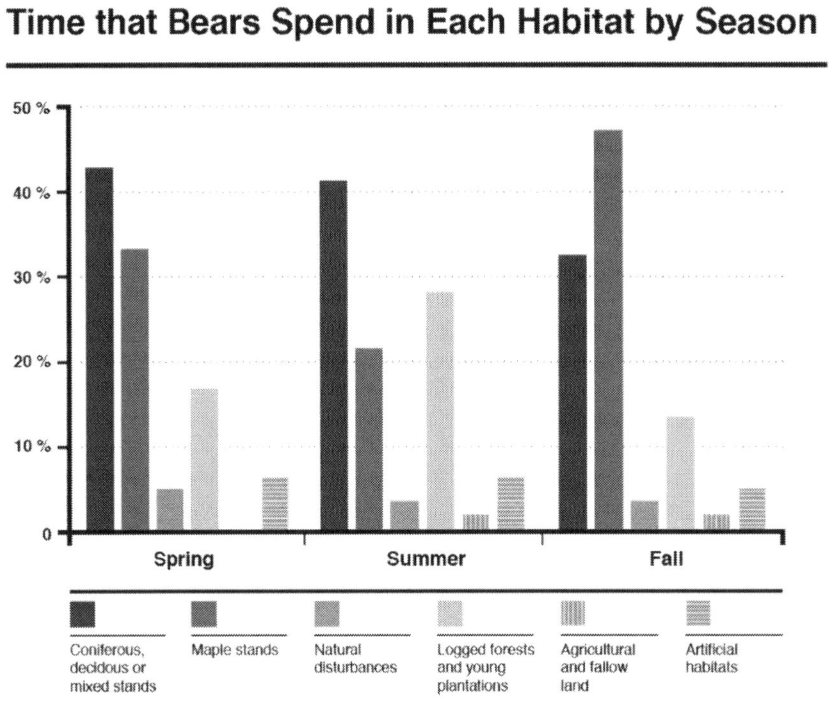

Bar graphs can also be horizontal, like the graph below.

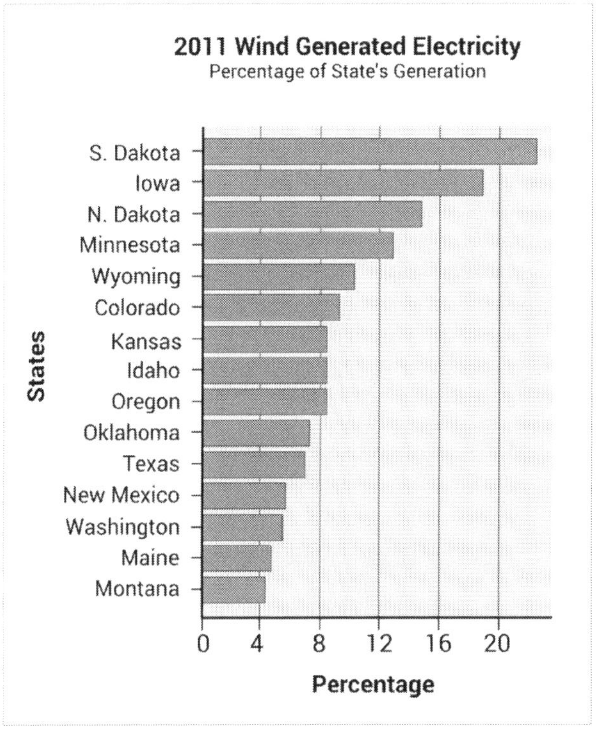

Scatter plots provide a visual representation of the passage data along the x- and y-axes. This representation indicates the nature of the relationship between the two variables. It is important to note that correlation doesn't equal causation. The relationship may be linear, curvilinear, positive, negative, inverse, or there may be no relationship. Questions may ask "What is the relationship between x and y?"

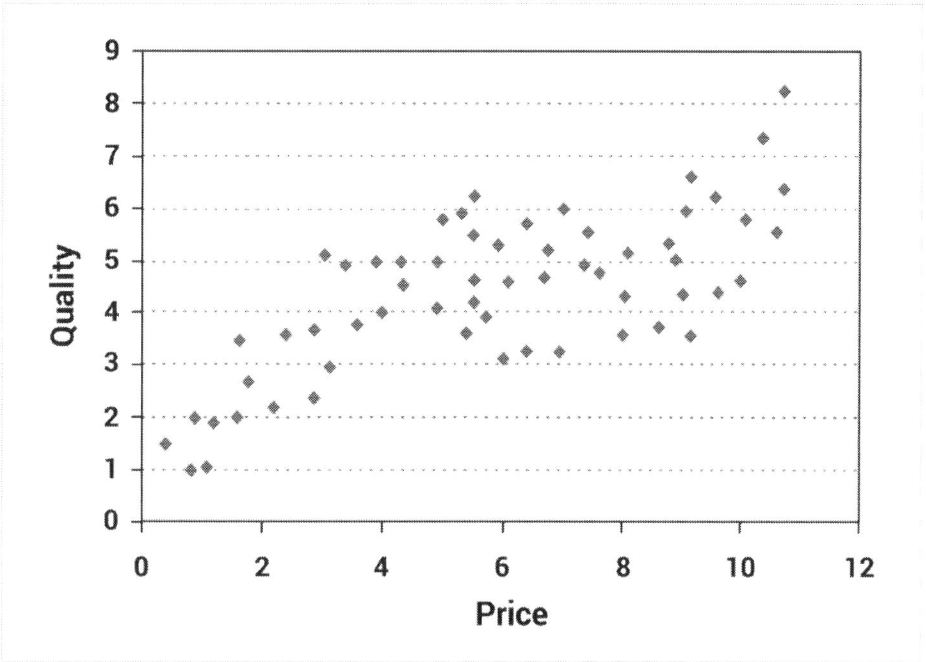

Line graphs are scatter plots that compare and contrast the relationships between two or more data sets. The horizontal axis represents the passage data sets that are compared over time. The vertical axis is the scale for measurement of that data. The scale points are equidistant from one another. There will always be a title for the line graph. Questions related to line graphs might ask," Which of the following conclusions is supported by the provided graph of tropical storms?"

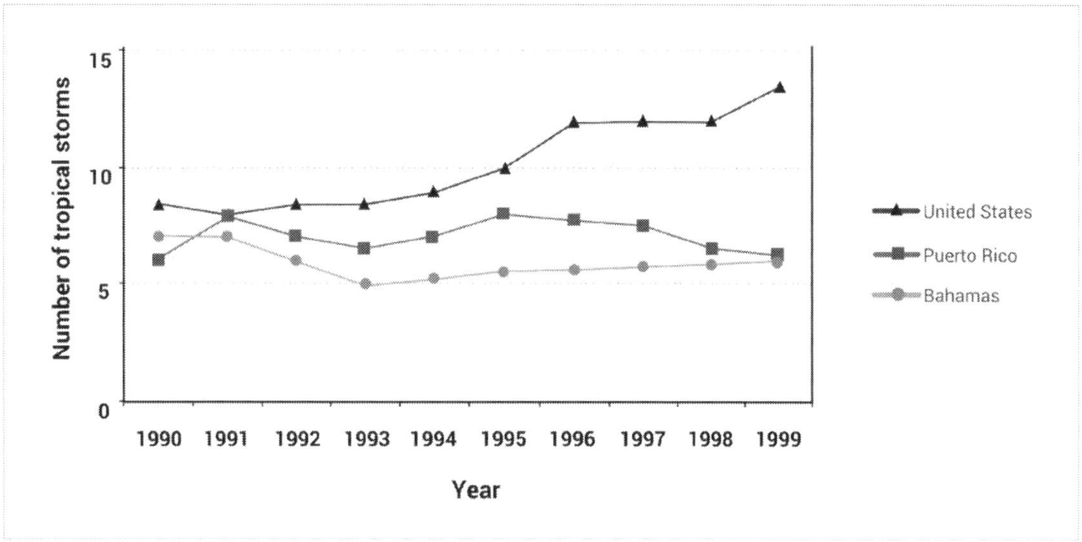

A **region graph** is a visual representation of the passage data set used to display the properties of a given substance under different conditions or at different points in time. Questions relating to this graph may ask, "According to the figure, what is the temperature range associated with liquid nitrogen?"

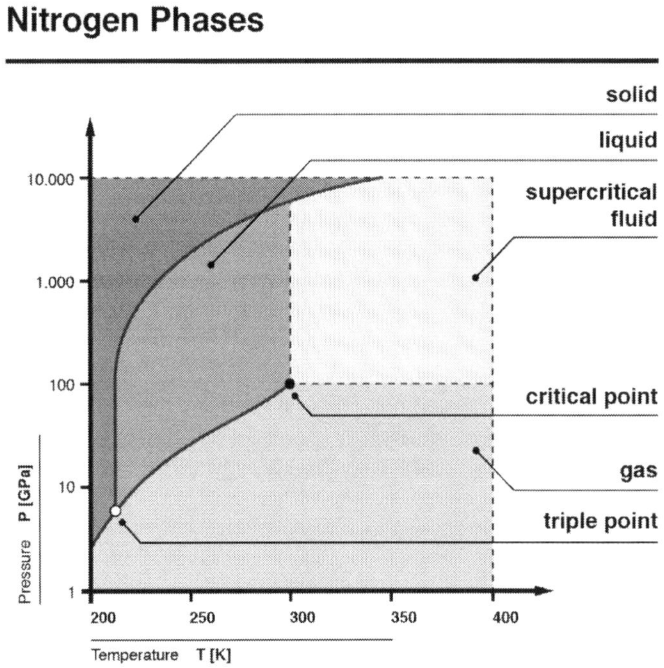

A **pie** or **circle graph** is used when the data sum to 100%, such as the percentage of students in each high school class interested in a trip to a local museum.

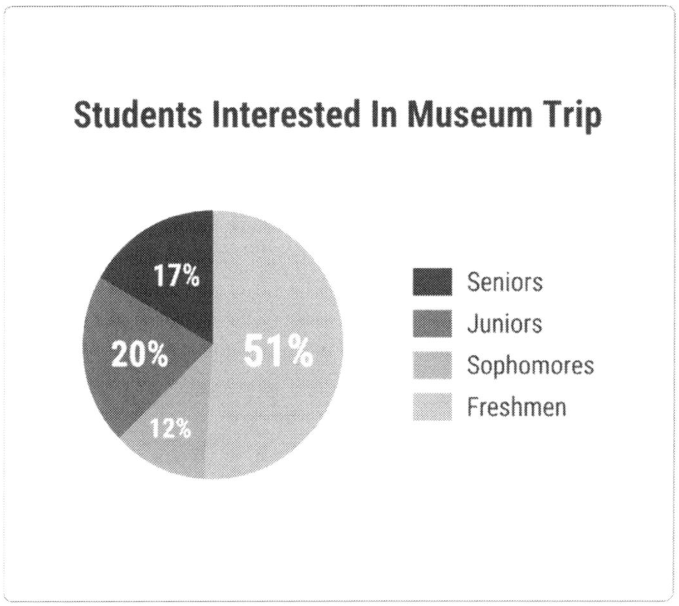

Systems of Measurement

Measurement is how an object's length, width, height, weight, and so on, are quantified. Measurement is related to counting, but it is a more refined process.

The United States customary system and the metric system each consist of distinct units to measure lengths and volume of liquids. The U.S. customary units for length, from smallest to largest, are: inch (in), foot (ft), yard (yd), and mile (mi). The metric units for length, from smallest to largest, are: millimeter (mm), centimeter (cm), decimeter (dm), meter (m), and kilometer (km). The relative size of each unit of length is shown below.

U.S. Customary	Metric	Conversion
12 in = 1 ft	10 mm = 1 cm	1 in = 254 cm
36 in = 3 ft = 1 yd	10 cm = 1 dm(decimeter)	1 m ≈ 3.28 ft ≈ 1.09 yd
5,280 ft = 1,760 yd = 1 mi	100 cm = 10 dm = 1 m	1 mi ≈ 1.6 km
	1,000 m = 1 km	

The U.S. customary units for volume of liquids, from smallest to largest, are: fluid ounces (fl oz), cup (c), pint (pt), quart (qt), and gallon (gal). The metric units for volume of liquids, from smallest to largest, are: milliliter (mL), centiliter (cL), deciliter (dL), liter (L), and kiloliter (kL). The relative size of each unit of liquid volume is shown below.

U.S. Customary	Metric	Conversion
8 fl oz = 1 c	10 mL = 1 cL	1 pt ≈ 0.473 L
2 c = 1 pt	10 cL = 1 dL	1 L ≈ 1.057 qt
4 c = 2 pt = 1 qt	1,000 mL = 100 cL = 10 dL = 1 L	1 gal ≈ 3.785 L
4 qt = 1 gal	1,000 L = 1 kL	

The U.S. customary system measures weight (how strongly Earth is pulling on an object) in the following units, from least to greatest: ounce (oz), pound (lb), and ton. The metric system measures mass (the quantity of matter within an object) in the following units, from least to greatest: milligram (mg), centigram (cg), gram (g), kilogram (kg), and metric ton (MT).

The relative sizes of each unit of weight and mass are shown below.

U.S. Measures of Weight	Metric Measures of Mass
16 oz = 1 lb	10 mg = 1 cg
2,000 lb = 1 ton	100 cg = 1 g
	1,000 g = 1 kg
	1,000 kg = 1 MT

Note that weight and mass DO NOT measure the same thing.

Time is measured in the following units, from shortest to longest: second (sec), minute (min), hour (h), day (d), week (wk), month (mo), year (yr), decade, century, millennium. The relative sizes of each unit of time is shown below.

- 60 sec = 1 min
- 60 min = 1 h
- 24 hr = 1 d
- 7 d = 1 wk
- 52 wk = 1 yr
- 12 mo = 1 yr
- 10 yr = 1 decade
- 100 yrs = 1 century

- $1{,}000 \text{ yrs} = 1 \text{ millennium}$

Some units of measure are represented as square or cubic units depending on the solution. For example, perimeter is measured in linear units, area is measured in square units, and volume is measured in cubic units.

Also, be sure to use the most appropriate unit for the thing being measured. A building's height might be measured in feet or meters while the length of a nail might be measured in inches or centimeters. Additionally, for SI units, the prefix should be chosen to provide the most succinct available value. For example, the mass of a bag of fruit would likely be measured in kilograms rather than grams or milligrams, and the length of a bacteria cell would likely be measured in micrometers rather than centimeters or kilometers.

Problems that involve measurements of length, time, volume, etc. are generally dependent upon understanding how to manipulate between various units of measurement, as well as understanding their equivalencies.

Identifying and utilizing the proper units for the scenario requires knowing how to apply the conversion rates for money, length, volume, and mass. For example, given a scenario that requires subtracting 8 inches from $2\frac{1}{2}$ feet, both values should first be expressed in the same unit (they could be expressed $\frac{2}{3}$ft & $2\frac{1}{2}$ft, or 8in and 30in). The desired unit for the answer may also require converting back to another unit.

Consider the following scenario: A parking area along the river is only wide enough to fit one row of cars and is $\frac{1}{2}$ kilometers long. The average space needed per car is 5 meters. How many cars can be parked along the river? First, all measurements should be converted to similar units: $\frac{1}{2}$km = 500m. The operation(s) needed should be identified. Because the problem asks for the number of cars, the total space should be divided by the space per car. 500 meters divided by 5 meters per car yields a total of 100 cars. Written as an expression, the meters unit cancels, and the cars unit is left: $\frac{500 \text{ m}}{5 \text{ m/car}}$ the same as $500 \text{ m} \times \frac{1 \text{ car}}{5 \text{ m}}$ yields 100 cars.

For an example manipulating time, Maria is scheduled to take a 90-minute test for her English class. It takes her 25 minutes to get ready and 40 minutes to ride the bus to school. If she begins to get ready at 1:10 p.m., what time will she be finished taking the test?

To find the ending time, all of the elapsed minutes must be totaled and then converted to hours.

$$25 + 40 + 90 = 155 \text{ minutes}$$

The conversion necessary for this problem is that 1 hour is equal to 60 minutes.

The total number of minutes must be converted into hours and minutes, by dividing the total number of minutes by 60.

$$155 \div 60 = 2 \text{ R } 35$$

The remainder is stated as minutes. So, the total elapsed time is 2 hours and 35 minutes. If Maria begins to get ready at 1:10 p.m., 2 hours from that time is 3:10 p.m., and an additional 35 minutes would add up to 3:45 p.m. Maria can expect to be finished with everything 2 hours and 35 minutes later, at 3:45 p.m.

When measuring length, choosing the right tool to perform the measurement requires determining whether United States customary units or metric units are desired, and having a grasp of the approximate length of each unit and the approximate length of each tool. The measurement can still be performed by trial and error without the knowledge of the approximate size of the tool.

For example, to determine the length of a room in feet, a United States customary unit, various tools can be used for this task. These include a ruler (typically 12 inches/1-foot-long), a yardstick (3 feet/1-yard-long), or a tape measure displaying feet (typically either 25 feet or 50 feet). Because the length of a room is much larger than the length of a ruler or a yardstick, a tape measure should be used to perform the measurement.

Converting Units of Measurement

Converting measurements in different units between the two systems can be difficult because they follow different rules. The best method is to look up an English to Metric system conversion factor and then use a series of equivalent fractions to set up an equation to convert the units of one of the measurements into those of the other. The table below lists some common conversion values that are useful for problems involving measurements with units in both systems:

English System	Metric System
1 inch	2.54 cm
1 foot	0.3048 m
1 yard	0.914 m
1 mile	1.609 km
1 ounce	28.35 g
1 pound	0.454 kg
1 fluid ounce	29.574 mL
1 quart	0.946 L
1 gallon	3.785 L

Consider the example where a scientist wants to convert 6.8 inches to centimeters. One method for converting units is to write and solve a proportion. The arrangement of values in a proportion is extremely important. The table above is used to find that there are 2.54 centimeters in every inch, so the following equation should be set up and solved:

$$\frac{6.8 \text{ in}}{1} \times \frac{2.54 \text{ cm}}{1 \text{ in}} = 17.272 \text{ cm}$$

Notice how the inches in the numerator of the initial figure and the denominator of the conversion factor cancel out. (This equation could have been written simply as $6.8 \text{ in} \times 2.54 \text{ cm} = 17.272 \text{ cm}$, but it was shown in detail to illustrate the steps). The goal in any conversion equation is to set up the fractions so that the units you are trying to convert from cancel out and the units you desire remain.

For a more complicated example, consider converting 2.15 kilograms into ounces. The first step is to convert kilograms into grams and then grams into ounces. Note that the measurement you begin with does not have to be put in a fraction.

So, in this case, 2.15 kg is by itself although it's technically the numerator of a fraction:

$$2.15 \text{ kg} \times \frac{1{,}000 \text{ g}}{\text{kg}} = 2150 \text{ g}$$

Then, use the conversion factor from the table to convert grams to ounces:

$$2150 \text{ g} \times \frac{1 \text{ oz}}{28.35 \text{ g}} = 75.8 \text{ oz}$$

Now suppose that a problem requires converting 20 fluid ounces to cups. To do so, a proportion can be written using the conversion rate of $8 \text{ fl oz} = 1 \text{ c}$ with x representing the missing value. The proportion can be written in any of the following ways:

$$\frac{1}{8} = \frac{x}{20} \left(\frac{c\,for\,conversion}{fl\,oz\,for\,conversion} = \frac{unknown\,c}{fl\,oz\,given} \right)$$

$$\frac{8}{1} = \frac{20}{x} \left(\frac{fl\,oz\,for\,conversion}{c\,for\,conversion} = \frac{fl\,oz\,given}{unknown\,c} \right)$$

$$\frac{1}{x} = \frac{8}{20} \left(\frac{c\,for\,conversion}{unknown\,c} = \frac{fl\,oz\,for\,conversion}{fl\,oz\,given} \right)$$

$$\frac{x}{1} = \frac{20}{8} \left(\frac{unknown\,c}{c\,for\,conversion} = \frac{fl\,oz\,given}{fl\,oz\,for\,conversion} \right)$$

To solve the proportion, the ratios are cross-multiplied, and the resulting equation is solved. When cross-multiplying, all four proportions above will produce the same equation: $(8)(x) = (20)(1) \rightarrow 8x = 20$. Divide by 8 to isolate the variable x, the result is $x = 2.5$. The variable x represented the unknown number of cups. Therefore, the conclusion is that 20 fluid ounces converts (is equal) to 2.5 cups.

Sometimes converting units requires writing and solving more than one proportion. Suppose an exam question asks to determine how many hours are in 2 weeks. Without knowing the conversion rate between hours and weeks, this can be determined knowing the conversion rates between weeks and days, and between days and hours. First, weeks are converted to days, then days are converted to hours. To convert from weeks to days, the following proportion can be written:

$$\frac{7}{1} = \frac{x}{2} \left(\frac{days\,conversion}{weeks\,conversion} = \frac{days\,unknown}{weeks\,given} \right)$$

Cross-multiplying produces: $(7)(2) = (x)(1) \rightarrow 14 = x$. Therefore, 2 weeks is equal to 14 days. Next, a proportion is written to convert 14 days to hours:

$$\frac{24}{1} = \frac{x}{14} \left(\frac{conversion\,hours}{conversion\,days} = \frac{unknown\,hours}{given\,days} \right)$$

Cross-multiplying produces: $(24)(14) = (x)(1) \rightarrow 336 = x$. Therefore, the answer is that there are 336 hours in 2 weeks.

History and Nature of Science

Types of Learning Experiences

Formal Learning Experiences

Formal learning experiences are typically employed in a teacher-led classroom – they are traditionally structured, compulsory, standardized, curriculum based, and driven by intended outcomes. The goal of formal learning experiences is empirically driven results.

Informal Learning Experiences

Informal learning experiences, while not bound to the classroom environment, typically take place outside the classroom environment – they are usually unstructured, voluntary, noncurricular based (i.e., experientially based or exploratory based), and driven by student choice. The goal of informal learning is not measurable outcomes, but rather positive experiences that might enhance measurable outcomes.

Enhancing Formal Scientific Learning with Informal Scientific Learning

Research supports using informal learning outside the classroom to bolster formal learning inside the classroom. Researchers have suggested that these two modes of learning actually enhance one another. Outdoor science projects and field lessons, for instance, can enhance students' understanding of scientific processes and/or concepts. Thus, these modes of learning should not remain mutually exclusive, but rather they should be aligned and integrated.

Hands-on Learning Experiences

Hands-on learning experiences, both inside and outside the classroom, can help "bridge the gap" between formal and informal learning. Hands-on learning experience may include laboratory activities inside the classroom (i.e., formal learning), or scientific experiments outside the classroom (i.e., informal learning). In both settings, these hands-on learning experiences are characterized by tactile, experiential, and kinesthetic activities.

Active Engagement in the Natural World

Students can only actively engage in the natural world if they are thrust outside the compulsory structures of formal learning environments. Field trips/lessons, service projects, nature walks, and outdoor labs are all examples of ways that students can informally engage with the world around them in order to enhance their classroom experience.

Student Interaction and Collaboration

While student interaction and collaboration can be a component of both formal and informal learning environments, social interactions tend to take precedence in informal learning activities. The social aspects of these activities can be used to create student discourse and ignite student curiosities with diverse perspectives. Most informal learning environments lend themselves to collaborative strategies that help clarify formal science terms and dispel scientific misconceptions.

Types of Scientific Tools

The use of scientific tools, including digital technologies, can enhance a student's ability to collect data, assess and measure scientific theories, and carry out various scientific tasks. As an extension of previously mentioned safety procedures and precautions, science educators must explicitly teach students appropriate uses for each tool. In general, the types of tools can be broken down into three categories: 1) Observation Tools, 2) Measurement Tools, and 3) Communication Tools. Additionally, as our society becomes increasingly digitized, a new overarching category has emerged: 4) Digital Tools.

Observation Tools: Used to capture or observe scientific phenomena, but not necessarily measure or communicate the findings

- Magnifying Glass: A traditional observation tool that magnifies small things, but not usually microscopic entities
- Microscope: A classic scientific tool that allows students to observe and analyze microscopic compounds and organisms
- Camera: Any device that records visual images or videos for documentation; a camera can be a standalone tool or can be attached to other tools such as microscopes or telescopes
- Telescope: Made famous by astronomers like Galileo, this popular observation tool allows scientists to observe things that are far away, such as stars and planets

Measurement Tools: Scientific tools that assist scientists with accurate and precise measurements of quantity, quality, length, weight, mass, and character

- Ruler: A primitive scientific tool that allows students to measure height, width, and length for mathematical calculations
- Scale: Another simple scientific tool that can help measure the weight or mass of an object by assessing the pull of gravity
- Thermometer: A basic scientific tool that measures temperature

Communication Tools: Help scientists communicate the findings they obtain through observation and measurement

- Writing: Writing is the foundation of all communication – handwritten or digital – in science; students will have to learn how to use writing as a tool to convey their ideas.
- Graphics and Visuals: Sometimes words need to be enhanced with graphics or visuals; these tools include tables, graphs, charts, and maps.
- Conceptual Diagrams or Models: Conceptual diagrams or models are visual representations of complex biological processes or chemical reactions.
- Photographs and Videos: Photographs and videos are the products of cameras, and can be used to communicate findings in a visual manner.
- Social Media and the Internet: In the digital world we live in, students and scholars are now able to communicate information seamlessly in a virtual setting.

Digital Tools: Any type of tool can be a digital tool so long as it uses computer-based technologies to enhance student observation, measurement, and communication. In fact, these digital technologies have led to the development of entirely new units of measurements. Recent developments in nanotechnology instruments, for instance, have enhanced the ways in which science classrooms can measure extremely small units of time, length, and mass. "Nano" means extremely small or dwarf-sized. In past decades, students would be unable to analyze small quantities of time, length, and math. Today, science students have digital nanotechnologies that allow them to measure one billionth of a meter (nanometer), one billionth of a second (nanosecond), and one billionth of a gram (nanogram).

These technologies include, but are not limited to, NanoGauges, electron microscopes, and nanosensors.

- NanoGauge: A device that carries out precision nanometer measurements without any complex procedures
- Electron Microscope: A microscope that produces images of microscopic organisms by using electron beams
- Nanosensor: A term used to describe any device that analyzes the characteristics or behaviors of nanoscale phenomena or particles

These nanotechnology measurement skills prepare students for all fields in science, technology, engineering, and mathematics. As nanotechnologies and telescopic technologies continue to advance, so does our understanding of measurements, which are getting infinitesimally smaller and larger with advancements in technology. Take a look at how the International System of Units (SI System) has been impacted by the changes in technological advancements in measurement over time:

Prefix	Symbol	10^n	Decimal	Short scale	Since
yotta	Y	10^{24}	1,000 000 000 000 000 000 000 000	Septillion	1991
zetta	Z	10^{21}	1,000 000 000 000 000 000 000	Sextillion	1991
exa	E	10^{18}	1,000 000 000 000 000 000	Quintillion	1975
peta	P	10^{15}	1,000 000 000 000 000	Quadrillion	1975
tera	T	10^{12}	1,000 000 000 000	Trillion	1960
giga	G	10^{9}	1,000 000 000	Billion	1960
mega	M	10^{6}	1,000 000	Million	1960
kilo	k	10^{3}	1,000	Thousand	1795
hecto	h	10^{2}	100	Hundred	1795
deca	da	10^{1}	10	Tenth	1795
		10^{0}	1	One	
deci	d	10^{-1}	0.1	Tenth	1795
centi	c	10^{-2}	0.01	Hundreth	1795
milli	m	10^{-3}	0.001	Thousandth	1795
micro	µ	10^{-6}	0.000 001	Millionth	1960
nano	n	10^{-9}	0.000 000 001	Billionth	1960
pico	p	10^{-12}	0.000 000 000 001	Trillionth	1960
femto	f	10^{-15}	0.000 000 000 000 001	Quadrillionth	1964
atto	a	10^{-18}	0.000 000 000 000 000 001	Quintillionth	1964
zepto	z	10^{-21}	0.000 000 000 000 000 000 001	Sextillionth	1991
yocto	y	10^{-24}	0.000 000 000 000 000 000 000 001	Septillion	1991

Making Systematic Observations and Measurements

When instructing the process of making systematic observations and measurements, one must understand the importance of observing and recording actions with specificity. Systematic observation requires the specification of actions and results so that all variables can be accurately recorded. The purpose of emphasizing this within science is to ensure that any observed results are reproducible if someone else were to attempt the same actions or experiments. When exploring new ideas in science, results may be an anomaly; therefore, making an experiment easily reproducible by systematically observing and recording the experiment is vital within science.

Another important aspect in teaching scientific ideas is to encourage students to pose their own investigative questions related to the topic. Putting students in groups to discuss ideas is a commonly used way within science courses to allow for further idea exploration and investigative inquiry. Teachers should also promote the use of critical thinking. The foundation of critical thinking is constantly asking questions. By analyzing information and evidence and asking more questions about a topic, conclusions can be reached more easily. Overall, critical thinking is applying logical principles to the evaluation of evidence, beliefs, and potential errors. Asking questions, analyzing data and observations, drawing conclusions, and asking questions are the bases for the scientific method.

Evaluating Different Explanations for Scientific Results and Understanding Sources of Error

The critical evaluation of scientific ideas, different perspectives, and specific arguments is vital for students' development as independent thinkers. Students should focus on completely understanding an experimental procedure or theory before analyzing and interpreting any results or conclusions. Teachers should emphasize the importance of considering all different points of view. Understanding contrary arguments and being able to argue effectively against them can greatly develop a student's ability to think critically and understand scientific theories or experiment results.

Another useful tool in teaching students to understand the scientific process is repetition of material. Educators can utilize different activities, experiments, and explanations around a single topic to promote a deeper understanding. In addition, teachers should instruct students to look for key terms or phrases that are repeated within literature about a particular subject. Researching important terms can make it easier to understand the broader topic being studied.

Lastly, an important aspect of scientific research is the ability to identify potential sources of error. The best technique for identifying sources of error within an experiment is to look for confounding variables. Confounding variables are factors that are not focused on in a study but influence the independent and dependent variables. A commonly used example is the association between ice cream consumption and sunburns. From the data alone it could appear that consuming ice cream causes sunburns, as when ice cream consumption increases, the number of sunburns increase. The confounding variable in this case is hot temperatures. The heat makes people consume more ice cream, and increased sun exposure results in more sunburns. Being able to identify these variables before beginning an experiment will show the potential sources of error.

Communicating Results

An important aspect of scientific inquiry is communicating scientific procedures and explaining results. Teachers should instruct students to communicate and defend their findings by having them discuss their investigative results with their peers or the instructor. This can also be done by allowing students to give presentations on the topic they are investigating. Presentations allow the possibility of other students asking questions, which makes the student defend and communicate what they found.

Some students may have difficulty with communicating and defending science verbally, so it is important to utilize written methods as well. A simple way for students to practice communicating and defending their results is through writing a laboratory report. Laboratory reports include a "results and conclusion" section, which is a good space for students to explain what they learned about a scientific subject. Additionally, a laboratory report allows space for them to defend their opinions against different perspectives and refutations.

With any of these strategies, it is important to instruct students to consider the audience with which they are communicating. A student must focus on communicating in a way that their specific audience would understand.

Principles of Scientific Ethics

Ethics refers to sets of values that a specific society follows. Ethics apply to all of life, including science. Before beginning research or an experiment, a scientist must determine whether what they plan on doing is ethical. Scientific ethics maintain the integrity of research and prevent immoral practices, plagiarism, and other forms of cheating.

There are many ethical principles that need to be accounted for when working in science. The most important are work for good, do no harm in research, obtain consent from participants, prevent any risk of harm to participants, protect participant anonymity, give participants the ability to withdraw from any activity, and avoid deceit. These general guidelines should always be considered in scientific research. When educating young students, many of these principles will likely not be relevant; however, it is important to educate students on what is considered unethical in science and why unethical practices should be avoided.

When beginning any kind of scientific research, one must consider whether the research will do any harm. An example of an experiment that failed in this principle of scientific ethics is the Manhattan Project, which created the first atomic bomb. After successfully creating the bomb, most of the scientists working on the project fought against the use of their work as they realized it was unethical because it would be used for harm.

Students first learning about principles of scientific ethics can begin practicing ethics in science by ensuring that they avoid plagiarism. Plagiarism is considered a deceitful practice and is therefore considered unethical in scientific studies, writing, and research.

Historical Development of Science

The very nature of scientific knowledge is that it continues to build upon itself with constant experimentation and newfound discoveries, throwing out old theories that have been proven false and replacing them with new ones. By using principles that have been developed and tested over hundreds of years, scientists and engineers have created today's technology.

Records of scientific experimentation date back as far as 400 B.C.E., although most significant discoveries didn't occur until the 17th century. A timeline of major accepted principles and models—which is by no means exhaustive—is listed below, and displays theories that were developed, discarded, and built upon:

- 1543—Nicolaus Copernicus developed the Heliocentric Model of the Solar System
- 1609—Galileo Galilei made telescopic observations of the solar system
- 1619—Johannes Kepler completed the laws of planetary motion
- 1622—Robert Boyle developed the law of ideal gas, which states that the pressure of an ideal gas is inversely proportional to the volume it occupies
- 1665—Robert Hooke discovered the biological cell
- 1672–1687—Sir Isaac Newton discovered that white light is a spectrum of different-colored rays, developed calculus, and created mathematical descriptions of force, gravity, and the laws of motion
- 1751—Benjamin Franklin discovered that lightning is electrical
- 1778–1798—Antoine Lavoisier discovered "phlogiston," later identified as oxygen; developed the law of conservation of mass and the basis for chemistry
- 1781–1800—William Herschel discovered Uranus, expanding the boundaries of the known universe and discovered infrared radiation
- 1820—Hans Christian Ørsted discovered the relationship between electricity and the magnetic field using a compass
- 1843—James Prescott Joule created the first law of thermodynamics
- 1858—Rudolf Virchow discovered that cells can only come from pre-existing cells
- 1859—Charles Darwin and Alfred Wallace developed the theory of evolution by natural selection
- 1864—James Clerk Maxwell developed the theory of electromagnetism
- 1865—Gregor Mendel identified the laws of genetic inheritance and provided the basis for genetics
- 1869—Dmitri Mendeleev created the periodic table of elements
- 1887—Alfred A. Michelson and Edward W. Morley disproved the existence of "the aether"
- 1896—Henri Becquerel, along with Marie and Pierre Curie, discovered radiation
- 1897—J. J. Thomson discovered the electron
- 1900—Max Planck created the law of black body radiation and the basis for quantum theory

- 1905–1915—Albert Einstein developed theories of special relativity, the photoelectric effect, and general relativity
- 1911—Ernest Rutherford discovered the nucleus
- 1912—Alfred Wegener proposed continental drift, the basis for plate tectonics
- 1913—Niels Bohr created a model of the atom
- 1924—Edwin Hubble realized the Milky Way is just one of many galaxies
- 1925–Cecilia Payne-Gaposchkin discovered that stars are composed of mainly hydrogen and helium
- 1925–1928—Major developments in quantum mechanics
- 1927—Georges Lemaitre proposed the Big Bang Theory
- 1928—Alexander Fleming discovered penicillin
- 1936—Inge Lehmann discovered the liquid inner core of the Earth
- 1938—Lise Meitner and Otto Frisch discovered nuclear fission
- 1944—Barbara McClintock discovered the existence of jumping genes
- 1952—Jonas Salk developed and tested the polio vaccine
- 1953—Rosalind Franklin, Francis Crick, and James Watson discovered the helical structure of DNA

1969—Dorothy Hodgkin discovered the structure of insulin

- 1983—Kary Mullis invented polymerase chain reactions
- 1997—Roslin Institute cloned the sheep Dolly
- 2001—First draft of the Human Genome Project was published
- 2006—Shinya Yamanaka generated the first induced pluripotent stem cells
- 2015—Traces of liquid water found on Mars

Certain discoveries that revolutionized scientific understanding deserve a deeper look.

Atomic Theory

Atomic theory—a philosophical concept in ancient Greece that solidified in the 19th century—states that the universe is made up of discrete units called **atoms**. Initially believed to have been one inseparable unit, the atom was discovered to be composed of subatomic particles—protons, electrons, and neutrons—in which the protons and neutrons comprise a dense nucleus and the electrons orbit around it at mind-boggling distances. The atom is now believed to be composed of mostly space.

The Heliocentric Model of the Solar System

Before Nicolaus Copernicus, people believed Earth was the center of the universe. Copernicus placed the Sun at the center of the solar system, with the other planets revolving around it. At the time, only Mercury, Venus, Earth, Mars, Saturn, and Jupiter were known. Evidence suggests that the ancient Greeks also used a heliocentric model of the solar system in the 3rd century B.C.E.

Gravity

Sir Isaac Newton recognized that gravity was responsible for objects falling toward the ground, which he extrapolated into a law that concluded that every object in the universe is attracted to another object through a force that is directly proportional to the product of their masses and inversely proportional to the square of the distance between them. This is called the law of universal gravitation and is expressed via the following formula:

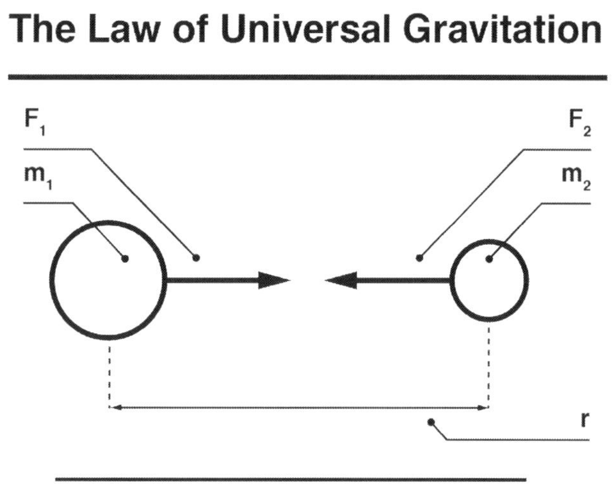

$$F_1 = F_2 = G\,\frac{m_1 \times m_2}{r^2}$$

Evolution

In 1859, Charles Darwin proposed the theory of evolution by natural selection, which explained how organisms developed *very* gradually over time as a result of mutations that enhanced an organism's ability to survive.

Key points of the theory of evolution include:

- There is genetic variation among species—meaning every species has a distinct arrangement of genes.
- Natural selection is the result of a random mutation that occurs in the genome and is favorable to the survival of the organism. For example, a random mutation that causes a moth's wings to appear white, making it harder for birds to eat them because they can't spot them against white tree branches, has a better chance of survival than dark moths. The birds eat the dark moths instead, and the white moth survives to pass on its mutation.
- The random mutation must be heritable—that is, it must be able to be passed on to its offspring.
- Natural selection is not the idea that organisms evolved to fit to their environment. For example, assuming that giraffes developed long necks to eat from tall trees is erroneous.

Contributions of Major Historical Figures

Many of the greatest contributors to the advancement of scientific knowledge were mentioned above. However, a brief overview of the most influential scientists is below.

Galileo Galilei

Galileo Galilei (1564–1642), considered by many to be the "Father of Modern Science," was an Italian astronomer, physicist, and philosopher. His telescopic investigations provided the basis for observational astronomy, in which he confirmed the phases of Venus, four of Jupiter's major moons, and sunspots.

Isaac Newton

Isaac Newton (1643–1727) was an English mathematician, physicist, astronomer, and philosopher. His most influential contributions were the theory of gravitation, the theory of color, the development of calculus, and the three natural laws of motion.

Charles Darwin

Charles Darwin (1809–1882) was an English biologist, whose major contributions include his theory of evolution as a result of natural selection, which provided a unifying theory for the genetic relationship and diversity of all species on Earth.

Max Planck

Max Planck (1858–1947) was a German physicist and the founder of quantum theory, a branch of theoretical physics that focuses on the relationships between subatomic particles.

Marie Curie

Marie Curie (11867–1934) was a Polish scientist who was a pioneer in the research of radioactivity. She was the only person to win the Nobel prize twice. She discovered the elements Radium and Polonium, and she also worked with early X-rays. It is believed that her death was caused by prolonged exposure to radiation.

Niels Bohr

Niels Bohr (1885–1962) was a Danish physicist primarily responsible for the creation of the nuclear model of the atom, which illustrates that electrons orbit around the atom's nucleus. His work received the Nobel Prize in Physics in 1922.

Albert Einstein

Albert Einstein (1879–1955), a German scientist, is possibly the most well-known scientist and contributor to modern physics. He is best known for his theory of mass-energy equivalence ($E = mc^2$) and his theories of special and general relativity. Einstein also received a Nobel Prize in Physics in 1921.

Rosalind Franklin

Rosalind Franklin (1920–1958) was an English Chemist known for her work with X-ray crystallography. Her work was vital to understanding the molecular structures of DNA, RNA, and more. Although she was unrecognized during her lifetime, her work was vital to the further development of molecular biology and all natural sciences.

Impact of Science

Application of Scientific Principles to Analysis and Decision Making

Scientific principles are explanations of a topic that are generally accepted throughout the scientific community. Within science, laws and principles can be easily confused, yet they are quite different. A scientific law refers to an event, and a principle explains why and how an event happens. An example of a scientific law is the law of gravity, which is a force of attraction between two objects with mass. It is considered a law because it is a universally observed and believed idea. It is a rule that is considered always true by all in the scientific community. An example of a principle is that human metabolism mainly functions through the oxidation of glucose. This is considered a principle because observation and study have shown that oxidation is a mechanism for the phenomenon of human energy production. When exploring a new idea in studies, it is useful to consider any scientific principle that may relate to the idea.

Additionally, scientific principles and the scientific method can be applied when decision-making. This can be done by making observations, studying and researching the observations, then deciding a course of action, just as one does within scientific research. Doing so may help illuminate efficacy of a decision or any viable alternatives. Applying scientific principles to any action can make any decision more credible and logical; however, there may be some disadvantages to this process. For example, scientific principles cannot credibly help explain concepts that are not completely understood scientifically, such as people's belief in the existence of a God or any other supernatural entity.

Application of Scientific Principles to Personal Choices

Many people focus heavily on researching how certain health and fitness habits will affect their longevity. The scientific process is heavily used in everyday society by people who care about their personal choices concerning health and fitness. Just as a scientist observes a phenomenon before researching it, someone who is trying to be conscious of their physical fitness often observes other people who are physically fit and what they do to become fit. After this, they follow the scientific process and research what they can about what they observed to determine if they believe that it is credible.

Before beginning a study, scientists research their observations to determine if it is something that has value to study, and they weigh the benefits and risks of what they will do. People also tend to determine the risks to their own health from certain actions, whether it be taking a supplement or contemplating utilizing a substance. Similar to a scientist, the next process is to test the hypothesis, which may be trying a new diet, changing a routine, adding a new workout, or eliminating something that may be harmful. Lastly, a person will examine their results and determine whether their actions were successful or not. If they are not successful, people will typically try to determine why and then start the process over again in a new direction, just as a scientist will change their research pursuit if their hypothesis was incorrect.

Additionally, the scientific process can be seen when someone is contemplating using a substance such as a drug. They should look at the effects of the drug, figure out what risks and benefits may be associated with its use, then determine if it is worth using. Many drugs can pose the risks of cardiovascular issues, overdose, and physical or mental impairment upon use. Additionally, many drugs result in tolerance that leads to addiction over time.

Human Population Growth

In recent years, the human population has grown by approximately 83 million people per year. In the year 1800, the human population was close to 1 billion, and in 2020, it was believed to be around 7.9 billion people. The growth of human population throughout known history appears to be growing exponentially, meaning that it is growing more and more rapidly every year.

There are many characteristics related to any population. Population density, dispersion, age structure, birth rate, and death rate all characterize the total population and changes in population. As the human population changes, so does the landscape of earth and the quality of life for an individual. The dispersion of humans into isolated communities over time has brought about groups of people who look and act differently and maintain distinct languages and customs.

Many scholars believe that the growth of the human population is not sustainable. With excessive increases in population, many issues may arise such as less access to food, which can result in starvation for many. Overgrowth of any population can overwhelm populations of other animals, causing their extinction. Also, increases in population are believed to have detrimental effects on our environment that could eventually destroy the earth if no solution is found. These negative effects include global climate change, pollution, decreasing availability of untouched natural land, less availability of fresh water, depletion of natural resources, and more. There are limits to population growth. At some point, if it continues to rise, the population will hit a point where it is no longer sustainable, causing the death rate to exceed the birth rate. This can be seen in deer populations in areas where predators have been removed from or hunted out of the area.

The Role of Science in Resolving Personal, Societal and Global Challenges

Science is essential to solving the issues faced on personal, societal, and global scales. On a personal scale, scientific research provides people with information on how to be more successful, how to stay safe, what to avoid, how to be healthy, and how to make decisions. Science teaches individuals how to question information, pursue answers, and put thought into action.

From a societal standpoint, science has brought advancements in medicine, food, entertainment, and much more. For example, research in electricity provided an understanding of how it can be used practically, and now most societies are fully powered, connected through the internet, and able to continue making machines that make life better. Additionally, science has taught societies to keep track of past data so it can be referenced in the future, and to solve problems logically using evidence and facts over feelings and emotions. On a global scale, the research of scientists has helped to identify and work towards solving challenges that the entire world population faces. For instance, scientists were able to identify the global threat posed by pollution and population growth, and they are actively trying to find ways to solve these problems so that future generations do not have to live with the consequences.

Concepts and Processes

Observations and Hypotheses

Human beings are, by nature, very curious. Long before the scientific method was established, people have been making observations and predicting outcomes, manipulating the physical world to create extraordinary things—from the first man-made fire in 6000 B.C.E. to the satellite that orbited Pluto in 2016. Although the history of the scientific method is sporadic and attributed to many different people, it remains the most reliable way to obtain and utilize knowledge about the observable universe. The scientific method consists of the following steps:

- Make an observation
- Create a question
- Form a hypothesis
- Conduct an experiment
- Collect and analyze data
- Form a conclusion

The first step is to identify a problem based on an observation—the who, what, when, where, why, and how. An **observation** is the analysis of information using basic human senses: sight, sound, touch, taste, and smell. Observations can be two different types—qualitative or quantitative. A **qualitative** observation describes what is being observed, such as the color of a house or the smell of a flower. **Quantitative** observations measure what is being observed, such as the number of windows on a house or the intensity of a flower's smell on a scale of 1–5.

Observations lead to the identification of a problem, also called an **inference**. For example, if a fire truck is barreling down a busy street, the inferences could be:

- There's a fire.

- Someone is hurt.
- Some kid pulled the fire alarm at a local school.

Inferences are logical predictions based on experience or education that lead to the formation of a hypothesis. A **hypothesis** is a testable explanation of an observed scenario and is presented in the form of a statement. It's an attempt to answer a question based on an observation, and it allows a scientist to predict an outcome. A hypothesis makes assumptions on the relationship between two different variables, and answers the question: "If I do this, what happens to that?"

In order to form a hypothesis, there must be an independent variable and a dependent variable that can be measured. The **independent variable** is the variable that is manipulated, and the **dependent variable** is the result of the change.

For example, suppose a student wants to know how light affects plant growth. Based upon what he or she already knows, the student proposes (hypothesizes) that the more light to which a plant is exposed, the faster it will grow.

- Observation: Plants exposed to lots of light seem to grow taller.
- Question: Will plants grow faster if there's more light available?
- Hypothesis: The more light the plant has, the faster it will grow.
- Independent variable: The amount of time exposed to light (able to be manipulated)
- Dependent variable: Plant growth (the result of the manipulation)

Once a hypothesis has been formed, it must be tested to determine whether it's true or false. (How to test a hypothesis is described in a subsequent section.) After it has been tested and validated as true over and over, then a hypothesis can develop into a theory, model, or law.

To test a hypothesis, one must conduct a carefully designed experiment. There are four basic requirements that must be present for an experiment to be valid:

1. A control
2. Variables
3. A constant
4. Repeated and collected data

The **control** is a standard to which the resultant findings are compared. It's the baseline measurement that allows for scientists to determine whether the results are positive or negative. For the example of light affecting plant growth, the control may be a plant that receives no light at all.

The **independent variable** is manipulated (a good way to remember this is *I* manipulate the *I*ndependent variable), and the **dependent variable** is the result of changes to the independent variable. In the plant example, the independent variable is the amount of time exposed to light, and the dependent variable is the resulting growth (or lack thereof) of the plant. For this experiment, there may be three plants—one that receives a minimal amount of light, the control, and one that receives a lot of light.

Finally, there must be constants in an experiment. A **constant** is an element of the experiment that remains unchanged. Constants are extremely important in minimizing inconsistencies within the experiment that may lead to results outside the parameters of the hypothesis. For example, some constants in the above case are that all plants receive the same amount of water, all plants are potted in the same kind of soil, the species of the plant used in each condition is the same, and the plants are stored at the same temperature. If, for instance, the plants received different amounts of water as well as light, it would be impossible to tell whether the plants responded to changes in water or light.

Once the experiment begins, a disciplined scientist must always record the observations in meticulous detail, usually in a journal. A good journal includes dates, times, and exact values of both variables and constants. Upon reading this journal, a different scientist should be able to clearly understand the experiment and recreate it exactly. The journal includes all **collected data**, or any observed changes. In this case, the data is rates of plant growth, as well as any other phenomena that occurred as a result of the experiment. A well-designed experiment also includes repetition in order to get the most accurate possible readings and to account for any errors, so several trials may be conducted.

Even in the presence of diligent constants, there are an infinite number of reasons that an experiment can (and will) go wrong, known as **sources of error**. All experimental results are inherently accepted as imperfect, if ever so slightly, because experiments are conducted by human beings, and no instrument can measure anything perfectly. The goal of scientists is to minimize those errors to the best of their ability. (Determining sources of error will be discussed in a subsequent section.)

Interactions Between Systems

A system is a collection of elements that work toward accomplishing a specific task. A subsystem is part of a system and is integral to its success. Subsystems can typically be divided further into individual parts that work together. Additionally, one system can be made up of many subsystems that all work together. Examples of systems and subsystems working together can be seen within a variety of different fields, from business and computers to biology and chemistry.

A physiological example of a system and its subsystems working together is the human body. The human body itself is a system with the overall main purpose of maintaining its own life. Within the human body are many organ subsystems that work in harmony so that the body can live. The respiratory system cycles gasses in and out, the lymphatic system defends against illness, the digestive system processes food, and all the other systems perform their specific tasks to maintain the life and wellness of the body.

Another example is an ecosystem. For example, the biosphere is a system with the main goal of maintaining balance to all life within it. The subsystems of the biosphere are the nutrient cycles; the carbon cycle, nitrogen cycle, water cycle, etc. all have their own unique tasks of recycling nutrients through the environment. Together, these cycles maintain the balance of life in the biosphere.

Applying Unifying Concepts to Explore Similarities

Though it may seem that various natural processes are unrelated, scientific research has discovered that many of them are actually connected. Examples of this idea can be seen throughout all scientific fields.

One example of two related natural phenomena is fire and rusting, which may appear to be completely different processes; however, they are united by oxidation. Oxidation occurs when oxygen atoms are combined with hydrogen and carbon to form carbon dioxide and water. When fire burns, oxidation happens rapidly and releases heat and energy. When rusting occurs, the oxidation process is also involved; it just happens much more slowly.

Another example of two unified natural phenomena can be seen in sunsets and rainbows. On some clear days when the sun is setting and it drops below the horizon, a green flash of light above the sun can be seen. This flash occurs when light is refracted into different frequencies. Rainbows occur when light refracts through water droplets, creating the full visible color spectrum across the sky.

Properties, Patterns, and Change in Systems

Scientists utilize the idea of systems to isolate specific topics so they will not be confused with other aspects of the complex world. When a system is isolated and separated from everything else, the effects of things outside of the system are viewed as forces acting on it or matter and energy flowing through it. Understanding how energy and mass can flow through a system is crucial in isolating it for further study. Additionally, observing how this occurs over time is crucial to understanding a system.

Observing how systems remain stable or change over time is a primary goal of many scientists and engineers. **Stability** refers to when an aspect of a system does not change for a period of time. Although many systems appear to be perpetually stable, no system will remain completely stable over long periods of time. The lack of stability is due to the always chaotic and perpetually expanding aspects of our universe. When forces act on a system, energy and matter flow in and out, and change will always occur.

Change within systems is always measured in differences of some aspect over time. These measurements of change are different depending on the rate that energy, matter, or anything else is acting on a system. Some specific situations can be observed where a system appears to be steady when things flow into and out of it at stable and equal rates. This concept of balance while constantly changing is referred to as dynamic equilibrium. An example of this could be the cycle of the moon. Although its orbit seems to be stable, it is a constantly cycling process of movement around the earth and through space.

Structure and function are complementary properties. The way that natural or built systems function is directly determined by their structures. For example, function depends on the shape of something and its relationship to the shape of what it interacts with; a simple explanation of this in a built system is a key and a lock. The structure of the key and the lock are required to match for their action to be accomplished.

Many examples of this relationship between form and function can be seen through all natural systems. One of the most obvious examples is a protein. Proteins known as enzymes facilitate reactions that occur in life to accelerate their rate. An enzyme has a region known as an active site that is shaped to perfectly bind to one or more specific structures known as substrates. When enzymes bind to a substrate, their physical shape will change to perform some action. Many enzymes in the human digestive system use their form to bind to a section of a food molecule and then break apart a bond in the food molecule.

Scientific Models

A model is something used to represent a system, object, or event. Models are utilized as tools to help people better understand the natural world. Models are best used to help visualize something unfamiliar in a more familiar way so that it can be better seen and understood. They are often used to communicate ideas, make predictions, understand processes, or make something more visible.

There are three different types of models: physical, mathematical, and conceptual. Physical models can be seen or touched, and they display something that is not easily seen with the eyes alone. A globe is a physical model of the earth. Physical models of molecules can be made with sticks and colored balls. Models can also be utilized to show the interior of something that cannot be seen without breaking it open. These types of physical models are often used in anatomy to display the inner structures of the human body.

Mathematical models are tools used to calculate mathematical equations and things that are far too difficult to calculate manually. Some mathematical models are so complex that they require a computer to complete their task. Computer models are utilized to study the movement of tectonic plates underground, aid cars in functioning properly, and predict weather outcomes based on a variety of atmospheric data. Mathematical computer models are most often utilized for predicting something that may happen in the future.

Lastly, conceptual models compare familiar things to aid in explaining an idea better. Conceptual models can be anything used to classify similar items, connect certain different ideas, and more. An example of a conceptual model is the classification of living organisms. Although it does not physically exist, there is a conceptual way to visualize the animal kingdom and identify a certain living organism by how it relates to other organisms. Another example of a conceptual model is the electron cloud model. The electron cloud model provides a way to visualize how an atom is arranged.

Students as Learners and Science Instruction

The Impact of Prior Knowledge and Experience on Science Learning

While teachers are undeniably instrumental catalysts in engaging students and sparking a love of science, research has found that a child's prior knowledge, experience, and perceived utility of science drive interest and aspirations in the field. The more positive students' prior experiences with science activities have been, the more students tend to view science education as useful and exciting. Children who have been encouraged to explore different scientific concepts will view science education with enthusiasm, as it provides a vehicle by which questions can be answered and the world can be better understood. This is true especially for the practical scientific concepts that allow students to experience the world around them, such as clouds, magnets, insects, plant growth, stars, and changing seasons.

Not every child has had parental support with their natural scientific curiosity and desire to explore. Early childhood educators should recognize the differing backgrounds and degree to which each child in their classroom has had opportunities to learn, discover, and develop a positive association with science. One benefit of teaching children who are at the early stages of their formal education is that the teacher has a greater ability to influence a child's attitude toward learning, even if they have limited positive background experiences, because the child is young and impressionable.

Differentiating Instruction

One of the greatest challenges for any classroom teacher is differentiating instruction to meet the needs of each student in the classroom. Every student, regardless of their background, has an equal right to learn in school, but each child is unique. Therefore, by differentiating teaching, one can ensure that every student in the classroom can learn the material, enjoy the process of learning, and reach their potential.

The teaching philosophy of differentiating instruction is based on the premise that the student differences should guide the "what" and the "how" teachers teach. Teachers should modify their instruction so that it meets the varying learning styles, readiness levels, interests, and abilities of the students in their classroom instead of applying a one-size-fits-all approach.

There are three primary components of the curriculum that teachers can differentiate: content, process, and products.

- **Content** is the knowledge, ideas, and skills that teachers wish to impart to students, and the means by which they choose to present these concepts and skills, such as through labs, lectures, demonstrations, readings, and videos. Every student, regardless of their level, should be provided the same core content. Emerging teachers sometimes make the common mistake of watering down content for struggling students. Instead, the same concept should be taught with a varying complexity of the explanation. Teachers should disseminate content in a variety of modes, like readings, experiments, and computer simulations, exposing each student to each at different times. For example, advanced learners might be given a challenging reading, while students who are struggling or ELLs might be given a video or a classroom demonstration to watch. The means by which content is taught is one key way to differentiate instruction for learners at different levels.

- **Process** involves the various activities that deliver the content and help students develop the knowledge and skills being taught. These activities can be modified by the teacher to alter their complexity. For example, additional scaffolding can be provided for students at lower levels. Reteaching, explicit step-by-step directions, or additional resources to supplement instruction are examples of ways to scaffold what is being taught.

- **Products** are the culminating assessments or projects students complete to demonstrate the things they have learned as well as how they can extend those concepts and skills. Products can be modified by altering the level of the assessment (multiple-choice test versus essay test or group project versus solo endeavor, etc.).

Other instructional methods that aid instructional differentiation are grouping students by current level or interest, providing different "stations" in the classroom, and compacting, which helps determine each student's initial level for a given concept.

Using Situations from Students' Daily Lives to Develop Instructional Materials

Science is all around us. The daily lives of students involve scientific concepts directly or things that can be explored via the scientific inquiry process, so teachers can develop lessons with practical instructional material. For example, the function and history behind inventions or discoveries that have impacted daily life could be investigated, including things like refrigerators, light bulbs, microscopes, plastic, computers, antibiotics, and the pasteurization process.

A lab investigating Earth's daily rotation could involve measuring and tracking the height of each student's shadow at set intervals of time throughout the day. Children can outline their shadows with different colors of chalk for each measurement so they can obtain a visual representation of the change. The chalk outlines can also help ensure the child returns to the exact same spot for every measurement. Teachers can use this lesson design to explain how it is Earth spinning around its axis, rather than the Sun moving across the sky, that causes the changes we see in daylight. Students could then be tasked with brainstorming ideas about how this knowledge can inform decisions. For example, once they understand that the sun is highest in the sky and casts maximal sunlight in the middle of the day, they might determine this would be the warmest time to play outside in cold winter months. The varying amount of sunlight and its influence on plant growth could also be discussed. Instructional material that uses everyday products or processes makes science seem useful and can help children "buy in" to the excitement and the utility of studying it.

Misconceptions in Science

Educators who have spent any time teaching science at the elementary level are likely well aware that students come into the classroom with many misconceptions regarding science. It then becomes the educator's role to erase the associated mental images and ideas from these misconceptions and replace them with correct information. In general, a **misconception** is a belief that contradicts current scientific theories, thinking, laws, evidence, and facts. The following list includes some common science misconceptions held by elementary school students:

- The Sun moves around Earth and across the sky.
- Seasons occur because Earth gets closer or farther from the Sun.
- The moon is only visible at night.
- The phases of the moon are due to Earth's shadow on the moon.
- A star's brightness is only influenced by its distance from Earth.
- Clouds are formed from cotton or smoke.
- Energy is not conserved because we are running out of it.
- Batteries contain electricity inside.

- When an object is at rest, there are no forces acting upon it.
- Rocks are always heavy.
- Continents don't move.
- Smaller magnets are weaker than larger ones.
- Rivers always flow north to south.
- Only water can melt and freeze.
- Mass and weight are different terms for the same thing.
- The heavier a pendulum bob, the faster it swings.
- A gas does not have mass.
- A viscous liquid is denser than a runny one.
- Heat and temperature are different terms for the same thing.
- Pupils are black spots on the surface of our eyes.
- Offspring can inherit acquired characteristics.

Misconceptions can result from preconceived notions, vernacular issues (wherein terms have different meanings in everyday and scientific language, such as "work"), or religious or cultural beliefs, among other reasons.

Refutational teaching is a pedagogical approach that teachers can employ to help students overcome their misconceptions. **Traditional teaching** starts and ends with instruction that provides the correct facts, information, and known evidence regarding that topic. For example, when teaching about seasons, educators would assert that we experience different seasons here on Earth because the planet is tilted on its axis (about 23.4 degrees) as it rotates around the Sun. The hemisphere experiencing summer is on the part of the planet that's tilted toward the Sun during that portion of the revolution, while the hemisphere experiencing winter is tilted away from the Sun.

Traditional teaching does not delve into any common misconceptions. Refutational teaching takes things a step further by bringing up a misconception about the topic (in this case, that summer occurs because Earth is closer to the Sun and winter occurs because Earth moves further from the Sun). The teacher must then explain why this is thinking is wrong. First, the correct information is shared, rationalized (why "right" is "right"), and then the preconceived notion is debunked (why "wrong" is "wrong"). Finally, the correct facts should be reiterated to form a sandwich of truth. Presenting things in this order helps ensure children do not tune out after initially hearing their misconception asserted and then erroneously thinking they must know all the rest of what will be said.

Hands-on Learning Experiences

Science instruction is often one of the most natural places in the elementary school day to incorporate hands-on learning activities. Many scientific concepts and principles can be readily explored through labs, experiments, field trips, and indoor and outdoor activities that require one or more of the five senses. In this way, teachers of science at the elementary level have the powerful tool of hands-on learning in their pockets.

Because many early elementary school students have yet to master reading, it's usually more developmentally appropriate to rely on alternative instructional materials, like labs and demonstrations, rather than readings or worksheets. Young children often prefer to learn by touching, moving, doing, exploring, and observing things, rather than simply listening or watching. Their inclination to question things lends itself quite well to the scientific inquiry process. Teachers can solicit ideas for topics that interest their students and make a list of scientific questions they have. From there, hands-on activities can be planned and implemented to help students discover the answers themselves with the supportive guidance of the teacher in the framework of a well-designed activity. This strategy can promote students' interest in the material and their understanding of the scientific process (making an observation, posing a research question, designing an experiment, gathering and analyzing data, etc.).

Higher-Level Thinking

When teachers use effective questioning strategies, they can help students achieve **higher-level thinking** and the ability to transfer concrete understanding to more abstract levels. It also can spark imagination, enhance inference skills, and provide sound critical thinking patterns that students can apply to their lives outside the classroom. While asking questions is an intuitive process, asking the "right" questions in the "right" way takes forethought and skill. Questions that are closed—answerable with a simple "yes," "no," or short response—typically are less effective at sparking further discussion and healthy debate, both of which are necessary to induce higher-level thinking. Instead of just restating facts, which is a more basic level of thinking, higher-level thinking requires students use those facts or knowledge for a secondary step. For example, students may need to connect and synthesize them, analyze them, categorize and group them, infer something from them, or apply them towards a novel situation.

Questioning strategies that promote higher-level thinking may involve the following:

- Posing open-ended questions
- Asking students to brainstorm alternative explanations to a problem or phenomenon
- Asking students to consider how some of these alternative explanations could be tested
- Tasking students with categorizing concepts and connecting previously-learned material with new ideas (what does this remind you of that we've already learned about?)
- Challenging students to make predictions and inferences (perhaps using language like "guesses" for young children) based on what has been observed

Accommodating and Inclusive Activities

As previously mentioned, all students should have an equal opportunity to learn in the classroom. Because each child has different needs, teachers should plan lessons to accommodate as many students as possible in the classroom. Although this can be a daunting challenge, accommodating the needs of all students is one of the teacher's key responsibilities. Differentiating instruction is the process by which educators can try and fulfill this responsibility. When educators shepherd students through the curriculum in lockstep, or attempt to teach to the "middle ground," many students may fail to gain the intended skills and concepts from the lesson. Students with greater competency may be bored and become distractors to peers. Additionally, they might monopolize class discussions and answer questions before other students have the chance to consider the idea and venture an answer. Students for whom the material is too complex will struggle to follow along and keep up.

A related issue concerns the delivery method of the content and its compatibility with the learning style of each child. For example, if a teacher exclusively relies on readings and worksheets to explain the water cycle, students who are auditory learners can miss out. For these students, videos, short lectures, think-pair-share discussions, and guest interviews are likely much more effective. Teachers should spend a significant amount of time and energy planning lessons that meet the curriculum standards and the needs of each student in the classroom.

Sequencing Learning Activities to Build on Prior Knowledge

Background knowledge enables a student to more readily absorb new related concepts. Students at the early elementary level likely have obtained their background knowledge from life experiences and resources in their homes and outside school (parents, siblings, museums, books read to them) rather than from in-class instruction. Because every child hails from a different background and living situation, early childhood educators often compete with a wide variety of background knowledge in their students.

Finding means to assess the background knowledge of students regarding a certain principle (for example, food webs), gives teachers an idea of the starting point to differentiate their instruction and build upon each student's background knowledge in an effective way. Lessons must be properly paced and sequenced to progress student understanding without being overly redundant or aggressive in their aims. Educators should help add to the background knowledge for students who have limited prior learning about a topic, or who possess misconceptions and inaccuracies. This can be accomplished through additional modules and activities, child-friendly websites that explain the fundamentals of the concept, videos, picture books, and paired work with students who have a deeper understanding of the principles. The latter strategy can simultaneously deepen advanced students' understanding. Hands-on experiments are another great way to expose emerging learners to new concepts and give them part of the responsibility in learning the material and discovering the "answers" themselves.

"Exit tickets" are a quick way educators can gauge student understanding after a lesson or activity so that appropriate sequencing can be followed when planning subsequent materials and activities. These short (typically 3 to 6 question), ungraded assessments provide teachers with an easy check-in with each student without taking much class time. For young children who cannot yet writepg , teachers will need to be more creative with how answers are captured. In these cases, the exit ticket administration may not be quite as brief, requiring some amount of oral expression or discussion, either in groups or as a class. For classrooms that are equipped with technology for every student (such as tablets for each student or tables of students grouped together), teachers can record audio prompts that children can then select and play, and then record their own verbal response. Teachers can use the results of these check-ins to determine the pace by which they can proceed to sequence lessons and build upon the knowledge already mastered.

Science Assessment

Types of Assessment

Although assessment and learning are often viewed as two separate entities in education, they should actually be viewed as two sides of the same coin. Assessment results should inform teachers what they should teach and what students need to learn, and assessments should be thoughtfully designed so that students learn from them. The science curriculum is largely dictated by state and national standards, but within this framework, educators have some latitude to select topics that they think will most interest their students. More importantly, the concepts and the ways in which they are taught should be mostly informed by students' prior knowledge, readiness level, and learning style.

Preliminary assessments, or formative assessments, can be used at the beginning of a new topic to gain insight into the starting place of each student in terms of their understanding of the topic. Lessons and teaching materials can be planned once results from these pretests are analyzed. Additionally, teachers can group students based upon mastery of concepts and needs. A more advanced group might be able to take on more complicated and complex explanations of the content, while novice students might need those same concepts packaged in more basic ways.

Ongoing assessments during various units of study can help teachers take the pulse on how well students are understanding the concepts and principles being taught. Results from these assessments can enlighten educators as to which ideas need further emphasis, reteaching, supplementary materials, and alternative instructional strategies, and which skills and principles have been learned.

Finally, **summative assessments** provide useful feedback as to what students have walked away with, what they are able to reiterate, and most critically, how they are able to apply concrete concepts taught to novel or abstract situations.

Students also have the opportunity to learn from these different stages and iterations of assessments. Sometimes, it is only by having to answer questions alone and without the aid of resources that it becomes clear to students what they know versus what they don't understand about a concept. Assessments can help students figure out where they still have confusion, what further questions they may have, and what strengths and weaknesses they are experiencing as a student of science.

Ongoing Assessment

In education, **assessment** is the process of systematically collecting and analyzing information about students' performance. Research has indicated that educators who employ a balanced system of ongoing, interrelated, specifically-designed assessments are able to most effectively reveal changes in students' learning and understanding over time. This has the dual benefit of informing instructional practice and motivating and instilling students' self-responsibility in their learning.

Teachers who design and administer interim assessments give themselves the opportunity to measure students' progress toward proficiency in the applicable standards and mastery of the skills and concepts being taught. This information should be used to inform instruction. If, for example, results indicate that many students are not grasping how atoms form bonds, the instructor can reteach that material, design a demonstration, or create some other alternative way to teach the concept. Interim assessments are also helpful in identifying struggling students who might need more individualized help or additional guidance and resources to learn the material.

For students, a system of ongoing assessments has multiple benefits. It gets them accustomed to the process of being evaluated, which can lessen the stress experienced when taking tests, giving oral reports, completing graded labs, and engaging in other activities where their performance will be measured. Interim assessments also provide students with feedback about their comprehension and skill attainment, which is an effective way to empower them to take responsibility for their learning and motivate them to seek additional help when necessary.

Products such as science projects, lab journals, rubrics, portfolios, student profiles, and checklists can be used as these ongoing assessments. It is important for educators to provide models of "success" so that students have an idea of what is expected and what to strive for. Finished lab reports that students can physically look at, for example, can help the teacher and students be on the same page regarding expectations.

Communicating Evaluation Criteria and Assessment Results to Students

Because elementary students are young, early in their educational careers, and still developing in every facet of their lives, educators may fail to see the importance and usefulness of involving their young students in the evaluation and assessment process. A common assumption is that children at these ages are unable to take responsibility in their learning and are uninterested in hearing what is expected of them. However, the truth is that most young pupils thrive on feeling like they have some ability to take care of themselves, make their own choices, and demonstrate their autonomy. Moreover, children tend to respond well when expectations and objectives are clear. For these reasons, it's not only effective, but also helpful, to communicate evaluation criteria and assessment results to students. The task of the educator is to communicate in a way that their young students can understand the purpose of evaluation in general, the specific criteria against which the students will be assessed and why, and how well an individual student is achieving the goals and what he or she can do to improve. Satisfying these outcomes will facilitate a successful assessment process and can help students develop their own self-assessment skills.

Scoring rubrics are particularly helpful in explicitly describing the evaluation criteria and the various benchmarks of performance along the continuum. Teachers should explain performance standards and use examples of anonymous or fabricated finished work to demonstrate models of the different levels of achievement of the standards. After using the rubric and evaluating a student's work or effort, the educator should take the time to explain the outcomes to each student. After several evaluation experiences, students should be given the opportunity to use the same rubric and practice evaluating their own work.

Teachers can lead this process by prompting students to consider what concepts they think they did well in, which concepts they are still working on, and what areas are particularly confusing. It is especially important to place significant evaluative emphasis on a student's effort and attitude in the early elementary years because it will plant the seeds of studiousness, the desire to learn, and self-efficacy in one's own learning. Students can then see that even if they aren't grasping concepts as readily or easily as peers, they aren't "failures." Finally, teachers who involve students in the evaluation process help them develop the ability to constructively critique the work of their peers. As students move through their schooling, the ability to gauge their comprehension becomes imperative for monitoring their mastery, identifying study needs, and learning when to seek additional help.

Forces and Motion

Gravitational, Electrical, and Magnetic Forces

Gravitational Forces

Gravity is known as the universal force of attraction, and it attracts any two forces with mass to each other. Any substance that has mass will experience gravitational forces and be attracted to any other substance with mass. Gravitational forces are directly proportional to the mass of the two objects interacting with one another. Therefore, objects of larger mass exhibit greater gravitational attraction. This explains why the planets orbit the sun. Because the sun is the most massive planetary body nearby, the other planets are attracted to its gravitational force. Likewise, objects with smaller mass see less gravitational attraction. Therefore, people do not feel gravitational forces to the objects around them; however, they do feel the gravitational pull of the Earth.

The theories on gravitational forces that are generally believed today were developed by Sir Isaac Newton and Albert Einstein. In Newton's original theory of gravitation, he concluded that the forces which keep the planets in their orbits are dictated by their masses and the distance between them. This is mathematically shown in the equation for universal gravitation: $F = G \frac{m_1 m_2}{r^2}$, where G is the gravitational constant, m_1 and m_2 are two masses, r is the distance between the masses, and F is the gravitational force between the two masses.

Electrical Forces

Electrical forces are attractive or repulsive forces between two different charged bodies. The majority of known information about electrical forces comes from the research of French scientist Charles Augustin Coulomb. Coulomb discovered ways to measure and estimate the attractive force between two very small, charged bodies. Like other forces, electrical forces can be described with Newton's laws of motion. Overall electrical forces are attractive forces between a negatively charged electron and a positively charged proton, or repulsive forces between bodies with the same charge. Charges within an empty space can create an electric field. Electric fields are the areas around a charged object where an electrical force is exerted on other charged objects. Electric charge is measured by the units called ampere and coulomb, which is an ampere per second. Additionally, the product of a charge's magnitude is directly proportional to the electric field it creates. Lastly, electrical forces are inversely proportional to the distance between the two charges, meaning that the further away they are from each other, the weaker the electrical forces are.

Magnetic Forces

Magnetic forces can occur naturally in certain types of materials. If two straight rods are made from iron, they will naturally have a negative end (pole) and a positive end (pole). These charged poles react just like any charged item: opposite charges attract and like charges repel. They will attract each other when set up positive to negative, but if one rod is turned around, the two rods will repel each other due to the alignment of negative to negative and positive to positive.

These types of forces can also be created and amplified by using an electric current.

The relationship between magnetic forces and electrical forces can be explored by sending an electric current through a stretch of wire, which creates an electromagnetic force around the wire from the charge of the current, as long as the flow of electricity is sustained. This magnetic force can also attract and repel other items with magnetic properties. Depending upon the strength of the current in the wire, a smaller or larger magnetic force can be generated around this wire. As soon as the current is cut off, the magnetic force also stops.

Magnetic Energy

Magnetic energy can be harnessed, or controlled, from natural sources or from a generated source (a wire carrying electric current). Magnetic forces are used in many modern applications, including the creation of super-speed transportation. Super-magnets are used in rail systems and supply a cleaner form of energy than coal or gasoline.

Forces and Motion

People have been studying the movement of objects since ancient times, sometimes prompted by curiosity, and sometimes by necessity. On earth, items move according to specific guidelines and have motion that is fairly predictable. In order to understand why an object moves along its path, it is important to understand what role forces have on influencing an object's movements. The term force describes an outside influence on an object. Force does not have to refer to something imparted by another object. Forces can act upon objects by touching them with a push or a pull, by friction, or without touch like a magnetic force or even gravity. Forces can affect the motion of an object.

In order to study an object's motion, the object must be locatable and describable. When locating an object's position, it can help to locate it relative to another known object, or put it into a frame of reference. This phrase means that if the placement of one object is known, it is easier to locate another object with respect to the position of the original object.

The measurement of an object's movement or change in position (x), over a change in time (t) is an object's speed. The measurement of speed with direction is velocity. A "change in position" refers to the difference in location of an object's starting point and an object's ending point. In science, the Greek letter Delta, Δ, represents a change.

Equation: $$\boldsymbol{velocity}\ (v) = \frac{\Delta x}{\Delta t}$$

Position is measured in meters, and time is measured in seconds. The standard measurement for velocity is meters/second (m/s).

$$\frac{\text{meters}}{\text{second}} = \frac{\text{m}}{\text{s}}$$

The measurement of an object's change in velocity over time is an object's acceleration. Gravity is considered to be a form of acceleration.

Equation: $$\boldsymbol{acceleration}\ (a) = \frac{\Delta v}{\Delta t}$$

Velocity is measured in meters/second and time is measured in seconds. The standard measurement for acceleration is meters/second^2 (m/s^2).

$$\frac{\frac{\text{meters}}{\text{second}}}{\text{second}} = \frac{\text{meters}}{\text{second}^2} = \frac{\text{m}}{\text{s}^2}$$

For example, consider a car traveling down the road. The speed can be measured by calculating how far the car is traveling over a certain period of time. However, since the car is traveling in a direction (north, east, south, west), the distance over time is actually the car's velocity. It can be confusing, as many people will often interchange the words speed and velocity. But if something is traveling a certain distance, during a certain time period, in a direction, this is the object's velocity. Velocity is speed with direction.

The change in an object's velocity over a certain amount of time is the object's acceleration. If the driver of that car keeps pressing on the gas pedal and increasing the velocity, the car would have a change in velocity over the change in time and would be accelerating. The reverse could be said if the driver were depressing the brake and the car was slowing down; it would have a negative acceleration, or be decelerating. Since acceleration also has a direction component, it is possible for a car to accelerate without changing speed. If an object changes direction, it is accelerating.

Motion creates something called momentum. This is a calculation of an object's mass multiplied by its velocity. Momentum can be described as the amount an object wants to continue moving along its current course. Momentum in a straight line is called linear momentum. Just as energy can be transferred and conserved, so can momentum.

For example, a car and a truck moving at the same velocity down a highway will not have the same momentum, because they do not have the same mass. The mass of the truck is greater than that of the car, therefore the truck will have more momentum. In a head-on collision, the vehicles would be expected to slide in the same direction of the truck's original motion because the truck has a greater momentum.

The amount of force during a length of time creates an impulse. This means that if a force acts on an object during a given amount of time, it will have a determined impulse. However, if the length of time can be extended, the force will be less, due to the conservation of momentum.

Consider another example: when catching a fast baseball, it helps soften the blow of the ball to follow through, or cradle the catch. This technique is simply extending the time of the application of the force of the ball, so the impact of the ball does not hurt the hand. As a final example, if a martial arts expert wants to break a board by executing a chop from their hand, they need to exert a force on a small point on the boards, extremely quickly. If they slow down the time of the impact from the force of their hand, they will probably injure their hand and not break the board.

Changes in Motion

Projectile motion describes the path of an object in the air. Generally, it is described by two-dimensional movement, such as a stone thrown through the air. This activity takes the shape of a parabolic curve. However, the definition of projectile motion also applies to free fall, or the non-arced motion of an object in a path straight up and/or straight down. When an object is thrown horizontally, it is subject to the same influence of gravity as an object that is dropped straight down. The farther the projectile motion, the farther the distance of the object's flight.

Friction is a force that opposes motion. It can be caused by several materials; there are even frictions caused by air or water. Whenever two differing materials touch, rub, or pass by each other, this can create friction, or an oppositional force. To move an object across a floor, the force exerted on the object must overcome the frictional force keeping the object in place. Friction is also why people can walk on surfaces. Without the oppositional force of friction to a shoe pressing on the floor, a person would not be able to grip the floor to walk—similar to the challenges of walking on ice. Without friction, shoes slip and are unable to help people push forward and walk.

When calculating the effects of objects colliding with each other, several things are important to remember. One of these is the definition of **momentum**: the mass of an object multiplied by the object's velocity. It is expressed by the following equation:

$$p = mv$$

Here, p is equal to an object's momentum, m is equal to the object's mass, and v is equal to the object's velocity.

Another important thing to remember is the principal of the **conservation of linear momentum**. The total momentum for objects in a situation will be the same before and after a collision. There are two primary types of collisions: **elastic** and **inelastic**. In an elastic collision, the objects collide and then travel in different directions. During an inelastic collision, the objects collide and then stick together in their final direction of travel. The total momentum in an elastic collision is calculated by using the following formula:

$$m_1v_1 + m_2v_2 = m_1v_1 + m_2v_2$$

Here, m_1 and m_2 are the masses of two separate objects, and v_1 and v_2 are their velocities, respectively.

The total momentum in an inelastic collision is calculated by using the following formula:

$$m_1v_1 + m_2v_2 = (m_1 + m_2)v_f$$

Here, v_f is the final velocity of the two masses after they stick together post-collision.

Example:

> If two bumper cars are speeding toward each other and collide head-on, they are designed to bounce off of each other and head in different directions. This would be an elastic collision.
>
> If real cars were speeding toward each other and collided head-on, there is a good chance their bumpers might get caught together and their subsequent direction of travel would be in the same direction together.

Circular motion takes place around an **axis,** which is an invisible line around which an object can rotate. This type of motion can be observed in the movements of a toy top. There is actually a point (or rod) through the center of a toy top on which the top can be observed as the spinning point for the top. This rod is called the axis.

When objects move in a circle by spinning on their own axis, or from being tethered around a central point (also an axis), they exhibit **circular motion**. In many ways, circular motion is similar to linear (straight line) motion. One difference is, when spinning an object on or around an axis, a force is created that feels like it is pushing out from the center of the circle. In reality, the force is actually pulling into the center of the circle, and the reactionary force is what is creating the feeling of pushing out. The inward force is the real force and is called **centripetal** force. The outward, or reactionary, force is called **centrifugal** force. The reactionary force is not the real force—it just feels like it is there. This has also been referred to as a **fictional** force. The true force is the one pulling inward, or the centripetal force. The terms *centripetal* and *centrifugal* are often mistakenly interchanged.

Example:

> A traditional upright-style washing machine spins a load of laundry to remove the water from the load. The machine spins a barrel with holes in a circle at a high rate of speed. A force is pulling in toward the center of the circle (centripetal force). At the same time, the force reactionary to the centripetal force is pressing the laundry up against the outer sides of the barrel, thus pushing the water through the small holes that line the outer wall of the barrel.

An object moving in a circular motion also has momentum. In a circular motion, this is called **angular momentum**. It is determined by rotational inertia, rotational velocity, and the distance of the mass from the axis of rotation, or center of rotation.

Objects exhibiting circular motion also demonstrate the conservation of angular momentum. This means that the angular momentum of a system is always constant, regardless of the placement of the mass. Rotational inertia can be affected by how far the mass of the object is placed with respect to the center of rotation (axis of rotation). The farther the mass is from the center of rotation, the slower the rotational velocity. Conversely, if the mass is closer to the center of rotation, the rotational velocity increases. A change in one affects the other, thus conserving the angular momentum. This holds true as long as no external forces act on the system.

Example:

> When ice skaters are spinning on one ice skate, they can extend their arms to slow their rotational velocity. However, when skaters bring their arms in close to their bodies (or shorten the distance between the mass and the center of rotation), their rotational velocity increases, and they will spin much faster. Some skaters extend their arms straight above their heads, which causes an extension of the axis of rotation, thus removing any distance between the mass and the center of rotation and maximizing their rotational velocity. In other words, they spin extremely fast.

The center of mass is the point that provides the average location for the total mass of a system. The word "system" can apply to just one object/particle or to many. The center of mass for a system can be calculated by finding the average of the mass of each object and multiplied by its distance from an origin point using the following formula:

$$x_{center\ of\ mass} = \frac{m_1 x_1 + m_2 x_2}{m_1 + m_2}$$

In this case, *x* is the distance from the point of origin for the center of mass and each respective object, and *m* is the mass of each object.

To calculate for more than one object, the pattern can be continued by adding additional masses and their respective distances from the origin point.

Force and Motion

A large amount of Isaac Newton's work was with discovering the relationships between force and motion. Newton created three laws of motion. The first law states that an object at rest stays at rest, and an object in motion stays in motion unless acted on by an unbalanced force. This means that an object will not move unless a force acts on it, and an object will not stop unless some countering force acts on it. The second law of motion states that acceleration depends on the net force that acts on an object. Newton's second law of motion is expressed in the equation $F_{net} = m \times a$, where F_{net} is net force, m is mass, and a is acceleration. The third law of motion, known as the law of action and reaction, says that when two objects interact, they apply forces to each other that are equal in magnitude and opposite in direction. An example of this could be a bird flying. The bird uses its wings to push down air, creating lift in the opposite direction.

The relationship between force and motion can be used to describe nearly everything in the known universe. Therefore, examples of it can be seen wherever one looks. An example from geology could be the force of pressure building up in a volcano, resulting in the explosive motion of magma being released from the volcano's crater. Within a simple machine, such as a pulley, force is applied to rope, which causes a weight to move upward. Any force applied to an object will cause an opposing reaction and may result in motion.

Physical and Chemical Properties

Physical and Chemical Properties

Both physical and chemical properties are used to sort and classify objects:

- Physical properties: refers to the appearance, mass, temperature, state, size, or color of an object or fluid; a physical change indicates a change in the appearance, mass, temperature, state, size or color of an object or fluid.

- Chemical properties: refers to the chemical makeup of an object or fluid

Solids, Liquids and Gases

States of matter refers to the form substances take such as solid, liquid, gas, or plasma. Solid refers to a rigid form of matter with a flexed shape and a fixed volume. Liquid refers to the fluid form of matter with no fixed shape and a fixed volume. Gas refers to an easily compressible fluid form of matter with no fixed shape that expands to fill any space available. Finally, plasma refers to an ionized gas where electrons flow freely from atom to atom.

> Examples: A rock is a solid because it has a fixed shape and volume. Water is considered to be a liquid because it has a set volume, but not a set shape; therefore, you could pour it into different containers of different shapes, as long as they were large enough to contain the existing volume of the water. Oxygen is considered to be a gas. Oxygen does not have a set volume or a set shape; therefore, it could expand or contract to fill a container or even a room. Gases in fluorescent lamps become plasma when electric current is applied to them.

Matter can change from one state to another in many ways, including through heating, cooling, or a change in pressure.

Changes of state are identified as:

- Melting: solid to liquid
- Sublimation: solid to gas
- Evaporation: liquid to gas
- Freezing: liquid to solid
- Condensation: gas to liquid

Physical and Chemical Changes in Matter

Reversible change (physical change) is the changing of the size or shape of an object without altering its chemical makeup. Examples include the heating or cooling of water, change of state (solid, liquid, gas), the freezing of water into ice, or cutting a piece of wood in half.

When two or more materials are combined, it is called a mixture. Generally, a mixture can be separated out into the original components. When one type of matter is dissolved into another type of matter (a solid into a liquid or a liquid into another liquid), and cannot easily be separated back into its original components, it is called a solution.

A chemical change refers to an alteration in the makeup of an object or fluid and forms a new solution or compound. Examples include burning, rusting, and combining solutions. If a piece of paper is burned it cannot be turned back into its original state. It has forever been altered by a chemical change.

Physical and Chemical Properties of and Changes in Matter

All matter is made up of various elements with unique chemical and physical properties. These properties include their reactivities with different elements, electronegativity, atomic radius (size), density, hardness, color, melting points, and boiling points. Many of these different properties affect how they interact with other matter around them. They also determine the formation of larger molecular structures.

Larger structures have some different properties. For example, molecules can be either hydrophobic or hydrophilic, meaning that they are either repelled by or attracted to water. Molecular structures of living things are organized in a way to utilize all their chemical and physical properties to enable the existence and maintenance of life. For example, proteins that pass through a cell's membrane are hydrophilic in their portions that are exposed to water but hydrophobic in their regions embedded in the cell walls.

The physical and chemical properties of matter can change in many situations. Physical properties of matter can change if their structure is forcibly changed, such as when something is put in a blender, heated to the point of boiling, or cooled to the point of freezing. Chemical changes to matter occur when chemical reactions take place. Burning, cooking, digesting, breathing, rotting, decomposing, thinking, and more involve chemical reactions.

Chemical and physical changes of matter can be observed everywhere on earth and in the expanse of space. With the progress of science and studies of the unknown in space, new states of matter, such as ionized plasma, are discovered. Plasma in space is a physical change in matter when extreme heat adds extra energy to gasses. Therefore, plasma is typically created by stars and is believed to make up over 99% of the visible universe. Additionally, through the study of states of matter in space, the possibility of other unknown concepts like dark matter, which is believed to be made of undiscovered subatomic particles.

Elements, Compounds, Mixtures, and Solutions

Everything that takes up space and has mass is composed of **matter.** Understanding the basic characteristics and properties of matter helps with classification and identification.

An **element** is a substance that cannot be chemically decomposed to a simpler substance, while still retaining the properties of the element.

Compounds are composed of two or more elements that are chemically combined. The constituent elements in the compound are in constant proportions by mass.

The basic building blocks of matter are **atoms,** which are extremely small particles that retain their identity during chemical reactions. Atoms can be singular or grouped to form elements. Elements are composed of one type of atom with the same properties.

Molecules are a group of atoms—either the same or different types—that are chemically bonded together by attractive forces. For example, hydrogen and oxygen are both atoms but, when bonded together, form water.

Ions are electrically-charged particles that are formed from an atom or a group of atoms via the loss or gain of electrons.

Mixtures

When a material can be separated by physicals means (such as sifting it through a colander), it is called a **mixture.** Mixtures are categorized into two types: heterogeneous and homogeneous. **Heterogeneous mixtures** have physically distinct parts, which retain their different properties. A mix of salt and sugar is an example of a heterogeneous mixture. With heterogenous mixtures, it is possible that different samples from the same parent mixture may have different proportions of each component in the mixture. For example, in the sugar and salt mixture, there may be uneven mixing of the two, causing one random tablespoon sample to be mostly salt, while a different tablespoon sample may be mostly sugar.

A **homogeneous mixture,** also called a **solution,** has uniform properties throughout a given sample. An example of a homogeneous solution is salt fully dissolved in warm water. In this case, any number of samples taken from the parent solution would be identical.

Chemical Reactions in Daily Life

Photosynthesis

One specific chemical reaction, photosynthesis, occurs everywhere in the world and provides oxygen and edible forms of energy. Plants utilize structures known as chloroplasts to complete photosynthesis, which converts carbon dioxide, water, and light into glucose and oxygen. Through this chemical reaction, carbon dioxide that humans produce is consumed, oxygen that humans need is released, and plants grow and can be used as food by other organisms.

Combustion Reactions

Humans utilize combustion reactions to produce energy. Combustion reactions occur when a high energy molecule, such as a hydrocarbon, reacts with oxygen to produce water, carbon dioxide and energy. The burning of wood or fossil fuels is considered a combustion reaction. Additionally, combustion reactions occur constantly in human bodies as they consume high energy molecules and oxygen to gain energy and release carbon dioxide.

Digestion

The digestive process utilizes thousands of chemical reactions. Most of these chemical reactions are enzymatic. Digestive enzymes have the function of breaking specific bonds in food molecules. For example, amylase, an enzyme in the saliva, breaks down starches into simpler sugars that can be absorbed and turned into energy molecules through glucose metabolism. Acid-base reactions also occur in digestion. Acid-base reactions are when an acid and a base neutralize one another to yield water and salt. A process based on this principle occurs in the stomach when hydrochloric acid reacts with consumed food.

Cellular Respiration

Cellular respiration is done within all living organisms; it converts digested food material into energy-carrying molecules. Cellular respiration uses broken down food and oxygen to produce ATP, which is what bodies use directly for energy. When ATP is used by cells, a reaction known as hydrolysis occurs. ATP hydrolysis is when ATP releases energy when it breaks apart into ADP and an inorganic phosphate.

Rusting

When iron is exposed to air and moisture, it will turn to rust through an oxidation reaction over time. Iron reacts with oxygen and water to form hydrous iron oxide, or rust. When a substance is made primarily of iron, rusting is often prevented by coating the surface with a material that does not interact with the air. This is why a car is more likely to rust in a location where its paint has been scratched.

Chemical Batteries

Electrochemical redox reactions are utilized in batteries. These reactions convert chemical energy into electrical energy that can be utilized to power electronics. These redox reactions work by transferring electrons from one chemical to another, creating a current of electricity. Recent and more advanced batteries such as lithium-ion batteries utilize redox reactions in the same way to produce electricity faster and for a longer time.

Energy and Interactions

Basics of Energy

The term **energy** typically refers to an object's ability to perform work. This can include a transfer of heat from one object to another, or from an object to its surroundings. Energy is usually measured in Joules. There are two main categories of energy: renewable and non-renewable.

- Renewable: energy produced from the exhaustion of a resource that can be replenished. Burning wood to produce heat, then replanting trees to replenish the resource is an instance of using renewable energy.
- Non-renewable: energy produced from the exhaustion of a resource that cannot be replenished. Burning coal to produce heat would be an example of a non-renewable energy. Although coal is a natural resource found in/on the earth that is mined or harvested from the earth, it cannot be regrown or replenished. Other examples include oil and natural gas (fossil fuels).

Temperature is measured in degrees Celsius (C) or Kelvin (K). Temperature should not be confused with heat. Heat is a form of energy: a change in temperature or a transfer of heat can also be a measure of energy. The amount of energy measured by the change in temperature (or a transfer) is the measure of heat.

First Law of Thermodynamics

The first law of thermodynamics is also known as the **conservation of energy.** This law states that energy cannot be created or destroyed, but is just transferred or converted into another form through a thermodynamic process. For example, if a liquid is boiled and then removed from the heat source, the liquid will eventually cool. This change in temperature is not because of a loss of energy or heat, but from a transfer of energy or heat to the surroundings. This can include the heating of nearby air molecules, or the transfer of heat from the liquid to the container or to the surface where the container is resting.

This law also applies to the idea of perpetual motion. A self-powered perpetual motion machine cannot exist. This is because the motion of the machine would inevitably lose some heat or energy to friction, whether from materials or from the air.

Second Law of Thermodynamics

The second law of thermodynamics is also known as the **law of entropy. Entropy** means chaos or disorder. In simple terms, this law means that all systems tend toward chaos. When one or more systems interacts with another, the total entropy is the sum of the interacting systems, and this overall sum also tends toward entropy.

Conservation of Matter in Chemical Systems

The conservation of energy is seen in the conservation of matter in chemical systems. This is helpful when attempting to understand chemical processes, since these processes must balance out. This means that extra matter cannot be created or destroyed, it must all be accounted for through a chemical process.

Potential Energy vs. Kinetic Energy

Potential energy (gravitational potential energy, or PE) is stored energy, or energy due to an object's height above the ground. Kinetic energy (KE) is the energy of motion. If an object is moving, it has some amount of kinetic energy.

Consider a rollercoaster car sitting still on the tracks at the top of a hill. The rollercoaster has all potential energy and no kinetic energy. As it travels down the hill, the energy transfers from potential energy into kinetic energy. At the bottom of the hill, where the car is going the fastest, it has all kinetic energy, but no potential energy. If energy losses to the environment (friction, heat, sound) are ignored, the amount of potential energy at the top of the hill equals the amount of kinetic energy at the bottom of the hill.

Mechanical Energy

Mechanical energy is the sum of the potential energy plus the kinetic energy in a system, minus energy lost to non-conservative forces. Often, the effects of non-conservative forces are small enough that they can be ignored. The total mechanical energy of a system is conserved or always the same. The amount of potential energy and the amount of kinetic energy can vary to add up to this total, but the total mechanical energy in the situation remains the same.

$$ME = PE + KE$$

$$Mechanical\ Energy = Potential\ Energy + Kinetic\ Energy$$

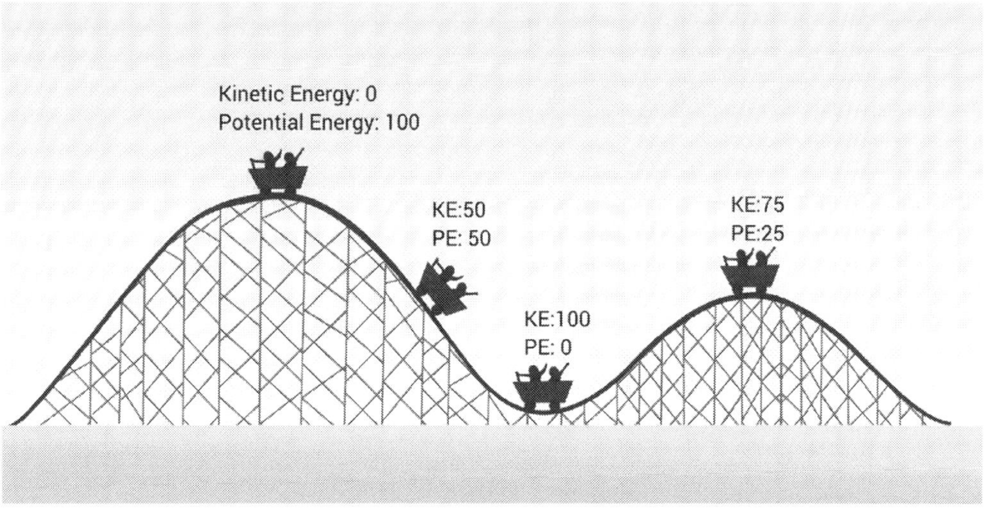

An illustration of a rollercoaster going down a hill demonstrates this point. At the top of the hill a label of $ME = PE$ describes the rollercoaster, halfway down the hill the label $ME = \frac{1}{2}PE + \frac{1}{2}KE$ describes the rollercoaster, and at the bottom of the hill, $ME = KE$ describes the rollercoaster.

Remember, energy can transfer or change forms, but it cannot be created or destroyed. This transfer can take place through waves (including light waves and sound waves), heat, impact, etc.

Other Forms of Energy

The following are forms of kinetic energy:

- **Radiant energy**: Represents electromagnetic energy, which usually travels in waves or particles. Examples of radiant energy include visible light, gamma rays, X-rays, and solar energy.
- **Thermal energy**: Refers to the vibration and movement of molecules and atoms within a substance. It is also known as heat. When an object is heated, its molecules and atoms move and collide with each other more quickly. Examples of thermal energy include geothermal energy from the Earth, heated swimming pools, baking in an oven, and the warmth of a campfire on a person's skin.
- **Sound energy**: Represents the movement of energy through a substance, such as water or air, in waves. Vibrations cause sound energy. Examples of sound energy include a person's voice, clapping, singing, and musical instruments.

- **Electrical energy**: Utilizes charged particles called electrons moving through a wire. Some examples of electrical energy include lightning, batteries, alternating current (AC), direct current (DC), and static electricity.

The following are forms of potential energy:

- **Chemical energy**: Represents the energy stored in the bonds of molecules and atoms. Chemical energy usually undergoes conversion to thermal energy. Examples of chemical energy include petroleum, coal, and natural gas.

- **Elastic energy**: Represents the energy stored in an object as its volume or shape is distorted. It is also known as stored mechanical energy. Examples of elastic energy include stretched rubber bands and coiled springs.

- **Gravitational energy**: Refers to the energy stored as a result of an object's place or position. Increases in height and mass translate into increased gravitational energy. Examples of systems using gravitational energy include rollercoasters and hydroelectric power.

- **Nuclear energy**: Refers to the energy stored in an atom's nucleus. Vast amounts of energy can be released through the combination or splitting of nuclei. An example of nuclear energy is the nucleus of the element uranium.

As stated by the conservation of energy, energy cannot be created or destroyed. If a system gains or loses energy, it is transformed within a single system from one type of energy to another or transferred from one system to another. For example, if the roller coaster system has potential energy that transfers to kinetic energy, the kinetic energy can then be transferred into thermal energy or heat released through braking as the coaster descends the hill. Energy can also transform from the chemical energy inside of a battery into the electrical energy that lights a train set. The energy released through nuclear fusion (when atoms are joined together, they release heat) is what supplies power plants with the energy for electricity. All energy is transferred from one form to another through different reactions. It can also be transferred through the simple action of atoms bumping into each other, causing a transfer of heat.

Heat Energy and Related Processes

Melting

In simple terms, melting is the conversion of a solid into a liquid when exposed to heat. The melting point of a substance is a temperature at which that substance will begin to melt from a solid into a liquid. When a substance is heated, its particles vibrate more rapidly and become more kinetic. Once the particles vibrate enough, their solid structure will break down and cause the substance to melt.

Evaporation

Evaporation is when a liquid converts to a gas. Like melting, when heat is applied to a liquid, the vibration of molecules continues to increase. As the molecules of a substance absorb more kinetic energy, they eventually reach a point when they can escape into the atmosphere as a gas.

Condensation

Condensation is the opposite process of evaporation. It is when a substance changes from a gaseous phase to a liquid phase. When a substance cools, the particles within it lose kinetic energy, which allows them to regain their attractions to each other. Therefore, when a gas cools, the vibration slows down, and the gas becomes a liquid.

Conduction

Conduction is the heating of one object by another through the actual touching of molecules, in order to transfer heat across the objects involved. A spiral burner on an electric stovetop heats from one molecule touching another to transfer the heat via conduction.

Convection

Heat transfer due to the movement/flow of molecules from areas of high concentration to ones of low concentration. Warmer molecules tend to rise, while colder molecules tend to sink. The heat in a house will rise from the vents in the floor to the upper levels of the structure and circulate in that manner, rising and falling with the movement of the molecules. This molecular movement helps to heat or cool a house and is often called convection current.

Radiation

The sun warms Earth through radiation or radiant energy. Radiation does not need any medium for the heat to travel; therefore, the heat from the sun can radiate to Earth across space.

Greenhouse Effect

The sun transfers heat into Earth's atmosphere through radiation traveling in waves. The atmosphere helps protect Earth from extreme exposure to the sun, while reflecting some of the waves continuously within the atmosphere, creating habitable temperatures. The rest of the waves are meant to dissipate out through the atmosphere and back into space.

Energy can be harnessed to operate objects, and this energy is obtained from various sources such as electricity, food, gasoline, batteries, wind, and sun. For example, wind turbines out in a field are turned by the natural power of the wind. The turbines then store that energy internally in power cells; that stored energy can be used to power the lights on a farm or run machinery.

Principles of Electricity

A **circuit** is a closed loop through which current can flow. A simple circuit contains a voltage source and a resistor. The current flows from the positive side of the voltage source through the resistor to the negative side of the voltage source. Note that if the switch is open or there is some other disconnected wire or break in continuity in the circuit, there will be no electromotive force; the circuit must be a closed loop to create a net flow of electrons from the voltage source through the wires and system.

Open and Closed Circuits

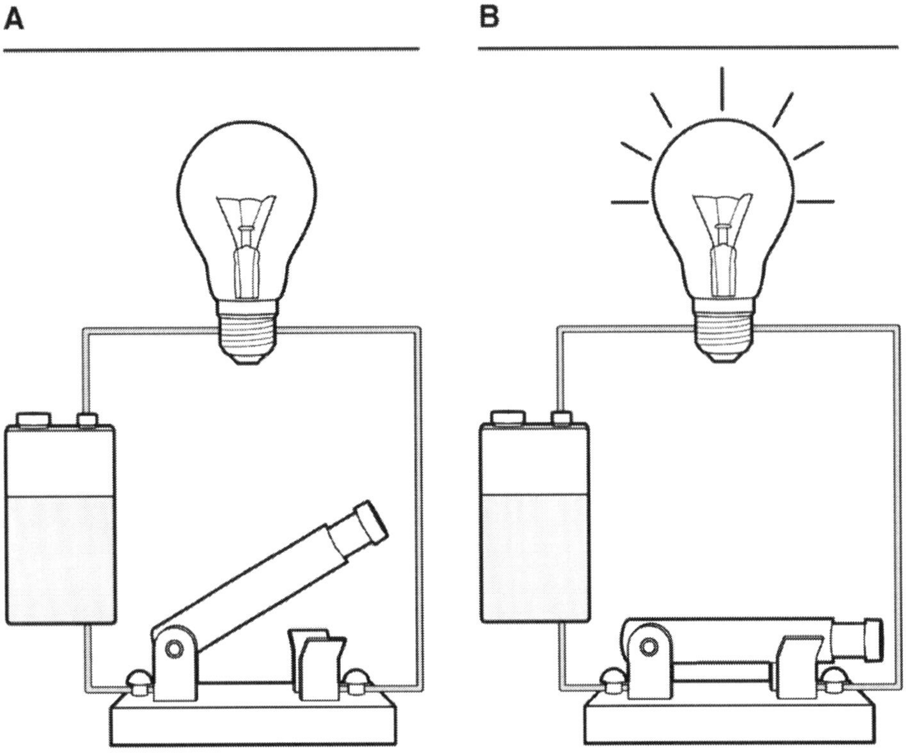

Open Circuit with no electric current

Closed Circuit with electric current flowing

Electrostatics is the study of electric charges at rest. A charge comes from an atom having more or fewer electrons than protons. If an atom has more electrons than protons, it has a negative charge. If an atom has fewer electrons than protons, it has a positive charge. It is important to remember that opposite charges attract each other, while like charges repel each other. So, a negative attracts a positive, a negative repels a negative, and similarly, a positive repels a positive. Just as energy cannot be created or destroyed, neither can charge; charge is transferred. This transfer can be done through touch.

If a person wears socks and scuffs their feet across carpeting, they are transferring electrons to the carpeting through friction. If that person then goes to touch a light switch, they will receive a small shock, which is the electrons transferring from the switch to their hand. The person lost electrons to the carpet, which left them with a positive charge; therefore, the electrons from the switch attract to the person for the transfer. The shock is the electrons jumping from the switch to the person's finger.

Another method of charging an object is through induction. Induction is when a charged object is brought near, but not touched to, a neutral conducting object. The charged object will cause the electrons within the conductor to move. If the charged object is negative, the electrons will be induced away from the charged object and vice versa.

Yet another way to charge an object is through polarization. Polarization can be achieved by simply reconfiguring the electrons on an object. If a person were to rub a balloon on their hair, the balloon would then stick to a wall. This is because rubbing the balloon causes it to become negatively charged and when the balloon is held against a neutral wall, the negatively charged balloon repels all of the wall's electrons, causing a positively charged surface on the wall. This type of charge would be temporary, due to the massive size of the wall, and the charges would quickly redistribute.

Electricity is a form of energy, like heat or movement, that can be harnessed to perform useful work. Electrical energy results from the electric force that exists between atoms and molecules with electrical charge, which is associated with the atomic structure of those substances. Atoms contain various subatomic particles. Protons, which are in the nucleus, carry a +1 charge. Electrons, which surround the outer part of an atom in orbitals or clouds, carry a –1 charge. Net charges of atoms or molecules occur when there is an imbalance in the number of electrons and protons. A net positive charge occurs when there are more protons than electrons, while a net negative charge results when there are more electrons than protons.

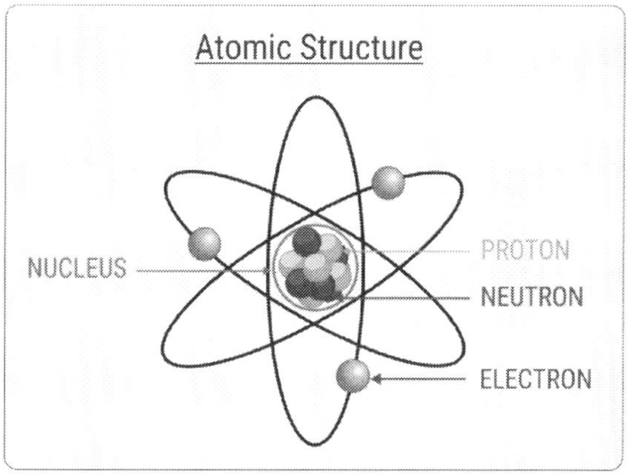

Atoms or molecules with electric charges that are the same experience a force that causes them to repel one another, while those with opposite charges attract each other. Therefore, two positive charges repel one another, two negative charges repel one another, but a positive and a negative charge attract one another. The unit of charge is denoted by C, the coulomb.

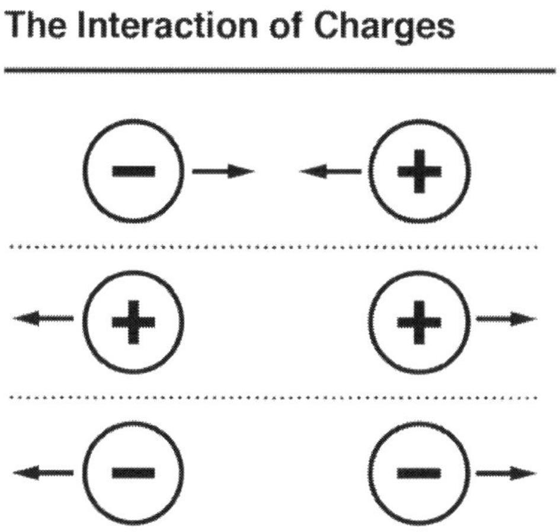

Similar to the Law of Conservation of Energy (which states that energy cannot be created or destroyed, only transferred from one form to another), there is a **conservation of charge** in the universe and in an isolated system. In a given isolated system, individual objects may experience a net loss or gain of charge with the transfer of charge from one object to another from within the system, but the overall charge within the system (or universe) cannot be created or destroyed. Individual positive or negative charges can be created or destroyed, but only in pairs (one positive with one negative), so that the net change in charge is zero.

The properties of any atom vary based on the number and arrangement of electrons in the cloud surrounding the nucleus. For example, electrons in the outer orbitals of metals are relatively free to drift between atoms because they are not pulled in strongly by their atom's own nucleus. These electrons, which carry a negative charge, move through conductive materials, such as other metals, by jumping quickly from atom to atom, creating an electrical flow. This electrical flow is energy that can be harnessed to do work.

The Flow of Electrons Creates Electrical Current

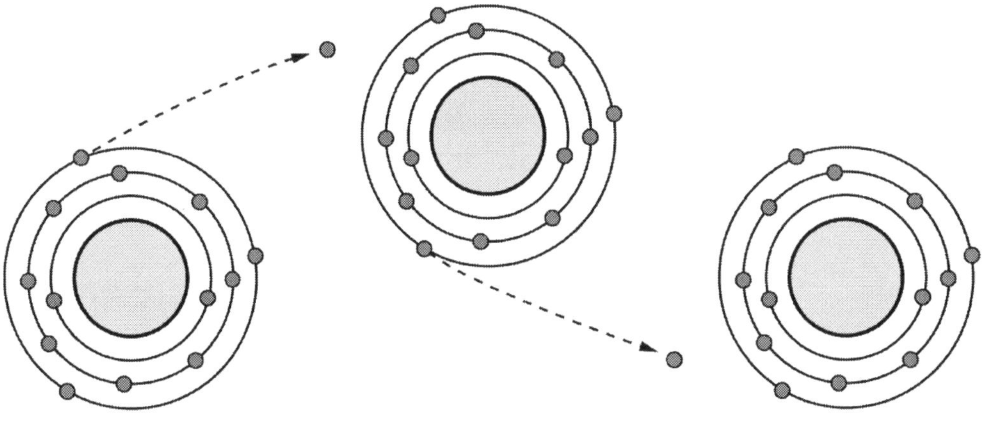

Current is the rate at which the electrical charge—or the number of electrons—flows through a conductive material. It is measured in amperes (A), with each ampere equal to approximately 6.24×10^{18} electrons per second.

Electric current carries energy much like pipes carry water. Water tanks serving an area are often elevated and have various pipes to transport the water down under ground, into each house, and then into smaller pipes leading to each sink, toilet, or shower. The purpose behind elevating the tank is to create pressure in the pipes carrying the water caused by the water above it pushing down. This pressure results in water flow, which can be equated to voltage (akin to pressure) that pushes electrons (the "water") through a circuit. With the water pipes, when the faucet is closed, water does not flow through the pipes, but water flows faster and faster the more the faucet is turned on to allow water in. The rate of water flow is analogous to current—the rate of electron flow through a circuit.

Voltage is the push, or potential, behind electrical work. It is measured in volts (V) and can be thought of as the electromotive potential. Voltage causes current, such that if there is a closed path for electrons and a voltage, current will flow. If there is a suitable path for electrons but no voltage, or voltage in the absence of a viable path, current will cease.

A voltage source is the general term used to describe anything that can be used to generate voltage, such as a battery or generator.

Electrical resistance, measured in ohms (Ω), is the amount of pressure inhibiting the flow of electrical current. Like friction, which slows the rate of movement, resistance dissipates energy and reduces the rate of flow or the movement of current. The amount of resistance that a given object contributes to a circuit depends on the properties of the object, particularly the material. Materials that are inherently more resistant inhibit the ease at which the electrons in the material's atoms can be displaced.

Some circuits have resistors built into them, which are specific electrical components designed to contribute a certain resistance to the circuit.

Resistance is inversely related to conductance, such that a highly conductive material has little resistance, and a material with high resistance has little conductance.

Materials vary in resistance because of the ease (or difficulty) with which electrons in the material's atoms can be displaced. The cross-sectional area and length of a given material also affect the resistance in a predictable relationship. The longer a given conductor is, the greater the resistance it provides; the greater the cross-sectional area (larger material), the less resistance there is. This relationship is quantitatively expressed as $R = \rho \cdot LA$, where ρ is the inherent resistivity of the specific conducting material, L is the length of the material, and A is the cross-sectional area.

Properties of Light and the Functioning of Optical Systems

The electromagnetic spectrum ranges from gamma rays with incredibly long wavelengths to radio waves with very short wavelengths. In the middle of that spectrum is the visible light that human eyes can perceive. Visible light ranges from 380 nanometer wavelength to 780 nanometer wavelength. When light comes in contact with materials, it can interact with the materials in different ways.

Light can be absorbed, reflected, and refracted. Dark surfaces, water, and metal absorb all wavelengths of light. Certain materials that are smooth and shiny, like mirrors, metals, and calm water, can bounce waves of light off their surfaces; this is known as reflection of light. Refraction of light is when light changes direction as it enters a transparent material. Refraction and reflection can be seen together in nature with rainbows. In rainbows, light refracts as it enters water droplets, is reflected by the back end of the droplet, then refracted again at different angles as it exits the droplet. Within optical systems, these properties of light are harnessed for a specific function.

A convex-shaped transparent material refracts light from all angles towards a single point on the other side of the transparent material known as a focal point. The lens of an eyeball utilizes this concept to focus light onto the retina in the eye so images can be resolved. Instruments like microscopes, telescopes, and cameras function in similar manners. They utilize convex lenses to focus light through them and magnify the images produced from the light. The distance between an object and the lenses of these instruments manipulates the image by changing the focal point.

Microscopes specifically use a series of glass lenses to refract and focus light, creating a magnified image. Light passes through a specimen being observed, then is focused and magnified through the convex lenses up to where it is viewed. Reflecting telescopes function in an opposite manner by using a concave mirror. Light from objects in the distance are reflected and focused to a single spot where it can be viewed. Traditional cameras operate by refracting light through a lens to focus on one spot of film.

Properties of Sound

Just like light, sound travels in waves and both are forms of energy. The transmittance of a sound wave produced when plucking a guitar string sends vibrations at a specific frequency through the air, resulting in one's ear hearing a specific note or sets of notes that form a chord. If the same guitar is plugged into an electric amplifier, the strength of the wave is increased, producing what is perceived as a "louder" note. If a glass of water is set on the amplifier, the production of the sound wave can also be visually observed in the vibrations in the water. If the guitar were being plucked loudly enough and in great succession, the force created by the vibrations of the sound waves could even knock the glass off of the amplifier.

Waves can travel through different mediums. When they reach a different material (i.e., light traveling from air to water), they can bend around and through the new material. This is called refraction.

If one observes a straw in half a glass of water from above, the straw appears to be bent at the height of the water. The straw is still straight, but the observation of light passing from air to water (different materials) makes the straw seem as though it bends at the water line. This illusion occurs because the human eye can perceive the light travels differently through the two materials. The light might slow down in one material, or refract or reflect off of the material, causing differences in an object's appearance.

In another example, imagine a car driving straight along a paved road. If one or two of the tires hit the gravel along the side of the road, the entire car will pull in that direction, due to the tires in the gravel now traveling slower than the tires on the paved road. This is what happens when light travels from one medium to another: its path becomes warped, like the path of the car, rather than traveling in a straight line. This is why a straw appears to be bent when the light travels from water to air; the path is warped.

When waves encounter a barrier, like a closed door, parts of the wave may travel through tiny openings. Once a wave has moved through a narrow opening, the wave begins to spread out and may cause interference. This process is called diffraction.

Energy Transformations and Conservation

Sources of Electrical Energy and Processes of Energy Transformation

Fossil Fuels

Fossil fuels are organic compounds from dead organisms that, when burned, produce energy. Through the pressure from rock layers above them, the heat emanating from Earth's mantle, and decomposition, these once-living organisms transform into oil, coal, and natural gas. Fossil fuels provide energy for the modern world, but there is a strong push to find other ways to harness energy.

Scientists are interested in finding renewable sources of energy, such as:

- Wind: Converting kinetic energy from wind into electrical energy using windmills (turbines) is inexpensive.
- Solar: Converting light energy from the sun using solar cells and panels is a more expensive option than wind energy, and effective storage solutions need to be developed for extended cloudy days.
- Geothermal: Converting heat energy that water picks up from Earth's surface into electricity requires expensive power stations that can only exist at geographical locations where water and heat converge (close to hot springs, for example).
- Hydroelectric: Converting kinetic energy from running water to electrical energy using water turbines has a major drawback. Hydroelectric power requires dams to hold water (to slow down its movement to maximize the energy production), which are expensive and can damage ecosystems.
- Biofuels/Biomass: Converting potential energy from decomposing organic material is currently expensive and also has the potential to damage ecosystems.

Solar Panels

Solar panels are made up of photovoltaic cells mounted onto a frame. The first steps toward the creation of solar panels were taken by Edmond Becquerel in 1839 when he discovered that certain materials could produce an electrical charge when exposed to light. Commercially created solar cells made of silicon were not manufactured until Bell Labs did so in 1954. Ever since, solar panels have been growing in popularity as a leading alternative to fossil fuel energy production.

The photovoltaic modules within the solar panels can create electricity through the phenomenon known as the photovoltaic effect. Despite the massive recent growth in popularity of solar panels for energy production, they only account for less than 5% of electricity produced in the world. The lack of complete use of solar panels for energy is due to a variety of issues. First, solar panels are rather expensive, so they cannot be readily available for everyone. Also, their storage capacity for the energy they produce is limited. Therefore, on cloudy days and winter seasons, they cannot rely on stored energy from the sunnier times. Lastly, they are currently not efficient enough to keep up with the demand for electricity. However, efficiency is projected to increase as it has already improved drastically over the past several years.

Hydroelectric Plants

The most utilized renewable energy production method is electricity produced from hydroelectric plants. Hydroelectric plants are made by blocking off water in a reservoir or man-made lake with a dam. Water is then released through the dam to spin turbines that generate the electricity. The blockage of a river or stream in the creation of a dam does have a significant environmental impact. This is due to the displacement of populations when water is built up in the reservoir, disruption of the ecosystem of the river involved, and erosion from the massive displacement of water. In addition to this, there is always a possibility of a dam failing, which could be catastrophic.

Aside from these concerns, hydroelectric plants still account for 70% of renewable energy production due to the fact that they are incredibly efficient and provide electricity for cheap. There are four different methods that hydroelectric plants use to produce energy: conventional dams, pumped storage, run-of-the-river, and tidal. Conventional dams funnel water from a reservoir through a turbine. Pumped storage allows control of water flow by pumping water into different reservoirs to save until demand for electricity is higher. Run-of-the-river plants don't require a reservoir and only take water from upstream. Lastly, tidal hydroelectric plants rely on the movement of tides to move water through the turbines.

Transfer of Energy

Energy is everywhere and is one of the few things in the universe believed to be constant. That means that in the whole universe, if all the energy could be measured (energy in all the stars, atoms, etc.), the amount of energy that was present at the beginning of time is exactly the same as it is now. The only difference is that energy has been converted into different forms. For example, a plant gets its energy from the Sun, using it to grow bigger and stronger; therefore, the Sun's energy is converted and stored inside the plant. Then a person eats the plant, using its stored energy. In this example, energy exists in the form of light, growth, and movement (picking the plant and chewing it).

Only with the energy food provides can organisms exist. Think of a construction team and a pile of bricks and mortar. The bricks are not going to just arrange themselves into a building. However, if a construction team uses their muscles and energy, the complex building can be built. If the construction team runs out of food, though, they will become exhausted and will be unable to construct the building.

The human body is the same way. Organs (heart, brain, stomach, etc.) are like the bricks. The chemical reactions in the body are like the workers. Energy is the food that the workers need to build the organism. The food of life is sugar, specifically glucose. A candy bar, soda, or a slice of birthday cake can provide a boost of energy because of all the sugar they contain. There are many bonds between the molecules of sugar, holding them in place (like the mortar holding the bricks in a building). When the bonds are broken in digestion, all that energy is released so that living things can invest that energy into chemical reactions.

Two chemical reactions are critical for living things: photosynthesis and respiration.

Photosynthesis

Any producer must have a chloroplast in order to convert light energy into food, usually in the form of a carbohydrate. Chloroplasts are organelles that look like little green beans because they contain the pigment chlorophyll, which is able to absorb the sunlight's energy in the form of photons, or light rays. Some prokaryotes are also photosynthetic, and although they don't have a chloroplast because they're too simple and don't contain organelles, they have a pigment in order to make their own food.

Plants need water and sunlight to live. Plants suck up water from their roots. The sunlight they need is absorbed by the chlorophyll in chloroplasts, which are clustered and concentrated in their leaves. Interestingly, the chlorophyll actually is able to absorb every color of light except for green, which is why leaves look green: they reflect green light. If the roots take in water and the leaves take in carbon dioxide and sunlight energy, why are stems important? The stems in plants are an example of how structure helps function. The stem is like a skeleton for plants; it holds the leaves high so they can be closer to the sun.

Plants are critical for life on earth because they absorb the energy from the sun and invest it in the bonds that make sugar. Sugar passes through the food chain to provide energy for all living organisms. Plants and other autotrophs can make their own energy, while heterotrophs (which cannot make their own energy) consume the sugar, break it down, and convert it into usable energy with their mitochondria.

Structure and Function of Living Things

Characteristics of Living Organisms

There are several common traits among all living organisms, including:

- They are comprised of cells
- They contain DNA, the genetic code of life
- They grow and develop
- They reproduce
- They need food for energy
- They maintain homeostasis
- They react to their surroundings
- They evolve as a population

There are two types of cells that make up living things: simple bacterial cells (**prokaryotes**) and the complicated cells of protists, fungi, plants, and animals (**eukaryotes**). All of these have a set of instructions, DNA, which codes for the proteins that allow organisms to grow. In the case of bacteria and single-celled eukaryotes, there is simple development, such as creating structures like DNA, **ribosomes** (protein factories), and a cell membrane. Bacteria do not have complex development because they simply divide once and make a new organism; however, multicellular organisms develop more complex structures—for examples, humans have hearts, stomachs, brains, etc. A human starts as one fused cell called a **zygote**. In nine months, that zygote has developed so much that it has all the internal organs needed to support life.

Organisms cannot live without energy to fuel the necessary reactions to grow and develop. They get the energy they need either by making it themselves (if they are **producers/autotrophs** like plants) or consuming it (like animals and fungi) from an outside source. Not only do organisms use that food to grow and develop, but they also use it to stay healthy and maintain homeostasis. For example, the human body has a constant temperature of 98.6 degrees. If the temperature goes above that, the body starts to sweat to cool off. Much below that temperature, the body will shiver in order to generate energy to heat up. For survival, all organisms must be highly regulated to function, kind of like a car. Every single part has to work together in harmony in order to function properly.

Living things, such as humans, respond to their surroundings. If someone hears a loud noise, his or her head turns toward it. If something gets thrown at one's face, the person will blink. Even plants grow towards sunlight. Living things also evolve as a population. Humans today are nothing like our ancestors of long ago because as a species, humans had to continually adapt to Earth's changing environment.

An extensive explanation of these characteristics of life is beyond an early childhood curriculum, but it's helpful for the teacher to know them because delineating living and nonliving objects can be tricky. A teacher needs to know why fire, a dead grasshopper, and a robot are not alive, because these are common student misconceptions. Although a fire can grow, it does not have DNA. Although a dead grasshopper is made of cells and has DNA, it can't grow or reproduce. A robot doesn't have DNA and isn't made of cells, although it can react to its environment. Conversely, some students don't believe that plants are alive because they don't walk around. To illustrate that they are alive, simple experiments can be used to show that they can reproduce, develop, and grow, such as planting seeds and using light-boxes to show that plants grow toward light.

Teachers must be able to explain that not all organisms move. Plants are alive because they are made of cells, have DNA, grow independently, and meet all of the other characteristics of life. Tiny germs are alive for the same reasons.

These nuances are complicated, but young students should be able to explain that living things grow and nonliving things don't. They should be able to identify mushrooms, plants, and animals as living, and fire, desks, and robots as nonliving.

Life Cycles

When we eat a hamburger, we're eating more than carbohydrates; we're also eating proteins and fats. Plants provide more than just carbohydrates when we eat them; they also are able to use the light energy to make proteins, fats, and, of course, their DNA, because if they didn't have DNA, they'd have no instructions to grow. The following organic compounds and their atoms don't magically appear in organisms—life has to either grab the nutrients from soil or seeds or eat them.

- Carbohydrates, proteins, fats, and DNA/RNA have carbon, hydrogen, and oxygen
- DNA, proteins, and fats also have phosphorus
- DNA and proteins also have nitrogen
- Proteins also can have sulfur

Plants need all of these elements to make food. Where do they get them? Remember that earth's atmosphere is a conglomerate of different gases, including nitrogen. Bacteria in the soil are able to convert that nitrogen into a usable form, and the roots of plants absorb the critical nitrogen. Carbon and oxygen get into the plant via photosynthesis (carbon dioxide), as does the element hydrogen, because plants take in water, which contains hydrogen. Phosphorus and sulfur are absorbed in plants through soil. Since heterotrophs cannot make their own food, they have to eat an autotroph (or eat something that ate an autotroph) in order to obtain these critical elements.

Cycles are a recurring pattern in science, and making food is no exception. When living things die, fungi and bacteria act as decomposers and break down the material. That's actually why dead things and rotten meat smell bad; the decomposers have broken them down so much that gases containing carbon, oxygen, phosphorus, nitrogen, and even smelly sulfur are released. Remember that sulfur is heavy in protein, and eggs are protein-rich. It makes sense that rotten eggs have an unpleasant smell as they release sulfur because they're mostly protein. Once living things decompose, all the elements eventually recycle back to the atmosphere or to the soil, and the atoms are available to construct molecules once again.

Human **development** starts when sperm fertilizes an egg to create a zygote, which will develop into an embryo. Pregnant women carry an **embryo** inside their bodies for nine months before giving birth to a live baby. Human reproduction is a concept best left for an older age, but mentioning that babies come from eggs that grow inside a mom is a concept that can be briefly discussed because all the organisms below develop from external eggs.

It will provide a good contrast to emphasize the following life cycles:

Chicken	Hens are female chickens, and they lay about one egg per day. If there is no rooster (male chicken) around to fertilize the egg, the egg never turns into a chick and instead becomes an egg that we can eat. If a rooster is around, he mates with the female chicken and fertilizes the egg. Once the egg is fertilized, the tiny little embryo (future chicken) will start as a white dot adjacent to the yolk and **albumen** (egg white) and will develop for 21 days. The mother hen sits on her clutch of eggs (several fertilized eggs) to incubate them and keep them warm. She will turn the eggs to make sure the embryo doesn't stick to one side of the shell. The embryo continues to develop, using the egg white and yolk nutrients, and eventually develops an "egg tooth" on its beak that it uses to crack open the egg and hatch. Before it hatches, it even chirps to let the mom know of its imminent arrival!
Frog	Frogs mate similar to the way chickens do, and then lay eggs in a very wet area. Sometimes, the parents abandon the eggs and let them develop on their own. The eggs, like chickens', will hatch around 21 days later. Just like chickens, a frog develops from a yolk, but when it hatches, it continues to use the yolk for nutrients. A chicken hatches and looks like a cute little chick, but a baby frog is actually a **tadpole** that is barely developed. It can't even swim around right away, although eventually it will develop gills, a mouth, and a tail. After more time, it will develop teeth and tiny legs and continue to change into a fully-grown frog! This type of development is called **metamorphosis.**
Fish	Most fish also lay eggs in the water, but unlike frogs, their swimming sperm externally fertilize the eggs. Like frogs, when fish hatch, they feed on a yolk sac and are called *larvae*. Once the larvae no longer feed on their yolk and can find their own nutrients, they are called **fry,** which are basically baby fish that grow into adulthood.
Butterfly	Like frogs, butterflies go through a process called **metamorphosis**, where they completely change into a different looking organism. After the process of mating and internal fertilization, the female finds the perfect spot to lay her eggs, usually a spot with lots of leaves. When the babies hatch from the eggs, they are in the larva form, which for butterflies is called a **caterpillar**. The larvae eat and eat and then go through a process like hibernation and form into a **pupa**, or a **cocoon**. When they hatch from the cocoon, the butterflies are in their adult form.
Bugs	After fertilization, other bugs go through **incomplete metamorphosis**, which involves three states: eggs that hatch, nymphs that look like little adults without wings and molt their exoskeleton over time, and adults.

All of these organisms depend on a proper environment for development, and that environment depends on their form. Frogs need water, caterpillars need leaves, and baby chicks need warmth in order to be born.

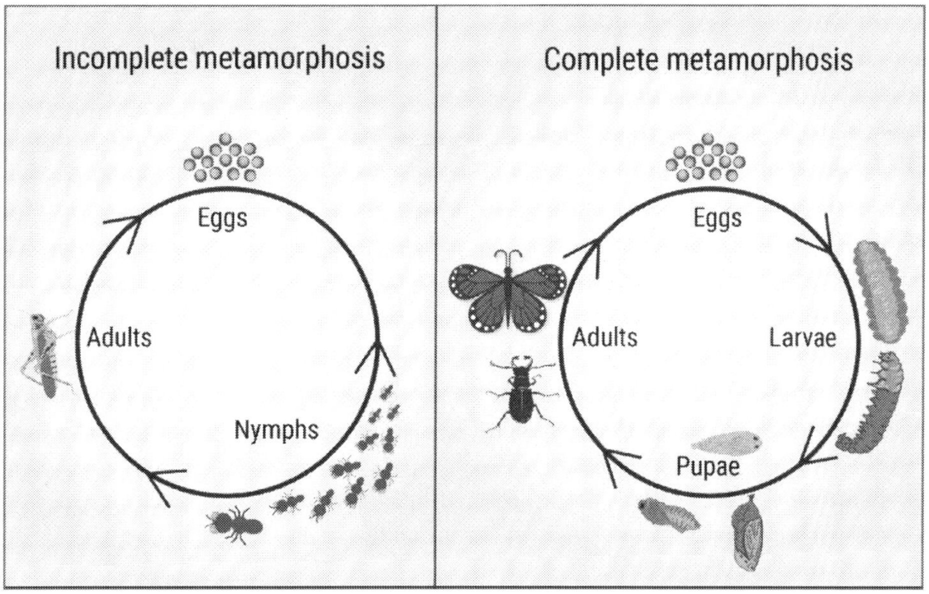

Engaging ways to introduce the life cycle are books like *Rainbow Fish* by Marcus Pfister and *The Very Hungry Caterpillar* by Eric Carle.

Structure and Function in Cells

Cell Theory

The cell is the main functional and structural component of all living organisms. Robert Hooke, an English scientist, coined the term "cell" in 1665. Hooke's discovery laid the groundwork for the cell theory, which is composed of three principals:

- All organisms are composed of cells.
- All existing cells are created from other living cells.
- The cell is the most fundamental unit of life.

Organisms can be unicellular (composed of one cell) or multicellular (composed of many cells). All cells must be bounded by a cell membrane, be filled with cytoplasm of some sort, and be coded by a genetic sequence.

The cell membrane separates a cell's internal and external environments. It is a selectively permeable membrane, which usually only allows the passage of certain molecules by diffusion. Phospholipids and proteins are crucial components of all cell membranes. The cytoplasm is the cell's internal environment and is aqueous, or water-based. The genome represents the genetic material inside the cell that is passed on from generation to generation.

Plant and Animal Cells

The two main classes of eukaryotes are plants and animals. Animal and plant cells contain many of the same or similar *organelles*, which are membrane enclosed structures that each have a specific function; however, there are a few organelles that are unique to either one or the other general cell type. The following cell organelles are found in both animal and plant cells, unless otherwise noted in their description:

- *Nucleus*: The nucleus consists of three parts: the nuclear envelope, the nucleolus, and chromatin. The **nuclear envelope** is the double membrane that surrounds the nucleus and separates its contents from the rest of the cell. The *nucleolus* produces ribosomes. *Chromatin* consists of DNA and protein, which form chromosomes that contain genetic information. Most cells have only one nucleus; however, some cells, such as skeletal muscle cells, have multiple nuclei.

- *Endoplasmic reticulum (ER)*: The ER is a network of membranous sacs and tubes that is responsible for membrane synthesis. It is also responsible for packaging and transporting proteins into vesicles that can move out of the cell. It folds and transports other proteins to the Golgi apparatus. It contains both smooth and rough regions; the rough regions have ribosomes attached, which are the sites of protein synthesis.

- *Flagellum*: Flagella are found only in animal cells. They are made up of a cluster of microtubules projected out of the plasma membrane, and they aid in cell mobility.

- *Centrosome*: The centrosome is the area of the cell where **microtubules,** which are filaments that are responsible for movement in the cell, begin to be formed. Each centrosome contains two centrioles. Each cell contains one centrosome.

- *Cytoskeleton*: The cytoskeleton in animal cells is made up of microfilaments, intermediate filaments, and microtubules. In plant cells, the cytoskeleton is made up of only microfilaments and microtubules. These structures reinforce the cell's shape and aid in cell movement.

- *Microvilli*: Microvilli are found only in animal cells. They are protrusions in the cell membrane that increase the cell's surface area. They have a variety of functions, including absorption, secretion, and cellular adhesion. They are found on the apical surface of epithelial cells, such as in the small intestine. They are also located on the plasma surface of a female's eggs to help anchor sperm that are attempting fertilization.

- *Peroxisome*: A peroxisome contains enzymes that are involved in many of the cell's metabolic functions, one of the most important being the breakdown of very long chain fatty acids. Peroxisomes produces hydrogen peroxide as a byproduct of these processes and then converts the hydrogen peroxide to water. There are many peroxisomes in each cell.

- *Mitochondrion*: The mitochondrion is often called the powerhouse of the cell and is one of the most important structures for maintaining regular cell function. It is where aerobic cellular respiration occurs and where most of the cell's adenosine triphosphate (ATP) is generated. The number of mitochondria in a cell varies greatly from organism to organism, and from cell to cell. In human cells, the number of mitochondria can vary from zero in a red blood cell, to 2000 in a liver cell.

- *Lysosome*: Lysosomes are responsible for digestion and can hydrolyze macromolecules. There are many lysosomes in each cell.

- *Golgi apparatus*: The Golgi apparatus is responsible for the composition, modification, organization, and secretion of cell products. Because of its large size, it was actually one of the first organelles to be studied in detail. There are many Golgi apparatuses in each cell.

- *Ribosomes*: Ribosomes are found either free in the cytosol, bound to the rough ER, or bound to the nuclear envelope. They manufacture proteins within the cell.
- *Plasmodesmata*: The plasmodesmata are found only in plant cells. They are cytoplasmic channels, or tunnels, that go through the cell wall and connect the cytoplasm of adjacent cells.
- *Chloroplast*: Chloroplasts are found only in plant cells. They are responsible for *photosynthesis*, which is the process of converting sunlight to chemical energy that can be stored and used later to drive cellular activities.
- *Central vacuole*: A central vacuole is found only in plant cells. It is responsible for storing material and waste. This is the only vacuole found in a plant cell.
- *Plasma membrane*: The plasma membrane is a phospholipid bilayer that encloses the cell.
- *Cell wall*: Cell walls are only present in plant cells. The cell wall is made up of strong fibrous substances including cellulose and other polysaccharides, and protein. It is a layer outside of the plasma membrane, which protects the cell from mechanical damage and helps maintain the cell's shape.

Cellular Organization and Organ Systems

Prokaryotes contain ribosomes, DNA, cytoplasm, a cell membrane, a cytoskeleton, and a cell wall. Eukaryotes vary between kingdoms but contain all of these structures except a cell wall because animal cells require so much mobility. Large, land-dwelling animals typically compensate with an exoskeleton (like insects) or an endoskeleton (like humans and other mammals, reptiles, and birds) for structure.

All bacterial cells are unicellular (existing as just one cell). Almost all types of protist and some species in fungi kingdom are unicellular, but they still have the complicated organelles of eukaryotes. A few protists, almost all fungi, and all plants and animals are multicellular. Multicellularity leads to development of structures that are perfectly designed for their function.

Cells combine to form tissue. Tissue combines to form organs. Organs combine to form organ systems, and organ systems combine to form one organism. The structures of all of these combinations allow for the maximum functionality of an organism, as demonstrated by the nervous system.

A neuron is a cell in the nervous system designed to send and receive electrical impulses. Neurons have dendrites, which are sensors waiting to receive a message. Neurons also have an axon, a long arm that sends the message to the neighboring neuron. The axon also has insulation known as myelin that speeds the message along. Many neurons combine to form a nerve, the tissue of the nervous system, which is like a long wire. The structure of this nerve is perfect—it is a long cable whose function is to send signals to the brain so the brain can process the information and respond. Nerve tissue combines with other tissue to form the brain, a complex structure of many parts.

The brain also has glands (epithelial tissue) that release hormones to control processes in our body. The brain and spinal cord together form the central nervous system that controls the stimulus/response signaling in our body. The nervous system coordinates with the circulatory system to make our heart beat, the digestive system to control food digestion, the muscular system to move an arm, the respiratory system to facilitate breathing, and all other body systems to make the entire organism functional. Cells are the basic building block in our bodies, and their structure is critical for their function and the function of the tissues, organs, and systems that they comprise.

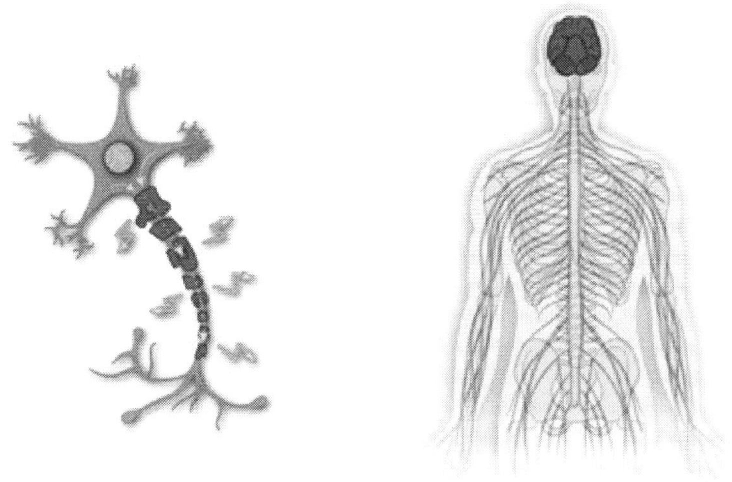

In the graphic above, the left depicts a neuron, and the right depicts the nervous system. A neuron is a nerve cell, and it is the basic building block of the nervous system. Cell, tissue, organ, and organ system structure are critical for function.

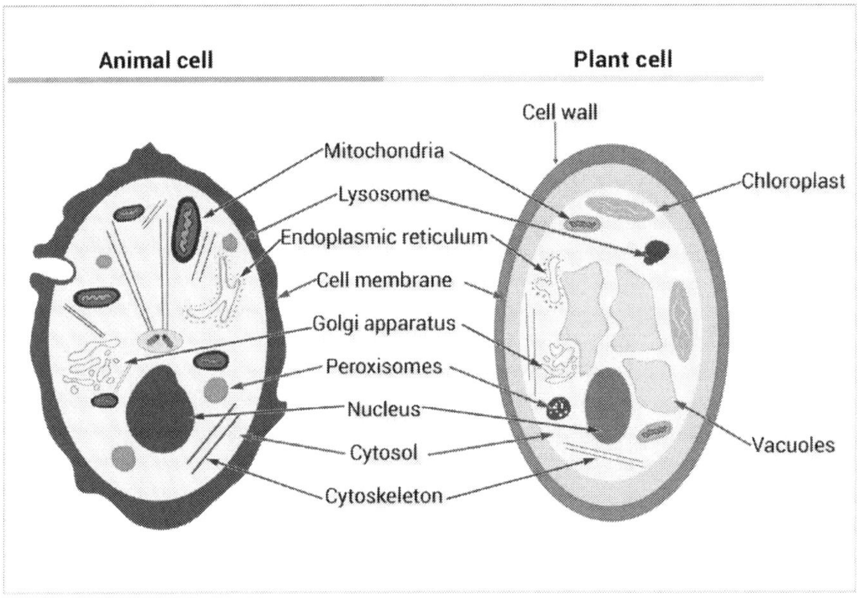

Although a human is noticeably different from a carrot, cells in these organisms have only a few differences. The main differences are the cell structure, appearance, and method of energy production.

Plant cells have a **cell wall** made of cellulose—a strong, fibrous material that adds bulk to stool because it's so hard to break down. This material must be strong in order to prevent the cell from bursting when water enters and increases the intracellular pressure. Animal cells don't have a cell wall. Instead, they have a **cell membrane** composed of several materials (which differ depending on cell type) embedded in a phospholipid bilayer. This bilayer is exactly what it sounds like: two layers of phospholipids stacked tail-to-tail. A **phospholipid** is a molecule with a glycerol (phosphate) head and two fatty acid (lipid) tails. This membrane is much weaker compared a plant's cellulose wall, so animal cells are much more susceptible to bursting from water pressure. And herein lies an important characteristic of the phospholipid bilayer: the tails inside the layer are actually **hydrophobic** (water-repellent) so they are able to prevent too much water from entering and killing the cell.

The shapes and sizes of plant and animal cells are also quite different. Plant cells have a consistent rectangular shape and are generally much larger, ranging from 10–100 micrometers. Animal cells vary in shape and are around 10–30 micrometers. Human liver cells (which are round) look completely different from nerve cells (which have a large cell body and long projections outward). The vacuoles are also different; plant cells tend to have just one large vacuole, while animal cells have several tiny ones.

The most important difference between plants and animals is how they create energy. Animals must consume energy from other living organisms. Plants have the amazing ability to use energy from the sun to power their growth and survival. The little organelles that make this possible are the **chloroplasts** in plants and **mitochondria** in animals. Both use carbon, oxygen, and water. Through photosynthesis, a chloroplast is able to extract carbon from the carbon dioxide (CO_2) in the air and combine it with water (H_2O) to make glucose ($C_6H_{12}O_6$) and oxygen (O_2). Glucose provides energy for animal cells. In the body, mitochondria use the energy embedded inside glucose molecules and combine them with oxygen to create carbon dioxide, water, and ATP (a form of useable energy for physiological processes). This process is called cellular respiration. Memorizing the chemical equations for these reactions may help with understanding these processes:

Photosynthesis: $6\ H_2O + 6\ CO_2 + \text{sunlight} \rightarrow C_6H_{12}O_6 + 6\ O_2$

Six molecules of water and six of carbon dioxide make one glucose molecule and six molecules of oxygen.

Cellular respiration: $C_6H_{12}O_6 + 6\ O_2 \rightarrow 6\ H_2O + 6\ CO_2 + \text{heat (energy)}$

Note that this is basically the reverse of photosynthesis.

Bacterial cells are a completely different story. There are a huge variety of bacteria, and they can actually share characteristics with both plant and animal cells. Some can utilize photosynthesis, some can only perform cellular respiration, and some can even do both or neither!

Human Body Systems and Functions

The following table lists organ systems in the human body:

Name	Function	Main organs
Nervous	Detect stimuli and direct response	Brain and spinal cord
Circulatory	Pump blood to deliver oxygen to cells so they can perform cellular respiration	Heart
Respiratory	Breathe in oxygen (reactant for cellular respiration) and release carbon dioxide waste	Lungs
Muscular	Movement	Heart and muscles
Digestive	Break down food so that glucose can be delivered to cells for energy	Stomach, small intestine, lots of others
Skeletal	Support and organ protection	All sorts of joints, skull, ribcage

Taxonomic Classifications

Due to the speciation that has occurred, the variety of organisms is astronomical. Scientists have identified about 2 million species, and they suspect that there are at least 8 million others out there.

A man named Carolus Linnaeus developed a naming system to try to create some order in classifying all species. For example, the classification of humans through the seven levels, from all-inclusive to the most specific, looks like this:

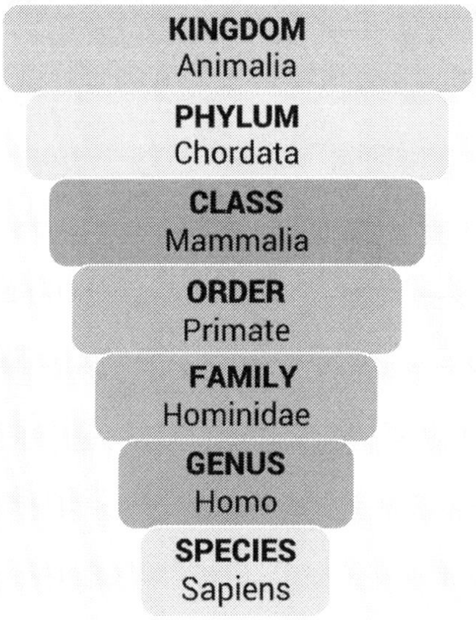

One benefit of this universal naming system is that because some organisms have different common names, like the roly-poly and doodlebug, or the cougar and panther, it allows scientists to have a common language. Due to the sheer magnitude of species, scientists need the seven levels, but when referring to organisms, their official names are just the last two: genus and species. Humans are simply referred to as *Homo sapiens*. This two-name system is called binomial nomenclature.

There are currently six kingdoms, although the prokaryotes (simpler cells) used to be lumped together into one kingdom called Monera. Currently, there are two prokaryotic kingdoms, Archaebacteria and Eubacteria.

Archaebacteria

Prokaryotes that have a cell membrane made of fats. They live in harsh places including extremely hot areas (volcanic vents or hot springs) and extremely salty locations (Utah's Salt Lake). These are the rarest prokaryotes.

Eubacteria

Common bacteria that have a cell membrane made of a protein-carbohydrate blend. They make up the vast majority of existing prokaryotes. An example is staphylococcus.

Protista

This kingdom consists of eukaryotes. Most are unicellular. This kingdom is the most diverse and can be divided into three types: fungus-like (including slime-molds), plant-like (including algae), and animal-like (including amoeba). Some scientists believe that there is so much diversity within the kingdom that they should be split into separate kingdoms, but so far, they remain in one group.

Animal-like protists are heterotrophs (they do not make their own food), and plant-like protists are autotrophs (they make their own food). Fungus-like protists are heterotrophs. Like actual fungi, these organisms externally digest their food by acting as parasites and decomposers. Animal-like protists ingest their food via phagocytosis (cell eating) or by absorbing it.

Depending on the particular protists, some produce asexually via mitosis and others reproduce sexually.

Fungi

Fungi are eukaryotic heterotrophs that digest their food externally. Many of them, including common mushrooms and toadstools, act as decomposers by breaking down dead organisms then absorbing the broken-down nutrients. Other fungi accomplish ingestion as parasites feeding off of living organisms, as in the case of a yeast infection. All fungi are multicellular with one exception—yeast. Fungi have cell walls made of a complex carbohydrate called chitin. Most fungi reproduce sexually and asexually.

Plantae

Plants are multicellular autotrophs like daisies, roses, and pine trees. They are closely related to the aquatic producer, algae, but different in that algae don't contain true roots, stems, or leaves. Plants are photosynthesizers, and their cells have surrounding cell walls made of the starch cellulose.

Animalia

Animals are multicellular heterotrophs, like fungi, except that animals move and internally ingest their food by consuming it. Animals are the only kingdom to not have cells with cell walls due to their flexibility and ability to move. The animal kingdom is very diverse and includes humans, jellyfish, and spiders, as well as all sorts of other organisms.

Reproduction and the Mechanisms of Heredity

Reproduction and Heredity

Cellular Reproduction

Unlike viruses, all living organisms can independently reproduce, but reproduction occurs differently between bacteria and the more complex kingdoms. Bacteria reproduce via binary fission, which is a simpler process than eukaryotic division because it doesn't involve splitting a nucleus and doesn't have a web of proteins to pull chromosomes apart. Prokaryotes have simpler DNA compared to cells that have a much larger number of individual chromosomes (humans have two sets of 23 chromosomes—one set from mom and one set from dad, for a total of 46 chromosomes). Think of going from class to class with two identical binders (like bacteria) versus going from class to class with 23 identical pairs of binders (humans); it would be much more difficult to organize the large set of binders than the smaller one.

Binary fission in bacteria is therefore relatively easy. Bacteria copy their DNA in a process called DNA replication, grow, and then the replicated DNA moves to either side, and two new cells are made.

Eukaryotic cell division is part of a well-defined cycle with the following phases:

- G1 phase: The cell is growing and working.
- S phase: The cell is getting too large, so it copies its DNA because it wants to make sure the two new cells have the full instruction manual that is DNA.
- G2 phase: The cell uses its workers to get ready for cell division.
- M phase: Chromosomes condense and line up in the middle of the cell. The copies are sent to either side.
- Cytokinesis: The moment when the cytoplasm is officially split in two, and then two identical daughter cells are produced and enter G1 phase.

The M phase has subdivisions because it quickly goes through a series of events. Each sub-phase of events is described and illustrated below.

PHASE	PHASE EVENTS	ANIMAL CELL DIAGRAM	PLANT CELL DIAGRAM
Interphase (G1, S, and G2)	DNA is loose and spread out and contained in nucleus. This is important because it is actively growing and needs access to its instructions to do chemical reactions correctly. Chromosomes are replicated (copied) in S phase so that they look like an X. Each side of the X has identical DNA.	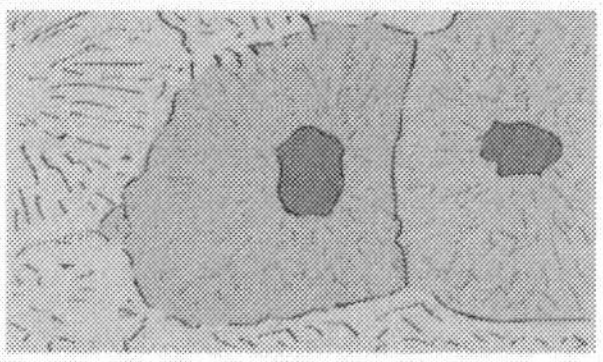	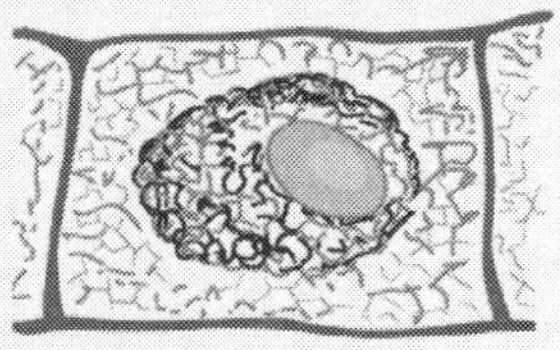
Prophase	Nucleus disappears and DNA condenses into chromosomes	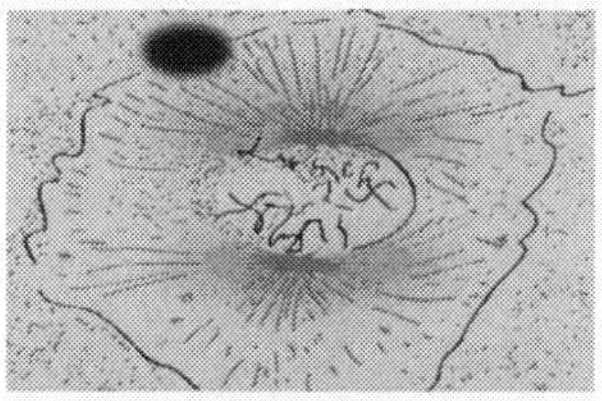	
Metaphase	Chromosomes line up in center and proteins from either side of cell attach to them	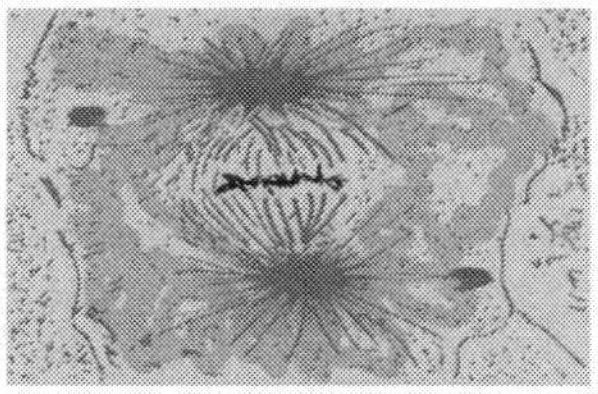	
Anaphase	Proteins shorten and pull chromosomes apart so that one half (either left side of X or right side of X) of DNA goes to each new cell		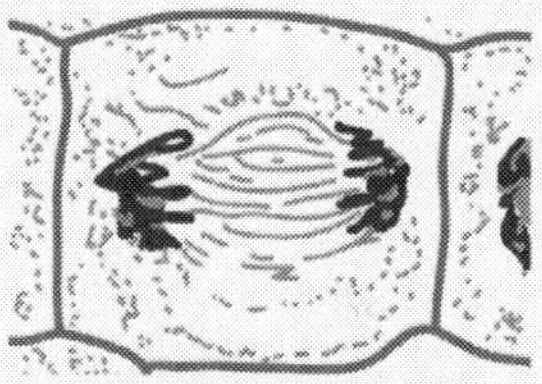
Telophase and Cytokinesis	Nuclei reform and chromosomes start to spread out **Animal cells**: cytoplasm to split in half **Plant cells**: cell plate (new cell wall) forms between daughter cells and extends (animal cells don't have a cell wall)	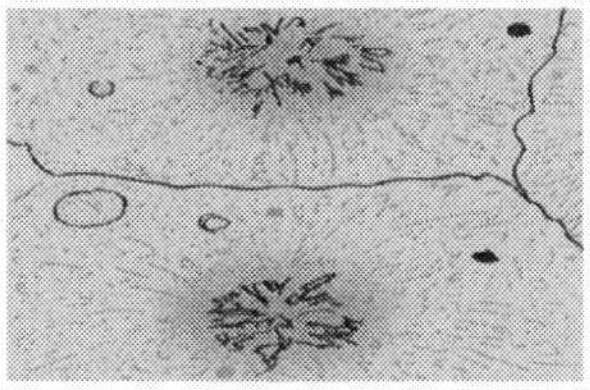	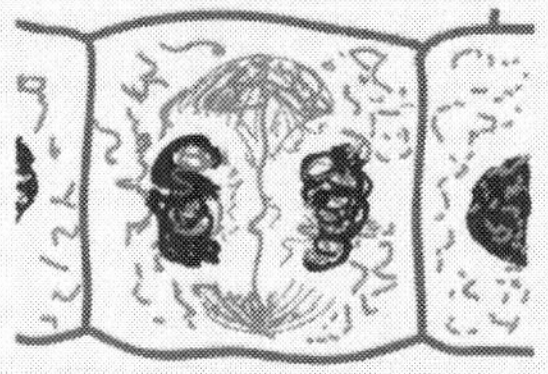

Organism Reproduction

For bacteria, cell reproduction is the same as organism reproduction; binary fission is an asexual process that produces two new cells that are clones of each other because they have identical DNA.

Eukaryotes are more complex than prokaryotes and can go through sexual reproduction. They produce gametes (sex cells). Females make eggs and males make sperm. The process of making gametes is called meiosis, which is similar to mitosis except for the following differences:

- There are two cellular divisions instead of one.
- Four genetically different haploid daughter cells (one set of chromosomes instead of two) are produced instead of two genetically identical diploid daughter cells.

- A process called crossing over (recombination) occurs, which makes the daughter cells genetically different. If chromosomes didn't cross over and rearrange genes, siblings could be identical clones. There would be no genetic variation, which is a critical factor in the theory of evolution of organisms.

In sexual reproduction, a sperm fertilizes an egg and creates the first cell of a new organism, called the zygote. The zygote will go through countless mitotic divisions over time to create the adult organism.

Heredity: Passing Genes Across Generations

All living things are a product of their DNA, specifically portions of their DNA called genes that code for different characteristics.

Learned behavior is not affected by DNA and is not hereditable. Changes in appearance like a woman painting her toenails, a bird whose feathers accidentally fall out due to a tornado, or a person getting a scar are also not heritable. Heritable characteristics are those coded by DNA like eye color, hair color, and height.

A man named Gregor Mendel is considered the father of genetics. He was a monk and a botanist, and through extensive experiments with pea plants, he figured out a great deal about heredity.

Our genetic code comes in pairs. Each chromosome contains many genes, and since we have one chromosome from our mom and one chromosome from our dad, we have two copies of each gene. Genes come in different forms called alleles. The two alleles work together, and when the cell reads them and follows their instructions, the way an organism looks or behaves is called a trait. For some traits, there are only two alleles: a dominant allele and a recessive allele. Even though eye color is a bit more complicated, pretend that brown eyes are dominant over blue eyes, and there are the only two alleles:

- B = Brown eyes
- b = blue eyes

A child inherits these alleles from his parents. There are three possible combinations a child can inherit, dependent on his parents' alleles:

- BB (homozygous dominant)
- Bb (heterozygous)
- bb (homozygous recessive)

The combination of genes above will determine the trait in the offspring. If the child gets any combination with a B, the more powerful allele, his eyes will be brown. Only the bb combination will give the child blue eyes. In this example, the combination of alleles is called a genotype, and the actual eye color the child has is called a phenotype.

Inherited Traits and Learned Characteristics

Inherited traits are aspects of a person that are inherited through genetics. Some examples of this include hair color, eye color, skin color, other physical appearances, and even some specific abilities like the ability to roll one's tongue, or the orientation by which one clasps their hands. Inherited traits are passed from parents to offspring following Mendelian genetics. All living organisms end up with half of their genes from one parent and half from another. For each specific trait, only the gene from one parent can be inherited.

For certain traits, the inherited result can be a mixture of two parents. A common example of this in Gregor Mendel's pea studies was when he bred two pink peas together. A quarter of the peas inherited both dominant alleles and had white flowers, a quarter of the peas received both recessive alleles and had red flowers, then the rest of the offspring peas had pink flowers that inherited both a dominant and a recessive allele.

A large number of recent studies are focusing how environmental factors can affect the expression of certain inherited traits. This field of study is known as epigenetics. Epigenetics shows that inherited traits can be expressed or blocked by certain environmental factors such as exposure to smoke, poor diet, and much more.

In contrast to inherited traits, learned characteristics, also known as acquired traits, are not inherited genetically but are learned over time. Acquired traits are picked up over time in one's family and interactions in society. Some examples of acquired traits can be a love for reading, liking specific foods, the ability to play guitar, swimming, and almost anything that can be learned. However, there might be somewhat of a genetic component to certain learned characteristics. An example of this would be talent in some sports. Although sports ability is improved through constant training and practice, exceptional eyesight, muscle mass, and height are inherited from parents.

Organization of Hereditary Material

Often the first thing that comes to mind when thinking about how genetic information is stored is deoxyribonucleic acid, or DNA. DNA is a molecule that is made up of coiled polynucleotide chains that carry all genetic information for every aspect of life. DNA is found within chromosomes, which are known for carrying genetic information. Eukaryotic organisms, like humans, have their chromosomes organized into many different strands that are found in the nuclei of the cells. Genes are found on specific parts of a chromosome in two copies. These two copies are not always the same, and when they are different, they are considered alleles. Therefore, both genes and alleles code for transmission of specific traits. A gene may have many different alleles, but there are only ever two alleles for a gene at any locus of a chromosome. A locus is the location of the DNA on a chromosome where a specific gene is found.

Although some traits are only coded by one gene, most traits are coded by many different genes. When a trait is determined by many different genes, it is known as a polygenic trait. Traits like ear lobes and a widow's peak are determined by only one gene, but traits like height and skin color are determined by many genes; these are called polygenic.

In some circumstances, multiple traits can be determined by a single gene. This single gene is known as a pleiotropic gene. An example of a pleiotropic gene in humans is Marfan Syndrome, which is a genetic disorder that affects the connective tissues in a human. It is caused by a mutation in a single gene and results in pleiotropy. Overall, genes come in pairs and are passed from parents to the offspring. Offspring will receive one copy of each gene to make up their complete genome.

Dominant and Recessive Traits

Since genes consist of two alleles, one of each is passed down from each parent to an offspring. The alleles can be considered either dominant or recessive. Dominant traits are carried by dominant alleles and recessive traits are carried by recessive alleles. Whenever a dominant allele is connected, the trait expressed will be dominant. Therefore, two dominant alleles paired together, as well as a dominant and recessive allele together, will display the dominant trait. For a recessive trait to be seen, both alleles paired must be recessive. When represented in literature, like research, dominant alleles are denoted by capital letters, whereas recessive alleles are denoted by lower case letters.

Probabilities in genetics are rather complex, but genetic outcomes can be predicted in many cases. The most valuable tool in predicting the outcomes of genetic combinations is the Punnett square. A Punnett square is a square with four boxes used to predict the outcome of breeding experiments. It is a way to better visualize the concepts of Mendelian genetics, researched by the Augustinian friar Gregor Mendel.

	Mother G	Mother g
Father G	GG	Gg
Father g	Gg	gg

Although Punnett squares are useful in many situations, they are not ideal for crosses of many genes. In addition to this, the product rule and the sum of probabilities can be utilized. With respect to genetic probabilities, the product rule is utilized to predict the chance of multiple outcomes occurring all together at once. This is done by simply multiplying the individual probabilities. Within studies of genetics, an individual may need to calculate the probability that only one of many different possibilities could occur. In this situation, the sum rule of probability can be used. The sum rule states that the probability of any of several possible outcomes occurring is equal to the sum of each individual probability.

Adaptations and Evolution

Adaptive Characteristics

The theory of **adaptation** is defined as an alteration in a species that causes it to become more well-suited to its environment. It increases the probability of survival, thus increasing the rate of successful reproduction. As a result, an adaptation becomes more common within the population of that species.

For examples, bats use reflected sound waves (echolocation) to prey on insects, and chameleons change colors to blend in with their surroundings to evade detection by its prey and predators. Adaptations are brought about by natural selection.

Adaptive radiation refers to rapid diversification within a species into an array of unique forms. It may occur as a result of changes in a habitat creating new challenges, ecological niches, or natural resources.

Darwin's finches are often thought of as an example of the theory of adaptive radiation. Charles Darwin documented 13 varieties of finches on the Galapagos Islands. Each island in the chain presented a unique and changing environment, which was believed to cause rapid adaptive radiation among the finches. There was also diversity among finches inhabiting the same island. Darwin believed that as a result of natural selection, each variety of finch developed adaptations to fit into its native environment.

A major difference in Darwin's finches had to do with the size and shapes of beaks. The variation in beaks allowed the finches to access different foods and natural resources, which decreased competition and preserved resources. As a result, various finches of the same species were allowed to coexist, thrive, and diversify. Finches had:

- Short beaks, which were suited for foraging for seeds
- Thin, sharp beaks, which were suited for preying on insects
- Long beaks, which were suited for probing for food inside plants

Darwin believed that the finches on the Galapagos Islands resulted from chance mutations in genes transmitted from generation to generation.

Theory of Natural Selection

The theory of natural selection is one of the fundamental tenets of evolution. It affects the phenotype, or visible characteristics, of individuals in a species, which ultimately affects the genotype, or genetic makeup, of those same individuals. Charles Darwin was the first to explain the theory of natural selection, and it is described by Herbert Spencer as favoring survival of the fittest. Natural selection encompasses three assumptions:

- A species has heritable traits: All traits have some likelihood of being propagated to offspring.
- The traits of a species vary: Some traits are more advantageous than others.
- Individuals of a species are subject to differing rates of reproduction: Some individuals of a species may not get the opportunity to reproduce while others reproduce frequently.

Over time, certain variations in traits may increase both the survival and reproduction of certain individuals within a species. The desirable heritable traits are passed on from generation to generation. Eventually, the desirable traits will become more common and permeate the entire species.

Selective Breeding and Mutation

Traits adapting over large periods of time is known as evolution. Evolution is an inevitable process where, within a population, heritable traits change to better ensure the health and reproducibility of organisms. There are four factors that affect evolution: mutation, gene flow, genetic drift, and natural selection. Mutations create new variations in the gene pool, and the mutations that affect evolution only occur in the gametes. Gene flow is when genes move in and out of a gene pool as a result of migration of organisms or movement of gametes. Genetic drift causes random fluctuations in the number of variants of genes in a given population. Natural selection is the process by which an organism adapts to an environment to survive and reproduce more successfully. Evolution is an incredibly slow process. It is believed that for a major change to occur and persist throughout a population, it could take up to a million years. However, for small changes to occur, or for new unique species to arise, it could only take a couple years.

In addition to evolution, there are other processes that allow organisms to adapt their traits. One of these processes is selective breeding. Selective breeding is when parents with desirable traits breed together to bolster the desirable trait in the offspring. Selective breeding is commonly done in many farming practices. For example, crops have been selectively bred for thousands of years to create better producing plants and plants that are more resistant to disease and predation.

Organisms and the Environment

Relationships Between Organisms and Their Ecosystems

An **ecosystem** consists of all living (**community**) and nonliving components (abiotic factors) in an area. **Abiotic factors** include the atmosphere, soil, rocks, and water, which all have a role in sustaining life. The atmosphere provides the necessary gasses, soil contains nutrients for plants, rocks erode and affect topography, and water has many different roles.

An ecosystem not only involves living things interacting with nonliving things, but also involves the community interacting with each other. **Food chains** depict one type of community interaction, like the one shown here:

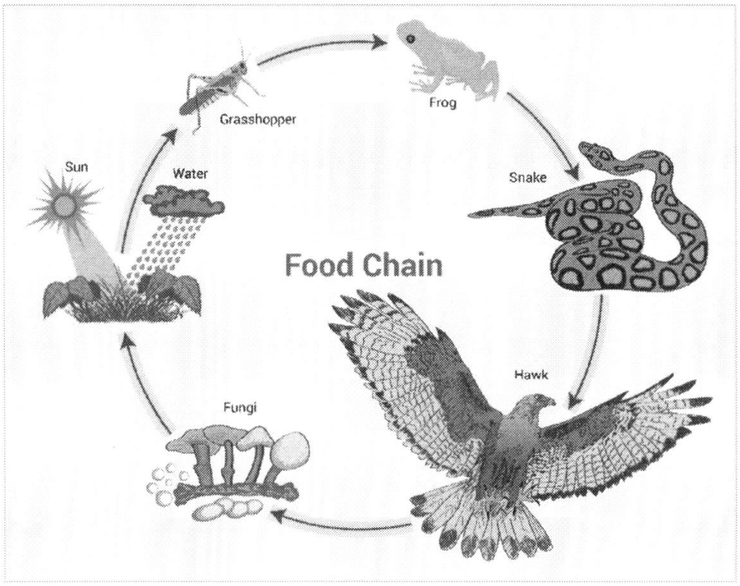

Food chains show the transfer of energy as one organism eats another. They also show an organism's eating habits. **Herbivores** eat plants and **carnivores** eat meat. A lion in grassland with no available animal prey will starve to death even though there is lots of grass because lions don't eat grass; that isn't their role in their habitat.

Food webs not only show predator-prey relationships, but they also show another relationship called **competition**.

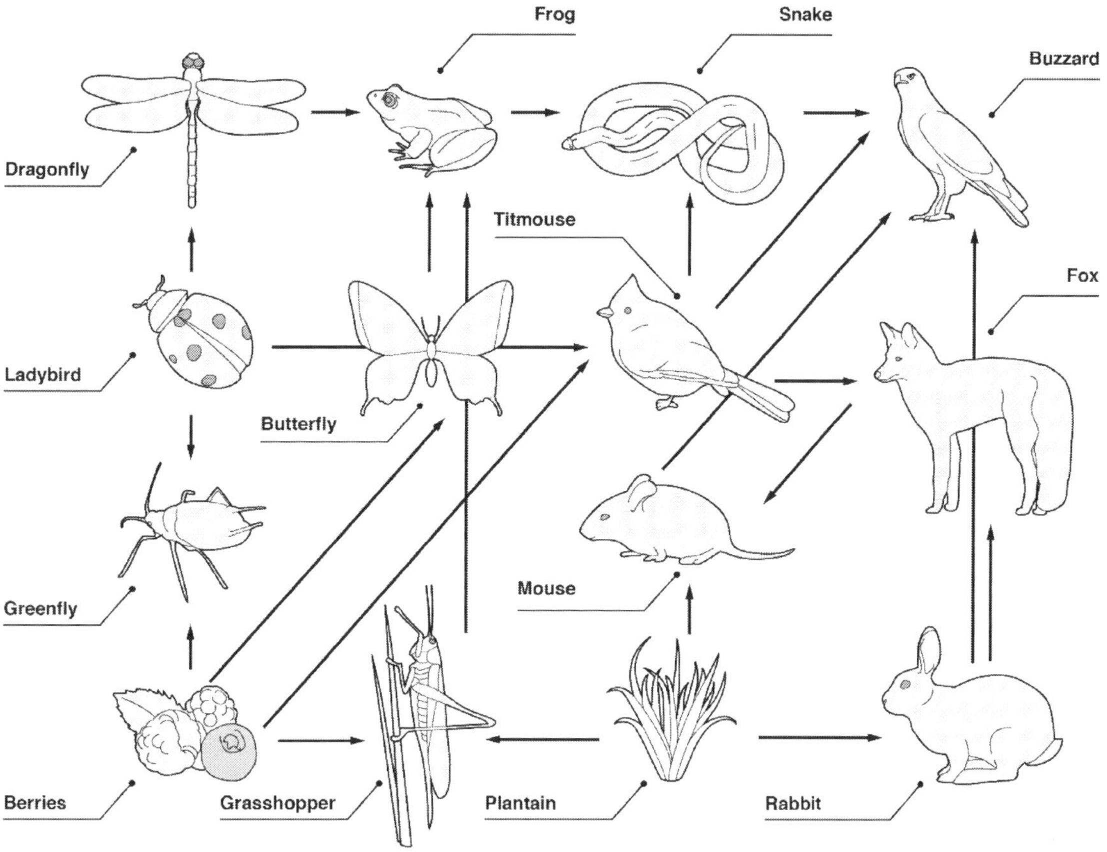

This food web shows that mice and frogs are competing for grasshoppers. If there is a scarcity of grasshoppers, the mouse and frog populations will decrease.

The final three types of community relationships all fall under the blanket term **symbiosis** and are described in the table below.

	Mutualism	**Commensalism**	**Parasitism**
Definition	Both organisms benefit from the relationship	One organism benefits from the relationship	One organism benefits from the relationship, and the other is harmed
Example	Birds and flowers	Whale and barnacle	Dog and flea
Explanation	Birds get nectar. Plants get pollinated.	Barnacle gets a free ride and access to food. Whale doesn't care because the barnacle is just latched on and isn't hurting anything.	Flea sucks dog's blood and gets nutrients. Dog is itchy and gets its blood drained.

The important knowledge for students to retain is:

- Plants need soil and sunlight to survive. This can be demonstrated by growing plants in the classroom.
- Animals in an area can have relationships other than predator-prey.
- Animals have niches in their environment. Some are herbivores (eat plants only), some are carnivores (eat meat only), and some are **omnivores** like humans (eat both plants and animals).

Interrelationships Among Organisms

All organisms work together so that life can exist. An organism represents one of a species, like the fish below, and all organisms serve a particular function. The fish's niche is to eat aquatic producers and excrete waste that acts as fertilizer.

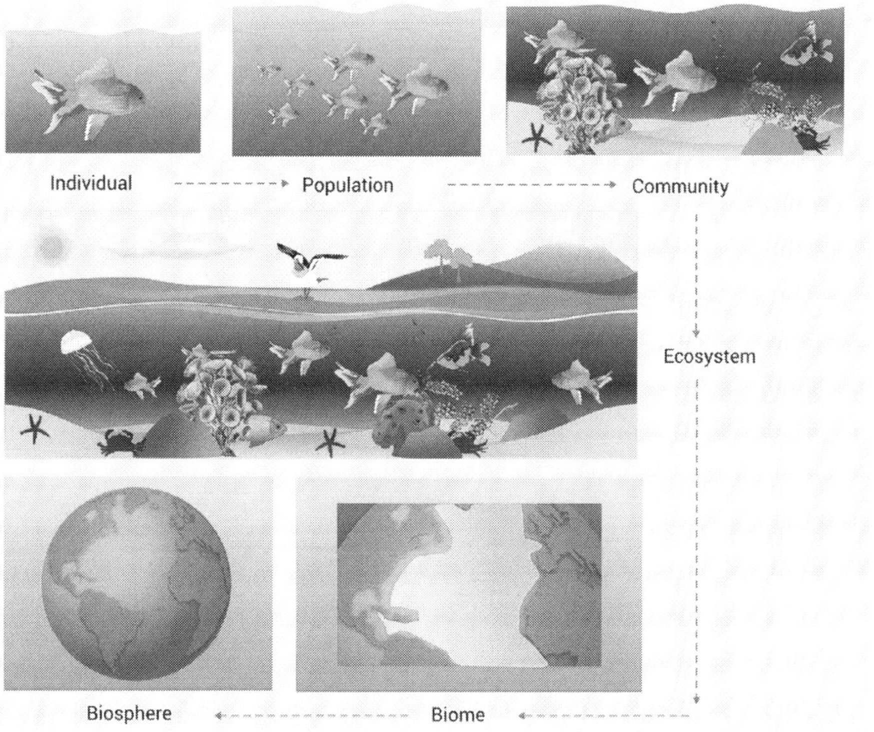

This fish is just one organism within a population. A population represents multiple individuals living in the same habitat. The community includes every biotic factor (living organism) within an ecosystem, in this case, the fish, jellyfish, algae, crab, bacteria, etc. An ecosystem includes all the biotic factors as well as the abiotic, which includes anything non-living—for the fish, that's a rock, a shipwreck, and a nearby glacier. For biomes, add weather and climate into the mix. The biosphere is all of Earth, which is the combination of all biomes.

We already discussed that producers (plants, protists, and even some bacteria) photosynthesize and make the food that provides energy required for all chemical reactions to occur and therefore all life to exist. A non-photosynthesizer must find and eat food, and this feeding relationship can be visualized in food chains. Consider this food chain:

The true source of the energy for every living organism is the sun. Plants absorb the sun's energy to make glucose and are on the first trophic level (feeding level). The grasshopper on the second trophic level is an example of an herbivore and is a primary consumer, as he is the first eater in the food chain. Unfortunately, he receives only 10 percent of the energy that the plant absorbed (this is known as the 10 percent rule) because the other 90 percent of energy was either used by the plant to grow or will be lost as heat.

The mouse on the third trophic level is the secondary consumer, or second eater. Food chains are not as inclusive as food webs, which show all feeding relationships in an ecosystem. Looking at this food chain suggests that mice are carnivores (eaters of animals), but mice also eat berries and plants, so they are actually considered omnivores (eaters of both plants and animals). The mouse only gets 10 percent of the energy from the grasshopper, which is actually only 1 percent of the original energy provided by the Sun. The snake on the fourth trophic level is a carnivore, as is the hawk on the highest trophic level.

The arrows in the food chain show the transfer of energy, and fungi as well as bacteria act as decomposers, which break down organic material. Decomposers act at every trophic level because they feed on all organisms; they are non-discriminating omnivores. Decomposers are critical for life, as they recycle the atoms and building blocks of organisms.

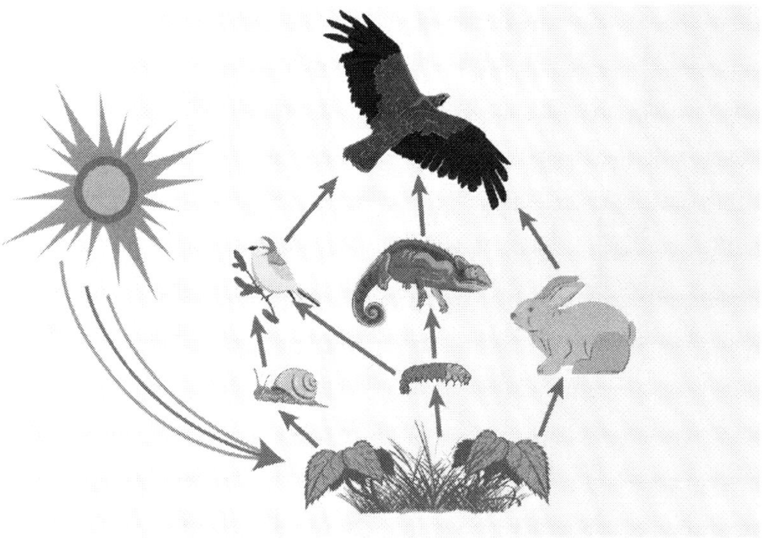

Feeding relationships and predator-prey relationships (hunter-hunted, like the hawk and the rabbit in the food web above) are not the only relationships in an ecosystem. There also can be competition within and between species. For example, in the food chain above, the rabbit and snail both eat grass, showing a relationship called competition, when two organisms want the same thing. Other relationships include symbiotic relationships, which represent two species living together.

Symbiosis comes in three varieties:

- Mutualism: an arrangement where both organisms help each other. An example is the relationship between birds and flowers. When birds consume the nectar that the flower produces, pollen rubs on the bird's body so that when it travels to a neighboring plant, it helps with fertilization. The plant helps the bird by providing food, and the bird helps the plant by helping it reproduce. This is a win-win.

- Parasitism: when one organism is hurt while the other is helped. Fleas and dogs are a prime example. Fleas suck the dog's blood, and dogs are itchy and lose blood. This is a win-lose.

- Commensalism: when one organism is helped and the other is neither harmed nor helped. For example, barnacles are crusty little creatures that attach themselves to whales. They don't feed on the whale like a parasite. Instead, they use the whale to give them a free ride so they have access to food. The whales don't care about the barnacles. This is a win-do not care.

How Adaptive Characteristics Aid in Survival

Many characteristics are inherited from the DNA obtained from an individual's parents, including skin color, eye shape, hair color, and color-blindness, among others. Learned behavior isn't related to genetics and is a result of training. For example, a dog catching a stick is learned. The overall intelligence of the dog, however, has to do with its genes.

An organism's survival depends on its **fitness** relative to the environment, and any trait that helps it survive is called an **adaptation**. Whale blubber and shark teeth are examples of adaptations. Blubber keeps whales warm, and a shark's many teeth ensures it's better able to capture prey. Whales don't decide to grow blubber, and sharks don't decide to grow teeth. These characteristics have been inherited from their parents.

Discussion of adaptations can involve showing pictures of various organisms and identifying which of their characteristics would be helpful and why. See below for some ideas for discussion.

Organism	Adaptation to identify	Why it's helpful
Cactus	Spikes	Help protect from water thieves
Peacock	Feathers	Help scare off predators (look like eyes); also help attract mates
Elephant	Trunk	Helps suck up water
Skunk	Smelly secretions	Help protect from predators

How Populations and Species Modify and Affect Ecosystems

Populations of different species can have various effects on an ecosystem, both negative and positive. For example, humans can both positively and negatively modify an ecosystem. There are many examples of how the human race positively modifies and affects an ecosystem. For example, humans typically make a point of preserving animal species that are on the brink of extinct, try to expand in a sustainable way, find ways to dispose of waste in a responsible manner, and much more. However, along with the positive ways humans affect an ecosystem, there are many negative ways as well. With growing populations, there's more pollution, fewer natural spaces available, and much more. With all of this, there is more erosion, deforestation, less clean water available, and poorer air quality.

All other organisms also have an impact on ecosystems. One organism that could have a negative impact on their ecosystems is the beaver. When beavers build dams, they can cause flooding to certain areas, which can kill flora and displace animals. However, along with the destruction of areas, the newly flooded areas can create brand new ecosystems where fish, insects, amphibians, and aquatic plants can reside. Another example of organisms that can strongly modify an ecosystem are invasive species. Invasive species, such as the zebra mussel, can cause the extinction of native species. Zebra mussels filter out algae that is a food source for native organisms, resulting in their extinction.

Structure and Function of Earth Systems

Structure of Earth

Earth's Layers

Earth has three major layers: a thin solid outer surface or **crust**, a dense **core**, and a **mantle** between them that contains most of Earth's matter. This layout resembles an egg, where the eggshell is the crust, the mantle is the egg white, and the core is the yolk. The outer crust of Earth consists of igneous or sedimentary rocks over metamorphic rocks. Together with the upper portion of the mantle, it forms the **lithosphere**, which is broken into tectonic plates.

Major plates of the lithosphere

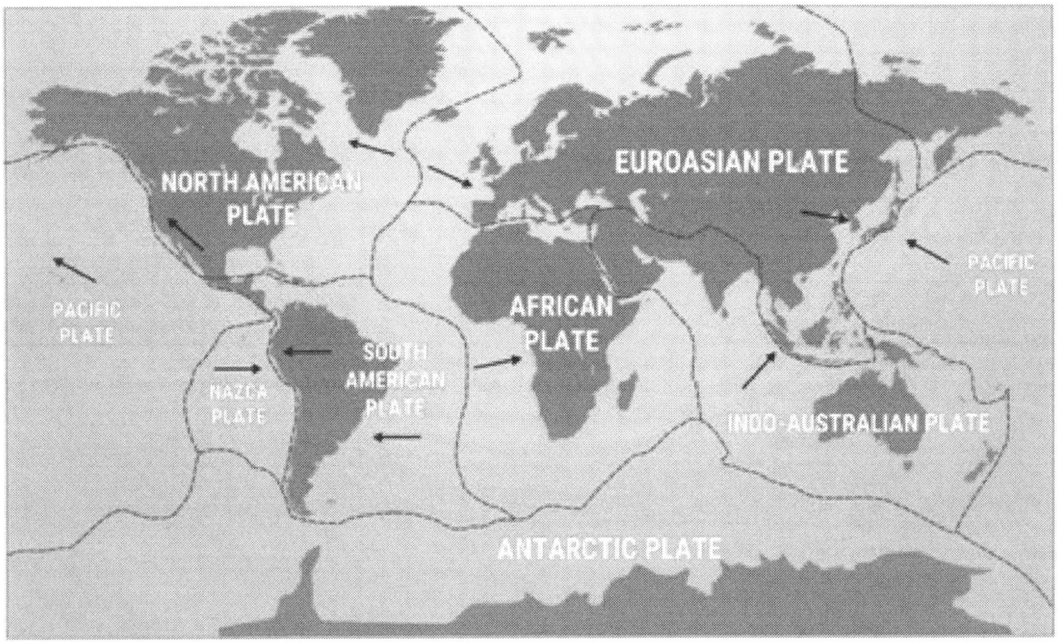

The mantle can be divided into three zones. The **upper mantle** is adjacent to the crust and composed of solid rock. Below the upper mantle is the **transition zone**. The **lower mantle** below the transition zone is a layer of completely solid rock. Underneath the mantle is the molten **outer core** followed by the compact, solid **inner core**. The inner and outer cores contain the densest elements, consisting of mostly iron and nickel.

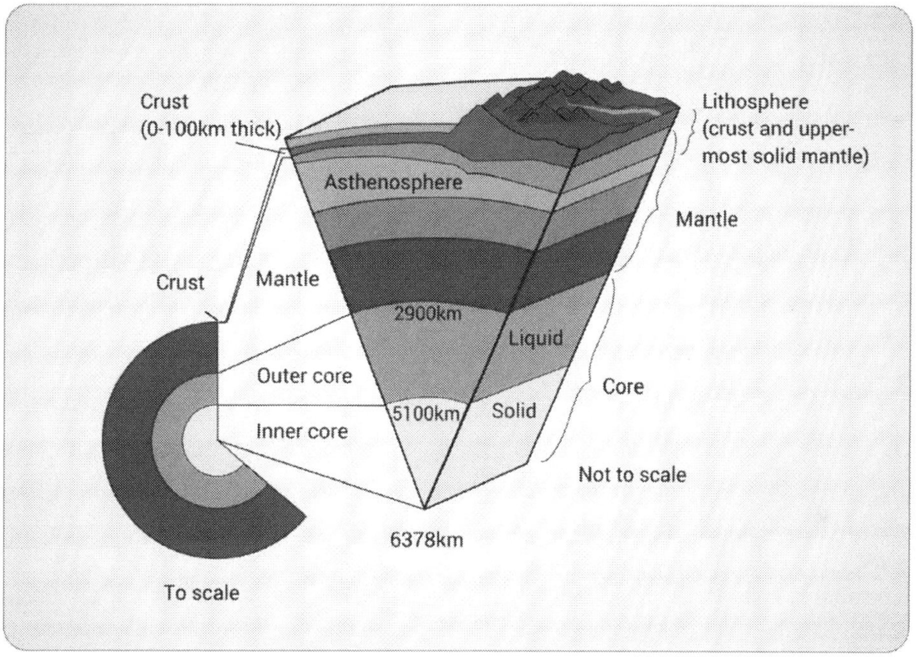

Shape and Size of Earth

Earth isn't a perfect sphere; it's slightly elliptical. From center to surface, its radius is almost 4,000 miles, and its circumference around the equator is about 24,902 miles. In comparison, the Sun's radius is 432,288 miles—over 1,000 times larger than Earth's—and the Moon's radius is about 1,000 miles.

Geographical Features

Earth's surface is dynamic and consists of various landforms. As tectonic plates are pushed together, **mountains** are formed. **Canyons** are deep trenches that are usually created by plates moving apart but can also be created by constant weathering and erosion from rivers and runoff. **Deltas** are flat, triangular stretches of land formed by rivers that deposit sediment and water into the ocean. **Sand dunes** are mountains of sand located in desert areas or the bottom of the ocean. They are formed by wind and water movement when there's an absence of plants or other features that would otherwise hold the sand in place.

Earth's Magnetic Field

Earth's **magnetic field** is created by the magnetic forces that extend from Earth's interior to outer space. It can be modeled as a magnetic dipole tilted about 10 degrees from Earth's rotational axis, as if a bar magnet was placed at an angle inside Earth's core. The **geomagnetic pole** located near Greenland in the northern hemisphere is actually the south pole of Earth's magnetic field, and vice versa for the southern geomagnetic pole. The **magnetosphere** is Earth's magnetic field, which extends tens of thousands of kilometers into space and protects Earth and the atmosphere from damaging solar wind and cosmic rays.

Plate Tectonics Theory and Evidence

The theory of **plate tectonics** hypothesizes that the continents weren't always separated like they are today but were once joined and slowly drifted apart. Evidence for this theory is based upon the fossil record. Fossils of one species were found in regions of the world now separated by an ocean. It's unlikely that a single species could have travelled across the ocean or that two separate species evolved into a single species.

Folding and Faulting

The exact number of tectonic plates is debatable, but scientists estimate there are around nine to fifteen major plates and almost 40 minor plates. The line where two plates meet is called a **fault.** The San Andreas Fault is where the Pacific and North American plates meet. Faults or boundaries are classified depending on the interaction between plates. Two plates collide at **convergent boundaries. Divergent boundaries** occur when two plates move away from each other. Tectonic plates can move vertically and horizontally.

Continental Drift, Seafloor Spreading, Magnetic Reversals

The movement of tectonic plates is similar to pieces of wood floating in a pool of water. They can bob up and down as well as bump, slide, and move away from each other. These different interactions create Earth's landscape. The collision of plates can create mountain ranges, while their separation can create canyons or underwater chasms. One plate can also slide atop another and push it down into Earth's hot mantle, creating magma and volcanoes, in a process called **subduction**.

Unlike a regular magnet, Earth's magnetic field changes over time because it's generated by the motion of molten iron alloys in the outer core. Although the magnetic poles can wander geographically, they do so at such a slow rate that they don't affect the use of compasses in navigation. However, at irregular intervals that are several hundred thousand years long, the fields can reverse, with the north and south magnetic poles switching places.

Characteristics of Volcanoes

Volcanoes are mountainous structures that act as vents to release pressure and magma from Earth's crust. During an **eruption**, the pressure and magma are released, and volcanoes smoke, rumble, and throw ash and **lava**, or molten rock, into the air. **Hot spots** are volcanic regions of the mantle that are hotter than surrounding regions.

Characteristics of Earthquakes

Earthquakes occur when tectonic plates slide or collide as a result of the crust suddenly releasing energy. Stress in Earth's outer layer pushes together two faults. The motion of the planes of the fault continues until something makes them stop. The **epicenter** of an earthquake is the point on the surface directly above where the fault is slipping. If the epicenter is located under a body of water, the earthquake may cause a **tsunami**, a series of large, forceful waves.

Seismic waves and Triangulation

Earthquakes cause **seismic waves**, which travel through Earth's layers and give out low-frequency acoustic energy. Triangulation of seismic waves helps scientists determine the origin of an earthquake.

Surface Water and Ground Water

Surface Water

Surface water is considered any water that is above ground. This includes lakes, rivers, oceans, wetlands, streams, and creeks. Surface water has a wide variety of functions. Surface water provides a home for all aquatic creatures on earth, is the source of hydration for every animal, is harnessed for energy uses with hydroelectric plants, and much more. Surface water is made and replenished from precipitation and runoff from snow and glaciers melting. Bodies of surface water lessen as they are increased. This occurs through draining into the ground and through the process of evaporation, where some water is lost to the atmosphere. Additionally, surface water is vital for many biological processes such as nourishing plants and aiding the nitrogen cycle, carbon cycle, and much more.

Ground Water

Ground water, on the other hand, is found under the surface of the earth. Portions of rock that yield water are known as aquifers. Ground water is harvested from wells or naturally released through springs. As ground water is often taken out of the earth, it must be replenished. This water is continually replenished by rainfall and snow melt running off and eventually draining through cracks and other openings of the earth's surface into the ground. In addition to this, surface water seeps into the ground perpetually. The use of ground water may cause some environmental issues as it is more difficult to access and clean.

Composition and Structure of the Atmosphere

The atmosphere is composed of various layers of gas surrounding the earth. The atmosphere of earth stays in place and does not simply dissolve due to the gravitational pull of earth and the low temperatures. The atmosphere of earth is composed of several different gasses. Most of the atmosphere is nitrogen (78%), oxygen (21%), argon (0.9%), and carbon dioxide (0.04%). The remainder of the atmosphere consists of small amounts of trace gasses. There are many different trace gasses in the atmosphere; the most common of them are neon, helium, methane, and hydrogen. In addition to the gasses in the atmosphere, there is also a considerable amount of vaporized water. The amount of water in the atmosphere varies based on the location. For example, there is more water vapor in the atmosphere in tropical regions than in temperate regions, and there is nearly no water vapor in polar regions.

The atmosphere of earth is divided into five different layers. From the surface to the sky, these layers are troposphere, stratosphere, mesosphere, thermosphere, then exosphere. In addition to this, the region known as the ionosphere extends through the mesosphere and thermosphere, and within the stratosphere there is the ozone layer where concentrations of ozone (O_3) are found. The troposphere contains 75% of the mass of the atmosphere, which is why air is said to become thinner at higher altitudes beyond the troposphere. The stratosphere is where the Jetstream forms from warm air meeting with cold air. The mesosphere is the coldest region of the atmosphere, and it is typically where objects falling into the atmosphere burn up. The thermosphere is where many free electrons and ions reside due to ionizing gas particles. Within the thermosphere, the ionosphere is where radio waves bounce off and the aurora borealis forms. Lastly, the exosphere is where satellites orbit earth.

Cycles in Earth Systems

The Rock Cycle

There are three primary types of rock: igneous, metamorphic, and sedimentary. Igneous rocks are created when molten rock cools down and solidifies, which is why volcanic rock is considered to be igneous rock. Igneous rock that is made on the earth's surface is known as extrusive igneous rock, and when it is formed inside the earth's crust, it is known as intrusive igneous rock. Metamorphic rocks are rocks that have changed from excessive heat and pressure. They are further classified as either foliated or nonfoliated. Foliated rocks have a crinkled sheet-like surface, and the patterns on them show the direction that pressure was applied on the rock.

Common types of foliated metamorphic rocks are slate, gneiss, and schist. Nonfoliated rocks are metamorphic rocks that do not have the layered look that foliated rocks have. Some common nonfoliated rock classifications are marble and quartzite. Sedimentary rocks form from the deposition of minerals and some organic particles. The process by which sedimentary rocks form is known as sedimentation. A large portion of the earth's surface is covered by sedimentary rock; however, it is only about 8% of what the earth's crust is composed of. Sedimentary rocks also form into large layers known as strata.

The rock cycle is the process of any type of rock converting into another type of rock. The different types of rock change through the processes of erosion, crystallization, melting, and metamorphism. Sedimentary rocks go through tectonic burial and metamorphism to become metamorphic rocks or erode to become different sedimentary rocks. Metamorphic rocks melt and crystalize to become igneous rocks or erode and become sedimentary. Igneous rocks erode and become sedimentary or melt and crystalize to become different igneous rock. This process is perpetually happening, and new rocks are constantly formed over time.

Minerals are inorganic compounds and elements that form specific crystalline structures when they are completely pure. Minerals form from rocks when they are heated to a point that specific atoms can move around and join with different atoms to form specific mineral molecules. Minerals dissolved in water can also be deposited onto surfaces. Soil is a thin layer covering the earth's surface. It is composed of various minerals, decomposed organic matter, gasses, water, and a variety of living organisms. Soil primarily forms when rocks are weathered and erode. The rocks are weathered and eroded by water, wind, pressure, organisms, and certain chemical interactions.

The Water Cycle

The water cycle is the cycling of water between its three physical states: solid, liquid, and gas. The sun is a critical component of the water cycle because its thermal energy heats up surface liquid water so much that parts of it evaporate. Transpiration is a similar process that occurs when the sun evaporates water from plant pores called stomata. As water vapor rises into the atmosphere through evaporation and transpiration, it eventually condenses and forms clouds heavy with liquid water droplets. The liquid (or solid ice or snow) will precipitate back to Earth, collect on land, and either be absorbed by soil or run-off to the oceans and lakes where it will accumulate, circulate, and evaporate once again.

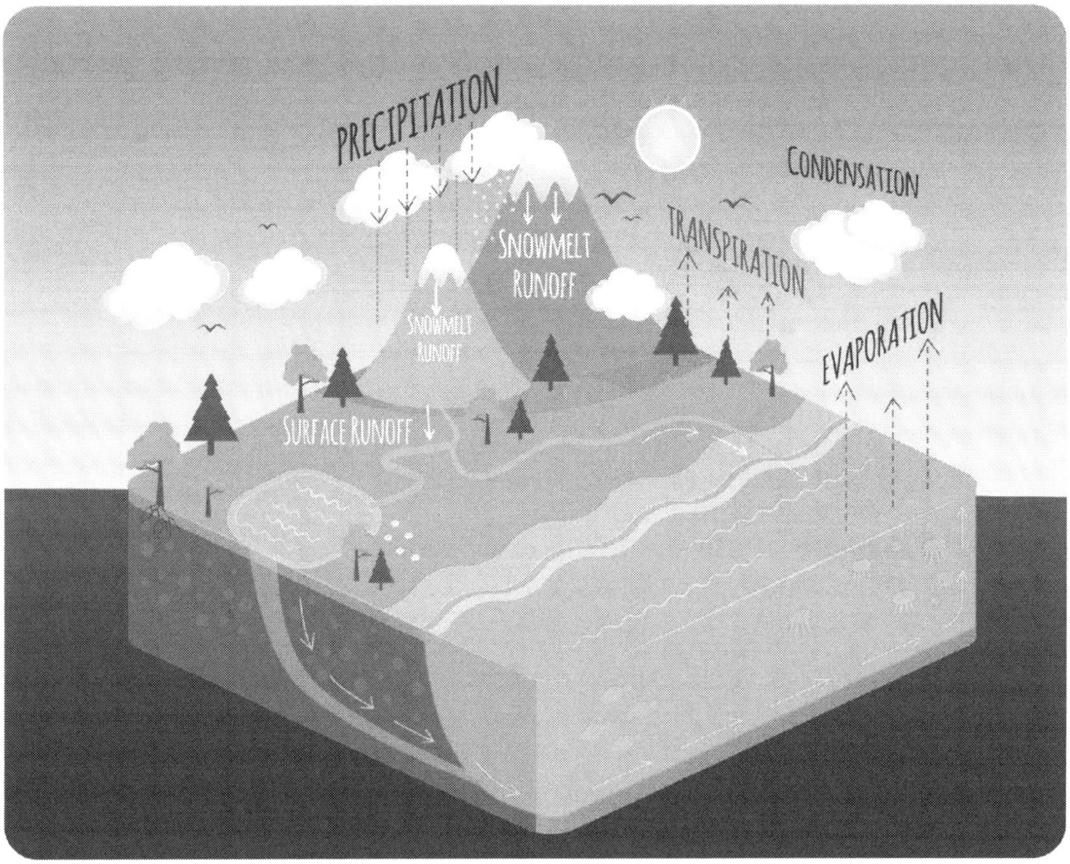

Clouds are condensed water vapor, which is water that has cooled from a gas to liquid, like the droplets on the outside of a glass of lemonade on a hot summer day. That water on the glass is water vapor that cooled enough to slow down the moving particles so that they become denser, forming a liquid. In the sky, water vapor combines in different ways so clouds appear in different forms.

Cloud height, shape, and behavior results in a variety of different types:

- **High-Clouds**
    - Cirrus: wispy and thread-like
    - Cirrostratus: like cirrus clouds, but wider and thicker sheets. They have a halo effect where sunlight and moonlight refract through.
    - Cirrocumulus: a cross between cirrus and cirrostratus clouds. These have rows of round puffs like a cotton-ball stretched out.
    - Contrails: clouds made by jets
- **Mid-Clouds**
    - Altostratus: thick, stretched clouds that block sunlight and are blue-grayish in color
    - Nimbostratus: a thick altostratus cloud accompanied by rain
    - Altocumulus: layered rolls of clouds
- **Low-Clouds**
    - Cumulus: white, round, puffy clouds
    - Stratus: wide, thick, stretched-out, gray clouds that may cause drizzle
    - Fog: lazy stratus clouds that have drooped so low that they reach Earth's surface
    - Cumulonimbus: the angry cloud that brings thunderstorms, hail, and tornadoes. It looks like a thick mountain.
    - Stratocumulus: stretched-out, grayish, puffy, cumulus clouds

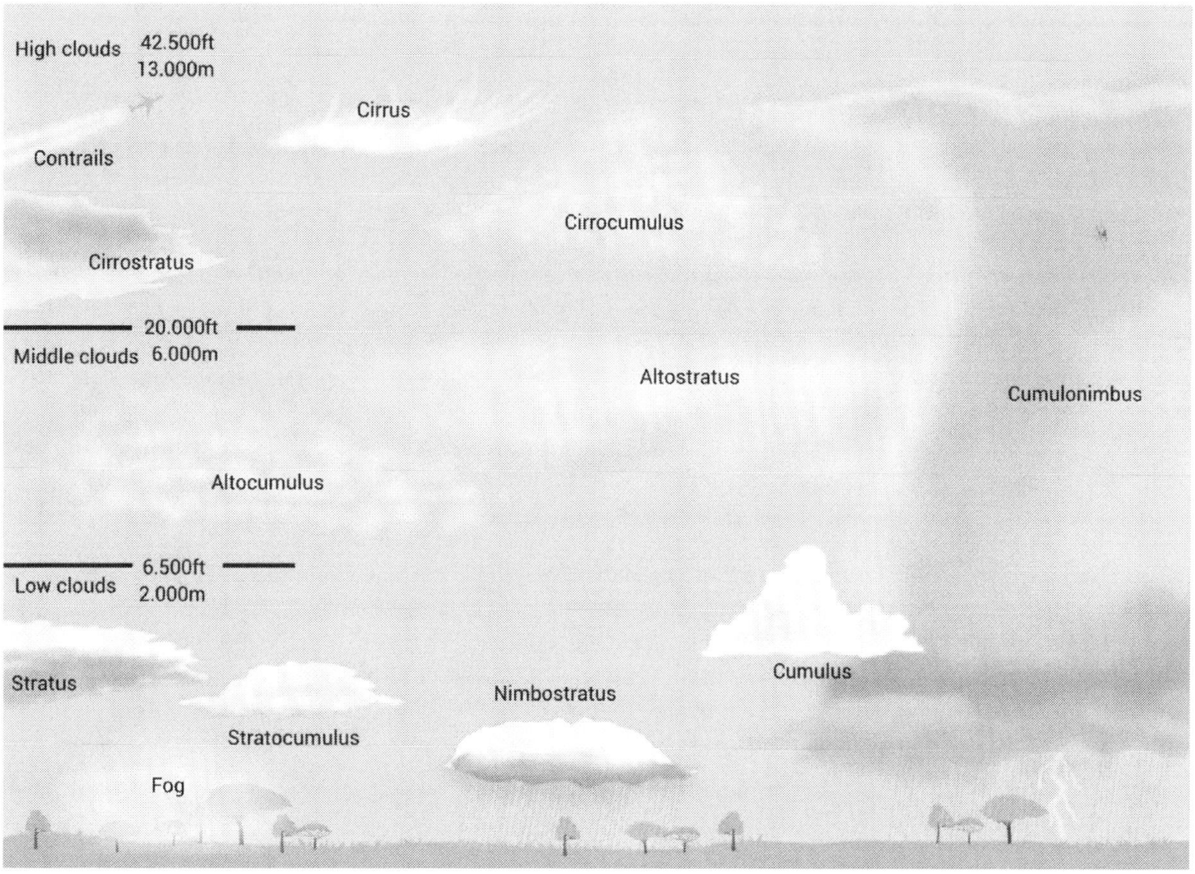

Precipitation comes in many different forms:

- **Rain** occurs due to water vapor condensing on dust particles in the troposphere. As more and more water condenses, the drops will eventually enlarge and accumulate mass, becoming so heavy that they fall to Earth.
- If the temperature is above the freezing point, rain remains liquid upon contact with the ground. However, when the temperature is below the freezing point and other conditions are right, rain can freeze upon contact with the ground or other surfaces, called **freezing rain**. This causes extremely dangerous driving conditions due to the slickness of the ice.
- **Sleet** freezes on its way down as opposed to freezing upon impact. Sleet starts as ice that melts as it falls through the atmosphere due to hitting spots of warmer temperature, and then it freezes again before hitting the ground.
- **Hail** is precipitation of balls of ice. Hail begins as ice at very cold temperatures in the atmosphere. Instead of precipitating sheets of ice like sleet storms, hailstorms precipitate ice that looks like rocks because hail is formed during thunderstorms. The massive winds throw hail up and down so more and more water vapor condenses and freezes on the original ice. Layer upon layer of ice combine, creating hail sometimes as large as golf balls.
- **Snow** forms as loosely packed ice crystals. Snow is less dangerous than the other frozen forms of precipitation and can produce beautiful snowflakes.

Even though seasons have predictable temperatures, there can be significant differences day to day. In the troposphere, the Sun's heat is trapped by the blanket of greenhouse gases and creates warm, low-pressure air. Because warm gas particles move faster and have less space between them, they are less dense than colder air, and they rise. Cool air moves below the warm air. This atmospheric movement is called general circulation and is the source of wind. Earth's spinning motion also causes wind.

Even more extreme weather includes tornadoes and hurricanes. Tornadoes are spinning winds that can exceed 300 miles per hour and are caused by changing air pressure and quick winds. Hurricanes, typhoons, and tropical cyclones (the same phenomenon with different regional names) are storms with spinning winds that form over the ocean. Hurricanes are caused by warm ocean water quickly evaporating and rising to a colder, lower-pressure portion of the atmosphere. The fast movement of the warm air starts a cyclone around a central origination point (the eye of the storm). Blizzards are also caused by the clash of warm air and cold air. They occur when the cold Arctic air moves toward warmer air and involve massive amounts of snow.

Precipitation and run-off are constantly affecting the surface of Earth, as the run-off weathers rocks or breaks them down from the original bedrock into pieces called regolith. Regolith sizes range from microscopic to large and quickly form either soil or sediment. *Weathering* is the process of breaking rock while *erosion* is the process of moving rock. Weathering can be caused by both physical and chemical changes. Mechanical forces such as roots growing, animal contact, wind, and extreme weather cause weathering. Another cause is the water cycle, which includes flowing water, moving glaciers, and liquid ice seeping into rocks and cracking them as water freezes and expands. Chemical weathering actually transforms the regolith into clay and soft minerals. One consequence of chemical weathering is corrosive acid rain.

The Nutrient Cycle

The nutrient cycle is a broad term that describes several natural processes of nutrients being recycled for reuse within ecosystems on the earth. It describes the processes of nutrients moving from the environment into living organisms, then back into the environment. It is a constant process of substances becoming a part of life within organisms, being removed from living organisms, and returning to the physical environment. The nutrient cycle is necessary for life and must stay stable and balanced for organisms to prosper. Overall, it operates through dead organisms decaying into soil, decomposing in the soil, being used by plants or released into the atmosphere, consumed by organisms, then constantly repeated. Each specific nutrient within the nutrient cycle has its own specific pathway for being recycled.

Nutrients are molecules and elements that are necessary for the growth of plants, animals, and microbes. The nutrients that are cycled through ecosystems in the largest amounts are carbon, hydrogen, and oxygen. They are primarily found in the forms of carbon dioxide and water. The other most important nutrients are nitrogen, phosphorous, potassium, magnesium, and calcium. Due to their importance, they are sometimes referred to as macro nutrients; however, they should not be confused with carbohydrates, fats, and proteins, which are macronutrients of the human diet. Additionally, there are micro nutrients that are cycled in small amounts. The most common micro nutrients include, but are not limited to, boron, copper, manganese, zinc, and chloride.

Because life on earth is carbon based, the carbon cycle is the specific nutrient cycle that is most taught and studied at all levels of education. Carbon is found in the air as gaseous carbon dioxide and is taken in by plants to be used in photosynthesis to be converted into energy molecules and mass growth of plants. Plants can then either die and decompose or be consumed by animals. When carbon goes into soil through decomposition, it can be taken up by microorganisms and released back into the atmosphere, or eventually converted into fossil fuels that can be burned for energy and released back into the atmosphere. If carbon is consumed by animals through a plant, it can be used as mass for an animal, then eventually decompose into soil, or be exhaled into the atmosphere as a byproduct of cellular respiration. Additionally, gaseous carbon consumed by phytoplankton goes through a similar process within oceans. Disruption of the carbon cycle, along with the other parts of the nutrient cycle, may be catastrophic.

Energy in Weather and Climate

Elements of Weather

Relative Humidity

Relative humidity is the ratio of the partial pressure of water vapor to water's equilibrium vapor pressure at a given temperature. At low temperatures, less water vapor is required to reach a high relative humidity. More water vapor is needed to reach a high relative humidity in warm air, which has a greater capacity for water vapor. At ground level or other areas of higher pressure, relative humidity increases as temperatures decrease because water vapor condenses as the temperature falls below the dew point. As relative humidity cannot be greater than 100%, the dew point temperature cannot be greater than the air temperature.

Dew Point

The **dew point** is the temperature at which the water vapor in air at constant barometric pressure condenses into liquid water due to saturation. At temperatures below the dew point, the rate of condensation will be greater than the rate of evaporation, forming more liquid water. When condensed water forms on a surface, it's called **dew**; when it forms in the air, it's called **fog** or **clouds**, depending on the altitude.

Wind

Wind is the movement of gas particles across Earth's surface. Winds are generated by differences in atmospheric pressure. Air inherently moves from areas of higher pressure to lower pressure, which is what causes wind to occur. Surface friction from geological features, such as mountains or man-made features can decrease wind speed. In meteorology, winds are classified based on their strength, duration, and direction. **Gusts** are short bursts of high-speed wind, **squalls** are strong winds of intermediate duration (around one minute), and winds with a long duration are given names based on their average strength. **Breezes** are the weakest, followed by **gales**, **storms**, and **hurricanes**.

Air Masses, Fronts, Storms, and Severe Weather

Air masses are volumes of air defined by their temperature and the amount of water vapor they contain. A **front** is where two air masses of different temperatures and water vapor content meet. Fronts can be the site of extreme weather, such as thunderstorms, which are caused by water particles rubbing against each other. When they do so, electrons are transferred, and energy and electrical currents accumulate. When enough energy accumulates, thunder and lightning occur. **Lightning** is a massive electric spark created by a cloud, and **thunder** is the sound created by an expansion of air caused by the sudden increase in pressure and temperature around lightning.

Extreme weather includes tornadoes and hurricanes. **Tornadoes** are created by changing air pressure and winds that can exceed 300 miles per hour. **Hurricanes** occur when warm ocean water quickly evaporates and rises to a colder, low-pressure portion of the atmosphere. Hurricanes, typhoons, and tropical cyclones are all created by the same phenomena, but they occur in different regions. **Blizzards** are similar to hurricanes in that they're created by the clash of warm and cold air, but they only occur when cold Arctic air moves toward warmer air. They usually involve large amounts of snow.

Development and Movement of Weather Patterns

A **weather pattern** is weather that's consistent for a period of time. Weather patterns are created by fronts. A **cold front** is created when two air masses collide in a high-pressure system. A **warm front** is created when a low-pressure system results from the collision of two air masses; they are usually warmer and less dense than high-pressure systems. When a cold front enters an area, the air from the warm front is forced upwards. The temperature of the warm front's air decreases, condenses, and often creates clouds and precipitation. When a warm front moves into an area, the warm air moves slowly upwards at an angle. Clouds and precipitation form, but the precipitation generally lasts longer because of how slowly the air moves.

Weather and Climate

Weather depends in a large part on temperature. Earth's equator is closest to the sun and receives more heat, so this area of earth is significantly warmer than the poles (Arctic and Antarctic). This warm air can form huge bubbles, as can the colder air at the poles. When warm air and cold air meet, the boundary is called a front. Fronts can be the site of extreme weather like thunderstorms, which are caused by water particles in clouds quickly rubbing against each other and transferring electrons, creating positive and negative regions. Lightning occurs when there is a massive electric spark due to the electrical current within a cloud, between two clouds, and even between a cloud and the ground.

While seasons are predictable trends in temperatures over a few months, climate describes the average weather and temperature patterns for a particular area over a long period of time, upwards of thirty years. While **fall** describes a season and **rain** describes weather, **rainforest** describes a climate. The climate of a rainforest, due to its proximity to the equator and oceans, consists of warm temperatures with humid air.

Making Weather Predictions

Weather forecasting nowadays is an incredibly complex process. To most accurately predict the weather, various aspects of science and technology are paired and utilized along with past data to figure out what the weather conditions will be at any time and place in the future. Historically, people have attempted to predict the weather since the nineteenth century. Before weather predictions can be made, massive amounts of data must be collected and analyzed. The data that is collected includes air temperature, atmospheric pressure, humidity, wind speed, wind direction, water currents, water temperatures, radar readings, and much more, all various altitudes. The instruments used to collect this raw data are thermometers, barometers, wind vanes, buoys, hygrometers, doppler radars, and much more. Additionally, visual data can be collected from satellite images that monitor cloud formation and movements.

With the technological advancements of today, all of this data is run through forecast models, which use a variety of different equations paired with past weather data to produce forecasts for meteorologists to utilize and analyze. In the past, meteorologists had to look at current data and compare all of the different readings to weather data of the past. They would look for patterns of weather data in the past that matches the present data to determine if weather similar to what happened in the past will happen again. Nowadays, the majority of human input in predicting the weather is determining which model will be most accurate given the current conditions. Although great strides have been made to increase the accuracy of predicting weather, it can still not be entirely accurate due to the chaotic and misunderstood nature of earth's atmosphere. In the future, weather forecasts will be improved by increasing the amount of data collected and increasing computing ability to model the weather further into the future.

How Transfers of Energy Between Earth Systems Affect Weather and Climate

The most important influence on the earth's weather and climate is the energy produced by the sun. The sun heats the earth in an unequal manner, as the earth is constantly rotating. The difference in temperatures causes air to rise and fall in different locations, which in turn creates wind across the earth's surface and within the upper atmosphere. The solar energy also dictates what water will either condense, freeze, or evaporate. The movement of different air temperatures with different energies create areas of the atmosphere with different densities known as convection cells. Convection cells create clouds and circular wind patterns. In addition to dictating the movement of air in the atmosphere, the energy from the sun affects the movement of water in the large bodies of water. Changes in solar energy cause water to evaporate into the atmosphere or condense back down to the surface. Solar energy also transfers into water as kinetic energy as it moves around changing currents.

Another big part of energy transfer's effect on the atmosphere and climate is the greenhouse effect. The greenhouse effect occurs when gasses and clouds trap the energy from the sun within the atmosphere. This results in increased heating within the atmosphere. Without the greenhouse effect, the earth would be far too cold to accommodate life. However, with increased gasses and pollutants in the atmosphere, the greenhouse effect becomes more pronounced and results in global heating that could drastically change what we view as normal weather and temperatures.

Effect of Earth's Position and Surface Features on Weather and Climate

Effects of Latitude, Geographical Location, and Elevation

The climate and seasons of different geographical areas are primarily dictated by their sunlight exposure. Because Earth rotates on a tilted axis while travelling around the Sun, different latitudes get different amounts of direct sunlight throughout the year, creating different climates. Polar regions experience the greatest variation, with long periods of limited or no sunlight in the winter and up to 24 hours of daylight in the summer. Equatorial regions experience the least variance in direct sunlight exposure. Coastal areas experience breezes in the summer as cooler ocean air moves ashore, while areas southeast of the Great Lakes can get "lake effect" snow in the winter, as cold air travels over the warmer water and creates snow on land. Mountains are often seen with snow in the spring and fall. Their high elevation causes mountaintops to stay cold. The air around the mountaintop is also cold and holds less water vapor than air at sea level. As the water vapor condenses, it creates snow.

Effects of Atmospheric Circulation

Global winds are patterns of wind circulation, and they have a major influence on global weather and climate. They help influence temperature and precipitation by carrying heat and water vapor around Earth. These winds are driven by the uneven heating between the polar and equatorial regions created by the Sun. Cold air from the polar regions sinks and moves toward the equator, while the warm air from the equator rises and moves toward the poles. The other factor driving global winds is the **Coriolis Effect.** As air moves from the North Pole to the equator, Earth's rotation makes it seem as if the wind is also moving to the right, or westbound, and eastbound from South Pole to equator.

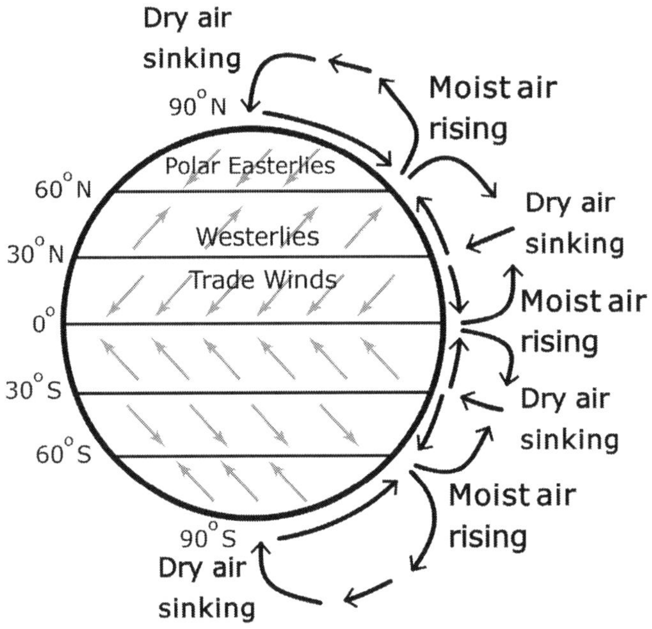

Global wind patterns are given names based on which direction they blow. There are three major wind patterns in each hemisphere. Notice the image above diagramming the movement of warm (dry) air and cold (moist) air.

Trade winds—easterly surface winds found in the troposphere near the equator—blow predominantly from the northeast in the Northern Hemisphere and from the southeast in the Southern Hemisphere. These winds direct the tropical storms that develop over the Atlantic, Pacific, and Indian Oceans and land in North America, Southeast Asia, and eastern Africa, respectively. **Jet streams** are westerly winds that follow a narrow, meandering path. The two strongest jet streams are the polar jets and the subtropical jets. In the Northern Hemisphere, the polar jet flows over the middle of North America, Europe, and Asia, while in the Southern Hemisphere, it circles Antarctica.

Effects of Ocean Circulation

Ocean currents are similar to global winds because winds influence how the oceans move. Ocean currents are created by warm water moving from the equator towards the poles while cold water travels from the poles to the equator. The warm water can increase precipitation in an area because it evaporates faster than the colder water.

Characteristics and Locations of Climate Zones

Climate zones are created by Earth's tilt as it travels around the Sun. These zones are delineated by the equator and four other special latitudinal lines: the Tropic of Cancer or Northern Tropic at 23.5° North; the Tropic of Capricorn or Southern Tropic at 23.5° South; the Arctic Circle at 66.5° North; and the Antarctic Circle at 66.5° South. The areas between these lines of latitude represent different climate zones. **Tropical climates** are hot and wet, like rainforests, and tend to have abundant plant and animal life, while polar climates are cold and usually have little plant and animal life. **Temperate zones** can vary and experience the four seasons.

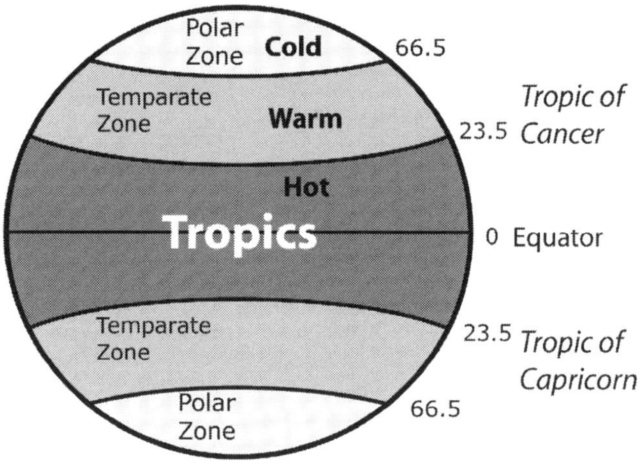

Effect of the Tilt of Earth's Axis on Seasons

In addition to the equator and the prime meridian, other major lines of latitude and longitude divide the world into regions relative to the direct rays of the Sun. These lines correspond with Earth's 23.5-degree tilt, and are responsible—along with Earth's revolution around the Sun—for the seasons. For example, the Northern Hemisphere is tilted directly toward the Sun from June 22 to September 23, which creates the summer. Conversely, the Southern Hemisphere is tilted away from the Sun and experiences winter during those months. The area between the Tropic of Cancer and the Tropic of Capricorn tends to be warmer and experiences fewer variations in seasonal temperatures because it's constantly subject to the direct rays of the Sun, no matter which direction Earth is tilted.

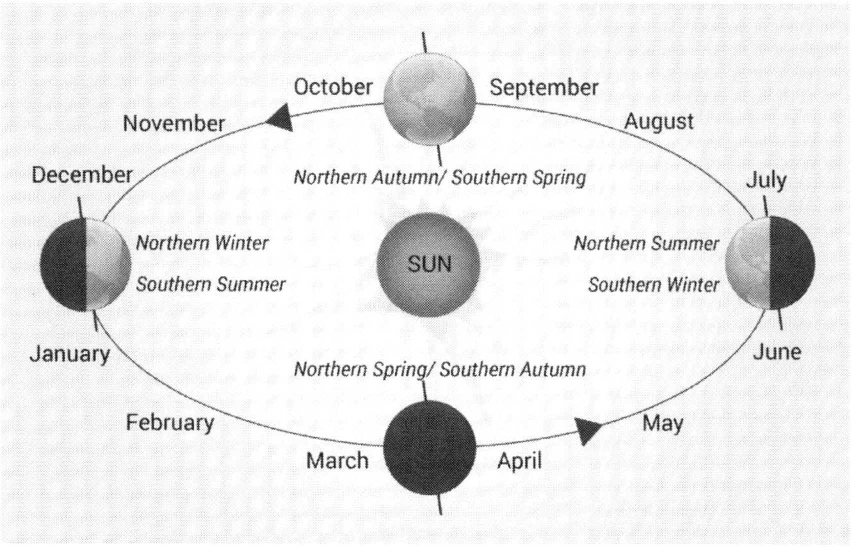

The area between the Tropic of Cancer and the Arctic Circle, which is at 66.5° North, and the Antarctic Circle, which is at 66.5° South, is where most of Earth's population resides and is called the **middle latitudes**. Here, the seasons are more pronounced, and milder temperatures generally prevail. When the Sun's direct rays are over the equator, it's known as an *equinox*, and day and night are almost equal throughout the world. Equinoxes occur twice a year: the fall, or autumnal equinox, occurs on September 22, while the spring equinox occurs on March 20.

Effects of Natural Phenomena

Natural phenomena can have a sizeable impact on climate and weather. Chemicals released from volcanic eruptions can fall back to Earth in acid rain. In addition, large amounts of carbon dioxide released into the atmosphere can warm the climate. Carbon dioxide creates the **greenhouse effect** by trapping solar energy from sunlight reflected off Earth's surface within the atmosphere. The amount of solar radiation emitted from the Sun varies and has recently been discovered to be cyclical.

El Niño and La Niña

El Niño and **La Niña** are terms for severe weather anomalies associated with torrential rainfall in the Pacific coastal regions, mainly in North and South America. These events occur irregularly every few years, usually around December, and are caused by a band of warm ocean water that accumulates in the central Pacific Ocean around the equator. The warm water changes the wind patterns over the Pacific and stops cold water from rising toward the American coastlines. The rise in ocean temperature also leads to increased evaporation and rain. These events are split into two phases—a warm, beginning phase called El Niño and a cool end phase called La Niña.

Solar System and the Universe

Characteristics of Objects in the Sky

Galaxies

Galaxies are clusters of stars, rocks, ice, and space dust. Like everything else in space, the exact number of galaxies is unknown, but there could be as many as a hundred billion. There are three types of galaxies: spiral, elliptical, and irregular. Most galaxies are **spiral galaxies**; they have a large, central galactic bulge made up of a cluster of older stars. They look like a disk with spinning arms. **Elliptical galaxies** are groups of stars with no pattern of rotation. They can be spherical or extremely elongated, and they don't have arms. **Irregular galaxies** vary significantly in size and shape.

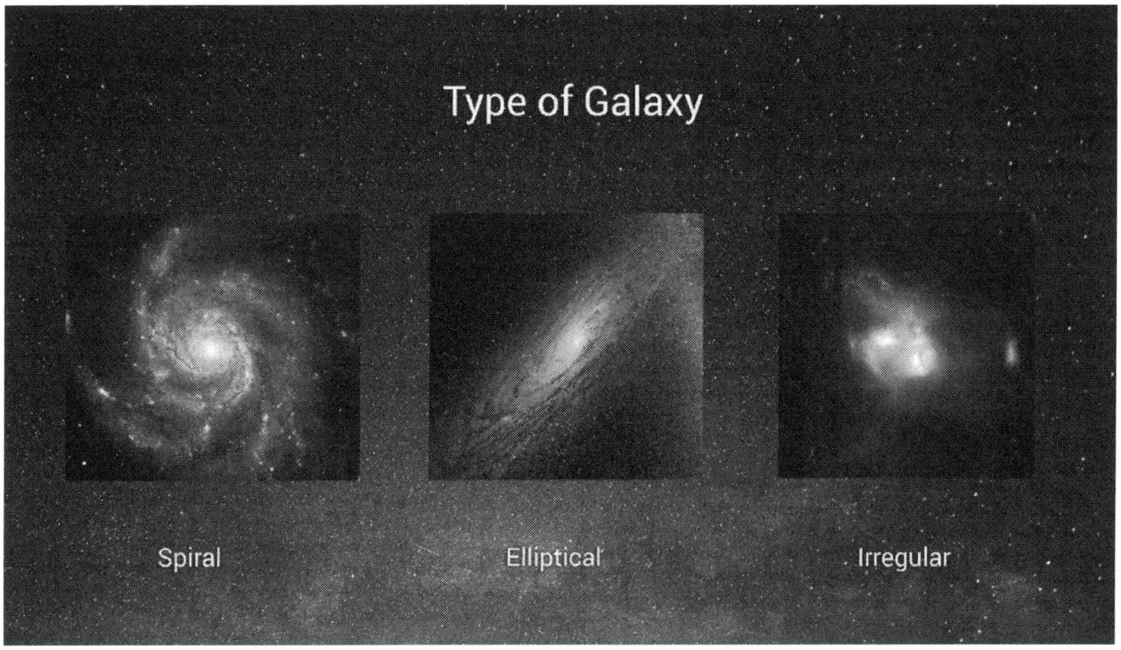

To say that galaxies are large is an understatement. Most galaxies are 1,000 to 100,000 parsecs in diameter, with one *parsec* equal to about 19 trillion miles. The Milky Way is the galaxy that contains Earth's solar system. It's one of the smaller galaxies that has been studied. The diameter of the Milky Way is estimated to be between 31,000 to 55,000 parsecs.

Characteristics of Stars and Their Life Cycles

Life Cycle of Stars

All stars are formed from **nebulae**. Depending on their mass, stars take different pathways during their life. Low- and medium-mass stars start as nebulae and then become red giants and white dwarfs. High-mass stars become red supergiants, supernovas, and then either neutron stars or black holes. Official stars are born as red dwarfs because they have plentiful amounts of gas—mainly hydrogen—to undergo nuclear fusion. Red dwarfs mature into white dwarfs before expending their hydrogen fuel source. When the fuel is spent, it creates a burst of energy that expands the star into a red giant. Red giants eventually condense to form white dwarfs, which is the final stage of a star's life.

Stars that undergo nuclear fusion and energy expenditure extremely quickly can burst in violent explosions called **supernovas**. These bursts can release as much energy in a few seconds as the Sun can release in its entire lifetime. The particles from the explosion then condense into the smallest type of star—a neutron star—and eventually form a **black hole**, which has such a high amount of gravity that not even light energy can escape. The Sun is currently a red dwarf, early in its life cycle.

Color, Temperature, Apparent Brightness, Absolute Brightness, and Luminosity

The color of a star depends on its surface temperature. Stars with cooler surfaces emit red light, while the hottest stars give off blue light. Stars with temperatures between these extremes, such as the Sun, emit white light. The **apparent brightness** of a star is a measure of how bright a star appears to an observer on Earth. The **absolute brightness** is a measure of the intrinsic brightness of a star and is measured at a distance of exactly 10 parsecs away. The **luminosity** of a star is the amount of light emitted from its surface.

Hertzsprung-Russell Diagrams

Hertzsprung-Russell diagrams are scatterplots that show the relationship of a star's brightness and temperature, or color. The general layout shows stars of greater luminosity toward the top of the diagram. Stars with higher surface temperatures appear toward the left side of the diagram. The diagonal area from the top-left of the diagram to the bottom-right is called the **main sequence**. Stars may or may not follow the main sequence during their life.

Dark Matter

Dark matter is an unidentified type of matter that comprises approximately 27% of the mass and energy in the observable universe. As the name suggests, dark matter is so dense and small that it doesn't emit or interact with electromagnetic radiation, such as light, making it electromagnetically invisible. Although dark matter has never been directly observed, its existence and properties can be inferred from its gravitational effects on visible objects as well as the cosmic microwave background. Patterns of movement have been observed in visible objects that would only be possible if dark matter exerted a gravitational pull.

Theory About the Origin of the Universe

The **Big Bang theory** is the most plausible cosmological model for the origin of the universe. It theorizes that the universe expanded from a high-density and high-temperature state. The theory offers comprehensive explanations for a wide range of astronomical phenomena, such as the cosmic microwave background and Hubble's Law. From detailed measurements of the expansion rate of the universe, it's estimated that the Big Bang occurred approximately 13.8 billion years ago, which is considered the age of the universe. The theory states that after the initial expansion, the universe cooled enough for subatomic particles and atoms to form and aggregate into giant clouds. These clouds coalesced through gravity and formed the stars and galaxies. If this theory holds true, it's predicted that the universe will reach a point where it will stop expanding and start to pull back toward the center due to gravity.

Earth–Moon–Sun System

The heat from the sun as well as the orbit and position of earth cause seasons. As discussed, earth rotates around the sun and spins on an axis. Earth is slightly tilted on its side. An imaginary line around the middle called the equator splits the earth into the northern and southern hemispheres.

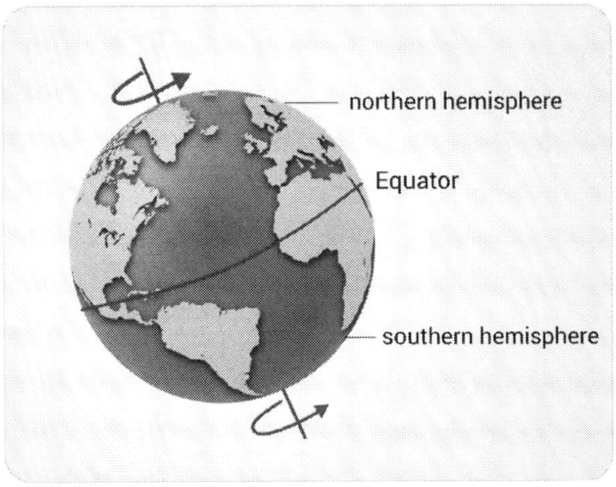

To understand seasons and the heating of the planet, refer to this picture:

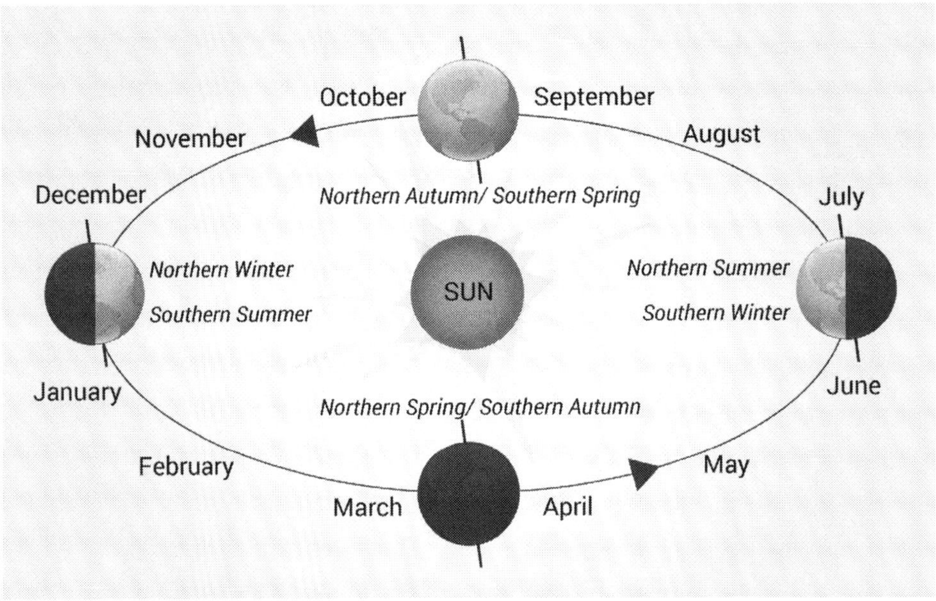

Observing July, these facts are apparent:

- Earth is tilted so that the northern hemisphere is pointing towards the sun. The southern hemisphere is pointed away.
- Because the north is tilted toward the sun, it gets more daylight in July than the southern hemisphere.

These observations explain why in July, the northern hemisphere experiences summer while the southern hemisphere experiences winter.

Notice in December that the opposite is true: the southern hemisphere gets more daylight compared to the northern hemisphere.

In spring and fall, both the north and the south get around the same sun exposure; therefore, those seasons have milder temperatures.

As the earth rotates, the distribution of light slowly changes, which explains why seasons gradually change. In June, the northern hemisphere experiences the summer solstice, the day with the most daylight. As the earth continues to orbit, its days will get shorter and shorter until the winter solstice, the shortest day of the year. Equinoxes occur in the fall and the spring and represent the days when the amount of daylight and darkness are relatively equal.

Just as the earth orbits the sun, the moon orbits the earth. The moon is much closer to earth than the sun. And even though the moon is so close to the earth, the moon contains no life because it lacks water and an atmosphere. Without greenhouse gases to blanket the sun's heat, temperatures on the moon are very low at night.

The moon is visible from the earth because it reflects sunlight at certain points in its orbit. The moon's orbit has a predictable pattern. It has two main phases, waxing and waning. When the moon is waxing, it goes from a new moon to a full moon. Notice that only the left side of the moon is dark during the waxing phase. The waning phase goes from full moon to new moon. Only the right side of the moon is dark when it is waning.

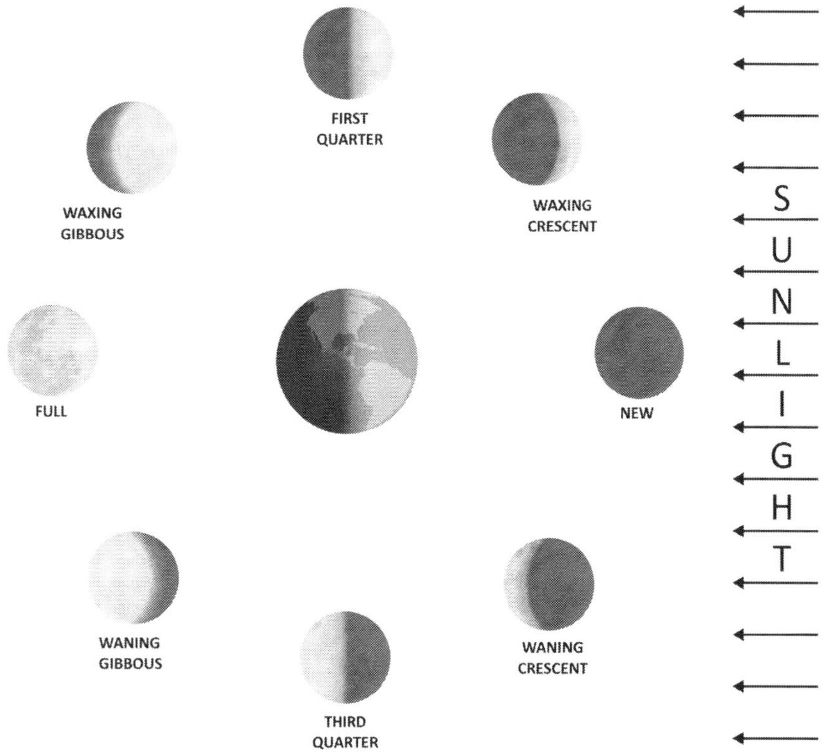

This picture shows that when the moon is behind the earth, then the moon's entire surface is reflected, and we see a full moon. When the moon is between the earth and the sun, it is invisible at night, which is called a **new moon**.

Half-moons are visible when the moon and the earth are in a line that is perpendicular to the direction of sunlight. Only half of the moon reflects light to the earth at night, as seen in the figure above.

A moon that looks larger than a half moon is called a **gibbous moon**, and a moon that looks smaller is called a **crescent moon**.

Eclipses occur when the earth, the sun, and the moon are all aligned—the earth blocks the others from seeing each other. If they are perfectly lined up, a total eclipse happens, and if they are only a little lined up, there is a partial eclipse.

There are two types of eclipses: lunar and solar. A lunar eclipse occurs when the earth interrupts the sun's light reflecting off of the full moon. Earth will then cast a shadow on the moon, and particles in earth's atmosphere refract the light so some reaches the surface of the moon, causing the moon to look yellow, brown, or red.

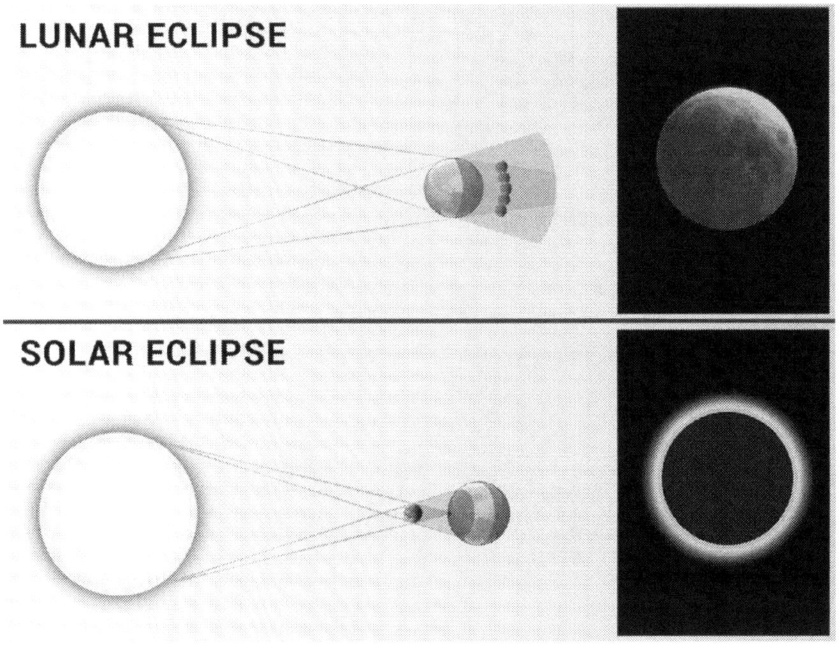

During a new moon, when the moon is between the earth and the sun, the moon will interrupt the sunlight, casting a shadow on earth. This is called a solar eclipse.

The moon also affects ocean tide due to gravity. Earth is much larger than the moon and has a very significant gravitational force that keeps us on the ground even though it is spinning very quickly. The moon is much smaller than earth, but because it is so close, it has a pulling effect on earth's oceans. When it is closest to earth, it pulls the water more, resulting in high tide. When the moon is farthest from earth, it pulls the ocean less and is called low tide.

Earth's Rotation and Orbital Revolution Around the Sun

Besides revolving around the Sun, Earth also spins like a top. It takes one day for Earth to complete a full spin, or rotation. The same is true for other planets, except that their "days" may be shorter or longer. One Earth day is about 24 hours, while one Jupiter day is only about nine Earth hours, and a Venus day is about 241 Earth days. Night occurs in areas that face away from the Sun, so one side of the planet experiences daylight and the other experiences night. This phenomenon is the reason that Earth is divided into time zones. The concept of time zones was created to provide people around the world with a uniform standard time, so the Sun would rise around 7:00 AM, regardless of location.

Time Zones

Longitudinal, or vertical, lines determine how far east or west different regions are from each other. These lines, also known as **meridians**, are the basis for time zones, which allocate different times to regions depending on their position eastward and westward of the prime meridian.

Effect of Solar Wind on Earth

Solar winds are streams of charged particles emitted by the Sun, consisting of mostly electrons, protons, and alpha particles. Earth is largely protected from solar winds by its magnetic field. However, the winds can still be observed, as they create phenomena like the beautiful Northern Lights (or **Aurora Borealis**).

Properties of the Components of the Solar System

Structure of the Solar System

The **solar system** is an elliptical planetary system with a large sun in the center that provides gravitational pull on the planets. It was formed 4.568 billion years ago from the gravitational collapse of a region within a giant molecular cloud that likely birthed other suns. This region of collapse is called a **pre-solar nebula**. As it started to collapse in the center, the nebula accumulated more energy and became hotter and heavier, providing more gravitational energy to the rest of the cloud, eventually becoming the Sun. The planets likely formed in a similar fashion, starting as small clumps called **protoplanets** that revolved around the Sun and then smashed together to form larger planets and, eventually, the solar system seen today.

Laws of Motion

Planetary motion is governed by three scientific laws called **Kepler's laws**:

1. The orbit of a planet is elliptical in shape, with the Sun as one focus.

2. An imaginary line joining the center of a planet and the center of the Sun sweeps out equal areas during equal intervals of time.

3. For all planets, the ratio of the square of the orbital period is the same as the cube of the average distance from the Sun.

The most relevant of these laws is the first. Planets move in elliptical paths because of gravity; when a planet is closer to the Sun, it moves faster because it has built up gravitational speed. As illustrated in the diagram below, the second law states that it takes planet 1 the same time to travel along the A1 segment as the A2 segment, even though the A2 segment is shorter.

Kepler's Laws of Planetary Motion

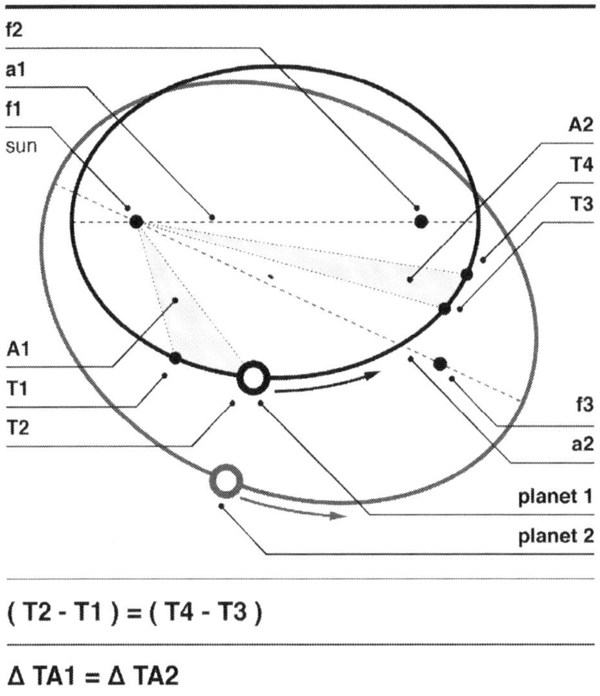

Characteristics of the Sun, Moon, and Planets

The Sun is comprised mainly of hydrogen and helium. Metals make up only about 2% of its total mass. The Sun is 1.3 million kilometers wide, weighs 1.989×10^{30} kilograms, and has temperatures of 5,800 Kelvin (9980 °F) on the surface and 15,600,000 Kelvin (28 million °F) at the core. The Sun's enormous size and gravity give it the ability to provide sunlight. The gravity of the Sun compresses hydrogen and helium atoms together through nuclear fusion and releases energy and light.

The Moon has a distinct core, mantle, and crust. It has elevations and craters created by impacts with large objects in the solar system. The Moon makes a complete orbit around Earth every 27.3 days. It's relatively large compared to other moons in the solar system, with a diameter one-quarter of Earth and a mass $\frac{1}{81}$ of Earth.

The eight planets of the solar system are divided into four inner (or **terrestrial**) planets and four outer (or **Jovian**) planets. In general, terrestrial planets are small, and Jovian planets are large and gaseous. The planets in the solar system are listed below from nearest to farthest from the Sun:

- Mercury: the smallest planet in the solar system; it only takes about 88 days to completely orbit the Sun
- Venus: around the same size, composition, and gravity as Earth and orbits the Sun every 225 days
- Earth: the only known planet with life
- Mars: called the Red Planet due to iron oxide on the surface; takes around 687 days to complete its orbit

- Jupiter: the largest planet in the system; made up of mainly hydrogen and helium
- Saturn: mainly composed of hydrogen and helium along with other trace elements; has 61 moons; has beautiful rings, which may be remnants of destroyed moons
- Uranus: the coldest planet in the system, with temperatures as low as -224.2 °Celsius (-371.56 °F)
- Neptune: the last and third-largest planet; also, the second-coldest planet

Asteroids, Meteoroids, Comets, and Dwarf/Minor Planets

Several other bodies travel through the universe. **Asteroids** are orbiting bodies composed of minerals and rock. They're also known as **minor planets**—a term given to any astronomical object in orbit around the Sun that doesn't resemble a planet or a comet. **Meteoroids** are mini-asteroids with no specific orbiting pattern. **Meteors** are meteoroids that have entered Earth's atmosphere and started melting from contact with greenhouse gases. **Meteorites** are meteors that have landed on Earth. **Comets** are composed of dust and ice and look like a comma with a tail from the melting ice as they streak across the sky.

Theories of Origin of the Solar System

One theory of the origins of the solar system is the **nebular hypothesis**, which posits that the solar system was formed by clouds of extremely hot gas called a **nebula**. As the nebula gases cooled, they became smaller and started rotating. Rings of the nebula left behind during rotation eventually condensed into planets and their satellites. The remaining nebula formed the Sun.

Another theory of the solar system's development is the **planetesimal hypothesis**. This theory proposes that planets formed from cosmic dust grains that collided and stuck together to form larger and larger bodies. The larger bodies attracted each other, growing into moon-sized protoplanets and eventually planets.

Practice Quiz

1. How many daughter cells are formed from one parent cell during meiosis?
    a. One
    b. Two
    c. Three
    d. Four

2. What is the total mechanical energy of a system?
    a. The total potential energy
    b. The total kinetic energy
    c. Kinetic energy plus potential energy
    d. Kinetic energy minus potential energy

3. What does the Lewis dot structure of an element represent?
    a. The outer electron valence shell population
    b. The inner electron valence shell population
    c. The positioning of the element's protons
    d. The positioning of the element's neutrons

4. Which rock is formed from cooling magma underneath the Earth's surface?
    a. Extrusive sedimentary rocks
    b. Sedimentary rocks
    c. Igneous rocks
    d. Metamorphic rocks

5. Which of the following is most abundant in the Earth's atmosphere?
    a. Carbon dioxide
    b. Oxygen
    c. Nitrogen
    d. Water

See answers on next page.

Answer Explanations

1. D: Meiosis has the same phases as mitosis, except that they occur twice—once in meiosis I and once in meiosis II. During meiosis I, the cell splits into two. Each cell contains two sets of chromosomes. Next, during meiosis II, the two intermediate daughter cells divide again, producing four total haploid cells that each contain one set of chromosomes.

2. C: In any system, the total mechanical energy is the sum of the potential energy and the kinetic energy. Either value could be zero, but it still must be included in the total. Choices *A* and *B* only give the total potential or kinetic energy, respectively. Choice *D* gives the difference between the kinetic and potential energy.

3. A: A Lewis dot diagram shows the alignment of the valence (outer) shell electrons and how readily they can pair or bond with the valence shell electrons of other atoms to form a compound. Choice *B* is incorrect because the inner shell does not help us understand how likely an atom is to bond with another atom. The positioning of protons and neutrons concerns the nucleus of the atom, which again would not relate to the likelihood of bonding.

4. C: Igneous rocks are formed from the cooling of magma, both on and below the Earth's surface, which are classified as extrusive and intrusive, respectively. Sedimentary rocks are formed from deposition and cementation on the surface, and metamorphic rocks are formed from the transformation of sedimentary or igneous rocks through heat and pressure.

5. C: Nitrogen is the most abundant element in the atmosphere at 78%. Carbon dioxide and water don't make up a large percentage. Oxygen makes up only 21% of the atmosphere.

Fine Arts, Health, and Physical Education

Visual Arts

Activities That Promote Enjoyment and Understanding of Visual Arts

As children progress through elementary school, they should be exposed to the basic foundations, creative expression and production of each type of art, and the ability to critically analyze a work of art and make connections within a cultural and historical context. Art education should build progressively during childhood so that older children are able to eventually take on these more sophisticated and advanced applications.

There are a wide variety of visual arts that can enhance a child's creativity and learning experience. It is optimal to expose young children to many different types of art – both as a creator and observer – for well-rounded cultural, creative, and comprehensive learning. Depending on the child's age, early childhood educators can tailor art assignments and activities to meet the child's interests, motor skills, attention, and needs.

Visual arts include things like drawing, painting, sketching, collage, sculpture, etc. Before the age of three, most artwork is produced less in an artistic way and more in a scientific and sensory way. Children at these youngest ages are more interested in the textures, colors, and shapes of what they create rather than expressing any sort of emotion or symbol. There are a variety of crafting activities that young children enjoy and can benefit from including finger painting, pasting, modeling with Play-Doh and clay, folding paper for origami, tracing and making models, and using a variety of craft supplies in creative ways including pom-poms, googly eyes, glitter, pipe cleaners, felt, and yarn. Craft activities help small children develop fine motor skills as they use instruments such as scissors and try to make precise movements like stringing beads and coloring within boundaries.

As children develop, they can focus for longer periods of time and can handle more precise movements with smaller materials and areas. For example, a three- to four-year-old child may make simple Play-Doh snakes or snowmen, while a six- to eight-year-old child can add spots, a tongue, and facial features to the snowman with smaller bits of material laid in more exact locations. Through arts and crafts, young children can learn about colors and observe colors in the world around them, recognizing things such as green grass and blue sky. Working on arts and crafts projects helps children develop skills in planning, attention and focusing, problem-solving, and originality. It also helps them learn how to observe the world around them, be appreciative of other people's interpretations and ideas, deal with frustrations when things do not go as planned, and develop hand-eye coordination.

Early childhood educators should strive to expose children to a vast array of arts and craft materials and different types of arts. Activities should be age-appropriate. For example, four- to five-year-old children are likely unable to use small beads and fine pencils and markers, and do better with wider drawing utensils and larger beads that are easier to grasp and manipulate. Children who are ten to twelve are able to work with more intricate objects and may be bored with crayons and coloring books. There are a variety of other art forms that students may view or try to create such as jewelry, pottery, stained glass, wire art, sewing, quilting, knitting, and decoupage.

Development of Perception

Perception is experiencing the world through one's senses. Humans take in and process information through hearing, seeing, touching, tasting, and smelling. We use this information to decide how we will act. Perception is developed in the following ways.

Observation

People learn by observing and copying (or avoiding) certain behaviors. This type of learning is sometimes called vicarious reinforcement. Children learn to behave by watching the adults in their lives, including parents, educators, and others.

Prior Knowledge

Observation and prior knowledge go hand in hand. After observing certain behaviors, we retain the information and apply it later. When we recreate behaviors, we are using prior knowledge that has been retained via observation. Prior knowledge includes content that students observe at home, including types of media, arts, and crafts.

Imaginative and Cognitive Processes

Cognition is how we learn and comprehend. Perception is actually one of several cognitive processes; others include language, memory, and imagination. We can improve our cognition by eating a healthy diet, exercising, practicing critical thinking, and seeking new opportunities to learn. Perception is learning information via our senses. The information received through perception is transformed into signals that our brains can comprehend.

Cognition and perception work together; cognition works through the mind while perception works through the senses. Students use these processes together in order to experience and evaluate art.

Imagination refers to a cognitive process that uses creativity and mental imagery. It occurs when we picture things that are not part of our immediate reality. Thinking, daydreaming, and dreaming are imaginative processes. Art is meant to engage the imagination. Imagination works hand in hand with perception; the way students perceive art (sight, sound, touch, etc.) ignites their imaginations. Likewise, each student's unique imagination will impact how they perceive art.

Multisensory Experiences

Multisensory experiences refers to the ability to perceive information via multiple senses simultaneously. Multisensory experiences occur when the senses work together, like hearing and watching a film, or using touch, taste, smell, and sight when preparing and trying out new foods.

Perception allows students to engage with and interpret their environments. As they age, their perception grows stronger. Meaningful and stimulating environments are key to perceptual development.

Environmental and Cultural Perception

Environmental Perception

Students can develop their perception and reflection skills through activities that involve observation. As they engage with their surroundings, they should be tasked with writing down their observations of the environment. Teachers can take the whole class on a walk outside or have students go around the classroom and write down what sticks out the most to them. Their descriptions should include colors, textures, and sounds.

Presenting students with a piece of artwork, whether it is a painting, drawing, or other visual medium, and then asking them to describe what they've seen is another activity teachers can introduce. They can give students five minutes or so to look over the artwork and write what they see and how the artwork makes them feel. Students can then share their observations with the class.

Cultural Perception

Students should also be exposed to a variety of artwork from multiple cultures. It helps them become more culturally aware and empathetic. Teachers should go over the history of each type of cultural artwork they present to students. For example, when presenting art inspired by Cinco de Mayo, they should teach the real history of Cinco de Mayo.

Students should be allowed to bring in art that represents their individual cultures. They can be asked to describe the history of the artwork, talk about the geography or region where that type of art is prevalent, and share their own cultural experiences with that type of art.

Visual art from other cultures isn't limited to drawings and paintings; it can also include theatre, dance, and instruments. For example, teachers can put students into groups and assign them stories; they can then ask the students to put on a mini performance to illustrate their understanding of the stories.

Educators should teach about a variety of cultural art throughout the school year. This regular exposure will help students learn to appreciate and respect other cultures.

Critical Thinking in the Perception of Artwork

Early childhood educators should use techniques that foster their students' ability to critically analyze a variety of art forms. Students should develop a toolbox with the appropriate language and terminology to be able to intelligently discuss artwork from a critical standpoint with others. Each form of art has its own unique terms that are important for students to understand, both for their own appreciation and fluency in the arts and for their ability to communicate with others about arts. As students mature and develop their own interests, they will become increasingly able to effectively talk about why they may or may not enjoy a piece of artwork and how it makes them feel. Educators should emphasize that the artistic process is creative and subjective and that each person will have his or her own opinions about various art forms, but that in every case, the universal principles of respect, diversity, and acceptance apply.

Although generally there is no "right or wrong" in art, the ability to critique creative works is a skill that takes time, maturity, exposure, and intellectual understanding and appreciation of art. Early childhood educators can best help students improve these skills through a broad exposure to many arts, detailed explanations about the intricacies of various types of artwork, and discussions about self-expression through art. For example, a young student may inherently not enjoy a classical piece of music arranged in a quartet, but he or she can learn to critique it from an unbiased position based on that type of music. By understanding the details taking place in the piece (such as how the composer changes the key from major to minor halfway through to invoke sadness or mystery, or how the cello and violin feed off each other as if conversing), students can become more impartial and able to understand art for art's sake.

Educators should instruct students to evaluate questions such as: what was the artist's purpose in creating the work, and is the purpose achieved? Is the style the artist chose appropriate for the expressed purpose of the work? Does the artist have a unique idea in their work? The dialogue underlying these lessons should always focus on showing respect for artwork and creative ideas that are different from the student's own and celebrating diversity of preferences and art forms.

Elements of Art

Early learners can focus on the basic vocabulary of visual art like identifying colors and shapes. Older students can be exposed to more nuanced terms in the world of visual art. Some visual art is **representational** and depicts objects as they appear in the real world. One visual tool that heightens the realistic accuracy of visual art is **perspective**, an artistic technique that creates the illusion of depth through the use of line (for example, lines in the foreground converge in the background), size and placement of objects (objects that are supposed to be closer to the viewer appear larger than objects that are further away), or color (for example, a hill that is close to the viewer is depicted in a vibrant green, while a distant mountain appears with a more muted, hazy color).

In contrast to representational art, other visual art is **abstract**. When artists use abstraction, they use line, color, and other elements to communicate the presence of objects and emotions rather than realistically portraying the objects. For example, a swirl of **warm colors** like red and orange might represent anger or anxiety; **cool colors** like blue and gray could communicate sadness or passivity. In this way, the artist's **palette**, or range of colors used in their work, can communicate a mood or emotion to the viewer. Some works are **monochromatic,** meaning that they only use one color (although the artist might use different shades of the same color—for example, dark blue and light blue). Different shades of color can also create the illusion of shape or represent different lighting.

Other tools of both abstract and representational visual art include **contrast** (the pairing of dissimilar elements to make each other stand out), **positive** and **negative space** (positive space refers to the areas of the artwork occupied by its subject, whereas negative space includes all the areas that do not contain any subject), **balance**, and **symmetry**. Some artistic techniques to introduce to students might include caricature, collage, painting, sculpture, portraiture, landscape, and still life. If educators are able to take students on museum field trips, students should know museum-related vocabulary terms like *gallery, exhibit,* and *curator.*

Principles of Art

Artists, regardless of medium, typically rely on the following six main principles in art: emphasis, rhythm, balance, contrast, harmony, and movement.

Emphasis

Artists often want to make one part of their work stand out from the rest and guide viewers to pay attention to specific components of their piece. For example, lines and textures in paintings and sculptures may direct viewers to specific details or target features, and altering the texture of one area may make it stand out in contrast to the rest of the work.

Rhythm

Rhythm involves repeating elements within a work such as colors, shapes, lines, notes, or steps to create a pattern of visual or auditory motion.

Balance

Balance is positioning objects or using size, color, shape and lighting in the artwork so that all of the elements are equally present with no particular component overpowering the rest. Symmetrical balance is when two halves of an image create a mirror image, so that if the work is folded in half, each half is the same. Balance can also be **asymmetrical,** wherein the composition is balanced but the two halves are not the same. For example, a large central object is balanced by a smaller figure on one edge.

Contrast

Contrast exemplifies differences between two unlike things such as loud and soft music, major and minor tones, fast and slow dancing movements, and light and dark colors.

Harmony

Somewhat opposite of contrast, **harmony** highlights the similarities in separate but related parts of a composition. Rather than emphasizing their dissimilarities, harmony shows that different things can actually be related to each other and blend together.

Movement

Artwork that contains a sense of motion or action has **movement**. Even stationary art, like painting and sculpture, can imply movement based on the positioning of objects or the artist's use of lines, which draw the viewer's eye to different areas of the artwork.

Various Functions and Techniques of Art

Art has **personal** (self-expression, gratification, narrative functions), **social** (collective meaning for a group of people, such as symbolic art honoring a god or political art), and **physical** (such as a pottery mug for tea) functions that often overlap within a single piece of work. As children go through elementary school, they become familiar with an increasing variety and complexity of visual art forms beginning with things like drawing, painting, and sculpting, then adding printmaking, sponge painting, film animation, and graphics in third and fourth grades, and dabbling in environmental design and art based on personal experience and observation by the fifth grade. They may also try computer-generated art, photography, metalworking, textile arts, and ceramics. Materials include scissors, brushes, papers, glue, beads, clay, film, and computers.

Art Throughout Cultures

It is imperative that early childhood educators focus on the fact that artwork has been used throughout history and in every culture as a means of expression and storytelling. Even seemingly new forms of art were not created out of nowhere, but rather, they have evolved from other previously existing forms of art. One of the best ways to discuss art is actually through embedding it in discussions of history and culture. The evolution of music can easily be discussed through various time periods. For example, the assassination of President John F. Kennedy, the Hippie movement, the Vietnam War, and the Beatles coexisted in the same time period, so students can find similarities and differences among these social and artistic ideals within their historical context.

Students can also study different time periods of art and architecture. In the **Classical period**, Greek artists focused on physical beauty and the human form, paying particular attention to Olympian gods and their idealized proportions in their works. The **Medieval period** that occurred in Europe from 500-1400 CE saw a flourish of Romanesque style art that shifted the emphasis from portraying realism to conveying a message, particularly symbolic Christian ideals.

Students should also learn about the history of art in other countries such as China, with its jade, pottery, bronze, porcelain, and calligraphy. Educators should focus on how various influences over time affected the predominant artwork each period. For example, Buddhism in the early first century BCE increased calligraphy on silks, the Song dynasty created landscape paintings that were popular, and the Ming and Qing dynasties developed color painting and printing with an evolution towards individualism. As China became increasingly influenced by Western society in the nineteenth and early twentieth centuries, social realism predominated.

In addition to covering other Asian nations, educators should expose students to traditional African art, which generally demonstrates moral values, focuses on human subjects, and seeks to please the viewer. Educators can also introduce art from the American Indians such as woodcarving, weaving, stitchery, and beading. Art in American Indian populations varies widely from tribe to tribe but tends to beautify everyday objects and create items of spiritual significance. Students should be exposed to music and theater from other cultures and observe the costumes, movements, instruments, and themes in performing arts from places like the Caribbean islands, Japan, Mexico, Australia, Africa, Italy, and Russia.

Integrating Visual Arts with Other Subjects

Visual arts can be used to teach other academic subjects. Using visual arts is a great way to keep students engaged and encourage classroom participation.

Some subjects, like geometry, use visuals already, such as geometric shapes. Topics like health or physical education could benefit from illustrations of the human body. Teachers can also ask students to draw and label parts of the body or use models of the body that can be taken apart to teach students about anatomy.

In English and language arts classes, some students may have trouble expressing themselves with words. It may benefit their understanding and engagement if they are able to express themselves with sketches.

Visual art is not limited to drawing and models; sculpture, printmaking, photography, and filmmaking are also types of visual art. For example, a physical education teacher could assign students workouts to do at home and ask them to film a few minutes of themselves doing those exercises. Teachers can also ask students to go out and photograph items that were discussed in class. For instance, if the class is learning about shapes, ask them to go out and photograph examples of those shapes.

Individually, Culturally, and Age Appropriate Instruction and Assessment

Cognitive skills help students understand the world around them. They develop those skills through thinking, observing, and doing. Art helps students learn to concentrate and increase their attention span. You can encourage students to develop these skills further by creating age-appropriate art instruction and assessments that meet each of your students' individual and cultural needs.

Individually and Culturally Appropriate Instruction

To create individually and culturally appropriate art instruction, differentiation is necessary. Differentiation addresses each student's particular interests or needs. Teachers may not have time to work with each student one-on-one, but they can make sure their lessons have enough variety to address students' various interests and backgrounds.

Carefully observe your students to ensure that the individualized and differentiated lesson plans are relevant. Take special note of your students' motor skills—pay attention to which students have developed skills, such as connecting dots, cutting along dotted lines, or coloring within the lines. For more advanced ages, take note of their ability to observe differences in light sources used in artwork. They should be able to identify differences in hue, texture, and color intensity.

To create culturally appropriate lesson plans, first consider your own values and how they shape your teaching. Then, research commonalities among different cultures, like storytelling traditions. Include artwork of diverse artists in the classroom. Most importantly, ask your students questions about their interests.

Age-Appropriate Instruction

It is never too early to introduce children to art. No matter their age group, simple instruction is usually the best. However, the more stimulating the art instruction is, the more students will pay attention.

For toddlers and preschoolers, hand-painting (impressing their hands in paint and then pressing their hands on paper) is ideal. Craft projects that involve cutting and folding paper are also appropriate for children in this age group. Outlining art (drawing dark lines around parts of a picture) and instructing them to stay inside the lines are good activities for kindergarteners and first graders. Teaching different drawing techniques and explaining color schemes are better suited for older children.

Assessment

Process art, which is choice-driven, allows children to pick art activities that they have the most interest in and perform them however they want. It is a great assessment of children's autonomy; it shows the teacher that they can make choices independently. Although it's mostly used for toddlers and preschoolers, process art can be used to assess older students and adults as well. Exploration and discovery are what process art is all about.

Older students should undergo performance-based assessments. To do this, the instructor should ask students to make a portfolio of their best artwork thus far and then schedule a meeting with them to provide feedback.

Feedback should highlight areas where the students used techniques properly, as well as areas where they could use more practice.

Music

Developing Music Literacy

Music literacy includes the listening, playing, reading, writing, speaking, viewing, and creation of music.

You can teach music literacy and have fun while doing it. For starters, make playing music in the classroom a daily habit. Choose a child-appropriate station on a music streaming platform or play CDs. Songs that encourage kids to clap their hands, sing along, or get up and dance are the best choices. You can also instruct students to draw the story happening in the songs they hear. This activity allows students to come up with their own creative interpretations of songs, which are fun to share with the class. Folk songs are especially great for this type of activity.

Authentic performance is the performance of music from another time period using instruments that were also common during that time. Giving students the opportunity to witness authentic performance is an educational tool to encourage musical literacy. It may spark them to ask questions about how instruments from other eras were traditionally played and how music has evolved over different time periods.

Teaching music history is another method of teaching music literacy. Instructors can present the biographies of different historical composers to teach music literacy as well. They can provide students with a list of interesting facts about each composer and play selections of their musical work, or assign students to research and report on a composer's biography. Teachers can also create a timeline of music eras to post in the classroom, readily available for students to refer to and learn from.

Another way is to provide students with worksheets that help them remember facts about music history. Some ideas for these worksheets include word searches or crosswords containing musical terminology, coloring sheets with pictures of instruments or musicians, or multiple-choice activities where students answer questions about different composers and types of music.

Music Terminology

Instruments used in the early education classroom typically fall into one of the following categories: **melodic instruments** (melody bells, xylophones, flutes, and recorders), **rhythmic instruments** (drums, triangles, tambourines, and blocks), or **harmonic instruments** (chording instruments such as the autoharp). The key elements of music include rhythm, melody, harmony, **form** (the structure or design of the music, usually referring to the music's different sections and their repetition, such as **binary** (AB), **ternary** (ABA), theme and variation and **rondo** (ABACA), and the musical phrases), and expression [**dynamics** (volumes) and timbre].

Students should be familiar with terms related to **meter,** which is the repeating pattern of stressed and unstressed sounds in a piece of music. While meter is a somewhat complex concept, students can easily understand the idea of a musical beat, which is the audible result of meter. In written music, meter is noted by a **time signature**, which looks like a fraction with one number on the top and one number on the bottom, like ¾. The bottom number expresses the **beat** as a division of a whole note (for example, the number four means that it is a quarter note), while the top number shows how many beats make up a **bar** (so ¾ means that three quarter note beats make up one bar).

In addition to patterns of stress, music also contains an arrangement of sounds, known as its melody. **Melody** refers to the development of a single tone; when many tones are combined simultaneously in a way that sounds pleasing to the listener, it is referred to as **harmony**. Other sound elements related to tone include **chords** (the combination of musical tones), **keys** (the principal tone in a piece of music), and **scales** (a series of tones at fixed intervals, either ascending or descending, usually beginning at a certain note). These elements can be described as either major or minor.

Words to describe the **tempo**, or the speed of a piece of music, include, from slowest to fastest: *largo, adagio, andante, allegro, vivace,* and *presto*. In terms of the intensity of the sound, **piano** refers to music that is played softly whereas **forte** means played with force. Students should also be familiar with vocabulary terms that describe different instruments, different genres of music, and different musical periods.

Musical Arrangement

Musical arrangement is the adaptation of musical composition to voices and/or instruments.

Teachers can guide their students to create simple song arrangements by having them come up with different ways to perform songs that they already know. For example, they can instruct the students to perform a song *a cappella*, change the tempo, or create new beats using body percussion, like clapping and tapping. Activities of this nature will usually get creative juices flowing.

After they recreate a song with different beats or vocal arrangements, assign the students to create songs that use the same beats as the songs they've already heard. Encourage them to be creative by adding in metal or wood instruments like harps or guitars. Use what you have! Instruments that are typically at a teacher's disposal include recorders, slide whistles, xylophones, castanets, triangles, hand drums, pianos, and rhythm blocks.

When students are creating music, ask them how they want the listener to feel when they hear it. Do they want the listener to feel romantic, heroic, or happy? This approach will help them determine their music's genre.

Students can also be taught to harmonize. Teachers should pick songs that have two-part harmony, then assign students to each part. Students should sing them separately at first and then simultaneously. Teachers should prompt students to repeat phrases or segments of songs until they sound right. They can also teach students when to raise or lower their voices for certain parts.

Music of Diverse Genres, Styles, and Cultures

Music education should be taught in a way that incorporates as many cultures and genres as possible. The United States is a multicultural nation, and the classroom needs to reflect that. To diversify their curriculum, teachers should do the following things.

Media and technology are right at your fingertips. Conduct a survey among students to see what types of music they grew up on and what they listen to currently. Then download or stream the different types of music they mentioned and play them for the class.

Students should be given the chance to experience music in different ways, from performing it themselves to attending concerts or performances. Teachers can take students on field trips to see local choirs or orchestras perform. If that isn't feasible, showing videos of musicals or concerts in the classroom works too.

When it comes to instrumental instruction, different students will be interested in different instruments. Therefore, it is necessary to have a variety of instruments for them to choose from. Many elementary classrooms begin with the recorder, but consider bringing in tambourines, triangles, drums, guitars, or any other instrument that is available for use.

Engagement is always key. Playing the same music or instruments, or having students sing the same songs repeatedly, gets boring very quickly. Variety is the best way to keep students on their toes and ready to participate.

Music's Relevance to Culture and Heritage

Music is integral to culture because it connects people and moves them in ways that nothing else can.

People listen to music everywhere they go: while at parties, driving, working out, relaxing at home, and during many other activities. They form memories centered around the music that was playing in the background during important life events. Perceptions, emotions, and actions can all be shaped by music.

Music is often reflective of the times. Cultural factors such as politics, fashion, or technology all have an influence on music.

It can also be used to teach other languages. English isn't everyone's native tongue in the United States. Listening to and singing along with songs in other languages is educational for children and adults.

Texas is the birthplace of many famous musicians. The state produced stars like Selena, Beyonce, Gary Clark Jr., Gene Autry, and Dale Evans. Many Texans were pioneers in music like western swing, Tejano, country, gospel, rock 'n' roll, jazz, and hip hop. These types of music all coexist in Texas, thanks in no small part to the state's diversity. One can even say that the diversity found in Texas is reflective of the United States as a whole.

Music plays a powerful role in society. People across time and nations have used it to express pain, victory, pride, and the whole spectrum of human emotion. It has been used to protest, confront societal issues, and forge individual identities. The history and heritage of the United States has been documented musically in songs such as "The Star-Spangled Banner," "America the Beautiful," and many more.

Music continually evolves as cultures grow and change. It will always be a mirror of the world.

Music-Related Careers

Instructors can teach students about a variety of musical genres by considering what types of music are popular on a global scale. Some of the top genres of music are classical, country, hip hop, pop, K-pop, R&B, and rock.

After selecting a few genres, teachers should define each one and provide examples by streaming songs or playing recordings or videos. The class can discuss the types of instruments and technology used to produce the different types of music.

Just as there are many types of music, there are also many career options in the music industry.

Performer

Professional musicians can come in many forms. Potential careers for the especially talented include singer, background vocalist, or member of a band, orchestra, or symphony.

Sound Engineer

Sound engineers schedule recording sessions, record the music performed in studios, and edit it to sound better. They also assist with any technical issues that occur while performers are recording.

Booking Agent/Manager

Booking agents handle all logistics involved in getting performances secured for artists. They take care of managing performance contracts, arranging accommodations, and procuring concert venues. Booking agents typically also handle marketing for performers.

Composer

Composers write and arrange music. They are not limited to writing for the music industry; they also arrange music for television shows, motion pictures, games, and commercials. Composers should be able to play at least one musical instrument and understand music theory.

Music Teacher

Music teachers don't just teach music to children in schools. They may offer private lessons or music workshops. They may teach students music theory, how to play instruments, or how to sing.

Evaluating and Critiquing Musical Performances

Here are some criteria teachers use to evaluate their students' musical performances:

- **Assess how they played**. To start, teachers need to observe whether students played the right notes and rhythms. Did they play the right tempo? Was the audience engaged?
- **Assess how they measure up.** Players usually have a standard to which they play. This means that they have a particular musical role model that they try to emulate. Teachers can listen to see if the students sound like the musicians they are trying to emulate and let them know if they are close or far off base.
- **Determine when they play best.** Do the students play better in an ensemble or individually? Do they perform songs that they've picked on their own better than ones that are assigned? Do they play better or worse while being conducted versus playing when and how they want to?

There are also specific assessment methods that teachers should use to critique musical performances.

- **Diagnostic assessment:** Teachers often use ratings and checklists for diagnostic assessments. They assign a list of tasks or goals for the student to reach based on their abilities. Each completed task receives a rating or a grade. Whether they use grades, like A through F, or a scale of 1 to 10 is up to each individual teacher.
- **Formative assessment:** This method of assessment occurs as students go along. Teachers provide them with feedback on a regular basis. Based on how students are performing at any given period, a teacher can change their lessons to reflect the areas in which students need more practice.
- **Summative assessment:** This assessment is conducted at the end of the learning process. Teachers review all the performances a student has completed, along with any relevant assignments they were given, to see if they improved.

Integrating Music with Other Subjects

Using music to teach other subjects is more common than people may think. Here are some other subject areas that teachers integrate music into and how they do it.

English and Language Arts

Literature that rhymes, like rhyming books or poetry, is a common way for English teachers to use music in the classroom. It gets children to read along to beats and count them. Teachers sometimes tell students to clap their hands or tap their feet with each beat.

Teachers can also assign children books about musicians. These books may introduce them to terminology that is commonly used in the music world, thereby expanding their vocabularies.

Social Studies

As students learn about history and geography in social studies, there are many songs that teachers can incorporate into the classroom to help students retain information. There are songs that list the 50 states, the state capitals, U.S. presidents, and more.

Science

Teaching the different elements of sound is as important in science as it is in music. One way that teachers can help their students to learn about sound is to emulate a thunderstorm. They can do this by using instruments and creating noise that resembles what they hear during a thunderstorm.

Expression

Music without expression can be boring, which is why it's important to teach students to use expression when they perform. Tone, phrasing, dynamics, and articulation are all tools that help performers be more expressive.

Tone refers to the quality of the music. Phrasing is how the music is emphasized. Dynamics is music volume. Articulation is the way notes are played. Students should be taught to use each of these tools to perform music that is expressive and engaging.

Teachers should lead by example and model expression. They can play an instrument in front of their classes and highlight each of the tools named above. They should also play songs two different ways: once with expression and once without. This will give students an idea of what their performances should look like.

Playing videos of performances or going to see live performances together is another way to show students how expression is used. Students should be asked which parts of the performances stood out to them the most. They should also be asked what they think performers were trying to express.

Color-coding music is another way to teach expression. An instructor can use different colors to highlight different notes or directions written on sheets of music. They can use one color to highlight a soft dynamic and another color to highlight a loud one.

Using storytelling to highlight musical expression is a fun activity for teachers and students. Most songs have a story to tell. A teacher can take a popular song, print out copies of the lyrics, and hand them to students. Then, they can go over each line and ask students what story they think is being told and how it makes them feel.

Health

Health Promotion and Disease Prevention

Early childhood educators should be able to incorporate health and physical education concepts into the classroom for the overall health, wellness, and growth of their students. Physical activity is especially important at young ages, and children need at least sixty minutes of moderate to vigorous physical activity daily according to the U.S. Surgeon General's Recommendations. There are five components of health-related **physical fitness**: cardiovascular fitness, muscular strength, muscular endurance, flexibility, and body composition. All five areas should be addressed in physical education classes.

With cardiovascular training, as the heart enlarges, the volume of the chambers increase, allowing for a greater **stroke volume** (the volume of blood ejected in each heartbeat) and cardiac output. This also enables the heart to be more efficient, with a resultant lowering of the resting and submaximal exercise heart rate and blood pressure, which increases the body's exercise duration and intensity tolerance. Blood volume—both in terms of plasma and hemoglobin—increases oxygen-carrying capacity and lactic acid metabolism improves, which allows the aerobic system to more effectively metabolize substrates for usable energy. Muscle glycogen storage, another important form of energy storage in the body, also increases. Vasculature increases as well, improving the blood perfusion of muscles.

Other positive results of physical fitness include increased bone mineral density, improvements in body composition, and neural adaptations. Resistance training, even with body weight alone (such as squats and push-ups), affords strength, power, and coordination improvements and leads to greater efficiency of the anaerobic metabolic systems. Nervous system adaptations occur quickly with training as **motor units** (connections between the spine and other muscles throughout the body) become conditioned to activate more quickly and more often. As a greater number of motor units activate together and coordinate with each other, a higher percentage of fibers in a muscle contract simultaneously, increasing strength. Over time, muscle fibers increase in size and bone mineral density increases in load-bearing bones. Flexibility training increases elasticity and resting length of muscle and connective tissues and joint range of motion (ROM) before the stretch reflex is initiated (muscle spindle adaptation), reducing injury risk.

Health education – even beginning at preschool ages – has been shown to have a significant positive impact on an individual for maintaining healthy behaviors as an adolescent and adult. Preschool children who receive high-quality physical and health education may have improved nutrition and exercise habits and are more likely to receive routine medical and dental care as adults. Early childhood educators can start laying the groundwork for a lifetime of healthier behaviors and attitudes by fostering an environment of enjoyment of physical activity, an understanding of nutrition and hydration, and methods of disease and injury prevention.

Educators can talk with older children about the types, causes, and characteristics of chronic, degenerative, communicable, and non-communicable diseases, as well as ways to detect and prevent them. Students can learn about modifiable risk factors for various diseases and conditions such as diabetes, coronary artery disease, cardiovascular disease, and obesity.

Areas of Health Instruction

The Relation Between Healthy Behaviors and a Healthy Person

Early childhood educators can introduce young children to a wide variety of healthy behaviors that will help improve overall health. An important concept to begin teaching students is that optimal health is brought about through routine practice of daily healthy behaviors and an overall commitment to a healthy lifestyle. For example, educators can discuss the importance of establishing regular physical activity and daily healthy eating habits and that, through these habits, students can control their body weight and help avoid obesity. Obesity is a modifiable risk factor for many diseases including insulin-resistant Type 2 diabetes mellitus and cardiovascular disease. It is important and empowering for children to start to understand their roles and responsibilities in healthy habits and disease prevention. By giving them the necessary knowledge and tools to put the information into practice in their lives, educators can increase the self-efficacy and behaviors of even young children. In this way, early childhood educators can be instrumental in bringing about a healthier generation of young children who have an awareness of their health and an understanding of their own influence on risk factors for certain diseases. The following are healthy behaviors that can lead to a healthy body and mind:

Nutrition

Children should be taught how to identify foods and the importance of consuming a daily variety of food within each healthy food group. The benefits of trying new foods, especially those from other cultures, can help students understand diversity and challenge their preconceived notions about different cultures and flavors. Older children can learn how to prepare simple foods, recognize the USDA recommended daily allowances of each food group in order to keep the body healthy, and classify foods based on their group and health benefits. Older students can also learn about the role of various nutrients in the body such as fat, fiber, and protein, and how to select nutrient-dense foods from a given list.

Children benefit from understanding what makes a food healthy and knowing options for healthy meals and snacks. By the third grade, students can start learning how to read nutrition labels, how to compare foods based on nutrition labels, and how to modify food choices to improve healthfulness, such as replacing low-fiber foods with higher fiber choices, like opting for apples instead of applesauce. When students are in the fourth grade, educators can start talking about portion sizes and the relationship between food consumption and physical activity on energy balance and weight control. In the context of introducing the basics about calories, prevention of obesity and the ramifications of an unhealthy diet can also be discussed. Children in the fifth and sixth grades can learn about the differences in types of fats, examples of common vitamins and minerals and food sources of these nutrients, the disadvantages of "empty-calories," and how to recognize misleading nutrition information.

Physical Activity

In childhood, regular physical activity improves strength and endurance, helps build healthy bones and muscles, controls weight, reduces anxiety and stress, increases self-esteem, and may improve blood pressure and cholesterol. Children should get at least sixty minutes of physical activity daily. Typically, young children are less concerned about their physical fitness and more concerned about having fun; therefore, physical education should center on fun and play as a means to engage the body in activity. Play-centered physical education programs are an effective means to promote children's movement development and meet their requisite activity needs for health. Early childhood educators should develop physical education programs that focus on the enjoyment of movement rather than sport-specific skill mastery for two reasons. Firstly, play-centered activity will help the child be more engaged and likely to adopt a positive attitude towards exercise; and secondly, in early childhood, basic general fitness and movement skills are more important than mastery of highly specialized skills unique to certain sports. Young children also tend to lack the gross and fine motor skills and perceptual abilities needed for such highly specialized skills, which can lead to frustration or simply an inability to perform the activity.

For optimal results, it is best for early childhood educators to establish an environment of student-centered learning in regard to physical education. Because young children at any given age can have vastly different motor and physical abilities from each other, it is imperative that the educator simply set standards of enjoyment, movement, and physical discovery rather than specific mastery of skills. This prevents boredom in more physically advanced children and bewilderment and demotivation in less skilled children. It is prudent for educators to provide a variety of options within every activity and game so that children can figure out what appeals and works for them at their own developmental level. This also starts children on the path to understanding themselves and evaluating choices at a young age within a fun, playful environment and begins to get their minds processing not just what to do but how to do it as well.

Educators should use simple instructions that are age-appropriate in terms of the steps and level of complexity, visual demonstrations of movements, and drills that help reinforce the skill. During practice and exploration of the new skill, educators should focus on positive feedback and evaluation to guide the children in learning. When teaching new skills, especially to toddlers and young children, instructions lasting longer than twenty seconds or that contain more than just a couple of steps will cause students to lose interest or get overwhelmed. It is typically advantageous to have very short instructional periods interspersed between longer breaks to play and try out the skills. To help manage a large group of small, active children, simple rules and expectations should be laid out with consequences for improper behavior.

Children should learn about the methods and benefits of a proper warm-up and cool-down, how to set goals to make exercise part of their daily routine, and the benefits of physical activity. Older children can learn about the effects of exercise on the heart and how to locate their pulse during and after exercise, how to stay physically active through more than just sports, and how to create a personal fitness plan.

Sleep

Early childhood educators should talk about the importance of sleep and why parents set a "bedtime," as well as healthy sleep hygiene and establishing a sleep schedule. Children can learn about how much sleep they need and ways to improve the quality of sleep, such as physical activity and avoiding screen time before bed. Young children who may experience nightmares can benefit from learning relaxation techniques as well as talking about their fears and feelings to trusted adults.

Stress Management

Students should be educated about stress management and exposed to techniques such as mental imagery, relaxation, deep breathing, aerobic exercise, and meditation. Children can be guided through progressive muscle relaxation and should be taught signs of excessive nervousness and stress, how to manage test and performance anxiety, and when and how to get help with excessive stress.

Healthy Relationships

Healthy family and social relationships are important to overall health and happiness. Studies have pointed to a negative impact of parental fighting on a child's wellbeing, including sleep and exercise habits, nutrition choices, stress, and social adjustment. Early childhood educators should talk about aspects of healthy relationships such as communication, emotional support, sharing, and respect. Younger children should learn skills that are helpful in making friends, cultivating relationships, and resolving conflict, especially as they relate to peers and siblings. Cooperation, taking turns, using words rather than physical means to communicate feelings, and exploring feelings are helpful concepts to instill. Older children should begin to be exposed to dating etiquette and forming healthy romantic relationships. Educators should work to create a classroom environment of inclusion where students have an awareness of peers who may feel left out and work to include everyone. Within discussions of healthy relationships, educators should talk about accepting and appreciating diversity, including differences in cultures, religions, families, physical appearance and abilities, interests, intellect, emotions, lifestyle, and, in older children, sexual orientations. Life skills – such as having self-esteem, making decisions, calming oneself when angry or upset, and using listening skills – should be addressed.

Hydration

Early childhood educators should teach students about the importance of hydration and signs of dehydration as well as healthy choices for fluids, with a special emphasis on water. Children and their parents should be encouraged to send kids to school with a water bottle, and classrooms or hallways should be equipped with water fountains that children can access and use with limited supervision or assistance.

Safety Behaviors

Children should learn basic safety behaviors and the importance of following rules to prevent common injuries. Basic safety behaviors include wearing sunscreen and sunglasses when going outdoors; wearing protective gear in sports such as bicycle helmets, reflective vests, appropriate pads and cups, etc.; and using a car seat and/or always wearing a seat belt. Young children should learn about household safety such as not touching burners and not putting their fingers in electrical sockets nor opening the door to strangers. Educators should have children practice the "no, go, and tell" procedure for unsafe situations. For example, if a stranger offers the child an unknown substance, the child should know how to firmly refuse, carefully leave the situation, and tell a trusted adult. In this lesson, educators should also help children to identify trusted adults in their families and communities.

Educators can also discuss community safety measures such as using sidewalks, contacting city services (police, fire, and ambulance) in emergencies, and crossing the street safely by using crosswalks, holding hands, and looking both ways before crossing. Children should also learn about the health consequences of smoking, how to avoid secondhand smoke, and how to identify and avoid poisonous household substances. Fire safety such as "stop, drop, and roll" and emergency evacuation procedures should be rehearsed. Older children can learn about safety rules for various types of weather and how weather affects their personal safety, what different traffic signs mean, water/swim safety rules, and the importance of weighing consequences before taking risks.

Hygiene

Young children should learn about germs and the spread of infections. Older children can learn about bacteria and viruses. The importance of washing hands (including appropriate demonstration) cannot be overstated in elementary and preschool classrooms.

Other aspects of hygiene such as covering the mouth while coughing and covering the nose while sneezing, not sharing cups, practicing clean bathroom habits, showering and bathing, and, in older children, using deodorants, antiperspirants, and facial cleansers should be included in the curriculum.

Hygiene Stickers Remind Students to Use Healthy Practices

Stages of Human Growth and Development

There are five stages of human growth and development: infancy, toddler, childhood, adolescence, and adulthood. Below are the markers of each. You will find that some stages overlap.

Infancy (Birth to One Year Old)

Social development is important during this stage. Smiling and interacting with others are signs of positive social development in infants. Their motor skills will also begin to develop as they start grabbing, holding things, crawling, standing, and walking. Babies start to recognize different objects around them and the voices of their caregivers. They need consistent care and affection.

Toddler (One to Five Years Old)

Children learn to talk during this stage, which is a sign of cognitive development. They will develop better physical skills like running, jumping, skipping, throwing, and cycling. They learn to share with others and how to collaborate. This is the stage where children start participating in games.

Childhood (Three to 11 Years Old)

During childhood, children begin to show more initiative and independence. However, they may show signs of emotional attachment to certain individuals. They begin to use their imaginations more often. It's important to teach them the difference between imagination and reality at this stage. They should be encouraged to learn new skills. They start to develop relationships with those around them.

Adolescence (12 to 18 Years Old)

Puberty begins in adolescence, sparking growth spurts and changes in the body and hormones. Boys experience changes in their voices and start growing body hair. Girls will also start growing body hair, but they experience other changes like their bodies becoming curvier, the development of breasts, and menstruation. Changes in hormones cause changes in temperament, which can lead to emotional and social stress. Adolescents start developing their self-image during this stage based on their environment. Romantic relationships start entering the picture during this stage, along with sexual activity.

Adulthood (18+)

By adulthood, people begin working on careers, mental health, and fitness. They may be in long-term partnerships, and they may have families of their own. They may continue their education by going to trade schools, colleges, or other educational institutions. Stress from school, work, relationships, and other factors may develop. They may learn to handle bereavement better than they would have in earlier stages.

Substance Use and Abuse

There is a plethora of addictive substances available today. Alcohol, tobacco, recreational drugs, and even caffeine can become addictive if misused.

Someone may be abusing substances if they use them to the point of impaired judgment; have regular hangovers; regularly miss work, school, or social events after consuming substances; or they have lost relationships due to their substance use.

Teachers should keep an eye out for warning signs that a student's caregiver(s) may be misusing substances at home. They need to pay attention to the student's behavior and note if they are regularly missing school and/or seem a bit withdrawn. These children could be experiencing psychological or physical abuse. Teacher can pull them aside to have a conversation. They should be open and friendly, letting the child know that they can be trusted. The teacher should start by asking the student how they are feeling before delving into questions about how things are going at home. If need be, they should refer the student to the school counselor, who will be better equipped at having these conversations with students.

Children are observant. Because children often mimic adults, they may not know what abusive use of substances looks like. They are more likely to repeat that behavior when they come of age (or even before). It's okay to be honest, tell them what misuse looks like, and explain to them that this behavior is to be avoided. They should also be taught to recognize commonly abused substances.

Here are some substances that people commonly abuse:

Nicotine

Like many other substances, many people smoke to relieve stress or to clear their heads. This becomes a problem when those people feel like they can't function without smoking. Nicotine is as hard to stop using as other major drugs, like heroin. Using it negatively affects hormones, the gastrointestinal system, and the heart. Common side effects of using nicotine are increased heart rate, higher blood pressure, nausea, and decreased appetite.

Caffeine

Surprised to see caffeine on this list? Don't be. Globally, caffeine is the most used mood-altering substance. It can cause acid reflux, anxiety and panic disorders, psychosis, and sleep disorders. It is possible to die or slip into a coma from consuming too much caffeine. The caffeine from a single cup of coffee can linger in the body for up to 12 hours. Because caffeine is a stimulant, combining it with other substances like alcohol can cause impairment.

Alcohol

Consuming alcohol blocks neurons from traveling to the brain, which leads to intoxication, poor memory, slurred speech, and decreased motor function. Drinking too much can lead to liver damage, such as scarring, inflammation, and even hepatitis.

Opioids

Opioids are usually prescribed to users for various pain disorders. Their misuse has become a huge problem. According to the Department of Health and Human Services, two out of three drug overdose deaths in 2018 were due to opioid misuse. Using opioids slows down a person's breathing and heart rate. Misuse can cause gastrointestinal problems, slow reflexes, drowsiness, and brain fog. Some types of opioids are oxycodone, codeine, methadone, and hydrocodone.

Herbal Supplements

Herbal supplements are made from plants and have been used for thousands of years. Common forms of these products are teas, tablets, oils, and ointments. They treat a broad range of issues. However, mixing herbal supplements with prescribed medications can cause serious health problems. Kratom and salvia are two types of herbal supplements that are often misused because they cause intoxication. Younger people who use them are more likely to try more serious drugs like alcohol, cigarettes, and narcotics.

Violence and Abuse

There are many types of violence and abuse. Below are descriptions of different types of violence and abuse, and ways to counter them and get help for victims.

Physical violence involves someone using part of their body to stop or control the actions of another person. Hitting, kicking, pushing, pulling, and more are forms of physical violence.

Sexual violence involves forcing someone to participate in sexual activity.

Psychological violence happens when one person threatens another and uses fear to control them.

Verbal abuse is using language to cause harm to another person.

Neglect is when a caregiver does not provide the care or assistance to someone they are in charge of.

Cultural violence is harming someone because of their cultural practices, traditions, or religion.

Preventing violence and abuse begins at home. However, educators have some tools at their disposal to help prevent violence and abuse in the classroom that could translate to children's home lives. The first step is providing a quality education. Assigning children to mentors and after-school programs is also a helpful way to protect them from violence and abuse, as these activities teach them what it's like to work with caring adults. These adults can also become trusted confidants if the children need someone to talk to about any violence or abuse that may occur in their homes.

Educators can help victims of violence and abuse by building bonds with students. Connecting them to mental health and health services is also vital. Children may need to be connected with a counselor to help them work through emotional challenges they face as a result of violence or abuse.

Safety, Accident Prevention, and Routine Care

Prevention of Common Injuries and Health Problems

One critically important component of health and safety education is the prevention of common injuries and illnesses. By practicing safety and exercising caution, many common injuries and illnesses can be avoided. For example, wearing helmets and seat belts can reduce the risk of injury during automobile or bicycle accidents. Washing hands thoroughly and frequently with antibacterial soap can help prevent the spread of germs, and thus safeguard against viral and bacterial infections. Even very young children should be encouraged to wash hands thoroughly before and after eating, after using the bathroom, after coming in from outdoor play, and when transitioning to a new activity. It is sometimes helpful to demonstrate how to wash in between each finger, under the fingernails, and up to the wrists, modeling not only how to wash hands but for how long. The common song "Row, Row, Row Your Boat" repeated three times is sometimes used to measure the appropriate length of time for hand washing.

By instilling an attitude of mindfulness and awareness, educators can help children to develop practices of safety, which will ultimately keep them healthy. Other longer-term behavioral and lifestyle principles – such as keeping a healthy weight through caloric balance and a healthy diet – will help prevent disease risk factors such as obesity, high triglycerides, hypercholesterolemia, and high blood sugar. Children should be informed about the dangers of smoking and the detrimental health consequences of tobacco products, including ingestion of secondhand smoke. Other simple safety practices include wearing proper footwear, practicing good hygiene, remaining alert when out in traffic, using sidewalks and pedestrian walkways, and wearing sunscreen.

Wearing Seat Belts and Helmets

Children should be informed that they should always wear a seat belt in the car. Children under eighty pounds should be in an appropriate car seat as well to maximize safety in moving vehicles. Many unfortunate traffic injuries and fatalities could have been prevented had the victim appropriately worn a seat belt. Riding bicycles, skateboarding, using scooters, and rollerblading are examples of excellent exercise and recreational pursuits; however, helmets and appropriate padding and protection on elbows and knees should always be worn. Children or their supervisors often neglect to fasten on a helmet when the child is simply trying out a skateboard or scooter around the driveway or park. This is quite dangerous because falls are inevitable in the learning process and even minor head bumps can be damaging.

Helmets should fit snugly with the band clipped securely under the chin and the dome of the helmet should cover the entire forehead. Helmets should not move freely on the head and should be snug enough to stay in place. They should be sized appropriately to the child's head with use of additional padding if necessary. Kneepads and shoulder pads are great adjuncts to safety gear for rollerblading, skateboarding, and scooters. Children riding in bicycle trailers should also wear helmets, and children should never ride on the handlebars of a bicycle. Although more stable, tricycles and bicycles with training wheels still require helmets with their use.

Drugs, Alcohol, and Tobacco

Drugs, alcohol, and tobacco are unhealthy substances that early childhood educators should begin informing young children about. Exposure to drugs, cigarettes, and alcohol happens at increasingly younger ages, particularly when children have older siblings. By educating children about the risks and consequences of such substances at young ages, teachers can begin to thwart the risks of unhealthy behaviors. The Drug Abuse Resistance Education (D.A.R.E.) program is often helpful at introducing such substances, their health consequences, and how to navigate social situations involving peer pressure. The difference between alcohol abuse and alcohol in moderation should also be discussed.

Routine Preventative Medical and Dental Care

By practicing routine medical and dental care and adhering to recommended guidelines regarding the frequency of preventative healthcare, certain risks for various diseases and dental issues (such as cavities and gingivitis) can be reduced. It is typically recommended the children see their pediatrician and get dental cleanings at least once every six months. In between these appointments, healthy habits continue to safeguard against health issues. Examples include thoroughly brushing teeth at least twice a day and flossing daily, getting at least sixty minutes of moderate to vigorous exercise a day, meeting healthy sleep requirements (the National Sleep Foundation recommends ten to thirteen hours for preschoolers and nine to eleven hours for elementary school children), consuming an adequate amount of water, and following nutritional guidelines. By keeping children on a routine schedule of preventive care with consistency in providers of that care, the health and wellbeing of each child can be tracked during their growth to ensure health issues do not slip through the cracks.

Food Preparation Choices

Early childhood educators should devote instructional attention to the methods of food preparation and how various choices in preparation affect the nutritive value of the food. For example, baking and steaming are healthier than pan frying, deep frying, and sautéing. Eating whole foods is healthier than eating their processed counterparts because the whole foods retain a greater percentage of the inherent nutrients. For example, apples are healthier than applesauce because applesauce strips away much of the fiber and the vitamins in the apple skin. Similarly, whole grain bread is healthier than refined white breads, which remove the bran from the grain, thereby reducing the fiber, protein, and B vitamin content. Foods that are organic do not have the pesticides and chemicals used with certain **conventional** (non-organic) foods. This is an important consideration for thin-skinned fruits and vegetables such as spinach, tomatoes, and berries, which can absorb harmful chemicals.

Coping Strategies

Coping with the unhealthy behavior of others can be difficult for anyone, but especially students who may not have the knowledge, experience, or resources to do so in a healthy manner. Students may be dealing with caregivers who neglect or abuse them, or who engage in other toxic behavior. The following are some coping techniques you can teach students for dealing with unhealthy environments:

Help students to recognize what stress looks like for them. Stress can make people forgetful, nervous, fidgety, or short tempered. Knowing how their stress manifests can help students deal with it.

Doing a relaxing activity is a good coping mechanism. Reading, going for a walk, or playing a game are some ways children can unwind.

Teach children mindfulness, such as breathing techniques that help them calm down. They can also be taught to choose a focal point and focus on it for a few seconds at a time to take their minds off their surroundings.

For smaller children, nap time is a good de-stressor. For older students, nap time in the classroom is not a possibility, so teaching them how to wind down and fall asleep at night is helpful.

Students should be taught that their emotions and feelings when experiencing unhealthy behaviors at home are acceptable. The teacher can show compassion and tell students it's okay to feel angry, sad, scared, etc.

Journaling is another healthy coping mechanism. Teachers can give students the opportunity to journal for a set time period in class. Some students may feel more comfortable disclosing what's happening at home in their journals than in a conversation.

Children can be taught early on the importance of asking for help. Creating a safe space in the classroom makes them feel more at ease in case they want to share about abuse or other negative situations faced at home.

Eating Disorders

Some indicators that a child may have an eating disorder include stunted growth, lack of weight gain, refusal to eat, eating less than normal, restlessness, and piqued interest in food related content, like cooking shows. The following are common eating disorders and their symptoms.

Bulimia

People with bulimia will overeat, or binge, large quantities of food and then attempt to purge that food . Purging includes vomiting, using enemas, taking laxatives or diuretics, or overexercising. Symptoms of bulimia are fear of weight gain, frequent binging, frequent purging, and self-esteem that is dependent on body image.

Anorexia

Someone with anorexia typically sees themself as overweight when they actually may be drastically underweight. Some signs that someone has anorexia include constantly weighing themself, restricting calories, avoiding certain foods, fear of weight gain, and inability to see that they are underweight.

Binge Eating

Someone who binge-eats consumes large portions of food in short intervals. They may feel like they are unable to control their eating. Symptoms of binge eating include eating until uncomfortable, eating when not hungry, and feelings of shame or guilt about overeating.

Pica

Pica is the eating of non-food items, like dirt, chalk, soap, hair, cloth, or other products. It is most common in people with mental disabilities, pregnant women, and children. People with pica run the risk of accidental poisoning, vitamin deficiencies, internal injury, and infection. The primary symptom of pica is the socially unacceptable consumption of a non-food item.

Effective Communication Skills

Early childhood educators are instrumental in developing effective communication skills in their students. Verbal and nonverbal communication skills are important in setting a positive, educational, supportive environment to optimize learning. They are equally important for students to master for use in their own daily lives. When communicating with others, students should be fully attentive, make eye contact, and use encouraging facial expressions and body language to augment positive verbal feedback. Postures including hands on hips or crossed over the chest may appear standoffish, while smiling and nodding enhance the comfort and satisfaction of the other party. **Active listening** is the process of trying to understand the underlying meaning in someone else's words, which builds empathy and trust. Asking open-ended questions and repeating or rephrasing in a reflective or clarifying manner is a form of active listening that builds a positive, trusting relationship.

In tandem with different communication styles, educators and students alike should be aware of different learning styles. **Auditory learners** learn through hearing, so the educator can use verbal descriptions and instructions. **Visual learners** learn through observation, so the educator can use demonstrations, provide written and pictorial instructional content, and show videos. **Kinesthetic learners** learn through movement, involvement, and experience, so the educator can prepare lessons with hands-on learning, labs, or games with a physical component.

An important skill for children is the ability to communicate effectively with adults, and developing this comfort from a young age will be helpful throughout life. Educators can facilitate this through providing experiences where children need to talk to adults in the community. For example, educators may take the class on a field trip to the local community library, where students must ask the librarian for help locating certain health resources. Students might also prepare a health fair and invite parents, community members, and those from senior centers to come learn from posters, demonstrations, and presentations. Children can also work on developing communication skills using an array of technologies such as telephone, written word, email, and face-to-face communication.

Responses to Illness or Injury

Parents entrust schools with keeping their children safe and protected. They trust that teachers are well equipped to respond to medical emergencies in the classroom. There are several things teachers should do to be prepared for such emergencies.

CPR certification is one of the best ways teachers can prepare for classroom emergencies. If their schools do not offer this type of training, they can seek out other organizations, like the Red Cross, to provide them with it. CPR training equips teachers with life-saving knowledge that they can use in the event of an emergency in the classroom.

Schools should inform teachers of what to do if a child is injured or becomes ill in class. Schools should have specific policies in place for emergencies, and teachers should know these policies well. Teachers should know who to contact and how to keep the ill or injured child comfortable until care can be provided. If there is a school nurse, teachers should figure out the best, least-alarming way to alert them of what's happening in the classroom. If the child can move, the teacher should walk them to the nurse's office. If that is not possible, they should call the nurse and inform them of what has happened.

Teachers should have established procedures for emergencies. These procedures might include locking the classroom door until help comes, sending a student to inform the nurse or principal of what's happened, or keeping other students away from the injured or ill student.

All classrooms should have equipment and supplies for medical emergencies. These supplies should include a first-aid kit with bandages and antiseptics. A medical professional should be called if the teacher suspects a concussion, broken bone, or major wounds.

Building Healthy Interpersonal Relationships

Building healthy interpersonal relationships is a necessary skill. Teaching children how to build these relationships helps them differentiate between healthy and unhealthy relationships.

A healthy relationship consists of trust, mutual respect, honesty, and good communication. It is positive and helps young people feel valued. Below are some tips for teaching children how to form healthy relationships.

Children should learn how to establish and respect boundaries. Boundaries protect people from mistreatment and help them meet their needs and those of others. To start, instructors should ask students about things that make them uncomfortable. They should articulate exactly why these things make them uncomfortable and what others can do to help. Students can be partnered up to discuss these things, then share with the class what they have learned. Teachers should establish classroom boundaries and enforce them, such as personal space, personal property, etc.

Teachers can also ask students how they'd like to be treated in relationships as well as how they would not like to be treated. Teachers should encourage students to verbalize these desires with classmates in an appropriate way. For example, if one student complains that a classmate is making distracting noises during class time, the teacher should encourage that student to ask the classmate politely to stop because it is hindering their ability to focus. The teacher should also address the distracting student, but encouraging students to address their own concerns first helps them practice healthy relationship development and vocalization of boundaries.

Communication is the most important part of relationships. One of the most important types of communication children should learn is conflict resolution. Teachers can demonstrate how changing a few words can resolve a disagreement. They can explain that in order to make the other person feel less defensive, it's best to avoid pointing fingers, using accusatory language, and only saying, "you did ________." Instead, students should practice saying "I feel ________ when you ________."

Teachers can have their students role-play to talk about their feelings. One scenario could involve one person feeling jealous of another. One person could express what is making them jealous and the other could respond by saying how that projected jealousy is affecting them.

Instructors should help students identify people they trust who will listen to them if they are having interpersonal issues. Children want to feel heard and not judged. These trusted people may be family, teachers, friends, clergy, or others.

Environmental Influences on Health

Health behaviors are heavily influenced by a child's environment, including family, friends, peers, media, and technology. These factors can shape the child's ideas of health, nutrition, and fitness, as well as influence subsequent health behaviors. It is important for educators to help children identify and cultivate positive influences while avoiding or modifying negative ones.

Educators should work with students to develop self-efficacy for healthy behaviors to help safeguard against any negative environmental influences. Children should learn about peer pressure, substance use, wearing seat belts, and how to make independent decisions and stick to them despite peer pressure or group dynamics. Discussed below are a few examples of potential environmental and situational influences.

Family

Family factors include health insurance status, safety and injury prevention education and care, nutritional meal planning and diet composition, family dynamics and stress, family culture during leisure time such as activity vs. inactivity, childcare situation, and parental and sibling modeled behavior.

Peers

The peer group that surrounds a child can affect his or her health behaviors depending on those of the group. Example behaviors and influences include the use of helmets and seat belts, interests and activities, inclusion on sports teams or during recess and physical education, aggression and bullying or teasing.

School and Community

Factors in this domain include things such as the availability and choices of food in vending machines, school breakfast and lunch programs, health education and screenings, first aid and AED (automated external defibrillator) access, bike paths and walking trails, parks and community fitness and sports programs, crosswalks, and non-smoking zones.

Public Policy and Government

Tobacco and alcohol sales and policies, seat belt and helmet enforcement, childcare laws, and other such regulations fall under the domain of public policy and governmental influences.

Media

Media use and exposure can have a significant impact on young minds. Children have not necessarily developed the critical thinking skills needed to evaluate the truthfulness of media claims. Television programming and commercials, PSAs, advertising, exposure to celebrities, knowledge of current events, and consumer skills all fall under this domain.

Technology

Technological factors including Internet access, handicap accessibility such as audio signals at crosswalks and wheelchair ramps and lifts, health technology apps, and pedometer availability can affect health behaviors.

Sources of Health Information

Providing students with quality health education helps them develop health literacy skills. There are many sources of health information on the market for teachers to draw from.

The Centers for Disease Control (CDC) provide resources for the health education of adolescents. Many of the tips in those resources can apply to younger children. They can be found at https://www.cdc.gov/healthyyouth/health-education/tool-training.htm.

One of those resources is the CDC's Healthy Schools, Characteristics of an Effective Curriculum page. This page states that a health curriculum should have clear health goals. It provides other criteria for health education, like using research-based information, addressing individual values, and personalizing information to engage students. This information can be found here: https://www.cdc.gov/healthyschools/sher/characteristics/index.htm.

Instructors can use the information they've learned to teach students about making health-related decisions. Healthcare decisions are largely influenced by individual lifestyle, which teachers must keep in mind when educating students. They should inform students that before they make any important decision regarding their health, they should ask questions. These questions may include:

What decision needs to be made?
Why does it need to be made?
Is there enough information available to help with this decision?
When does the decision need to be made?
What specific treatments, exercises, dietary restrictions, etc., are involved?
What are the options?
What are the pros and cons?

Healthy literacy is important. Everyone needs to understand where to find health information and how to use it.

Learning to Seek Health Care

Early childhood educators can play an instrumental role in the lifelong practice of seeking routine medical and dental care as well as medical support during illness and injury by setting positive attitudes towards such care and explaining the benefits to young children. Not all children will necessarily have health insurance, so information regarding local free and affordable options should be made available to parents. It is important that children learn to identify signs of illness and injury such as sore throats, headaches, stomachaches that do not go away, swelling, etc.

Consistent Feelings of Sadness, Anxiety, Loneliness, and Stress

Just as it is important to get professional help for medical issues, it equally important to seek help with mental and emotional issues. Educators should talk about feelings and emotions and how it is normal to feel sad or anxious at various times, but that if such feelings persist, help may be necessary. Teachers can lead the class through stress management techniques to combat anxiety and talk about the role of physical activity, sound nutrition, and good sleep for mood stabilization. Young children should learn about identifying and communicating their emotions.

Lingering Pains or Aches

Children should be instructed to tell a trusted adult when they have pains, aches, or symptoms that persist for several days so that the adult can help determine if medical attention is needed. Children can also learn basic first-aid such as how to wash a cut and put on a Band-Aid or when and how to use **RICES** (Rest, Ice, Compression, Elevation, and Stabilization) after an injury.

Health Content and Curriculum Based on the Texas Essential Knowledge and Skills

Chapter 115 of the Texas Essential Knowledge and Skills (TEKS) for Health Education lays out the requirements for health education curriculum. The following are some of the requirements for early childhood through grade six.

The chapter starts off by naming the essential skills children should learn, no matter their age, from health education. These skills include maintaining healthy relationships, decision making, goal setting, problem solving, and seeking help and support.

Across all ages, students should learn about the following key areas in their health education classes:

Physical Health and Hygiene

Maintaining physical health and practicing good hygiene are habits children will need throughout their lives. Curricula should highlight how maintaining physical health and hygiene have lifelong positive outcomes. Students should learn the foundations for physical health and hygiene, along with information about body systems.

Mental Health and Wellness

The curriculum for mental health and wellness should teach students skills to manage their emotions and reactions. Teachers must go over topics such as how to identify mental health and wellness concerns, risks and protective factors, and healthy self-image. Students should be taught tips for self-regulating their behavior in reaction to their feelings and thoughts. They should also learn to resolve interpersonal conflicts with their peers.

Healthy Eating and Physical Activity

The curriculum must explain the connection between nutrition, physical activity, and healthy lifestyles. Students should be taught how to apply critical thinking skills to help them make healthy choices. They must learn about the various food groups, portion control, and the benefits of physical activity. They must also be taught the connection between eating healthy, being physically active, and disease prevention.

Injury and Violence Prevention

The curriculum should focus on preventing bullying, what to do in the event of an altercation, where to seek first aid, and exercising discernment to identify safe and unsafe situations. The goal of this education is to teach students how to keep themselves and their peers safe.

Physical Education

Key Concepts in Physical Education

Cardiovascular Endurance

The heart's ability to endure periods of physical activity is called cardiovascular endurance. According to the American Heart Association, American children's cardiovascular endurance has consistently fallen six percent per decade since 1970. However, endurance can be improved, and physical education teachers can help by incorporating aerobic exercises into their lesson plans. These exercises can include jogging, walking, jumping rope, or playing sports like basketball, soccer, or volleyball. Jumping jacks, sprints, and swimming are also forms of aerobic exercise that students can take part in.

Muscular Strength

Muscular strength is how long muscles can work and how strong they are. Pushing, supporting, and pulling are ways to test muscular strength. Strong muscles also help strengthen the bones. Walking up hills, dancing, weightlifting, pushups, squats, and sit-ups are all exercises that assess muscular strength. Some other muscular strength exercises for children are crab walks, calf raises, cartwheels, hip bridges, planks, squat jumps, and side leg raises. Developing muscular strength is important because it helps people perform everyday activities and improves fine motor skills. Improving muscular strength has also been proven to increase metabolism.

Flexibility

Flexibility measures the body's range of motion without pain or stiffness. Stretching is the best way to assess flexibility in children. It is important at all grade levels. Stretching can improve performance and prevent injury. It keeps ligaments and tendons flexible, eases sore muscles, improves posture, helps with blood circulation, and reduces stress. Anyone who sits for long periods of time can benefit from improving flexibility. Being flexible helps people move comfortably all day. Types of stretches include toe touches, neck circles, shoulder circles, arm circles, side bends, lunges, child's pose, and sit-and-reach.

Weight Control

Healthy eating habits and exercising are the best ways to maintain weight control. Controlling weight gain helps children grow and develop normally. Teachers can help students develop tools for weight control by explaining the pros of making healthy choices versus the cons of inactivity and eating unhealthy food. Teachers should highlight the importance of eating fruit, vegetables, whole grains, and lean meats, as well as drinking water. They should also go over exercises that are easy for students to practice at home to maintain physical activity.

Conditioning

Conditioning is the development of physical fitness through various exercises. Muscular endurance/strength, cardiovascular endurance, and flexibility are all components of conditioning. Conditioning will make children's bodies stronger. Teachers can show students how to condition through aerobic exercise and strength training. Conditioning exercises for children include planks, low squats, split jacks, push-ups, mountain climbers, inchworms, skips, sprints, and speed skaters.

Safety

Exercising safely is important because it prevents injuries. A common mistake people make is pushing their bodies to a point where they experience pain or injury. Teachers can show students how to exercise safely in several ways. Teachers must ensure that students are using proper form. Performing exercises in the incorrect position is unsafe, and children could wind up hurting themselves. Using the right equipment for various exercises is also important. Equipment can include comfortable clothing or the right tools for performing exercises, like weights, stretch bands, etc. Some other ways children can practice exercise safety is by warming up, stretching, drinking water, taking their time, resting, and cooling down.

Stress Management

Teachers should help students identify their sources of stress and teach them ways to manage and/or avoid it. They should describe the importance of leading a healthy lifestyle to help prevent stress. Some signs of stress in children include excessive worrying, inability to relax, recurring fears, clinginess, lost appetite, bedwetting, and trouble sleeping. To combat stress, teachers should go over the importance of sleeping well, exercising, talking about issues, quiet time, going outside, and mindfulness.

Nutrition

When teaching children about nutrition, provide them with clear facts about how what they put in their bodies affects them mentally and physically. Learning about nutrition starts in the home, but teachers can expand upon what students have learned already. One of the first things students need to learn is that healthy eating is a routine; eating nutritiously must become a habit. Teachers should show students what a nutritious meal looks like. Photos of plates filled with fruit and vegetables are ideal. Teachers should talk about portion control and limiting unhealthy foods, like sweets.

Benefits of an Active Lifestyle

The youngest students enjoy being physically active for the fun of movement itself, and they particularly enjoy non-structured activities in moderate and high intensities followed by sufficient rest. By the end of second grade, students will likely voluntarily incorporate activities from physical education class to leisure time activity and, although they are not typically concerned with structured exercise or activity recommendations for health, they do recognize the physical and mental benefits of activity and they self-select game-like play they enjoy. They are able to recognize the physiologic indicators of exercise such as elevated heart rate, sweating, and heavy breathing; they have a general understanding that physical fitness improves health, and they know that there are five components of health-related fitness: cardiovascular endurance, muscular strength, muscular endurance, flexibility, and body composition.

By the end of fifth grade, students should be aware that participation in regular physical activity is a conscious decision, and they should choose activities based on both enjoyment and health benefits. At this age, they begin to develop an awareness of resources and opportunities in the school and community to support activity and may become more interested in healthy food choices, realizing that personal responsibility and their own choices can affect their health. They also become more aware of their body and voice in a complex dynamic environment with others, and have greater focus towards controlling parts of their body and their movements within an environment with others. Students should also begin to take an interest in improving aspects of fitness for better sports' performance or health indicators, and should apply the results of fitness assessments to gain a deeper understanding of their own personal fitness and health compared with peers and standards. Older students also understand that success comes with practice and effort, and they also enjoy broadening their skills and activities by learning new sports and skills based on prior mastery. They can engage in mutual physical activity with students of differing ability levels.

Methods for Evaluating, Monitoring, and Improving Fitness Levels

Below are some methods for evaluating physical fitness in children. Each activity should be completed multiple times over the school year to track students' progress.

Walk or run one mile: To do this, teachers usually take students to a track or a large, safe, paved area and give them a set number of times to run or walk around it to complete a mile. Students will be timed and evaluated by how quickly they complete the mile. To encourage students, the teacher can walk the course with them and give them tips for preserving energy.

Sit-and-reach: This exercise measures the flexibility of the hamstring muscles and lower back. It is usually performed with a specific sit-and-reach box, but a ruler or meter stick placed between the students' feet can also be used. Students should take their shoes off and place the soles of their feet against the box or other flat surface. With their palms facing down, they extend their arms and reach as far as they can. The ruler measures how far they can reach.

Pull-up test: This exercise is sometimes referred to as the chin-up test. To perform it, students take hold of an overhead bar and pull their bodies up until their chins are above the bar. This exercise measures upper-body strength. Students with weak upper-body strength may not be able to complete a pull-up at all.

Stork test: To perform this exercise, students should stand with their feet firmly on the ground. Then, they should bend and lift one leg up until their ankle rests on the inside of the opposite leg's knee. The teacher then records how long the student can hold this pose before dropping the other foot back down to the floor.

Flexed arm hang: To perform the flexed arm hang, students stand on a stool or step and grab a bar overhead. Their grip can be overhand (palms facing down) or underhand (palms facing up). The student should then jump up from the stool or step and, with their arms flexed, hold themselves up, chin above the bar, for as long as they can. Teachers may need to assist students by lifting them up.

Pedometers: A pedometer can monitor children's fitness levels by measuring the number of steps they take over a selected period of time. The teacher should come up with a target number of steps for the students to complete during a given time period. Target rates should be different for children with different levels of physical ability.

Heart rate monitors: These devices measure pulse rates while participating in physical activity. Target heart rates should be individualized for each student. The targets should challenge students, but should not be too difficult for them to reach.

Motor Development

Educators should be familiar with physical and neurological development, especially in terms of motor skills and development, to provide developmentally appropriate motor movement tasks. As young children grow and mature, they develop the ability to handle increasingly complex motor skills. Children learn to move and move to learn and, for this reason, physical activity is especially important in the classroom for young children. As children grow, their physical abilities gradually increase, and educators can begin to modify lessons and activities to continue to challenge and improve new movement patterns and abilities. What looks like "play" actually consists of meaningful movement patterns that help the child move his or her body and use large muscle groups to develop physical competency. This is known as movement education.

Children should learn basic movement patterns and skills for daily life so that they can maneuver safely and appropriately in their environment in relation to other people and objects. After basic skills are mastered, more specific sport-related skills can be achieved. Movement competency is the successful ability of the child to manage his or her body in both basic and specialized physical tasks despite obstacles in the environment, while perceptual motor competency includes capabilities involving balance, coordination, lateral and backward movements, kinesthetic sense, and knowledge of one's own body and strength.

Educators should be able to assess the level at which students can control specific movements and identify patterns of physical activity that have been mastered. This information can be used to plan developmentally-appropriate movement tasks and activities. In addition, early childhood educators can be helpful in identifying students who seem to be lagging behind in age-appropriate motor abilities. In such cases, early intervention programming and resources may be beneficial.

There are three general categories of basic skills: locomotor, non-locomotor, and manipulative skills; more complex movement patterns combine skills from multiple categories. **Locomotor skills** – such as walking, running, jumping, and skipping – are the movement skills that children need to travel within a given space or get from one space to another. **Non-locomotor skills** are typically completed in a stationary position – such as kneeling, pushing, twisting, bouncing, or standing – and help control the body in relation to gravity. **Manipulative skills** usually involve using the hands and feet, although other body parts may be used. These skills help the child handle, move, or play with an object. Manipulating objects helps advance hand-eye and foot-eye coordination so that the child can more successfully participate in sports activities like throwing, batting, catching, and kicking.

Young children can begin to learn these skills with balls and beanbags at a less challenging level and progress to more difficult levels and activities with practice and development. Early stages usually involve individual practice first and then progress to involve partners and groups. Throwing and catching are actually quite complex skills that can be as challenging to teach as they are to learn. Early childhood educators should emphasize skill performance and principles such as opposition, following objects with the eyes, weight transfer, follow through, and, eventually, striking targets. **Motor planning** is the ability of the child to figure out how to complete a new motor task or action and depends on both the sensory motor development of the child as well as his or her thinking and reasoning skills.

Typical motor development milestones for various age groups are as follows:

Ages three to four: have mastered walking and standing and are now developing gross motor skills such as single foot hopping and balancing, unsupported ascent and descent of stairs, kicking a ball, overhand throwing, catching a ball off of a bounce, moving forward and backward with coordination, and riding a tricycle. Fine motor skills begin to progress including using scissors with one hand, copying capital letters and more complex shapes, and drawing basic shapes from memory.

Ages four to five: tackling increasingly complex gross motor skills that require some coordination and multiple movement patterns combined together such as doing somersaults, swinging, climbing, and skipping. They also can use utensils to eat independently, dress themselves with clothing containing zippers and buttons, and begin to tie shoelaces. Mastery of fine motor skills begins to progress more rapidly, including cutting and pasting, and drawing shapes, letters, and people with heads, bodies, and arms. They tend to engage in long periods of physical activity followed by a need for a significant amount of rest. Physically, bones are still developing. Girls tend to be more coordinated while boys are stronger, but both sexes lack precise fine motor skills and the ability to focus on small objects for a long time.

Children Enjoy Exercise with Games Like Tag

Age six to eight: skating, biking, skipping with both feet, dribbling a ball. By the end of grade two, children should be able to make smoother transitions between different locomotor skills sequenced together. They can also accomplish more complicated manipulative skills such as dribbling a soccer ball with their feet and can better control their bodies during locomotion, weight-bearing, and balance. Students can begin to use feedback to hone motor skills from a cognitive perspective.

Ages nine to eleven: Children begin to get stronger, leaner, and taller as they enter the pre-adolescent stage and growth accelerates with the beginnings of secondary sex characteristics. Attention span and gross and fine motor skills improve. By the end of grade five, most children can achieve more performance-based outcomes such as hitting targets and can complete specialized sports skills such as fielding baseballs and serving tennis balls. They are also able to combine movements in a more dynamic environment such as moving rhythmically to music. From a cognitive perspective, they can begin to take concepts and feedback learned in other skills or sports and apply them to a new game. An example of this is increasing body stability by bending the knees to lower the center of gravity in basketball during a pick drill; this skill can also be reapplied on the ski slope. Additionally, children begin to observe peers more and can provide feedback to others.

Modifying Instruction Based on Differences in Growth and Development

To make physical education classes more inclusive, instructors need to modify their lessons based on students' individual physical differences. Teachers need to be aware of students with disabilities and differentiate their instruction so that these students can participate and succeed in physical education class.

Instructors need to get to know their students to determine their strengths and areas that need improvement. They should not make assumptions about students' abilities, especially if those students have disabilities. Over time, teachers will figure out what strategies work best for each student.

One of the first ways to learn how to differentiate instruction is to speak with specialists, such as physical therapists, occupational therapists, or adapted physical education teachers. These professionals can provide instructors with advice for how to assess students and prepare specialized physical education.

Modifying activities is the next step. There are various ways to modify physical education activities for students of all abilities, like the following:

- Eliminating time limits
- Modeling to demonstrate the activity
- Decreasing the number of players on teams
- Allowing students to partner up
- Using lightweight equipment
- Providing balance support
- Slowing down the activity's pace
- Using balls of varying sizes
- Allowing for rest periods

Teachers can adapt rules of certain games so that students can remember them easily. Instructions for all activities should be clear, especially boundaries. Fewer rules can make activities easier to follow, especially for younger students. The instructions can also be written on white boards so that students can refer to them as needed.

Improving Teamwork

It is important that educators continually address the issues of personal and social behavior, especially as it relates to accepting and respecting differences in abilities, ideas, lifestyles, cultures, and choices. By the end of second grade, students should know how to follow the rules and safety procedures in physical education classes and during activities with little to no need for reinforcement. They also understand the social benefits of playing with others and how activities are more fun while interacting with other people. They should be able to effectively communicate during group activities in a respectful way, and enjoy working collaboratively with others to complete motor tasks or goals by combining movements and skills from many people together. By the end of fifth grade, students should be able to work independently or in small or large groups during physical activities in a cohesive and agreeable manner, understanding that the group can often achieve more than the individual alone. However, individually, the student should understand that he or she is also responsible for personal health behaviors and movements.

Promoting Active Engagement

Students who do not think physical education is relevant to their lives tend to disengage. Teachers must find ways to engage these students by making the activities fun and encouraging them to work with other students. Instructors can start by asking students upfront what activities they'd like to learn and play. This feedback should be used to inform the curriculum. Additionally, students are more likely to engage when they are in smaller groups or partnered up. Researchers from the National Center for Biotechnology Information (NCBI) have found that students are more likely to enjoy participating in activities when they do not feel like they are on display.

Instead of doing the same activities from week to week, physical education teachers need to mix up their schedules. There are numerous possibilities for classes of all ages, so there is no reason to play the same games all the time. At some point, each student is bound to find an activity that they like. Changing up the game lineup also keeps students from getting bored with the curriculum.

Playing music in the gym is another fun way to engage students and promote a positive environment. Upbeat music can improve students' moods and get them more excited about what they're doing. Playing age-appropriate music for each class is key. When students hear music that they like, they tend to be more interested in class than they would be listening to something that is irrelevant or unfamiliar to them or their age group.

Providing students with regular positive reinforcement helps keep them interested in class. Teachers should focus on what students do well and compliment them on it. Positive reinforcement is considered a teacher's most valuable tool.

Diverse Learning Needs

To address diverse learning needs, teachers need to eliminate rigid teaching patterns. There must be some flexibility in their lesson plans to accommodate the needs of each student. While accommodating the needs of each student, teachers must be careful not to single anyone out.

The Universal Design for Learning (UDL) is a system that allows teachers to personalize their instruction based on the ways that different humans learn. To implement UDL in the classroom, teachers can do the following:

Present content in different ways. Not everyone learns well via lecture. When creating a lesson plan, teachers should come up with different ways to present information to students. This could include slide shows, video clips, social media, podcasts, or visuals.

Provide students with options. To help them retain information, instructors can come up with different projects for students to complete. Instead of assigning students specific projects, allow them to pick and choose from a few options. These options might include role-playing, playing games, constructing models, creating videos, or making a presentation.

Accommodate every student. Only accommodating the needs of a few students could make them feel isolated. Teachers should consider modifications that could benefit all students. This could include making class presentations accessible for students who may not be good at taking notes or who are absent from class. This information could be posted on classroom management websites for parents or students to log in and download. Another method is offering the option of listening to certain assignments rather than reading them.

Theatre

Development of Perception Through Theatre

Certain conventions of theatre can help students further develop their perception skills. Developing these skills helps students become more aware of their surroundings and helps them make more informed decisions. Performing involves physical and cognitive processes.

Some examples of theatre conventions are:

- Using slow motion
- Adding narration
- Breaking into song
- Choruses commenting on actions
- Flashbacks and flash-forwards
- Spoken thought
- Split focus

Dramatic arts help students make connections between their environment, creative thinking, and human interaction. Perception is a combination of the students' performance and expectations.

These are some dramatic conventions that can help develop perception:

- Performing a soliloquy (a solo speech that provides insight into what an actor is thinking)
- Including narration in which an actor tells what is happening in a scene
- Using asides in which characters directly address the theatre audience
- Performing split roles or multi-roles*

*A role is called a split role when more than one actor plays the same character. An actor playing more than one character is a multi-role. A famous example of a multi-role is that of Dr. Jekyll and Mr. Hyde.

Perception is integral to acting. Getting into character helps students see from different perspectives. They experience a variety of emotions, often involving conflict and resolution. Theatre requires children to take risks, further developing cognitive skills.

Theatre also mirrors real life. Each time a child meets someone new, they present a persona. With theatre personas, children get to be different people. They must figure out how these people think and speak. This allows children to expand their worldview. Theatre also helps children practice empathy. The semantics used in theatre are said to help develop children's perception as it pertains to decision making.

Instructional Strategies

Theater-in-Education (TIE)

This is performed by teachers and students using curriculum material or social issues. Participants take on roles that enable them to explore and problem-solve in a flexible structure that is also educational. TIE productions are conducted with clear educational objectives, such as teaching facts or communicating a lesson to the audience.

Puppetry

Puppetry can be used for creative drama with either simple puppets and stages made of bags, cardboard, socks, or more elaborate, artistic materials. Using puppets in theater allows students to tell stories about a wide variety of characters and settings without requiring large and complex costumes, props, or sets. Telling stories with puppets also allows children to develop their motor skills.

More formal theater works for children are typically product-oriented and audience-centered, and children can be either participants or audience members. Such forms may include the following:

Traditional Theater
Actors use characters and storylines to communicate, and the audience laughs, applauds, or provides other feedback. The performers and audience are separate entities and the acting takes place on a stage, supported by technical workers.

Participation Theater
Students can engage their voices or bodies in the work by contributing ideas, joining the actors, or contributing in other ways. This is more interactive than traditional theater.

Story Theater
Often told with simple sets, story theater can take place easily in the classroom with minimal scenery and costumes. Due to the sparse use of sets, props, and costumes, story theater often incorporates improvisational strategies to communicate character and setting to the audience. The actors function as characters and narrators and play multiple parts, often commenting on their own actions in their roles.

Readers' Theater
Readers perform a dramatic presentation while reading lines (typically from children's literature), enabling performance opportunities in the absence of elaborate staging or script memorization. This allows students to focus on emotional expression and speaking skills while reading their lines. The students can sit or stand but no movement is needed.

Readers' Theater

Elements of Theatre, Theatre Occupations, and Creating Theatrical Productions

Elements of Theatre
The elements of theatre are:

Dramatic play: Assuming and performing various roles
Expressive movement: Using the body to express a story
Voice: Communicating through speech and song
Characterization: Creating fictional characters

Dramatic play, or sociodramatic play, is when students role-play. For example, one child pretends to be a doctor while another pretends to be a patient. The children imitate actions that they've observed someone else doing.

Children can practice expressive movement through dance. This can be done through dancing freely, allowing children to express their own creativity through their movements, or they can learn choreographed actions or dances that are often used to tell stories or evoke emotion.

An actor's voice tells the audience many things about them. It expresses tone, attitude, personality, and more. The use of inflection is an integral part when telling stories. Students should learn how to express a variety of emotions with their voices.

Characterization, or the creation of fictional characters, involves assigning specific traits, movements, gestures, and voices to each performer. When students are assigned a character, they should be taught to emulate that character in each of these ways. Remind students that one of the goals of theatre is to engage the audience in the story, which can only be done effectively when the characters are portrayed consistently and convincingly.

Theatre Occupations

For children interested in pursuing theatre when they grow up, it's helpful to inform them of the different occupations available. They should know that there are several roles other than actors, such as playwrights, set designers, stage crew members, lighting technicians, producers, directors, stage managers, marketing strategists, choreographers, and sound engineers. Other careers include box office staff, ticket agents, shop attendants, and drama therapists.

Once students learn about the various careers, teachers can assign them projects to research the details of each role and present their findings to the class. Once they understand the roles these different occupations play in creating theatrical productions, they will be able to put together productions of their own.

Putting on a Production

When putting on a production with an entire class, assign students different jobs so that they understand how those jobs work. Choose actors, choreographers, sound engineers (for smaller children, this could just be using musical instruments like drums, triangles, etc.), and directors. Put some children in charge of marketing the play; this could just mean making signs for the play or writing mock emails about the performances.

Theatrical performances help children develop self-confidence, develop problem-solving skills, and learn to work in teams. It also allows them to use their imaginations and be creative. Giving them a task like putting on a play improves their language and communication skills, and it also makes them practice concentration.

Integrating Theatre with Other Subjects

Integrating theatre into other subjects can make them more digestible and enjoyable for students. For example, performing skits to teach children other languages helps them remember terminology by creating concrete images. Students can also put on their own in-class plays to demonstrate their knowledge of languages by dressing up in costumes and using props to tell stories.

Performing can help children prepare for vocabulary tests. Teachers can assign students words and put them into groups, then ask them to write and put on performances that use the words correctly. This helps enforce their knowledge of the terms.

Using improv to teach novels is a fun activity for teachers and students. Teachers can select scenes from age-appropriate texts and ask students to improvise how they think that scene would have gone in real life. Improv can also be used to write new scenes that they think should be added to the storylines.

Acting helps children demonstrate reading comprehension. Students can be put into groups and then act out a particular scene in a book to show how they interpreted it. The teacher can then assess whether the students understood what was happening in the story. This same method can be used in history and science classes. It encourages interaction and collaboration between students and demonstrates their knowledge of each topic.

Technical Elements of Theatre

The technical elements in theatre are everything that make a staged production possible. Lighting, scenery, sound, costumes, and props all work together to create the setting and mood of a play. If one of these elements is incomplete, it can ruin the quality of the entire production. Putting on a production is an exercise in collaboration for students of all ages.

In theatre, everyone has a job. To help students identify and use technical elements properly, they should be assigned specific jobs in production. These jobs can be to control the sound, turn on the lights, build and design the set, or assign costumes.

Characterization, mood, theme, and setting are important elements of performance that are affected by the technical side of theatre. Characterization is the creation of fictional characters. Mood is the overall feeling or state of mind. The theme is the primary topic of the play. Setting is where the story takes place. Students must be able to define these elements in order to create a story.

To help students remember the definitions of story elements, teachers can use flash cards and writing exercises to teach them to students. They can also have students put on small performances and then ask their peers to identify the story elements when they are finished.

Technical theatre helps shy students come out of their shells. By putting them in social situations where they'll have to interact with the rest of the production crew, they'll exercise communication skills and develop friendships.

Practice Quiz

1. Non-locomotor skills are best defined as what?
    a. Skills that move an individual from one point to another
    b. Skills used to propel or receive an object
    c. Skills of stability that require little or no movement
    d. Skills that include responding and moving with the beat, tempo, or pitch of music

2. Which of the following techniques is NOT proven to help maximize participation in physical education?
    a. Activity modification
    b. Multiactivity designs
    c. Punitive discipline measures
    d. Differentiated forms of grouping

3. Which of the following factors affect a student's development and fitness?
    a. Societal influences
    b. Psychological influences
    c. Cultural influences
    d. All of the above

4. What is the best definition of *expressive movement* in theater?
    a. Responding with your body to rhythm or using facial expressions to communicate
    b. Clothing and accessories worn by actors to portray a character
    c. Any articles used as part of a production
    d. Theatrical equipment, such as backdrops and platforms

5. Setting clear expectations is one way teachers can help foster healthy relationships with students and parents. Which of the following is NOT a strategy that teachers should employ to foster positive relationships?
    a. Consistent positive reinforcement
    b. Closed lines of communication
    c. Encouraging active listening
    d. Practicing empathetic listening

See answers on next page.

Answer Explanations

1. C: Non-locomotor skills do not require much movement. Locomotor skills, Choice *A*, move an individual from one point to another. Manipulative skills, Choice *B*, are used to propel or receive an object. And rhythmic skills, Choice *D*, include responding and moving with the beat, tempo, or pitch of music.

2. C: Punitive discipline measures can actually stunt any kind of educational growth. Choices *A* (activity modification), *B* (multiactivity designs), and *D* (differentiated forms of grouping) are all best practices in physical education.

3. D: Choices *A* (societal influences), *B* (psychological influences), and *C* (cultural influences) all affect a student's development and fitness.

4. A: Responding to your body with rhythm or using facial expressions to communicate is the definition of *expressive movement.* Choice *B* (clothing and accessories worn by actors to portray a character), Choice *C* (any articles used as part of a production), and Choice *D* (theatrical equipment, such as backdrops and platforms) are not examples of expressive movement.

5. B: Closed lines of communication can shut students and parents out. Choices *A* (consistent positive reinforcement), *C* (encouraging active listening), and *D* (practicing empathetic listening) can all help foster healthy relationships with students and parents.

TExES 391 Practice Test #1

English Language Arts and Reading

1. What contributes the most to schema development?
   a. Reading comprehension
   b. Structural analysis
   c. Written language
   d. Background knowledge

2. Which of the following is NOT an essential component of effective fluency instruction?
   a. Spelling
   b. Feedback
   c. Guidance
   d. Practice

3. The Directed Reading Thinking Activity (DRTA) method helps students to do what?
   a. Build prior knowledge by exploring audiovisual resources before a reading
   b. Predict what will occur in a text and search the text to verify the predictions
   c. Identify, define, and review unfamiliar terms
   d. Understand the format of multiple types and genres of text

4. A teacher assigns a writing prompt in order to assess her students' reading skills. Which of the following can be said about this form of reading assessment?
   a. It is the most beneficial way to assess reading comprehension.
   b. It is invalid because a student's ability to read and write are unrelated.
   c. It is erroneous since the strength of a student's reading and writing vocabulary may differ.
   d. It is the worst way to assess reading comprehension.

5. When does scaffolded reading occur?
   a. A student hears a recording of herself reading a text in order to set personal reading goals.
   b. A student receives assistance and feedback on strategies to utilize while reading.
   c. A student is given extra time to find the answers to predetermined questions.
   d. A student is pulled out of a class to receive services elsewhere.

6. What are the three interconnected indicators of reading fluency?
   a. Phonetics, word morphology, and listening comprehension
   b. Accuracy, rate, and prosody
   c. Syntax, semantics, and vocabulary
   d. Word exposure, phonetics, and decodable skills

7. Which of the following about effective independent reading is NOT true?
   a. Students should read texts that are below their reading levels during independent reading.
   b. Students need to first demonstrate fluency before reading independently.
   c. Students who don't yet display automaticity should whisper to themselves when reading aloud.
   d. Students who demonstrate automaticity in decoding should be held accountable during independent reading.

8. Timed oral reading can be used to assess which of the following?
   a. Phonics
   b. Listening comprehension
   c. Reading rate
   d. Background knowledge

9. Syntax is best described as what?
   a. The arrangement of words into sentences
   b. The study of language meaning
   c. The study of grammar and language structure
   d. The proper formatting of a written text

10. What do informal reading assessments allow that standardized reading assessments do NOT allow?
   a. The application of grade-level norms toward a student's reading proficiency
   b. The personalization of reading assessments in order to differentiate instruction based on the needs of individual students
   c. The avoidance of partialities in the interpretation of reading assessments
   d. The comparison of an individual's reading performance to that of other students in the class

11. When building a class library, a teacher should be cognizant of the importance of what?
   a. Providing fiction that contains concepts relating to the background knowledge of all students in the class.
   b. Utilizing only nonfictional text that correlates to state and national standards in order to reinforce academic concept knowledge.
   c. Utilizing a single genre of text in order to reduce confusion of written structures.
   d. Including a wide range of fiction and nonfiction texts at multiple reading levels.

12. Samantha is in second grade and struggles with fluency. Which of the following strategies is likely to be most effective in improving Samantha's reading fluency?
   a. The teacher prompts Samantha when she pauses upon coming across an unknown word when reading aloud.
   b. The teacher records Samantha as she reads aloud.
   c. The teacher reads a passage out loud several times to Samantha and then has Samantha read the same passage.
   d. The teacher uses read-alouds and verbalizes contextual strategies that can be used to identify unfamiliar words.

13. Reading fluency is best described as the ability to do what?
   a. Read smoothly and accurately
   b. Comprehend what is read
   c. Demonstrate phonetic awareness
   d. Properly pronounce a list of words

14. Poetry is often an effective device when teaching what skill?
   a. Fluency
   b. Spelling
   c. Writing
   d. Word decoding

15. A teacher needs to assess students' accuracy in reading high frequency and irregular sight words that are grade-appropriate. Which of the following strategies would be most appropriate for this purpose?

a. The teacher gives students a list of words to study for a spelling test that will be administered the following week.
b. The teacher allows students to bring their favorite books from home and has them read their selected text aloud independently.
c. The teacher administers the Stanford structural analysis assessment to determine students' rote memory and application of morphemes contained within the words.
d. The teacher records how many words each student reads correctly when reading aloud a list of teacher-selected, grade-appropriate words.

16. What type of texts are considered nonfiction?

a. Folktales
b. Memoirs
c. Fables
d. Short stories

17. What is a summative assessment?

a. A formal assessment that is given at the end of a unit of study
b. An informal assessment that is given at the end of a unit of study
c. An assessment that is given daily and is usually only a few questions in length, based on the day's objective
d. An assessment given at the end of the week that is usually based on observation

18. How are typographic features useful when teaching reading comprehension?

a. Typographic features are graphics used to illustrate the story and help students visualize the text.
b. Typographic features give the answers in boldfaced print.
c. Typographic features are not helpful when teaching reading comprehension and should not be used.
d. Typographic features such as boldface, italics, and subheadings can be used to highlight important vocabulary or content or indicate changes in topics.

19. What do English language learners need to identify prior to comprehending text?

a. Vocabulary
b. Figurative language
c. Author's purpose
d. Setting

20. What kind of assessment is most beneficial for students with special needs?

a. Frequent and ongoing
b. Weekly
c. Monthly
d. Summative assessments only at the end of a unit of study

21. Which is NOT a reason why independent reading is important for developing reading comprehension?

a. To develop a lifelong love of reading
b. To encourage students to read a genre they enjoy
c. So that students can read at their own pace
d. To visit the reading corner, which is an area of the classroom that is restful and enjoyable

22. Why are purposeful read-alouds by a teacher important to enhance reading comprehension?
    a. They encourage students to unwind from a long day and reading lesson.
    b. They encourage students to listen for emphasis and tone.
    c. They encourage students to compare the author's purpose to the teacher's objective.
    d. They encourage students to work on important work from earlier in the day while listening to a story.

23. Which of the following is the study of what words mean in certain situations?
    a. Morphology
    b. Pragmatics
    c. Syntax
    d. Semantics

24. What is "text evidence" when referring to answering a comprehension question?
    a. Taking phrases directly from the text itself to answer a question
    b. Using a variety of resources to find the answer
    c. Using technology and websites to locate an answer
    d. Paraphrasing and using a student's own words to answer the question

25. What allows readers to effectively translate print into recognizable speech?
    a. Fluency
    b. Spelling
    c. Phonics
    d. Word decoding

26. Which of the following is the MOST important reason why group-based discussions in the classroom enhance reading comprehension?
    a. They promote student discussions without the teacher present.
    b. They promote student discussions with a friend.
    c. They promote student discussions so that those who didn't understand the text can get answers from another student.
    d. They give all students a voice and allow them to share their answers, rather than one student sharing an answer with the class.

27. Which of the following is NOT useful when initially helping students understand and comprehend a piece of text?
    a. Graphic organizers
    b. Note-taking
    c. Small intervention groups
    d. Extension projects and papers

28. Why are intervention groups important to advanced learners?
    a. They are not useful, as they do not need intervention in a particular skill.
    b. They can be used to teach struggling students.
    c. They can be given more advanced and complex work.
    d. They can be given tasks to do in the classroom while others are meeting for intervention.

29. Which of the following can be useful when working with intervention groups of struggling readers?
    a. Having the teacher read aloud a text to the students while they take notes
    b. Having students read the text silently
    c. Assigning independent work and explaining the directions in detail
    d. Providing games for them to play while the teacher observes

30. What should be taught and mastered first when teaching reading comprehension?
   a. Theme
   b. Word analysis and fluency
   c. Text evidence
   d. Writing

31. What is the method called that teachers use before and after reading to improve critical thinking and comprehension?
   a. Self-monitoring comprehension
   b. KWL charts
   c. Metacognitive skills
   d. Directed reading-thinking activities

32. When a student looks back at a previous reading section for information, he or she is using which of the following?
   a. Self-monitoring comprehension
   b. KWL charts
   c. Metacognitive skills
   d. Directed reading-thinking activities

33. Which choice of skills is NOT part of Bloom's Taxonomy?
   a. Remembering and understanding
   b. Applying and analyzing
   c. Listening and speaking
   d. Evaluating and creating

34. What is the spelling stage of a student who looks at a word and is able to tell the teacher that the letters spell C-A-T, but who cannot actually say the word?
   a. Alphabetic Spelling
   b. Within Word Pattern Spelling
   c. Derivational Relations Spelling
   d. Emergent Spelling

35. Predicting, Summarizing, Questioning, and Clarifying are steps of what?
   a. Reciprocal teaching
   b. Comprehensive teaching
   c. Activation teaching
   d. Summative teaching

36. When a student asks, "What do I know?", "What do I want to know?", and "What have I learned?" and records the answers in a table, he or she is using which of the following?
   a. Self-monitoring comprehension
   b. KWL charts
   c. Metacognitive skills
   d. Directed reading-thinking activities

37. What technique might an author use to let the reader know that the main character was in a car crash as a child?
    a. Point of view
    b. Characterization
    c. Figurative language
    d. Flashback

38. A graphic organizer is a method of achieving what?
    a. Integrating knowledge and ideas
    b. Generating questions
    c. Determining point of view
    d. Determining the author's purpose

39. A student is trying to decide if a character is telling the truth about having stolen candy. After the student reads that the character is playing with an empty candy wrapper in her pocket, the student decides the character is guilty. This is an example of what?
    a. Flashback
    b. Making inferences
    c. Style
    d. Figurative language

40. What is the method of categorizing text by its structure and literary elements called?
    a. Fiction
    b. Nonfiction
    c. Genre
    d. Plot

41. A reader is distracted from following a story because he's having trouble understanding why a character has decided to cut school, so the reader jumps to the next page to find out where the character is headed. This is an example of what?
    a. Self-monitoring comprehension
    b. KWL charts
    c. Metacognitive skills
    d. Directed reading-thinking activities

42. Phonemic Awareness, Phonics, Fluency, Vocabulary, and Comprehension are the five basic elements of what?
    a. Bloom's Taxonomy
    b. Spelling instruction
    c. Reading education
    d. Genre

43. A child reads the story "Little Red Riding Hood" aloud. He easily pronounces the words, uses an apprehensive tone to show that the main character should not be leaving the path, adds a scary voice for the Big Bad Wolf, and reads the story at a pace that engages the class. What are these promising signs of?
    a. Reading fluency
    b. Phonemic awareness
    c. Reading comprehension
    d. Working memory

44. A student is trying to read the word *preferred*. She first recognizes the word *red* at the end, then sounds out the rest of the word by breaking it down into "pre," then "fer," then "red." Finally she puts it together and says "preferred." This student is displaying what attribute?

a. Phonemic awareness
b. Phonics
c. Fluency
d. Vocabulary

45. A class silently reads a passage on the American Revolution. Once they are done, the teacher asks who were the two sides fighting, why were they fighting, and who won. What skill is the teacher gauging?

a. Orthographic development
b. Fluency
c. Comprehension
d. Phonics

Mathematics

1. Simplify: $\frac{4a^{-1}b^3}{a^4b^{-2}} \times \frac{3a}{b}$?

a. $12a^3b^5$
b. $12\frac{b^4}{a^4}$
c. $\frac{12}{a^4}$
d. $7\frac{b^4}{a}$

2. What is the product of two irrational numbers?

a. Irrational
b. Rational
c. Irrational or rational
d. Complex and imaginary

3. The graph shows the position of a car over a 10-second time interval. Which of the following is the correct interpretation of the graph for the interval 1 to 3 seconds?

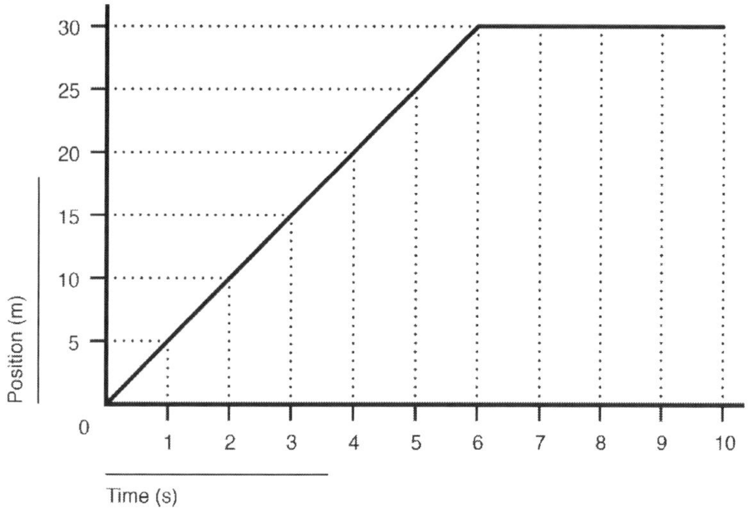

a. The car remains in the same position.
b. The car is traveling at a speed of 5m/s.
c. The car is traveling up a hill.
d. The car is traveling at 5 mph.

4. The number –4 can be classified as which of the following?
a. Real, rational, integer, whole, natural
b. Real, rational, integer, natural
c. Real, rational, integer
d. Real, irrational

5. $4\frac{1}{3} + 3\frac{3}{4} =$
a. $6\frac{5}{12}$
b. $8\frac{1}{12}$
c. $8\frac{2}{3}$
d. $7\frac{7}{12}$

6. Five of six numbers have a sum of 25. The average of all six numbers is 6. What is the sixth number?
a. 8
b. 10
c. 11
d. 12

7. 4.67 miles is equivalent to how many kilometers to three significant digits? Use the conversion 1 mi=1.609 km.
a. 7.514 km
b. 7.51 km
c. 2.90 km
d. 2.902 km

8. If $\frac{5}{2} \div \frac{1}{3} = n$, then n is between:

a. 5 and 7
b. 7 and 9
c. 9 and 11
d. 3 and 5

9. A closet is filled with red, blue, and green shirts. If $\frac{1}{3}$ of the shirts are green and $\frac{2}{5}$ are red, what fraction of the shirts are blue?

a. $\frac{4}{15}$
b. $\frac{1}{5}$
c. $\frac{7}{15}$
d. $\frac{1}{2}$

10. Shawna buys $2\frac{1}{2}$ gallons of paint. If she uses $\frac{1}{3}$ of it on the first day, how much does she have left?

a. $1\frac{5}{6}$ gallons
b. $1\frac{1}{2}$ gallons
c. $1\frac{2}{3}$ gallons
d. 2 gallons

11. How would $\frac{4}{5}$ be written as a percent?

a. 40%
b. 125%
c. 90%
d. 80%

12. What are all the factors of 12?

a. 12, 24, 36
b. 1, 2, 4, 6, 12
c. 12, 24, 36, 48
d. 1, 2, 3, 4, 6, 12

13. At the beginning of the day, Xavier has 20 apples. At lunch, he meets his sister Emma and gives her half of his apples. After lunch, he stops by his neighbor Jim's house and gives him 6 of his apples. He then uses $\frac{3}{4}$ of his remaining apples to make an apple pie for dessert at dinner. At the end of the day, how many apples does Xavier have left?

a. 4
b. 6
c. 2
d. 1

14. How would the number 847.89632 be written if rounded to the nearest hundredth?
   a. 847.90
   b. 900
   c. 847.89
   d. 847.896

15. What is the sum of $\frac{1}{3}$ and $\frac{2}{5}$?
   a. $\frac{3}{8}$
   b. $\frac{11}{15}$
   c. $\frac{11}{30}$
   d. $\frac{4}{5}$

16. Add and express in reduced form: $\frac{5}{12} + \frac{4}{9}$
   a. $\frac{9}{17}$
   b. $\frac{1}{3}$
   c. $\frac{31}{36}$
   d. $\frac{3}{5}$

17. Divide and reduce: $\frac{4}{13} \div \frac{27}{169}$
   a. $\frac{52}{27}$
   b. $\frac{51}{27}$
   c. $\frac{52}{29}$
   d. $\frac{51}{29}$

18. Express $54/15$ as a mixed number, reduced to lowest terms.
   a. $3\frac{3}{5}$
   b. $3\frac{1}{15}$
   c. $3\frac{3}{54}$
   d. $3\frac{1}{54}$

19. In the problem $5 \times 6 + 4 \div 2 - 1$, which operation should be completed first?
   a. Multiplication
   b. Addition
   c. Division
   d. Subtraction

20. Express $8\ 3/7$ as an improper fraction.
   a. $\frac{11}{7}$
   b. $\frac{21}{8}$
   c. $\frac{5}{3}$
   d. $\frac{59}{7}$

21. Express $11\ 5/8$ as an improper fraction.
   a. $\frac{55}{8}$
   b. $\frac{93}{8}$
   c. $\frac{16}{11}$
   d. $\frac{19}{5}$

22. Round to the nearest tenth: 8.067.
   a. 8.07
   b. 8.1
   c. 8.00
   d. 8.11

23. When rounding 245.2678 to the nearest thousandth, which place value would be used to decide whether to round up or round down?
   a. Ten-thousandths
   b. Thousandths
   c. Hundredths
   d. Thousands

24. Simplify $1.2 \times 10^{12} \div 3.0 \times 10^{8}$ and write the result in scientific notation.
   a. 0.4×10^{4}
   b. 4.0×10^{4}
   c. 4.0×10^{3}
   d. 3.6×10^{20}

25. You measure the width of your door to be 36 inches. The true width of the door is 35.75 inches. What is the relative error in your measurement?
   a. 0.7%
   b. 0.007%
   c. 0.99%
   d. 0.1%

26. The phone bill is calculated each month using the equation $c = 50g + 75$. The cost of the phone bill per month is represented by c, and g represents the gigabytes of data used that month. What is the value and interpretation of the slope of this equation?
   a. 75 dollars per day
   b. 75 gigabytes per day
   c. 50 dollars per day
   d. 50 dollars per gigabyte

27. Mom's car drove 72 miles in 90 minutes. How fast did she drive in feet per second?
   a. 0.8 feet per second
   b. 48.9 feet per second
   c. 0.009 feet per second
   d. 70.4 feet per second

28. $3\frac{2}{3} - 1\frac{4}{5} =$
   a. $1\frac{13}{15}$
   b. $\frac{14}{15}$
   c. $2\frac{2}{3}$
   d. $\frac{4}{5}$

29. 20 is 40% of what number?
   a. 50
   b. 8
   c. 200
   d. 5,000

30. Which equation is NOT a function?
   a. $y = |x|$
   b. $y = x^2$
   c. $x = 3$
   d. $y = 4$

31. What is the domain for the function $y = \sqrt{x}$?
   a. All real numbers
   b. $x \geq 0$
   c. $x > 0$
   d. $y \geq 0$

32. Jessica buys 10 cans of paint. Red paint costs $1 per can, and blue paint costs $2 per can. In total, she spends $16. How many red cans did she buy?
   a. 2
   b. 3
   c. 4
   d. 5

33. Which of the following is NOT a way to write 40 percent of N?
   a. $(0.4)N$
   b. $\frac{2}{5}N$
   c. 40
   d. $\frac{4}{10}N$

34. Four people split a bill. The first person pays for $\frac{1}{5}$, the second person pays for $\frac{1}{4}$, and the third person pays for $\frac{1}{3}$. What fraction of the bill does the fourth person pay?

a. $\frac{13}{60}$
b. $\frac{47}{60}$
c. $\frac{1}{4}$
d. $\frac{4}{15}$

35. 6 is 30% of what number?

a. 18
b. 20
c. 24
d. 26

36. $52.3 \times 10^{-3} =$

a. 0.00523
b. 0.0523
c. 0.523
d. 523

37. Which of the following numbers has the greatest value?

a. 1.4378
b. 1.07548
c. 1.43592
d. 0.89409

38. The value of 6×12 is the same as:

a. $2 \times 4 \times 4 \times 2$
b. $7 \times 4 \times 3$
c. $6 \times 6 \times 3$
d. $3 \times 3 \times 4 \times 2$

39. This chart indicates how many sales of CDs, vinyl records, and MP3 downloads occurred over the last year. Approximately what percentage of the total sales was from CDs?

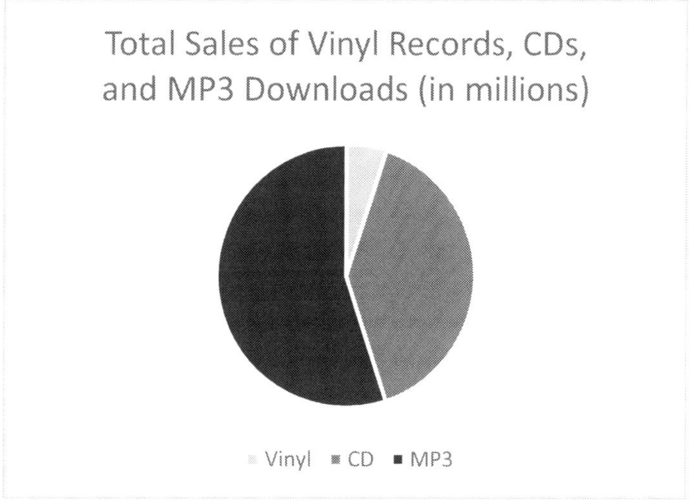

a. 55%
b. 25%
c. 40%
d. 5%

40. After a 20% sale discount, Frank purchased a new refrigerator for $850. How much did he save compared to the original price?

a. $170
b. $212.50
c. $105.75
d. $200

Social Studies

1. Which of the following correctly lists the Thirteen Colonies?

a. Connecticut, Delaware, Georgia, Maryland, Massachusetts, New Hampshire, New Jersey, New York, North Carolina, Pennsylvania, Rhode Island, South Carolina, Virginia
b. Carolina, Connecticut, Delaware, Maryland, Massachusetts, New Hampshire, New Jersey, New York, Ohio, Pennsylvania, Rhode Island, Virginia, West Virginia
c. Connecticut, Delaware, Georgia, Maine, Massachusetts, New Hampshire, New Jersey, New York, North Carolina, South Carolina, Pennsylvania, Vermont, Virginia
d. Canada, Connecticut, Delaware, Georgia, Florida, Maryland, Massachusetts, New Hampshire, New York, North Carolina, Rhode Island, South Carolina, Virginia

2. Which of the following was NOT an issue contributing to the American Revolution?

a. Increased taxes on the colonies
b. Britain's defeat in the French and Indian War
c. The stationing of British soldiers in colonists' homes
d. Changes in class relations

3. The election of a presidential candidate from which party led to the Civil War?
   a. Democrat
   b. Whig
   c. Republican
   d. Federalist

4. Which of the following was NOT an important invention in the twentieth century?
   a. Airplanes
   b. Telegraph
   c. Television
   d. Computers

5. Which of the following sets includes a primary cause and effect of the American Revolution?
   a. A cause was the taxation of the colonies, and an effect was the civil rights movement.
   b. A cause was the Declaration of Independence, and an effect was the Constitution.
   c. A cause was the French and Indian War, and an effect was the Bill of Rights.
   d. A cause was the debate over slavery, and an effect was the Seven Years' War.

6. What are the two main parts of the federal legislative branch?
   a. President and vice president
   b. Federal and state
   c. District court and court of appeals
   d. Senate and House of Representatives

7. What was a concern that George Washington warned of in his Farewell Address?
   a. The danger of political parties
   b. To be prepared to intervene in Europe's affairs
   c. The abolition of slavery
   d. To protect states' rights through sectionalism

8. What is NOT a responsibility for citizens of democracy?
   a. To stay aware of current issues and history
   b. To avoid political action
   c. To actively vote in elections
   d. To understand and obey laws

9. Which of the following statements is true?
   a. Times zones are defined by their latitude.
   b. Eastern and Western hemispheres are defined by the prime meridian.
   c. A place is constant, while a location is changeable with the movement of people.
   d. A continent is one of six especially large landmasses in the world.

10. Which of the following statements is true?
   a. Water usage has largely shifted from appropriation to riparian.
   b. Native Americans lived in harmony with nature by never disrupting it.
   c. Cities are fully isolated environments.
   d. Invasive species can have catastrophic impacts on ecosystems.

11. Which of the following are reasons that geography is important to the examination of history?

I. Historians make use of maps in their studies to get a clear picture of how history unfolded.
II. Knowing the borders of different lands helps historians learn different cultures' interactions.
III. Geography is closely linked with the flow of resources, technology, and population in societies.
IV. Environmental factors, such as access to water and proximity of mountains, help shape the course of civilization.

a. I, II, and III only
b. II, III, and IV only
c. I, II, and IV only
d. I, III, and IV only

12. Which of the following statements is true?
a. All Native American tribes are matrilineal.
b. Japan is struggling to manage its high birthrate.
c. Shi'a Muslims traditionally follow imams.
d. Mexico's culture is deeply tied to its Protestant roots.

13. Which of the following advancements was NOT invented by Greek culture?
a. The alphabet
b. The Hippocratic Oath
c. Democratic government
d. Theater

14. Which of the following was an important development in the 20th century?
a. The United States and the Soviet Union officially declared war on each other in the Cold War.
b. The League of Nations signed the Kyoto Protocol.
c. World War I ended when the United States defeated Japan.
d. India violently partitioned into India and Pakistan after the end of colonialism.

15. Which of the following is NOT an example of cross-cultural interactions?
a. Egyptian and Mayan pyramids
b. The Spanish language
c. Styles of sushi
d. Study of Chinese culture

16. Which of the following is true?
a. The barter system no longer exists.
b. Economic resources can be divided into four categories: natural, capital, manufactured, and nonrenewable.
c. Individuals help to determine the scarcity of items through their choices.
d. According to the law of supply, as the price of a product increases, the supply of the product will decrease.

17. What is NOT an effect of monopolies?
a. Promote a diverse variety of independent businesses
b. Inhibit developments that would be problematic for business
c. Control the supply of resources
d. Limit the degree of choice for consumers

18. Which method is NOT a way that governments manage economies in a market system?
    a. Laissez-faire
    b. Absolute monarchy
    c. Capitalism
    d. Self-interest

19. Which of the following nations did NOT establish colonies in what would become the United States?
    a. Italy
    b. England
    c. France
    d. Spain

20. Which of the following statements about the US Constitution is true?
    a. It was signed on July 4, 1776.
    b. It was enacted at the end of the Revolutionary War.
    c. New York failed to ratify it, but it still passed by majority.
    d. It replaced the Articles of Confederation.

21. Which of the following locations was NOT subjected to American imperialism?
    a. Philippines
    b. Puerto Rico
    c. Canada
    d. Guam

22. What is a power that Congress has?
    a. To appoint the cabinet
    b. Right of nullification
    c. To impeach the president
    d. To interpret laws through courts

23. Which of the following is true?
    a. The Emancipation Proclamation ended slavery in the United States.
    b. President Wilson called for the foundation of the United Nations in his Fourteen Points.
    c. The Constitution of 1787 and the Bill of Rights were ratified simultaneously.
    d. The Declaration of Independence was primarily concerned with the colonists' complaints against King George III.

24. "The entire Roman Empire was destroyed in the fifth century AD." Is this statement true or false?
    a. True; it was conquered by barbarians in that era.
    b. True; it was destroyed by a civil war during that time period.
    c. False; the western half survived as the Holy Roman Empire.
    d. False; the eastern half, known as the Byzantine Empire, survived until 1453 AD.

25. Which of the statements about the United Nations is false?
    a. It ensured the continuance of an alliance between the United States and Soviet Union.
    b. It was based on the idea for the League of Nations.
    c. It helps to promote human rights.
    d. It includes many former colonies from around the world.

26. Which of the following gentlemen was NOT instrumental in leading the charge for discussion at the Constitutional Convention held in Philadelphia in 1787?
    a. George Washington
    b. Alexander Hamilton
    c. Thomas Jefferson
    d. James Madison

27. Which American Indian tribe led a nomadic lifestyle and lived in teepees that were easily moved from place to place?
    a. Plains
    b. Southwest
    c. Eastern
    d. Northwest

28. What was Britain's first permanent settlement in North America?
    a. Plymouth, Massachusetts
    b. Roanoke, Virginia
    c. Jamestown, Virginia
    d. L'Anse Meadows, Newfoundland

29. What was the controlling act imposed by the British on American colonists that taxed imported lead, glass, paints, paper, and tea, and prompted the colonies to unite against British rule?
    a. The Stamp Act
    b. The Sugar Act
    c. The Currency Act
    d. The Townsend Act

30. Where did the first shot of the American Revolution take place?
    a. At the Boston Massacre
    b. During the Boston Tea Party
    c. On Lexington Green
    d. At the Battle of Trenton

31. The Revolutionary War's final battle took place on October 19, 1781, when British General Lord Cornwallis surrendered to Washington's troops at what location?
    a. Yorktown, Virginia
    b. Valley Forge, Pennsylvania
    c. Trenton, New Jersey
    d. Saratoga, New York

32. What important US structure was burned during the War of 1812?
    a. The Washington Monument
    b. Independence Hall
    c. The White House
    d. The Statue of Liberty

33. Who was elected President of the Confederate States of America during the Civil War?
    a. Robert E. Lee
    b. Jefferson Davis
    c. William T. Sherman
    d. Abraham Lincoln

34. The period of business and industrial growth from 1876 through the turn of the 20th century was deemed by author Mark Twain as what?

a. Manifest Destiny
b. The Columbian Exchange
c. The New Deal
d. The Gilded Age

35. When did World War I begin?

a. 1915
b. 1917
c. 1914
d. 1918

36. Which of the following countries was a US ally during World War II?

a. The Soviet Union
b. Italy
c. Germany
d. Japan

37. The North Atlantic Treaty Organization (NATO) was formed between which countries or regions?

a. Canada, the US, and South America
b. Western Europe, the US, and Canada
c. The US, Western Europe, Canada, and the Soviet Union
d. Asia, the US, and Western Europe

38. Which of these events was not a driving force for the passage of the Civil Rights Act in 1964?

a. *Brown vs. the Board of Education*
b. Freedom Rides
c. The G.I. Bill
d. The Montgomery bus boycott

39. What program launched by the US government under President Ronald Reagan was designed to shield the US from nuclear attack by the Soviet Union?

a. The Strategic Arms Limitation Talks (SALT I and II)
b. The Strategic Defense Initiative (SDI)
c. The Iran-Contra Affair
d. Glasnost

40. After the terrorist attacks initiated by Islamic fundamentalist Osama bin Laden on September 11, 2001, President George W. Bush ordered bombing raids on various locations in what country in an attempt to bring down bin Laden and his al-Qaeda network?

a. Afghanistan
b. Iraq
c. Kuwait
d. Pakistan

Science

1. At what point in its swing does a pendulum have the most mechanical energy?
    a. At the top of its swing, just before going into motion
    b. At the bottom of its swing, in full motion
    c. Halfway between the top of its swing and the bottom of its swing
    d. The same amount of mechanical energy throughout its path

2. What does the scientific method describe?
    a. How to review a scientific paper
    b. How to organize a science laboratory
    c. The steps utilized to conduct an inquiry into a scientific question
    d. How to use science to earn money in society

3. The energy of motion is also referred to as what?
    a. Potential energy
    b. Kinetic energy
    c. Solar energy
    d. Heat energy

4. Burning a piece of paper is what type of change?
    a. Chemical change
    b. Physical change
    c. Sedimentary change
    d. Potential change

5. A ramp leading up to a loading dock would be considered which type of simple machine?
    a. Screw
    b. Lever
    c. Inclined plane
    d. Pulley

6. Who is credited for simplifying the laws of motion?
    a. Einstein
    b. Hawking
    c. Copernicus
    d. Newton

7. The heat transfer due to the movement of gas molecules from an area of higher concentration to one of lower concentration is known as what?
    a. Conduction
    b. Convection
    c. Solarization
    d. Radiation

8. Which of the following is true of an object at rest on earth?
    a. It has no forces acting upon it.
    b. It has no gravity acting upon it.
    c. It is in transition.
    d. It is in equilibrium.

9. When researching a problem in science, what are the best sources to use?
   a. People you have seen on television
   b. Anyone with a Ph.D.
   c. Accredited laboratories and universities
   d. Any source with an internet webpage

10. What is a change in state from a solid to a gas called?
   a. Evaporation
   b. Melting
   c. Condensation
   d. Sublimation

11. The forces acting upon an object can be illustrated using what?
   a. A Venn diagram
   b. A periodic table
   c. A force diagram
   d. A stress-strain diagram

12. Which is NOT a form of Energy?
   a. Light
   b. Sound
   c. Heat
   d. Mass

13. A projectile at a point along its path has 30 Joules of potential energy and 20 Joules of kinetic energy. What is the total mechanical energy for the projectile?
   a. 50 Joules
   b. 30 Joules
   c. 20 Joules
   d. 10 Joules

14. What factors can prompt scientific inquiry and progress?
   a. Curiosity
   b. Competition
   c. Greed
   d. All of the above

15. Which of the following is considered a force?
   a. Weight
   b. Mass
   c. Acceleration
   d. Gravity

16. Why would a pencil appear to bend at the water line in a glass of water?
   a. The wood of the pencil becomes warped from being in the water.
   b. It appears to bend because of the refraction of light traveling from air to water.
   c. The pencil temporarily bends because of its immersion into separate mediums.
   d. The reflection of the light from water to a human's pupil creates the illusion of a warping object.

17. Which of the following is NOT one of Newton's three laws of motion?
    a. Inertia: an object at rest tends to stay at rest, and an object in motion tends to stay in motion
    b. $E = mc^2$
    c. For every action there is an equal and opposite reaction
    d. $F = ma$

18. The law of the conservation of energy states which of the following?
    a. Energy should be stored in power cells for future use.
    b. Energy will replenish itself once exhausted.
    c. Energy cannot be created or destroyed.
    d. Energy should be saved because it can run out.

19. Which of the following is true regarding magnets?
    a. Opposite charges attract.
    b. Like charges attract.
    c. Opposite charges repel.
    d. Like charges do not repel or attract.

20. Running electricity through a wire generates which of the following?
    a. A gravitational field
    b. A frictional field
    c. An acoustic field
    d. A magnetic field

21. When an ice skater spins on one skate in a circle, what happens if they extend their arms out like the letter *T*?
    a. They spin faster.
    b. They spin slower.
    c. They stop spinning.
    d. Nothing changes.

22. For circular motion, what is the name of the actual force pulling toward the axis of rotation?
    a. Centrifugal force
    b. Gravity
    c. Centripetal force
    d. No force is acting.

23. Which is NOT a method for transferring electrostatic charge?
    a. Polarization
    b. Touch
    c. Election
    d. Induction

24. What does the re-radiation of solar waves trapped in earth's atmosphere contribute to?
    a. Global warming
    b. Greenhouse effect
    c. Climate change
    d. All of the above

25. Velocity is a measure of which of the following?
  a. Speed with direction
  b. The change in distance over the change in time
  c. Meters covered over seconds elapsed
  d. All of the above

26. Which of the following sources of energy are non-renewable?
  a. Wind energy
  b. Solar energy
  c. Fossil fuel energy
  d. Geothermal energy

Use the following image to answer question 27.

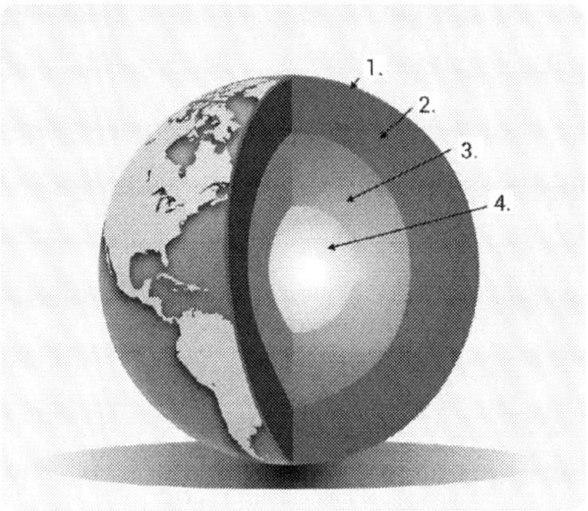

27. Which choice describes layer 4?
  a. Inner core: solid
  b. Inner core: liquid
  c. Outer core: solid
  d. Outer core: liquid

28. Which type of rock accumulates in layers at the bottom of the ocean due to run-off?
  a. Igneous
  b. Sedimentary
  c. Metamorphic
  d. Minerals

29. The water cycle involves phase changes. Which example below is evaporation?
  a. Clouds forming in the sky
  b. Rain, snow, or ice storms
  c. River water flowing to the ocean
  d. Sunlight's effect on morning dew

30. Which of the following is NOT directly caused by tectonic plate movement?
  a. Spreading of the ocean floor
  b. Earthquakes
  c. Mountain formation
  d. Precipitation

31. Which of the following statements is false?
    a. Magma circulates in the upper mantle.
    b. All volcanoes have explosive eruptions.
    b. Igneous rocks are formed by crystallized lava.
    c. Igneous rocks recycle and form magma.

Use the following image to answer questions 32 and 33.

32. Which fossil is the oldest?
    a. Dinosaur head
    b. Seashell
    c. Skeleton
    d. Grass

33. The fossils in the figure are embedded in which type of rock?
    a. Metamorphic
    b. Igneous
    c. Sedimentary
    d. Magma

Use the following image to answer question 34.

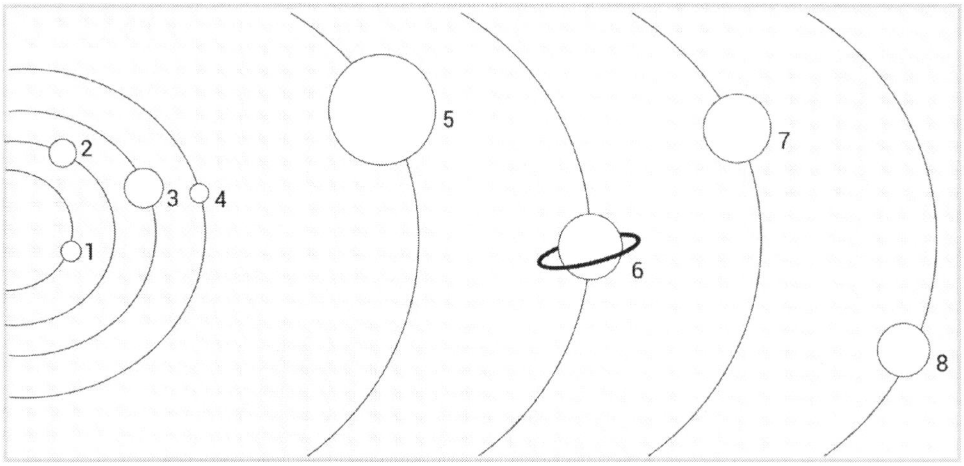

34. Where is the asteroid belt located in the figure above?
    a. Between structures #2 and #3
    b. Between structures #3 and #4
    c. Between structures #4 and #5
    d. Between each planet

35. Why is a year on Mars shorter than a year on Jupiter?
    a. Mars is much smaller than Jupiter.
    b. Mars is a rocky planet, while Jupiter is made of gas.
    c. Mars has a smaller orbit around the Sun.
    d. Mars is inside the asteroid belt.

Use the following image to answer question 36.

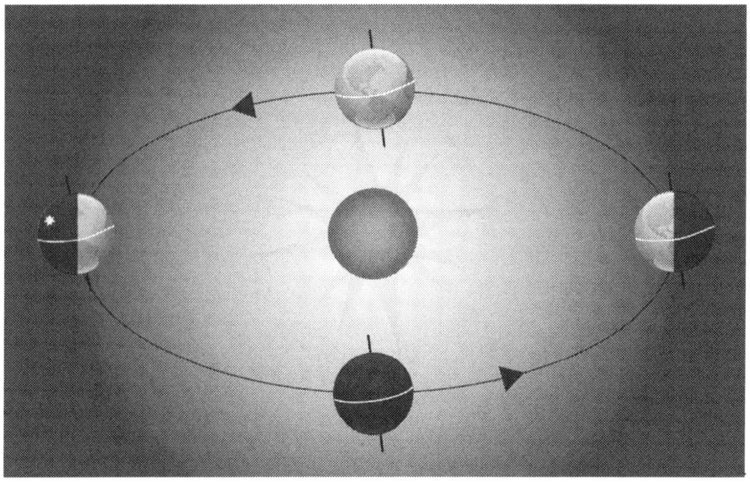

36. The figure above illustrates earth's orbit around the sun. What season is it where the dot is located?
    a. Summer
    b. Winter
    c. Fall
    d. Spring

37. Which statement(s) are true about the phases of the moon?
    a. Full moons are farther away from the sun than new moons.
    b. Crescent moons are smaller than half moons.
    c. Gibbous moons are larger than half moons.
    d. All of the above are true.

38. Why are greenhouse gases important?
    a. They allow UV rays to penetrate the troposphere.
    b. They insulate earth and keep it warm.
    c. They reflect light so that the sky looks blue.
    d. They form clouds and directly participate in the water cycle.

39. How is a theory different from a hypothesis?
    a. Theories are predictions based on previous research, and hypotheses are proven.
    b. Hypotheses can change, while theories cannot.
    c. Theories are accepted by scientists, while hypotheses remain to be proven.
    d. Hypotheses are always wrong, while theories are always true.

40. Which scientist is correctly paired with what he or she studies?
    a. Paleontologist: earth's crust
    b. Meteorologist: fossils
    c. Seismologist: earthquakes
    d. Geologist: weather

41. What part of most plants performs photosynthesis?
    a. Root
    b. Stem
    c. Leaf
    d. Flower

42. Which definition describes an ecosystem?
    a. One individual organism
    b. Rocks, soil, and atmosphere within an area
    c. All the organisms in a food web
    d. All living and nonliving things in an area

Use the following image to answer questions 43 and 44.

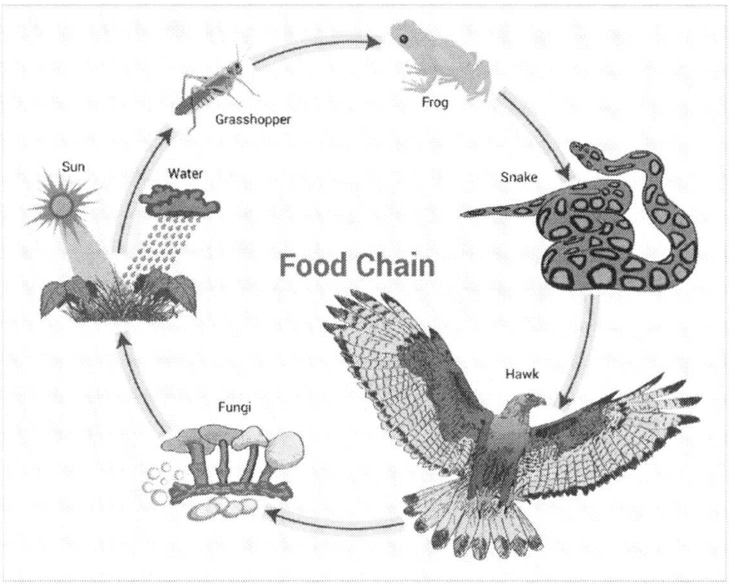

43. Which is the decomposer in the food chain above?
    a. Sun
    b. Grass
    c. Frog
    d. Fungi

44. Which is the herbivore in the food chain above?
    a. Grass
    b. Grasshopper
    c. Frog
    d. Fungi

45. What is a product of photosynthesis?
    a. Water
    b. Sunlight
    c. Oxygen
    d. Carbon dioxide

Fine Arts, Health, and Physical Education

1. Which of the following is a primary reason to provide guidance and scaffolds for art activities for children?
    a. To create an unstructured framework so students are encouraged to experiment and improvise
    b. To give students a sense of direction and purpose
    c. To help students develop of sense of how to use art supplies appropriately
    d. To set expectations that push students to become the best artists they can be

2. Throwing a tennis ball at various targets is an effective and appropriate physical education activity for students in which grade level?
   a. Pre-K
   b. First grade
   c. Third grade
   d. Fifth grade

3. Which of the following is NOT one of the five components of health-related physical fitness?
   a. Body composition
   b. Cardiovascular fitness
   c. Agility
   d. Muscular strength

4. Which of the following is true regarding neural adaptations to fitness training?
   a. Neural adaptations to fitness training are slow because it takes a long time for the body to develop additional motor units and improve coordination of existing units.
   b. Increases in muscle fiber size are the primary cause of initial strength gains, and as training progresses, motor units become more coordinated.
   c. In the early stages of training, the body will experience increases in the ease of activation and coordination of motor units.
   d. Neural adaptations to fitness training are rapidly achieved because the elasticity and resting length of muscles and connective tissues decrease and shorten, respectively, in the early stages of training.

5. Which of the following is NOT an advantage of having a completed model of an art project to show prior to the students engaging in the project themselves?
   a. It helps give the student a frame of reference from which they can work for the activity.
   b. It helps the teacher determine an appropriate timeframe for the activity.
   c. It helps students visualize the step-by-step process that will go into the activity.
   d. It helps establish an enticing end-goal for students and can engage them in the activity.

6. A teacher is developing an art activity to demonstrate the concept of unity. She uses Vincent van Gogh's *Starry Night* (1889) painting as an example and as launch pad to discuss his contributions to the art world. The design of this lesson can best be described as which of the following?
   a. An implicit activity
   b. An explicit activity
   c. An emphasis activity
   d. A balance activity

7. The analyzing part of the performance sequence of art is best described as which of the following?
   a. The process where the performer learns as much as possible about the chosen piece.
   b. The process where the artist engages in practice and self-criticism for improvement.
   c. The process where the artist makes the piece distinct and their own.
   d. The process where the artist uses their judgment to make meaning out of the work and make it their own.

8. Young students' skills regarding responding to art is thought to be augmented effectively by which of the following evaluation methods?
   a. Formative evaluations
   b. Summative evaluations
   c. Formal assessments
   d. Self-assessments

9. Which of the following would NOT be included on a list of nutrition recommendations for children?
   a. Replace higher fat foods with lower-fat alternatives
   b. Replace higher fiber foods with lower-fiber options
   c. Reduce intake of sugary beverages
   d. Replace refined foods with foods in their more natural form

10. The optimal physical education curriculum for five- to six-year-old children should focus on which of the following?
   a. Movement for enjoyment
   b. Sport-specific skills
   c. Hand-eye coordination
   d. Low intensity, endurance activities

11. Which of the following is true regarding classroom instruction of new movement skills for young children?
   a. It should occur in one long session at the beginning of the class, followed by time for children to play and attempt the skill.
   b. It should contain many small steps for the children to keep track of during play.
   c. It should be limited to short twenty-second stretches of instruction interspersed with long periods of play.
   d. It should be given in written form so children can read it at their leisure.

12. Which of the following is a healthy lifestyle habit for children?
   a. Getting eight hours of sleep every night
   b. Keeping their emotions to themselves
   c. Following safety procedures like wearing a seat belt
   d. Brushing their teeth once a day before bed

13. Educators should teach students about the importance of visiting a doctor for all EXCEPT which of the following reasons?
   a. Routine medical care and check-ups
   b. Consistent feelings of sadness, anxiety, loneliness, and stress
   c. Pains or aches that do not go away
   d. When insurance coverage changes

14. Health insurance status, safety and injury prevention education and care, nutritional meal planning and diet composition, social dynamics and stress, and culture around leisure time are all potential health behavior influences related to which factor?
   a. Family
   b. Peers
   c. School
   d. Media

15. Which of the following is true regarding motor skill development in children?
   a. Motor skill development shouldn't begin until after kindergarten.
   b. Sports skills are learned more readily than generalized body movements such as skipping.
   c. Gross motor skills are mastered before fine motor skills.
   d. Students benefit from formal movement training rather than free play.

16. Which of the following is NOT a general category of basic movement skills?
    a. Locomotor skills
    b. Sports-specific skills
    c. Non-locomotor skills
    d. Manipulative skills

17. In a kindergarten classroom, physical education should include a focus on all EXCEPT which of the following?
    a. Hitting targets
    b. Weight transfer
    c. Following objects with the eyes
    d. Running and stopping

18. Which of the following age groups is likely to be most interested in the health-based benefits of physical activity?
    a. Two- to four-year-old children
    b. Five- to seven-year-old children
    c. Seven- to nine-year-old children
    d. Nine- to twelve-year-old children

19. Which of the following are the major categories of the arts that educators should focus curricular activities on?
    a. Music, dance, theater, visual arts
    b. Music, performing arts, visual arts, sculpture
    c. Painting, drawing, woodworking, visual arts
    d. Language arts, music, theater, visual arts

20. The youngest children just beginning in art tend to create art with a focus on which of the following?
    a. Self-expression
    b. Narrative storytelling
    c. Scientific and sensory observations
    d. Creative and artistic ideas

21. Which of the following is true of art education for children?
    a. Children should focus on learning about art from their own culture and time-period.
    b. It is important for children to see professional art before creating their own works.
    c. It is important for children to study art theory before beginning their own projects.
    d. Children should experiment with a variety of methods and materials to create art.

22. Which of the following is a way for young students to easily learn rhythm in music class?
    a. Have students memorize each song on multiple instruments.
    b. Have students sit still and focus intently on the music.
    c. Have students read the lyrics before they listen to the music.
    d. Have students accompany music with simple instruments like tambourines.

23. Which of the following is performed by teachers and students using curriculum material or social issues?
    a. Puppetry
    b. Participation Theater
    c. Reader's Theater
    d. Theater-in-Education (TIE)

24. The main skills in theatrical arts for children include all EXCEPT which of the following?
   a. Staging
   b. Literary
   c. Technical
   d. Performance

25. A three- to four-year-old child would likely create a drawing emphasizing which of the following?
   a. The emotions expressed in their work.
   b. The figural accuracy of the drawing.
   c. The symbolic meaning of their work.
   d. The colors they use and how they look.

26. Which of the following is a technique used to make flat objects look as though they have depth?
   a. Balance
   b. Perspective
   c. Optical illusion
   d. Abstraction

27. Art serves all EXCEPT which of the following main functional categories?
   a. Religious functions
   b. Personal functions
   c. Social functions
   d. Physical functions

28. Which of the following is a principle in art that highlights the similarities in separate but related parts of a composition?
   a. Contrast
   b. Harmony
   c. Movement
   d. Balance

29. What has contemporary research found about breakfast and children?
   a. Breakfast is damaging to school attendance.
   b. Breakfast spikes blood sugar in students and causes behavioral problems.
   c. Breakfast helps students do well on tests.
   d. There is no link between breakfast and student academic achievement.

30. According to the literature, why are educators being encouraged to incorporate art into the curriculum?
   a. To develop students' fine motor skills, and facilitate metacognition and abstract thinking
   b. Because there are many career opportunities in art
   c. To expose students to other cultures
   d. To offer discipline and structure

31. When developing an art activity, instructors are encouraged to do what first?
   a. Develop a model of the finished artwork or project.
   b. Establish clear learning objectives.
   c. Get clear on the overriding concept or idea that is embedded in the lesson.
   d. Offer praise and constructive criticism to the students.

32. What are the four parts of creating art?
    a. Conceptualizing, making, evaluating, and refining
    b. Imagining, planning, making, and presenting
    c. Developing, assessing, sharing, recreation
    d. Creating, revising, producing, and entertaining

33. Which word is NOT a part of the four-part process of responding to art?
    a. Selection
    b. Analysis
    c. Evaluation
    d. Assessment

34. In visual media, how is a line typically looked at or understood?
    a. A framework that can be used to provoke emotions and paint mental pictures for the viewers
    b. As the outline of a three-dimensional object, the edge of a two-dimensional object, and the path of a moving point
    c. As the outline of a two-dimensional object, the side of a three-dimensional object, and the path of a static point
    d. A symbol that represents the continuation of time and the timelessness of art

35. What is the best way to create rhythm in visual art?
    a. By repeating visual movement
    b. By the manipulation of lines and figures
    c. Through the use of illusion
    d. None of the above

36. Which color is NOT a primary color?
    a. Yellow
    b. Blue
    c. Green
    d. Red

37. What helps to create unity in a piece of artwork?
    a. An artist's intention
    b. Shape, focus, and repetition
    c. Colors, theme, pattern, and texture
    d. The reader's perception

38. Which is an example of contrast in art?
    a. Large vs. small shapes
    b. Rough vs. smooth surfaces
    c. Black vs. white
    d. All of the above

39. The speed of music is best described as what?
    a. Pitch
    b. Tempo
    c. Rhythm
    d. Range

40. The psychological benefits of physical activity include which of the following?
   a. Relief of stress
   b. Better self-concept
   c. Improved capability to handle some stressors
   d. All of the above

Answer Explanations #1

English Language Arts and Reading

1. D: A schema is a framework or structure that stores and retrieves multiple, interrelated learning elements as a single packet of knowledge. Children who have greater exposure to life events have greater schemas. Thus, students who bring extensive background knowledge to the classroom are likely to experience easier automation when reading. In this way, background knowledge and reading comprehension are directly related. Likewise, students who have greater background knowledge are able to learn a greater number of new concepts at a faster rate.

2. A: Practice is an essential component of effective fluency instruction. A student's accuracy and rate will likely increase if a teacher provides opportunities to learn words and use word-analysis skills. Oral reading accompanied by guidance and feedback from teachers, peers, or parents has a significant positive impact on fluency. In order to be beneficial, such feedback needs to target specific areas in which students need improvement, as well as strategies that students can use in order to improve in those areas. Such feedback increases students' awareness so that they can independently make needed modifications to improve fluency.

3. B: DRTA, or directed reading-thinking activity, incorporates both read-alouds and think-alouds. During a DRTA, students make predictions about what they will read in order to set a purpose for reading, give cognitive focus, and activate prior knowledge. Students use reading comprehension in order to verify their predictions.

4. C: A student's reading ability will most likely differ when assessed via a reading assessment versus a writing sample. There are five types of vocabulary: listening, speaking, written, sight, and meaning. Most often, listening vocabulary contains the greatest number of words. This is usually followed by speaking vocabulary, sight reading vocabulary, meaning vocabulary, and written vocabulary. Formal written language usually utilizes a richer vocabulary than everyday oral language. Thus, students show differing strengths in reading vocabulary and writing vocabulary.

5. B: Scaffolded opportunities occur when a teacher helps students by giving them support, offering immediate feedback, and suggesting strategies. In order to be beneficial, such feedback needs to help students identify areas that need improvement. Much like oral reading feedback, this advice increases students' awareness so they can independently make needed modifications in order to improve fluency.

Scaffolding is lessened as the student becomes a more independent reader. Struggling readers, students with reading difficulties or disabilities, and students with special needs especially benefit from direct instruction and feedback that teaches decoding and analysis of unknown words, automaticity in key sight words, and correct expression and phrasing.

6. B: Key indicators of reading fluency include accuracy, rate, and prosody. Phonetics and decodable skills aid fluency. Syntax, semantics, word morphology, listening comprehension, and word exposure aid vocabulary development.

7. A: Once students become fluent readers, independent reading can begin. Students who don't yet display automaticity may need to read out loud or whisper to themselves during independent reading time. Independent silent reading accompanied by comprehension accountability is an appropriate strategy for students who demonstrate automaticity in their decoding skills. Also, each student should be provided with a text that matches his or her reading level.

8. C: The most common measurement of reading rate includes the oral contextual timed readings of students. During a timed reading, the number of errors made within a given amount of time is recorded. This data can be used to identify if a student's rate is improving and if the rate falls within the recommended range for his or her grade level.

9. A: Syntax refers to the arrangement of words and phrases to form well-developed sentences and paragraphs. Semantics has to do with language meaning. Grammar is a composite of all systems and structures utilized within a language and includes syntax, word morphology, semantics, and phonology. Cohesion and coherence of oral and written language are promoted through a full understanding of syntax, semantics, and grammar.

10. B: Informal reading assessments allow teachers to create differentiated assessments that target reading skills of individual students. In this way, teachers can gain insight into a student's reading strengths and weaknesses. Informal assessments can help teachers decide what content and strategies need to be targeted. However, standardized reading assessments provide all students with the same structure to assess multiple skills at one time. Standardized reading assessments cannot be individualized. Such assessments are best used for gaining an overview of student reading abilities.

11. D: Students within a single classroom come with varied background knowledge, interests, and needs. Thus, it's unrealistic to find texts that apply to all. Students benefit when a wide range of fiction and nonfiction texts are available in a variety of genres, promoting differentiated instruction.

12. D: This answer alludes to both read-alouds and think-alouds. Modeling of fluency can be done through read-alouds. Proper pace, phrasing, and expression of text can be modeled when teachers read aloud to their students. During think-alouds, teachers verbalize their thought processes when orally reading a selection. Teachers' explanations may describe strategies they use as they read to monitor their comprehension. In this way, teachers explicitly model the metacognition processes that good readers use to construct meaning from a text.

13. A: Reading fluency is the ability to accurately read at a socially acceptable pace and with proper expression. Phonetic awareness leads to the proper pronunciation of words and fluency. Once students are able to read fluently, concentration is no longer dedicated toward the process of reading. Instead, students can concentrate on the meaning of a text. Thus, in the developmental process of reading, comprehension follows fluency.

14. A: The rhythmic sounds and rhyming words of some poems help build a child's phonemic awareness.

15. D: Word-reading accuracy is often measured by counting the number of errors that occur per 100 words of oral reading. This information is used to select the appropriate level of text for an individual.

16. B: Nonfiction texts include memoirs, biographies, autobiographies, and journalism. Choices *A*, *C*, and *D* are all examples of fictional prose.

17. A: Summative assessments are formal assessments that are given at the end of a unit of study. These assessments are usually longer in length. They are not completed daily. These summative assessments shouldn't be confused with informal assessments, which are used more frequently to determine mastery of the day's objective. However, summative assessments may be used to determine students' mastery, in order to form intervention groups thereafter.

18. D: Typographic features that help students locate key ideas or understand the structure of a piece of text are important when teaching reading comprehension.

19. A: English language learners should master vocabulary and word usage in order to fully comprehend text. Figurative language, an author's purpose, and settings are more complex areas; figurative language is culture-based, and inferences about purpose and setting may be difficult for those with a different cultural background. These areas can be addressed once ELL students understand the meanings of words.

20. A: Assessments should always be frequent and ongoing for all students, but especially for those with special needs. These assessments may be informal, but given daily after direct instruction and modeling. Summative assessments are important, but this should not be the first and only assessment during a unit of study, as these types of assessments are given at the end of a unit of study. Weekly and monthly assessments are not frequent enough for instructors to identify struggling areas and for successful remediation and intervention.

21. D: Although the reading corner should be a restful and enjoyable place to encourage students to read independently, it does not enhance reading comprehension directly. Choices *A*, *B*, and *C* all encourage enhancement of reading comprehension. Giving students a chance to read independently allows them to choose books they enjoy, read at their own pace, and develop a lifelong enjoyment of reading.

22. B: Purposeful teacher read-alouds allow students to listen to a story for voice emphasis and tone. This will help students when they are reading independently as well. Although students may find this time restful or a chance to catch up on old work, neither is the main purpose. Students may use this time to take notes on the reading, but students should only be listening to the story being read and not doing other work.

23. B: Pragmatics is the study of what words mean in certain situations. Choice *A*, morphology, involves the structure and formation of words. Choice *C*, syntax, refers to the order of words in a sentence. Choice *D*, semantics, addresses the distinct meanings of words.

24. A: "Text evidence" refers to taking phrases and sentences directly from the text and writing them in the answer. Students are not asked to paraphrase, nor use any other resources to address the answer. Therefore, Choices *B*, *C*, and *D* are incorrect.

25. C: Phonics allows readers to effectively translate print into recognizable speech. If children lack proficiency in phonics, their ability to read fluently and to increase vocabulary will be limited.

26. D: Group-based discussions, like think-pair-share, encourage all students to speak rather than having just one student share an answer. Each student is given time to collaborate with another student and share their thoughts. It is not intended for one student to give another student the answers, which is why Choice *C* is incorrect. Although Choices *A* and *B* might be correct, they are not the MOST important reason that group-based discussions are useful in the classroom.

27. D: Extension projects and papers should be used to challenge advanced learners, not learners developing comprehension skills. Graphic organizers, taking notes, and small intervention groups can aid reading comprehension. Graphic organizers and taking notes are great ways for a student to outline key parts of the text. Small intervention groups set up by the instructor can then focus on individual needs.

28. C: Advanced students can benefit from intervention groups by allowing the students to be challenged with more complex assignments. These assignments can be worked on independently and can include more difficult questions or higher-level vocabulary. Even short projects may be beneficial for these advanced students to work on throughout the week.

29. A: Small intervention groups can benefit from a teacher reading a text or small book aloud while students listen and take notes. This helps struggling students to focus on reading comprehension rather than having to decode words. Intervention time is not meant for a teacher to give independent work nor to just provide observation without support.

30. B: Word analysis and fluency should be mastered before teaching theme, text evidence, and writing. For English Language Learners and struggling readers, word analysis and fluency are often difficult barriers, which is why comprehension skills are not initially mastered. Theme is often a complex and inferential skill, which is developed later on. Text evidence is pulling answers to comprehension questions directly from a text and cannot be accomplished until readers can fluently read and understand the text. Writing skills generally come after comprehension skills are underway.

31. D: Teachers use directed reading-thinking activities before and after reading to improve critical thinking and reading comprehension. Metacognitive skills are when learners think about their thinking. Self-monitoring is when children are asked to think as they read and ask themselves if what they have just read makes sense. KWL charts help guide students to identify what they already know about a given topic.

32. C: Asking oneself a comprehension question is a metacognition skill. Readers with metacognitive skills have learned to think about thinking. It gives students control over their learning while they read. KWL charts help students to identify what they already know about a given topic.

33. C: Listening and speaking are not part of Bloom's Taxonomy. The six parts are remembering, understanding, applying, analyzing, evaluating, and creating.

34. D: During the Emergent Spelling stage, children can identify letters but not the corresponding sounds. The other choices are all fictitious.

35. A: Reciprocal teaching involves predicting, summarizing, questioning, and clarifying. The other choices are all fictitious.

36. B: KWL charts are an effective method of activating prior knowledge and taking advantage of students' curiosity. Students can create a KWL (*Know/Want to know/Learned*) chart to prepare for any unit of instruction and to generate questions about a topic.

37. D: Flashback is a technique used to give more background information in a story. None of the other concepts are directly related to going back in time.

38. A: Graphic organizers are a method of integrating knowledge and ideas. A graphic organizer can be one of many different visual tools for connecting concepts to help students understand information.

39. B: Making inferences is a method of deriving meaning in writing that is intended by the author but not explicitly stated. A flashback is a scene set earlier than the main story. Style is a general term for the way something is done. Figurative language is text that is not to be taken literally.

40. C: Genre is a means of categorizing text by its structure and literary elements. Fiction and nonfiction are both genre categories. Plot is the sequence of events that make a story happen.

41. A: Scanning future portions of the text for information that helps resolve a question is an example of self-monitoring. Self-monitoring takes advantage of students' natural ability to recognize when they understand the reading and when they do not. KWL charts are used to help guide students to identify what they already know about a given topic. Metacognitive skills are when learners think about their thinking. Directed reading-thinking activities are done before and after reading to improve critical thinking and reading comprehension skills.

42. C: The five basic components of reading education are phonemic awareness, phonics, fluency, vocabulary, and comprehension.

43. A: If a child can accurately read text with consistent speed and appropriate expression while demonstrating comprehension, the child is said to have reading fluency skills. Without the ability to read fluently, a child's reading comprehension, Choice *C*, will be limited.

44. B: Phonics is the ability to apply letter-sound relationships and letter patterns in order to accurately pronounce written words. Phonemic awareness is the understanding that words are comprised of a combination of sounds.

Fluency is an automatic recognition and accurate interpretation of text. Vocabulary is the body of words that a person knows.

45. C: Comprehension is the level of content understanding that a student demonstrates after reading. Orthographic development is a cumulative process for learning to read, with each skill building on the previously mastered skill. Fluency is an automatic recognition and accurate interpretation of text. Phonics is the ability to apply letter-sound relationships and letter patterns in order to accurately pronounce written words.

Mathematics

1. B: The first step is to make all exponents positive by moving the terms with negative exponents to the opposite side of the fraction. This expression becomes $\frac{4b^3b^2}{a^1a^4} \times \frac{3a}{b}$. Then the rules for exponents can be used to simplify. Multiplying the same bases means the exponents can be added. Dividing the same bases means the exponents are subtracted. Thus, after multiplying the exponents in the first fraction the equation becomes $\frac{4b^5}{a^5} \times \frac{3a}{b}$. Therefore, we can first multiply to get $\frac{12ab^5}{a^5b}$. Then, dividing yields $12\frac{b^4}{a^4}$.

2. C: The product of two irrational numbers can be rational or irrational. Sometimes the irrational parts of the two numbers cancel each other out, leaving a rational number. For example, $\sqrt{2} \times \sqrt{2} = 2$ because the roots cancel each other out. Technically, the product of two irrational numbers is a complex number, because real numbers are a type of complex number. However, Choice *D* is incorrect because the product of two irrational numbers is not an imaginary number.

3. B: The car is traveling at a speed of 5 meters per second. On the interval from 1 to 3 seconds, the position changes by 10 meters. This is 10 meters in 2 seconds, or 5 meters in each second.

4. C: The terms "whole numbers" and "natural numbers" include all the ordinary counting numbers $(1, 2, 3, 4, 5, \dots)$, and sometimes zero depending on the definition used, but no negative numbers. The term "integers" includes all those numbers, their negatives, and zero. So –4 is not a whole number or a natural number, but it is an integer. It is also rational because it can be written as a ratio of two integers $\left(-\frac{4}{1}\right)$; all integers are rational. It is a real number because it does not have an imaginary component (symbolized by the letter i); all integers are real numbers.

5. B: $4\frac{1}{3} + 3\frac{3}{4} = 4 + 3 + \frac{1}{3} + \frac{3}{4} = 7 + \frac{1}{3} + \frac{3}{4}$. Adding the fractions gives $\frac{1}{3} + \frac{3}{4} = \frac{4}{12} + \frac{9}{12} = \frac{13}{12} = 1 + \frac{1}{12}$. Thus, $7 + \frac{1}{3} + \frac{3}{4} = 7 + 1 + \frac{1}{12} = 8\frac{1}{12}$.

6. C: The average is calculated by adding all six numbers, then dividing by 6. The first five numbers have a sum of 25. This scenario can be expressed by the equation $\frac{(25+n)}{6} = 6$, where n is the unknown number. After multiplying both sides by 6, we get $25 + n = 36$, which means $n = 11$.

7. B: The answer choices for this question are tricky. Converting to kilometers from miles will yield the choice 7.514 kilometers when using the conversion $1 \text{ mi} = 1.609 \text{ km}$. However, because the question asks for an answer with three significant digits, 7.51 kilometers is the correct answer. Choices *C* and *D* could seem correct if someone flipped the conversion upside-down—that is, if they divided by 1.609 instead of multiplied by it.

$$4.67 \text{ mi} \times \frac{(1.609 \text{ km})}{(1 \text{ mi})} = 7.51 \text{ km}$$

8. B: $\frac{5}{2} \div \frac{1}{3} = \frac{5}{2} \times \frac{3}{1} = \frac{15}{2} = 7.5$.

9. A: The total fraction taken up by green and red shirts will be $\frac{1}{3}+\frac{2}{5}=\frac{5}{15}+\frac{6}{15}=\frac{11}{15}$. The remaining fraction is $1-\frac{11}{15}=\frac{15}{15}-\frac{11}{15}=\frac{4}{15}$.

10. C: If she has used $\frac{1}{3}$ of the paint, she has $\frac{2}{3}$ remaining. $2\frac{1}{2}$ gallons is the same as $\frac{5}{2}$ gallons. The calculation is:

$$\frac{2}{3}\times\frac{5}{2}=\frac{10}{6}=\frac{5}{3}=1\frac{2}{3}\text{ gallons}$$

11. D: To convert a fraction to a percent, we can first convert the fraction to a decimal. To do so, divide the numerator by the denominator: $4\div 5=0.8$. To convert a decimal to a percent, multiply by 100: $0.8\times 100=80\%$.

12. D: A given number divides evenly by each of its factors to produce an integer (no decimals). To find the factors of 12, determine what whole numbers when multiplied equal 12. 1×12, 2×6, and 3×4 are all the ways to multiply to 12 using whole numbers, so the factors of 12 are: 1, 2, 3, 4, 6, 12.

13. D: This problem can be solved using basic arithmetic. Xavier starts with 20 apples, then gives his sister half, which is 20 divided by 2.

$$20-\frac{20}{2}=20-10=10$$

He then gives his neighbor 6, so 6 is subtracted from 10.

$$10-6=4$$

Finally, he uses $\frac{3}{4}$ of his remaining apples to make a pie, which mean he has $\frac{1}{4}$ left:

$$\frac{1}{4}\times 4=1$$

14. A: The hundredths place value is located two digits to the right of the decimal point (the digit 9 in the original number). To decide whether to round up or keep the digit, examine the digit to the right, and if it is 5 or greater, round up. In this case, the digit to the right is 6, so the hundredths place is rounded up. When rounding up, if the digit to be increased is a 9, the digit to its left is increased by one and the digit in the desired place value is made a zero. Therefore, the number is rounded to 847.90.

15. B: Fractions must have like denominators to be added. The least common multiple of the denominators 3 and 5 is found. The LCM is 15, so both fractions should be changed to equivalent fractions with a denominator of 15. To determine the numerator of the new fraction, the old numerator is multiplied by the same number by which the old denominator is multiplied to obtain the new denominator. For the fraction $\frac{2}{5}$, multiplying both the numerator and denominator by 3 produces $\frac{6}{15}$. When fractions have like denominators, they are added by adding the numerators and keeping the denominator the same: $\frac{5}{15}+\frac{6}{15}=\frac{11}{15}$.

16. C: To find a common denominator, look for a number that has both denominators (12 and 9) as factors. 36 works. Multiply the top and bottom of each fraction by whatever number will make the denominator 36:

$$\frac{5}{12}\times\frac{3}{3}+\frac{4}{9}\times\frac{4}{4}=\frac{15}{36}+\frac{16}{36}$$

Now add the numerators, keeping the same denominator.

$$\frac{15+16}{36}=\frac{31}{36}$$

The top and bottom do not have any factors in common (31 is prime), so this fraction can't be reduced.

17. A: $\frac{52}{27}$

Set up the division problem.

$$\frac{4}{13}\div\frac{27}{169}$$

Flip the second fraction and multiply.

$$\frac{4}{13}\times\frac{169}{27}$$

Simplify the fractions before multiplying to make numbers simpler to work with.

$$\frac{4}{1}\times\frac{13}{27}$$

Multiply across the top and across the bottom to solve.

$$\frac{4\times 13}{1\times 27}=\frac{52}{27}$$

18. A: Divide 54 by 15:

$$\begin{array}{r} 3 \\ 15\overline{)54} \\ -45 \\ \hline 9 \end{array}$$

The result is 3 with a remainder of 9, which is equivalent to $3\frac{9}{15}$. Reduce the fraction $\frac{9}{15}$ for the final answer, $3\frac{3}{5}$.

19. A: Using the order of operations, multiplication and division are computed first from left to right. Multiplication is on the left; therefore, multiplication should be performed first.

20. D: $\frac{59}{7}$

The original number was $8\frac{3}{7}$. Multiply the denominator by the whole number portion. Add the numerator and put the total over the original denominator.

$$\frac{(8\ \times 7)+3}{7}=\frac{59}{7}$$

21. B: $\frac{93}{8}$

The original number was $11\frac{5}{8}$. Multiply the denominator by the whole number portion. Add the numerator and put the total over the original denominator.

$$\frac{(8 \times 11) + 5}{8} = \frac{93}{8}$$

22. B: To round 8.067 to the nearest tenths place, use the digit in the hundredths place.

6 in the hundredths place is greater than 5, so round up in the tenths place.

8.<u>0</u>67

0 becomes a 1.

8.1

23. A: We use the place value to the right of the thousandths place, which would be the ten-thousandths place. The value in the thousandths place is 7. The number in the place value to its right is greater than 4, so the 7 is bumped up to 8. Everything to its right is removed, giving us 245.268.

24. C: It may help to look at this problem as a fraction: $\frac{(1.2\times10^{12})}{(3.0\times10^{8})}$. We can calculate $\frac{1.2}{3} = 0.4$, and using the rules of exponents, we can see that $\frac{10^{12}}{10^{8}} = 10^{12-8} = 10^{4}$. This gives us an answer of 0.4×10^4, which is Choice A, but our answer is not yet in scientific notation because the first term, 0.4, is not between 1 and 10. We can rewrite 0.4×10^4, multiplying the first term by 10 and subtracting 1 from the exponent, which gives 4.0×10^3, Choice *C*.

25. A: The relative error can be found by finding the absolute error and making it a percent of the true value. The absolute error is $36 - 35.75 = 0.25$. This error is then divided by 35.75—the true value—to find 0.7%.

26. D: The slope from this equation is 50, and it is interpreted as the cost per gigabyte used. Since the g-value represents the number of gigabytes and the equation is set equal to the cost in dollars, the slope relates these two values. For every gigabyte used on the phone, the bill goes up 50 dollars.

27. D: This problem can be solved by using unit conversions. The initial units are miles per minute. The final units need to be feet per second. Converting miles to feet uses the equivalence statement 1 mile equals 5,280 feet. Converting minutes to seconds uses the equivalence statement 1 minute equals 60 seconds. Setting up the ratios to convert the units is shown in the following equation:

$$\frac{72 \text{ miles}}{90 \text{ minutes}} \times \frac{1 \text{ minute}}{60 \text{ seconds}} \times \frac{5{,}280 \text{ feet}}{1 \text{ mile}} = 70.4 \text{ feet per second}$$

The initial units cancel out, and the new, desired units are left.

28. A: First, convert the mixed numbers to improper fractions: $\frac{11}{3} - \frac{9}{5}$. Then, use 15 as a common denominator:

$$\frac{11}{3} - \frac{9}{5} = \frac{55}{15} - \frac{27}{15} = \frac{28}{15} = 1\frac{13}{15}$$

29. A: Setting up a proportion is the easiest way to represent this situation. The proportion is $\frac{20}{x} = \frac{40}{100}$, and cross-multiplication can be used to solve for x. Here, $40x = 2{,}000$, so $x = 50$.

30. C: The equation $x = 3$ is not a function of x because it does not pass the vertical-line test: if any vertical line can intersect the equation's graph at more than one point, the equation is not a function. This test comes from the definition of a function, in which each x value in the domain must be mapped to no more than one y value. This equation is a vertical line, so the x value of 3 is mapped to an infinite number of y values.

31. B: The domain is all possible input values, or x-values. For this equation, the domain is every number greater than or equal to zero. There are no negative numbers in the domain because taking the square root of a negative number results in an imaginary number.

32. C: We are trying to find x, the number of red cans. The equation can be set up like this:

$$x + 2(10 - x) = 16$$

The left x is actually multiplied by \$1, the price per red can. Since we know Jessica bought 10 total cans, $10 - x$ is the number of blue cans that she bought. We multiply the number of blue cans by \$2, the price per blue can.

That should all equal \$16, the total amount of money that Jessica spent. Working that out gives us:

$$x + 20 - 2x = 16$$

$$20 - x = 16$$

$$x = 4$$

33. C: $40N$ would be 4,000% of N. It's possible to check that each of the others is actually 40% of N.

34. A: To find the fraction of the bill that the first three people pay, the fractions need to be added, which means finding the common denominator. The common denominator will be 60. $\frac{1}{5} + \frac{1}{4} + \frac{1}{3} = \frac{12}{60} + \frac{15}{60} + \frac{20}{60} = \frac{47}{60}$. The remainder of the bill is $1 - \frac{47}{60} = \frac{60}{60} - \frac{47}{60} = \frac{13}{60}$.

35. B: 30% is $\frac{3}{10}$, so if 6 is 30% of some number n, we can write this as $6 = \left(\frac{3}{10}\right)n$. To solve for n, multiply both sides by the reciprocal: $n = \left(\frac{10}{3}\right) \times 6 = \frac{60}{3} = 20$.

36. B: Multiplying by 10^{-3} means moving the decimal point three places to the left, putting in zeros as necessary.

37. A: Compare each numeral after the decimal point to figure out which overall number is greatest. In Choices *A* (1.43785) and *C* (1.43592), both have the same value in tenths (4) and hundredths (3). However, the thousandths place is greater in Choice *A* (7), so Choice *A* has the greatest value overall.

38. D: $6 \times 12 = 72$, so we can calculate the values of all four choices and find that only Choice *D* equals 72. That makes sense, because we can rearrange and group these four numbers to make the factors of the original two numbers: $(3 \times 2) \times (4 \times 3) = 6 \times 12$.

39. C: The total percentage of a pie chart equals 100%. We can see that CD sales make up less than half of the chart (50%) but more than a quarter (25%), and the only answer choice that meets these criteria is Choice *C*, 40%.

40. B: Since \$850 is the price after a 20% discount, \$850 represents 80% (or 0.8) of the original price. In other words, $850 = 0.8x$ (where x is the original price). Solving this, we find $x = \frac{850}{0.8} = 1{,}062.5$. Now, to find the savings, calculate the original price minus the sale price: $\$1{,}062.50 - \$850 = \$212.50$.

Social Studies

1. A: Carolina is divided into two separate states—North and South. Maine was part of Nova Scotia and did not become an American territory until the War of 1812. Likewise, Vermont was not one of the original Thirteen Colonies. Canada remained a separate British colony. Finally, Florida was a Spanish territory. Therefore, by process of elimination, *A* is the correct list.

2. B: Britain was not defeated in the French and Indian War, and, in fact, disputes with the colonies over the new territories it won contributed to the growing tensions. All of the other options were key motivations behind the Revolutionary War.

3. C: Abraham Lincoln was elected president as part of the new Republican Party, and his plans to limit and potentially abolish slavery led the southern states to secede from the Union.

4. B: Out of the four inventions mentioned, the first telegraphs were invented in the 1830s, not in the twentieth century. In contrast, the other inventions had considerable influence over the course of the twentieth century.

5. C: The Declaration of Independence occurred during the American Revolution, so it should therefore be considered an effect, not a cause. Similarly, slavery was a cause for the later Civil War, but it was not a primary instigator for the Revolutionary War. Although a single event can have many effects long into the future, it is also important to not overstate the influence of these individual causes; the civil rights movement was only tangentially connected to the War of Independence among many other factors, and therefore it should not be considered a primary effect of it. The French and Indian War (which was part of the Seven Years' War) and the Bill of Rights, on the other hand, were respectively a cause and effect from the American Revolution, making Choice *C* the correct answer.

6. D: The president and vice president are part of the executive branch, not the legislative branch. The question focuses specifically on the federal level, so state government should be excluded from consideration. As for the district court and the court of appeals, they are part of the judicial branch. The legislative branch is made up of Congress, which consists of the House of Representatives and the Senate.

7. A: George Washington was concerned that sectionalism could destroy the United States, and he warned against it. He also advised that Americans avoid getting involved in European affairs. He did not make abolition a theme in his Farewell Address.

8. B: To avoid involvement in political processes such as voting is antithetical to the principles of a democracy. Therefore, the principal responsibility of citizens is the opposite, and they should be steadily engaged in the political processes that determine the course of government.

9. B: Time zones are determined by longitude, not latitude. Locations are defined in absolute terms, while places are in part defined by the population, which is subject to movement. There are seven continents in the world, not six. On the other hand, it is true that the prime meridian determines the border for the Eastern and Western hemispheres.

10. D: Riparian water usage was common in the past, but modern usage has shifted to appropriation. While often practicing sustainable methods, Native Americans used fire, agriculture, and other tools to shape the landscape for their own ends. Due to the importance of trade in providing essential resources to cities, a city is never truly separated from the outside world. However, invasive species are a formidable threat to native environments, making *D* the correct answer.

11. C: Historians make use of maps in their studies to get a clear picture of how history unfolded, knowing the borders of different lands helps historians learn different cultures' interactions, and environmental factors, such as access to water and the proximity of mountains, help determine the course of civilization. The phrase "Geography is closely linked with the flow of resources, technology, and population in societies" is a characteristic of economics.

12. C: While many Native American tribes are matrilineal, not all of them are. Japan is currently coping with an especially low birthrate, not a high one. Mexico's religion, like that of Spain, is primarily Roman Catholic rather than Protestant. On the other hand, Shi'a Islam is based on the view that imams should be honored as Muhammad's chosen heirs to the Caliphate, making *C* correct.

13. A: Although Greeks used the alphabet as the basis for their written language, leading to a diverse array of literature, they learned about the alphabet from Phoenician traders. All the other options, in contrast, were invented in Greece.

14. D: The partition into Hindu India and Islamic Pakistan led to large outbreaks of religious violence. The Cold War was never an official war; the United States and the Soviet Union instead funded proxy conflicts. The Kyoto Protocol was signed by members of the United Nations; the League of Nations was long since defunct. Japan fought on the side of the Allies in World War I; its defeat by the Allied powers occurred at the end of World War II.

15. A: Although Egyptian and Mayan civilizations are an interesting subject for comparisons, the two cultures never interacted. The other answers are all examples of interactions between different cultures; a study of Chinese culture, for instance, would require examination of the multiple ethnic groups throughout China.

16. C: Although monetary systems were invented to solve problems with barter systems, it is wrong to assume that barter systems have ceased to exist; bartering remains a common practice throughout the world, albeit less common than money. The four main categories for economic resources are land, labor, capital, and entrepreneurship. The law of supply says that supplies will increase, not decrease, as prices increase. The correct answer is *C,* as scarcity is determined by human choice.

17. A: Rather than competition, a monopoly prevents other businesses from offering a certain product or service to consumers.

18. B: Absolute monarchies often use command system economies, but they do not represent a way that governments manage economies. Laissez-faire, capitalism, and self-interest, in contrast, are all fundamental concepts behind the market system.

19. A: England, France, and Spain all established North American colonies that would later be absorbed into the United States, but Italy, despite Christopher Columbus' role as an explorer, never established a colony in America.

20. D: The Constitution was signed in 1787; the Declaration of Independence was signed in 1776. It was successfully ratified by all the current states, including New York. Finally, the Articles of Confederation were established at the end of the American Revolution; the Constitution would replace the articles years later due to issues with the government's structure.

21. C: Although American forces made several early attempts to take Canada from Britain, the United States was never able to successfully seize this territory. On the other hand, the United States did control the Philippines, Puerto Rico, and Guam.

22. C: The executive branch determines the cabinet, while the judicial branch has the responsibility of interpreting the Constitution and laws. Even so, the legislative branch can check the president's power by impeaching him.

23. D: The Emancipation Proclamation only freed slaves in Confederate-held territories; southern states still loyal to the Union kept their slaves for the time being. Although Wilson succeeded in instituting the League of Nations, the United Nations would not emerge until decades later. The Bill of Rights was ratified after the Constitution to provide additional protection for individual liberties. However, it is true that the main body of the Declaration of Independence consisted of grievances that the colonies had against British rule.

24. D: While it is true that Rome fell to barbarians in the fifth century AD, it would be inaccurate to say the Roman Empire had been completely destroyed. The Byzantine Empire considered itself the heir of the Roman Empire. The western sections, on the other hand, certainly collapsed; the later Holy Roman Empire tried to draw on Rome's past glory but was not a true successor.

25. A: Based on the prior League of Nations, the United Nations included many nations in postcolonial Africa and Asia and worked to support human rights. However, it failed to maintain the World War II alliance between the United States and the Soviet Union, leading to the unofficial Cold War.

26. C: At the time of the Constitutional Convention, Thomas Jefferson was in Paris serving as America's foreign minister to France. George Washington led the meeting, and Alexander Hamilton and James Madison set the tone for debate, rendering *A*, *B*, and *D* incorrect.

27. A: Plains Indians followed the buffalo across the prairies, living in tent-like teepees that were easily moved from place to place. Choice *B* is incorrect because Native Americans in the Southwest relied on farming for much of their food and built adobes, which are houses made out of dried clay or earth. Native Americans in the Eastern and Northwest sections of North America survived by hunting, gathering, farming, and fishing, and lived in wooden longhouses, plank houses, or wigwams. Thus, Choices *C* and *D* are incorrect.

28. C: Established in 1607, Jamestown, Virginia was the first permanent British settlement in the New World. Plymouth was founded a bit later in 1620 when a group of Pilgrims founded the first permanent European settlement in New England, making Choice *A* incorrect. Choice *B* is incorrect because although the Roanoke Colony was founded in 1585, it isn't considered permanent – the colony's leader, John White, went back to England for supplies two years later, and he returned to find that all of the colonists had mysteriously disappeared. Choice *D* is incorrect because L'Anse Meadows was an area in Newfoundland that was briefly settled by Scandinavian Vikings around 1000 AD.

29. D: The British issued the Townsend Act in 1767, which taxed imported lead, glass, paints, paper, and tea, and increased the colonists' anger and further strained the relationship between England and the colonies. Choice *A*, the Stamp Act of 1765, taxed printed items, including playing cards and newspapers printed in the colonies. Choice *B*, the Sugar Act of 1764, placed import duties on items such as molasses, sugar, coffee, and wine. Choice *C*, the Currency Act, banned the issuing of paper money in the colonies and mandated the use of gold in business dealings.

30. C: The first shot took place on Lexington Green. When the British heard that colonists were stockpiling weapons, they sent troops to Concord to seize them. However, a group of approximately seventy Minutemen confronted the British soldiers on Lexington Green. British troops killed five protesting colonists during the Boston Massacre in 1770, but this is not considered the first shot of the Revolution. Thus, Choice *A* is incorrect. Choice *B* is incorrect because the Boston Tea Party was when colonists dumped 342 chests of expensive tea into the Boston Harbor in defiance of the tea tax. The Revolution had already started when the Battle of Trenton took place on December 25, 1776, making Choice *D* incorrect.

31. A: British General Lord Cornwallis surrendered to Washington's troops at Yorktown, Virginia. No battles occurred at Valley Forge, but Washington's troops suffered major losses as a result of starvation, disease, and exposure to the cold, making Choice *B* incorrect. Choice *C* is incorrect because the Battle of Trenton was the first major battle of the Revolution, which occurred when Washington led his troops across the Delaware River to wage a surprise attack on British and Hessian soldiers stationed in Trenton on December 25, 1776. Choice *D,* Saratoga, New York, was the site of a major victory by General John Burgoyne in October 1777 and prompted European countries to help support the American cause.

32. C: British soldiers burned the White House during the War of 1812. Neither the Washington Monument nor the Statue of Liberty—Choices *A* and *D*—were built at the time, and Philadelphia's Independence Hall, Choice *B*, escaped conflict during this war.

33. B: Jefferson Davis was elected president of the Confederate States of America in November 1861. Choice *A*, General Robert E. Lee, was the leader of the Confederate Army. Choice *C*, William T. Sherman, was a union general famous for his march through Georgia and the burning of Atlanta in 1864. Choice *D*, Abraham Lincoln, was President of the US during the Civil War.

34. D: This period was called the Gilded Age since it appeared shiny and golden on the surface but was fueled by undercurrents of corruption led by big businessmen known as robber barons. Choice *A*, Manifest Destiny, is the concept referring to the pursuit and acquisition of new lands by the US. The Columbian Exchange, Choice *B*, was an era of discovery, conquest, and colonization of the Americas by the Europeans. The New Deal, Choice *C*, was a plan launched by President Franklin Delano Roosevelt to help rebuild America's economy after the Great Depression.

35. C: World War I began in 1914 when a Serbian assassin killed Archduke Franz Ferdinand of Austria and prompted Austria-Hungary to declare war on Serbia. 1915, Choice *A*, is the year when German submarines sank the passenger ship *Lusitania*, killing 128 Americans and leading many to support US efforts to enter the war. 1917, Choice *B*, is the year the US entered World War I, declaring war on Germany. 1918, Choice *D*, signaled the end of the war when American troops helped defeat the German army that September. Fighting ended in November after Germany signed a peace agreement.

36. A: The Soviet Union was invaded by Germany in 1941 and allied with Britain. Subsequently, the U.S. President Roosevelt, British Prime Minister Winston Churchill, and Soviet director Joseph Stalin met in 1945 to plan their final assault on Germany and discuss postwar strategies. Germany aligned with Italy and Japan in 1940 to form the Axis Alliance. Their goal was to establish a German empire in Europe and place Japan in control over Asia. Thus, Choices *B*, *C*, and *D* are incorrect.

37. B: The North Atlantic Treaty Organization (NATO) was formed between Western Europe, Canada, and the US in defense of Soviet hostility after the Soviet Union introduced Communism into Eastern Europe. The Soviet Union countered by creating the Warsaw Pact.

38. C: The G.I. Bill was a government program started in the 1950s that gave military veterans a free education. In the revolutionary 1954 case, *Brown vs. the Board of Education,* the Supreme Court ruled that school segregation was illegal, thereby setting the Civil Rights Movement in motion, making Choice *A* incorrect. Freedom rides, Choice *B*, and the Montgomery bus boycott, Choice *D*, were among the non-violent protests against segregation that took place in the US in the 1960s.

39. B: President Reagan advocated peace through strength, building up the US military and launching the Strategic Defense Initiative (SDI), also called Star Wars. Choice *A*, the Strategic Arms Limitation Talks (SALT I and II), negotiated between 1972 and 1979, resulted in limits on nuclear weapons for both the US and Russia. Choice *C*, the Iran-Contra Affair, was a scandal involving the secret sale of weapons to Iran in exchange for American hostages. Choice *D*, Glasnost, was a policy of political openness launched by Soviet leader Mikhail Gorbachev.

40. A: Afghanistan was the site of the bombing raids. Bush invaded Iraq, Choice *B*, in 2003 when Iraqi dictator Saddam Hussein defied the terms of the truce agreed upon in 1991 after the Gulf War. Kuwait, Choice *C*, was invaded by Iraq in 1990, sparking the Gulf War. Pakistan, Choice *D*, is where Osama bin Laden was killed by a group of Navy SEALs under orders from President Obama.

Science

1. D: It has the same amount of mechanical energy throughout its path. Mechanical energy is the total amount of energy in the situation; it is the sum of the potential energy and the kinetic energy. The amount of potential and kinetic energy both vary by the position of an object, but the mechanical energy remains constant.

2. C: The scientific method refers to how to conduct a proper scientific inquiry, including recognizing a question/problem, formulating a hypothesis, making a prediction of what will happen based on research, experimenting, and deciding whether the outcome confirmed or denied the hypothesis.

3. B: Kinetic energy is energy an object has while moving. Potential energy is energy an object has based on its position or height. Solar energy is energy that comes from the sun. Heat energy is the energy produced from moving atoms, molecules, or ions, and can transfer between substances.

4. A: A chemical change alters the chemical makeup of the original object. When a piece of paper burns it cannot be returned to its original chemical makeup because it has formed new materials. Physical change refers to changing a substance's form, but not the composition of that substance. In physical science, *sedimentary change* and *potential change* are not terms used to describe any particular process.

5. C: An inclined plane is a simple machine that can make it easier to raise or lower an object in height. Simple machines offer a mechanical advantage to performing tasks. While a screw, a level, and a pulley are also simple machines, they would be used to offer a mechanical advantage in other situations.

6. D: Sir Isaac Newton simplified the laws of motion into three basic rules, based upon his observations in experimentation and advanced mathematical calculations. Albert Einstein was known for his theories involving electricity and magnetism, relativity, energy, light, and gravitational waves. Stephen Hawking is known for his theories and studies of space, dark matter, black holes, and relativity. Copernicus was known for his observations and theories regarding the movements of the planets in our universe—specifically, that the sun was the center of our solar system, not earth.

7. B: Convection is the transfer of heat due to the movement of molecules from an area of higher concentration to that of lower concentration; this is also how heat can travel throughout a house to warm each room. Conduction is the transfer of energy from one molecule to another molecule through actually touching or making contact with each other. Radiation is how the sun warms Earth; no medium is needed for this type of transfer.

8. D: An object at rest has forces acting upon it, including gravitational, normal, and frictional forces. All of these forces are in balance with each other and cause no movement in the object's position. This is equilibrium. An object in constant motion is also considered to be in equilibrium or a state of balanced forces.

9. C: When conducting scientific research, it is best to rely on sources that are known for honest, ethical, and unbiased research and experimentation. Most laboratories and universities must have their work validated through independent means in order to publish or claim results. Anyone can publish things on the Internet—it does not mean their work has been validated, and therefore, their work may not be correct.

10. D: Sublimation is a change in state from a solid to a gas. Evaporation is a change in state from a liquid to a gas, melting is a change in state from a solid to a liquid, and condensation is a change in state from a gas to a liquid.

11. C: A force diagram shows all of the forces acting upon an object in a situation. The direction of arrows pointing around the object shows the direction of each force. A Venn diagram is used to show mathematical sets, a periodic table shows how the elements are categorized, and a stress-strain diagram is used in engineering.

12. D: Mass refers to the amount or quantity there is of an object. Light, sound, and heat are all forms of energy that can travel in waves.

13. A: The mechanical energy is the total (or sum) of the potential energy and the kinetic energy at any given point in a system.

$ME = PE + KE; 50 \text{ Joules} = 30 \text{ Joules} + 20 \text{ Joules}$

14. D: Scientific inquiry can be prompted by simple curiosity as to how or why something works. As seen in the race to enter outer space, scientific progress can be driven by competition. Many inventors are motivated by the idea of finding a better, faster, or more economical way of doing or producing something so that they can prosper from their discovery.

15. A: Using Newton's equation for motion, $F = ma$, and substituting gravity in for acceleration (a), the weight, or force could be calculated for an object having mass (m). Weight is a force, mass is the amount of a substance, and acceleration and gravity are rate of speed over time.

16. B: It appears to bend because of the refraction of light traveling from air to water. When light travels from one material to another it can reflect, refract, and go through different materials. Choice *A* is incorrect, as the pencil does not actually become warped but only appears to be warped. Choice *C* is incorrect; although the pencil appears to bend because of its immersion into separate mediums where speed is different, the pencil does not become temporarily warped—it only appears to be warped. Choice *D* is incorrect; it is the refraction of light, not reflection. The latter happens within the same medium, which makes the answer choice incorrect.

17. B: While this is Einstein's application of Newton's theory to that of light, it is not one of Newton's original three laws of motion. Newton's three laws are $F = ma$, the law of inertia, and for every action there is an equal and opposite reaction.

18. C: This is a fundamental law of thermodynamics. Energy can only transfer, transform, or travel. The amount of energy in a system is always the same.

19. A: The ends (or poles) of a straight magnet are different charges. One end is positive, and one end is negative. Therefore, the positive end of magnet #1 would attract the negative end of magnet #2 and repel magnet #2's positive end.

20. D: When electricity is run through a wire, it is carrying current, and current has a charge. Therefore, there is a charge running down the wire, which creates a magnetic field that can attract and repel just like any magnet.

21. B: The ice skater is demonstrating the conservation of angular momentum. This means that the amount of momentum for the situation will remain the same. If the skater is redistributing the mass (their arms), then the angular speed will compensate for that alteration. In this case, the mass is extended out away from the axis of rotation, so the rate of rotation is slowed down. If their arms were brought back in near their body, then the rate of rotation would increase, making the skater spin faster.

22. C: This is the actual force recognized in a rotational situation. The reactive force acting opposite of the centripetal force is named the centrifugal force, but it is not an actual force on its own. A common mistake is to interchange the two terms. However, the real force acting in a rotational situation is pulling in toward the axis of rotation and is called the centripetal force.

23. C: Electric charge can be transferred through touch of one physical object to another, induction by bringing a charged object near another object, and polarization, or the forcing of one charge to the end of an object in a centralized area.

24. D: The solar waves from the sun warm Earth. Many of the waves are meant to reflect back off of the atmosphere to keep Earth warm, and the rest of the waves are meant to reflect back out into space through the atmosphere. This is known as the greenhouse effect. However, when the atmosphere has become too dense (polluted by gases), the waves meant to escape are trapped and re-radiate in Earth's atmosphere, causing an overall warming of the climate, known as global warming.

25. A: Velocity is a measure of speed with direction. To calculate velocity, find the change in position over the change in time. Choices *B* and *C* are incorrect because they are both equations for speed, and do not imply a direction. A standard measurement for velocity is in meters per second (m/s).

26. C: Wind energy from turbines, solar energy from sun panels, and geothermal energy are all considered renewable and preferable alternatives to fossil fuel, of which there is a limited supply.

The following image is the answer to question 27.

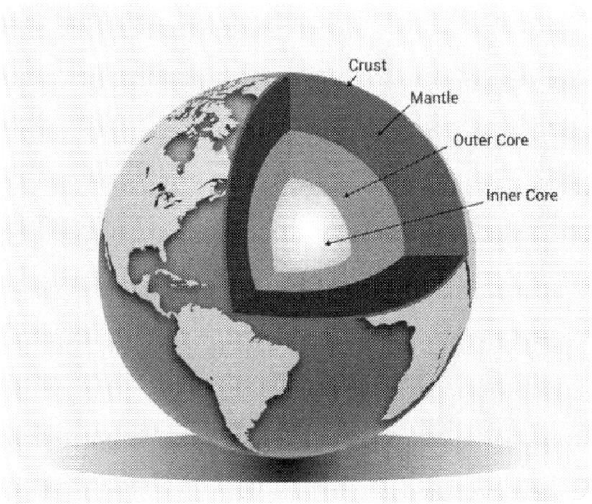

27. A: Layer 4 is the inner core; therefore, Choices *C* and *D* are incorrect. The inner core is solid due to the intense pressure upon it, making Choice *B* incorrect.

28. B: Sedimentary. Choice *A* (igneous) is incorrect because that is crystallized magma found on land. Choice *C* (metamorphic) is incorrect because that is unified, solid rock close to earth's mantle. Choice *D* (minerals) isn't a type of rock, but what composes rock.

29. D: Sunlight evaporates dew from plants. Choice *A* is incorrect because cloud formation is condensation. Choice *B* is incorrect because rain, snow, and ice storms are different forms of precipitation. Choice *C* is incorrect because rivers flowing into the oceans are examples of run-off.

30. D: Precipitation has nothing to do with plate tectonic theory. Plate movement causes ocean floor spreading, mountain formation, and earthquakes; therefore, all other answer choices are true.

31. B: It is not true that all volcanoes have explosive eruptions; shield volcanoes have thin magma that oozes out gently. Choice *A* is true because magma circulates in the upper mantle. Choice *C* is true because igneous rock is cooled lava. Choice *D* is true because igneous rock goes through the rock cycle and will eventually become magma again.

The following image is for questions 32 and 33.

32. B: The oldest rock layer is on the bottom. Choice *D* doesn't show a fossil—the grass is a living organism. Choices *A* and *C* show fossils in higher layers, so these are not the correct answers.

33. C: Fossils are only found in sedimentary rock. Igneous rock, metamorphic rock, and liquid magma don't contain fossils, so Choices *A*, *B*, and *D* are incorrect.

The following image is for question 34.

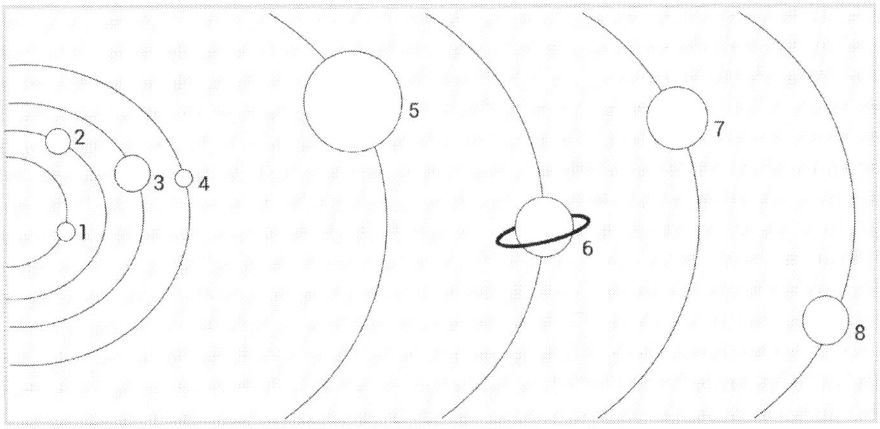

34. C: The asteroid belt is rock orbiting between the inner, solid planets and the outer, gassy planets. More precisely, it is between Mars (planet #4) and Jupiter (planet #5). It is not Choice *A* (between Venus and Earth), nor is it Choice *B* (between Earth and Mars). Choice *D* is incorrect since it is not between every planet.

35. C: Mars has a smaller orbit around the Sun. This question requires critical thinking because every answer choice is true, but only one of them has to do with orbiting time. A year is the time it takes a planet to orbit the Sun, and because Mars is closer to the Sun and has a smaller orbit, its year is significantly shorter than a year on Jupiter.

The following image is for question 36.

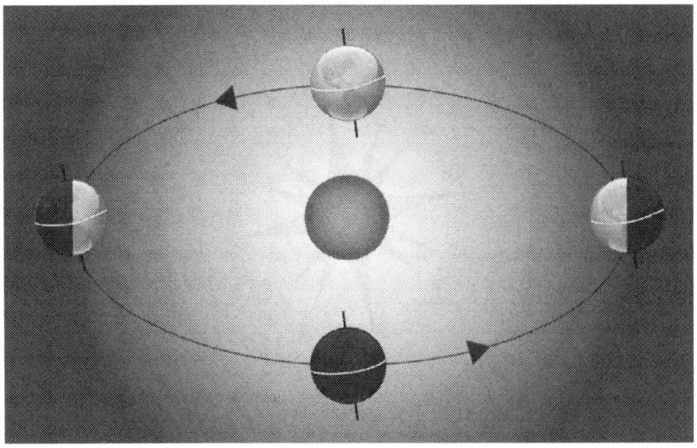

36. B: Students must identify the lateral equator and know the difference between North and South. They should recognize that because the top hemisphere is tilted away from the Sun; it would be winter at that time. Spring and fall, Choices *D* and *C*, are incorrect because both hemispheres have the same exposure to the sun, and summer, Choice *A*, is incorrect since the top hemisphere is tilted toward the sun.

37. D: All choices are true. New moons are closest to the sun and full moons are farthest, Choice *A*. Crescent moons are smaller than half-moons, Choice *B*, and gibbous moons are larger than half-moons, Choice *C*.

38. B: Greenhouse gases insulate earth and keep it warm; they serve as a blanket and allow earth to exist at livable temperatures. Choice *D* is incorrect because greenhouse gases do not form clouds; clouds are formed by condensed water vapor. Choice *C* is incorrect because while it is true that particles in the atmosphere reflect light so that the sky appears blue, this isn't an important function of the particles in the troposphere. The blue appearance is just cosmetic. Choice *A* is incorrect because ozone in the stratosphere actually prevents UV rays from passing.

39. C: Theories are accepted by scientists, while hypotheses remain to be proven, making Choice *C* correct. Choice *A* is incorrect because theories are far more than predictions; they are actually highly supported and accepted as truth. Choice *B* is incorrect because theories can change with new technology and understanding. Choice *D* is also incorrect because theories may not always be true and can change. Also, hypotheses can be and often are supported.

40. C: A seismologist studies earthquakes. All other choices have been mixed up. Paleontologists study fossils, meteorologists study weather, and geologists study Earth's crust.

41. C: Leaf. Leaves are the part of the plant that contain chloroplast (due to their green appearance), thus they are the parts that perform photosynthesis. Roots, Choice *A*, suck up water. Flowers are reproductive structures, Choice *D*.

42. D: All living and nonliving things in an area. Choice *C* (all the organisms in a food web) describes feeding relationships and not symbiosis. Choice *B* (rocks, soil, and atmosphere in an area) includes nonliving factors in an ecosystem. Choice *A*, one organism, is too small to be considered an ecosystem.

The following image is for questions 43 and 44.

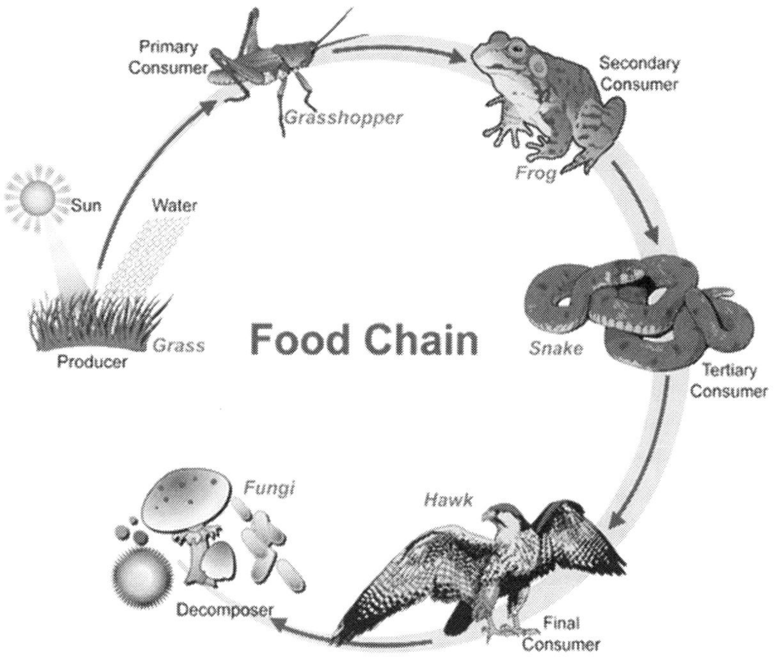

43. D: Choice *A* (the sun) is not even a living thing. Grass (*B*) is a producer, and the frog (*C*) is a consumer. The fungi break down dead organisms and are the only decomposer shown.

44. B: An herbivore is an organism that eats only plants, and that's the grasshopper's niche in this particular food chain. Grass, Choice *A*, is a producer; the frog, Choice *C*, is a consumer; and the fungi, Choice *D*, is a decomposer.

45. C: Water, Choice *A*, is a reactant that gets sucked up by the roots. Carbon dioxide, Choice *D*, is a reactant that goes into the stomata, and sunlight, Choice *B*, inputs energy into the reaction in order to create the high-energy sugar.

Fine Arts, Health, and Physical Education

1. B: It is recommended that teachers offer clear, understandable guidance and scaffolds for art projects when working with children because it helps them gain a sense of direction and purpose in the activity. While some degree of flexibility and openness to the framework should be included so that children can experiment and engage their creativity, a structured environment helps define the goals and purpose of the activity. Choice *A* is incorrect because guidance and scaffolds create a structured, not unstructured, framework. Choice *C* may be a fringe benefit to guiding the activity, particularly if finished models are presented, but it is not the primary reason to provide guidance. Choice *D* is incorrect; the goal of art instruction at the early education levels is not to turn each student into the best student he or she can be, but rather to introduce the central concepts of art and its variety of functions, such as self-expression, communicating social ideas, exploring emotions, relating to the world, and creating usable pieces.

2. D: Throwing a tennis ball at various targets involves significant hand-eye coordination, fine-motor skills, and manipulative skills. It also is considered a performance-based skill, rather than a process-based skill. These criteria make it an inappropriate activity for young children because they have yet to develop these skills. Activities for younger children should focus on foundational movement patterns and developing a life-long love of moving. While children in the first and third grades do start to develop fine motor skills, the hand-eye coordination needed to hit targets is not typically present. To this end, process-based outcomes, such as the proper body position and follow through when throwing a ball, should take precedence over performance-based ones, like nailing a specific target with a pitch. However, by the end of fifth grade, most children's motor development is such that these skills are possible. Moreover, they are more developmentally ready to achieve some performance-based outcomes.

3. C: The five components of health-related physical fitness are cardiovascular fitness, muscular strength, muscular endurance, flexibility, and body composition. While agility is an important sports-specific, performance-based skill, one's agility does not significantly impact physical health.

4. C: Adaptations to the nervous system occur quickly with fitness training. The initial increases in strength are due to the conditioning of motor units to activate more quickly and more frequently. The number of motor units that activate in unison results in a higher percentage of muscle fibers in a muscle that contract with one neural impulse. As training continues over weeks and months, the size of muscle fibers increases, furthering improving strength. Choice *A* is incorrect because neural adaptations usually occur quickly after a fitness training program has been started. Choice *B* reverses the order of primary adaptations to the nervous system. Lastly, Choice *D* states the elasticity and resting length of muscles and connective tissues decrease and shorten, respectively, in the early stages of training, when in truth, particularly with regular flexibility training, they increase. These changes help improve range of motion and can prepare the tissues to handle higher loads without inducing injury.

5. C: Having an on-hand model of the planned art activity that is fully completed offers a variety of benefits. It helps give the student a tangible frame of reference from which they can work for the activity. In this way, it can build excitement and interest in the activity because it gives students a concrete representation of what they can create. When the teacher goes through the process of making a model of the finished product, it allows them to figure out how much time is needed for the activity and to note any difficult steps that might require additional explanation. Because the model represents a finished product, it does not readily demonstrate the individual steps of the activity; therefore, Choice *C* is not a primary function of a completed model.

6. B: Art activities can be either explicit, implicit, or both. For example, an art activity that is explicitly designed may help students understand the biography and work of a particular artist, such as in the activity described in the question. To add an implicit component to the activity, teachers can educate students about the history of the period during which the artist worked and the social world that the artist lived in. Choices *C* and *D* are not defined types of art activities. The balance and emphasis are concepts of artwork, which can be explored through various art activities, either in isolation or in combination with other concepts like unity (the focus of the teacher's lesson in the question), texture, rhythm, color, movement, and contrast.

7. A: The performance sequence of art has five parts: selecting, analyzing, interpreting, rehearsing/evaluating/refining, and presenting. In the analyzing stage, the performer does research on the chosen piece, so that he or she can learn as much as possible about it. Doing so can enable the artist to become more immersed in the work, which can further enhance the interpretation. Choice *B* describes the rehearsing/evaluating/refining stage. This is also the stage where the artist hones their skills and perfects the piece for its eventual performance. Choices *C* and *D* both describe the interpreting stage, which follows the analyzing stage.

8. D: While formative, summative, and formal evaluations all have merit in the learning process, they are typically not the ideal assessments for art education at the early elementary levels. Art is highly subjective, and thus these more objective evaluations lack the same utility they carry for subjects like math or history. One of the primary objectives of art education for young children is to develop their sense of how to assess, interpret, and respond to art. The artistic process, particularly the aspects revolving around artistic interpretation and responding to art, can aid deep learning, including learning about society, the world, and oneself. Self-assessment, or the process of evaluating one's own art, is an effective means by which young students can learn to better assess art created by others.

9. B: Nutrition recommendations for children include replacing higher fat foods with lower-fat alternatives, reducing the intake of sugary beverages, and replacing more refined foods like applesauce with foods in their natural form, such as a fresh, whole apple. Answer Choice *B* is incorrect because fiber is beneficial in the diet because it increases the feeling of satiety, which can lower caloric intake, and fiber can also reduce LDL cholesterol by binding to it and helping the body excrete it. Lower fiber refined grains have the bran stripped away and should be replaced by higher fiber options.

10. A: The optimal physical education curriculum for five- to six-year-old children should focus on movement for enjoyment. Children at this age are motivated by fun and playing and will be active if it is fun. They are not necessarily ready to focus on sports-specific skills requiring significant hand-eye coordination. They do best with moderate- and high-intensity activities with adequate rest.

11. C: When teaching new skills, especially to toddlers and young children, instructions lasting longer than twenty seconds or containing more than just a couple of steps or cues will lead students to losing interest or getting overwhelmed. It is typically advantageous to have very short instructional periods interspersed between longer breaks to play and try out the introduced skills. Reading material is likely not appropriate for this age group, many of whom do not yet know how to read.

12. C: Following safety procedures like wearing a seatbelt is the best choice. Experts recommend that children get over nine hours of sleep per night. Also, children should brush their teeth after every meal, not just before bed. Finally, it is important for children to learn how to express their emotions in a healthy way and let a trusted adult know if they are struggling with persistent feelings of sadness or anxiety.

13. D: Teachers should educate students on the importance of visiting doctors for routine medical care and check-ups (every six months or so); consistent feelings of sadness, anxiety, loneliness, and stress; and pains or aches that do not go away. Research has found that even at the preschool level, talking about the importance of visiting the doctor can positively impact health behaviors in adulthood.

14. A: Family influences on health behaviors include health insurance status, safety and injury prevention education and care, nutritional meal planning and diet composition, social dynamics and stress, and the family's culture around leisure time.

15. C: Gross motor skills are mastered before fine motor skills. Students begin developing basic motor skills like walking, balancing, and manipulating objects from a very early age. They master gross motor skills before they move on to fine motor skills. Sports skills are not learned more readily than generalized body movements, because sports skills require more fine motor skills, complex motions, and cognitive abilities (e.g. locating and aiming for targets). Also, what looks like play actually helps children develop movement patterns and abilities.

16. B: The general categories of basic movement skills include locomotor skills like walking, running, and skipping; non-locomotor skills such as squatting and twisting; and manipulative skills such as throwing and catching.

17. A: In a kindergarten classroom, hitting targets is not an appropriate focus for physical education because children at this age have not mastered the fine motor abilities and complex skills to aim and hit targets. Hitting targets is more appropriate for fifth grade students. In kindergarten, activities should focus on foundational skills such as weight transfer, balance, following objects with the eyes, and basic skills like jumping and skipping.

18. D: Of the listed age groups, nine- to twelve-year-old students are likely to be more interested in health-based benefits of physical activity than younger children, who are primarily interested in movement for fun and enjoyment. As children mature, they gain a deeper understanding of physiology and healthy lifestyle choices and they become more interested in the health benefits of exercise.

19. A: Educators should focus curricular activities on the major categories of arts: music, dance, theater, and visual arts (painting, drawing, sculpture, pottery, etc.).

20. C: The youngest children tend to create art with a focus on the scientific and sensory aspects of the project rather than artistic creativity, self-expression, or conveying a narrative or story. They enjoy art more as a means to which explore the textures they make (for example, making texture rubbings with crayon on paper), the contrast of colors they use, and the various shapes they make as they move the drawing utensil around (although they are not making shapes for symbolic reasons, they are simply enjoying and exploring what they make when they use the supplies).

21. D: Children should experiment with a variety of methods and materials to create art. Educators should provide children with a wide range of materials like finger paint, glitter, and felt so that children experiment with different textures. *A* is not the best answer because art education should expose students to the historical and cultural context of art beyond that of their everyday experiences. Students can learn about famous artists and art history, but those lessons can be incorporated into creative coursework; they are not a prerequisite for student experimentation.

22. D: Have students accompany the music with simple instruments like tambourines. Students can easily beat along to simple songs using rhythmic instruments like tambourines, maracas, or small drums. Young children enjoy moving around more than sitting and focusing on one thing for an extended time, so learning rhythm through actions like shaking rhythmic instruments or stomping and clapping is more effective for students at this age. Also, *C* is not the best answer because many young children are not yet strong readers.

23. D: Theater-in-education (TIE) is performed by teachers and students using curriculum material or social issues. Participants take on roles, which enable them to explore and problem-solve in a flexible structure, yet in an educational theatrical way. In Readers' Theater, readers perform a dramatic presentation sitting on stools reading the lines typically from children's literature, enabling performance opportunities in the absence of elaborate staging or script memorization. Puppetry can be used for creative drama with either simple puppets and stages made of bags, cardboard, socks, or more elaborate, artistic materials.

24. A: The main skills in theatrical arts for children include literary (reading and writing the script and memorizing lines), technical (includes the staging, lighting, sound effects, etc.), and performance elements (such as the set design and the musical score). Staging is part of the technical elements.

25. D: A three- to four-year-old child's drawing usually emphasizes his or her color choices. At this young age, children typically do not use art for self-expression, symbolism, or realistic figural accuracy. These are all artistic skills that students develop when they are older. Young students tend to focus on sensory exploration involving color, shape, and texture.

26. B: Perspective is a technique used to make flat objects look as though they have depth. Balance is using size, position, color, shape and lighting in the artwork so that all of the elements are equally present with no particular component overpowering. Abstraction is unrealistic artwork that typically has geometric lines or patterns.

27. A: Art has personal (self-expression, gratification, narrative functions), social (collective meaning for a group of people such as symbolic art honoring a god or political art), and physical functions (such as a pottery mug for tea) that often overlap in a project. Religious functions fall under the realm of social functions.

28. B: Harmony is a principle in art that highlights the similarities in separate but related parts of a composition to show how different things can actually be similar and blend together. Balance is positioning objects or using size, color, shape and lighting in a way that makes all of the elements equally present. Contrast is exemplifying differences between two unlike things such as loud and soft music, major and minor tones, fast and slow dancing movements, and light and dark colors.

29. C: Breakfast helps students do well on tests. Choice *A* is incorrect; on the contrary, breakfast is *integral* to school attendance. Choice *B* is incorrect; eating a sufficient amount of nutrition in the morning helps students stay focused and awake. Choice *D* is incorrect because the link between breakfast and student academic achievement is that breakfast aids in academic achievement.

30. A: Educators are incorporating art into the curriculum to develop students' fine motor skills and facilitate metacognition and abstract thinking. Though there are many career opportunities for artists, Choice *B*, this is not cited as a driver for its incorporation into current curriculum. Exposing students to other cultures, Choice *C*, may be a second order consequence of art curriculum, though not a driver. Finally, Choice *D* is incorrect. Art offers as much, if not more, freedom and creativity than it does discipline and structure.

31. C: Educators are encouraged to get clear on the overriding concept or idea that is embedded in the lesson. Developing a model project, Choice *A*, has value because it gives students an example of the finished expectations. Yet, it is not the first order of business when designing a lesson for children. Establishing learning objectives, Choice *B*, is imperative, but it is not the first step when developing an art activity. Choice *D*, offering praise and constructive criticism, should happen after the activity is done, not before.

32. B: There is a four-step process to making art that includes imagining, planning, making and presenting. The third step, *making*, also includes *evaluating* and *refining*, both of which aren't mentioned in the question. Choices *A*, *C*, and *D* may be synonymous to the process of creating, but they are not listed specifically in the guide.

33. D: Assessment is a word that is not a part of the four-part process reviewed in the literature. Choice *A*, Selection, is the process where the person viewing the art chooses the type of art that they want to experience. Choice *B*, Analysis, is the process where the viewer assesses or makes meaning or judgments about the work, what they liked about it, what they did not like about it. Choice *C*, Evaluation, is where the consumer is capable of expressing a judgment about the quality of the work/performance. Interpretation is the fourth part, which involves the process of formulating a judgment or interpretation about the work, in part or whole.

34. B: A line can be best looked at as the outline of a three-dimensional object, the edge of a two-dimensional object, and the path of a moving point as found in the literature. In Choice *A*, art can be described as a framework that can be used to provoke emotions and paint mental pictures for the viewers. However, the best answer is *B* when it comes to how a line is looked at or viewed. Choice *C* is incorrect; "three-dimensional object" should replace "*two*-dimensional object;" "the edge of a two-dimensional object" should replace "the *side* of a *three*-dimensional object;" and "the path of a moving point" should replace "the path of a *static* point." Although Choice *D* is not absolutely incorrect, as a line could be viewed as representing the continuation of time, it is not the best answer for this question.

35. A: The best way to create rhythm in visual art is via repeating visual movement. Manipulating lines and figures, Choice *B*, can effectively create the appearance of rhythm in visual art; yet, repetition needs to be included into the process. Illusion, Choice *C*, is created in this form of artistic impression, but it is an effect of the process rather than the means to achieve it. Choice *D*, none of the above, is incorrect.

36. C: Green is not a primary color. The three primary colors are Choices *A, B*, and *D*: yellow, blue, and red.

37. C: Colors, theme, pattern, and texture help an artist create unity in their work. Intention, Choice *A*, can be the starting point, but to actually achieve unity, the answers in Choice *C* must be applied. Choice *B*, shape, focus, and repetition, are not wholly relevant to the answer. Choice *D* is incorrect; the reader's perception can help to create unity after the fact, but the use of colors, theme, pattern, and texture are the best answer regarding creating the artwork.

38. D: Choice *A*, large vs. small shapes, Choice *B*, rough vs. smooth surfaces, and Choice *C*, black vs. white are all examples of the principle of contrast found in art. Thus, Choice *D* is the correct answer.

39. B: The speed of music is its tempo. Pitch, Choice *A*, is a frequency of sound in something like a musical note. Rhythm, Choice *C*, refers to the number of beats per measure and the differences between note lengths that generate patterns. Choice *D*, range, is the scope of notes that a voice or instrument can produce.

40. D: Exercise often leads to psychological benefits like relief of stress, better self-concept, and improved capability to handle stressors.

TExES 391 Practice Test #2

To keep the size of this book manageable, save paper, and provide a digital test-taking experience, the 2nd practice test can be found online. Scan the QR code or go to this link to access it:

testprepbooks.com/bonus/texes-core

SCAN ME

The first time you access the tests, you will need to register as a "new user" and verify your email address.

If you have any issues, please email support@testprepbooks.com.

Dear TExES Core Subjects EC-6 Test Taker,

We would like to start by thanking you for purchasing this study guide for your exam. We hope that we exceeded your expectations.

Our goal in creating this study guide was to cover all of the topics that you will see on the test. We also strove to make our practice questions as similar as possible to what you will encounter on test day. With that being said, if you found something that you feel was not up to your standards, please send us an email and let us know.

We have study guides in a wide variety of fields. If you're interested in one, try searching for it on Amazon or send us an email.

Thanks Again and Happy Testing!
Product Development Team
info@studyguideteam.com

FREE Test Taking Tips Video/DVD Offer

To better serve you, we created videos covering test taking tips that we want to give you for FREE. **These videos cover world-class tips that will help you succeed on your test.**

We just ask that you send us feedback about this product. Please let us know what you thought about it—whether good, bad, or indifferent.

To get your **FREE videos**, you can use the QR code below or email freevideos@studyguideteam.com with "Free Videos" in the subject line and the following information in the body of the email:

a. The title of your product

b. Your product rating on a scale of 1-5, with 5 being the highest

c. Your feedback about the product

If you have any questions or concerns, please don't hesitate to contact us at info@studyguideteam.com.

Thank you!

SCAN HERE

Made in the USA
Coppell, TX
27 March 2024

30613168R10232